THE PATTERNING INSTINCT

THE PATTERNING INSTINCT

A Cultural History of Humanity's Search for Meaning

JEREMY LENT

Guilford, Connecticut

An imprint of Globe Pequot, the trade division of
The Rowman & Littlefield Publishing Group, Inc.
4501 Forbes Blvd., Ste. 200
Lanham, MD 20706
www.rowman.com

Distributed by NATIONAL BOOK NETWORK

British Library Cataloguing in Publication Information Available

Library of Congress Cataloging-in-Publication Data

Names: Lent, Jeremy R., 1960– author.
Title: The patterning instinct : a cultural history of humanity's search for meaning / by Jeremy R. Lent.
Description: Amherst, New York : Prometheus Books, 2017. | Includes bibliographical references and index.
Identifiers: LCCN 2016036581 (print) | LCCN 2016057101 (ebook) | ISBN 9781633882935 (hardback) | ISBN 9781633882942 (ebook) | ISBN 9781633887596 (paper)
Subjects: LCSH: Ethnophilosophy. | Meaning (Philosophy) | Social norms. | Sustainability—Social aspects. | Human ecology. | BISAC: SOCIAL SCIENCE / Anthropology / Cultural.
Classification: LCC GN468 .L46 2017 (print) | LCC GN468 (ebook) | DDC 306.4—dc23
LC record available at https://lccn.loc.gov/2016036581

™ The paper used in this publication meets the minimum requirements of American National Standard for Information Sciences—Permanence of Paper for Printed Library Materials, ANSI/NISO Z39.48-1992

To Future Generations

CONTENTS

LIST OF ILLUSTRATIONS

FORMATTING CONVENTIONS

An asterisk has been added to any endnote that contains significant information beyond a listing of textual sources, as an indicator to the reader that it may be worthwhile to turn to that particular note.

This book follows the convention established in the field of cognitive linguistics of using small capitals when referring to cultural metaphors such as CONQUEST OF NATURE.

FOREWORD

When I went to high school in Austria in the 1950s, history was taught exclusively as military history, which I found utterly boring and studied only minimally, just enough to pass my exams. My main academic interests were literature, foreign languages, and, above all, science and mathematics. Then, a decisive moment came when, as a young physics student, I read Werner Heisenberg's *Physics and Philosophy*, his classic account of the conceptual revolution triggered by quantum physics and relativity theory.

Heisenberg's book had a tremendous influence on my thinking and determined the trajectory of my entire career as a scientist and writer. One passage, in particular, planted a seed in my mind that would mature, more than a decade later, into a systematic investigation of the limitations of the Cartesian worldview and the wide range of its scientific, philosophical, social, and political implications. "The Cartesian partition," wrote Heisenberg, "has penetrated deeply into the human mind during the three centuries following Descartes, and it will take a long time for it to be replaced by a really different attitude toward the problem of reality."

This passage also triggered in me a new interest in history, but this time in the history of ideas, a subject that has fascinated me ever since. The history of ideas is endlessly captivating because well-known sequences of political and cultural events of the past, again and again, appear in a new light when we look at them through a different narrative lens. I have no doubt that this is the reason for the tremendous success of books like Jared Diamond's *Guns, Germs, and Steel* and Yuval Harari's *Sapiens*, and of documentaries like Kenneth Clark's *Civilisation* and Jacob Bronowski's *The Ascent of Man*.

The Patterning Instinct by Jeremy Lent continues this tradition of broad interdisciplinary historical narratives, written in nontechnical language, eminently readable, entertaining, yet sophisticated and intellectually fascinating. In this book, the author introduces a new perspective, which he calls "cognitive history." Instead of the traditional approach of assuming that the direction of history is determined, ultimately, by material causes—geography, economy, technology, and the like—he argues that, following the fundamental human urge to endow our surroundings with meaning, "different cultures construct core metaphors to make meaning out of their world" and "these metaphors forge the values that ultimately drive people's actions."

By calling his approach "cognitive history," the author implies that he traces the human search for meaning through the lens of modern cognitive science, a rich interdisciplinary field that transcends the traditional frameworks of biology, psychology, and epistemology. The key achievement of cognitive science, in my view, is that it has overcome the Cartesian division between mind and matter that has haunted scientists and philosophers for centuries. Mind and matter no longer appear to belong to two separate categories but are seen as representing two complementary aspects of the phenomenon of life: process and structure. At all levels of life, mind and matter, process and structure, are inseparably connected.

The Santiago theory of cognition, in particular, identifies cognition (the process of knowing) with the very process of life. The self-organizing activity of living systems at all levels of life is "mental" or cognitive activity. Thus, life and cognition are inseparably connected. Cognition is embedded in matter at all levels of life. Moreover, the theory asserts that cognition is not a representation of an independently existing world but rather a "bringing forth" or "enacting" of a world through the process of living.

Jeremy Lent applies this insight to history, recognizing the power of the human mind to construct its own reality and arguing that "the cognitive frames through which different cultures perceive reality have had a profound effect on their historical direction." Engaging the reader in an "archaeology of the mind," he shows how, in different epochs of history, dominant cognitive frames can be defined in terms of certain fundamental patterns of meaning: "everything is connected," "the hierarchy of the gods," "split cosmos, split human," "the harmonious web of life," "NATURE AS MACHINE," and so on.

From this cognitive perspective, Lent proposes new answers to some age-old questions of human history: Is it our true nature to be selfish and competitive, or empathic and community-minded? How did the rise of agriculture set the stage for our current ecological crisis? Why did the Scientific Revolution take place in Europe and not in Chinese or Islamic civilization? What are the root causes of our modern global culture of rampant consumerism, and is there a way we can change that culture?

In our time of global crisis, which desperately needs guidance through new and life-affirming metaphors, the answers to these questions are more important than ever.

Fritjof Capra, physicist, author of *The Systems View of Life*

Preface

A COGNITIVE HISTORY OF HUMANITY

This book takes an approach to history that recognizes the power of the human mind to construct its own reality. It offers a simple thesis: culture shapes values, and those values shape history. While this might appear selfevident to some, it's an approach at odds with some widely accepted principles of modern historical interpretation. There are good reasons why contemporary historians have denied the importance of culture in shaping history, but this has led to an unnecessarily limited understanding of our past. In today's world, reeling from global crises and transfixed by the dazzle of technology, it is more important than it has ever been to understand how values have shaped history and, consequently, how they might also shape our future.

The book introduces an approach I call *cognitive history*. In the broadest terms, cognitive science is the analytical study of the human mind. It is an interdisciplinary tradition that began in the decades following World War II and has since expanded in many directions, leading to important insights in fields as diverse as neuroscience, linguistics, and anthropology. Like these other fields, cognitive history analyzes its subject with reference to the cognitive structures of the human mind. In this book, it attempts to interpret historical phenomena such as the rise of agriculture, the Scientific Revolution, and our current world system from a cognitive perspective. In doing so, it recognizes the enormous complexity of human culture and draws from recent advances in systems thinking to develop an interpretative framework.

For those interested in the book's methodological underpinnings, this preface places it in the context of modern interpretations of history and shows how the systems approach to understanding complexity can be usefully applied to the field of history.

Truth and Reason . . . Or Geography and Greed?

As a teenager growing up in London, I remember sitting in the living room and watching television with my father as we avidly soaked up *The Ascent of Man*, an award-winning BBC documentary series produced by Dr. Jacob Bronowski. For my father, it was a splendid exposition of how "Man" (there were no qualms in those days about giving humanity a male gender) climbed from peak to peak in his ascent to the pinnacle of modern scientific achievement. In contrast to animals, which merely adapt to their environment, Bronowski explained triumphantly, Man is "not a figure in the landscape; he is the shaper of the landscape."[1]

I didn't know it at the time, but I was watching a view of history that fit snugly within the cultural metaphor of CONQUEST OF NATURE. Inspired by the discoveries of Europe's scientific revolution, historians had spent centuries extolling the inexorable march of progress that, in their view, culminated in the glorious achievements of Western civilization. The conquest of nature was paralleled by an equally ambitious conquest of the rest of the world by European powers, leading to the decimation of indigenous populations and the rise of empires that spanned the globe. By the early twentieth century, the supremacy of the "white man" galvanized a pseudoscientific, racist interpretation of history with a grand narrative describing the evolutionary progress of humanity from its origins (which, it was thought, could still be seen in the "brutal Hottentot" of Africa) to its culmination in modern European culture. By the time Jacob Bronowski took the stage, the aftermath of the totalitarian horrors of the mid-twentieth century had muted some of the overt racism of this narrative and added some ambivalence to the triumphalist storyline, but the core thesis remained the same.[2]

In the postwar generation, the West had the magnanimity to invite the "Third World" nations to a seat at its table, as long as they learned to play by its rules. Underlying these rules was a cognitive framework that went something like this: the Truth has been discovered by Science, which leads to continual Progress as a result of Man using his unique faculty of Reason for the benefit of all. While other cultures might have something to offer, they were generally viewed as complementing the rule of Reason as defined by Western civilization. In 1946, American philosopher F. S. C. Northrop kicked off a new globalist era with his book *The Meeting of East and West*, envisaging a world civilization combining the "theoretically scientific philosophy" of the West with the "aesthetic component which the Orient has mastered." In the following decades, countless visionaries offered their own versions of this synthesis of East and West, generally with the West playing the role of rational investigator of scientific truth and the "Orient" offering various complementary perspectives based on some form of mysticism or spiritual insight deemed more difficult for the logical, scientific mind of the Westerner to access.[3]

However, in the 1970s, while Bronowski was eulogizing the Ascent of Man, a new generation of intellectuals set out to challenge the assumptions underlying this narrative. In his book *Orientalism*, Edward Said showed how centuries of cultural prejudice had shaped the West's romanticized image of Oriental mystique. A series of critiques by a school of French philosophers coalesced into a movement known as postmodernism, which attacked the notion that objective truths could be applied universally under the rubric of such capitalized abstractions as Truth, Science, Reason, and Man. Included in this attack was the tradition of "cultural essentialism," by which Northrop and those who followed him had sought to ascribe a particular set of universal characteristics to the Orient, the West, or, for that matter, any racial or cultural stereotype.[4]

In contrast to the modernist view of the world, which had emerged with the Scientific Revolution, the postmodernists proposed that reality is constructed by the mind and can never therefore be described objectively. Each culture, they argued, develops its own version of reality that arises from its specific physical and environmental context. If you try to "essentialize" a culture's frame of reality and compare it with that of another culture, you risk decontextualizing it and therefore invalidating its unique attributes. The postmodernists accused Westerners who had attempted to do so of engaging in a form of cultural imperialism, seeking to appropriate what seemed valuable in other cultures for their own use while ignoring its historical context. A more useful investigation, according to the postmodernist critique, would be to recognize the multiplicity of discourses created by various cultures and, rather than try to distill some essential meaning from them, trace how certain social and political groups used these discourses to maintain or enhance their own power relative to others.[5]

The postmodernist critique has had a profound effect on the social sciences, and even when it hasn't been fully accepted, some of its principles have helped shape the current norms of many academic disciplines, including history. A major step in establishing this new standard was the publication by Jared Diamond of *Guns, Germs, and Steel* in 1997. This book, which has deservedly become a modern classic, investigates one of the crucial questions of history: why have the Eurasian civilizations been so successful in establishing hegemony over the people of other continents? Diamond claims the reasons can be found not in genes or culture but in geography. For example, the broad east-west axis of Eurasia meant that newly domesticated crops could easily spread across zones with similar climates, whereas the north-south axis of the Americas prevented it. Similarly, new infectious diseases that arose in humans from animal domestication spread in waves across Eurasia, leaving survivors with immunity. All this led to the Eurasian population developing the tools of civilization before the rest of the world, resulting in the guns, germs, and steel that permitted them to dominate other continents.[6]

Eurasia, however, includes not just Europe but China, Russia, and India. If geography caused Eurasia's rise, why was it Europe that eventually established empires throughout the world? There are no end of different explanations offered for this conundrum, but a prominent one again fingers geography as the cause. Historian Kenneth Pomeranz argues in his acclaimed book *The Great Divergence* that it was England's easily accessible coal deposits and the proximity of Europe to the New World that gave it the impetus to achieve an industrial revolution and thereby dominate the rest of the globe.[7]

Something these, and other influential modern histories, have in common is a rejection of cultural essentialism. It's assumed there are no intrinsic behavioral differences between the people of various parts of the world, and, therefore, we need to look to environmental factors to explain how each developed in different ways. This approach is an admirable improvement over the racist assumptions of Western superiority that previously infused theories of history, but it inevitably creates its own form of cultural imperialism by implicitly assuming a new set of human universals. The distinctive values and beliefs about human nature that form the bedrock of Western thought are silently assumed to be those that drive people all over the world and throughout history. When investigating, for example, why Europe rather than China experienced an industrial revolution, most historians take it for granted that this was a wholly desirable goal that China "failed" to achieve before Europe. Similarly, when asking why Europe, not China, conquered the New World, it's generally assumed that if Chinese navigators had reached the Americas before the Europeans, they would have plundered the continents in the same way the Europeans did. The underlying values that drove Europeans into these historical pathways are simply taken to be universal human norms, leaving the only remaining question: who got there first?[8]

This reductionist approach to history—arguing that all the reasons for the direction of history can ultimately be reduced to material causes—reached a kind of nadir in a book published in 2010 by Ian Morris entitled *Why the West Rules—For Now*, in which the author offers his own Morris Theorem to summarize the universal cause of social change in history: "Change is caused by lazy, greedy, frightened people looking for easier, more profitable, and safer ways to do things." To Morris, "culture, values, and beliefs were unimportant" in explaining the great currents of history, and instead we need to look for "brute, material forces," specifically those arising from geography.[9]

A Cognitive Approach to History

This book takes an entirely different approach from historical reductionism. Instead, it offers a cognitive approach to history, arguing that the cognitive frames through which different cultures perceive reality have had a profound effect on their historical direction. The worldview of a given civilization—the implicit beliefs and values that create a pattern of meaning in people's lives—has, in my opinion, been a significant driver of the historical path each civilization has taken. But, at the same time, I disavow any affinity with the old triumphalist view of history, which posits some characteristic of the Western mindset that made it somehow superior to that of other cultures and, therefore, led to the West's "success" over the rest of the world. Instead, as the book unfolds, it reveals an underlying pattern to Western cognition that is responsible for its Scientific and Industrial Revolutions—as well as its devastating destruction of indigenous cultures around the world and our current global rush toward possible catastrophe. In this respect, the book shares much with the postmodern critique of Western civilization, recognizing those capitalized universal abstractions such as Reason, Progress, and Truth to be culture-specific constructions. In fact, a significant portion of the book is devoted to tracing how these patterns of thought first arose and then infused themselves so deeply into the Western mind-set as to become virtually invisible to those who use them.

An obvious question arises to challenge this point of view: if Western cognition was responsible for the Scientific and Industrial Revolutions, how come the rest of the world (especially Asia) has been so adept at catching up with—and now, in many ways, surpassing—Western achievements? And aren't China, India, and other so-called developing countries partly responsible for the world's impending environmental catastrophe? My answer is based on the premise that cognitive frames, while deeply influencing the direction of a society, are not permanently fixed. When drastic change occurs to a given society, its cognitive structures—and, ultimately, its entire worldview—can change equally drastically within a generation or two. When the Western powers installed their empires throughout the globe, humiliating traditional leaders and undermining established hierarchies, they overwhelmed the old cognitive patterns with new values and measures of success, which people in the conquered societies aspired to achieve. Through this process, I would argue that—especially since the mid-twentieth century—what had once been the Western worldview has now become the dominant worldview of those in positions of wealth and power who drive our global civilization, from Bangkok to Beijing and from Mumbai to Mexico City.

For cognitive history, there's an important lesson to learn from this, which applies to the entire sweep of human experience from the evolution of *Homo sapiens* to the present: the relationship between cognition and history is not one-way but reciprocal. The cognitive patterns of humans living their day-to-day existence are continually affected by what goes on around them, and the consequent actions they take are continually affecting whatever is around them. It's a perpetual, bidirectional feedback loop. From this perspective, the currently fashionable reductionist view of history is half right: it captures a one-way causative flow from environment to cognition but misses the reciprocal causative flow in the other direction.[10]

Creating Our Own Reality (Without Really Trying)

The thought of tracing feedback loops winding back on themselves can feel intimidating, and it's easy to see the attraction of a simpler view, such as historical reductionism, that just focuses on one direction of causality. However, I've written this book in the belief that important insights can be gained by investigating how these reciprocal loops can transform societies and ultimately shape the course of history. Fortunately, some valuable research in recent decades has shed light on how these feedback loops work. Their findings inform this book's methodology and merit a brief overview.

A good place to begin is the theory of evolution. Like the reductionist view of history, the traditional approach to evolution was based on a one-way flow: an environment poses a set of "problems" to organisms, and the organisms best adapted to "solve" the problems leave the most offspring, leading to the process of natural selection. The particular way in which an organism finds its own survival strategy, whether it's spiders weaving webs or bees turning nectar into honey, is called an evolutionary niche. However, in recent years, researchers have suggested there's really a two-way flow going on, which they call "niche construction." As organisms adapt to their environment, they are not just finding their niche but actively constructing it, and, by doing so, they are shaping the environment for themselves, their offspring, and the other organisms around them. As they shape their environment, these organisms also take an active role in eventually shaping their own genome as their descendants evolve specialized attributes to thrive in the niche they've constructed. As spiders, for example, became expert at constructing their webs, they also evolved an array of techniques for camouflage, protection, and communication that work specifically for their web niche.[11]

What was the niche that humans constructed for themselves as they evolved? Many evolutionary biologists have come to agree it was an entirely different kind: it was a cognitive niche, a result of using their unique cognitive powers to learn to cooperate with others and collectively discover new ways to manipulate their environment. Gradually, hominids began to invent tools to hunt animals stronger or faster than them and process foods that would otherwise be inedible. A crucial outcome of this cognitive niche was the power it unleashed by allowing them to work together as a group. While some might use teamwork to hunt prey, others could forage for plant food, all of which would later be shared within the community, enabling everyone to enjoy a more nutritious diet. The importance of this social aspect of human evolution has led some researchers to argue that the human niche might instead be called a sociocognitive or cultural niche.[12]

From this cognitive niche, human culture emerged as a set of shared symbols and practices that ties a group together and is passed down from one generation to the next. And here we have a new feedback loop to consider: in a process known as gene-culture coevolution, culture has shaped the human niche so profoundly that it's caused changes within the human genome, affecting the very direction of human evolution. This may have begun as far back as two million years ago, when our prehuman ancestors first figured out how to use fire to cook their food. Because cooking frees up more energy from food for our bodies to digest, new generations relied increasingly on cooked food, leading eventually to physiological changes that caused their descendants to depend on cooking in much the same way spiders depend on their webs. Much later in history, when cattle were first domesticated, a few lucky people had genes that allowed them to drink milk as adults, known as lactose tolerance. With the extra nutrition available to them, they flourished, leaving more offspring, until their genes spread through virtually the entire population of Europe, making dairy farming even more important than before.[13]

And the feedback loops kept turning: From culture to genes to livelihood. And then, from livelihood back to culture. As various populations developed different forms of agriculture, the requirements of their work influenced the cultural patterning of each society. Social psychologists have discovered, for example, that people who herd animals for a living tend to lead more independent and mobile lives, resulting in more individualistic values. Farmers, on the other hand, who lead more settled lives and rely on each other to help with planting and harvesting, develop more collectivist cultures. Even within farming, important cultural variations have been shown to arise from the kind of crops that are cultivated. A recent study, for example, has found that Chinese provinces that rely on rice, which requires a great deal of mutual cooperation within the community, have a more holistic outlook than those provinces that rely on wheat, where farmers can manage more easily by themselves.[14]

How do these cultural differences get passed on from one generation to the next? There are some who speculate it's through genetic changes, even in the more recent past.[15] However, a more convincing explanation—and one that forms a foundation of this book—is that each society shapes the cognitive structure of individuals growing up in its culture through imprinting its own pattern of meaning on each infant's developing mind.

The most important way in which a growing infant's mind is molded by her culture is through language. Anthropologists in the early twentieth century became so entranced by the power of language to shape cognitive structures that they sometimes overstated the case, asserting that our native language forces us to think in certain ways and prevents us thinking in other ways. This theory, the Sapir-Whorf hypothesis, was witheringly attacked in the later twentieth century as researchers showed how people from a particular culture were able to adapt their cognition to culturally different ways of thinking even as adults. More recently, however, a plethora of new evidence has convincingly demonstrated a more refined version of the Sapir-Whorf hypothesis: that the language we speak from birth—although it doesn't prevent us thinking in different ways—establishes structures of cognition that influence us to perceive, understand, and think about the world according to certain patterns. Or, in its simplest terms: language has a patterning effect on cognition.[16]

And in yet another feedback loop, the patterning each person uses to impose meaning on the world ultimately affects the actions and choices they make in the world. When aggregated to an entire civilization, these patterns of meaning shape history and fundamentally alter the world around us. In the words of cognitive linguist George Lakoff, "metaphorical concepts. . . . structure our present reality. New metaphors have the power to create a new reality." When, for example, European thinkers began to conceive of the natural world as a complex machine, this inspired them to discover how the machine worked in order to manipulate it more effectively for their benefit, leading ultimately to our present era of genetic engineering and synthetic biology.[17]

Making Sense of Complexity

These reciprocal feedback loops are not just complicated—they're also complex. In everyday language, we tend to use these two words interchangeably, but, in the world of systems theory, they're very different. A system can be complicated but not complex, no matter how large, if each of its components and the way they relate to each other can be completely analyzed and given an exact description. A jumbo jet, an offshore oil rig, and a snowflake are all examples of complicated systems. A complex system, on the other hand, arises from a large number of nonlinear relationships between its components with feedback loops that can never be precisely described. Any living thing, or system comprising living things, is complex: a bacterium, a brain, an ecosystem, a financial market, a language, or a social system.[18]

In this book, I've taken the view that human culture itself can be viewed as a certain type of complex system. Thinking about culture in this way makes it easier to understand some of the critical transitions that have taken place in history. With this in mind, it helps to consider how systems theorists try to make sense of complexity.

Complex systems have some indicative characteristics. They have a large number of elements, each of which interacts with and influences other elements within the system through nonlinear feedback loops. They constantly interact with their environment, and, frequently, they contain smaller systems within them while themselves being nested within bigger systems. They are never in equilibrium but are continually in flux, evolving through time as a result of both their previous conditions and the environment around them.[19]

One important attribute of a complex system is a special type of reciprocal causality: each part of the system has an effect on the whole, while the system as a whole affects each part. Because of this, a complex system can never be fully understood by reducing it to its component parts. An example of this kind of reciprocal causality can be seen in a tropical rain forest. As a forest becomes dense and large, the roots of its trees interconnect to create a healthy network of root fungus in the soil; the foliage creates more shade, which keeps the undergrowth moist; and the evaporation from its leaves creates its own cloud system, increasing the rainfall. The forest system as a whole thus affects each tree, while each tree affects the entire system.[20]

The reciprocal causality of complex systems has a profound impact on the nature of change in the system. Within certain parameters, a complex system can be highly resilient, adapting to and accommodating changes both within itself and in its external environment. However, at a certain point, the cohesive set of reciprocal causal relationships that form the system can rapidly become unraveled, and when that happens, the system undergoes what's known as a critical transition, leading to a new stable state that can be either more or less complex than the previous one. When this happens, it's very difficult for the system to shift back to the state it was in previously, a characteristic known as hysteresis. For example, in the case of the tropical forest, once the system forms its root network, its shady foliage, and its own rain clouds, it's likely to remain in that stable state for millennia. If, however, something drastic happens to it—such as humans cutting down trees and thinning out the forest—at a certain point, it reaches a critical threshold. There's no longer enough foliage to keep the ground cover moist and not enough evaporation to form rain clouds. In a relatively short time, the tropical forest turns into a new, stable state of arid scrubland, and it's now very difficult for the system to shift back to its previous state.[21]

The entire four-billion-year history of life on earth can be understood in terms of these critical transitions with hysteresis. The emergence of life itself, in the form of single-celled organisms such as bacteria, was the first such critical transition. Another occurred when cells developed a nucleus, leading to all other forms of life. Other transitions include the emergence of multicellular organisms, such as animals and plants; colonies of organisms, such as ants and bees; and the evolution of humans with language. In each case, once the newly complex, stable system emerged, the earth's ecosystem never reverted to its previous state.[22]

Given that human societies are themselves complex systems, can we use this framework to understand the great critical transitions in our history? I believe we can, with the caveat that when we apply this framework to human society, there is yet another crucial feedback loop to consider. Because of our unique cognitive capacity, human social systems need to be understood as a pair of two tightly interconnected, coexisting complex systems: a tangible system and a cognitive system. The tangible system refers to everything that can be seen and touched: a society's tools; its physical infrastructure; and its agriculture, terrain, and climate, to name just some of its components. The cognitive system refers to what can't be touched but exists in the cognitive network of the society's culture: its language, myths, core metaphors, know-how, hierarchy of values, and worldview. These coupled systems interact dynamically, creating their own feedback loops, which can profoundly affect each other and, consequently, the direction of the society. Sometimes the cognitive system might act to inhibit change in the tangible system, leading to a long period of stability. At other times, the cognitive and tangible systems might each catalyze change in the other system, leading to a powerful positive feedback loop that causes dramatic societal transformation.[23]

Much of this book is devoted to tracing these complex feedback loops. In some of the most significant transitions of human history—the appearance of language, the rise of agriculture, and the Scientific and Industrial Revolutions—we'll see how the cognitive and tangible systems of the period interacted with each other, causing a newly coherent system to emerge and usurp what had gone before. I think it's a fascinating story in its own right, but this approach gains extra relevance when we turn to our present era. There seems little doubt that we are currently in the midst of one of the great critical transitions of the human journey, and yet it is not at all clear where we will end up once our current system resolves into a newly stable state. The final chapter uses this systems framework to explore some of the possibilities we face. My hope in writing this book is that it can offer a valuable framework for readers to come to their own assessment of humanity's future path—and their own potential role in shaping it.

Introduction

SHAPING OUR HISTORY

In 1405, Admiral Zheng set off from China with a glorious armada, leading three hundred magnificent ships on a thirty-year odyssey to distant lands as far afield as Africa. Everywhere he went, Zheng—a Muslim by birth whose father had completed a pilgrimage to Mecca—heightened the prestige of the empire. He left such a fine impression that, in some parts of Southeast Asia, he was even deified, with temples still venerating him to this day. His ships inspired awe in those he visited—not surprisingly, since his crew of twenty-seven thousand men was larger than the entire population of many ports of call. Indeed, his fleet was the greatest the world had ever seen, dwarfing the technological capabilities of Europe at that time. Zheng's largest ships had as many as nine masts and luxurious cabins with balconies, while his armada included troop and horse transports, patrol boats, warships, and tankers holding fresh water.[1]

Later that century, Christopher Columbus set sail from Spain with a crew of ninety men in three threadbare boats, each of which could have fit ten times into one of Zheng's. After just three days, one of their rudders broke, and they had to stop in the Canary Islands for repairs.

And yet, in spite of this enormous technological chasm, it was Columbus's voyage that would change the course of history, while Zheng's armada left virtually no imprint on the world. Why?

In this book, we'll try to get inside the minds of people like Zheng and Columbus to gain a new perspective on this and other crucial questions of history: Is it our true nature to be selfish and competitive, or empathic and community-minded? How did the rise of agriculture set the stage for our current ecological crisis? Why did the Scientific Revolution take place in Europe and not in Chinese or Islamic civilization? What are the root causes of our modern global culture of rampant consumerism, and is there any way we can change it?

Pioneering the new field of cognitive history, this book will show how different cultures construct core metaphors to make meaning out of their world and how these metaphors forge the values that ultimately drive people's actions.

We will discover why a hunter-gatherer tribe insulted the anthropologist who gave them a fat ox for Christmas, why a great Muslim scholar received fifty lashes for his scientific research, and what drove a prominent church father to castrate himself.

The book is based on a simple but compelling theme: culture shapes values, and those values shape history. It will show the layers of values that form the norms of mainstream Western culture and how these continue to shape our world today. That is why, although this book focuses on history, it can help us understand not just where we came from but where we're headed.

There has never been a more important time to contemplate this question.

Imagine a satellite being launched into orbit, but its controls aren't working too well. If the trajectory gets too steep, it will break through the earth's gravity field and soar into outer space. If it accelerates too rapidly, atmospheric resistance will cause it to come crashing down in a fiery ball. Only if everything is managed with great care will the satellite achieve a stable orbit. The trajectory of our civilization is a lot like that of the satellite. At the accelerating rate of technological innovation, artificial intelligence may soon transcend our own, and human DNA might be re-engineered to produce a genetically enhanced species—akin to the satellite leaving its home planet forever. On the other hand, the rate at which we're exploiting the earth's resources is unsustainable: in addition to climate change, there's a rapidly accumulating list of equally daunting crises, such as capacity limits in crucial resources, deforestation, and a massive extinction of species. If the convergence of these multiple threats becomes too much to handle, our global civilization could face a total collapse—akin to the satellite hitting too much resistance and crashing down.

To me, and perhaps to you too, neither of these scenarios is attractive. But is it possible for our civilization to manage its trajectory capably enough to reach a stable orbit? What would it take to achieve that? If we want to steer our future toward a sustainable path, it's important to know how we got into this unstable and potentially disastrous trajectory to begin with. The operating system of that satellite is buried deep within the values that shape our civilization. That's what we'll be unearthing in this book.

An Archaeology of the Mind

Each of us conducts our lives according to a set of assumptions about how things work: how our society functions, its relationship with the natural world, what's valuable, and what's possible. This is our worldview, which often remains unquestioned and unstated but is deeply felt and underlies many of the choices we make in our lives. We form our worldview implicitly as we grow up, from our family, friends, and culture, and, once it's set, we're barely aware of it unless we're presented with a different worldview for comparison. The unconscious origin of our worldview makes it quite inflexible. That's fine when it's working for us. But suppose our worldview is causing us to act collectively in ways that could undermine humanity's future? Then it would be valuable to become more conscious of it.[2]

We can think of a society's worldview like a building that's been constructed layer by layer over older constructions put together by generations past. Imagine the mainstream Western worldview, with its implicit beliefs in science, progress, and economic growth, as a house we're living in comfortably. As in a regular house, we're used to seeing the walls, decorations, and furnishings every day—but only rarely, if something goes wrong, are we called upon to probe through the masonry and inspect the house's infrastructure. Rarer still are those times when we need to delve into the house's foundations. But now we've learned we're living in an earthquake zone: there's a growing awareness that we may be creating our own Big One in the form of climate change, resource depletion, and species extinction. If our worldview is built on shaky foundations, we need to know about it—we need to find the cracks and shore up the weaknesses before it's too late.

Unlike modern houses, in which the foundations are part of the blueprint and constructed specifically for the house, the foundations of a worldview comprise the earlier worldviews of previous generations. As we probe further into history, we excavate deeper into the cognitive layers of our ancestors. That's why we can think of this exercise as an archaeology of the mind.

It's a matter of delving deeper not just in time but also into the underlying structures of human cognition: the entire set of processes, conscious and unconscious, we rely on to know our world and respond to it. In recent decades, cognitive scientists have made important discoveries into how we learn, as infants, to make sense of the reality around us. They've shown that our worldview is based on root metaphors we use to frame other aspects of meaning without even realizing we're doing so. These core metaphors, which arise from our embodied existence, structure how we conceptualize our world. HIGH is better than LOW; LIGHT is better than DARK; our life is a JOURNEY along a PATH. Throughout this book, we'll see how root metaphors have played a crucial role in structuring the worldviews of different cultures.[3]

What causes us to create these root metaphors in the first place? As we dig deeper into the archaeology of the mind, we find that, unlike other mammals, we humans possess an insatiable appetite to find meaning in the world around us. In the words of a little doggerel:

> Fish gotta swim; bird gotta fly.
> Man gotta sit and say why? why? why?[4]

As far as we know, asking why is something only humans do, so if we want to know *why* we ask why, it helps to look to the source of what makes us uniquely human. Fortunately, in recent decades, cognitive neuroscientists have come a long way in their efforts to answer this. They've identified the prefrontal cortex (PFC) as the part of our brain primarily responsible for our thinking and acting in ways that differentiate us from other animals. The PFC mediates our ability to plan, conceptualize, symbolize, make rules, and impose meaning on things. It controls our physiological drives and turns our basic feelings into complex emotions. It enables us to be aware of ourselves and others as separate beings and to turn the past and the future into one coherent narrative.[5]

The Patterning Instinct

Think of whatever we do that animals don't do: talking, reading, driving a car, planning for retirement, or making music. These uniquely human activities require the involvement of our highly developed PFC, especially during the period when we're learning them for the first time. Because they involve conceptualizations, these PFC-mediated modes of thought may be called our *conceptual consciousness*. Now think of what we share with other mammals: hunger, sexual urges, pain, aggression, desire for warmth, caring for our offspring—we can call this collection of cognitive experiences our *animate consciousness*. While many of the PFC's advanced functions exist to some degree in other creatures—chimpanzees, dolphins, and parrots, for example—their predominance in humans is overwhelmingly different in magnitude and scope, accounting largely for our current domination of the world.[6*]

How does our PFC allow us to think this way? Cognitive neuroscientists tell us the PFC is the most connected part of the brain, and one of its primary functions is to make sense of all the inputs it receives from other parts of the nervous system: the senses, primary emotions, feelings, and memories. One important way it does this is to detect patterns in what it receives: What's new? What's recurrent? What's important? What correlates with something else? Out of these patterns, as infants, we begin to make sense of our surroundings: recognizing family members, picking up on speech formations, and gradually learning to become members of our community. As we grow older, we continue to rely on our PFC to make meaning of all the different events we experience and to construct models for how to live our lives.[7*]

Through the capabilities of the PFC, our species has evolved a *patterning instinct*: an instinct unique to humans that lends its name to the title of this book. It deserves to be called an instinct because it emerges in human behavior at the earliest stages of development, well before any cultural learning has taken place. In fact, this instinct is what's responsible for an infant's ability to engage in cultural learning. As we'll see in a later chapter, when an infant is only nine months old, she has already begun to identify the unique phonetic patterns of her native language, and by twelve months she's learned to ignore phonetic units that don't exist in her own language. No one tells her to do this; she does it by instinct. This human instinct for patterning is embedded in our cognition, maintaining its activity throughout our lives. We create narratives about our past and future; we construct identities for ourselves; we categorize things, putting more value on some and less on others. And, just like our distant ancestors, we continually search for meaning in our lives and in the world around us.[8]

Before cognitive neuroscience, astute observers of the human condition already understood the drive for meaning to be a defining characteristic of humanity. The father of evolutionary theory, Charles Darwin, saw it as a natural consequence of human cognition, writing that "as soon as the important faculties of the imagination, wonder, and curiosity, together with some power of reasoning, had become partially developed, man would naturally crave to understand what was passing around him, and would have vaguely speculated on his own existence." Anthropologist Clifford Geertz recognized something similar, describing a human being as a "symbolizing, conceptualizing, meaningseeking animal," whose "drive to make sense out of experience, to give it form and order, is evidently as real and as pressing as the more familiar biological needs." Geertz saw religion, art, and ideology as "attempts to provide orientation for an organism which cannot live in a world it is unable to understand."[9]

Somehow, though, this drive to make sense of the world around us, while it's given us so much we value, has also brought our civilization to the brink of collapse. How could this have happened? Is it an inevitable result of human nature, or is our present situation culturally driven: a product of particular structures of thought that could conceivably be repatterned? The answer to this question—and its implications—may be one of the most important factors affecting the future direction of the human race.

Core Patterns of Meaning

The path from the earliest human search for meaning to our current precarious situation is what we'll be tracing in this book. It's a fascinating journey, offering up new possibilities to understand our human condition along the way, while occasionally challenging some of our deepest assumptions. The path can be segmented into different periods, each characterized by the core pattern of meaning by which people made sense of their world. These periods, with their patterns of meaning, give the book its structure. Here's what they look like.

Part 1. Everything Is Connected

What makes us uniquely human? Is it our true nature to be competitive or cooperative? The answers to these key questions can be found in our earliest history, and we'll begin by considering the surprising recent findings by scientists that overturn prevailing views of human nature. We'll discover how prehumans developed a nonverbal form of communicating with each other, using mime, laughter, chanting, and communal dancing, well before language came on the scene. We'll examine how, when it finally did, a new form of mythic consciousness arose, causing our ancestors to find meaning in every aspect of their daily existence and that of the animals and plants around them.

We'll see how this new consciousness led early hunter-gatherers to form their worldview around the first pattern of meaning: EVERYTHING IS CONNECTED. The natural world was infused with spirits, while the earth was seen as intimately involved with humans' daily activities, like a parent. Were their lives really nasty, brutish, and short (in the famous words of Thomas Hobbes) or did they enjoy ease and plenty? With the light cast on this question by modern anthropologists, we'll gain insight into how hunter-gatherers saw each other and their universe and how, in spite of their connection with the natural world, they conducted their own form of mass extinctions around the globe.

Part 2. Hierarchy of the Gods

Hierarchies and wealth. Property and land ownership. These things seem like they've been part of the human experience since time immemorial, but we'll see that's not the case. These new notions only arose when foragers began settling in one place, beginning about ten thousand years ago. We'll discover how, as they domesticated animals and plants, humans were themselves domesticated by the emergence of agriculture. Was this something our ancestors chose, or was it an inexorable process in which they were unwitting participants? As we answer this question, we'll explore how, along with its benefits, agriculture also brought an unprecedented level of anxiety into the human condition.

The hierarchical structure of agrarian societies helped shape a new conception of the universe. In agrarian civilizations around the world, a HIERARCHY OF THE GODS emerged, stratified and distant from ordinary people, mediated by priests. People still viewed themselves as connected with the natural world, but now they believed their own active participation was required to keep the cosmos running. We'll see how prayer, worship, and sacrifice became crucial parts of the human endeavor to propitiate the gods, who could take terrible retribution on those who failed to honor them.

While early civilizations everywhere shared important cognitive patterns, they also began to distill different meanings from the cosmos. We'll investigate some of these patterns of meaning spanning the globe—from China to Mesopotamia and from Egypt to Harappa. And we'll discover the unlikely culture on the fringes of the great civilizations that was destined to outlast nearly all of them and leave the greatest imprint on the cognitive structures of our modern world.

Part 3. The Patterns Diverge

Western Pattern: Split Cosmos, Split Human

Eastern Pattern: Harmonic Web of Life

In ancient Greece, a radically new way of thinking about the universe emerged. We'll discover what caused Greek philosophers to split the human experience into two by proposing a divided cosmos, with a heavenly domain of eternal abstractions and a worldly domain polluted with imperfection. And we'll see how this SPLIT COSMOS was paralleled by a SPLIT HUMAN, composed of an eternal soul temporarily imprisoned in a physical body destined to die.

Where did God come from? Recent discoveries have transformed our understanding of who really wrote the Old Testament, when they did it, and—perhaps most importantly—why they did it. We'll review these astonishing findings and trace how Christianity combined the Hebrew vision of a single all-powerful god with the divided cosmos of the ancient Greeks to create the world's first systematic dualistic cosmology. We'll glimpse the agonies of the early Christians struggling with the self-hatred and existential fragmentation arising from their new conception of humanity. And we'll watch how the metaphor of a SPLIT COSMOS led to a new understanding of the world as merely a desacralized theater for the human drama to be enacted.

Meanwhile, in China, a very different pattern of meaning evolved. We'll explore how the early Chinese saw themselves embedded in a HARMONIC WEB OF LIFE, which led to the view of a cosmos where the purpose of life was not to seek everlasting salvation but to harmonize one's existence within the hierarchical network of family, society, heaven, and earth.

We'll explore the gulf between the dualistic view of the cosmos that developed in Europe and the integrated cosmology of China. As we do so, we'll dive into one of the most acrimonious debates of modern academia: whether language affects the patterns of thought of its native speakers or not. We'll find how the front lines of this battle have recently shifted and review startling evidence that the ancient divergence of worldviews between Europe and China still continues to structure different ways of thinking between modern East Asians and Westerners.

Part 4. Conquest of Nature

China was more advanced technologically in the eleventh century than Europe in the seventeenth century. Yet it was in Europe that the Scientific Revolution occurred, fundamentally transforming the human experience across the globe. Why Europe and not China? We'll explore this crucial question, arriving at an answer that challenges prevailing theories of history. As part of our inquiry, we'll see how the language of the Old Testament, giving mankind dominion over the animals, was perceived in Europe as a clarion call for the scientific CONQUEST OF NATURE, framing the pattern of meaning that has encompassed the world through the present day.

In modern times, the clash between science and religion may seem like the inevitable result of two fundamentally contrasting worldviews. However, we'll discover that, far from being diametrically opposed, the Christian worldview served for centuries as an incubator for scientific cognition, which might never have flourished without it. By shining light on these deep linkages, we'll discover certain hidden beliefs underlying mainstream scientific thought that usually remain unquestioned, even by some of the greatest scientific minds of our age. Meanwhile, we'll take a look at an alternative form of scientific understanding—the systems way of thinking—and discover its fascinating parallels with the traditional cosmology of China.

More recently, the Western capitalist model has enveloped the globe, catalyzing a dramatic increase in the consumption of natural resources, with its implicit promise that the future offers greater prosperity and happiness for all. In recent decades, this rampant consumption has begun to take its toll, raising such specters as a massive extinction of species, a global freshwater crisis, and runaway climate change. Equipped with our learnings from history, we'll take a look at patterns of meaning in the prevalent modern mind-set and identify some faulty underpinnings driving our global civilization on its unsustainable course.

Part 5. The Web of Meaning?

The fifth pattern has not yet emerged. The book concludes by examining some of humanity's possible future trajectories, spanning the grimmest to the most dazzling. We'll investigate how earlier civilizations drove themselves to collapse, and we'll ask what lessons might apply to us. Will technology be our savior? We'll savor some of the breathtaking possibilities offered by artificial intelligence and genetic enhancement and ask: How would that affect our experience of being human? Would it exacerbate the chasm already existing in today's world between the haves and have-nots, possibly even leading humanity to bifurcate as a species? Finally, we'll explore an alternative scenario: a transformation of global norms based on a realization of our intrinsic connectedness with each other and with the natural world. Might a greater understanding of our cognitive patterns help us to construct a more integrated worldview that could put humanity on a sustainable path? I've written this book in the hope that this is indeed the case.

Part 1

EVERYTHING IS CONNECTED

Chapter 1

HOW WE BECAME HUMAN

A Story That Matters

It's a film clip that's captured the imagination of millions. At the beginning of the classic movie *2001: A Space Odyssey*, a band of prehistoric hominids has been driven from a water hole by another clan. In a moment of inspiration, one of them picks up a bone and realizes he can wield it as a weapon. He and his band use their newfound power to beat one of the other clan members to death. It works. They get their water hole back. It's the Dawn of Man. The ape-man genius throws the bone up into the sky, where—in a flash of cinematic brilliance accompanied by a grandiose soundtrack—it morphs into a satellite orbiting the earth.

It's a bittersweet story. But is it true? Are competition and conflict really the ultimate source of human ingenuity? The story of how we became human is an important one, not just from a scientific point of view but because it infuses our beliefs about human nature. Our view of humanity's origin has always been shaped by the cultural lens through which we see it, and, as that lens shifts, so does our perception of what really makes us human. Is it our true nature to be selfish and competitive, or empathic and cooperative? This matters because what we believe about ourselves has a way of becoming a self-fulfilling prophecy.

There's another story to be told about the origin of the human species. It's been painstakingly put together by archaeologists and anthropologists working diligently over the past few decades. It's one that can, perhaps, offer us a sense of hope and inspiration for the future. That's the story we'll be uncovering in this chapter.

This story begins roughly eight million years ago. There was a certain species of primates swinging around the branches in the forests of Africa. In an area known as the Great Rift Valley, massive tectonic shifts caused mountain peaks to rise in the west, blocking off much of the rainfall further east. A vast forested region gradually turned into open savannah with a more variable climate. The primates stranded there had to learn new ways to adapt to their dangerous and changeable surroundings. They were now more vulnerable to the giant saber-toothed cats prowling the terrain. Food wasn't as easy to procure. Many perished, but a lucky few survived and developed new skills. The descendants of the primates that remained in the western forests are known today as chimpanzees and bonobos. The descendants of those that survived the new challenges of their unpredictable landscape are known today as humans.[1]

The Birth of Mimetic Culture

The last common ancestor that humans shared with chimpanzees and bonobos is thought to have lived about six million years ago. In the evolutionary time scale, this is roughly the same time frame in which horses and zebras, lions and tigers, and rats and mice also shared their common ancestors. If you look at a physical comparison between humans and chimpanzees, that seems fairly reasonable. But if you look at the massive contrast in what we've accomplished, there's clearly something else going on. So what, specifically, was the change that led humans to populate the world with seven billion of us, building cities, surfing the internet, and sending rockets into space, while chimps and bonobos still live in the jungle and face the threat of extinction?[2]

There are plenty of biological differences between humans and other primates that offer some clues. We walk upright on two legs. We're capable of fine manipulation with our hands and can throw things accurately and powerfully. We have much smaller upper canine teeth. We have larger brains relative to the size of our bodies. The iris of our eye is surrounded by white, making it more visible. Our infants are helpless for years, relying entirely on adult support. Females don't show outward signs when they're ovulating. And we're virtually hairless, except for our heads and genitals. Do these seemingly unrelated differences have anything in common? If so, what clues might they hold to whatever it was that led humanity on the road to worldwide domination?[3]

If we think of the community of early hominids stranded in the eastern side of the Great Rift Valley as a complex system, we can begin to trace a network of feedback loops that tie together each of these biological differences into a cohesive story of how humans and other primates began to diverge. As the trees became sparser, the hominids who were able to get around more easily on the ground were better adapted to the new terrain, leaving offspring who gradually became bipedal. Walking on two legs freed up the hands for new possibilities, such as holding sticks or throwing stones to defend against predators. Losing bodily hair allowed them to sweat more easily and stay cool in the hot sun. But these physical changes alone weren't enough to save the stranded hominids. Crucially, this new, precarious environment required them to work more closely together than when they were in the forest. Without trees to protect them from the big cats, they found that defending themselves as a group was more effective than each member simply looking out for himself.[4]

The other great apes of Africa live in strictly hierarchical communities with an alpha male that exercises sexual dominance over the other males in the group. The alpha male rules by force, leaving the other males frequently resentful, but there's nothing they can do until an upstart rises from the ranks, conquers the dominant one, and replaces him as the new alpha male. This was very likely the societal structure of the primates that were our last common ancestors six million years ago. In the challenging environment of the savannah, the stranded prehominids began shifting toward a new, more effective, form of social interaction. They began to cooperate extensively with each other. When they went out scavenging for carrion or foraging for plant food, they would do so in teams. When they found a good cache of food, instead of eating whatever they could and moving on, they would use their hands—freed up by their bipedal locomotion—to carry any surplus back to the band and share it with them. While this form of social cooperation wasn't always in the best shortterm interest of each individual, it turned out to be invaluable to the group as a whole, with the result that those groups that cooperated more tended to be the ones to survive, leaving more descendants.[5]

Gradually, the large canine teeth of the males, once so crucial for intergroup battles for dominance, became less important in the new social order. However, the rivalry between males for sexual access to females continued to be a source of conflict within the group, occasionally leading to a breakdown in social cohesion. This rivalry would get especially intense over females seen to be ovulating. In those groups where the females' overt signs of ovulation were diminished, the intergroup rivalry was lessened, with improved results for the groups' long-term survival.[6]

With their cooperative habits, the groups increased in both size and social complexity. A new form of cultural bonding emerged, one that cognitive neuroscientist Merlin Donald has called "mimetic culture." This was a complex network of multiple forms of nonverbal communication between individuals, incorporating such activities as eye contact, dancing, rhythmic chanting, body language, gesturing, facial expressions, and varying tones of voice. Different kinds of calls most likely developed to express different needs and situations: a predator alarm call, a request for help, the availability of food, communication between mother and infant, and perhaps complex vocalizations to express the more subtle emotions these hominids were beginning to experience. Rhythm likely played an increasingly important part in community cohesion. When two rivals were facing off, others may have reduced the tension by chanting and dancing, creating a warm feeling of camaraderie. By moving and vocalizing in rhythm with others, these early hominids could feel engaged with their community like never before.[7]

What's fascinating about this mimetic phase is that we modern humans have never left it behind. We've added language on top of it, but our mimetic communication is still the most powerful form of interaction between us, shaping our identity with others. You can get a feeling for the power of mimetic expression when you think of our own nonverbal forms of expression: prayer rituals; dancing; chanting and cheering in a sports stadium; expressions of contempt or praise, intimacy or hostility. Mimetic culture, Donald notes, is so allencompassing that it "underlies all modern cultures and forms the most basic medium of human communication."[8]

Social Brain (Selfish Gene)

As anyone knows who has misread nonverbal cues in a social situation, mimetic culture is far from straightforward. In many ways, it's more nuanced and complex than spoken language. In early hominid societies, as the complexity of social interaction became more pronounced, the most successful in passing on their genes to future generations were those who navigated skillfully through the maze of mimetic signals, understanding the needs of others and conveying their own needs effectively. Over thousands of generations, hominids evolved a greater ability to put these diverse signals together into a pattern of meaning through increased use of their PFC, which—as we saw earlier—is the most connected part of the brain and integrates inputs from feelings, memories, sensations, and thoughts.

The idea that the human brain grew in size and intelligence as a result of social complexity is known as the "social brain hypothesis" and has emerged from decades of studying humans and other animals. Scientists have discovered that species of monkeys and apes that typically live in larger groups have a larger neocortex (the more recently evolved part of the brain that contains the PFC). This correlation exists even with nonprimates. A study of hyenas, for example, found that the spotted hyena, which lives in more complex societies, has a larger cerebral cortex than other hyena species. With humans, though, the relative size of the cerebral cortex is far greater than in other animals.[9]

The increased capability of the PFC has led humans to a more complex understanding of the relationship between ourselves and others than any other creature has likely achieved. Perhaps the most important step in this understanding is the recognition that other people have minds like we do, and that, by thinking about how we ourselves respond to things, we can make predictions about how they might respond. This realization is known as "theory of mind," and it forms the basis of much of our social existence. While chimpanzees have been shown to have some inklings of a theory of mind, it appears to be only a partial and hazy capability. It doesn't come easily even to human children. It's usually not until a child is three or four years old before a full theory of mind emerges. When that happens, a child realizes, for example, that her parents can be wrong, and that there are some things they can only know about if she tells them. Before too long, she will begin to experiment with lying and deception.[10]

Lying and deception. That seems to take us right back to the *2001: A Space Odyssey* story of human nature. And, in fact, when the social brain hypothesis first emerged in the 1970s, this was exactly how it was presented. What was unique about humans was said to be our "Machiavellian Intelligence" (from the title of one book on the subject). In the view of an influential thinker, Richard Alexander, as hominids became more dominant in their ecology, they no longer needed to evolve better capabilities to deal with the natural environment. Instead, they developed new cognitive skills to outcompete each other. In this way, we became (in his words) our own "hostile force of nature," entering into a "social arms race" with each other. Alexander saw our ancestors as playing a "mental chess game" with the other members of their group, "predicting future moves of a social competitor . . . and appropriate countermoves":

> In this situation, the stage is set for a form of runaway selection, whereby the more cognitively, socially, and behaviorally sophisticated individuals are able to out maneuver and manipulate other individuals to gain control of resources in the local ecology and to gain control of the behavior of other people.[11]

Outmaneuvering, manipulation, and control: are these, then, our defining characteristics after all? When Charles Darwin published his theory of evolution in the *Origin of Species*, one of his chapters was entitled "Struggle for Existence," and that phrase was readily picked up by the followers of Alexander. The evolution of human intelligence, to them, represents a "special kind of struggle with other human beings for control of the resources that support life and allow one to reproduce."[12]

While Alexander was honing his theory of the "social arms race," another biologist, Robert Trivers, was explaining how, from an evolutionary perspective, even altruism was really just a sophisticated form of selfishness, based on the principle of "I'll scratch your back and you scratch mine." In a much-cited paper, he described what he called "reciprocal altruism" as an ancient evolutionary strategy that could be seen in the behavior of fish and birds, and he interpreted human altruism in the same way. "Under certain circumstances," he wrote, "natural selection favors these altruistic behaviors because in the long run they benefit the organism performing them."[13]

This approach is consistent with what's become known as the "selfish gene" interpretation of evolution, as popularized by biologist Richard Dawkins. In this view, all evolution can be explained by the "selfish" drive of our genes to replicate themselves. And those special human virtues we value so highly are no exception. "Let us try to teach generosity and altruism," Dawkins suggests, "because we are born selfish." Alexander comes to a similar conclusion, proposing that "ethics, morality, human conduct, and the human psyche are to be understood only if societies are seen as collections of individuals seeking their own self-interest."[14]

It's a powerful story, and one that fits with the prevailing philosophy underlying our global free-market economy. Our very genes are selfish; all creatures in nature are ultimately selfish; we humans are merely unique in having taken our selfishness to new levels of Machiavellian manipulation. Even Alexander admitted his ideas seemed "repugnant," but he felt it was even more repugnant "to deny men the possibility of seeing themselves as they are." The geopolitical history of the twentieth century seems to have borne out this philosophy: communism failed, we are told, because it was founded on an unrealistic view of human nature, whereas capitalism succeeded because it's based on harnessing the selfish nature of each individual for the ultimate good of society.[15]

A powerful story, indeed, but one that has been shown in recent decades to be erroneous at each level of its narration. While the idea of the "selfish gene" still holds currency in the popular imagination, it has been extensively discredited as a simplistic interpretation of evolution. In its place, theorists offer a view of evolution as a series of complex, interlocking systems, in which the gene, organism, community, species, and environment all interact with each other in a variety of ways over different time frames. And, regarding our intrinsic human nature, a new generation of scientists has pointed to our ability to cooperate, rather than compete, as our defining characteristic.[16]

Competition and Cooperation

The next time you have an opportunity to watch young children playing together, take a few moments to observe how they interact. Before too long, you'll probably notice one of them pointing or gesturing to an object, holding something up to show it or offer it to another, bringing another child to a location to see something there, and perhaps intentionally teaching a new game. Developmental psychologist Michael Tomasello has pointed out that these are all behaviors humans naturally do that chimpanzees don't. He believes that's because chimps don't understand others as intentional agents in the way we do. In his view, the major difference between our cognition and that of chimpanzees is that humans identify more deeply with others of our species. It's from this "one uniquely human, biologically inherited, cognitive capacity," he suggests, that all the other distinctively human traits emerged.[17]

According to Tomasello, it's chimpanzees, not humans, that are obsessed with competing against each other. "Among primates," he writes, "humans are by far the most cooperative species, in just about any way this appellation is used." The instinct for social competition, he argues, may have driven the evolution of primate intelligence, but the cognitive skills that have enabled humans alone to develop language, culture, and civilization have been driven by social cooperation. Tomasello focuses on a uniquely human capability he calls "shared intentionality": our ability to realize that another person is seeing the same thing we are, but from a different perspective. This enabled early hominids to work collaboratively on complex tasks and transform their mimetic culture into cognitive communities that enabled them to share values and practices.[18]

There's a major flaw, however, to the theory that cooperation was the evolutionary driver of human uniqueness: the free-rider problem. What happens to a community when most people are sharing their resources but some are just going along for the ride, taking advantage of the others? Evolutionary researchers have modeled this problem extensively using game theory, testing real examples in the lab, and have discovered that it takes only a few selfish players to undermine the cooperation of others who trust each other. Some other ingredient, they realized, would have been needed for cooperation to become an evolutionarily successful strategy for early humans. But what?[19]

Imagine you're sitting alone in a room. In the next room is someone else, whom you don't know. You're never going to meet each other. A researcher walks in holding a hundred dollars and tells you this sum will be split between you and the stranger in the other room. And the good news is, you're allowed to decide exactly how you want to split it. But there's a catch: you can only propose one split. The person in the other room will be told the split and can either accept it or reject it. If he accepts it, the money is shared accordingly. If he rejects it, you'll both get nothing.

Welcome to the ultimatum game. If you're like most people, you'll decide to split the hundred dollars down the middle, so you get fifty, the other person will accept his fifty, and you'll both be ahead. Researchers view the ultimatum game as convincing evidence that refutes the earlier view of humans as fundamentally self-interested. If that were the case, then you (the proposer) would be more likely to keep, say, ninety dollars and offer ten to the other stranger (the responder). The responder would accept ten dollars because, being self-interested, he would be happier with that than nothing. But that's not what people do. Responders, in fact, frequently reject offers below thirty dollars, and the most popular amount offered by proposers is fifty.[20]

It seems we humans have evolved a powerful sense of fairness. So powerful, in fact, that we would rather walk away with nothing than permit someone else to take unfair advantage of us. Researchers call this "altruistic punishment." These results, and others like them, suggest that, over thousands of generations, our social intelligence was molded by cooperative group dynamics to evolve an innate sense of fairness and a drive to punish those who flagrantly break the rules, even at our own expense. This intrinsic sense of fairness is, in the view of some researchers, the extra ingredient that led to the evolutionary success of our species and created the cognitive foundation for values in our modern world such as freedom, equality, and representative government.[21]

It is, however, abundantly clear from any casual perusal of the daily news, not to mention the calamities of history, that cooperation is not the only force driving human affairs. Where, then, does the human drive for power fit in?

Anthropologist Christopher Boehm, who has researched social behavior in both primates and humans, offers a convincing theory that places both our competitive and cooperative drives into a cohesive framework. Our understanding of human nature, Boehm suggests, is only complete when we recognize it as intrinsically ambivalent, with our primate competitive drive and more recent cooperative instinct pushing in opposite directions.[22]

The form of society that emerged with early humans—and predominated for the vast majority of human history—was the nomadic hunter-gatherer band, which is overwhelmingly egalitarian in structure. Boehm has studied how these small bands manage to maintain their egalitarian nature in the face of the more ancient instinct for domination that inevitably prevails in some individuals. He discovered that, in virtually all hunter-gatherer societies, people join together to prevent powerful males from taking too much control, using collective behaviors such as ridicule, group disobedience, and, ultimately, extreme sanctions such as assassination. He names this kind of egalitarian society a "reverse dominance hierarchy" because "rather than being dominated, the rank and file itself manages to dominate."[23]

As long as humans lived as nomadic hunter-gatherers, the social structure that prevailed was distinctly egalitarian. What changed? Why does the history of the past few millennia differ so drastically from a system that had been stable for so long? This change was one of humanity's great critical transitions, and its implications reverberate throughout this book. Before we can begin to understand what happened, though, we need to investigate further those characteristics of our evolution that helped make us uniquely human.[24]

The Emergence of Symbolic Thought

Archaeologists have some helpful clues in piecing together a picture of how early hominids changed over time in the form of the tools they left behind. It was once believed that tool use was a defining attribute of humans. Then, in the 1960s, Jane Goodall discovered that chimpanzees also use primitive tools, such as stalks of grass placed in termite holes or rocks to crack open nuts, and, since then, a small cottage industry has sprung up to study tool use by chimps and other primates. For the first few million years after humans diverged from our common ancestor, they likely used tools in ways similar to how modern chimps use them. Then, something happened. Around 2.5 million years ago, hominids began chipping away at stones to make tools that were sharper and more useful than ever before. These are known by archaeologists as Oldowan artifacts, after the Olduvai Gorge in East Africa where they were first found, and the species that produced them is called *Homo habilis*, or "handy man," for their achievement. An Oldowan tool doesn't look like much, but it can't be made by a chimpanzee, even one that's trained for the task. A captive bonobo named Kanzi, famous for his advanced linguistic skills, was apprenticed for three years in the art of making a simple Oldowan stone tool but was unable to do so.[25]

These tools give archaeologists a good idea of how our ancestors might have procured their food. They would now have been able to dig up termite colonies or scavenge big game carcasses in the savannah, cutting through bones into the nutritious marrow. The extra calories available to them would have fueled the development of their larger brains, which demanded more metabolic energy. Their larger brains, in turn, gave them the social intelligence to thrive in their newly complex societies, creating a positive feedback cycle, leading to the evolution of even more powerful brains capable of developing more complex tools.[26]

It was, at first, a tediously slow feedback effect. For a million years, hominids got by just fine on their Oldowan technology, but then a breakthrough occurred. A new species of hominid, *Homo erectus*, began producing far more elaborate tools, with sharp points and bilateral symmetry, known as the Acheulean industry. Unlike the Oldowan, an archaeologist can look at an Acheulean tool and make an educated guess from its shape whether it was likely used as a hand ax, a cleaver, a pick, or a knife.[27]

A number of cognitive breakthroughs were necessary for *Homo erectus* to have achieved this new technology. First, they needed to conceptualize the tool they wanted in advance and hold that idea in their minds. Then, they would have had to logically think through each step that would be required and maintain their goal orientation to follow through. This entire sequence of steps would have required what is known in cognitive science as "mental time travel": using one's imagination to create a vision of a hypothetical future—in this case, a future when it would be worthwhile to have a completed tool. With that future image beckoning, they developed a new capacity for self-control, suppressing other claims on their attention while focusing on the ultimate goal of constructing their tool.[28]

All these mental capacities have been shown by cognitive neuroscientists to be mediated by the PFC—the same part of the brain that correlates in size with a species' cultural complexity. Is this mere coincidence? Most likely not.

Tomasello and others argue convincingly that the expansion of the PFC's capabilities as a result of increased social complexity led to a greater capacity for it to develop these other functions.[29]

What is it about the PFC that could transform a set of social skills into an array of such varied capabilities? One critical factor is that the PFC is connected to virtually all other parts of the brain, which gives it a unique capability to merge different inputs—such as vision and hearing, instinctual urges, emotions, and memories—into one integrated story. As humans diverged from other primates, their PFCs evolved far greater connectivity, with a 70 percent increase in the number of possible neuronal connections compared to that of a chimpanzee. This connectivity forms the basis of the human patterning instinct.[30]

Researchers have identified three discrete regions in the modern human PFC, each of which is more activated by certain cognitive tasks: the ventromedial region is more involved in emotional and social processing; the dorsolateral region activates more strongly in abstract, logical processing; and the orbitofrontal is crucial to repressing instinctual drives for a future goal. However, none of these regions works in isolation from the others. Each has its own specialized capabilities while, at the same time, remaining functionally integrated with the other regions.[31]

Could it be the integration of these different domains of PFC processing that led to the emergence of modern humans? Archaeologist Steve Mithen has proposed an influential theory of human evolution that lends support to this possibility. He begins with the premise that early hominids developed specialized, or "domain-specific" skills. For example, they may have developed social intelligence, technical intelligence for tool making, or increased knowledge about the natural world, but at first they were unable to connect these intelligences together. Imagine these domain-specific intelligences like the blades and tools of a Swiss Army knife. You can use each of them, but you'd be hard-pressed to use them all together at the same time. But, Mithen suggests, at some time in the development of the modern human mind, we developed what he calls "cognitive fluidity," whereby we started combining these domain-specific intelligences into an integrated meta-intelligence.[32]

Modern humans achieve much of this cognitive fluidity by using a particular capability of the PFC known as "working memory": the ability to consciously hold a variety of things in our mind for a short time. For example, if someone tells you a phone number and you have to go across the room to write it down, you'll use your working memory to hold it in your mind until it's down on paper, at which point your memory is freed up for something else. But working memory is more than just short-term memory. Comparable to the random access memory of a computer, it's the process used by the mind to keep enough discrete items up and running so they can be combined to arrive at a new understanding or a new plan. It's sometimes referred to as a "global workspace" for the brain, or "the blackboard of the mind."[33]

Having a "blackboard" in your mind is clearly a helpful way of keeping disparate bits of information available for your PFC to construct a new pattern of meaning out of them. But what happens when the blackboard gets filled up? A widely known fact about our working memory capacity is that it can only hold about seven pieces of information at one time. That might be barely enough to construct an Acheulean tool, but it could hardly cope with the "cognitive fluidity" arising from merging the different domains of human intelligence. The solution to this capacity constraint came in the form of a cognitive breakthrough that has allowed humans to think in a way that, most likely, no other creature on earth has ever achieved: symbolic thought.

A symbol is something that has a purely arbitrary relationship to what it signifies, which can only be understood by someone who shares the same code. To get a feeling for the unique power of a symbol, imagine it's time to feed your pet dog. You open the can, and your dog comes running because he smells the food. But now, suppose that instead of giving your hungry dog the food, you write on a piece of paper "FOOD IN TEN MINUTES" and put it in your dog's bowl. The piece of paper and the writing have no intrinsic connection with the food. They are merely a symbolic representation. Clearly, your dog doesn't understand symbols, and now he's pawing at the pantry door trying to get to his food.[34]

Thinking in symbols allows humans to break through the capacity constraints of working memory and construct the elaborate patterns of meaning that shape our lives. To understand how it can do this, imagine for a moment our working memory as a literal blackboard. Now, imagine a teacher asking twenty-five children to come up and write on the blackboard what they had to eat that morning before they came to school. The blackboard would quickly fill up with words like "cereal" and "eggs," "pancakes" and "waffles." Now, suppose that, once the blackboard's filled up, the teacher erases it all and just writes on the blackboard the word "BREAKFAST." That one word, by common consent, symbolizes everything that was previously written on the blackboard. And now it's freed up the rest of the blackboard for anything else.

That's the powerful effect the use of symbols has on human cognition. But there's another equally powerful aspect of writing that one word, "BREAKFAST," on the blackboard. Every schoolchild has her own experience of what she ate that morning, but, by sharing in the symbol BREAKFAST, she can rise above the specifics of her own particular meal and understand that there's something more abstract being communicated, referring to the meal all the kids had before they came to school, regardless of what it was. For this reason, symbols are an astonishingly powerful means of communicating, allowing people to transcend their individual experiences and share them with others.[35]

Of all the characteristics that differentiate humans from other primates, it's probably our capacity for symbolic thought that is the most crucial, forming the basis for everything, both good and evil, that humans have achieved in our time on the earth. In the memorable words of philosopher Ernst Cassirer, "No longer in a merely physical universe, man lives in a symbolic universe. Language, myth, art, and religion are parts of this universe. They are the varied threads which weave the symbolic net, the tangled web of human experience. All human progress in thought and experience refines upon and strengthens this net."[36]

So what do we make of this new, science-based story of how we became human? Are we really competitive, selfish, and Machiavellian at heart? That certainly describes one aspect of our nature, one that is evolutionarily ancient, which we share with other primates. Are we intrinsically cooperative and empathic, defined by our shared intentionality? In a sense, that's a more accurate description of human uniqueness, since these traits evolved only after our ancestral line bifurcated from that of other primates. Ultimately, though, perhaps the uniquely defining characteristic of humanity is the patterning instinct we evolved along the way, which allowed us to develop the capacity for symbolic thought, and which incessantly drives us to construct patterns of meaning in everything we experience. It's through these patterns that we're able to look back over our history and try to make sense out of it, to look forward to our future and try to direct where it will take us.

There was, however, a crucial ingredient required before any patterns of meaning could be shared between one person and another. As we've noted, symbols are an arbitrary form of communication. Symbolic thought could only be communicated with others if each individual could agree on the code to be used in referencing what they meant. It had to be a code that everyone could learn and that could be communicated very easily, taking into account the vast array of different things that could carry symbolic meaning. In short, it needed language—that all-encompassing network of symbols that we'll explore in the next chapter.

Chapter 2

THE MAGICAL WEAVE OF LANGUAGE

Vervet monkeys, which live in the forests of eastern Africa, are unbearably cute. They have little black faces with eyes that peer out through a shock of lighter-colored fur. They also have a trick that has earned them a special place among language researchers. The monkeys have three important natural predators—leopards, eagles, and pythons—each of which has a different way of attacking them: jumping at them, swooping down from the sky, or lunging up from the ground. Back in 1980, researchers discovered that the vervet monkeys use different vocalizations to warn their group of each predator: short tonal calls for leopards, low-pitched staccato grunts for eagles, and high-pitched "chutters" for snakes. When the monkeys hear the leopard call, they climb up in the trees; an eagle call causes them to look up or run into dense bush; and a snake call has them looking down at the ground around them. The researchers could induce the different behaviors in the monkeys simply by playing tape recordings of each call. These smart monkeys have found a way to categorize their primary threats and use arbitrary sounds to distinguish them. As we saw in the last chapter, that means they are communicating in symbols to each other. So does that mean they have language?[1]

To answer this question, let's turn from the African forest to somewhere in the United States and consider the following sentence:

> You remember that guy from New York we met at the cocktail party the other day, who told us that if the Fed doesn't ease the money supply, stocks would fall?

It seems like a simple enough sentence, but there's a lot going on under the surface. As we investigate how language emerged among early humans in this chapter, we'll find in the difference between that sentence and the calls of the vervet monkeys some crucial ingredients that allowed our ancestors to begin to pattern meaning into their world.

Language has a central role to play in the story of humanity's patterning instinct. Without it, there would be no way for one person to transmit their particular patterns of meaning to another. We would all live in islands of experience, connected to each other by our feelings but unable to share with anyone else whatever constructions of meaning arose within our own consciousness. Language is the primary vehicle for how a culture's values get transmitted to each new generation—and, consequently, how the direction of history gets determined. We need to understand some essentials about how language works before we can make further sense of the history of humanity's search for meaning.

For something we all use every day of our lives, there is an astonishing amount of disagreement among the experts about language. Some believe it evolved slowly beginning millions of years ago; others believe it appeared suddenly, perhaps as recently as forty thousand years ago. Some famous theorists have proposed we have a "language instinct," a specialized set of neural pathways that evolved to comprehend the unique attributes of language. Other researchers argue back that this is impossible, and what's intrinsic to human brains is something more fundamental than language. This chapter will untangle some of the debates about language that continue to exercise the experts and, in doing so, will uncover some insights into the very nature of how we think.

What's Special about Language?

When a vervet monkey looks up and gives a low-pitched grunt, she's not really saying the word "eagle." She's saying, with that one grunt, "There's an eagle coming, and we'd all better head for the bushes." If she grunted twice, that wouldn't mean "two eagles." And if she followed her grunt with a chutter, that wouldn't mean, "An eagle just attacked a snake." Smart as they are, vervet monkeys can't rise above the context of their particular situation or combine their sounds to make new meanings. Each vocalization stands alone and causes a predictable response in the other monkeys.

When humans talk, on the other hand, we are constantly linking words together to create meanings that emerge in new and sometimes unexpected ways. This combinatory power, which can create an infinite array of meanings from a finite set of words, is an essential part of language that sets it apart from the vervet calls and is known as syntax.[2]

Let's go back to that earlier example sentence and begin with the words "cocktail party." A cocktail means a mixed drink. A party is a group of people getting together. But we all know that "cocktail party" refers to a specific type of party. It isn't necessary for anyone to actually be drinking a cocktail to make it a "cocktail party." Hosts might serve wine and champagne, but we wouldn't call it a "wine and champagne party." This crucial element of language takes two completely separate aspects of reality—a mixed drink and a social gathering—and blends them together, just like the ingredients of a cocktail, to create a brand-new concept—a process that's referred to as conceptual blending.[3]

The complexity really gets going when we come to phrases like "ease the money supply" and "stocks would fall." Here, we meet one of the crucial aspects of modern language: the use of metaphors to convey abstract meaning. We're so used to these metaphors in our daily language that we don't even consider them as such. But ponder for a moment what it means to "ease the money supply." There's an implicit image of some kind of reservoir of liquid, perhaps water, that would normally flow out to people. But someone's hands are on a lever of some sort, keeping the supply controlled. Now, to let everyone have a little more of the liquid, this person—the Fed—eases up on the lever, allowing more to flow out. Similarly, stocks don't really fall. People, animals, or things might fall off a table or out of a tree. But, of course, when something falls, it goes from a high position to a lower position. So, we naturally understand that a falling stock is one whose price is moving from higher to lower, and we get so accustomed to this form of conceptual blending that we stop thinking about where the metaphor originally came from.[4]

There's still more amazing complexity to that simple sentence. Notice that it's referring to someone we met "the other day." He's not there talking to us now. It all happened in another place and time, but, through language, we can bring the past back to the present in a matter of seconds, and we can whisk people or things from anywhere in the universe to be present in our minds with just a few words. This uncanny power of language to refer to absent entities is known as displacement.[5]

The wizardry of language goes even further. Consider that we were being asked to imagine a scenario in which stocks would fall if the Fed didn't ease the money supply. This is something that hasn't actually happened. It may never happen. But we can still talk about the scenario with as much ease as if it were happening right now. This ability of language to create hypothetical situations out of thin air is known as a counterfactual.

There's already a lot to be impressed about in that one sentence, but the coup de grace of this sentence—and most other sentences in every language of the world—is its syntax. If language is like a net of symbols, we can think of syntax as a magical weave that can link each section of the net to any other section at a moment's notice. Look at how many miraculous conceptual leaps we make while still holding a meaningful narrative together in our minds. (1) "You remember" (in a questioning tone): *access our memory*; (2) "that guy": *focus on the category of male humans*; (3) "from New York": *narrow down that category based on where the person is from*; (4) "we met at the cocktail party the other day": *create a mental image of the party;* (5) "who told us": *shift from a mere recall of the person to a recollection of the conversation;* (6) "if the Fed doesn't ease the money supply . . .": *abrupt transition from an image of the cocktail party to a hypothetical financial scenario.*

This magical weaving that we pull off incessantly without even being aware of it is known as recursion and is the most powerful and characteristic feature of modern language. How and when did it first appear? As we know from the previous chapter, there's one part of the human brain that's uniquely connected to permit the cognitive fluidity required for recursion: the prefrontal cortex. Does it hold some clues to the emergence of human language?[6]

The PFC hasn't historically enjoyed much press regarding language. There are two areas in the left hemisphere of the brain—known as Broca's and Wernicke's areas, after the physicians who discovered them—that have attracted most of the attention and are generally viewed as the brain's language centers. However, while these areas are indispensable for language, they are also actively used by other nonlinguistic primates. Broca's area is adjacent to the part of the brain that controls our mouth, tongue, and larynx, and Wernicke's area is adjacent to our auditory cortex. Most likely, these areas evolved as key nodes in the language network of the brain, enabling us to speak the right words and understand what we hear, which would explain why people lose the ability to speak normally when these areas are damaged. Essential for language, undoubtedly, but not necessarily pointing us to the source of its uniqueness in humans.[7]

In recent years, though, cognitive scientists have begun to recognize the PFC's central role in the emergence of language. With its unique ability to integrate so many different inputs from various parts of the brain, only the PFC seems capable of creating symbolic associations through words and then weaving them into the wondrous web of syntax, thus constructing meaning out of all the disparate elements.[8]

If the PFC was, in fact, a central driver of the emergence of language, what light does that shed on those raging debates about when and how language evolved and whether there is something that can be called a "language instinct"? To answer that, we need to understand a little more about the social context in which language emerged.

From Grooming to Gossip

Imagine you're standing in a cafeteria line. You hear multiple conversations around you: "I heard she bought it in . . .", "Can you believe what Joe did . . .", "How much did that cost you . . .", "So I said to him. . . ." Random, meaningless gossip. But don't be so quick to dismiss it. What you're hearing may be the very foundation of human language and, as such, a key to our entire human civilization.

This is the remarkable and influential hypothesis of anthropologists Leslie Aiello and Robin Dunbar. It begins with the well-recognized fact that chimpanzees and other primates use the time spent grooming each other as an important mode of social interaction through which they form and maintain cliques and social hierarchies. Aiello and Dunbar ingeniously calculated how much time different species needed to spend grooming for their social group to remain cohesive. Larger groups required significantly more time, with some populations spending as much as 20 percent of their day grooming. Based on the group sizes early humans probably lived in, they would have had to spend 30–45 percent of their day grooming to maintain social cohesion—probably an unsustainable amount of time. Gradually, mimetic forms of communication—gestures, grunts, and other vocalizations—would have become more significant, offering a more efficient form of social interaction than grooming, until finally developing into language.[9]

Language, then, can be understood as a network enabling enhanced communication. In fact, the emergence of language offers an ancient parallel to the recent growth of the internet. One person could no more come up with language than one computer could create the internet. In each case, the individual node—a human brain or a computer—needed to develop enough processing power to participate in a meaningful network, but, once it got going, the network itself became far more important as a driver of change than any single node.[10]

Another interesting parallel between language and the internet is that, in both cases, their growth was self-organized, an integrated network emerging from a vast assemblage of unique interactions without a preordained design. Just as the complexity of the internet quickly surpassed anything one individual could devise, so the complexity of language was far greater than any individual mind could have conceived. Language was an emergent phenomenon of the increasingly elaborate social interaction of early human communities, comparable to other emergent phenomena arising from complex group interactions in the natural world, such as the intelligence of beehives and ant colonies, or the majestic patterns in the sky created by flocks of starlings.[11]

Language Evolution: "Gradual and Early" or "Sudden and Recent"?

It seems, at first sight, straightforward. If language evolved socially as a sophisticated substitute for grooming, then it must have happened gradually and a long time ago. It's therefore no surprise that Aiello and Dunbar are proponents of the "gradual and early" language hypothesis, arguing that there was a transition from mimetic forms of communication beginning as far back as two million years ago. They, along with other leading anthropologists, believe that language most likely "crossed the Rubicon" to its modern state about three hundred thousand years ago, shortly before the appearance of anatomically modern humans.[12]

There is, however, a troubling issue with this theory. Once we recognize that language is a network of symbols, it becomes clear that whoever could produce language must have been thinking symbolically and, therefore, would likely have produced other material expressions of symbolism. It seems reasonable to expect that language users would have left some trace of symbolic artifacts, such as painted shells, figurative carvings, cave paintings, and maybe even musical instruments.

The archeological evidence does indeed point to a time when all these expressions of symbolic behavior suddenly emerged. There's just one problem. That time was not three hundred thousand years ago but around forty thousand years ago in Europe, when a veritable explosion of symbolic expression occurred, known as the Upper Paleolithic revolution (which will be discussed in more detail in the following chapter). Archaeologists have found a vast array of remains from that time, including body decorations, sophisticated hunting gear, ritual artifacts, beautiful cave paintings, and—yes, even musical instruments. Was this, then, the period when language made a sudden and recent appearance in human history?[13]

Those who emphasize the symbolic nature of language are, not surprisingly, the strongest proponents of the "sudden and recent" school of language emergence. Notable among them is the psychologist-archaeologist team of Bill Noble and Iain Davidson, who argue that modern language permitted the sophisticated information flows and generation of new ideas that enabled the crescendo of Upper Paleolithic creativity.[14]

The disagreement is not just a matter of timing. It's also about how language arose. Noble and Davidson, along with other theorists, believe that because of the networked nature of language, you can no more have a "half language" than you can be half pregnant. The logic is powerful. In much the same way that the internet is rapidly transforming the modern world, once a group of humans realized that a symbol (i.e., a word) could relate to another symbol through syntax, the sky was the limit. Any word could work. All they needed was the set of neural connections to make the realization in the first place. Once a large enough community stumbled upon this miraculous power, there would have been no going back. Once symbols were woven into language, this would have rapidly reinforced other symbolic networks, such as art, religion, and tool use, which, in turn, would have made the use of language even more indispensable.[15]

It's a powerful argument. And one that seems incompatible with the "gradual and early" camp. How should we make sense of it? Perhaps there's another way to approach the problem, by turning to that other controversy about whether or not there's a "language instinct." Surely this would help resolve the issue? After all, if there is a language instinct, it must be embedded so deeply in the human psyche that we would have been talking to each other at least a few hundred thousand years ago. So let's see what light this other debate sheds on the problem.

A Language Instinct?

The Language Instinct is a popular book written by renowned cognitive scientist Steven Pinker. Pinker's title says it all, and he makes no bones about his position in the language debate. "Language is not a cultural artifact that we learn the way we learn to tell time or how the federal government works," he writes. "Instead, it is a distinct piece of the biological makeup of our brains." He uses the word "instinct," he explains, "because people know how to talk in more or less the sense that spiders know how to spin webs." Drawing a clear line in the sand, Pinker makes his case: "Language is no more a cultural invention than is upright posture. It is not a manifestation of a general capacity to use symbols."[16]

Pinker follows a widely respected tradition begun by Noam Chomsky, considered the father of modern linguistics. Chomsky believes every human being has an innate knowledge of language, which he calls a "universal grammar." Differences in languages around the world merely reflect superficial variations in how the universal grammar is interpreted by different cultures. Pinker calls this universal grammar "mentalese," explaining that knowing a language is simply "knowing how to translate mentalese into strings of words and vice versa. People without language would still have mentalese."[17]

If language were in fact an instinct, that would surely support the "gradual and early" camp of language evolution, and here Pinker makes himself equally clear, arguing that "there must have been a series of steps leading from no language at all to language as we now find it, each step small enough to have been produced by a random mutation or recombination."[18]

This theory has been widely influential for many years. However, a barrage of criticism has recently been leveled against it based on the premise that language is far too intricate and rapidly changing for any combination of genes to have evolved to control for it specifically. It seems to make more sense to look for the underlying capabilities that evolved to enable language than to view language itself as a natural product of evolution.

To take an extreme example for the sake of clarity, if someone argued there was a "driving instinct" because of the ease with which most people learn to drive a car, we'd probably argue back that we should instead look for the underlying human traits that permitted driving to become ubiquitous, such as our ability to see things far away, to respond quickly to changes in the line of vision, to rapidly assess changes in speed, and to employ sophisticated hand-eye-foot coordination. Just as automobiles and roads took their shape as a result of human traits and capabilities, so language evolved as a function of what our brains were capable of doing. In the words of one team of researchers, "Language is easy for us to learn and use, not because our brains embody knowledge of language, but because language has adapted to our brains."[19]

An important breakthrough in this debate has been achieved by researcher

Patricia Kuhl, who studied how infants distinguish between the different sounds they hear when people speak to them. Kuhl discovered that long before infants have any idea that such a thing as language exists, they are already able to distinguish the different phonetic units that make up human speech. An infant, in her first six months, will discriminate between all kinds of phonetic units, regardless of the language used. However, by nine months, she's already more interested in the phonetic units of her particular language. American infants listen longer to English words, while Dutch infants show a preference for Dutch words.

By twelve months, the infant has learned to ignore phonetic units that don't exist in her native language and can no longer discriminate their phonetic contrasts. From the very beginning, Kuhl theorizes, an infant's mind looks for patterns in the sounds she hears, locking into the more frequent sound patterns. As time goes on, the infant becomes increasingly adept at distinguishing the sound patterns of her own language and ignoring those that don't fit into the patterns she's already identified. This amounts to strong evidence that humans in fact possess a patterning instinct rather than a language instinct. Because all infants grow up in societies where language is spoken, this underlying patterning instinct locks into the patterns of language, and it's this second-order application of the patterning instinct that Chomsky and Pinker have seen as a language instinct.[20]

Kuhl's research points to something beyond this particular language debate. It shows, in her words, that "language experience warps perception." By a very early age, an infant's brain has literally been shaped by the language she hears around her, causing her to notice some distinctions in sounds and ignore others. This early shaping quickly hardens, like a resin, and is set for the rest of her life. As an example, Kuhl describes how Japanese speakers are unable to distinguish between the sounds /r/ and /l/, even though to a Western speaker the distinction seems obvious.[21]

If we have a patterning instinct, and the sounds we hear as infants affect the sound patterns we hear for the rest of our lives, what does that mean for other kinds of patterns in language? After all, language is not just about sounds; it's also about symbols and meaning. Is it possible that language shapes our perception, not just of the sounds we hear, but of the very symbols we perceive as having meaning? If this is the case, it implies that language may have been instrumental in shaping how we think, perhaps even how the connections evolved within our brains.

The Coevolution of Language and the PFC

Over the past three million years, the size of the human brain in proportion to the body has steadily increased, with the PFC showing even more rapid growth. Did language have a part to play in this evolutionary path? If so, what came first, language or a more powerful PFC? Which is the chicken, and which is the egg?

Imagine the world of our hominid ancestors over those three million years. It was a mimetic, highly social world with increasingly complex group dynamics. Communication probably involved a combination of touching, gesturing, facial expressions, and complex vocalizations, including the many kinds of grunts, growls, shrieks, and laughs that we still make to this day. Applying Kuhl's findings, we can imagine how a prehuman growing up in mimetic society would hear, see, and feel the complex communication going on around her, and how her PFC would shape itself accordingly. Those infants whose PFCs were able to make the best connections would be more successful at realizing how the complex mélange of grunts, rhythms, gestures, and expressions around them patterned themselves into social meaning. As they grew up, they would be better integrated within their community and, as such, more likely to pass on their genes for enhanced PFC connectivity to the next generation. The adaptive effect of language would have been especially powerful at a group level: groups more effective at using language would have outcompeted others and, consequently, left more descendants. It was no longer the biggest, fastest, or strongest prehumans who were most successful, but the ones with the most advanced PFCs.[22]

All this could have taken place before the emergence of modern language with syntax and recursion. However, when modern language did eventually emerge, it's easy to imagine how it would have drastically ratcheted up the evolutionary growth of the PFC. It would have enabled societies to reach new levels of social complexity, rewarding the individuals and groups that mastered it best and would therefore have been more successful in passing their PFC-enhanced genes to the next generation. In this way, we can understand language and the PFC to have coevolved, each ratcheting up enhancements in the other.[23]

How does this help us settle the debate about when language emerged? The evidence for both the "early and gradual" and the "recent and sudden" camps seems powerful. Is it possible that somehow they could both be right?

Three Stages of Language Evolution

There is at least one expert who thinks so: linguist Ray Jackendoff, who suggests that language may have evolved in different stages, with major transitions occurring between them. In a paper published in 1999, Jackendoff takes the role of peacemaker, noting that his proposal could "help defuse a long-running dispute." He points out that if his theory became widely accepted, it would no longer be meaningful to ask whether one or another hominid "had language." Rather, the question should be "what elements of a language capacity" a particular hominid had.[24]

Jackendoff proposed nine different phases of language development, which can be condensed into three clearly demarcated stages. These three stages can be correlated to different levels of tool technology found in the archaeological record, so an approximate time frame can be applied to each stage. The last stage, the transition to modern language, would be contemporaneous with the Upper Paleolithic revolution and therefore solve the conundrum posed by the "sudden and recent" camp. Using the analogy of language as a "net of symbols," we can visualize each stage as a different kind of net: the first stage like a small net that you might use to catch a single fish in a pond; the second stage analogous to a series of small nets tied together; and the third stage as the vast kind of net that a modern trawler uses to catch fish on an industrial scale. Here's how each stage looks.

Stage 1: Mimetic language. This stage probably began several million years ago, and it continued until slightly before the advent of modern *Homo sapiens*, around two hundred thousand to three hundred thousand years ago. Concurrent with the mimetic stage of human development, it would have involved single words that could be used in different contexts, thus differentiating them from the vervet calls discussed earlier, which only have meaning in a particular context. Examples of these words could be *shhh*, *yes*, *no*, or *hot*. Jackendoff gives the example of a toddler first learning language who says the single word *kitty* to draw attention to a cat, ask where it is, call it, or point out something that resembles it. At a campfire a million years ago, a hominid may have pointed to a stone next to the fire and said "hot!" and then might later have caused his friends to laugh by using the same word to describe how he felt after running on a sunny day.[25]

The correlative level of technology would have been the Oldowan and Acheulean stone tools that persisted over millions of years. Interestingly, a recent study employed brain scanning technology to analyze what parts of the brain people use when they make these kinds of stone tools. Oldowan toolmaking showed no PFC activity at all, while Acheulean tools required limited use of the PFC, activating an area that mediates hierarchically organized action sequences.[26]

Stage 2: Protolanguage. This stage most likely emerged around three hundred thousand years ago (when Aiello and Dunbar believe language "crossed the Rubicon") and would have involved chains of words linked together in a simple sentence, but without modern syntax. Going back to our Stone Age campfire, imagine that the fire's gone out, but an early human wants to tell his friends the stones from the fire are still hot. He might point to the area and say "stone hot fire" or "fire hot stone" or even "hot fire stone." Different concepts are now being placed together to create a far more valuable emergent meaning, but the words are still chained together without the magical weave of syntax. The order of the words does not affect the meaning.[27]

Notably, it was around three hundred thousand years ago that new advances in stone tool technology left behind the old Acheulean stagnation. These innovative techniques, known as Levallois technology, show an order-of-magnitude increase in complexity, with differences between geographical regions suggesting the emergence of particular cultural traditions. One anthropologist notes that they required the kind of complex problem-solving, planning, and coordination that is mediated by the PFC and that may have influenced its evolution.[28]

Stage 3: Modern language. This stage may have begun to emerge around a hundred thousand years ago, but it probably only achieved the magical weave of full syntax around the time of the Upper Paleolithic revolution, about forty thousand years ago. By this time, our human ancestor could have told his friend, "I put the stone you gave me in the fire, and now it's hot," with syntax and recursion. The correlative level of technology is the sophisticated grinding and pounding tools, spear throwers, bows, nets, and boomerangs associated with the Upper Paleolithic revolution. The same brains that could handle syntax and recursion could also handle the complex planning required to conceptualize and make these advanced tools.

But the Upper Paleolithic revolution involved more than sophisticated tools. It also delivered the first evidence of human behavior that was not purely functional but had symbolic significance. For the first time, humans were creating art, regularly decorating their bodies, and constructing musical instruments and ritual artifacts. These innovations may correlate with one particular aspect of language that also likely emerged at this time: the use of metaphor.

The Metaphoric Threshold

We generally think of metaphor as a technique used by poets, not necessarily a part of our everyday speech. However, in a groundbreaking book published in 1980, cognitive philosophers George Lakoff and Mark Johnson show how virtually every aspect of our normal speech uses hidden metaphors to communicate abstract ideas and concepts. We saw earlier how simple statements like "stocks falling" or "easing the money supply" utilize metaphors that work below our conscious awareness. If you examine your regular speech, you will soon discover that it is virtually impossible to say something with any level of abstraction without using a metaphor that usually relates to something more concrete.[29]

Here are some simple examples of how these unconscious metaphors work:

"I gave you that idea"—AN IDEA IS AN OBJECT
"My spirits rose"; "I fell into a depression"—HAPPY IS UP; SAD IS DOWN
"He broke under cross-examination"—THE MIND IS A BRITTLE OBJECT
"I've had a full life"—LIFE IS A CONTAINER
"She gave me a warm smile"—FACIAL EXPRESSION IS A GIFT; INTIMACY IS WARMTH.

The examples are limitless; it's fascinating to observe your own language and that of others around you, to discover the full extent of our reliance on metaphors. In the Upper Paleolithic example, this new form of thought might have enabled our human ancestor to turn to his friend and say, "Since I lost my son, my heart has turned to stone."

Without the use of metaphor, we are simply unable to conceptualize and communicate abstract thoughts about feelings or ideas. Therefore, the first use of metaphor in language was not just another milestone in the increased sophistication of human linguistic abilities. It was the threshold that human thought had to cross to achieve abstract thought of any kind, including the search for meaning in life and the creation of mythic and religious ideas. In short, the crossing of this metaphoric threshold opened the floodgates to the power of the patterning instinct and catalyzed the Upper Paleolithic revolution.

This, in turn, led to the emergence of a new mythic consciousness in human thought, imposing meaning on the natural world based on a metaphoric transformation of the tangible qualities of everyday life, using them as scaffolding for more abstract conceptions. The patterning instinct that evolved through community would now be applied to the vast universe about which early humans were becoming aware. The new world of mythic consciousness that emerged will be the subject of the next chapter.

Chapter 3

THE RISE OF MYTHIC CONSCIOUSNESS

The Great Leap Forward

In September 1940 in southern France, four boys entered a cave their dog had discovered some days earlier, and they stumbled upon a breathtaking spectacle. There, on the cave walls, were mysterious ancient paintings featuring all kinds of strange animals in motion. These boys were the first modern humans to cast their eyes on what turned out to be the most dramatic spectacle of Paleolithic cave art in the world. The Lascaux Cave, along with several hundred others scattered around Europe, contains more than six hundred magnificent paintings of aurochs (the wild ancestor of domestic cattle), horses, and deer, some as big as fifteen feet long. Even more astonishing than the size and number of paintings is their stunning sophistication and beauty. This is no mere "primitive" art but an expression of the power and mystery of the natural world that awes us today as much as the greatest art of more recent times (figure 3.1). What did these images mean to those early humans who spent so many painstaking hours on their creation? We'll never know for sure, but, in this chapter and the next, we'll explore the new mythic consciousness emerging among our ancestors at that time—and perhaps sneak a few insights into what they might have been expressing on those cave walls.[1]

The Lascaux Cave paintings have been dated to approximately seventeen thousand years ago, which means that, ancient as they are, they were part of a tradition that had already been flourishing for about fifteen thousand years. Recently, a site named Hohle Fels in Germany has yielded a slew of magnificent carved ivory specimens, dating as far back as thirty-five thousand years ago, including a bird figurine; a "Venus" figure with huge breasts and carefully carved genitalia; three "Lion-men" with human bodies and lion heads; and the world's earliest known musical instrument, a bone flute complete with well-spaced holes (figures 3.2 a-d). These beautiful objects were constructed with as much aesthetic sophistication as the Lascaux paintings, powerfully demonstrating that the first modern humans in Europe were already highly accomplished artists.[2]

Figure 3.1: Aurochs cave painting from Lascaux Cave

When you look at these intense artistic expressions, it's easy to understand what archaeologists mean when they say this was the time that humans achieved "cultural modernity." We may not understand the precise significance of the Venus or the Lion-man, but there's no doubt they held symbolic meaning to their makers. This revolution in symbolic thought occurred across virtually every aspect of human behavior. For the first time, humans were sewing garments with fine needles; using kilns to bake ceramic figures; engaging in long-distance trade; utilizing storage facilities; and organizing their homes just like we do today, with different spaces for kitchens, sleeping areas, and eating. This period in history has been aptly summed up by Jared Diamond as humanity's "Great Leap Forward."[3]

It's an impressive moment in history. However, some archaeologists have recently looked past these spectacular accomplishments to ask why it didn't happen sooner. It's generally agreed that humans were anatomically modern 150,000 years ago or earlier. Why did it take so long for symbolic thinking to get going? This rather awkward question was first framed by archaeologist Colin Renfrew, who referred to it as the "sapient paradox."[4]

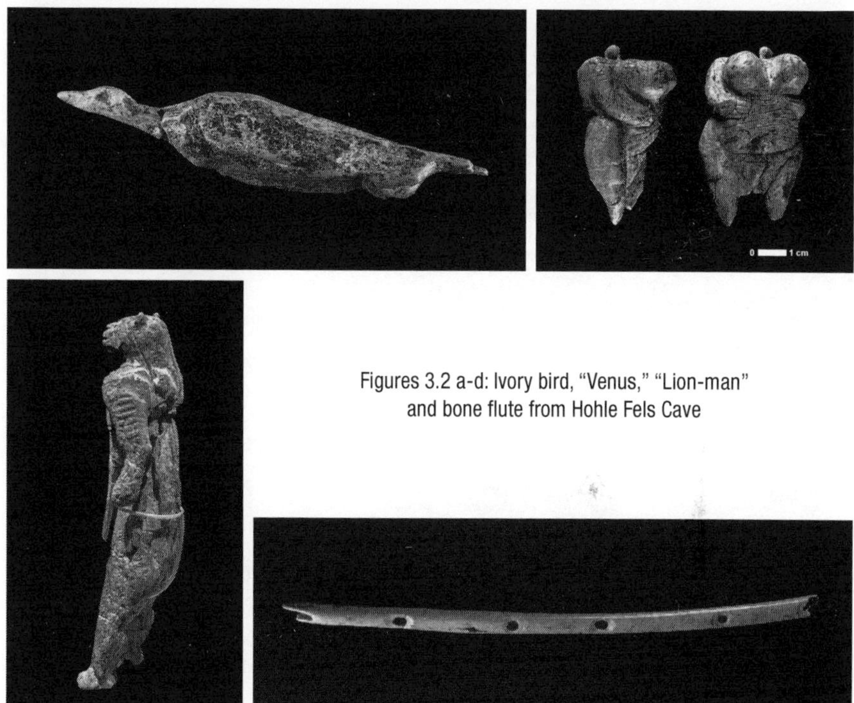

Figures 3.2 a-d: Ivory bird, "Venus," "Lion-man" and bone flute from Hohle Fels Cave

Out of Africa

According to a growing number of experts, it actually did happen sooner. A lot sooner. In fact, there's evidence that the beginnings of cultural modernity may have occurred at least seventy-five thousand years ago. It's just that these early stirrings of modernity showed up not in Europe but in southern Africa. In recent years, excavations at Blombos Cave on the coastline of South Africa have uncovered startling new evidence of early symbolic behavior by our human ancestors. The findings include engraved ostrich eggshells probably used as personal ornaments, but the most striking treasure unearthed to date has been one particular piece of ochre engraved with a series of complex cross-hatches (figure 3.3). Renfrew and fellow archaeologist Paul Mellars feel certain that this deliberate patterning represents "the earliest unambiguous forms of abstract 'art' so far recorded" and suggest that "the human revolution developed first in Africa . . . between 150,000 and 70,000 years ago."[5]

Figure 3.3: Ochre with cross-hatching from Blombos Cave

What does that say, then, about the Great Leap Forward? Doesn't it begin to seem like a series of steps rather than a great leap? Two archaeologists who think so, Sally McBrearty and Alison Brooks, have caused a stir arguing exactly this point, calling it "the revolution that wasn't." Granted, some cross-hatching and engraved eggshells are not as impressive as the later explosion of symbolic thinking in Europe, but they are valuable clues to the origins of modern humans.[6]

In place of the Great Leap Forward, another epic story has moved into the foreground. The story, called by some "Out of Africa," has emerged through advances in DNA analysis, which have enabled scientists to provide accurate time estimates regarding the migrations of different groups. Around seventy thousand years ago, a certain lineage of humans expanded throughout Africa, reaching as far north as Ethiopia. A small contingent, no more than a few hundred strong, then migrated across the mouth of the Red Sea, through Arabia and eastward along southern Asia until reaching Australia. At some point during this migration, a splinter group headed north into western Asia, eventually arriving in Europe, where their descendants would instigate the Upper

Paleolithic "revolution." A couple of startling implications arise from this epic journey. The first is that all non-Africans alive today are descendants of the small group that made its way across the Red Sea. Second, because of this, there is far wider genetic diversity among different African populations than among all other non-Africans on the planet.[7]

It's a grand story, but it still doesn't explain the sapient paradox. If humans were already modern in their behavior, why is there so little to show for it in the archaeological record until the explosion of artifacts in Europe forty thousand years ago? Some argue for a genetic mutation that occurred then, allowing for the flourishing of symbolic thought. An alternative view is that a slight increase in the efficiency of hunting technology, along with expanded trading networks between different groups, may have led to a sustained growth in population, creating a positive feedback loop in which innovations would, in turn, be copied by other communities. This could have led to a cultural ratchet effect, with each improvement building on the previous one until a whole new level of technological sophistication was reached.[8]

Neither of these theories, however, is a sufficient explanation for the timing of the Upper Paleolithic revolution. The population densities in Europe were initially no greater than those in Africa, and those who made it to Europe were the same genetic group as those remaining in Ethiopia. So is there any other way to resolve the sapient paradox? An important clue might be found in what these migrants encountered when they arrived in Europe.

When modern humans first showed up in Europe, the continent was already populated by Neanderthals, close cousins of *Homo sapiens* who had diverged genetically a few hundred thousand years earlier. The Neanderthals had withstood more than two hundred thousand years of climatic fluctuations in the cold reaches of Ice Age Europe, and, with their heavyset bodies, they would have seemed better equipped than the *Homo sapiens* arriving from Africa to handle Europe's freezing climate. But ten thousand years after *Homo sapiens* appeared on the scene, the Neanderthals were extinct.[9]

To many anthropologists, the evidence seems cut-and-dried: the Neanderthals were outcompeted and driven to extinction by their cognitively superior cousins. There's even been mention of a "Pleistocene holocaust," prompting some observers to look at our more recent history and speculate that if we're so intolerant of other races, how much more ruthless might we have been to a competing species?[10]

Others argue that the situation was not so simple. In fact, they claim, the

Neanderthals also showed evidence of symbolic behavior. Traditionally, when bone tools and ornaments were dug up from Neanderthal sites, they were dismissed with arguments that the Neanderthals were just mimicking the *Homo sapiens* invaders without understanding the true meaning of these items. But, recently, the same kind of ornaments have been discovered dating back to thousands of years before modern humans arrived, offering powerful evidence of Neanderthal symbolic thought. So what should we make of that?[11]

A possible solution arises if we consider the three stages of language evolution proposed in the previous chapter. Under that hypothesis, the Neanderthals may have reached the second stage, which correlates with their Levallois stone-working technology, but been unable to make the leap across the metaphoric threshold to modern language with recursion. It's easy to imagine how a group that could say to each other "fire stone hot" would be outcompeted by another group that could say "I put the stone that you gave me in the fire, and now it's hot."[12*]

Could the encounter between *Homo sapiens* and Neanderthals have been the catalyst that sparked the dramatic achievements of the Upper Paleolithic revolution? The competition between the two species was probably fierce and likely endured for thousands of years. As we know from modern history, warfare is frequently the grim handmaiden of major technological innovation, and it's reasonable to believe the same could have been true of that much earlier conflict. Another possibility is that the challenges of the Ice Age in Europe forced the physically vulnerable *Homo sapiens* to develop new coping strategies, requiring the greater social complexity that may have launched a cultural transformation. We may never completely settle this question, but one thing we know for sure is that by thirty thousand years ago, the Neanderthals were extinct. There was only one subspecies of *Homo* left in the world, from which we are all descended.[13*]

The Tragedy of Cognition

The power of the patterning instinct, even in this early stage of history, was impressive. The PFC's unique connectivity was responsible for theory of mind, which allowed people to see others as independent agents; for creating hierarchies of thoughts, leading to complex tools and the recursion of language; and for crossing the metaphoric threshold that permitted humans to think and communicate abstract thoughts. But these powers came at a terrible cost, something that has been fittingly named the "tragedy of cognition."[14]

Once you understand that those around you are thinking and feeling people like you, a disturbing crescendo of implications is likely to occur in your mind when somebody dies. It's clear that the life force previously animating that person has vanished. As that happens to those around you, you soon realize this will eventually be your own fate, leading to profound dread at the inevitable future reality of your own death.[15]

It seems reasonable to assume there's some connection between that dread of death and the earliest signs of our ancestors burying their dead. The first deliberate burials discovered date back to about ninety-five thousand years ago, before even the cross-hatched ochre from Blombos Cave, and there's clear evidence the Neanderthals also buried their dead. So this tragedy of cognition seems to have materialized from an early phase in our symbolic thought, which has been aptly described as "the birth of metaphysical anguish."[16]

There has been a long tradition proposing this fear of death as the ultimate source of religious thought. Twentieth-century anthropologist Bronislaw Malinowski theorized that religion is the "affirmation that death is not real, that man has a soul and that this is immortal," which has since inspired a school of thought called "terror management theory." In this view, just as an infant gains comfort and security from the authority of her parents, so as she grows up and becomes aware of death, she is comforted by the notion of deities, who are frequently patriarchal or matriarchal figures.[17]

This makes sense, as far as it goes. However, since the fear of death extended all the way back to Neanderthals and other prehumans, it doesn't seem like enough to account for the complexity of religious beliefs. Was there something else in the symbolic breakthrough of the Upper Paleolithic revolution that could have been responsible for the emergence of religious thought as we now know it? Several cognitive anthropologists have proposed that this is, indeed, the case.

Religion as a Spandrel

If you pay a visit to St. Mark's Cathedral in Venice, someone will probably draw your attention to its great central dome. Look up, and you will see beautiful mosaics covering not just the central circle of the dome but also the arches holding it up, along with the triangular sections where two arches meet each other at right angles (figure 3.4). These sections are called spandrels, and two evolutionary biologists, Stephen Jay Gould and Richard Lewontin, once used them to illustrate an influential evolutionary theory. A spandrel doesn't, by itself, serve any purpose. It simply exists as an architectural by-product of the arches that hold up the dome. But if someone looked at the beautifully decorated spandrels without knowing anything about architecture, they would see them as an integral part of the architectural design. The living world, according to Gould and Lewontin, is full of evolutionary spandrels: features or functions that seem to have evolved for a specific purpose but, on closer evaluation, turn out to have been a superfluous by-product of something else.[18]

Figure 3.4: Spandrels in St. Mark's Cathedral, Venice

For some cognitive anthropologists, religion is a spandrel. By *religion*, they mean not just the organized religions we know in the modern world but the entire set of mythic constructions that virtually every culture has used from the earliest times to make sense of the universe. To understand how religion evolved, they believe, you need to look at some of the key functions of the modern human mind, and you will find that religion developed as their byproduct. We're already familiar with several of these functions from what we know about the workings of the PFC, such as theory of mind, displacement (our ability for thinking about people even though they're distant from us), and our capacity to hold counterfactuals in our mind: things we can consider even though we know they're not true.[19]

To see how a religious spandrel arises, let's consider an example, such as the ubiquitous belief that a spirit exists separately from a body. How could our capacity for displacement give rise to this idea? As infants, we quickly learn that people can disappear and then reappear, sometimes minutes, hours, or even days later. From this, we realize that people continue to exist even while they have disappeared. This soon becomes an essential ingredient of our social intelligence, allowing us to imagine, for example, what others would feel or think *if* they were here. It's a relatively simple step to apply the same practice of displacement to the thoughts and feelings of a dead person. Given the central role of social intelligence in human cognition, it may be easier for us to think of someone still existing but not being physically present than to conceive of that person ceasing to exist altogether. And the tendency for the deceased to reappear to us in dreams adds another important node to this particular pattern of meaning.[20]

To explore this, a group of researchers presented kindergarten-age children with a puppet show in which an anthropomorphized mouse was killed and eaten by an alligator. When the children were asked about whether he still needed to eat or relieve himself, they were clear that this was no longer the case. Yet, when they were asked whether the dead mouse was still thinking or feeling, most children answered yes, suggesting it may be our default cognitive position to believe that a dead person still exists in some form.[21]

Besides believing in spirits, little children also intuitively believe everything exists for a purpose, a viewpoint known as teleology, which is inextricably intertwined with religious thought. Psychologist Deborah Kelemen has conducted studies of children's intuitive beliefs—with some intriguing results. When a group of seven- and eight-year-olds were asked why prehistoric rocks were pointy, they rejected physical explanations such as "bits of stuff piled up for a long period of time" for teleological explanations such as "so that animals wouldn't sit on them and smash them" or "so that animals could scratch on them when they got itchy." Similarly, the children explained that "clouds are for raining" and rejected more physical reasons even when told that adults explained clouds this way.[22]

As we get older, we may accept other reasons for pointy rocks, but we never completely overcome the powerful drive in our minds to assign agency to inanimate objects and actions. If we're home alone on a dark, stormy night and hear a door creaking open in the other room, our first reaction is fear that it might be an intruder, not the thought that it's just the wind blowing the door open. We have, explains anthropologist Scott Atran, "a naturally selected cognitive mechanism for detecting agents—such as predators, protectors, and prey." It's clear how this served a powerful evolutionary purpose: there's no harm in mistaking the wind for an intruder, but mistaking an intruder for the wind could cost you your life.[23]

This agency-detection system is so deeply ingrained that it causes us to attribute agency to all kinds of natural phenomena, such as anger in a thunderclap or voices in the wind, resulting in our universal tendency for anthropomorphism. Stewart Guthrie, author of *Faces in the Clouds: A New Theory of Religion*, argues that "anthropomorphism may best be explained as the result of an attempt to see not what we want to see or what is easy to see, but what is *important* to see: what may affect us for better or worse." Because of our powerful anthropomorphic tendency, "we search everywhere, involuntarily and unknowingly, for human form and results of human action, and often seem to find them where they do not exist."[24]

When our anthropomorphism is applied to religious thought, it's notably the mind, rather than the body, that's universally applied to spirits and gods. In the diverse cultures of the world, gods come in all shapes and sizes, but one thing they always share is a mind with the ability to think symbolically, just like a human. This makes sense in light of the critical importance of theory of mind in the development of our social intelligence: if other people have minds like ours, wouldn't that be true of other agents we perceive to act intentionally in the natural world?[25]

Our patterning instinct, honed over millions of years to find meaning in the complex experience of daily life, plays a crucial role in this drive to imbue our own mental characteristics into the world around us. In prelinguistic times, its powers helped early humans successfully navigate their increasingly sophisticated communities. With the emergence of language, it drove infants to impute meaning into the cacophony of sounds with which they were bombarded. With its unrelenting compulsion for patterning, its prowess was then applied to look for meaning in the otherwise seemingly chaotic occurrences of the universe.

The human patterning instinct used the intuitive reflexes of social cognition as scaffolding for a new mythic consciousness in much the same way that it had used embodied experiences as scaffolding for the metaphors that enabled abstract thought. The cognitive processes of toolmaking, for example, by which things were designed and constructed for a particular purpose, may have inspired the belief that natural objects were also created for a purpose. Similarly, the intuitive sense of fairness that was crucial to the stability of hunter-gatherer societies would have implied the need to maintain equally harmonious relationships with the spirits of the natural world.[26]

Culture as Sculptor

Powerful as our own patterning instinct is, there is an even more potent force shaping the particular patterns we perceive around us. It's what anthropologists call *culture*. Just as language shapes the perception of an infant as she listens to the patterns of sounds around her, so the mythic patterns of thought informing the culture a child is born into will literally shape how that child constructs meaning in his world. Every culture holds its own worldview: a complex and comprehensive model of how the universe works and how to act within it. This network of beliefs and values determines the way in which each child in that culture makes sense of his universe.

To see how this happens, we need to understand how an infant's brain matures. In recent years, neuroscientists have discovered that early brain development is essentially a pruning process. In the embryo and newly born infant, massive amounts of neuronal connections known as synapses form spontaneously. As the infant gets used to certain behaviors, such as grasping, nursing, or cooing, the synaptic junctions that enable a successful behavior get strengthened by increased usage. The connections that are never used gradually wither away. As the infant grows, this synaptic reinforcement continues until some pathways are massively strengthened, while countless others that turned out to be useless have died out. A useful analogy is an uncultivated field of tall grass through which people walk to get to various places. At first, everyone's beating about the bush, but, after a while, certain trails appear in the grass as the most successful routes become more popular, causing the grass to get flattened down until, eventually, clear pathways emerge through the field. The clearer the pathway, the more likely it is to be used by the next person, thus leading to a positive feedback cycle.[27]

Because of this process of synaptic pruning, a human born in the modern world might be virtually identical genetically to one of our ancestors born before the Upper Paleolithic revolution, but if a brain scan could be performed on both individuals at maturity, they would look very different. The differences would not be in the general layout and gross structure of the brain but rather in the fine, dense mesh of synaptic connections that have been systematically pruned and shaped since infancy.[28]

It's through this process that we arrive at the notion of culture as sculptor. We can think of each distinct culture as the cumulative network of meaning constructed by countless generations of minds within a given tradition. The neural network of each person born into that tradition is sculpted by the previous accumulation of meanings and then may contribute its own unique interpretations to modify the culture incrementally for the next generation. In this way, the relationship between an individual and a culture is, to a certain degree, mutually interactive, although the impact of the culture on the individual is far greater than vice versa.[29]

Every human interaction subtly shapes the neural network of a growing child as she learns to integrate into her culture. The words her parents speak to her, their responses to different behaviors, the games she plays, the rituals she participates in are all continually sculpting her own perception of the world, shaping how she patterns meaning into the universe. This process takes place mostly below the level of conscious control. Rarely does someone consciously try to explain their worldview to the infant, and rarely does she consciously try to make sense of it all. However, in a process known as deep enculturation, she inevitably grows up with a set of beliefs and values about the world embedded within her unconscious, which shapes how she conceptualizes virtually every aspect of her experience.[30]

We can thank this process of deep enculturation for the entire spectrum of human progress since *Homo sapiens* first evolved. Without enculturation, no human being would be capable of staying alive for long, and even a community working together could barely survive without the inherited wisdom of its cultural traditions. The integration of symbolic meaning between individuals and their culture has allowed the human race to effectively "pool their cognitive resources," both from each other and from the past, and thus achieve the dominance over the rest of the world that we experience today.[31]

Culture's Power Tool

Culture has been sculpting the human brain ever since our earliest ancestors began living complex social lives millions of years ago. However, with the advent of the Upper Paleolithic revolution, it began using a new power tool that has transformed the human experience ever since. When humans arrived in Europe and constructed their first symbolic artifacts, they were crafting external manifestations of the network of meaning held by their collective mythic consciousness. Cognitive neuroscientist Merlin Donald calls this cultural power tool "external symbolic storage": the entire set of physical objects constructed by humans to hold and communicate a symbolic meaning beyond mere utilitarian function. The most obvious examples include cave art, sculptures, personal ornamentation, and musical instruments, but external symbolic storage can also refer to more subtle symbolic signaling, such as stonework styles and even the spatial patterns of how a campsite is used.[32]

Through external symbolic storage, culture no longer resides merely in the shared network of people's minds. It has taken up permanent residence in a set of concrete symbols that remain fixed, outliving those who constructed them and communicating stable symbolic meaning to countless new generations.[33]

The power of external symbolic storage to shape the human mind arises from its fixed and stable attributes: its nature is different from the meaning that arises solely within a human mind. The biological memory records created within the brain, Donald explains, "are impermanent, small, hard to refine, impossible to display in awareness for any length of time, and difficult to locate and recall. . . . In contrast, external symbols give us stable, permanent, virtually unlimited memory records."[34]

Consider a common abstraction, such as patriotism. Each time you think of your country, your mind will produce something slightly different than the previous time. The concept arises within a tangled, momentary web of feeling, emotion, symbol, memory, and narrative. Now, think of your nation's flag. The information stored in this external symbol is far more stable. The next time the flag is unfurled, it will store virtually the same symbolic information it held the previous time. Over extended periods, even the information of external symbols may evolve or disappear. During the Vietnam era, war protesters burned the US flag in a conscious effort to change its symbolic significance. We no longer know what the Lascaux Cave paintings symbolize. But it is their relatively fixed nature that gives external symbolic storage the power to influence each new generation of human minds.

By stabilizing meaning within a group, external symbolic storage permits communities to expand massively in size and complexity while maintaining a cohesive framework of values and beliefs. Institutions we take for granted in today's society, such as marriage, money, and government, exist only because their reality is grounded in a common understanding that relies on external symbolic storage to maintain consistent meaning. In our modern world, the sheer volume of external symbolic storage has, of course, expanded vastly, incorporating virtually everything around us, including books, newspapers, the internet, television, music, architecture, interior design, fashion, road signs—the list is endless. Without external symbolic storage, human civilization could never have developed. However, its power severely limits the autonomy each of us has in constructing our own pattern of meaning from the world.

"Ensnared in an Inescapable Web"

To what extent has our culture shaped our minds so that we can only think in the patterns we've inherited from the past? Donald warns that our cultural storage systems have "assumed a certain autonomy" and, in many ways, act like an organism with its own volition:

> Our cultures invade us and set our agendas. . . . Big Brother culture owns us because it gets to us early. As a result, we internalize its norms and habits at a very basic level. We have no choice in this. Culture influences what moves us, what we look for, and how we think for as long as we live.[35]

Like an alien force from a sci-fi movie, our culture maintains its existence outside any one of us and yet, at the same time, pervades our minds. While its tangible expressions affect our daily lives, its ultimate power derives from the intangible conceptualizations that lie below, out of sight. The abstract concepts of culture have shaped the course of world history more profoundly than any of its physical manifestations. Beliefs in God, heaven and hell, liberty and progress, communism and capitalism have all profoundly affected the human experience over the millennia. In the words of anthropologist Terrence Deacon:

> The symbolic universe has ensnared us in an inescapable web. Like a "mind virus," the symbolic adaptation has infected us, and now by virtue of the irresistible urge it has instilled in us to turn everything we encounter and everyone we meet into symbols, we have become the means by which it unceremoniously propagates itself throughout the world.[36]

This hidden force has real and tangible implications for the future of the human race and the planet on which we reside. Far more powerful than any individual or group, its abstractions engender the values that drive our collective behavior, leading our global civilization on a trajectory that may not be of our choosing.

When one realizes the immense power our culture has had in shaping the very structure of our minds, it's tempting to surrender to it and merely accept the network of meaning in which we're enmeshed. However, daunting as the task may be, it's not impossible to regain at least some autonomy. Even our brain's neural network, sculpted from infancy by our cultural influences, can be literally reshaped to a certain degree. Modern neuroscience has demonstrated that the adult brain remains plastic, thus permitting us to consciously resculpt some of the structures of thought that our culture has instilled in us from infancy.[37]

Going back to the analogy of the brain's neural organization as a field of tall grass: even after the main thoroughfares have been laid down, it's still possible to find new ways through the bush. Finding a different pathway through the tall grass can be inconvenient, messy, and even scary, so it's something you'll do only if you discover the old paths no longer lead you to places you want to go.

The rest of this book will identify some of the foundational structures of thought that have shaped our own cultural patterning and examine how they may be taking our civilization to places we don't want to go. It is only through a clear identification of these underlying structures that we can perceive them in our own minds, thereby gaining some freedom to disentangle ourselves from the "inescapable web"—and ultimately, perhaps, to influence the shape of the culture that will sculpt the minds of future generations.

Chapter 4

THE GIVING ENVIRONMENT: THE WORLD OF THE HUNTER-GATHERERS

The Riddle of the Scrawny Ox

Christmas was approaching, and anthropologist Richard Lee wanted to give the best gift he could procure to the band of !Kung foragers with whom he'd been living. The !Kung, whose idea of Christmas was a celebration to "praise the birth of white man's god-chief," found the season particularly appealing because of their trading neighbors' custom of slaughtering an ox for them to feast on. Lee decided to make them a gift of the biggest ox he could find: a fat, meaty giant. However, instead of gratitude, Lee was nonplussed to receive nothing but insults: it was the skinniest "sack of guts and bones," they told him, that they had ever seen. Even while they spent two days feasting on it, they continued to mock his ox, complaining, "It was too thin to bother eating," and, "It gives us pain to be served such a scrawny thing."[1]

What was going on? Hunter-gatherers think and act in ways that are very different from and sometimes incomprehensible to our modern sensibilities. Realizing this, social commentators have for hundreds of years used their behavior as a demonstration of intrinsic human nature to make political points. Back in the seventeenth century, Thomas Hobbes kicked off the debate with his famous claim that the life of man in a "state of nature" was "solitary, poor, nasty, brutish, and short." In the following century, the diametrically opposed myth of the "noble savage," associated with French philosopher Jean-Jacques Rousseau, took hold of the European imagination. Nowadays, the references are more sophisticated, but the underlying themes remain. While some emphasize the sharing mentality of hunter-gatherer societies, others continue the Hobbesian line, pointing to the endemic warfare of many precivilized cultures.[2]

In reality, any attempt to understand the hunter-gatherer worldview through the lens of a modern value system is doomed to draw a distorted picture. Such perspectives are, by their very nature, anachronistic, using more recent conceptual structures that our hunter-gatherer ancestors could never have dreamed about. Can we even use observations about modern foragers like the !Kung to draw inferences about the primordial hunter-gatherer worldview all the way back to Upper Paleolithic days? Modern anthropologists are well aware of this challenge. After all, not only is there the question of how hunter-gatherer cultures may have evolved over millennia, but there's also the inevitable influence from the agricultural communities that surround those few forager societies that still remain. Nevertheless, other than the cave paintings those earliest human communities left behind, the patterns of thought exhibited by modern foragers provide the best clues for piecing together how they made sense of the world.[3]

Is there even a common hunter-gatherer worldview that can be described? How could a group of forest dwellers deep in the heart of the Amazon see the world in the same way as a community of Inuit up in the Arctic Circle? Their languages and the specific attributes of their environment differ drastically: one culture may be oriented around a river, another around the migration of a particular animal. But many decades of research have unearthed what anthropologist Bruce Trigger calls "cross-cultural uniformities in human behavior." The uniformities tend to exist under the surface, leading to underlying patterns of thought that are remarkably similar across cultures, even while their manifestations in each culture's beliefs and practices are profusely variable.[4]

These uniformities hint at the foundations of the hunter-gatherer worldview that we'll be exploring in this chapter, giving us a glimpse of how our earliest ancestors made sense of their world. As we examine how they oriented themselves in their cosmos, we'll also see how Richard Lee's experience brought him face to face with one of the unexpected ways in which hunter-gatherers weave their own complex web of meaning into their lives.

Everything Is Connected

Probably the most pervasive underlying pattern in the hunter-gatherer worldview is the belief that all aspects of the world—humans, animals, ancestors, spirits, trees, rocks, and rivers—are related parts of a dynamic, integrated whole. The natural environment is, for hunter-gatherers, fully alive. Anthropologist Richard Nelson writes evocatively how the Koyukon people of Alaska's boreal forest "live in a world that watches, in a forest of eyes. A person moving through nature—however wild, remote, even desolate the place may be—is never truly alone. The surroundings are aware, sensate, personified."[5]

The sentience of nature is frequently manifested in the spirits perceived to exist all around. They form an integral part of the natural world as much as humans and other animals do. Like humans, spirits possess emotions and intelligence; they can be male or female and have families. Some are tied to specific places, while others roam around. Some are friendly, some hostile, and they may be very sensitive to how they are regarded. "They feel," writes Nelson. "They can be offended. And they must, at every moment, be treated with proper respect." Those aspects of life that we define as "religious" permeate all the daily activities of hunter-gatherers, who generally have no word for religion because their relationship to the spirit world pervades everything they do.[6]

The Dreamtime of the Australian Aboriginals is a tradition that powerfully demonstrates the interconnectedness of aspects of life that we tend to keep separate. The Aboriginals understand the world as having been brought into being by creative entities called the Dreamings, who crisscrossed the continent, crawling, walking, flying, hunting, fighting, and copulating, leaving tracks of their activities in the landscape. They continually shifted their shapes from animal to human and back again, changing their language and songs while they did so. They were the original ancestors of all the humans and animals in the world.[7]

Through the Dreamtime, Aboriginals integrate not only the human, natural, and spiritual domains but also the past, present, and future. We are used to creation myths describing events that occurred long ago, but, for the Aboriginals, the Dreamtime exists in the present as much as the past. The creative ancestors may connect with humans in dreams, but also in other ways. For example, in a phenomenon known as "conception Dreaming," it's believed that the spirit of the place where a woman conceives enters the fetus and remains a part of the infant when she's born. Thus, a network of meaning is formed in which everything relates to everything else, whether it's tangible or intangible, past, present, or future. In the words of Aboriginal storyteller Daisy Utemorrah:

> All these things, the plants and the trees, the mountains and the hills and the stars and the clouds, we *represent* them. You see these trees over there? We represent them. I might represent that tree there. Might be my name there, in that tree. Yes, and the reeds, too, in the waters . . . the frogs and the tadpoles and the fish . . . even the crickets . . . all kinds of things . . . we *represent* them.[8]

We saw earlier how the recursive property of language created a magical weave, connecting previously separate ideas to permit new meanings to emerge. Similarly, in the mythic consciousness of the hunter-gatherer worldview, all aspects of life participate to form an integrated web of meaning, in which nothing exists in isolation and each human activity resonates with everything else.

The Giving Earth

The earth itself forms the hub of this web of connectivity. As Aboriginal elder Hobbles Danaiyarri describes it, "Everything come up out of ground—language, people, emu, kangaroo, grass." The terrain is filled with sacred places where different forms of Dreaming, such as kangaroo or wild fig, have existed since the beginning of time. When a person dies, their spirit is believed to return to the earth and join with the ancestors. This leads to such an intimate relationship with "country" (as Aboriginals call their ancestral lands) that many Aboriginal groups speak directly to the "old people" when they go into the bush. They call or sing out loud to the Dreamings, the other living beings and the ancestors, treating them as though they're fully living members of an extended family. Sometimes, they will use a visit to "country" as an opportunity to introduce new arrivals such as youngsters or newly married spouses to the ancestors.[9]

This interweaving of earth, spirits, and family is shared by hunter-gatherer societies across the world. The Ojibwa of North America refer to the natural spirits as "our grandfathers." In the forested Gir Valley of South India, Nayaka foragers regularly invite the local spirits to visit them and share their food. They view them as part of their family, calling them "our relatives" and referring to particular spirits as "grandmother" or "grandfather."[10]

Anthropologist Nurit Bird-David, who has studied the Nayaka extensively, identifies a root metaphor in the Nayaka worldview of FOREST AS PARENT, which affects every aspect of life down to the most mundane detail. The Nayaka, she explains, "look on the forest as they do on a mother or father. For them, it is not something 'out there' that responds mechanically or passively but like a parent, it provides food unconditionally to its children." This leads to a relationship of trust with the natural environment, rather than one characterized primarily by anxiety or fear. Unlike the religious traditions most of us are used to, huntergatherers don't worship their gods; rather, they converse with the spirits as they would with their own elders. Just as a Nayaka parent may punish a misbehaving child with a spanking but would never dream of withholding food, so the spirits of the forest may inflict aches and pains on an errant Nayaka but would still provide them with means of nourishment. Through this root metaphor, the Nayaka, like many hunter-gatherers, view their world as a "giving environment."[11]

Continual Transformation

Generally, when we hear a metaphor, we recognize that it's not the real thing. When we hear that "stocks are falling," we don't listen for the sound of them hitting the floor. However, a root metaphor can become so embedded in the collective consciousness of a culture that it's no longer viewed as a metaphor but as reality. For hunter-gatherers, the spirits surrounding them are not *like* family—they *are* family. Similarly, as anthropologist Graeme Barker points out, "nonhuman animals are not just *like* humans, they *are* persons." The natural world is filled with persons, regardless of whether their shape is mammal, reptile, or plant, each linked to human foragers through common ancestry and each possessing their own intelligence, feelings, and moral conscience.[12]

When we remember from the previous chapter that the one common feature applied to spirits around the world is the human mind, it makes sense that the body of a spirit is capable of total transformation, even death, while its sentience remains constant. According to this logic, as Barker explains, "killing a plant or animal is not murder but transformation." For this reason, many hunter-gatherers have elaborate sacred rituals around hunting animals, believing that although the flesh of the animal has been made available to them, its spirit remains alive and must be treated with due respect.[13]

Virtually everything in the hunter-gatherer environment has this potential for transformation. Here's how an early-twentieth-century Inuit woman, Nalungiaq, described her people's beliefs in the original transformative capability of both humans and animals:

> In the very earliest time when both people and animals lived on earth, a person could become an animal if he wanted to and an animal could become a human being. Sometimes they were people and sometimes animals and there was no difference.[14]

As with the Aboriginal Dreamtime, for most hunter-gatherer cultures, these transformations did not merely happen in the distant past but continue within their own community. Not everyone is considered capable of managing this metamorphosis at will, but specific individuals are believed to have the power to transform themselves and journey to a world where direct communication with the spirits is possible. These individuals are known as shamans, and the set of beliefs and practices around their spirit journeys goes by the name of shamanism.[15]

Journeying to the Spirit World

In hunter-gatherer communities, a shaman is believed to have the ability to mediate between the everyday world and the spirit worlds (usually an upper world in the sky and a lower world beneath the earth). The mediation generally takes the form of a journey in which the shaman's spirit leaves his body to visit the other worlds. To embark on this journey, the shaman must put himself into an ecstatic trance, something he does through a combination of chanting, fasting, hyperventilating, prolonged rhythmic dancing, or ingesting hallucinogens. Often, the journey's initiation is a community event, in which others join in the chanting or dancing, but it can also be the shaman's solitary experience. While the shaman is on the journey, his body will sometimes be seen shaking and "talking in tongues," while his spirit may take the form of another animal. Once in the spirit world, the shaman will engage in the (often terrifying) experience of communicating with the spirits, usually with a specific goal for the community, such as healing, controlling the activities of the wild animals, or influencing the weather.[16]

The first Westerners who observed shamanism were travelers in Central Asia, and the word comes from a Siberian tribe in which the central figure of the community was called the *saman*. Since then, extensive studies have shown similar practices occurring in virtually every forager community worldwide. The significance of shamanism goes beyond its hunter-gatherer origins: it influenced agrarian cultures around the world, and elements of it can be seen in Indian Yoga, certain practices of ancient Chinese culture, and in the Aztec and Mayan civilizations of Mesoamerica.[17*]

Why would shamanism be prevalent all around the world? There are two possible explanations. It could be because it was originally practiced by the early humans who took the first epic journey out of Africa. The original Upper Paleolithic immigrants to Europe would have brought shamanistic beliefs with them, as would their fellow travelers who migrated throughout Asia. Some of those Asian settlers then crossed the Bering Strait around thirteen thousand years ago, making it all the way down to South America within a couple of thousand years. Another explanation could be that shamanism is an inevitable part of human mythic consciousness and that, wherever humans evolved, the same set of beliefs would evolve with them. It seems likely that both explanations are true: shamanism probably is an intrinsic part of early mythic consciousness, and its beliefs diffused with the original Out of Africa migration. In this case, shamanism might have something important to tell us about the evolving role of the patterning instinct in the early human mind.[18]

We're fortunate that the settlers who arrived in Europe some thirty-five thousand years ago left behind a treasure trove of evidence of their beliefs, in the form of their sculptures and cave art. What clues might these hold about how they made sense of their world? If we consider the three Lion-men with human bodies and lion's heads, it's easy to see some linkage with shamanistic beliefs: they seem like a graphic illustration of Nalungiaq's story of animalhuman metamorphosis. How closely linked, in fact, are they?

Archaeologist David Lewis-Williams has conducted a detailed investigation of Upper Paleolithic cave art from a shamanistic perspective. "The ancient expression of shamanism," he suggests, "would in all probability not have been *identical* to any of the historically recorded types of shamanism, but it would have had comparable features." He surmises that the cave paintings may be images of what shamans saw and experienced during their trances. The shamans wouldn't have painted these in that state but would have recreated their ecstatic visions later, perhaps to share them with the rest of the community.[19]

Lewis-Williams points out that the vast majority of cave paintings are of animals rather than humans, which would make sense if the shamans were depicting the experience of leaving their body for an animal form during the spiritual journey. Interestingly, the few humanlike figures found on the cave walls are known as "wounded men" because they tend to have lines radiating from their bodies, which are generally seen as sticks or spears. Lewis-Williams interprets these images as symbolizing not real spears but rather the symbolic death of the shaman as he leaves his body behind for the journey.[20]

The idea of the shaman's spirit journey requiring the symbolic death of the body is an important motif in shamanism. It is powerful evidence of the belief, prevalent throughout the hunter-gatherer world, in a spirit's separate existence from the body. Just as the spirit can escape the body during a shaman's trance, it is also believed to survive the body's death, at which point it merely rejoins the ancestors in the spirit world. For hunter-gatherers, the spirit world is every bit as real as the day-to-day world—and, in some ways, more important because it maintains its continuity throughout the transformations and birth-death cycles of the regular world. The spirit world links each individual with the natural environment and the ancestors, permitting him to join the ancestors inhabiting the cosmos even after his body has died.[21]

The "Affluent Forager"

"Our modern skulls house a stone age mind." These are the words of evolutionary psychologists Leda Cosmides and John Tooby, who argue that, in order to understand the psychology of people living in today's world, we must realize that our minds evolved in hunter-gatherer societies for 99 percent of our species' history. "The key to understanding how the modern mind works," they tell us, is to realize that it wasn't designed to deal with the challenges of urban life but rather "to solve the day-to-day problems of our hunter-gatherer ancestors." For example, it's easier to deal with groups roughly the same size as a foraging band than with crowds of thousands. For the same reason, we instinctively fear a snake rather than an electric socket, even though electric shocks pose far greater risk to us. Similarly, in conducting an archaeology of the mind, we must examine the core values of hunter-gatherers if we want to understand the foundations of our modern value system.[22]

When European explorers first came across pristine hunter-gatherer cultures, they were shocked by their ingenuousness. When Christopher Columbus arrived on the island of Hispaniola, he wrote in his journal:

> They are so artless and free with all they possess, that no one would believe it without having seen it. Of anything they have, if you ask them for it, they never say no; rather they invite the person to share it, and show as much love as if they were giving their hearts; and whether the thing be of value or of small price, at once they are content with whatever little thing of whatever kind may be given to them.[23]

If this sounds suspiciously like the "noble savage" myth, it's important to bear in mind that it was written hundreds of years before Rousseau and by a man known more for his ruthlessness to indigenous people than his romantic idealization.

A couple of centuries later, Captain James Cook came across the natives of what is now New South Wales in Australia and marveled with equal wonder at their lifestyle:

> They live in a Tranquillity which is not disturb'd by the Inequality of Condition: The Earth and sea of their own accord furnishes them with all things necessary for life, they covet not Magnificent Houses, Household-stuff etc. . . . In short they seem'd to set no value upon any thing we gave them, nor would they ever part with any thing of their own for any one article we could offer them; this in my opinion argues that they think themselves provided with all the necessarys of Life and that they have no superfluities.[24]

As the age of imperialism got underway, the Hobbesian view of savages living lives that were "poor, nasty, brutish, and short" was more convenient for the justification of Western colonial policies and became the predominant European viewpoint. So it came as a shock to the academic establishment when anthropologist Marshall Sahlins proposed in 1968 that hunter-gatherers comprised the "original affluent society." Sahlins explained this radical notion by observing that there are two paths to affluence. There's the modern course of market economies, which assumes that human needs are considerable and that the more an economy produces, the closer it comes to meeting those needs. Then, there's what Sahlins called the "Zen strategy," based on the notion that human material needs are few, and there is therefore very little to do to fulfill those needs. Foragers, Sahlins argued, follow the "Zen road to affluence" because they need very little and they don't have to work too hard to get it. Further research on the !Kung people provided concrete evidence for Sahlins's viewpoint, showing that each adult !Kung typically spends only two to three hours a day on the basic needs of food and shelter.[25]

Hunter-gatherers might have few possessions, but they are not poor. Poverty itself is an invention of a different kind of society. This perspective is borne out by another early explorer, seventeenth-century French Jesuit Pierre Biard, who lived for a while with the Micmac tribe in what's now Nova Scotia (again, long before the "noble savage" myth got going). Describing how the tribe moved camp, he wrote that they "start off . . . with as much pleasure as if they were going on a stroll or an excursion . . . in order to thoroughly enjoy this. . . . They are never in a hurry. Quite different from us, who can never do anything without hurry and worry."[26]

Not only did hunter-gatherers have more leisure time, they were also much healthier than the farmers who came after them. Foragers tend to enjoy a wide variety of food sources providing sufficient amounts of protein, vitamins, and minerals. Early farmers, on the other hand, would often concentrate on a few principal crops that grew more readily, providing a narrower range of nutritional needs. Also, for a farmer, a crop failure might result in famine, whereas foragers could simply move to someplace else where another food source was more plentiful. Most importantly, early hunter-gatherers enjoyed a life virtually free of infectious disease. Most diseases that became endemic, such as plague, smallpox, tuberculosis, or cholera, were originally acquired by humans from their farm animals, and the diseases only achieved critical mass on account of the high population densities of towns and cities that sprang up following the rise of agriculture.[27]

The superior health of ancient hunter-gatherers is demonstrated by the study of ancient human skeletons, which shows that, at the end of the last Ice Age, hunter-gatherers in Europe had an average height of around five feet ten for men and five feet six for women. After the adoption of agriculture, by about 4,000 BCE, the average height had fallen to five feet three for men and five feet one for women. These studies reveal agriculturalists as far more disease ridden, with skeletal remains showing more rickets, scurvy, dental cavities, and lesions from leprosy and tuberculosis.[28]

However, we'd be wrong to view these statistics as unequivocal, though they might seem so at first. It's important to remember that the foraging nomadic lifestyle offers no safety net if someone becomes sick or injured. There is no permanent shelter for someone to rest and be cared for. This applies even more drastically to infants: a study of modern hunter-gatherers found that infanticide is regularly carried out in the vast majority of the societies examined. One study estimates that an infant born into a forager society has a 15–50 percent chance of being killed. So perhaps one reason those ancient hunter-gatherers were so healthy was that the weak and sick had already been killed.[29]

Giving and Taking

Even the hunter-gatherer largesse that so impressed Columbus turns out to be rather different from our modern view of generosity. Anthropologist Nicolas Peterson describes how nonplussed a visitor might be arriving at an Aboriginal settlement, where someone might come up to her and say, "I want to owe you five dollars." Peterson calls this typically assertive style "demand sharing" and contrasts it with the Western sense of altruistic giving. The insistent demand for sharing is not limited to prosperous visitors from outside but is a normal part of hunter-gatherer interaction. James Woodburn, describing the social pressure on foragers to give up anything they might have, tells how a Hadza man lucky enough to get his hands on a ball of tobacco, a shirt, or a cloth is "unlikely to keep it for long unless he is very determined and willing to make himself unpopular. He will be asked for it endlessly."[30]

Even more exasperating, from a modern perspective, is that once a forager has received the gift he's been demanding, he treats it with an outright lack of respect. Woodburn relates how he was repeatedly pressed by the Hadza to get them some hoop iron from which they could make arrowheads. Finally, with difficulty, he obtained the iron and handed out a piece to every man in the camp, only to discover later that they had simply thrown away all the iron they couldn't immediately use.[31]

At least Woodburn didn't suffer the humiliation of Richard Lee, whose Christmas gift of the fat ox caused him such consternation. Only later did Lee discover that this is the !Kung's normal response when a hunter returns with a big kill. Rather than boasting about his kill, the hunter is expected to announce, "Ah, I'm no good for hunting. I saw nothing at all . . . just a little tiny one," while the group that carries the meat back to camp cries out, "You mean to say you have dragged us all the way out here in order to make us cart home your pile of bones?" Lee's informant explained to him how this elaborate, counterintuitive ritual is designed to prevent the rise of arrogance in a hunter: "When a young man kills much meat he comes to think of himself as a chief or a big man, and he thinks of the rest of us as his servants or inferiors. We can't accept this. We refuse one who boasts, for someday his pride will make him kill somebody. So we always speak of his meat as worthless. This way we cool his heart and make him gentle."[32]

We can see from this story how behavior that, at first sight, seems bizarre is actually a sophisticated form of social engineering that promotes sustainable community living.

In fact, the sharing ethic of hunter-gatherer society can be seen as a sensible long-term insurance strategy. Anthropologist Polly Wiessner was studying a group of !Kung during a long drought that began to cause serious hunger. Suddenly, she saw them prepare gifts and begin a trek to a region the drought had spared, where other !Kung lived. There, they were treated as extended family and invited to share in the available food. This system of pooling risk through a network of social obligations, known as *hxaro,* is long established in !Kung culture.[33]

The insurance aspect of hunter-gatherer sharing also works within a particular group. When Daniel Everett discovered that the Pirahã, a forager group living deep in the Amazon, knew how to preserve meat by smoking, drying, and salting, he asked them why they didn't do it. "I store my meat in the belly of my brother" was the answer. Everett saw this play out in the person of an old man who could no longer contribute to the camp but was nevertheless provided with ample food. When he asked some Pirahã if they minded sharing with someone who couldn't contribute back, they responded that "he had fed them when they were too young to feed themselves, and therefore they were pleased to feed him and help him." When the old man got lost in the jungle, the entire village searched for him tirelessly for three days. They were emotional when they finally found him, calling him their "parent," hugging him, and giving him food as soon as they got back to the village.[34]

A World without Boundaries

It's not surprising that the Pirahã treated the old man with such respect, given what we know of the hunter-gatherer worldview. After all, when he died, he would become one of the ancestral spirits watching them in the forest. We can see here how the mutual reciprocity informing a hunter-gatherer's relationship with other members of the group becomes the basis for their relationship with the spirit world. These values can equally be seen flowing from the spirit world to the everyday world. The generosity of the spirits in allowing animals to be hunted and fruit to be picked implies that any selfish behavior within the human community, such as hoarding, should be frowned upon. The ethic of sharing is so central to hunter-gatherer culture that it imbues their sense of kinship. A Nayaka, for example, is expected to share with anybody who is present, regardless of any prior relationship they may have with them, and if they share with that person for long enough (even a non-Nayaka like an anthropologist), they begin to refer to that person as *sonta*, which means "relative."[35]

A common principle that emerges from each aspect of the hunter-gatherer worldview is the blurring of boundaries between domains. Whether it's between the living and dead, the everyday and the spirit world, human and animal, owning and giving, or family and nonfamily, fluidity in relations is a universal feature of hunter-gatherer societies. Even the bond between husband and wife or parent and child is characterized by this lack of clear boundaries. Among the Hill Pandaram of South India, once children reach the age of five or six, they loosen their emotional ties with their parents, even though they still may be affectionate with each other. During the dancing and singing that occurs at the full moon, Pirahã adults, even those who are married, engage openly in sexual relations with other partners. Sometimes, when a man and woman become newly attracted to each other, they might disappear into the forest for a few days while their spouses call and search for them. When they return, they might set up a new household or return to their spouses, from whom they almost never receive any retaliation.[36]

This lack of boundaries is reflected in the hunter-gatherer view of their own territory. For them, the land also has no fixed borders. The !Kung define territory in terms of where the important wild plants grow and the paths of animal migrations. Lee writes of them having a "boundaryless universe," with vague perimeters that they don't think of defending.[37]

Parochial Altruism

With their sharing ethic, disregard of worldly possessions, and tolerance of sexual freedom, it's easy to see how hunter-gatherer societies might be held up by modern-day Rousseaus as a model of how society ought to be. This ideal, however, hits a serious snag on the topic of aggression, an issue that takes us right back to the heart of the debate between the Hobbesian and Rousseauian camps: were hunter-gatherer communities fundamentally more peaceful than us?

This issue took center stage in anthropological circles in 1996, when Lawrence Keeley published *War before Civilization: The Myth of the Peaceful Savage*, which systematically chronicled the grim and unremitting archaeological evidence proving that, in his words, "homicide has been practiced since the appearance of modern humankind." While many researchers have argued that war only began with the rise of agriculture, Keeley traced it all the way back to the earliest hunter-gatherer societies, claiming that "the vast majority of . . . hunter-gatherer groups did engage in warfare and . . . there is nothing inherently peaceful about hunting-gathering or band society."[38]

The question of when war really began, though, is a semantic one. Given a certain level of aggression among human males, the issue might be viewed more meaningfully through tracing the gradations of organization, scale, and necessity by which aggression turns into war. Anthropologist Peter Wilson offers a helpful perspective on this, explaining that "violence is not unknown in nomadic societies and is greatly feared. Fights occur, and excessive, abnormal, or pathological violence tends to be countered by violence: men whose violent dispositions make them a threat to the peaceful life of a camp are reported as being ambushed and killed. But no modern ethnography gives an indication of such violence either being organized permanently or getting out of hand."[39*]

It's helpful to remember how the !Kung would insult a successful hunter's kill to prevent his pride getting the better of him. Also, the members of a hunter-gatherer band are frequently changing, and if someone feels antagonized in a particular group, he can "vote with his feet" and simply join another band. Additionally, without being tied down to a particular piece of land, a group of foragers can quickly move to a different territory if another band threatens them. For all these reasons, a number of anthropologists continue to refute Keeley's position, arguing that warfare only emerged among domesticated communities.[40*]

Behavioral scientist Samuel Bowles offers a valuable insight into the question of hunter-gatherer aggression by describing what he calls "parochial altruism." Bowles views the willingness of a warrior to fight to the death to protect his group as an extreme form of the altruistic instinct that evolved in early humans. Imagine two early forager societies fighting each other, with one group of fighters only looking out for themselves, while the other group consists of fighters willing to risk their own lives for the sake of their community. It's not hard to imagine how the group-oriented fighters would be more successful in battle. The altruism of these warriors, though, only extended to the boundary of their particular group, which is why Bowles calls it "parochial." If these parochial altruists kept beating the self-interested groups in battle, they would, over time, become the predominant population. Bowles speculates that this new form of altruism might have been responsible for the rapid expansion of modern humans out of Africa and the consequent extinction of the Neanderthals.

"Paradoxically," he writes, "the grisly evidence of our warlike past may help explain our distinctly cooperative nature."[41]

Exploiting Nature's Easy Pickings

If the parochial altruism of hunter-gatherers calls into question any claim that they represent an aspirational model for human behavior, their approach to the sustainability of their environment explodes it to smithereens. In fact, our hunter-gatherer ancestors were responsible for mass extinctions of some of the most spectacular species that have lived on the earth. The forager view of the natural world as a giving environment was only too literal. The environment gave and gave, and our hunter-gatherer ancestors took and took, until they had wiped out the natural world's easy pickings.

Geoscientist Paul Martin first proposed the idea in the 1960s that the mass extinctions known to have occurred in North and South America and Australia may have been the result of human activity. Until then, the predominant theory had pointed to climate change. After decades of persistent accumulation of evidence, a large portion of the scientific community now supports what Martin calls the "overkill hypothesis."[42]

The statistics behind it are starkly compelling. Beginning roughly a hundred thousand years ago, half the 167 genera of large mammals across the world became extinct. The first extinctions occurred in Africa, but far more dramatic numbers occurred in Australia when humans first arrived, about fifty thousand years ago. Giant marsupials, reptiles, and flightless birds once inhabited Australia, including a rhino-sized wombat, a giant horned tortoise, and a marsupial lion that preyed on them, but twenty-three out of twenty-four of these megafauna disappeared in the first few thousand years of human settlement. The next areas to be affected, around thirteen thousand years ago, were North America—losing thirty-three out of forty-five genera of megafauna—and South America, which lost forty-six out of fifty-eight genera. Some of the creatures lost included camels; giant ground sloths; several types of elephants, including mammoths and mastodons; an armadillo the size of a van; and predators such as saber-toothed tigers and giant running bears. The same story unfolds for each of the large islands as they became colonized. Giant tortoises and hippos disappeared from Madagascar; in New Zealand, fifteen species of moas—the tallest birds that ever lived—vanished within a few centuries of the

Maoris' arrival; in Cyprus, the pygmy hippopotamus and pygmy elephant disappeared (figure 4.1).[43]

Megafauna extinctions, in relation to *Homo sapiens* arrival

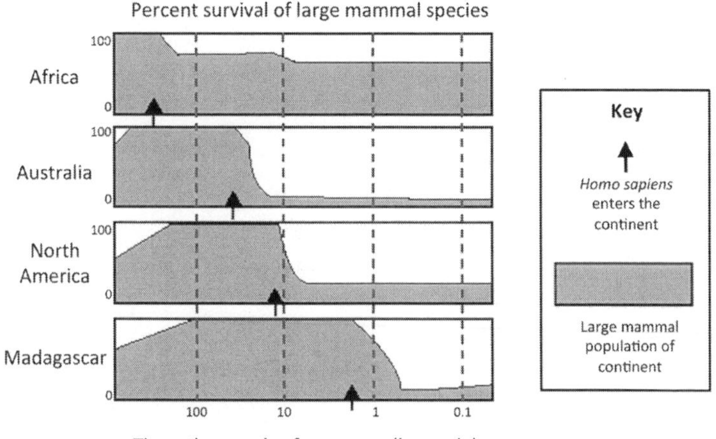

After Elin Whitney Smith, based on Martin P. S. (1989). "Prehistoric overkill: A global model." In *Quaternary Extinctions: A Prehistoric Revolution* (ed. P.S. Martin and R.G. Klein). Tucson, AZ: Univ. Arizona Press. pp. 354–404.

Figure 4.1: Megafauna extinctions by continent.

With such overwhelming evidence, it's not hard to see why this overkill has been called "one of the swiftest and most profound biological catastrophes in the history of the earth." But why exactly did this happen? One clue is that Africa (and, to a limited extent, Asia) is the only continent where megafauna still exist plentifully. In these areas, hominids evolved alongside the megafauna, so the animals had millions of years to evolve an instinctive fear of humans. However, by the time of the exodus from Africa, the new capabilities arising from the patterning instinct were already fully developed, causing a precipitous imbalance in the ecological equilibrium that had previously existed. Our ancestors used strategy and advanced weapons on creatures that had never come across humans before and, therefore, had never evolved any reason to fear them.[44]

Most likely, the herbivores were hunted down by humans, while the predators died out after their natural prey disappeared. While the overkill looks dramatic to us in hindsight, it would have been imperceptible to the foragers arriving in a new continent. One researcher has calculated that hunting down and killing juvenile megafauna at rates as low as one kill per person per decade would have led to these massive species extinctions over a period of several thousand years. From the foragers' perspective, nature's bounty would have seemed limitless.[45]

Thus, while the hunter-gatherers' worldview caused them to respect the spirits of the natural world and trust nature to be a giving environment, the power of the patterning instinct propelled them unwittingly into an unsustainable cycle of exploitation. For generation after generation, the world presented itself to them as a universe without boundaries (both literally and conceptually), without hierarchies, without ownership, without existential angst. It was a world of continual transformation, but, gradually, as the easy pickings all got picked, this world transformed into a different one: a world of limitations, a world of anxiety, a world where their capabilities for technological and conceptual invention were increasingly required for survival. The giving environment had given way to the world of agriculture.

Part 2

HIERARCHY OF THE GODS

Chapter 5
AGRICULTURE AND ANXIETY

Enkidu and the Temptress

In the Mesopotamian *Epic of Gilgamesh*, one of the most ancient myths to have survived to modern times, a character named Enkidu becomes a close friend of the hero Gilgamesh. Enkidu was created by the gods as a wild man with matted hair covering his body, oblivious of mankind and knowing nothing about civilization. He eats grass in the hills with the gazelles and drinks with the herds of wild game at the watering holes. One day, the civilized folk, terrified of Enkidu, decide to corrupt him with a "harlot from the temple of love," who waits for him at the watering hole and tempts him with her "woman's art." Enkidu makes love with her for six days and seven nights, forgetting his home in the hills. When he's done, he goes back to the wild beasts, but now everything is different. When the gazelles and other wild creatures see him, they bolt. He tries to run after them, but his body feels bound, as though with a cord, and his knees give way. His swiftness has gone. Enkidu has grown weak, we are told, "for wisdom was in him, and the thoughts of a man were in his heart." He goes back to the harlot, who persuades him to accompany her to the city, saying, "You are wise, Enkidu, and now you have become like a god. Why do you want to run wild with the beasts in the hills? Come with me. I will take you to strong-walled Uruk."

Enkidu follows her to Uruk, where he puts clothes on for the first time and learns how to eat bread and drink wine. There, he engages in hand-to-hand combat with Gilgamesh until he's finally thrown, after which they embrace and become inseparable friends. Enkidu doesn't look back on his old free life until he's lying on his deathbed, when a pang of regret takes hold and he curses all those who corrupted him. "I was once in the wilderness," he laments, "with all the treasure I wished."[1]

This disconcerting tale, echoing across the millennia, contains deep insights into the most profound transition in human history. For millions of years, foraging was the only way our ancestors could satisfy their hunger from one day to the next. Then, about ten thousand years ago, a radically different way of relating to the natural world emerged and set humankind on a course we've been following ever since. We crossed a Rubicon from which there was no turning back. As the story of Enkidu suggests, there was much that we gained but also a poignant loss.[2]

Why did this happen? What made hunter-gatherers settle down and start sowing their own seeds, preparing the soil, and doing the countless other backbreaking jobs involved in agriculture, when they had been blithely foraging for untold generations? How did agriculture take over across the entire world? In exploring these questions, we'll see how the rise of agriculture engendered a new constellation of values, hitherto unknown in human society, which we implicitly accept nowadays. And we'll see how the agrarian worldview transformed the hunter-gatherer's sense of nature as a giving environment into one of a cosmos demanding far more from its human participants, giving birth to a world filled with the existential anxiety that has remained with us ever since.

Storing the Barley

Strangely enough, the story of agriculture begins with a people known as Natufians, who, as far as we know, never sowed a seed nor tamed a wild animal. They lived in the Eastern Mediterranean, in what is now Israel, Jordan, Syria, and Lebanon. During the last Ice Age, around twenty thousand years ago, the Natufians foraged in small bands of fifteen to fifty people, hunting deer and gazelle and gathering tubers and nuts in what was at that time a treeless landscape. As the climate became warmer, woodlands of olives, pistachios, and oaks sprang up, along with fields of wild barley and wheat. Gradually, the Natufians began to do something no humans had done before: they settled down. Instead of wandering from place to place, they began building permanent houses of stone and wood, and their communities grew to several hundred people. They began behaving differently from other foragers, burying their dead with elaborate rituals within their settlements and grinding the wild cereals with mortars and pestles. The Natufians continued to forage and hunt for their food. They never actually took up agriculture, but what they did was perhaps the most radical change of all: they began the sedentary lifestyle that eventually made agriculture possible.[3]

Sedentism is the name given to the lifestyle of living in permanent dwellings, and it's considered by many to have been the most important step in prehistory. It's easy to see why sedentism may have occurred. There are, after all, many downsides to a nomadic lifestyle: the work of setting up and dismantling camp, the physical difficulties for the aged and infirm, and the burden of carrying infants and family possessions from place to place. We can imagine a point when the Natufians realized that, for them, nature had become an unconditionally giving environment, and there was simply no need to get up and move on to find the next season's food. There was enough food to gather and hunt from one place all year round.[4]

However, something happens to a community that becomes sedentary. Material things take on new importance. As we saw in the previous chapter, when an anthropologist gave hoop iron to the nomadic Hadza foragers, they simply threw away what they couldn't use. But if you're living in one place, why not keep the hoop iron you can't use now and store it for later? For that matter, if you're lucky enough to have found a lot of barley that week while foraging, why not pick more than you can eat now and store it for later, too? These are the revolutionary new ideas that occur to a sedentary group, which nomads would never consider.

Sedentary communities are sometimes referred to as "delayed-return" societies because people plan ahead, setting aside food and other supplies for later. In delayed-return societies, accumulation of property leads inevitably to inequalities between people. Someone who decides to work extra hard to gather surplus wheat will not be happy to give it away later to someone who was too lazy to do so. This leads to what anthropologist Alain Testart has called a "change in ideology." The foraging principle of food sharing has to be transformed or given up. There is less reliance on kinship and friendship for protection when things go wrong, and more reliance on building up your own stores of wealth. Attitudes toward time begin to change: the past (when you accumulated your goods) and the future (when you might need them) become more important, replacing a simple, consistent focus on the present. Attitudes toward work also shift: rather than doing just what you need to feed yourself that day, there's an incentive to work harder to invest in the future. This all leads to a changed view of nature, with people relying on their own planning and storage rather than an ever-providing natural world. "Thus," Testart writes, "storage expresses a distrust of nature."[5]

Although sedentism seems to have been a prerequisite for agriculture, it didn't inevitably lead to it. For example, the west coast of North America was inhabited for millennia by sedentary foragers, who exhibited many characteristics usually associated with agricultural societies, such as magnificent ceremonial houses and pronounced inequality, with some societies divided into chiefs, commoners, and slaves. But they never turned to agriculture. What, then, was the catalyst that led some sedentary societies to take that extra step to farming?[6]

The Domestication of the Human

The climate probably played a part. Beginning fifteen thousand years ago, the Northern Hemisphere suffered a severe period of cold and dry conditions known as the Younger Dryas. Then, about 11,500 years ago, conditions warmed up considerably, setting the scene for the milder climatic period, the Holocene, that we're still enjoying today. The Holocene wasn't just warmer—it was also wetter and less variable, and many experts believe it was this reliability that helped farming gain a foothold.[7]

Some researchers see increased population pressure as another catalyst of agriculture, as foragers killed off the easy pickings. But it certainly doesn't tell the whole story. For example, agriculture developed autonomously in the tropics of the New World, but there is no evidence in that region that preagricultural populations approached the land's carrying capacity.[8]

Perhaps the most important thing to recognize about the rise of agriculture is that it wasn't preplanned. It's very unlikely that anyone ever made a decision to stop foraging for food and begin planting seeds for themselves. Most likely, agriculture emerged as the result of a powerful dynamic between humans and the wildlife they relied on, with the result that—like Enkidu—it was humans who got domesticated as much as the plants and animals.

To understand how this happens, it's helpful to look at the example of cereals such as wheat and barley. In the wild, wheat and barley plants have weak husks that spontaneously shatter, dropping their seeds to the ground, where they germinate and grow into the next generation. Occasionally, a mutation causes the husks to grow stronger and prevents them from shattering. While this mutation would be lethal for a wild plant, it's highly convenient for human gatherers because the seeds remain in the plant and are more available to be harvested. Over generations, humans collected these seeds; brought them back to camp, occasionally spilling some on the ground; and gradually increased the population of these mutant crops relative to the wild variety. However, as people relied increasingly on these nonshattering varieties, they had to take over the job of planting them each year because the plants had become unable to propagate themselves. They then had to weed the fields they had planted, to keep out the stronger, wild varieties.[9]

A similar dynamic occurred with the wild dogs, goats, sheep, and cattle that became domesticated. In each case, humans would select the smaller and gentler animals, and, over generations, these genetic traits would predominate until the species became too weak to survive by itself in the wild. Now, humans were responsible for protecting these domesticated animals from predators, something their wild predecessors had been able to do for themselves. In this way, humans who had once had the freedom to wander wherever they chose were forced to stay put and care for the crops and animals that had previously looked after themselves.[10]

Light from the Near East?

One consequence of agriculture was a dramatic population explosion. Plants could be grown in gardens and orchards at a much higher density than in the wild. Heavy technology, such as presses and forges, could be utilized in a sedentary community to make food preparation more efficient. Cereals could be turned into easily digestible foods to wean infants much earlier, as a result of which women's fertility increased. And although many of the world's epidemic diseases arose from domesticated animals, these would not have appeared at first, so the early farmers would have been just as healthy, if not healthier, than those who continued foraging. As a result, it's estimated that the population of Southwest Asia, ground zero for agriculture, increased from just a hundred thousand people to five million between 8000 and 4000 BCE.[11]

This population growth put severe pressure on both the environment and the social equilibrium. Assaulted by forest clearance, soil tillage, and animal pasturing, the fragile environment of Southwest Asia quickly degraded. On the periphery of agricultural territories, these pressures led to population dispersal, with generations of young pioneers heading off yonder, staking out virgin land to create a new future for themselves. In central regions, where pioneering wasn't an option, these pressures led to ever-increasing complexity of social organization, ultimately resulting in the early civilizations of Mesopotamia and Egypt.[12]

What happened when these farming trailblazers ventured into territory already occupied by foragers? Was it an ancient version of the Wild West myth, in which the pioneers were periodically set upon by the locals but eventually conquered them? Or was it a more tolerant exchange of cultures in which hunter-gatherers gradually took up agricultural techniques themselves? This question has been the subject of much controversy.

Archaeologist Gordon Childe set the tone for the debate in the early twentieth century with a theory known as *ex oriente lux*, or "light from the Near East." In his view, over thousands of years, farmers from Southwest Asia colonized Europe, bringing their domesticated plants and animals along with ceramics and tools. The hunter-gatherers already there could do very little to resist the advance.[13]

In recent decades, however, some researchers have argued against this model of aggressive colonization. Rather, in their view, it was the foragers themselves who gradually took up agriculture in a process of cultural diffusion. "The last hunters," they claim, "were the first farmers."[14]

There's more at stake here than just an academic debate. This is a question about the founding dynamics of our ancestry. Are we virtually all descendants of violent, colonizing aggressors, or do we come from an ancient tradition of cultural tolerance and diffusion?

Those who argue for the colonizing theory point to the fact that, in historical times, hunter-gatherers who lived in fertile lands have shown no interest in adopting agriculture. Woodburn describes some Hadza who were forced to live in government-run settlements and trained to become farmers. Those few who applied themselves and obtained a good crop had their fields raided by other Hadza, and, once they harvested the remaining grain, they were under relentless pressure to share it rather than keep it stored until the next harvest. He concludes that "even the successful farmer is likely to give up," and if it's so difficult to switch to agriculture even under government supervision, it's "even less likely that they would have been able to convert to agriculture in the past."[15]

The cultural diffusion proponents counter with the example of southern Scandinavia, where sedentary hunter-gatherers known as the Pitted Ware culture lived side by side with farmers for more than a thousand years. As we saw earlier, sedentary foragers would be expected to develop values more akin to farmers, so this may be an explanation for their relatively peaceful coexistence.[16]

In recent years, advanced DNA analysis seems to have settled the dispute in favor of the colonizing theory. Even the Pitted Ware foragers, it turns out, are not actually the direct ancestors of modern Scandinavians: their genes never made it down the line. It seems that agriculture was, in fact, disseminated throughout the world by the brute force of colonizing farmers. Analysis of modern European populations has found that most male chromosomes descend from Near Eastern farmers, whereas maternal lineages are mostly from hunter-gatherers, indicating that farming males had a reproductive advantage over their foraging rivals. Similar male-female patterns of DNA have been associated with the Bantu agricultural expansion in Africa and the spread of agriculture in both India and Japan. Whether you interpret these findings as evidence of ancient conquest and rape on a massive scale or as a more genteel narrative of forager women being attracted to high-prestige farmers as husbands, the message seems clear: agriculture conquered.[17]

A Revolution in Values

When the first farmers conquered their way across the world, they brought with them a different collective consciousness. Agrarian culture emphasized a new suite of values such as accumulation of property, hierarchies, and planning for the future while inhibiting the urge for instant gratification. Imposing their willpower over short-term gratification would have been particularly necessary during difficult times, when farmers would have to force their families to go hungry rather than let them eat the seed grain and breeding stock required for the next season. The very word "agriculture" suggests a radically new process where the wild field (*ager*) is cultured and turned into a human construct. The first farmers didn't just transform the wild; they also invented the notion of home as a domain separate from wilderness. In this sense, they literally domesticated themselves.[18]

For the first time, humans saw themselves as different from the rest of the world and imposed their own symbolic forms on nature. Archaeologist Jacques Cauvin sees this cognitive shift as the most important aspect of the rise of agriculture, calling it the Symbolic Revolution. He points to the transition in Southwest Asia, after the emergence of agriculture, from circular dwellings to square and rectangular houses. The natural world is filled with circular or curved shapes, but squares and rectangles are almost entirely human constructions. Once villages became permanent, those born into these settlements would have developed a new view of human patterns and structures as different from the unruly patterns of the wild. It is here, Cauvin writes, "that we find the roots of the present state of the human race, not only in its domination and exploitation of the environment, but also . . . in the very foundations of our culture and mentality."[19]

Along with squares and rectangles, boundary lines emerge, separating not just farmland from the wild but also one farmer's landholding from another. The land itself—previously free—becomes a valuable asset, permitting those who own it to become even wealthier by growing more crops. Wealth becomes an intrinsic value, and those who don't have any are seen as worthless. Significant hierarchical inequalities emerged over the first few thousand years of agriculture. In a grave site in Sudan dating to 4000 BCE, most people are buried with nothing, but a few are buried with more than a hundred pots and bracelets of elephant and hippopotamus ivory. A famous cemetery in Varna, Bulgaria, from around the same time has yielded the first known high-prestige gold and copper artifacts, along with other impressive goods.[20]

Once material possessions have value, they can be compared with each other and bartered or traded, leading to new levels of economic and social complexity. For the first time, people could specialize in crafts rather than producing their own food and make a living by trading what they made for other things they needed. In this way, farming was the precondition for the first great civilizations and every civilization since, including our own.[21]

The new emphasis on wealth and hierarchy made its way into the most intimate aspects of the human experience, influencing relationships within the family. In forager cultures, familial relationships were as fluid and unstructured as everything else. The Hadza, for example, have no household heads, and the children tend to do what they want rather than obey their parents. In an agrarian society, however, someone who has spent his life building up wealth and prestige doesn't want to see it all evaporate on his death. The issue of inheritance emerges, requiring rules for how possessions get passed from one generation to the next. The authority of the patriarch becomes paramount. Women are perceived as commodities, like land and food sources, that males can utilize to further enhance their wealth into the distant future, even beyond their own life span. New values emphasizing hitherto unknown concepts of honor, virginity, and sexual fidelity now become major issues dominating people's lives.[22]

Ancient Mesopotamia, so much closer in time to this transformation, bears witness to the revolution in values. In a fertility ceremony dating back at least six thousand years, *The Marriage of Inanna and Dumuzi*, Inanna, the goddess of sexual love and fertility, has to decide between marrying a farmer or a shepherd. Dumuzi, one of her regal suitors, woos her by convincing her of his background and rank. She finally gives herself to him with the following incantation:

> Inanna: As for me, my vulva, . . .
> Me—the maid, who will plow it for me?
> My vulva, the watered ground—for me,
> Me the Queen, who will station the ox there?
> Dumuzi: Oh Lordly Lady, the king will plow it for you,
> Dumuzi, the king, will plow it for you
> Inanna: Plow my vulva, man of my heart!
> Chorus: Plants rose high by his side,
> Grains rose high by his side.[23]

It's hard to imagine a more dramatic expression of the fusion of agriculture, social status, sexuality, and abundance into one combined set of values.

Anxiety and Authority

There was one tremendous downside to the new agrarian emphasis on material possessions: you could lose them. This fundamental vulnerability of the agricultural system profoundly influenced the way farmers related to the cosmos. For foragers, sustained by a wide variety of foods, it was of no great concern if the climate acted unpredictably—they could simply shift their diet to other tubers, grubs, nuts, or berries. If things didn't improve, they could move to another territory. Farmers, by contrast, were committed to a narrow range of staples and had given up the option of moving on. No matter how diligently they worked, they were dangerously vulnerable to natural forces outside their control, such as drought, flood, or crop failure.

This led, in the words of archaeologist Graeme Barker, to "a very different kind of spirituality characterized by a separation from and distrust of nature," which generated "the anxiety over cosmic disorder that seems to lie at the core of all the agrarian religions." No longer was nature a generous, giving parent; instead, it was increasingly something to "control and appropriate rather than be part of."[24]

The theme of control becomes central. On the one hand, the very idea of agriculture opens the possibility of humans controlling their destiny through their actions. On the other hand, the parameters under human control remain painfully limited. A sure recipe for distress. Agrarian views of the universe arise directly from the habitual patterns of agricultural life—and, as a result, the twin themes of control and anxiety are never far away.

As humans exerted increasing control over other animals, their gods took on a more human form. In older forager times, deities were associated primarily with animals. When shamans journeyed to other worlds, their spirits would take on the forms of those animals. But, as early as the Natufians, images of animals began to be superseded by human forms, primarily female "mother goddess" figurines.[25]

These new gods take on a position of authority, a concept unknown to nomadic foragers. Images of deities begin to show humans around them with their arms raised in the position of supplication. As Cauvin puts it, "The theme of the 'supplicant' introduces an entirely new relationship between god and man . . . a new distinction at the heart of the human imagination between an 'above' and a 'below', between an order of a divine force, personified and dominant, and that of an everyday humanity." Gone are the days of nature as mother and father providing food unconditionally to their children. Instead, nature now provides food only in return for the right conduct. If the ancestral spirits receive the correct sacrifices given with the appropriate rituals, they will reward their descendants with a good harvest. If not, they might cause the crops to fail in retribution.[26]

The increasing complexity of human society was reflected in ever more elaborate notions of how the divine world connected with the human domain. The relationship between people and their gods was taken over by priests, mediating a communication that had once been direct. As people began living in urban settlements, it became increasingly difficult to conceive of deities existing only in the natural world. How could people now communicate with them? The emergence of idols solved this problem. Now, just as a natural object such as a tree could hold a divine essence, an idol could too.[27]

Everyone, from peasant to king, had a part to play in this elaborate network of cosmos, society, and individual. No role was more crucial than that of the king, who, by performing the required rituals, could maintain the order of the cosmos—which, in turn, transferred to political and social stability. But while the king was central to the cosmic network, each citizen gained his own sense of identity through his interactions with the social and cosmic order.[28]

Spirits Everywhere

Separated now from the wilderness, agriculturalists saw the natural world as a mysterious place filled with cosmic power. The Aztecs believed this divine presence, called *teotl*, was physically manifested in a lake, a thunderstorm, or a mountain. The Yoruba called this force *ase*, which they believed brought all things into existence. For the Inca, there were sacred places in the earth known as *huacas*, such as rocks, springs, valleys, or mountains, where the cosmic force was particularly concentrated.[29]

Across the world, each agrarian culture saw the natural objects around them as intrinsically divine. In ancient Egypt, the sun was a god whose rising and setting were acts of will; the Nile was another deity who deliberately chose to bestow floodwaters each year to the people. Every hill, tree, and stream had its own guardian spirit that needed to be placated before it could be dug into, cut down, or dammed.[30]

Humans themselves were understood to contain spirits that animated them. Across the globe, the sense of the wind as cosmic breath bestowing a life force became a powerful element of agrarian mythic consciousness. In many cultures of prehistory, the word for breath is the same as for wind and for the life force animating a living being. The ancient Indians used *prana* with each of these meanings; the Chinese used *qi*; for the Hebrews, the analogous words were *ruah* and *nephesh*; and the early Greeks used *pneuma* and *psyche* to capture the same ideas.[31]

These agrarian notions of the human spirit were very different from the modern idea of a soul. In our era, pervaded by monotheistic thought, any discussion of the soul is likely to assume that it exists in a nonphysical dimension with no tangible qualities. This concept was unknown to early cultures, where the human soul was presumed to have a material, if somewhat evanescent and numinous, quality. Even though the spirit survived the body after death, it still maintained a quasimaterial existence and could itself die. In China, the departed spirit was understood to shrink gradually with time, so the spirit of a newly dead person was believed to be heavier than that of an old one.[32]

Virtually every early culture saw humans as having more than one spirit: usually two or three, and sometimes more. Paralleling the modern distinction in cognitive neuroscience between conceptual and animate modes of consciousness, one spirit was frequently related to the mind and another to the life force animating the body. In ancient Egypt, the *ba*, which existed independently from the body, was associated with a person's individuality, whereas the *ka* was seen as a vital force inherited from the parents. The *ba* was crucially related to the practice of mummification because the Egyptians felt that if they could preserve the body, the *ba* would have a chance to reunite with it after death. The Chinese, similarly, believed that two main spirits, *hun* and *po*, made up a human being. The *hun*, like the Egyptian *ba*, represented a person's intellect and ascended to the sky as a shining spirit after death, while the *po* remained in the tomb for about three years, after which it traveled to the mythical Yellow Springs, where it was recycled into a new life force.[33]

In contrast to hunter-gatherers, who believed spirits of the deceased became part of the natural world, recently departed spirits in agrarian communities tended to remain in the home, where they were thought to continue to eat and sleep with the family, causing nightmares and calamities if they weren't treated with sufficient respect. This led to the development of elaborate sacrificial rituals, with reverential worship of individuals from several generations back and a more general veneration of the entire ancestral family.[34]

Actively Participating in the Cosmos

Through agriculture, people learned a new way to interact with nature: actively manipulating it to accomplish their goals. In the same way, their cosmology led them to attempt to manipulate the gods as well.

In today's world, if a high-tech entrepreneur has an idea he wishes to capitalize on, he needs more than just the technology to work. He also requires extensive intangible support for his goals, such as financing and regulatory approvals. Similarly, an early farmer planning to sow a field with a new crop would feel the need for approval from the appropriate deities to maximize his chances for success. And just as a modern businessperson needs to make sure her payroll taxes are filed accurately and on time, so the early farmer would devote himself meticulously to the performance of the correct rituals if he expected to stay in the gods' good graces.[35]

Appeasing the gods wasn't just a matter of following the rules. There was also a sense that if you used the right techniques, you might even get those cosmic rules to bend a little for your benefit, just as a modern executive might donate money to a political cause that could help her industry. Consider this Egyptian spell to heal serpent and scorpion bites, in which the physician-priest threatens to cause the sun's sailing vessel to come to a standstill and describes the consequences:

> Springs are blocked, plants wither
> Life is taken from the living,
> Until Horus recovers for his mother Isis
> And my patient also recovers.

The priest brings his patient into the midst of the cosmic drama, attempting to take control of the resonance between the affairs of the deities and that of his patient.[36]

Over time, this perception that humans had some partial control over their destiny through their relationship with the gods led to a broader sense of active participation in the cosmos—a defining characteristic of agrarian cosmologies worldwide. The agricultural lifestyle may again be seen as the source of this conviction. Foragers never felt any responsibility to keep their world abundant. Farmers, on the other hand, grew accustomed to a systematic, never-ending schedule of tasks, such as plowing, sowing, irrigation, weeding, and harvesting, all of which needed to be conscientiously performed, or disaster might ensue. Is it any wonder, then, that they should apply these habits of thought to their worldview, believing that cosmic order could only be preserved if they diligently and continuously worked on it?

Early civilizations around the world shared this weighty sense of responsibility. The Maya believed that their rituals helped the gods carry their burdens along the cycles of time and that the universe would not function properly without them. Cosmic responsibility was even more onerous for the Aztec, who believed the sun could only be kept in motion if it were fueled with the vital energy of human blood. This was the source of the notorious Aztec tradition of human sacrifice, which caused their military to carry out a continual program of conquests, using the blood of their captives to keep the sun god on his course. While the ancient Egyptians didn't follow the path of human sacrifice, they held an equally powerful notion of cosmic order, called *ma'at*, which they believed translated directly into political and social order and could only be maintained by continuous attention.[37]

The rituals themselves paralleled the agricultural seasons with their recurrent cycles. There was a strong sense shared around the world that, at the beginning of the universe, the gods performed actions in certain ways, and it was the sacred duty of humans to repeat those actions on a cyclical basis. "We must do what the gods did in the beginning," says one of the ancient Vedic scriptures of India. In Egypt, the power of priestly invocation was drawn from the fact that the god Thoth had created the world through his own spoken words. The Judeo-Christian Sabbath derives from this same ancient formula: in Genesis, we are told that "God blessed the seventh day and made it holy, because on it he rested from all the work of creating that he had done."[38]

From Asia to Mexico, from Central America to Egypt, there is a remarkable similarity in the conceptual substrata of the worldviews of agrarian civilizations, traceable to the new behaviors and anxieties that agriculture brought to the collective human consciousness. But equally significant are the different directions these cultures took as they elaborated their views of the universe. This leads us to an important turning point. Until now, the channels of thought sculpted by the patterning instinct have been equally applicable to societies across the globe. From this point on, the world's great cultural traditions begin going their own ways. In the following chapters, we'll investigate how different civilizations created their own unique worldviews and how these ultimately led to the profound divergence in patterns of thought that has characterized human history ever since.

Chapter 6

GOING THEIR OWN WAYS: EARLY CIVILIZATIONS

If an extraterrestrial explorer had visited Earth around the year 1500 BCE, she'd have found an array of different cultures in the Eurasian landmass, ranging from great civilizations to scattered tribespeople. If she'd made a wager with her crew members as to which cultures would leave the greatest imprint on the future of the human species, she'd likely have put her galactic dollars on those that were the most organized and built the grandest monuments. She'd probably have given short shrift to a bunch of illiterate horsemen herding their cattle on the plains. But she'd have been wrong.

In this chapter, we'll investigate five cultural complexes that flourished in the second millennium BCE. We'll trace the fascinating way each turned its common heritage—agrarian mythic consciousness—into a distinct way of imposing meaning onto the mysterious fluctuations of the universe. As we watch these early thought traditions emerge, we'll be able to identify embryonic forms of ideas about the universe that have come to structure our current world. However, as that visiting extraterrestrial would have discovered, the relative contributions of these cultures to our modern ways of thinking were anything but predictable.

In the ensuing millennia, three of the most advanced civilizations we'll investigate turned to dust, only to be rediscovered by modern archaeologists. The culture that was most successful in bequeathing its pattern of thought to modern times had not even achieved literacy. And only one of those early civilizations would remain intact through the thirty-five hundred years to the present day. That one was China.

China: The Orderly Cosmos

Separated from the rest of the Eurasian landmass by the Himalayas, China's thought traditions evolved in virtual isolation from the developments going on elsewhere. This may have contributed to China's unique cultural stability. While the beliefs and languages of other regions have changed out of all recognition, Chinese culture has maintained enough cohesion through the millennia that it can rightly claim to have the oldest continuous civilization in the world.[1]

In the second millennium BCE, the priests of the Shang dynasty used a particular divination method to communicate with their gods. They took turtle shells and scapulae (shoulder blades) of cattle, carved questions into them, and placed them in a fire until they cracked. They would read the cracks as guidance from the gods. Thanks to their careful archiving of these inscriptions, more than a hundred thousand shells and scapulae have been found, enabling archaeologists to piece together an extensive understanding of what was important to the Shang rulers.[2]

The picture we get of Shang thought is a classic agrarian cosmology, replete with spirit worship, sacrifice, and ritual. What is unique to the Shang is how they turned the tradition of ancestor worship into a comprehensive, orderly system that structured their entire worldview. While it gave due attention to the spirits of the mountains, trees, and rivers, the Shang religion was primarily a cult of the ancestors. The power and authority held by the patriarch of the family continued unbroken after his death—only now they were exercised through supernatural forces, which could endow wealth and prosperity on those who came after, as long as they demonstrated their respect through the correct rituals and sacrifices. The perpetuation of the family line was allimportant. Filial piety evolved as a core value of Chinese civilization, establishing the primacy of patriarchy in the living family and infusing the worship of the ancestors.[3]

The shamanic relationship with the spirit world, an integral part of the hunter-gatherer experience, was transformed by agrarian values into a hierarchical and specialized set of practices. As before, shamans used their rituals to converse with the spirits, only now they worked for those who held political power. The king himself was seen as the highest shaman, who could determine and influence the will of the ancestral spirits through divination, prayer, and sacrifice. The primordial power of shamanism had merged with the hierarchical values of agriculture to create the new legitimacy of kingship.[4]

Back in forager days, no sacrifice was required to communicate with the spirit world. In the centralized hierarchy of the Shang, sacrifice and ritual became entrenched as a way to influence the deities. The spirits of the ancestors were believed to rely on the offerings of grain, wine libations, and animal—even human—sacrifices to maintain their strength. These sacrifices served another political purpose: sometimes involving several hundred cattle at a time, they impressed all around with the awe-inspiring power of the dynasty through its relationship with the spirit world.[5]

With one king commanding the state, the spirit world was also believed to have a supreme ruler, Ti, who held power over all the ancestral spirits. Just as, in the court, a commoner might try to gain access to a nobleman who had the king's ear, so the cosmic system worked the same way. The king communicated directly with his own ancestors, who, in turn, communicated with Ti.[6]

This process became tightly systematized, with a rigid sacrificial schedule and particular sacrifices required for specific responses. The inscriptions on the priestly scapulae show tremendous concern for the correct numbers and ratios for the sacrifices: Two or three sheep? What proportion of male to female animals? Shang historian David Keightley sees a bureaucratic mindset emerging: in place of ad hoc bribery to the gods to achieve a particular purpose, a kind of salary system appears, with particular payments required of the right number of cattle to the right ancestors on the right day.[7]

Just as bureaucracies thrive on systems of seniority, so, too, did Shang cosmology. The senior ancestors exercised their power impersonally on statewide issues such as harvests, whereas a recently deceased ancestor would stick closer to home, possibly plaguing a living individual who had known him when he was still alive. Ti's jurisdiction, most impersonal of all, incorporated such factors as rain and warfare.[8]

The Shang worldview envisaged an orderly cosmos, a rational universe that responded to the appropriate human actions. Of course, things could go wrong, such as a particular ancestor feeling malevolent, but, even then, there was the belief that a specific action could be divined to propitiate him. Ultimately, there was a conservative optimism at the heart of the Shang world, a belief that the universe—just like the bureaucracy of the imperial court—could work for all people's benefit if everyone played their part correctly.[9]

Egypt: The One and the Many

The struggle for *ma'at*

Thousands of miles to the west, the ancient Egyptians had their own profound sense of order in the universe, called *ma'at*. However, the Egyptian conception of *ma'at* was more conflicted than the bureaucratic optimism of the Shang. Egyptian civilization rose from the fertile floodwaters of the Nile, and the annual floods that gave life to their society provided a natural structure to their view of the cosmos. Ancient Egyptian history is characterized by long periods of prosperity punctuated by occasional devastating episodes of collapse, usually following years in which the Nile floods failed. Perhaps this pattern embedded itself into the cultural consciousness of the Egyptians, leading to the sense that *ma'at* could never be wholly relied on.[10]

Ma'at literally means "base," as in the base of a throne, and it was understood by the Egyptians as the foundation of the entire world order. It governed every aspect of life but was continually being disturbed, and the combined efforts of humans and gods alike were required to preserve it. If these efforts failed, the dreaded alternative was *isfet*, or "lack"—a lack of order that manifested in disease, scarcity, violence, injustice, and death.[11]

If the ancient Egyptians missed out on some of the Shang optimism about life in this world, they outdid themselves with optimism regarding the next. The Shang were interested in the world of the ancestor spirits only insofar as it affected their own; they rarely, if ever, speculated on their own individual paths upon entering the spirit world. By contrast, the Egyptians viewed the afterlife as the most important sphere, with their current life merely a kind of dream preparing them for the next. When they died, Egyptians took up permanent residence in the Field of Hetep, a fertile paradise with abundant harvests, where both rich and poor alike could cultivate crops on their own plots of land.[12]

However, this egalitarian immortality was not for everyone. A ticket to the Field of Hetep was only available to those who had lived their lives in accordance with *ma'at*. It was believed that when you died, you faced a trial with a judge (usually the god Osiris), counsel for the prosecution and the defense, and witnesses. At this point, your heart was weighed by the jackal-headed god Anubis, with a feather representing *ma'at* on the other side of the scales. If you failed the trial, the crocodile-headed Amamet, the "Gobbler," stood by, ready to devour you. We see here, for the first time in recorded history, what scholar

Robert Wright calls a "morally contingent afterlife," ordaining that your actions in this life have a direct effect on your experience of the next. A chapter in the *Book of the Dead* tells you what to say when arguing your case with Osiris:

> I have brought no evil. . . .
> I have not oppressed servants.
> I have not scorned any god.
> I have not defrauded the poor of their property. . . .
> I have not caused pain.
> I have caused no man to hunger.
> I have not added weights to the scales to cheat buyers.
> I have not stolen milk from the mouths of children.

These "negative confessions" suggest that, for the Egyptians, two negatives made a positive: a lack of *isfet* in your life meant you had fulfilled your contribution to maintaining *ma'at*.[13]

One god or many gods?

With its moral linkage between this world and the next, Egyptian cosmology broached a theme that became central to later monotheistic thought. Additionally, many Egyptian texts had a way of referring to particular gods as "the greatest of all gods" or the "one god that created all others." It's therefore not surprising that the Europeans who first deciphered Egyptian hieroglyphs in the nineteenth century enthused over what they saw as an early version of monotheism in Egyptian thought.[14]

However, modern Egyptologists have shown that the Egyptian view of the universe was more nuanced. To begin with, it's easy to misinterpret simple flattery for monotheism. If you're praying to a god with power over your destiny, there is no harm in showering him with praise and telling him he's unequalled throughout the universe. Scholars have pointed out that a laserlike focus on one particular god might also go beyond the realm of flattery. With enough concentration on the greatness of the god you're praying to, the other gods could begin to disappear from view. One way to understand this is to imagine being in a dimly lit room when someone shines a flashlight in your face. All you can see is the beam of light from the flashlight. The rest of the room has been obliterated from your sight, even though you know it's still there.[15]

There was, though, a time when Egyptian thought did lurch toward monotheism, a dramatic episode that has been traced by Egyptologist Jan Assmann. Around 2200 BCE, the Old Kingdom—a peak of civilization that produced the Great Pyramid of Giza—suffered decades of drought. Catastrophic failures of the Nile floods resulted in the collapse of the Old Kingdom into anarchy. The very foundation of beliefs about the cosmos was shaken during this time, resulting in a crisis of faith regarding whether *ma'at* could be maintained. During this epoch, people began to wonder whether their destiny was, in fact, driven by what Assmann calls "the inscrutable will of a hidden god."[16]

In the Coffin Texts, dated to the period following the Old Kingdom's collapse, the traditional names of the most powerful gods are avoided, and in their place are phrases such as "one who came into existence by himself." As the centuries wore on, ancient Egypt recovered and emerged even stronger during a period known as the New Kingdom. A new theology developed, centered around the great temple complex at Karnak, which worshipped a god called Amun-Re in terms that seem to approach the totality of monotheism. In the *Hymn to Amun-Re*, the entire universe, including all other gods, is described as Amun-Re's creation. Here is a passage from around 1600 BCE:

> You are the sole one, who has created all that is,
> The single sole one who created what exists;
> From whose eyes humankind came forth,
> From whose pronouncement the gods came into existence.

Amun-Re was no longer competing with the other gods but rather absorbed them into his own essence.[17]

The evolution of Egyptian thought took a drastic turn during the short reign of Akhenaten from 1353 to 1336 BCE. Akhenaten was the father of the famous boy pharaoh Tutankhamen, whose mummified remains have traveled the world, but he has a far greater claim to fame than his celebrity son. Akhenaten was the first person to introduce true monotheism to human history. In a dramatic power play, he abolished any worship of Amun-Re and imposed the worship of the sun god known as the Aten. This was a huge disruption to the traditional lives of the people, and Akhenaten enforced his new theology with unprecedented brutality, terrorizing the population and hacking Amun's image out of every monument in the land. "The monotheistic revolution of Akhenaten," Assmann writes, "was not only the first but also the most radical and violent eruption of a counter-religion in the history of humankind."[18] The hymns to the Aten take the earlier tradition eulogizing Amun-Re and—substituting the Aten as the supreme god—extend it even further:

> The earth comes into being at your nod, as you have created it. . . .
> You are lifetime itself: one lives through you. . . .
> You are the One yet a million lives are in you.

With Akhenaten, a new intolerance entered Egyptian theology. If, in fact, there is just one god responsible for everything, then, surely, worshipping other gods is an insult to the one true god? The connection of monotheism with intolerance will be explored later, but it is noteworthy that the first appearance of monotheism in history brought with it such brutality and persecution.[19]

Another characteristic of monotheism, seen here for the first time, is a shift in the source of sacredness from the world up to the heavens. Until now, all cosmologies—shamanic or agrarian—saw the natural world and the spirit world as intrinsically interconnected. The spirits of the animals and trees, the storms and the sun, all participated in orchestrating the cosmos. Now, with a single transcendent creator god, the natural world begins to be seen as merely the recipient of the god's beneficence rather than the source itself of such powers.[20]

Reconciling the one and the many

Akhenaten's revolution barely outlasted his own life. Tutankhamen was just nine years old when he ascended the throne, and the traditional Amun-Re priesthood quickly reasserted itself. Akhenaten's new royal capital was abandoned along with the monotheistic worship of the Aten. But this brief, convulsive episode of Egyptian history sheds light on key conceptual difficulties that can arise when people are driven by their patterning instinct to attempt a more systematic representation of the universe.[21]

Traditional forager and agrarian worldviews don't try to systematize their myths into a comprehensive whole. Their worldviews comprise a set of patterns that don't necessarily cohere. For example, when anthropologist Roger Keesing attempted to pin down the Kwaio of the Solomon Islands about their ancestors, he noted that people were "remarkably vague" and "not even very precise about the process whereby a living person becomes an ancestor. The few who bother to think about such matters only do so as a result of being prompted by an anthropologist, and they have wildly divergent representations of the process." The ancient Egyptians, however, attempted to turn their mythic patterns into a comprehensive system and, in so doing, uncovered what Assmann has called the "cognitive dissonance" that results from an attempt to resolve the relationship between unity and diversity.[22]

In a traditional polytheistic cosmology, there's no need for a worldview to be systematic. Each god may have unique powers that are not necessarily consistent with those of another god. However, once we conceive of a sole creative power in the universe, the gods that previously represented natural forces and creatures are no longer the source of divinity. They become mere recipients of the creative force of the one god; they are now just intermediaries between the one transcendent god and ordinary human beings.

The patterning instinct compels an attempt to understand the system this creator has bestowed: if the universe, which seems so variegated, is really a unified entity, then isn't this unity the true wellspring of meaning? Trying to reconcile a universe composed of "the one" and "the many" was a massive conceptual challenge, one that has been described as a "meltdown" in polytheistic mythology.[23]

One solution to this meltdown was that promulgated by Akhenaten: the imposition of a systematic monotheism forcefully excluding any other form of worship. In Assmann's words, it "resolved the cognitive dissonance . . . of the relationship between unity and diversity by abolishing diversity."[24]

Monotheism is one solution. But it's not the only one. Assmann describes how, in the post-Akhenaten era, known as the Ramesside period, a new pantheistic cosmology arose that explained the various deities as different aspects and forms of a single transcendent creator god, thus making it possible "to conceive of the diversity of deities as the colorful reflection of a hidden unity."[25]

This new pantheistic god didn't just create the universe—he *was* the universe, in all its variegated forms. The ultimate source of sacredness came back down from the heavens to inhabit the earth. Here's a Ramesside prayer demonstrating the new pantheism:

> Your two eyes are the sun and the moon,
> Your head is the sky,
> Your feet are the netherworld.
> You are the sky,
> You are the earth,

You are the netherworld,
You are the water,
You are the air between them.

Another hymn from this period hails "the One who makes himself into millions," and, in another text, he's actually referred to as "million of millions."[26]

These two choices for a coherent cosmological system held significance beyond ancient Egypt. As we'll see, centuries after Akhenaten's revolution, the civilizations of ancient Greece and India came across the same cognitive dissonance and chose different paths: Greece laying the framework for monotheism and India choosing a form of transcendent pantheism. In later Chinese thought, philosophers grappled with similar questions about the one and the many, leading to a sophisticated new understanding of the universe. In the struggles of ancient Egypt, we glimpse the first attempts to arrive at systematic cosmological solutions that have come to structure the thought patterns of much of the human race today.

Mesopotamia: Tidying Up the Cosmic Mess

A cosmos of grinding insecurity

For all their differences, both the Shang and the Egyptians shared a view of a cosmos that was orderly, as long as you worked hard enough to maintain it. How the Mesopotamians would have loved that sense of order! For thousands of years, the inhabitants of the valley formed by the Tigris and Euphrates labored to create the earliest and, in many ways, the most innovative civilization of ancient times, but they did so under the never-ending threat of chaos and devastation, both in their daily lives and in their understanding of the cosmos.

The Mesopotamian worldview, like the Egyptian and Chinese, may have been influenced by their geography. The territory of Mesopotamia was dry and inhospitable, with few minerals and barely any trees. Even the rivers refused to cooperate like the Nile: in late summer, when newly planted crops needed the most water, they were at their lowest levels. So how did this barren region become the incubator of the world's first great civilization? In one word: irrigation. By digging an increasingly elaborate system of canals, the early inhabitants of the region were able not only to sustain themselves but to create an agricultural surplus that permitted them to trade for the raw materials they lacked—and eventually develop the most complex society the world had ever seen.[27]

Mesopotamian civilization lasted for an impressive three thousand years, but the political history of the region was characterized by incessant instability and plagued by warfare and invasions, leading to the rise and fall of a series of different empires. A sense of dread was never far away from its dogged citizens.[28] Perhaps no distinction is more striking between Egypt and Mesopotamia than their views of the afterlife. In dire contrast to the idyllic Field of Hetep, the Mesopotamian epic *The Descent of Ishtar* describes the gloomy underworld waiting for the deceased, who journey through demon-infested lands

> . . . to the house whose entrants are bereft of light,
> Where dust is their sustenance and clay their food.
> They see no light but dwell in darkness,
> They are clothed like birds in wings for garments,
> And dust has gathered on the door and bolt.[29]

With this mournful view of the afterlife, it's not surprising that the typical Mesopotamian turned his attention to what could be accomplished in this life. In contrast to the Egyptian focus on the rewards of the next world, the Mesopotamian relationship to the gods was concerned entirely with benefits that were currently available. In a poem called *Ludlul*, a man thrown into misfortune remembers when times were better and his piety was well compensated:

> For myself, I gave attention to supplication and prayer:
> To me prayer was discretion, sacrifice my rule . . .
> The day of the goddess's procession was profit and gain to me.[30]

Unfortunately for the Mesopotamians, the linkage between piety and reward seemed painfully capricious. Mesopotamian cosmology appears to have been modeled directly on the hierarchical structures of their own society, as a result of which, life for the gods was no more predictable than it was for humans. Just as human plans were subject to the whims of the king, so the plans of the gods were dependent on the favor of the chief god. During the third millennium BCE, as villages grew into cities and then into empires, the institution of kingship became increasingly powerful. The majestic king, exercising supreme authority over his people, became the core metaphor for the cosmos.

Here, for example, is a hymn to the god Enlil with imagery taken directly from the royal palace:

> When the honorable Enlil sits down in majesty
> On his sacred and sublime throne,
> When he exercises with perfection
> His power as Lord and King,
> Spontaneously the other gods prostrate [themselves] before him
> And obey his orders without protest![31]

The gods were subject to the vicissitudes of life just like their human supplicants. They plotted, fought each other, and could become sick and die. This cosmic turbulence had direct implications for the daily lives of the Mesopotamians. You could pray to your god and perform all the right rituals, but if that god was outmaneuvered in the cosmic sphere, there was nothing you could do about it. You were out of luck. In one inscription, the goddess of the city Ur laments her powerlessness to defend her city after the divine assembly agreed it should be destroyed:

> Dread of the storm's floodlike destruction weighed on me . . .
> Upon my couch at night no dreams were granted me . . .
> Because (this) bitter weeping had been destined for my land
> And I could not, even if I scoured the earth—a cow seeking her calf—
> Have brought my people back.[32]

How different from the orderly bureaucracy enjoyed by the Shang ancestors!

Matters were made worse by the fact that no one really knew how to maintain a good relationship with the gods anyway. The author of *Ludlul* utters a plaintive lament for the existential confusion that reigned over the relationship between god and human:

> I wish I knew that these things were pleasing to one's god!
> What is proper to oneself is an offense to one's god,
> What in one's own heart seems despicable is proper to one's god.
> Who knows the will of the gods in heaven?
> He who was alive yesterday is dead today. . . .

> I am appalled at these things; I do not understand their
> significance.[33]

Perhaps it's because of this grinding insecurity felt by Mesopotamians, this sense that no amount of piety could secure your position in this world, and the next world didn't even bear thinking about, that their civilization went on to create some of the greatest innovations the world has ever seen. If you can't rely on the gods to do it for you, they seemed to believe, you may as well accomplish what you can on your own.

Mesopotamian firsts

It was in the turbulent cities of Mesopotamia that many of the conceptual foundations of modern civilization were invented. The Mesopotamians were responsible for the first libraries and maps and for devising new disciplines such as mathematics, medicine, chemistry, botany, and zoology.[34]

Perhaps their most resounding achievement was the invention of writing, the first in human history. In contrast to the Shang, whose writing system revolved around divining the intentions of the ancestors, and the Egyptians, whose hieroglyphs record prayers to the gods, the earliest cuneiform of the Mesopotamians had a more prosaic purpose: bookkeeping. The Mesopotamians came up with writing as an ingenious form of keeping track of things, of making lists of such items as receipts of tribute, itemization of war booty, distribution of rations, and payments to officials.[35]

In their attempts to organize the world around them, the Mesopotamians were far ahead of any other civilization. In addition to their written lists, they devised a form of counting known as the sexagesimal system, using the base of sixty, that survives to this day. Every time we measure the degrees of an angle or look at a clock to tell the time, we're using a system we inherited from Mesopotamia. When the Mesopotamians looked up at the night sky, they arranged the stars into constellations and developed a tradition to divine future events based on the positions of the sun, moon, planets, and constellations, which survives today in the form of astrology. These careful observations of the night sky can also lay claim to be the ancestor of modern science and astronomy.[36]

Mesopotamians came up with many of the original formulations we still use to structure human activities. They invented dictionaries, legal documents such as sales and deeds, and codes of law. They were the first culture to create a separation between what we nowadays think of as religious and secular domains and to create concepts, such as equity and freedom, that have resounded through the millennia to become integral parts of the modern conception of society.[37]

Justice to the oppressed

In the third millennium, warfare between different city-states intensified, causing new warrior kings to take power while remaining precariously vulnerable to being toppled by other figures who might emerge from neighboring city-states. In contrast to Egyptian or Shang civilizations, where the centralized ruler was virtually indistinguishable from the gods, the insecure kings of Mesopotamia made no attempt to assert divinity. The most they could claim was to act as stewards of the gods, and everyone recognized they would be punished by military defeat if they failed to do their job well. This separation of the king from divinity led to a process of secularization, during which the political domain was gradually recognized as separate from the cosmological.[38]

In this more fragmented society, high-ranking officials and other successful citizens began to carve up land allotments until eventually it became the aspiration of all Mesopotamians to own some arable land for themselves. It was in this environment, where people could buy and sell land using legal contracts, and where debtors might lose everything to creditors if things went wrong, that the Babylonian king Hammurabi instituted his famous Code of Laws containing more than 280 laws written on twelve tablets, most of which survive to this day.[39] The remarkable feature of Hammurabi's Code was its sense of fairness and social welfare. If, for example, a debtor couldn't make payments because of a crop failure caused by natural events, then his debts would be waived. Hammurabi explained that these laws were promulgated

> . . . that the strong might not oppress the weak,
> That justice might be dealt the orphan (and) the widow. . . .
> I wrote my precious words on my stela . . .
> To give justice to the oppressed. . . .[40]

We see, again, the Mesopotamians recognizing that the gods alone could not be relied on to ensure order in society, and, therefore, they had better come up with some human guidelines.

This is not to suggest that the Mesopotamians saw their laws as separate from the cosmic order of things; rather, Hammurabi's Code implied that humans had been delegated by the gods to play a bigger role in managing their own destiny. Hammurabi declared that Shamash, the god of justice and commerce, had bestowed on him something known as *kittum*, which can be translated as "truth" or "natural law," a kind of universal law that transcends human idiosyncrasies.

The revolutionary and far-reaching implication of this concept was that a ruler couldn't just do whatever he wanted with his power. His responsibility was to ensure that *kittum* was implemented with justice and equity. Its significance becomes clear when contrasted with the Egyptian notion of *ma'at*. Instead of trying to maintain a cosmic order with the reward of a blessed afterlife, the Mesopotamians' goal was to execute *kittum* in the here and now, in the day-to-day activities of the marketplace and people's lives. If implemented well, the end result wasn't eternal paradise but, hopefully, a more equitable and just society for everyone.[41]

Faced with a cosmological mess and never-ending threats to their security, generations of Mesopotamians turned their attention to making their chaotic world a little more manageable. They bravely took the cosmic chaos they observed and attempted to make as much sense of it as they could through their dictionaries, mathematics, astronomical calculations, and codes of law. In doing so, these pioneers of civilization realized some of the most astounding achievements of any people in history.

Harappa: Explorations of the Mind?

The Mesopotamians imported valuable resources such as copper, gold, ivory, and cotton from a faraway, prosperous country they called Meluhha. While Meluhha's whereabouts have not been verified, most scholars are convinced it refers to an extensive civilization that grew up in the Indus Valley and prospered during the third and second millennia BCE.[42]

For more than a century, archaeologists busily excavated the ruins of Mesopotamia and Egypt without having the slightest idea that a contemporaneous Indus Valley civilization had even existed. Then, in 1924, archaeologists announced the discovery of two great cities—Mohenjo-daro and Harappa—located six hundred kilometers away from each other in an area that was then part of the British Empire and is now spread over Pakistan and India.[43]

Following the excitement of discovering an unknown civilization, the general reaction to the archaeological sites of the Indus Valley cities became one of disappointment. There were no pyramids, no great amphitheaters, palaces, or sculptures. Over the decades, it emerged that what became known as Harappan civilization was fundamentally different from its contemporaries. Its most striking feature seems to have been its degree of standardization. Everything was manufactured according to strict standards of quality and size that remained unchanged through generations: weights and measures, bricks, even road widths. Streets are twice the width of side lanes, while the main arteries are twice the width of streets, most of which are laid out along a straight grid pattern and run north–south or east–west. These patterns were retained through different phases of rebuilding, lasting many centuries. This organized approach may have led to a high quality of life for the inhabitants, who enjoyed advanced water and sewage systems rivaling those of Rome. Impressively, the standards were maintained throughout the entire territory of Harappan civilization, which covered a greater area than the Old Kingdom of Egypt or the Sumerian civilization in Mesopotamia.[44]

The rigid conformity of Harappan civilization has elicited strong reactions over the years. Scholars have pondered the "intense conservatism" of what they perceive as a "faceless sociocultural system." One archaeologist expresses his repulsion in no uncertain terms, seeing "a terrible efficiency about the Harappa civilization" reflecting "an isolation and a stagnation hard to parallel in any known civilization of the Old World."[45]

Others interpret the lack of august monuments and palaces very differently, seeing a clue that perhaps here was a great civilization that avoided the extreme hierarchical inequalities of its contemporaries, one that focused on its citizens' quality of life. "This was an enormously innovative civilization," suggests archaeologist Michael Jansen. "Rather than spend their time on monuments as in Egypt, they built practical things that benefited the inhabitants." Indus Valley specialist Gregory Possehl speculates that the lack of Harappan temples suggests a different form of religious consciousness. "The Harappans expressed their belief," he writes, "without the need for massive, large-scale religious edifices. Religion seems to have been an individualized, private practice, largely undertaken in the household by individuals or family groups. It may not have involved priests, high priests and an institution of religious specialists."[46]

One tantalizing clue that seems to support the notion of a unique Harappan approach to religious experience is a seal showing a figure sitting in a classic seated yoga posture (figure 6.1). A number of observers have interpreted this to suggest that Harappan civilization may have been a source of India's unique spiritual tradition. If this linkage is indeed valid, writes scholar Eknath Easwaran, "it would imply that the same systematic attitude the Indus Valley dwellers applied to their technology was applied also to study of the mind." It is intriguing to consider the possibility that this vanished civilization might have formed the basis for a practice that continues to influence millions of people throughout the modern world.[47]

Figure 6.1: Harappan seal showing a seated yoga posture

For reasons not entirely clear but probably related to climate change, Harappan civilization began declining around 1800 BCE. Their decline was likely exacerbated by an invasion from the north of a group of illiterate, horse riding pastoral warriors. These people, who called themselves Aryans, emerged from a culture known today as Proto-Indo-European. Together with their brethren heading west into Europe, this unlikely crew would have a more profound effect on the shape of world history than would any of the great civilizations we have yet encountered.[48]

Proto-Indo-Europeans: Might Is Right

A language looking for a homeland

In 1783, a respected British barrister, Sir William Jones, arrived in Calcutta on an important mission. The British government wanted to bring some order to the chaotic relationship between English merchants and the local Indians. The Indians conducted business under the age-old system of Hindu law, and the British realized the need to integrate their legal system with it. The problem was that Hindu law was written in the ancient language of Sanskrit, which no Englishman understood. Jones, one of the most respected linguists in Europe, seemed the perfect man for the job.

During the three years Jones spent at a venerable Hindu university studying ancient Sanskrit texts, a startling realization gradually formed in his mind, which he announced to the Asiatic Society of Bengal in 1786. Sanskrit, he declared, bears a "stronger affinity" to Greek and Latin "than could possibly have been produced by accident; so strong indeed, that no philologer could examine them all three, without believing them to have sprung from some common source, which, perhaps, no longer exists." Jones went on to make the astounding claim that not only Greek and Latin but also Persian, Celtic, and German belonged to the same family of languages as Sanskrit.[49]

Since then, generations of linguists have confirmed Jones's original hypothesis. Twelve distinct branches of Indo-European have been identified, incorporating the vast majority of European languages as well as languages such as Armenian, Kurdish, and Persian. Using sophisticated models analyzing subtle changes in sounds and meanings, linguists have concurred that all these branches can be traced back over thousands of years to a common source, which has been called Proto-Indo-European (PIE). This hypothesized language has been so scrupulously studied that dictionaries exist that detail its reconstructed vocabulary, which contains more than fifteen hundred separate roots.

As the PIE language emerged from the shrouds of time, it was logically surmised that a particular people must have spoken it at a particular place and time. This much is generally agreed upon. But what group? Where? And when? These questions remain the source of heated debate to this day.[50]

The controversy centers on two opposing theories with contrasting geographies and timelines. One theory, the Anatolian farming hypothesis, proposes that the PIE language goes back to the original influx of agriculture into Europe, as farmers advanced northwest from Anatolia beginning around 6000 BCE. Opponents of this theory, however, point out what may be a fatal flaw: many crucial root words in the PIE lexicon refer to developments and technologies that occurred thousands of years after the birth of agriculture. For example, the word for horse appears frequently, but the horse was probably only domesticated in the fourth millennium BCE. The same is true of the word for wagon, an object known to be a fourth-millennium phenomenon. Similarly, metals such as silver, as well as crops that were not available to the first Anatolian farmers, are referred to across the PIE family of languages.[51]

So if not Anatolia at the birth of agriculture, then where and when? The predominant theory, known as the Kurgan hypothesis (named for the burial mounds that have been a source of much archaeological evidence), places the PIE homeland in the steppes north of the Black Sea at around 3500–3000 BCE. (See figure 6.2.) A major advantage of this theory is that the archaeological and linguistic evidence appear to support each other, indicating that this was the time and place where the horse was first domesticated, where wagons were first used extensively, and where large herds of cows became the central focus of a new pastoral way of life. The Kurgan hypothesis is also strongly supported by recent DNA evidence and, although still unproven, will form the basis of any references to the PIE question for the remainder of this book.[52]

PIE migrations

To the terrified Harappans standing on their city ramparts, defending the remnants of their civilization against marauding bands on horseback, it really didn't matter where they came from. What mattered was that a new, ascendant culture was entering the Indian subcontinent. The invasion of India by the Aryans is considered the earliest documented mass migration in history. The documentation comes to us in the form of the *Rig Veda*, a collection of hymns chanted by priests at sacrifices where a psychedelic beverage, soma, was drunk.

Since the early Aryans had no writing, the *Rig Veda* was originally transmitted orally across the generations until it was written down hundreds of years later.[53]

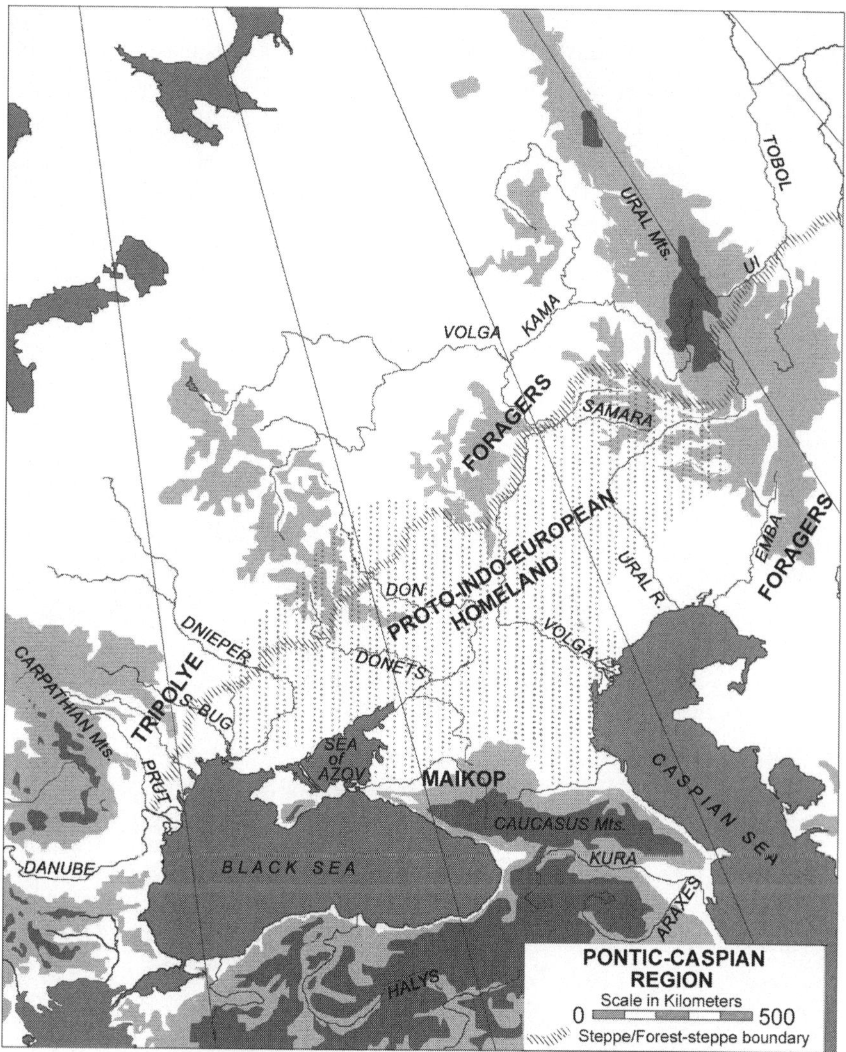

Figure 6.2: The PIE homeland according to the Kurgan hypothesis

The *Rig Veda* is clearly the work of an invading people. Two of its early books refer to places in eastern Iran and Afghanistan on a direct path from the Black Sea to the Harappan cities. Another book recounts the feats of two clans who journeyed long distances; crossed many rivers; and fought a dark-skinned people called the *Dasa*, who are described as "nose-less," presumably referring to the facial features of the indigenous Dravidian population of India. The *Rig Veda* is filled with references to the horses and chariots of the Aryans and invokes divine support for the destruction of their enemies and the storming of their citadels, in all likelihood those of Harappa, Mohenjo-Daro, and whatever else remained of the civilization that had once prospered there.[54]

The migration of the Aryans into India probably took place in waves over several centuries. Gradually, Aryan culture merged with that of the indigenous Harappan population, and, over the ensuing millennium, the newly synthesized culture spread south and east, reaching the Ganges and, eventually, all the way to the southern tip of India.[55]

The social structure of this new culture clearly showed the military and social dominance of the Aryans. This was the source of the rigid caste system that has structured Indian life ever since, with the priesthood or *Brahman* as the highest caste, followed by the land-owning *Kshatriya*, while the lowest-caste slaves, the *Dasa*, were reduced to tilling the land. In the millennia that have followed, these rigid distinctions have remained astonishingly enduring.[56*]

While one group of Aryans established themselves in the Indian subcontinent, other groups settled down farther west, naming their land "Realm of the Aryans," or Iran. This group went on to develop Zoroastrianism. Meanwhile, still more nomads from the PIE homeland journeyed southwest of the Black Sea. These people, called the Achaeans, would go on to found the culture of ancient Greece.[57]

A profoundly important, but little recognized, fact of early civilization is the close affinity between the religious and philosophical traditions of Greece and India as a result of their derivation from a common PIE source. These cultures shared many of the same gods, as well as common terms for weapons such as bow and arrow, and both even used the same term for a specific ritual known as the hecatomb, which involved the sacrifice of a hundred cows.[58]

These different branches of the original PIE culture shared a perspective on the fundamental nature of the universe. For example, a central concept in the *Rig Veda*, ancient Greek thought, and Zoroastrianism is a notion of truth/order/righteousness, called *rta* in Vedic writings, *dike* in Greek, and *asha* in Zoroastrian scriptures. Another shared term, with important implications, refers to a liberating kind of knowledge providing a direct insight to spiritual wisdom, called *jnana* in Sanskrit and *gnosis* in Greek. In both cultures, this fundamental idea set up a chain of linked concepts that would help structure both Greek and Indian cosmologies.[59]

"Might is right"

Who were these tribespeople whose linguistic structures underlaid both Indian and Greek civilizations and would, in turn, become the foundation of modern Western thought? What were their values and daily concerns? The path to understanding the mentality of the PIE nomads begins with the cow, which was fundamental to their society and became equally central to their set of values. The primary symbols of prosperity were milk and butter, which, along with the cows, became sacrificial offerings to the gods. The *Rig Veda* praises the war god, Indra, for heroically breaking into other people's cow pens and stealing their cattle.[60]

The other bulwark of the PIE economy was the horse. The PIE herdsmen in the steppes of central Asia were almost certainly the first people in the world to domesticate the horse and harness its power. This major breakthrough was most likely the key to the astonishing success of PIE culture in spreading throughout Europe and southern Asia. Loading their horse-driven wagons with tents and supplies, herdsmen could take their cattle out onto the open steppes for months at a time, turning what was once wild land into pasture for their increasingly large herds.[61]

Cattle, however, can be easily stolen, leading inevitably to armed conflict between different groups. "Under these circumstances, brothers tend to stay close together," PIE specialist David Anthony wryly notes. "The connection between animals, brothers, and power," Anthony explains, "was the foundation on which new forms of male-centered ritual and politics developed among Indo-European-speaking societies." The male orientation of their culture extended up to the heavens: PIE tribespeople expressed thanks to a god called the Sky Father for their sons, fat cattle, and swift horses.[62]

Along with this male-centered value system came a high regard for military prowess. In the PIE warrior ethos, every able-bodied male was expected to be a fighter, and the king himself was primarily a warlord. The PIE root word for king was **reg-*, which led to the Sanskrit word *raj* as well as the Latin *rex* and English *royal*. This root word expanded into a fascinating constellation of meanings that have passed into PIE-based cultures ever since. Across IndoEuropean languages, the root word **reg-* forms the foundation for words such as *right*, *straight*, *correct*, *ruler*, and *regulate*—suggesting a conceptual underpinning that links power with right and associates the strong right hand with regulating what is correct, and which may be summarized by the phrase "might is right."[63] Another deep-rooted cultural inheritance passed on by the PIE horsemen of the steppes is a dualistic pattern of thinking about the universe. The original

PIE creation myth involves two brothers, Man and Twin, and tells how the universe was created when Man sacrificed Twin. A binary opposition between right and left is extended through the PIE language to form a systematic pattern of opposites, with concepts of healthy, strong, and dexterous on one side and unfavorable, weak, and sinister (the Latin word for left) on the other side. The right side is associated with males and the left with females.[64]

The Kurgan expansion

How did this group of illiterate nomads leave such a profound imprint on the thought patterns of billions of us living today? This question is often posed by those arguing against the Kurgan hypothesis, who claim that "it is hard to understand (perhaps even inconceivable) how steppe pastoralists could have imposed their language on so much of Europe west of the steppes."[65]

The answer emerges in the PIE warriors' superior military technology in the form of the horse. With more horses and larger horses than anyone else around, and more skillful horsemanship, they could terrorize the enemy while advancing and retreating from raids faster than warriors on foot. The military superiority of the PIE horsemen led, according to researcher Maria Gimbutas, to waves of migrations from around 4000 to 2500 BCE known as the "Kurgan expansion," which fundamentally altered the face of Europe forever. Gimbutas proposes that the first settled inhabitants of Eastern and Central Europe were peaceful farmers living in egalitarian, matriarchal societies, worshipping a mother goddess, who were brutally conquered by the PIE invaders.[66]

We need to be careful of the stereotyping arising from Gimbutas's account: the peaceful, matriarchal farmers versus the warlike, patriarchal PIE invaders. After all, most civilizations we've encountered were patriarchal and constantly at war, so it seems unlikely that PIE warriors invented these traits. However, the essential part of Gimbutas's theory, suggesting waves of PIE invasions across Europe over fifteen hundred years, is solidly supported by the archaeological and linguistic evidence; and it does seem that the PIE horsemen combined values of patriarchy and aggression in a unique and devastating way.[67]

The PIE conquest of Europe was different from the Aryan invasion of India. No caste system ever developed in Europe that was in any way comparable to that of India. Anthony suggests it might have been "more like a franchising operation," with an initial PIE penetration accomplished through military force, leaving a small group of warriors in each new location. With their higher prestige as conquerors, their myths, rituals, and language would have spread across the communities until they gradually overwhelmed the indigenous culture.[68]

Zoroaster's struggle of Good and Evil

In the plains of northern Iran, the earliest waves of PIE pastoralists settled down and formed stable communities that relied on those bulwarks of PIE prosperity, the horse and the cow. Their stability, however, was threatened by new waves of advancing tribespeople more interested in cattle raiding than cattle rearing. It was into this society of settled cattle breeders assailed by fearsome raiders that Zoroaster was born, the man who would found the world's first dualistic religion based on the cosmic struggle between good and evil.[69]

Growing up in a world that seemed to him utterly divided between the peaceful ways of the cattle breeders and the violent incursions of nomadic raiders, Zoroaster generalized this split between good and bad into a chasm dividing the entire cosmos. He referred to his own supporters as "followers of Truth" and his enemies as "followers of the Lie," described in Zoroastrianism's holy book, the *Avesta*, as "the evil-doer who cannot earn a livelihood except by doing violence to the husbandman's herds and men, though they have not provoked him."[70]

Virtually everything in Zoroaster's cosmos is characterized by the fundamental divide he perceived between good and evil, which he traced back to the very creation of the universe. Zoroaster turned the original PIE creation myth of Man sacrificing Twin into a primal struggle between good and evil. When these two primordial spirits first encountered each other, he taught, they created "life and notlife." The name of the good spirit, who became the Zoroastrian god, was Ahura Mazda; his evil opponent was Angra Mainyu. Everything in the universe could be understood by the conflict between these two spirits. The entire cosmos became an arena for the struggle between the True and the False, a battle involving everyone and pervading every aspect of life, no matter how big or small.[71]

As Zoroaster saw it, Ahura Mazda had created a perfect universe, and anything that was a blemish to that perfection, such as dirt, disease, mold, or decay, was the work of Angra Mainyu and his followers. Even the animal world was divided into good and evil, with creatures such as scorpions, wasps, or toads considered part of Angra Mainya's countercreation and therefore unclean.[72]

The fundamental cleavage of the universe between good and evil created a form of dogmatic thought that permitted no compromise. Good is equated with Truth, and Evil with Falsehood. The devout Zoroastrian must affirm publicly, "I believe in whatever this religion says or thinks." In a chilling precursor to the intolerance that later versions of monotheism would bring, the word for free choice came to mean heresy—exactly paralleling the evolution of the Greek word *hairesis* in Christianity.[73]

Zoroaster claimed that Ahura Mazda had given him the clarity of vision to determine the path between Truth and Falsehood, and those who found themselves on the wrong side of his determination could expect no accommodation. All opponents were evil incarnate. In a disturbing passage, Zoroaster expresses his hardline policy, stating that each person "should show kindness to the follower of Truth, but should be evil to the follower of the Lie," for the man "who is most good to the follower of the Lie is himself a follower of the Lie."[74]

Zoroastrianism remained a potent force within Iran until the conquest of the region in the seventh century CE by the Arabs, after which its influence gradually dwindled. However, during the Babylonian exile of the Jewish people in the sixth century BCE, prominent Jewish thinkers were influenced by the core ideas of Zoroastrianism, including the conception of Ahura Mazda as a creator god and the cosmic struggle between good and evil. As we'll see later, some of the most important sections of the Old Testament were written during the Jewish exile in Babylon and likely inspired by Zoroastrian beliefs.[75]

While Zoroaster was forming his dualistic conception of the universe, other branches of Indo-European-speaking nomads were settling into their new homelands in Greece and India. The hypothetical extraterrestrial traveler visiting Earth around 1500 BCE would have been surprised at what transpired. The Egyptians may have bequeathed to us their cosmological speculations; the Mesopotamians handed down their scientific achievements; but the PIE cattle herders were the ones who set both Indian and European thought patterns on the courses they eventually took, passing on to us their notions of a fixed natural law, a binary conception of right and wrong, and a dualistic universe. The farreaching legacy of these PIE tribespeople will be examined in the next two chapters, as we explore the Greek and Indian cosmological speculations that would ultimately structure the beliefs of much of the world's population today.

Part 3

THE PATTERNS DIVERGE

Western Pattern: Split Cosmos, Split Human

Eastern Pattern: Harmonic Web of Life

Chapter 7

THE BIRTH OF DUALISM IN ANCIENT GREECE

The young philosopher, shattered by the trial and execution of his mentor, fled Athens to join his companions in the neighboring city of Megara. What was to be done? Socrates, the revered sage who had taught them how to question traditional beliefs, had been accused by the Athenian patricians of corrupting the minds of the youth. The year was 399 BCE. Sentenced to death, Socrates had chosen to take poison rather than escape and flee Athens. The young philosopher, horrified by the injustice he had witnessed, now had to find his own way in life. He spent years traveling the known world, drawn particularly to southern Italy, where the disciples of another great philosopher, Pythagoras, had settled. The young philosopher's name was Plato, and he would go on to take sweet revenge on those who had condemned his mentor to death. At age forty, he returned to Athens to found an academy that would last for hundreds of years. The vision of the cosmos that he taught there, a brilliant synthesis of ideas he ascribed to the persona of Socrates, would become the foundation of European thought for the two and a half millennia that followed.[1]

The influence of Plato's thought is so pervasive that it led philosopher Alfred North Whitehead to comment famously that the European philosophical tradition "consists in a series of footnotes to Plato." Nevertheless, while Plato's impact on Western thought is monumental, he was just part of a dramatic transformation in cognition that occurred in ancient Greece and has shaped the world ever since.[2]

It's been called the "Greek miracle." Over the course of just a couple of hundred years, a few city-states in the Eastern Mediterranean set Europe on the course that led to today's technological civilization. New ways of thinking sprang up, giving birth to a stunning range of disciplines that nowadays we take for granted. Philosophy, as we now conceive of it, emerged there. Concepts such as democracy and tragedy were developed. Logic was invented. The practice of systematic and empirical thinking that eventually led to modern science began there.

Along with these wonders came other innovations in thought. The concept of pure abstraction appeared, bringing with it the previously unimagined notion of an eternal God with infinite presence in time and space. The citystates of ancient Greece bequeathed to us not only the scientific tradition but also the thought structures that made monotheism possible in the form that has taken over much of the world. It's difficult to consider the Greek contribution to humanity without being impressed, even awed. But it's not quite true to call it the "Greek miracle," if we take that to imply something inexplicable. The Greek transformation was unique, but it can be understood best as a magnificent flowering of branches of thought that in fact sprouted from earlier traditions.

It was also not the only foundational system of thought to emerge during the middle of the first millennium BCE. In the few centuries from roughly 750 to 350 BCE, the other great cultural edifices that structure our world were also being formed. In China, Confucius and Lao-Tzu left their legacy. In India, ancient Vedic traditions were crystallizing, while the Buddha offered revolutionary new ways of thinking about one's life. In Israel, Hebrew prophets were compiling the Old Testament. Philosopher Karl Jaspers was so struck by these contemporaneous breakthroughs that he called this period the Axial Age: these systems of thought can be seen as the axis, or pivot, from which modern structures of cognition ultimately derive. In the following chapters, we'll explore some features of this axis that has given rise to today's world.[3]

A Miracle of Convergence

The Greeks were descendants of PIE invaders known as Mycenaeans, who had migrated to the region between 2000 and 1650 BCE, bringing with them the linguistic core of PIE-based thought structures that was the underpinning of all subsequent developments. As the Mycenaeans settled over the next millennium to form the Greek population, new cultural influences took root on that PIE core. Greek-speaking city-states were spread out across the Eastern Mediterranean, occupying what is today not only Greece but also southeastern Italy and the west coast of Turkey. Living on the periphery of the two great civilizations of Persia and Egypt, these city-states were in constant communication and competition with each other.[4]

The Eastern Mediterranean in the middle of the first millennium BCE was a vibrant, multicultural zone, a result of the unusual cultural tolerance of the massive Persian Empire, which stretched from Libya in the west to the Indus river valley in the east. (See figure 7.1.) The Greeks seem to have taken advantage of this tolerant environment, with merchants, mercenaries, and artists traveling widely, absorbing different cultural influences and bringing them back to their own city-states. Arising from this cultural mélange, the "Greek miracle" was really a marvel of convergence and emergence: a convergence of multiple worldviews, leading to the emergence of a synthesis of these views as a new, comprehensive system of thought.[5]

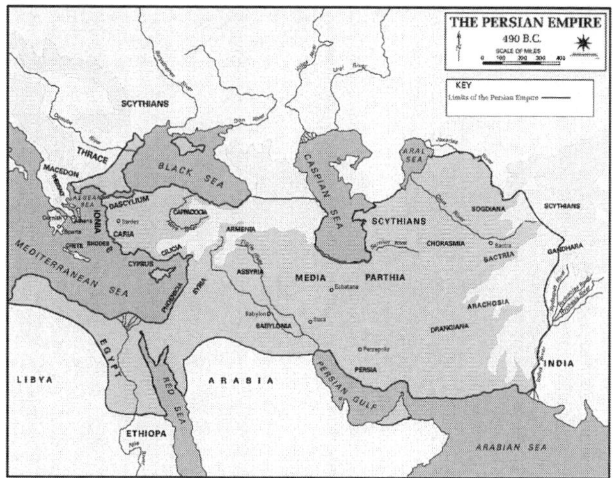

Figure 7.1: The extent of the Persian Empire around 500 BCE

It's only in recent decades that the extent of Greek indebtedness to other Near Eastern civilizations has been fully acknowledged. In 1992, Walter Burkert published an important work, *The Orientalizing Revolution*, which demonstrated how extensively the ideas of the Greeks had been influenced by eastern models. The Greeks themselves might not have argued with Burkert. Their own historian, Herodotus, described how Pythagoras had traveled to Egypt, where he was captured and taken to Babylon, as a result of which he learned both the Egyptian and Babylonian approaches to mathematics. Even the Greek alphabet, from which all Western alphabets evolved, was derived from that of the Phoenicians, who had themselves taken it from other Semitic sources.[6]

Shamanic Sources

As much as Greek culture borrowed from other civilizations of the Eastern Mediterranean, it owed perhaps even more to earlier shamanic traditions. Thales, the man considered to be the world's first philosopher, thought—like hunter-gatherers worldwide—that "all things are full of gods." Another important shamanic borrowing was the notion of a spirit that travels outside the body, which would become a central theme in the development of Greek thought.[7]

Another viewpoint the earliest Greek philosophers (known as the Presocratics) shared with their hunter-gatherer predecessors was that the universe was in a state of continual transformation. Thales's successor, Anaximander, saw the cosmos as a vortex in eternal motion. The Presocratic philosopher Heraclitus believed that the most fitting metaphors for the universe came from dynamic forms such as fire and water. In one fragment of his writings, he proposes that "this cosmos . . . always was and is and will be one everlasting Fire, kindled in measure and in measure quenched." Because of its ever-changing, dynamic nature, Heraclitus declares that a fixed view of the universe is not possible. Like an ever-flowing river, as soon as you fix a perception of what it looks like, it's already changed. "It is impossible," he says, "to step into the same river twice." The only thing you can rely on is the continual flow, the realization that "all things are momentary and pass away." Heraclitus doesn't mean that you should give up trying to understand the universe. Rather, in his words, "wisdom consists in one thing, to know the principle by which all things are steered through all things."[8]

Empedocles, who lived a generation after Heraclitus, continued the tradition of explaining the universe in terms of ever-changing flux. For Empedocles, the universe was composed of the four elements of fire, air, earth, and water. Far from being fixed, these elements were continually metamorphosing into each other in a state of dynamic tension driven by opposing forces: a connecting principle of love and a separating principle of strife.[9]

However, these early Presocratic views, rooted in the ancient traditions of mythic consciousness, eventually lost out to a particular characteristic of Greek thought that would shape its unique contribution to human civilization: what historian H. D. F. Kitto has called "a passion for generalizing."[10]

The Discovery of Abstraction

The emergence of symbolic thought in our conceptual consciousness, as we saw in chapter 1, is part of what made us uniquely human. By creating higher-level generalizations from a mass of concrete specifics, symbolic thought permitted language to evolve and drove the development of early humanity's mythic consciousness. In a period of just a few generations, the ancient Greeks nurtured this faculty for symbolic thinking and brought it to an entirely new level of sophistication.

Abstracting a general rule from an assortment of details is the defining characteristic of Greek thought. The Greeks weren't content merely to record what happened around them. Instead, they created categories and generated rules for why things happened, with the ultimate objective of explaining them and perhaps even predicting what would happen next. Things made more sense to the Greeks the more they were part of a general theory.[11]

An example of this process in action can be seen in a speech given by a politician called Diodotus to the Athenian assembly. The city of Mytilene had rebelled unsuccessfully against the Athenian empire, and there was a proposal to massacre its residents in retribution. Diodotus, arguing for a more moderate approach, concludes his speech as follows:

> This is the advantageous policy and the strong policy, because the party which deliberates wisely against his enemy is more formidable than the one which acts with a violence borne of recklessness.

Diodotus had already made the empirical arguments for his position, but here he is appealing to the higher authority of theory. He offers a general rule of engagement which supports his position, claiming that this universal principle is the reason why he is right. It is the generalization that proves his point.[12]

The Greek passion for generalizing was embedded within the very structure of their language. The Greeks were the first to use the definite article as a significant part of their grammar. For example, every language might have an adjective such as "good" to describe things. The Greek innovation was to arrive at a concept of "*the* Good" as an abstract generalization of all good things. Regardless of the different ways in which things can be good, the definite article posits the idea that "the Good" exists independently. This forms the linguistic basis for what one scholar has called "the birth of the very idea of abstraction."[13]

After twenty-five hundred years of concepts like "the Good" floating around Western thought, we might think such an abstraction would have always been readily available to the human mind. But this kind of thought was literally invented by generations of brilliant Greek thinkers, each daring to take his ideas one step further from the realm of the concrete toward a realm of pure idealization. By the end of the Greek era, European culture would have a new toolbox comprising forms of systematic and abstract thought, which would eventually launch the Scientific Revolution.

Using this toolbox of abstraction, the Greeks created a radically new conception of the cosmos that was a function of humanity's own unique capacity for systematic reasoning. One by one, leading Presocratic thinkers pushed the envelope of abstraction further and further until it formed its own parallel universe quite apart from the empirical world of the senses. Abstraction itself was deified.

Anaximander initiated this process with the suggestion that the world was originally formed from what he called the *apeiron*, usually translated as "infinite" or "undefined." This extraordinary concept of an immaterial dimension from which the universe came into being has been called by historian Thomas McEvilley "the first purely philosophical idea . . . a first daring incursion into the realm of the abstract."[14]

Some decades later, Xenophanes applied Anaximander's notion of the abstract to a radical critique of traditional mythologies, claiming that people viewed their gods merely as fanciful representations of themselves. He mocks the simple anthropomorphic view of the gods in a statement that remains fresh through the ages:

> Mortals consider that the gods are born, and that they have clothes and speech and bodies like their own. The Ethiopians say that their gods are snub-nosed and black, the Thracians that theirs have light blue eyes and red hair. But if cattle and horses or lions had hands, or were able to draw with their hands and do the works that people can do, horses would draw the forms of the gods like horses and cattle like cattle, and they would make their bodies such as they each had themselves.[15]

Xenophanes offers an alternative viewpoint on divinity, conceptualizing a mind existing without a body:

> One god, greatest among gods and men, in no way similar to mortals either in body or in thought. Always he remains in the same place, moving not at all; nor is it fitting for him to go to different places at different times, but without toil he shakes all things by the thought of his mind. All of him sees, all thinks, and all hears.[16]

Xenophanes is really employing another—if more sophisticated—form of anthropomorphism by projecting a disembodied mind onto his god. By separating the mind from the constraints of the body, he permits a conception of the mind as an infinitely powerful vehicle, thus initiating the Greek process of deifying the power of pure thought.

A few decades later, Anaxagoras further developed the notion of a pure mind ruling the cosmos. He believed that "Mind" must be composed of a different substance than the rest of the universe in order to have control over it. "All other things," he writes, "have a portion of everything, but Mind is infinite and self-ruled, and is mixed with nothing but is all alone by itself. . . . Mind controls all things, both the greater and the smaller, that have life."[17]

Other Presocratic philosophers took the idea of the divinity of Mind in another direction, emphasizing the distinction between the mind and the senses and concluding that if the mind were all-powerful, then the senses could not be trusted as a source of knowledge. For one of them, Democritus, only knowledge obtained through the intellect was legitimate. In one of the earliest recorded statements of a viewpoint that would establish the primacy of reason over the senses for millennia, he says: "Of knowledge there are two forms, one legitimate, one bastard. To the bastard belong all this group: sight, hearing, smell, taste, touch. The other is legitimate, and separate from that."[18]

One result of this emphasis on the power of the mind was an ever-increasing reliance on conclusions reached through the rigorous application of systematic thought. In fact, while some philosophers were nudging ever closer to the realm of pure abstraction, others were applying humankind's conceptualizing faculty to develop the thought structures that would lead eventually to the scientific revolution that formed our modern world.

The Birth of Scientific Methodology

Once you believe the entire cosmos is the creation of a rational Mind, it's natural to conclude that the world must work according to a set of rational laws created by that Mind. This was the underlying logic that led the Greeks to search for systematic laws of the universe.[19]

From the earliest days of Greek civilization, centuries before the Presocratic philosophers, Homer's *Iliad* and *Odyssey* referred to a cosmic order called *ananke*, meaning "Necessity," a force so powerful that not even the gods could affect it. As we've seen, this belief in a fixed universal law can be traced back even earlier than Homer to the original PIE belief system encapsulated in the Greek language, which also shows up in Vedic and Zoroastrian thought.[20]

The idea of a power surpassing even the gods is a crucial one. If you believe, as did the Mesopotamians, that the universe is directed by capricious gods choosing on a whim how they will affect your life, then it makes sense to try to understand what motivates these gods and act accordingly. If you believe, like the Greeks, that the universe is not capricious but obeys fixed laws, it makes sense to try to understand what these universal laws are.[21]

For the Greeks, the paradigmatic example of the orderliness of nature was to be found in mathematics, in which something once proven to be true remains unchanging and independent of the imperfect world around it. Generations of Greek philosophers viewed the pure, fixed nature of mathematics as convincing proof that Heraclitus's idea of a changing universe was fundamentally wrong. Gradually, the shamanic sense of a universe in continual flux was replaced by a newly imagined cosmos containing a predictable, orderly world where things behaved according to fixed laws.[22]

It was Pythagoras, whose teachings the young Plato would seek out, who first conceptualized an orderly world with all parts coexisting harmoniously. An example the Pythagoreans used to demonstrate the beautiful symmetry of natural laws was the fact that the musical note produced by a string is exactly one octave lower than the note produced by a string exactly half that length, and thus the two notes harmonize perfectly. To them, this was no coincidence but rather evidence of the essential harmony of nature, discoverable by mathematics. Based on their faith in nature as a harmonious unity, they believed they could find a mathematical basis for everything, including morality and religion.[23]

When the Pythagoreans used the example of the musical string to support their claims about the universe, they pioneered another breakthrough in the development of scientific methodology: using empirical research to prove or disprove a theory. The annals of ancient Greece offer stunning examples of an empirical approach to scientific investigation that would be highly regarded in a modern research establishment. Empedocles used a wineskin to demonstrate that air is a material substance. Xenophanes formulated a theory of geological change based on the existence of seashells on mountains. Two heroes of empiricism, Euctemon and Meton, set out to prove by observation that the two equinoxes fall at the exact midpoints of the periods between them. When their observations showed, to their surprise, that the periods were slightly unequal, rather than fudging the results, they stuck by their numbers and rejected their hypothesis. In a similar vein, Hippocrates, the founder of the principles of modern medicine, writes in his *Precepts*: "In Medicine one must pay attention not to plausible theorizing, but to experience and reason together. . . . Conclusions drawn by the unaided reason can hardly be serviceable; only those drawn from observed fact."[24]

At times, the Greeks were painfully aware of the vast amount of knowledge still out of their grasp as they pursued their empirical approach. Democritus sums up this sense of frustration: "But in reality we know nothing; for truth is in the depths. . . . It will be clear that to really know what each thing is like is beyond our power." Showing his passionate desire for scientific understanding, he exclaims that he "would rather find one natural explanation than win the kingdom of Persia."[25]

Thinking about Thinking

If the Greeks were at times frustrated by the limitations of their empirical knowledge, they more than made up for this by establishing a set of rules for how to think about this knowledge. In the politically fragmented cities of ancient Greece, where ideas were freely discussed, criticized, and defended in public forums, philosophers had to compete with each other in an open marketplace. If they wanted to succeed, they had to consider how best to defend their ideas against attack, without recourse to some external authority. This competitive environment encouraged Greek philosophers to draw up general principles and rules about thinking itself, culminating in the development of systematic, formal logic.[26]

An early adopter of this systematic logic, Parmenides, showed how easy it is to become intoxicated by its power. He argued that nothing new could ever come into existence, since "it must either come from something, in which case it already existed, or from nothing, which is impossible, since nothing does not exist." Using this logic, Parmenides concluded that everything is fixed and "change is impossible."

Parmenides put his new intellectual power to use by destroying Heraclitus's cosmology of change, which, in one place, proposes, "We both are and are not." A paradox like that no longer holds water in the systematic world of logic. As McEvilley observes, "Parmenides renounces the world of sense in favor of the principles of logic; Heraclitus renounces the principles of logic in favor of the world of sense." In this battle for the soul of Western thought, Parmenides won handily. Systematic logic henceforth became the defining characteristic of scientific truth.[27]

It was Aristotle, living about a century after Parmenides, who completed the victory for systematic thinking. One of Aristotle's most important contributions to Western thought was his invention of the formal syllogism, the deductive mode of thought whereby two related premises lead to an irrefutable conclusion. An example of a syllogism is "All humans are mortal. All Greeks are humans. Therefore, all Greeks are mortal." This is the basic building block of logical discourse, forming the very foundation of the Western concept of truth.[28]

But perhaps the greatest gift Aristotle gave Western civilization was his synthesis of the empirical mode of investigation with the systematic process of logic. Unlike Parmenides, Aristotle didn't reject the world of the senses. On the contrary, he embraced it passionately. He personally dissected animals to understand their internal parts. He examined chick embryos by breaking an egg open every day and observing the progress, noticing, for example, that, on the third day, "the heart appears, like a speck of blood in the white of the egg." It was Aristotle's embrace of both empiricism and logic that laid the foundation for what would ultimately become scientific methodology.[29]

Aristotle's accomplishments in formulating a systematic, empirical approach to knowledge would, however, be eclipsed by a competing tradition of Greek thought that arrived at an utterly different conception of truth. This tradition, following Democritus and Parmenides, separated the soul from the body and distilled abstract ideals from worldly forms, assigning truth only to one and not the other. It was this approach to truth that Plato championed in his Academy. While Aristotle's crowning achievement was to synthesize different modes of thinking into the foundations of science, Plato's great accomplishment involved synthesizing ideas about the separation of body and soul into a dualistic framework that would become the foundation of monotheistic thought.

The Journey of the Soul

The earliest recorded writings of the ancient Greeks shared the ubiquitous agrarian belief that humans are made up of multiple spirits with some kind of tangible properties. Homer's epics describe two types of soul: *psyche*, which escapes from a person's mouth at the moment of death, and *thymos*, the source of energy and courage, which is found in the blood. In the sixth century BCE, the philosopher Anaximenes described how "our soul, being air, holds us together and controls us," just like the "wind and air enclose the whole world."[30]

However, in the same century, a movement was afoot in Greece that, from its unlikely beginnings, would set the Western world down an entirely new path. Priests from a popular cult called Orphism would appear at the doors of the wealthy and claim to possess sacred powers to cleanse any injustice they might have done. Although held in contempt by the elite, their rituals mesmerized the general populace with intense emotional expression and passionate spectacles. Topping off their attractions, the Orphics captivated followers by claiming to have a simple, if somewhat bizarre solution, to the problem of death.[31]

Each human soul, they explained, was undergoing punishment for a crime it had once committed. The punishment was to be confined in a series of human bodies and repeatedly subjected to cycles of pain, decay, and death. The body was described as the tomb of the soul, as if the soul were buried alive in it. The death of the body was thus a temporary release for the soul until its incarceration in the next body.[32]

If these beliefs had stayed within the Orphic sect, perhaps nothing much would have come of them. But a similar set of beliefs was taken up by the highly respectable philosopher Pythagoras, who turned them into a comprehensive system, settling in the Greek colony of Croton in southern Italy to teach his ideas to a secret sect of disciples.[33]

A crucial difference between Pythagoras and the Orphics was stylistic: the emotional intensity of Orphism was replaced by cool contemplation. Instead of spectacle and passion, Pythagoras taught serene contemplation of a permanent, rational truth, leading to a way of life that he called *philosophia*: the pursuit of wisdom. For Pythagoras, the soul didn't need the body's death for liberation; by relinquishing emotions and bodily desires, a person could achieve release of the soul even while the body was alive.[34]

Pythagoras taught his followers that every human possessed an immortal soul that ascended to heaven for divine judgment after the body's death. Depending on the judgment, the soul would be reincarnated into another being, either human or animal. The clear implication, for Pythagoras, was that all living beings were kindred spirits. A famous story tells of Pythagoras walking past someone beating a dog, at which he turned and said, "Stop, and beat it not; for the soul is that of a friend; I know it, for I heard it speak." This led to a firm prohibition within the Pythagorean sect against the slaughter of animals and, consequently, to a strictly vegetarian diet. Many have noticed the striking similarity of this Pythagorean doctrine to common precepts of Indian faiths—something we'll explore further in the next chapter.[35]

By the time Plato was fleeing Athens, the ideas of Pythagoras had begun to infiltrate the progressive edge of Greek speculation. However, the notion of an immortal soul existing separately from the body was still an esoteric doctrine, inexplicable to most people of the time. Plato's astounding achievement was to take the body-soul dualism of Pythagoras, combine it with the new concept of pure abstraction, and infuse all this with the mathematical sense of divine order in nature. By weaving together these different strands of thought, he would create a radically new, comprehensive cosmology that would serve as the underpinning for more than two thousand years of theological, philosophical, and mathematical speculation in the Western world.[36]

The Conflict of Body and Soul

Plato's view of the soul and body incorporates the same general themes as Orphism and Pythagoreanism, envisaging the body as a prison or tomb in which the soul is confined. In one of his writings, Plato offers an allegory of men imprisoned in a deep cave, facing a wall and chained so they can't move their heads. Behind these men is a fire, in front of which other people and animals move. The prisoners can only see the changeable shadows on the wall cast by the flickering light of the fire. Because these unfortunate prisoners haven't seen anything else since their infancy, they mistake the shadows they're seeing for reality. Plato explains that our souls are like these prisoners, imprisoned in a world of sense experience, unable to see reality directly, and mistaking these illusory shadows for the truth.[37]

Plato's metaphors reveal a strong, visceral distaste for the body. In one work, he describes how the part of the soul that attends to the body's appetite is "tethered . . . like a beast untamed" to the area of the navel, which serves as the "manger for the body's nourishment." It is stationed here, as far as possible from the head, which houses the pure part of the soul, so that "always feeding at its stall . . . it might cause the least possible tumult and clamour and allow the highest part to take thought in peace for the common profit of each and all."[38]

Polluted by physical desires, the body-oriented part of the soul is in conflict with the pure, mind-oriented aspect of the soul. In the *Republic*, Plato gives an example of someone trying not to drink despite being thirsty: "There is in their soul that which bids them drink, and also something else which forbids them, and prevails over the other." The part that tells a person to drink is desire, and the other part is reason. What Plato calls reason can be mapped onto what modern neuroscientists call cognitive control, which has been shown to be a crucial function of the PFC.[39]

In a well-ordered person, Plato explains, desire obeys reason, just as, in a well-organized state, the lower orders obey the rulers. Virtuous people are those whose reason controls their desires, whereas those who don't have self-control inevitably perform bad actions. Here, setting a course that Western thought would follow for millennia, Plato suggests a theory of human consciousness in terms of a conflict between the benevolent force of the reasoning faculty and the unruly force of physical desire.[40]

Only when the soul distances itself as far as possible from the tumultuous world of the body can it glimpse true reality. In one dialogue, the *Phaedo*, Plato has Socrates describe this process:

> The soul can best reflect when it is free of all distractions such as hearing or sight or pain or pleasure of any kind—that is, when it ignores the body and becomes as far as possible independent, avoiding all physical contacts and associations as much as it can, in its search for reality. . . .
>
> The body intrudes . . . into our investigations, interrupting, disturbing, distracting, and preventing us from getting a glimpse of the truth. We are in fact convinced that if we are ever to have pure knowledge of anything, we must get rid of the body and contemplate things by themselves with the soul by itself.[41]

The philosopher's primary occupation, Socrates goes on, is therefore to separate the soul from the body in order to arrive at pure knowledge. In the twenty-first-century language of cognitive neuroscience, it is as though truth is only available through separating the PFC-mediated conceptualizing faculty from all other parts of human cognition.[42]

What is this pure knowledge attained by thought once it is freed of the senses? Socrates explains that when the soul is freed to look by itself, it perceives true reality composed of "the pure, the eternal, the immortal, the unchanging." The soul can then "cease its wanderings," and, through its contact with eternal truth, it too becomes eternal. This, he avers, is the soul's true nature, a condition called wisdom.[43]

In describing this eternal truth perceived by the soul, Plato expands his dualistic philosophy beyond the soul-body split to conceive a cosmos split into two different domains: an ideal world known only by the soul, and the changeable, material world experienced by the body. This form of thought is known in philosophy as substance dualism, positing a universe composed of two entirely different substances. It is a radically new type of cosmos, different from any of the agricultural or hunter-gatherer cosmologies discussed so far. And it forms the basis for much of Western thought to this day.[44]

A Cascade of Dualism

The core of Plato's worldview, known as the theory of Forms, is that for everything existing in the material world, there exists an ideal form of that thing in another dimension, the immutable world of Ideas. For example, while there may be countless types of chairs, in different shapes, sizes, and materials, there is one ideal form of Chair, of which each actual chair is an ephemeral representation. Plato's theory gains more resonance when it moves into ideas such as Beauty or the Good. People may be beautiful in different ways, but there is only one ideal of Beauty. There may be countless ways to be good, but, in the end, there is only one true ideal of the Good.[45]

Plato's theory of Forms relies ultimately on generalization. Identifying true reality requires ignoring the particular differences between things and focusing on what they have in common as a category. It is remarkable how precisely his theory of Forms maps onto an essential element of the human patterning instinct: the rule-making function of the PFC. When an infant begins to detect patterns in the speech around her, when a growing child acquires the behaviors of his unique culture, and when an adult learns a new profession, in each case, their PFC is primed to detect what is common about a set of experiences and categorize the common factors as abstract concepts with general principles and rules.[46]

In formulating his dualistic cosmos, Plato took this uniquely human capability and turned it into the basis for both understanding reality and imposing a value system on it. A crucial aspect of this split cosmos of ideal Forms and material reality is the unequivocal value judgment Plato applies to the different domains. "The soul," he writes, "is most like the divine, immortal, intelligible, uniform, indissoluble, unchangeable Idea," whereas the mortal body is part of the unintelligible, perpetually changing material world.[47]

At times, Plato tries to work out what happens at the contact point between the purity of the ideal and the messiness of the real world. His descriptions utilize the metaphor of pollution, visualizing something that belongs in the clear air and, when dipped in the muddy, infected swamp of the world, loses its clarity. The further from the swamp, the clearer the air. When the Idea becomes embodied, Plato tells us, it gets "infected with human flesh and colours and all sorts of mortal rubbish."[48]

The eternal soul, Plato explains, knew all about the immutable world of Ideas before it was incarnated. At birth, when the soul is forced to leave the world of Ideas and become fused with a mortal body, it forgets most of its previous knowledge. Thus, the goal of philosophy, in purifying the soul from the body's pollution, is not to learn new truths but to rediscover the Truth that was already known to the soul prior to its incarnation. Indeed, Plato suggests, the very act of thinking about bodily senses is what makes a person mortal, whereas knowledge of the eternal Truth of the world of Ideas is equivalent to attaining immortality.[49]

Here, in Plato's cosmology, is the beginning of the cascade of dualism that would structure the European tradition of thought about the nature of humanity and the universe all the way to the present. In this constellation of ideas that would become endemic throughout Western civilization, the human capacity for abstract thought is linked with the soul, which, in turn, is linked with truth, and truth with immortality. The body, as part of the changeable material world, is associated with sensory appetite, ignorance, and death.

This cosmology would, by itself, have been a major turning point in human thought. But Plato doesn't leave things there. He goes on to link the world of Ideas with another theme he inherited from the Pythagoreans: the conception that mathematics provides the key to eternal truth. The original creator god, according to Plato, formed a world soul, dividing up an unformed chaos in a rigorously mathematical way, creating squares and cubes blended in perfect ratios with each other. Geometry was so central to Plato's cosmology that the entrance doors to his Academy were inscribed with the statement "Let no one unacquainted with geometry enter here." As with so many of Plato's other speculations, this mathematical view of nature has become a foundation stone for European thought.[50]

The Deification of Reason

Plato imagined his creator god as a benevolent mathematician who formed an ordered and beautiful world by imposing rational principles on a primordial mess. Whereas the Presocratic philosophers had looked for patterns of organization intrinsic to the universe, Plato assumed that the universe originally was utter chaos, and only the benevolence of the creator gave it regularity. For Plato, the order of the universe was not, therefore, intrinsic but had to be imposed by an outside agent.[51]

Just as humans use their patterning instinct to impose meaning on the otherwise chaotic world, so Plato imagined the creator using his own patterning instinct to impose meaning on the unformed chaos that had previously existed, bringing it "from disorder into order, since he judged that order was in every way the better." The creator god imposed order through a benevolent impulse, the desire "that all things should be good." With this creation myth, Plato adds the characteristic of goodness to the soul-eternity-truth-mathematics thought constellation. It's not just that the universe is constructed according to eternal principles of mathematical order; the harmonious and symmetrical construction of the cosmos is also the ultimate good.[52]

Given that the universe was created as an act of goodness, it's not surprising that knowledge of the Good—the abstract Idea of goodness—is described by Plato as "the greatest thing we have to learn." It is man's reason that connects him to the Good. (In those days, virtually all recorded thought about humanity was male gendered.) Man can become divine himself, to the extent he can produce in his own nature the order and harmony that the creator originally imposed on the universe. This is the beginning of the deification of reason that would become a central theme in European thought.[53]

Once someone has attained pure knowledge of the Good, Plato believes he will naturally put this knowledge into practice in his everyday life. No longer will there be a conflict between reason and the "baser" desires. In terms of cognitive neuroscience, a truly virtuous man, for Plato, is one whose executive function has established complete cognitive control over the rest of his consciousness. The domination of reason is what makes a man divine, is what permits him to achieve immortality.

Plato set up his famous Academy to teach his philosophy, an institution that would last hundreds of years until it was destroyed by the Romans. One of his first pupils—and his most famous—was Aristotle. Although Aristotle would develop a view of the cosmos that differed in important ways from Plato's, one powerful idea they shared was the divinity of man's faculty of reason.[54]

Aristotle asserts, in the *Nicomachean Ethics*, that the life of reason "will be the perfect wellbeing of man." This life of reason is "higher than the measure of humanity," and a man would choose to follow it "in virtue of something divine within him." Aristotle goes on to conclude, "If, then, Reason is divine in comparison with man, the life of Reason is divine in comparison with human life."[55]

From Plato and Aristotle onward, the divinity of reason became the foundation for theories about human nature in the Western world. For several centuries that followed, until the beginning of the Christian era, a philosophy known as Stoicism became influential. While Stoicism held some views that differed substantially from Plato's, it again affirmed the faculty of reason as the pinnacle of all human experience. For the Stoics, explains scholar E. R. Dodds, the exercise of reason was necessary for moral perfection, and any "passions" felt by a man were merely "errors of judgment." For the founder of the Stoic movement, Zeno, "man's intellect was not merely akin to God, it *was* God, a portion of the divine substance in its pure or active state."[56]

In just a few generations, the philosophers of ancient Greece revolutionized human thought. The senses and emotions were no longer to be trusted. Reason and abstraction would henceforth be the source of what was good in the human experience. Only through the power of the intellect could a person connect to the divine. In the words of classicist F. M. Cornford, "the intellect had become a deity."[57]

Chapter 8

DUALISM AND DIVINITY IN ANCIENT INDIA

When Alexander the Great crossed the Indus River and entered India in the spring of 334 BCE on his expedition of world conquest, he and his men encountered the strange sight of naked men wandering around. These men weren't outcasts but ascetics who had chosen to renounce worldly things in pursuit of spiritual insight. Alexander was so intrigued by these "gymnosophists"—Greek for "naked philosophers"—that he tried to persuade one of them, Dandamos, to join his company. Dandamos refused, asking Alexander why he had bothered to travel so far in his drive for fame and power. He told Alexander:

> I have just as much of the earth as you and every other person; even if you gain all rivers, you cannot drink more than I. Therefore, I have no fears, acquire no wounds and destroy no cities. I have just as much earth and water as you; altogether I possess everything. Learn this wisdom from me: wish for nothing and everything is yours.[1]

This episode, along with other fascinating stories of gymnosophists, made it back to Greece, where it was recorded with relish by contemporary chroniclers. As far back as Alexander's time, a chasm had already appeared between the customary values of Europe and those of India, a cultural gap wide enough to be a source of wonder for the Greeks. This story, and countless others like it, became fodder for what has since emerged as one of the great cultural clichés of history: the mysterious and exotic Orient as a source of spiritual wisdom.

A cliché, perhaps, but one that continues to be grounded in some reality. To this day, even while India claims its position as one of the leading nations of the globe politically, economically, and culturally, there are still enough "gymnosophists" wandering around the countryside to provide fabulous footage for the occasional National Geographic special. The unbroken connection of modern India with its past extends beyond the wandering sadhu; it's rooted deep in the shared cognition of the Indian people, many of whom regularly discuss the details of legends thousands of years old and continue to worship gods with hymns composed even earlier.[2]

When the Indo-European horsemen thundered from their original homeland into Greece and India thousands of years ago, they brought with them a shared set of ideas about the cosmos. What was it that led one tradition to create the "Greek miracle," laying the foundation for the modern scientific worldview, while another became known for its spiritual investigation into humanity's place in the cosmos? As we explore this question, we'll identify some surprising elements both traditions continued to hold in common. Understanding their common foundations, as we'll see, allows insights into each of these two great cultures that would otherwise remain concealed.

The Harappan Synthesis

A common theme to both cosmologies was the sense of an impersonal, transcendent force that ruled the universe. While the Greeks called it *ananke*, it is referred to as *ṛta* in the *Rig Veda*. The Greeks' belief in impersonal laws of nature formed the basis for their exploration of those laws, as in Plato's vision of a creator god using geometry to turn primordial chaos into the harmony of the universe. Plato, like the ancient Egyptians, had struggled with the cosmic riddle of how the One and the Many can coexist, arriving at a very different resolution than the Egyptians' transcendent pantheism.

The Aryans also puzzled over how the universe could exhibit both unity and diversity at the same time, a conundrum that became a central theme in their quest to understand the cosmos. Their worship of the fire god Agni offers a glimpse of how they grappled with the problem of the One and the Many. They were fascinated by the way fire can exist in many separate manifestations but always remains the same. The fire in the family hearth is the same as the fire of the sacrifice and the fire that could blaze through a forest. Agni seemed manifested in all these fires everywhere at the same time. In one *Rig Veda* hymn, echoing the Egyptian worship of Amun, Agni is elevated above all other deities and said to contain—or be one with—them all: "You, O Agni, are Indra, you are Vishnu. . . . You, O Agni, are King Varuna. . . . You are Mitra. . . . You are Aryaman. . . . You, O Agni, are Rudra."[3]

The *Rig Veda* was composed during the period of the Aryans' conquest of

India. Once the Aryans settled there, they came face to face with the ancient culture that was the legacy of Harappan civilization. Was it the synthesis of the Harappans' cosmological speculations with the Aryans' PIE-based thought structures that led to the unique worldview that arose in the Indian subcontinent during the first millennium BCE? As we saw earlier, tantalizing archaeological fragments unearthed from Harappan cities suggest an already existing tradition akin to yoga. It seems possible that the Harappans contributed more than yoga to what became known as the Vedic tradition: they are, in fact, a likely source of the idea of reincarnation that forms the backbone of Vedic cosmology.

The Aryans who composed the *Rig Veda* asked deep questions about the cosmos but had not yet formulated systematic answers. A notable passage wonders about the creation of the universe, pondering how something could have come from nothing:

> Then even nothingness was not, nor existence.
> There was no air then, nor the heavens beyond it.
> What covered it? Where was it? In whose keeping? . . .
> Then there was neither death nor immortality . . .
> There was that One then, and there was no other. . . .
> The gods themselves are later than creation,
> So who knows truly whence it has arisen?[4]

Here, around 900 BCE, the biggest questions about the universe were being raised, but answers were not yet forthcoming. Then, sometime before the sixth century BCE, in a series of texts known as the Upanishads, references are made to multiple reincarnations of a person's soul as it goes through a cosmic cycle of death and rebirth. An answer to some of the profound metaphysical questions of the Aryans was beginning to take shape.[5]

Reincarnation is never mentioned in the *Rig Veda*, but it becomes central to Vedic thought from the sixth century onward. There is a shamanic undertone to the reincarnation myth, with the primordial notion of a spirit that journeys between earth and heaven while taking the form of different animals. This shamanic theme may have been an important part of the Harappan tradition. Many yoga postures, even today, are named after animals and inspired by their characteristic forms. When the Aryan invaders settled among the postHarappan indigenous population of northwest India, they imposed their values and beliefs on those they had conquered. But, powerful as the Aryans were, they would have been significantly outnumbered by the native population. Over generations, some elements of Harappan culture would have inevitably been absorbed and reinterpreted to form the Vedic synthesis. There is a strong possibility that this included the idea of reincarnation.[6]

How can we explain the appearance of reincarnation in Greek thought during the same period? After all, Pythagoras, who lived in the later part of the sixth century BCE, espoused the same idea of the soul's cycle of reincarnation. In ancient Greece, however, the original idea is associated with one man—Pythagoras—who was believed to have travelled to both Egypt and Babylon. Although the idea was further developed by leading Greek intellectuals including Plato, it never became widely accepted and rapidly vanished from the Western tradition.

The momentum of the concept in India is utterly different. Several Upanishads mention reincarnation in the sixth century BCE, and, before long, the idea is dispersed widely throughout India. This rapid diffusion would be more consistent with a notion already ingrained in the culture of the population, as opposed to an alien idea imposed from outside. As it was gradually absorbed into Aryan beliefs, it evolved further and crystallized into the system that became foundational to Hindu, Buddhist, and Jainist thought.[7]

In addition to yoga and reincarnation, another theme central to Vedic thought may plausibly be ascribed to Harappan sources: the shift of religious focus from external rituals to a person's internal experience. The early Aryan invaders were obsessed by their sacrificial rituals. Specialized priests, *brahmin*, officiated at the sacrifices by placing valued objects, such as cattle or clarified butter, into great ritual fires. Over the centuries, as the Aryans settled in their new land, a change in the proceedings occurred. Wealthy tribespeople would pay the priests to perform the sacrifices for them while they sat separately, silently reciting prayers to themselves.[8]

Gradually, a notion arose of what became known as the Five Great Sacrifices: offerings to the gods, to the ancestors, to animals, and to other people, and the offering of one's own study of sacred truths. This last form of sacrifice eventually eclipsed the others. As an early Upanishad puts it, "What people call 'the sacrifice' is really the disciplined life of a seeker of sacred knowledge."[9]

This shift indicated a fundamental reorientation of thinking about the link between humans and divinity, but why ascribe it to Harappan influence? As described earlier, the archaeological remains of the Harappan cities are unique for their complete lack of grand monuments and temples, which has led archaeologists to speculate that Harappan religion was a private affair, conducted in the home without priests. It could be pure coincidence that this shift in Vedic religious orientation just happened to occur in the remains of a civilization unique for its lack of monumental architecture, but a simpler explanation might be that the interior focus of Harappan culture was influential in this change.[10]

Atman Equals Brahman

As the ideas of reincarnation, yoga, and interiority gradually spread throughout India, the ancient concept of *ṛta* underwent a transformation. Scholar William Mahony explains that the literal translation of *ṛta* means "that which has gone before," implying a dynamic, cosmic harmony. By the sixth century BCE, the word *ṛta* was replaced by *Brahman*, which was "in a way a restatement" of *ṛta*, except that some of the flowing nature of *ṛta* has disappeared, and in its place has arisen the view of Brahman as "the unchanging ground of being that pervades and supports all things."[11]

There was another, unique characteristic of Brahman: the sages of that time had begun to practice the disciplined system of meditation they called Yoga and had come to experience a stillness within themselves that they associated with the unchanging, all-pervasive unity of Brahman. At some point, these sages made the extraordinary breakthrough of conceiving that what they felt inside wasn't merely *like* the eternal nature of Brahman—it really *was* Brahman. In one of the most radical and powerful ideas in the history of human thought, they established an identity between their core inner experience of consciousness and the universal nature of reality. The word for self in their language, Sanskrit, was *atman*, so they came up with a simple and profound equation: *atman* equals Brahman.[12]

How could an individual possibly contain all of reality? The solution goes back to the "one and many" concept that had evolved around Agni. Just as one little flame contained the essence of fire as much as a blazing furnace, so within one single individual, the essence of universal reality burned its own eternal flame.[13]

This idea of *atman's* identity with Brahman is widely recognized as the single most important element of Indian thought. Everything else may be seen as arising from this core concept, which is neatly summarized in a famous expression, *tat tvam asi*, meaning "That art thou." The self that is identical to universal reality, however, is not the daily self that most of us are aware of: the self that goes to work, gets hungry, eats dinner, and feels happy or sad. It's a self that can only be discerned by looking deeply inside, piercing through all the layers of daily life. It might be difficult to do, but discovering this eternal, unchanging self is seen as the ultimate goal of human existence, allowing a person to merge with divinity. One early text entices readers by telling them, "Whoever knows thus, 'I am Brahman', becomes this all. Even the gods cannot prevent his becoming thus, for he becomes their self."[14]

The path of this profound transformation of thought can be traced back to the ninth century BCE, when small groups of people would occasionally leave their regular lives in the village to meditate in the forest. These early predecessors of Dandamos developed teachings that were eventually written down in texts known as the Aranyakas, or "forest-books." As these insights became more systematic, a new set of teachings arose: the Upanishads, a name that literally means "sitting down near." This etymology gives a valuable glimpse into that time, suggesting a forest clearing where a teacher imparts his secret wisdom to the select few seated at his feet.[15]

There are a couple of hundred Upanishads in total, spanning several centuries, and virtually all of them draw from the same basic synthesis of the ideas of reincarnation, Yoga, and the *atman*/Brahman identity. A basic summary of this comprehensive view of the cosmos might go as follows: There is an eternal, unchanging reality beyond the world of change. Our souls are continually born and reborn into the world of change as creatures and humans as part of an endless cycle of reincarnation. We humans, by following the discipline of Yoga, are able to realize the unchanging, eternal reality within ourselves. Through this realization, we can become one with the infinite and, by doing so, experience liberation from the cycle of reincarnation.[16]

The Gateway to the Infinite

Since Brahman exists beyond the changeable world of normal human experience, the composers of the Upanishads frequently chose to define it by what it is not. They describe it as "neither gross nor fine, neither short nor long, neither glowing red like fire nor adhesive like water" and "incomprehensible for it cannot be perceived." At roughly the same time, thousands of miles to the west, Anaximander was initiating the Greek discovery of abstraction with his concept of the *apeiron* or the "undefined" from which the world was originally formed.[17] The similarities between Vedic and Greek speculations about the cosmos are extensive. While Anaxagoras explored the notion of a god composed of pure mind, "infinite and self-ruled," that controlled the universe, Brahman was conceived in India as "the all-seeing, the all-powerful, the Lord, the maker and creator."[18]

Perhaps the most striking similarity between Greek and Indian thought is that they both saw an eternal essence within the individual as the gateway to the infinite reality of the universe. When Plato described the soul as pure, eternal, and unchanging, he could almost have been quoting from Katha Upanishad, which describes *atman* as follows:

> The all-knowing Self [*atman*] was never born,
> Nor will it die. Beyond cause and effect,
> This Self is eternal and immutable.
> When the body dies, the Self does not die. . . .
> The supreme Self is beyond name and form,
> Beyond the senses, inexhaustible,
> Without beginning, without end, beyond
> Time, space, and causality, eternal,
> Immutable.[19]

Given the split in both cosmologies between eternal soul and mortal body, it's not surprising that they also shared the idea of the soul's liberation from the body at death. When Socrates was condemned to death, he comforted his followers by explaining that although his body would perish, his immortal soul would move on. The Bhagavad Gita, perhaps the greatest expression of classical Indian thought, expresses Socrates's idea with sublime style:

> The body is mortal, but he who dwells in the body is immortal and immeasurable. . . .
>
> You were never born; you will never die. You have never changed; you can never change. Unborn, eternal, immutable, immemorial, you do not die when the body dies.
>
> As a man abandons worn-out clothes and acquires new ones, so when the body is worn out a new one is acquired by the Self, who lives within.

We can only imagine how Socrates's followers might have been comforted by this poetic vision![20]

While both cosmologies saw the body's death as a liberation of the soul, they also shared the idea that the right practices could lead to liberation even while the body was alive—along with the accompanying notion of the body itself as something bad, which shackled the soul to mortality and suffering. One Upanishad summarizes this as follows:

> The mind may be said to be of two kinds,
> Pure and impure. Driven by the senses
> It becomes impure; but with the senses
> Under control, the mind becomes pure.
> It is the mind that frees us or enslaves.
> Driven by the senses we become bound;
> Master of the senses we become free.
> Those who seek freedom must master their senses.
> When the mind is detached from the senses
> One reaches the summit of consciousness.[21]

The stark mind-body contrast of this passage clearly parallels Plato's view of the body as an infected swamp, polluting the soul's purity.

The Chariot and the Horse

The affinity between Greek and Indian views of the soul-body split extends to their larger understanding of the cosmos. Plato's theory of Forms, which sees the tangible world as merely ephemeral representations of abstract Ideas, is mirrored in the Upanishadic concept of *maya*, a word frequently used in the Upanishads to describe the illusory world of changing form as a veil preventing a person from seeing the true, eternal world of Brahman.[22]

It follows logically, if the world of the senses is just an illusion, that the wise path would be to reject that world and focus on what is real: the knowledge of *atman*/Brahman. This message is repeatedly affirmed throughout the Upanishads, which promise that *atman* will "never wither and decay"; it "knows no aging when the body ages; knows no dying when the body dies."[23]

It's largely for this reason that renunciation of worldly affairs plays such a central part in the Indian spiritual tradition. The desires arising from the body's senses are viewed in the Upanishads—every bit as much as by Plato—as mere impediments to immortality. A verse in the Katha Upanishad states:

When all desires which cling to the heart fall away
Then the mortal becomes immortal,
And in this life finds a Brahman.
When all the earthly ties of the heart are sundered,
Then the mortal becomes immortal.
This is the end of all instruction."[24]

Those living in the world of *maya* might consider renunciation of worldly things in terms of what is given up. But for the seeker of *atman*/Brahman, the bliss awaiting is far greater than anything the tangible world offers. The term for the liberating spiritual wisdom awaiting the mystical seeker is *jnana*, a word of special importance in comparing Greek and Indian thought: it shares the same root as the Greek word *gnosis,* with a virtually identical meaning. Here we see powerful evidence of the shared linguistic and conceptual sources of the Greek and Indian systems of thought. After more than a millennium of separation, both traditions still shared a vision of the liberating insight arising from renunciation of the senses.[25]

Patanjali, one of the principal synthesizers of the Indian spiritual tradition, laid out the yogic path to liberation through rejection of the body in a classic known as the *Yoga Sutra*, which bears a striking resemblance to Plato's approach. Matching Plato's desire to avoid associating with the body, Patanjali writes that "from physical purity [arises] disgust for one's own body and disinclination to come into physical contact with others."[26]

Such is the shared conceptual core of this mind-body split that both traditions even utilize the same root metaphors to describe it. Both Plato and the Katha Upanishad use the relationship between a horse and chariot to illuminate the mind-body duality. A close look at the way the metaphor is treated in each culture shows their deep connection but, at the same time, offers an insight into their differences.[27*]

In Plato's *Phaedrus*, Socrates describes a chariot with two winged horses: a noble horse, representing the soul, wants to fly up to heaven; the other horse, "of ignoble breed," representing the bodily appetites, aims for the ground. The charioteer, the human reasoning faculty, inevitably experiences "a great deal of trouble" driving his chariot.[28]

The chariot metaphor in the Katha Upanishad is more elaborate. It envisages *atman* as lord of the chariot, the body as the chariot itself, the discriminating intellect as charioteer, the mind as the reins, and the senses as the horses. When the mind is undisciplined, "the senses run hither and thither like wild horses," but they "obey the reins like trained horses when one has discrimination." The section concludes triumphantly by stating how those

> Who have discrimination, with a still mind
> And a pure heart, reach journey's end,
> Never again to fall into the jaws of death.
> With a discriminating intellect
> As charioteer and a trained mind as reins,
> They attain the supreme goal of life
> To be united with the Lord of Love.[29]

Both metaphors see an essential split in the human entity: one faculty driving and one being driven. Plato, however, sees another split between the two horses pulling in diametrically opposing directions, with the troubling job of managing this split left in the hands of the reasoning faculty. The Katha Upanishad offers a more detailed and potentially harmonious system for managing the entire enterprise. The Katha horses are not predestined to move in opposite directions: if trained properly, they will pull together and take the chariot to "journey's end."

This distinction points to key elements that differentiate the Indian system of thought from that of the Greeks. The Indian system offers a systematic vision of how the different parts of the human experience can be integrated, and it promises that harmonious integration is, in fact, possible, whereas Plato's chariot suggests that conflicting drives are an inevitable part of the human experience. How does the Indian system achieve that integration? The contrasting chariot metaphors offer another important clue.

Peeling the Onion

The divergent horses of body and soul pulling the Greek chariot are driven by the divine faculty of reason, described by Aristotle as "in the highest sense, a man's self." The Katha chariot, however, has two occupants: the reasoning faculty is merely a charioteer in the service of the ultimate lord, *atman*. This encapsulates a crucial difference between the two systems regarding the role of reason in attaining liberation. It is at this point that if a debate were taking place between the two systems, the Indian debater might openly contradict the Greek. In fact, the Kena Upanishad essentially does that, stating that only "the ignorant think *atman* can be known by the intellect." The Katha Upanishad concurs, declaring:

> The Self [*atman*] cannot be known through study
> Of the scriptures, nor through the intellect,
> Nor through hearing learned discourses.[30]

The highest state of knowledge, the Katha asserts, can only be achieved by ceasing activity in both the senses *and* the intellect:

> When the five senses are stilled, when the mind
> Is stilled, when the intellect is stilled,
> That is called the highest state by the wise.[31]

What is left in consciousness when even the intellect is stilled? The Indian tradition offers a systematic approach to resolving this mystery: Yoga.

The system of Yoga represents a crucial difference between the Greek and Indian approaches to the human experience. When the Greeks tried to understand the mysteries of the universe, they relied entirely on their reasoning faculty. The natural focus of their attention became those areas where reason excelled: searching for general properties of the natural world or for systematic laws of logic. This led the Greeks to launch some of the great Western traditions such as geometry, analytical philosophy, and empirical thinking. The Indians, however, saw the intellect as merely a stepping stone on the way to true knowledge. The yogic system was founded on the core identity of *atman* and Brahman: within the self lies the entire universe. Therefore, the natural object of attention within Yoga became *atman*, concealed beneath the various layers of consciousness. Knowledge of *atman* would give the successful practitioner true knowledge of the entire universe.

For many in the Western world, the word "yoga" has become synonymous with the ubiquitous postural practices offered in exercise classes. In ancient India, *Yoga* meant something far more profound. The first clue to its meaning lurks in the word itself, which comes from the root *yuj*, "to yoke." This concept, of course, takes us right back to the Katha metaphor with the horses yoked to the chariot. Yoga, then, can be understood as the process by which the charioteer (the intellect) learns to use the reins (the trained mind) to control and direct the wild horses of the senses, thus bringing the whole enterprise successfully to journey's end.[32]

In those early times, while the postures or *asanas* that are taught nowadays were an important part of the process, the central aspect of Yoga was *dhyana*—the practice of meditation focusing attention on the inner layers of consciousness. The aspiring yogi also learned various breathing techniques, *pranayama*, which aided the mind to reach states of consciousness more conducive to knowledge of the inner self. It's notable that while both Plato and Patanjali agreed that true knowledge could only be attained by transcending the body, Patanjali gave detailed instruction on meditation and *pranayama*, whereas neither of these techniques is mentioned anywhere in Plato.[33*]

The practices of Yoga were difficult to master, but the Upanishads repeatedly emphasize that it is well worth the effort. One Upanishad describes how a yogi who has mastered his practice will finally hear his "inner voice of divinity" and even offers a preview: "I am the breath of life," says the voice. "I am the wise Self. As such, meditate on me as the life-force. Meditate on me as immortality." The bliss arising from consciousness of the truth—*satcitananda*—is the reward for all those years spent in the yogic discipline. It's a reward arising from mind and body being united to such an extent that the separations between them have disappeared, as described in this verse from the Maitri Upanishad:

> The oneness of the breath and mind,
> And likewise of the senses,
> And the relinquishment of all conditions of existence—
> This is designated as Yoga.[34]

The realization of oneness in breath, mind, and the senses seems a long way from the Platonic notion of the separation of mind and body. In fact, an influential school of classical Indian thought is known as *advaita*, which literally means "not two" and is frequently translated as "nondualism." Does this mean, then, that the principles of Yoga transcend the dualistic mind-body split that Indian civilization inherited from its PIE forebears? Further investigation shows this is not in fact the case.[35]

First, we need to consider what the term *advaita* refers to. Is it saying that body and mind are not two, that they are really just different aspects of one entity? Not really. Its core teaching is based on the foundational idea that *atman* equals Brahman, that the world of *maya* is illusory, and that although things seem separate from each other, if you keep peeling the onion and look to the inner reality, you will see that everything is ultimately part of Brahman. Rather than resolving the mind-body split, *advaita* teaches that relinquishing the body and all other conditions of existence is necessary to realize the true identity of *atman* and Brahman.[36]

This peeling of the onion can be seen in the meditative technique known as *neti-neti*, which means literally "not this, not this," and is applied to thoughts, feelings, and ideas as they arise. By progressively withdrawing attention from whatever arises, the meditator peels away those layers of conceptualizations generally considered to form a person's identity until there is nothing left, at which point he recognizes what remains as *atman*/Brahman. A recitation invokes this:

> *Om*. I am not reason, intuition, egoity, or memory. Neither am I hearing, tasting, smelling, or sight; neither ether nor earth; fire or air. I am Shiva, in the form of Consciousness-Bliss. I am Shiva.[37]

In this case, Shiva refers to the Absolute God or Brahman. The teaching of *advaita* is clear: the ultimate realization that *atman* is Brahman, that the inner self is identical with the absolute nature of the universe, can only be achieved by rejecting the world of the senses inhabited by the body.

Gods Everywhere

There is, however, another crucial aspect of Indian thought that, far from renouncing the physical world, embraces it in all its sensual overload. When the Aryans arrived in the Indian subcontinent, they may have imposed their language and conceptual structures on the indigenous populations, but they didn't succeed in eliminating some of the shamanic and pantheistic ideas that were already there.

Indigenous Indian pantheism, the remembrance of an earlier hunter-gatherer worldview, never really accepted defeat from the Aryan invaders. Rather, it permeated the dualistic patterns of Aryan thought, with the result that, instead of the ascetic rejection of the world proposed by Yoga, the prevailing characteristic of Indian civilization is in fact a joyous celebration of all aspects of worldly affairs, including the most sensual parts of life.

The Upanishads themselves embrace tangible qualities of the world, even while they propose the yogic path of renunciation. This embrace is imbued with the idea that Brahman's divinity is manifested in each and every tangible part of the universe. Here is how one Upanishad describes the manifestations of Brahman:

> He is fire and the sun, and the moon
> And the stars. He is the air and the sea. . . .
> He is this boy, he is that girl, he is
> This man, he is that woman, and he is
> This old man, too, tottering on his staff.
> His face is everywhere.[38]

Just as the Aboriginal storyteller Daisy Utemorrah reflects how her own spirit represents the plants, mountains, stars, and tadpoles, so the Katha Upanishad describes how *atman* exists in all aspects of the world:

> He dwells in human beings, in gods, in truth,
> And in the vast firmament; he is the fish
> Born in water, the plant growing in the earth,
> The river flowing down from the mountain.[39]

The similarities are striking. In both cases, the heavens, plants, and animals are intrinsically connected. The difference is that for Utemorrah, a human directly represents the natural world; for the Katha Upanishad, the all-pervasive force of Brahman is the ultimate cause of that connection. This transcendent form of pantheism, which sees the source of connection in an all-encompassing, universal power, found sublime expression in the Bhagavad Gita when Krishna, an incarnation of Brahman, describes himself to Arjuna:

> I pervade the entire universe in my unmanifested form. All creatures find their existence in me, but I am not limited by them. Behold my divine mystery! These creatures do not really dwell in me, and though I bring them forth and support them, I am not confined within them. They move in me as the winds move in every direction in space.[40]

Here we see a remarkable synthesis of the hunter-gatherer view of interconnected nature with the original PIE idea of *ṛta*, the transcendent force of the universe. These two cosmologies merged to form the transcendent pantheism of the Upanishads.

In this fusion, we see another important difference between the Indian and Greek traditions. When the Greek philosophers used their new tools of reason and logic to understand the world, one of the first casualties was the original pantheon of gods. Zeus, Poseidon, Aphrodite, and their cohorts became worthy subjects of literature but increasingly separated from any authentic search for meaning. In India, the opposite was true. The archaic gods of the indigenous common people became inextricably linked with the cosmological nexus of *atman* and Brahman.[41]

There are far-reaching implications to this split between the Greek and Vedic traditions. When the Greek philosophers identified reason, a uniquely human faculty, as the link to divinity, this meant that other living creatures, lacking reason, missed out on divinity. This dichotomy between humans and the rest of the natural world went on to become a central theme of Western thought.

In the Vedic tradition, by contrast, reason was merely a tool in the service of true divinity. This permitted the rest of the natural world also to partake in divinity, whether or not they possessed the faculty of reason, as summed up in the following Upanishadic verse:

> He [Brahman] has thousands of heads, thousands of eyes,
> Thousands of feet; he surrounds the cosmos
> On every side. This infinite being
> Is ever present in the hearts of all.
> He has become the cosmos.[42]

There is a remarkable similarity between this passage and the Egyptian hymn to the god Amun, "the One who makes himself into millions," which proclaims:

> You are the sky,
> You are the earth,
> You are the netherworld,
> You are the water,
> You are the air between them. . . .[43]

What is the significance of this intriguing parallel in the language of divinity between two civilizations with so little else in common? It suggests, perhaps, that transcendent pantheism is one natural outcome of the human search for meaning, combining the shamanic sense that everything is connected with the patterning instinct's drive to find a unifying cosmological system.

In India, unlike Egypt, transcendent pantheism never died, only to be rediscovered by archaeologists. On the contrary, it thrived in popular culture, becoming a pervasive characteristic of the subcontinent through the millennia. Here is the colorful observation of a twelfth-century Indian poet, Basavanna, on its consequences:

> The pot is a god. The winnowing fan is a god. The stone in the street is a god. The comb is a god. The bowstring is also a god. The bushel is a god and the spouted cup is a god.
>
> Gods, gods, there are so many there's no place left for a foot.[44]

How did Vedic culture reconcile the two opposing tendencies toward asceticism and transcendent pantheism? Or were they ultimately irreconcilable? An answer lurks in this passage from the Upanishads, which describes how *atman* exists within everything:

> The universe is loved not for its own sake, but because the Self
> [*atman*] lives in it. . . .
> Creatures are loved not for their own sake, but because the Self
> lives in them.
> Everything is loved not for its own sake, but because the Self
> lives in it.[45]

The implicit metaphor suggests that everything is a kind of worthless container that holds value only because of the divinity buried within it. In fact, this CONTAINER metaphor extends to the practice of Yoga. Recall the technique of *neti-neti*, in which the practitioner systematically peels away the layers of identity until she arrives at the realization of her infinite existence. Those external layers had no value in themselves; they existed in the world of *maya*. Only when the practitioner has pierced through those layers can she glimpse the core of divinity concealed deep within.

This pervasive metaphor, suggesting that everything in the universe contains a hidden core of divinity where its true nature resides, offers a solution to the conundrum of the Upanishads. Within this cosmological metaphor, renunciation is required to find the absolute reality of *atman*/Brahman. You must discard the layers of *maya*, the illusion that most of us take as reality, to see the true sanctity within. But because everything contains that divine essence, an enlightened person will see all aspects of creation as manifestations of the infinite, as expressions of the all-encompassing *atman*/Brahman.

The belief in the divinity of everything in the universe ultimately differentiates Indian thought from that of the Greeks. In Greek dualism, only humans possess the faculty of reason that enables them to achieve the lofty heights of divinity. For the Greeks, the ultimate Truth attained by reason is to be found *above* the world, separate from the world, in a dimension of eternal abstraction. In the Indian cosmos, dualism took a different form: the source of meaning is both *above* material things and hidden deep *within* them, and is glimpsed by piercing through both the reasoning faculty and the senses.

While looking in different directions for the ultimate source of meaning, both traditions agree that it's not to be found in the tangible world. It is in this respect that both are dualistic. In the next chapter, we will explore an alternative understanding of the universe. In the ancient civilization of China, untouched by the migrations of Indo-European tribespeople, an unbroken tradition evolved from shamanic roots into a cosmology that demonstrated, by its very structure, how the human quest for meaning can take an altogether different approach.

Chapter 9

THE SEARCH FOR HARMONY IN ANCIENT CHINA

The Nameless Uncarved Wood

Two learned Chinese gentlemen were walking through a cultivated garden. It was the fourth century BCE, and China was undergoing a long stretch of political turbulence known as the Warring States period. Thoughtful people were casting about, searching for the underlying causes of life's vicissitudes. One gentleman, Master Tung-kuo, turned to the other and asked:

> "This thing called the Tao—where does it exist?"
> "There's no place it doesn't exist," came the answer.
> "Come," said Tung-kuo, "you must be more specific!"
> "It is in the ant."
> "As low a thing as that?"
> "It is in the grass."
> "But that's lower still!"
> "It is in the tiles and shards."
> "How can it be so low?"
> "It is in the piss and shit!"
> Stunned, Master Tung-kuo made no reply.[1]

The gentleman taking such delight in answering Tung-kuo's questioning was Zhuangzi (Master Zhuang), one of the most brilliant philosophers in Chinese history and a proponent of what became known as Taoism. The *Tao Te Ching*, the greatest classic of Taoism, offers a similar—if less startling—approach to finding the Tao:

Tao everlasting
Is the nameless uncarved wood.
Though small,
Nothing under heaven can subjugate it.[2]

What a difference from the Greeks and Indians! For them, reality was nowhere to be found in the material world. For the Taoists, reality informed everything around them, no matter how lowly. The Tao didn't exist in an abstract Idea of wood, as Plato was suggesting. It wasn't concealed *within* the wood, as the Indians conceived *atman*. Instead, it quite simply *was* the wood. "You must not expect to find the Tao in any particular place," Master Zhuang explained to his companion. "There is no thing that escapes its presence!"[3]

Unlike the Greek and Vedic cosmologies, the Chinese model of the universe never posited a transcendent dimension of eternal meaning. Whereas the Greek and Vedic worldviews both sprang from a common PIE source, the Chinese approach grew organically from its shamanic roots. In the Chinese cosmos, there was no eternal soul; no pure, abstract mind creating and directing the universe. Instead, the Chinese found the most profound source of meaning within the everyday, material dimension of life. As we explore the traditional Chinese interpretation of the cosmos in this chapter, we'll gain a glimpse into a very different pattern of meaning, the implications of which remain as relevant to today's world as they were to that of the Warring States period.[4*]

The Interplay of *Yin* and *Yang*

While the early Greeks and Indians were pondering the concept of nothingness, imagining an immaterial dimension that generated the tangible world, the Chinese conceived an alternative ground of existence, an all-pervasive energy force they called *qi* (pronounced "chee.") Like other agrarian cultures, the Chinese used this one word to refer to breath, a creature's life force, and the underlying energy animating the entire world.

The most ancient Chinese symbol for *qi* denotes vapor arising from rice cooking. We can imagine early Chinese thinkers noticing steam rising from the pot, smelling the rice essence, and associating it with their own breath that seemed to contain their life's essence. At death, breath no longer emanated from the nostrils. A certain energetic life force seemed to leave the body. This force, whether in its manifestation as wind, the vapors of cooked food, or a person's spirit, seemed to be common to all things. That commonality was their *qi*.[5]

Qi was both material and spiritual in nature. It could be perceived, and yet it was also the imperceptible living essence of a person. Unlike Plato's substance dualism, which posited two separate kinds of reality—spiritual and physical—and became the foundation for Western thought, *qi* presented a cosmological framework in which there was only one kind of stuff—*qi* stuff—which was both spiritual and physical at the same time.[6]

In the traditional Chinese creation myth, the universe was originally an unformed mass of *qi* that became differentiated. The lighter, more ethereal *qi* wafted up to form the heavens, while the denser *qi* congealed as the earth. Between these extremes, certain forms of *qi* self-organized with an undulating type of harmony to generate life. This is the basis for the central theme of traditional Chinese medicine that good health arises from proper regulation of one's *qi*, whereas illness is the result of a *qi* imbalance. Ultimately, life and death are to be understood in terms of *qi*. As Zhuangzi puts it, "Living is the gathering of *qi*. Death is the separation of *qi*."[7]

An all-important aspect of *qi* is its continual dynamism. *Qi* is never still, forming a universe of perpetual motion similar to the one Heraclitus postulated in ancient Greece. The ideas of Heraclitus, the "philosopher of flux," never gained traction against the hard logic of Parmenides and Plato's dualistic vision. In China, on the other hand, the notion of a universe in continual flux became the basis for each of the major thought traditions that would ensue. Some of the earliest Chinese thinkers, trying to understand how to flourish in a world where everything was continually changing, identified certain principles within this system of change, which they compiled into one of the great classics of Chinese culture, *The Book of Changes* or *I Ching*.[8]

The core principle of the *I Ching*, and much of Chinese philosophy ever since, is that *qi*, in all its forms, exhibits a never-ending interplay of polarities known as *yin* and *yang*. The *yin* principle represents softness, wetness, darkness, femininity, and receptivity; the *yang* principle represents hardness, dryness, light, masculinity, and activity. While *yin* and *yang* are opposites, they are very different from the cosmic opposites emerging from a dualistic cosmology. Beginning with Zoroaster, the Western dualistic tradition viewed opposites such as good and evil as antagonistic, necessitating a continual struggle in which good, associated with properties such as light and transcendence, tries to conquer evil, which is associated with darkness.[9]

Yin and *yang*, however, are not antagonistic to each other, and one is not considered better than the other. The *yin-yang* relationship is based, rather, on mutual harmony. A useful way of thinking about it is to consider the positive and negative poles of an electric current, or the relationship between the north and south poles of the earth. Each is a necessary part of an integrated system, and neither can exist without the other. This complementarity is summed up beautifully in the *Tao Te Ching*:

> The difficult and easy complement each other,
> The long and short shape each other,
> The high and low lean on each other,
> Voices and instruments harmonize with one another,
> The front and rear follow upon each other.[10]

When *yin* and *yang* are applied to the perpetually moving patterns of *qi*, they form the dynamic cycles that are ubiquitous throughout the natural world: the waxing and waning of the moon; the cresting and falling of a wave; the rhythms of day and night, of summer and winter, growth and decline, birth and death. A profound insight of this system is that each pole of the cycle always contains the other within it. *Yin* is always becoming *yang*, while *yang* is always becoming *yin*. The famous *yin-yang* sign (figure 9.1) exhibits this, showing each side containing a seed of the other.[11]

Figure 9.1: The classic Chinese symbol of yin and yang.

The Chinese saw this insight as a fundamental law of the universe, permeating their entire sense of how to live their lives. A famous story tells of a Taoist sage and prime minister, Chang Liang, who assisted his emperor in overthrowing the previous tyrannical ruler. At the peak of his power, enjoying the greatest reputation of anyone in the empire save the emperor himself, Chang Liang disappeared from court to become a hermit. He had realized the profound truth that there was nowhere to go from his peak except down. Sure enough, the emperor soon began killing off all the other ministers in a fit of suspicion. Because of the way he embodied the principles of *yin* and *yang*, Chang Liang is viewed as one of the wisest men in Chinese history.[12]

Blending the Broth

The *I Ching* attempted to systematize this interplay of *yin* and *yang* by considering sixty-four different configurations of the universe, each represented by a hexagram of six stacked lines, either broken or unbroken. Six unbroken lines represented the extreme of *yang* (heaven), while six broken lines represented the *yin* extreme (earth). The sixty-two other hexagrams represented everything in between (figure 9.2). Just as the simple combination of ones and zeros in binary computer code can produce full-color videos on our latest high-tech gadget, so the ancient Chinese viewed the configurations of *yin* and *yang* as explaining the dynamics of all natural phenomena. An ancient text, the *Great Commentary to the I Ching*, summarizes this, observing, "The alternation of *yin* and *yang* make up the Tao."[13]

True to its name, the *Book of Changes* recognized that each part of the natural world had a fluctuating, interactive effect on every other part, and it attempted to trace this complex interplay. As the *Great Commentary* puts it, "Movement and rest have constant patterns. . . . Through the easy and simple means [of the *I Ching*] the inner structures of the world may be grasped, and one's position established in their midst." The heavens and earth were seen as resonating with each other, creating a kind of universal web in which the slightest movement of one part could cause undulations throughout the entire network. Everything was related dynamically to everything else.[14]

A useful way to understand this connectivity is to consider what in music is called sympathetic resonance. If a musician strikes a tuning fork, any nearby violin string tuned to a similar frequency will resonate. We experience sympathetic resonance when a plane flying overhead causes the windows of the room we're in to rattle because the plane engine's sound waves resonate with the glass. Similarly, we can imagine the myriad movements of *yin* and *yang* throughout the cosmos as a form of wave action, only this time, the waves are the dynamic action of the entire universe.[15]

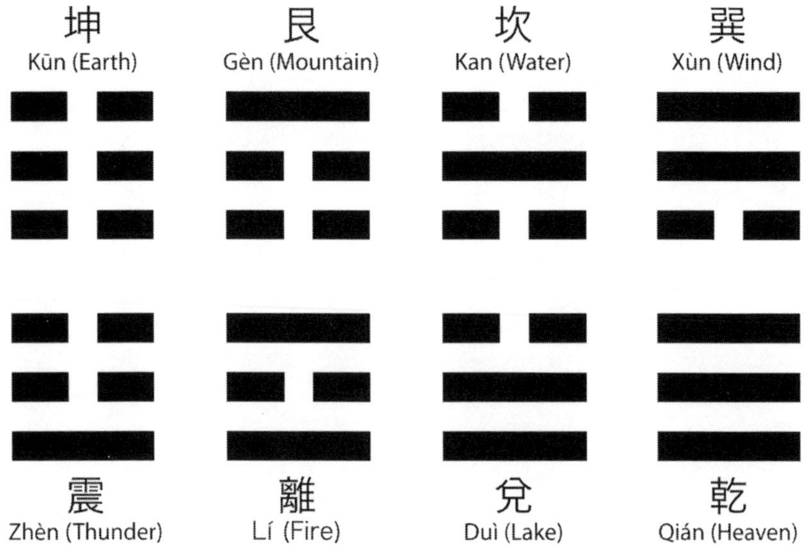

Figure 9.2: Examples of *I Ching* hexagrams

This notion of a universe working through resonance led to an altogether different understanding of cosmic order than the one developing contemporaneously in Greece. Plato visualized his god as the personification of reason, constructing the universe out of primordial chaos on geometric principles. In the Chinese world, by contrast, as described by renowned scholar of Chinese science Joseph Needham, "the harmonious cooperation of all beings arose, not from the orders of a superior authority external to themselves, but from the fact that they were all parts in a hierarchy of wholes forming a cosmic pattern, and what they obeyed were the internal dictates of their own natures."[16]

The sense of intrinsic cosmic harmony extended to the dynamics of human society as well as the great forces of nature. As an ancient commentator on the *I Ching*, Wangbi, observed: "We do not see Heaven command the four seasons, and yet they never swerve from their course. So also we do not see the sage ordering the people about, and yet they obey and spontaneously serve him."[17]

In his seminal multivolume work *Science and Civilisation in China*, Needham broke new ground by recognizing traditional Chinese thought as "organismic": a cosmology based on the root metaphor of the world as one gigantic organism. This underlying metaphor of the cosmos had far-reaching implications for Chinese thought. It is also consistent with modern scientific accounts of the selforganized complexity of the natural world, found in biological systems as small as a single cell or as large as an entire ecosystem. What was originally used in China as a root metaphor to understand the universe is increasingly validated by modern scientific research as a more explanatory model of the natural world than the mechanistic framework that has dominated Western thought.[18]

Conceiving of the entire universe as a single organism has implications for how people choose to live their lives. In ancient Greece, where reason was deified, the primary objective of a philosopher was the cultivation of the intellect. In ancient India, the goal of Yoga was to shed the illusory layers of consciousness until a person could arrive at his own inner truth. In ancient China, where cosmic harmony was seen as the way of the universe, the ultimate intention of the sage was to learn from nature's ways and live according to those same harmonious principles.[19]

How does one go about this process? It begins with the principle of sympathetic resonance connecting what the Chinese understood as the three central nodes of the universe: heaven, earth, and humanity. If you are constantly being buffeted by waves of *yin* and *yang* from across the universe, it seems sensible to try to harmonize with those waves in a compatible way: to avoid being so brittle that a dissonant wave could cause you to shatter, and to resonate with concordant waves in ways that could lead to health and happiness. The universe as a whole seemed to act in harmony, and it became the goal of Chinese sages to live their own lives according to that same principle. In the words of the great philosopher Confucius, "Let the states of equilibrium and harmony exist in perfection, and order will prevail throughout Heaven and Earth, while all things will be nourished and prosper."[20]

For the Chinese, there was no separate, abstracted human soul trying to escape the pollution of the changeable world. Rather, each human being was seen as a natural system embedded dynamically within the network of the cosmos, intertwined between heaven and earth. Humanity did not exist separately from nature but was intrinsically connected to it. There was no sense in trying to conquer nature; rather, humans should harmonize with it.[21]

The pursuit of harmony applied equally to social relations. Harmony, in this case, didn't necessarily mean agreement. You could disagree with someone while still maintaining harmony. In one delightful passage from a Chinese classic, the contrast between harmony and agreement is explained through the analogy of blending different flavors in a broth.

> The Marquis of Qi said, "Only Chü is in harmony with me!"
>
> Yen Tzu replied, "All that Chü does is agree with you—wherein is the harmony?"
>
> "Is there a difference between 'harmony' and 'agreement'?" asked the Marquis.
>
> Yen Tzu replied, "There is. Harmony is like making broth. One uses water, fire, vinegar, sauce, salt, and plum to cook his fish and meat, and burns firewood and stalks as fuel for the cooking process. The cook blends these ingredients harmoniously to achieve the appropriate flavor. Where it is too bland, he adds flavoring, and where it is too concentrated, he dilutes it with water. When you partake of this broth, you feel most content. The relationship between ruler and minister is the same. . . .
>
> "Now Chü is not acting accordingly. Whatever you say is right, Chü also says is right; whatever you say is wrong, Chü also says is wrong. If you add water to flavor water, who can eat it?"[22]

In the down-to-earth approach typical of Chinese thought, harmonizing with the universe is discussed in terms of blending ingredients of a broth. In a cooking school, everyone might share the goal of making the food tasty and healthy, but there might be different recipes to make a meal from the same set of ingredients. Similarly, in the different schools of philosophy that arose in ancient China, there was general agreement about the need to achieve harmony among heaven, earth, and humanity, but differences arose over the best technique to arrive at that harmony. Of these, the two that would become most important throughout the remainder of Chinese history, and which we'll now explore, were the schools of Taoism and Confucianism.[23]

"Not by Decree, but by Spontaneity"

The *Tao Te Ching* begins with a warning. "The Tao that can be spoken of," it declares, "is not the Everlasting Tao. The name that can be named is not the everlasting name." In spite of this, many have attempted throughout history to describe the Tao. The word *tao* literally means "way" or "path," and the idea of the Tao (pronounced "*dao*" and often spelled like that) is as central to Chinese thought as *qi* or *yin* and *yang*.[24]

The Taoist school of thought in ancient China was dedicated to understanding this pathway and learning how to live one's life according to it. The *Tao Te Ching*, second only to the Bible as the most translated book in history, was its foundational text. Legend has it that it was written by Lao-Tzu (whose name literally means "old master"), but it more likely represents the collective wisdom of an ancient tradition dating back into the mists of time, finally captured in written form during the third century BCE.[25]

In approaching the *Tao Te Ching*, it's helpful to look more closely at its title. The word *ching* means a classic text, so the title can be translated as "The Classic of Tao and *Te*." We know that Tao means way, so what about *te*? Translator Ellen Chen explains that *te* (pronounced "duh") refers to the universal power of nature as well as "the power inherent in each individual being determining its unfolding from within . . . the resident creativity in the natural world." Here's how the *Tao Te Ching* describes the two forces:

> Tao gives birth,
> *Te* rears . . .
> Therefore the ten thousand things,
> None do not respect Tao and treasure *te*.
> Tao is respected,
> *Te* is treasured,
> Not by decree,
> But by spontaneity.
> Therefore Tao gives birth,
> *Te* keeps, grows, nurtures, matures, ripens, covers and buries.[26]

The key here is the phrase "not by decree, but by spontaneity." There is no external lawmaker creating universal laws of nature. Instead, there is an underlying principle that harmony arises from each entity following its own nature spontaneously. "When things follow *tao* and *te*," Chen explains, "they follow the freedom and spontaneity of their own natures."[27]

It's useful to consider the deeper meaning of *te* within the context of the Chinese metaphor of THE UNIVERSE AS AN ORGANISM. Think about how your own body works. Each organ performs its complex activities, not because anyone is telling it what to do but because it evolved to perform its functions spontaneously.

Within each organ, every cell acts according to its own intrinsic needs, and, in so doing, it participates in the cellular network that creates the processes permitting the organ—and, ultimately, your entire body—to live and thrive. Similarly, each living entity is seen by the Taoists like a cell within the body, following its own *te* to create the vast, interconnected web of life that constitutes the Tao.

This emphasis on the power inherent within the natural world has led many to note that Taoism is ultimately a life-affirming philosophy. The ancient Greeks viewed the human body as a tomb in which the soul is imprisoned. The Upanishads gave the promise of immortality to those who renounced the illusory world of *maya*. The Taoists, on the other hand, put their attention into how to live in this world rather than prepare for another one.

The Chinese were just as aware of death as the Greeks and Indians and longed for immortality as much as they did. However, their search for immortality was characteristically rooted in their embodied lives. Rather than seek immortality through an abstraction such as the eternal soul or *atman*, they looked for more practical ways to extend life indefinitely. As far back as 1000 BCE, bronze inscriptions show that the most popular blessing people entreated their ancestors to bestow upon them was longevity.[28]

By the time the *Tao Te Ching* was written, this focus on longevity had become, in some circles, an inordinate preoccupation, and one branch of Taoism developed all kinds of bizarre approaches to this end. The renowned Emperor Qin, the first to unify China, was so obsessed by his search for immortality that he died in 210 BCE from ingesting mercury pills that were supposed to be the elixir of life.[29]

Wu-Wei: Effortless Action

For those who couldn't afford mercury pills, the *Tao Te Ching* offered another, more reliable approach to enjoying a long and happy life, in the form of *wu-wei*. The word *wei* means action, and *wu* signifies a negative, so the traditional translation of *wu-wei* is "non-action." Here is how the *Tao Te Ching* introduces the subject:

> To pursue [*wei*] learning one increases daily.
> To pursue [*wei*] Tao one decreases daily.
> To decrease and again to decrease,
> Until one arrives at not doing [*wu-wei*].
> Not doing [*wu-wei*] and yet nothing is not done.[30]

Here is a paradox. How can you do nothing and yet leave nothing undone? Modern scholars have pointed out that instead of translating *wu-wei* as nonaction, it's more accurate to view it as effortless action, the kind of activity that avoids "going against the grain of things." Ancient texts observed how the sun and moon followed each other effortlessly and ceaselessly: "Without any action being taken [*wu-wei*], all things come to their completion; such is the Tao of Heaven." Every entity in nature, by acting according to its *te*, seemed to demonstrate this kind of effortless action. Achieving a state of *wu-wei* was, for many philosophers of ancient China, the secret to harmonizing with the universe and, therefore, life's most important goal. Why, they asked, did *wu-wei* seem so difficult to accomplish?[31]

One way to answer this is to consider its opposite: *yu-wei* or purposive action. One classical text explains that if you tried using a fire to dry up a well, or forced water uphill to irrigate a mountainside, that would be acting contrary to nature and thus would be *yu-wei*: acting with a definite purpose in mind. When we act in harmony with the way things naturally are, when we "go with the flow," we attain *wu-wei*. Zhuangzi encapsulated this idea by kicking off his book on Taoism with a chapter entitled "Going Rambling without a Destination." Without a predetermined destination, you are free to make the most of whatever presents itself and adapt yourself accordingly. Once you establish a final goal, you've moved into the zone of *yu-wei*, your actions become purposive, and you may miss out on the finer qualities of your journey.[32]

Acting purposively, however, is a fundamental attribute of humanity. Humans, as we've seen, are driven by a different kind of *te*: our patterning instinct resulting from the unique capabilities of our PFC. The purposive, goal-oriented faculties of the PFC gave us symbolic thought, language, and control over the natural world. The PFC's planning capability permitted the first farmers to make the radical shift toward cultivating crops, putting in backbreaking hours of work tilling and planting, and delaying instant gratification for the sake of future plans. It is our uniquely human patterning instinct that causes us to target a destination rather than ramble about and that eventually led to the invention of a steam engine that could literally drive water uphill to irrigate a mountainside.[33]

The ancient Taoists, of course, had no idea about the PFC and its function in the human brain. If they had, they might have seen it as the ultimate source of disharmony. The *Tao Te Ching* views civilization as a decline from the original state of nature when humans lived in harmony with the Tao. And it identifies the analytical part of the mind—the same part that's responsible for building civilization—as the culprit for the loss of the Tao. "Eliminate learning," it declares, "so as to have no worries." It points out how the mind's discriminating faculty creates distinctions of good and bad, of beauty and ugliness—dualities arising from conceptualizations that only the human brain, with its patterning instinct, is capable of making:

> When all under heaven know beauty as beauty,
> There is then ugliness;
> When all know the good [as] good
> There is then the not good.[34]

Identifying the Tao with the "nameless, uncarved wood," the *Tao Te Ching* recognizes language as a fundamental step in the loss of human connection with the Tao:

> At the beginning of institution names come to be.
> Once there are names,
> One must know when to stop.
> One who knows when to stop does not become exhausted.[35]

This, according to the *Tao Te Ching*, is why the purposive action catalyzed by our patterning instinct—*yu-wei*—is the ultimate source of disharmony and failure:

> One who desires to take the world and act [*wei*] upon it,
> I see that it cannot be done.
> The world is a spirit vessel,
> Which cannot be acted upon.
> One who acts on it fails,
> One who holds on to it loses. . . .[36]

Here is a fundamental difference between the Taoist view of the PFC's unique faculties in human consciousness and the views of Greek and Indian civilizations. For the Greeks, reason itself was divine, and the human ability to create abstractions was the pathway to divinity. For the Indians, the "discriminating intellect" was the charioteer driving *atman* to enlightenment, harnessing the wild horses of the senses. For the Taoists, the discriminating, reasoning faculty was the source of *yu-wei*, the rise of civilization, and the loss of the harmony available to humans through effortless action.

Power and Responsibility

China's Warring States era generated a maelstrom of philosophical ideas. Virtually everyone shared with the Taoists the aspiration to harmonize with the Tao, but many disagreed vehemently with them on how to do it. One of these was Confucius, whose name has become almost synonymous with Chinese culture and whose ideas remain integral to Chinese thought to this day.

Instead of viewing civilization as causing an inevitable loss of the Tao, Confucius turned his attention to how the Tao was actually manifested in society. Confucius agreed with the Taoists that there had been a precipitous decline in values from an earlier golden age, but, for Confucius, that golden age was defined not by absence of culture but rather by a more harmonious and morally upright culture that had since become corrupted.

While the Confucian and Taoist approaches had significant differences, they were sometimes seen not as opposing philosophies but as complementary methods of harmonizing with the Tao. Whereas Taoism focused on how an individual might shed his cultural conditioning to achieve *wu-wei*, Confucianism focused on the individual's relationship with society, with the goal of attaining social harmony. Some people professed both philosophies at the same time, considering themselves Confucianists in their social conduct and Taoists when enjoying more solitary pursuits. Others embraced one philosophy or the other at different stages in their lives, acting as community-oriented Confucianists while building their careers, only to become more solitary Taoists during retirement—or perhaps after losing out in a power struggle.[37]

The Confucian framework of culture and society is embedded within the ancient belief in the emperor's crucial role of mediating the relationship between heaven and earth. Because of the dynamic resonance between heaven and earth, if something were out of harmony in one domain, this was believed to cause disharmony in the other. The emperor was viewed as the fulcrum within this setup, and, as such, his role was essential in maintaining balance between the two domains.[38]

This is one of the earliest documented ideas in history. As far back as 1046

BCE, the small state of Chou managed to conquer the Shang dynasty and establish its own dynasty in its place. Its regent, the Duke of Chou, made a famous announcement to the Shang people to explain how they could have been vanquished, even though their ancestors in heaven should have had the power to protect them. The reason, he explained, was that:

> Your last Shang king abandoned himself to indolence, disdained to apply himself to government, and did not bring pure sacrifices. Heaven thereupon sent down his ruin. . . . But our king of Chou treated well the multitude of the people, was able to practice virtue, and fulfilled his duties to the spirits and to Heaven. Heaven instructed us, favored us, selected us, and gave us the Mandate of *Yin*, to rule over your numerous regions.[39]

Thus began the so-called Mandate of Heaven, a doctrine declaring that as long as the emperor ruled his people responsibly, the ancestral spirits in heaven would endorse him and maintain his position. While this might sound like no more than a cynical rationalization made by a conqueror to legitimize power, it cut both ways. There was an implicit threat to the ruler that if he failed to carry out his role diligently, he would lose the mandate and get toppled himself. The mandate was as much a responsibility as a right.[40]

This idea remained so stable in Chinese culture that, a full two thousand years later, in 1085 CE, a leading statesman wrote in his memoirs:

> Heaven responds to the deeds of the ruler. If he continuously cultivates himself and treats his people justly . . . then Heaven sends prosperity, and the Son of Heaven receives the realm for all times. There will be no misfortune and nobody will create trouble. If he, however, neglects the deities, ill-treats his people, and does not fear the Mandate of Heaven, there will be misfortune.[41]

The astonishing consistency of this idea may be linked to the fact that the Chinese words for "to care for" and "to govern" are the same. In the traditional Chinese cosmos, the rights and responsibilities of power are so inextricably linked that they are in fact one and the same thing.[42]

Nowhere is this fusion of rights and responsibilities more apparent than in the traditional Chinese family. Each family was seen as a microcosm of the entire empire, with every family member obliged to carry out his or her particular duties; otherwise, disharmony would arise and lead to misfortune for the entire family. Each member's role in the traditional Chinese family was far more structured than is conceivable to the Western mind, and it continues in this way to the present day. Most families, for example, give specific names to each generation, so that every brother, sister, and cousin has one name in common, with the result that, simply by hearing someone's name, people know where they fit in the generational hierarchy.[43]

This sense of knowing exactly where you stand within a complex network of relationships, rights, and obligations pervades the Confucian cultural framework. A person's identity arises from his or her particular cluster of connections within the network: being a son or daughter, a parent, a student or teacher, an official or an employee. An individual's moral responsibility is to reconcile and balance these relationships for the well-being of the entire nexus.[44]

Where a conflict might arise between the family unit and the state, Confucius seemed to think that the family was ultimately the more important nexus. The *Analects*, the classic compilation of Confucius's teachings, tells a story of a duke who boasts how morally upright his state is, giving the example of a man who turned in his father for stealing a sheep. Confucius is not impressed. "In my country," he responds, "the upright are different from this. A father will screen his son and a son will screen his father." Confucius is not condoning stealing; rather, he is saying that the sacred family ties must be preserved at all costs.[45]

The roots of this Confucian emphasis on the importance of family go back to the ancient agrarian view of the family as a continuum spanning heaven and earth, with the ancestors in heaven holding the power to affect the lives of the current generation. The best way someone could look after their living family was therefore to pay their respects as diligently as possible to those who had passed on to heaven. Attention to the appropriate rituals for the ancestors was, indeed, a guiding tenet of traditional Chinese life and a core principle of Confucianism.

Enlarging the Tao

When a diligent family member paid respects to the ancestral spirits, he was performing his own version of harmonizing with the Tao, hoping to persuade the powers of the spirit world to harmonize with his own needs. It is here that we find the source of the Confucian approach to the resonance of heaven and earth. A line in the *Analects* succinctly illuminates it: "Man is able to enlarge the Tao," says Confucius, "it is not that the Tao enlarges man."[46]

This is the key point of divergence between Taoism and Confucianism. While the Taoist practice of *wu-wei* encouraged a person to shed the accoutrements of civilization and become like the uncarved piece of wood, for Confucius, there were elements of civilization that enabled humanity to "enlarge the Tao," essentially improving on nature. The specific tools for enlarging the Tao were available in the form of ritual observances, known as *li*, which were seen as a kind of cosmic resonance, a sacred acting out by humans of the overarching principles of the universe.[47]

The importance of *li* to the Confucian worldview cannot be overstated: they form the bedrock of all other aspects of Confucian thought. "If one departs from the *li*," states an ancient text, "one will be destroyed. Is not *li* the greatest of all principles?" The scope of *li* gradually expanded beyond sacred rituals, such as sacrifices, to cover the whole range of human activity, governing such subjects as how to relate to your parents, how long to mourn after they died, what articles of clothing to wear in various contexts, and how to act toward others in your community.[48]

In our modern world, it is common to think of ritual as form rather than substance, significant only insofar as it represents a deeper reality. The traditional Chinese didn't make this distinction. The *li* were detailed prescriptions for behavior that bound them together as a community and linked them with the ancestors. Each individual held a sacred responsibility to perform the *li* properly and thus maintain harmony for everyone else.[49]

The *li* referred to not just the ritual acts themselves but the authentic manner in which they were performed. Insincerity could turn the right behavior into something potentially destructive. "Respect without *li* becomes tiresome," Confucius observes. "Caution without *li* becomes timidity; courage without *li* becomes disorderly conduct; straightforwardness without *li* becomes rudeness."[50]

The notion of truly authentic behavior, known as *cheng*, was the Confucian alternative to *wu-wei* as the best practice for those who aspired to harmonize with the Tao. Rather than shedding layers of civilization, the Confucian sought to integrate them with his true nature. It is as though the Confucianists, recognizing that human nature incorporates the unique capabilities of the PFC, used the *li* as a means to integrate the patterning instinct with the rest of the natural world. Thus, in an ancient work attributed to Confucius's grandson, it is written, "*Cheng* is the Tao of heaven; to apply oneself to *cheng* is the Tao of man."[51]

Those who succeeded in the lifelong task of applying themselves to *cheng* could attain a state of *ren*: the Confucian ideal of an enlightened person behaving authentically in every way. *Ren* is associated with a range of virtues such as filial piety, courage, and loyalty, but its scope expands to cover what we might call love. It is sometimes translated as "humanity," but we need to understand this in a more expansive way than the word is generally used: as a true fulfillment of the possibilities intrinsic to the state of being human. It was in response to someone asking Confucius for a definition of *ren* that he gave the original version of what has become known worldwide as the Golden Rule: "Do not do to others what you would not wish for yourself."[52]

The Path or the Road?

Imagine a river making its way from a mountain range down to the plains and, finally, to the ocean. The river finds its path, meandering here and there, based on the natural effects of gravity, terrain, and the water's flow. Now suppose that, over time, human beings begin to settle there. They would gradually create their own pathways between their settlements, following the meandering terrain the river valley offered them. As civilization progressed, these pathways would develop into more direct roads and ultimately, perhaps, even a freeway. The difference between the Taoist and Confucian approaches may be seen in terms of the contrast between a meandering path along the river valley and a straighter, paved road. Is the Tao best understood as the path or the road? Which is more beneficial to human life and offers the greatest sense of meaning?

Two leading scholars, David Hall and Roger Ames, argue in their book *Thinking through Confucius* that, for Confucians, to realize the Tao was to interpret and extend the way of life already established by their predecessors and thus to provide a road map for future generations. Confucian Tao, according to their interpretation, is almost synonymous with culture. "The human being is not only heir to and transmitter of tao," they write, "but is, in fact, its ultimate creator. Thus . . . the tao emerges out of human activity. As the metaphor 'road' would suggest, tao, at least for Confucius, is ultimately of human origin."[53]

How different from the Taoist notion of the uncarved piece of wood! The *Tao Te Ching*, in fact, barely conceals its distaste for the very *li* that Confucius saw as sacrosanct. Only when Tao, *te*, and *ren* are all lost, it asserts, "then there is *li*. As to *li*, it is the thin edge of loyalty and faithfulness, and the beginning of disorder." For the Confucians, *li* was the key to harmonizing with the Tao; for the Taoists, it was the last step of calamitous decline in the quality of human experience. For the Confucians, the goal was to integrate the artificial constructions of the human patterning instinct; for the Taoists, it was to deconstruct what the patterning instinct had forged.[54]

While the Chinese were the first major civilization to develop these contrasting views of the consequences of the patterning instinct, they were not the only ones. In Europe, the Romantic movement, which began in reaction to the Enlightenment values of the new scientific age, shared much with Taoism, rejecting the artifice of civilization with the iconic notion of the "noble savage" and the elevation of imagination over reason. The split between Romantic and Enlightenment values, however, followed the split between emotion and reason inherited ultimately from Platonic dualism, and, to this day, much of the debate in the West is couched in these dualistic terms.

The Chinese tradition took a different and arguably more illuminating path. As we'll explore later, a school of philosophy known as Neo-Confucianism subsequently developed a model of the cosmos that synthesized principles of both the Taoist and Confucian schools to create an integrated system of meaning that holds important implications for us today.

Even with their differing views on the Tao, the Confucians and Taoists agreed that harmonizing with it was their ultimate objective. The Chinese search for meaning, in all its variations, was based on an entirely different foundation than the Vedic and Greek traditions, which saw the source of meaning as transcendent, separate from the physical realities of human experience. Far from being mere theoretical distinctions, these differences have influenced the structures of thought of every generation since ancient times and continue to elicit profound differences in how Westerners and East Asians think to this day.

The next chapter will delve more deeply into these contrasts and trace how these divergent cognitive frameworks led to structural differences in language, thought, and even the neural pathways through which people from these two cultural complexes continue to perceive themselves and the world around them.

Chapter 10

THE CULTURAL SHAPING OF OUR MINDS

Does Language Shape Our Minds?

In the far north of Queensland, Australia, live a few hundred Aboriginals who speak a language called Guugu Yimithirr. Theirs is the language that gave us the word "kangaroo," but they have another claim to fame. Instead of using words such as "right," "left," "in front," or "behind," they use the cardinal directions of north, south, east, and west. If a Guugu Yimithirr speaker wants you to move back from a table, she may ask you to "move a bit to the east." If she wants you to make room in a car, she might say, "Move over to the west." Guugu Yimithirr speakers maintain their orientation to the points of the compass no matter whether they are standing still or moving around, indoors or outdoors, in the deepest forest or the thickest fog. Just as people with perfect pitch can tell you exactly what note they hear without knowing why, the Guugu Yimithirr automatically know their cardinal directions every moment of their lives.[1]

The Guugu Yimithirr are not alone in their extraordinary skill. Languages that rely on geographic coordinates have been discovered in Mexico and Polynesia as well as other parts of Australia, and, in each case, the speakers demonstrate a spatial sensory faculty that is missing for the vast bulk of humanity.[2] The ability of these speakers to locate themselves in a way that is impossible for the rest of us is only the most dramatic in an array of discoveries that are causing a revolution in the world of linguistics. Researchers point to the Guugu Yimithirr as *prima facie* evidence supporting the argument that the language you speak affects how your cognition develops. As soon as they learn their first words, Guugu Yimithirr infants begin to structure their orientation around the cardinal directions. In time, their neural connections get wired accordingly until this form of orientation becomes second nature, and they no longer even have to think about where north, south, east, and west are.[3]

The idea that language—and its corresponding cultural framework—

affects the way we think is a key premise of this book. The reason it's important to investigate the root metaphors of ancient cultures such as Greece, India, and China is that they have framed the patterns of thought each of us inherits as we grow up, thus affecting how we construct meaning in our lives. If we each determined our own ways of thinking independently of our language and culture, we wouldn't need to delve into the past to understand our patterns of cognition. In this chapter, we'll take a look at the theoretical underpinning of this premise and trace how ideas about the cosmos that developed thousands of years ago in Greece and China still affect how billions of us think about our place in the universe today.

For many of us, the idea that the language we speak affects how we think might seem self-evident, hardly requiring a great deal of scientific proof. However, for decades, the orthodoxy of academia has held categorically that the language a person speaks has no effect on the way they think. To suggest otherwise could land a linguist in such trouble that she risked her career. How did mainstream academic thinking get itself in such a straitjacket?[4]

The answer can be found in the remarkable story of one charismatic individual, Benjamin Whorf. In the early twentieth century, Whorf was a student of anthropologist-linguist Edward Sapir, whose detailed study of Native American languages had caused him to propose that a language's grammatical structure corresponds to patterns of thought in its culture. "We see and hear and otherwise experience very largely as we do," Sapir suggested, "because the language habits of our community predispose certain choices of interpretation."[5]

Whorf took this idea, which became known as the Sapir-Whorf hypothesis, to new heights of rhetoric. The grammar of our language, he claimed, affects how we pattern meaning into the natural world. "We cut up and organize the spread and flow of events as we do," he wrote, "largely because, through our mother tongue, we are parties to an agreement to do so, not because nature itself is segmented in exactly that way for all to see."[6]

The crux of Whorf 's argument was the contrast between the subject-verbobject grammatical structure of Indo-European languages and that of Native American languages such as Hopi. Indo-European grammar, Whorf argued, forced Westerners to think about everything that happened in terms of some person or thing doing something to some other person or thing. But this is not necessarily how nature actually works, he suggested, nor is it how other cultures understood the natural world. He extended his arguments to the IndoEuropean tense structure of past-present-future. Once again, he claimed, this structure "colors all our thinking about time," even though the natural world is not necessarily organized in this way. "For if we inspect consciousness," he went on, "we find no past, present, future, but a unity embracing complexity." In Hopi, he explained, verbs had entirely different tenses. One tense, for example, denotes that the speaker is reporting a situation, while other forms denote different degrees of duration.[7]

Whorf was brilliant but highly controversial. He had a tendency to use sweeping generalizations and dramatic statements to drive home his point. "As goes our segmentation of the face of nature," he wrote, "so goes our physics of the Cosmos." Sometimes he went beyond the idea that language affects how we think to a more strident assertion that language literally forces us to think in a certain way. "The forms of a person's thoughts," he proclaimed, "are controlled by inexorable laws of pattern of which he is unconscious." This rhetoric led people to interpret the Sapir-Whorf hypothesis as a theory of linguistic determinism, claiming that people's thoughts are inevitably determined by the structure of their language.[8]

A theory of rigid linguistic determinism is easy to discredit. All you need to do is show a Hopi Indian capable of thinking in terms of past, present, and future, and you've proven that her language didn't ordain how she was able to think. The more popular the Sapir-Whorf theory became, the more status could be gained by any researcher who poked holes in it. In time, attacking Sapir-Whorf became a favorite path to academic tenure, until the entire theory became completely discredited.[9]

In place of the Sapir-Whorf hypothesis arose what is known as the nativist view, which argues that the grammar of language is innate to humankind. As discussed earlier, the theory of universal grammar, proposed by Noam Chomsky in the 1950s and popularized more recently by Steven Pinker, posits that humans have a "language instinct" with grammatical rules coded into our DNA. This theory has dominated the field of linguistics for decades. "There is no scientific evidence," writes Pinker, "that languages dramatically shape their speakers' ways of thinking." Pinker and other adherents to this theory, however, are increasingly having to turn a blind eye—not just to the Guugu Yimithirr but to the accumulating evidence of a number of studies showing the actual effects of language on people's patterns of thought.[10]

Frustration . . . or *Stenahoria*?

In the deepest recesses of the Amazonian rain forest, by the bank of the Maici River, lives a tribe of a few hundred people known as the Pirahã. Their language is highly unusual, lacking recursion, a past tense, color terms, numbers of any kind, and any concept of counting or quantification.[11]

Psychologist Peter Gordon saw an opportunity to test the most extreme version of the Sapir-Whorf hypothesis with the Pirahã. If language predetermined patterns of thought, then the Pirahã should be unable to count, in spite of the fact that they show rich intelligence in other forms of their daily life. He performed a number of tests with the Pirahã over a two-year period, and his results were convincing: as soon as the Pirahã had to deal with a set of objects beyond three, their counting performance disintegrated. His study, he concludes, "represents a rare and perhaps unique case for strong linguistic determinism."[12]

The Guugu Yimithirr, at one end of the spectrum, show the extraordinary skills a language can give its speakers; the Pirahã, at the other end, show how necessary language is for basic skills we take for granted. In between these two extremes, an increasing number of researchers are demonstrating a wide variety of more subtle ways the language we speak can influence how we think.

One set of researchers illustrated how language affects perception. They used the fact that the Greek language has two color terms—*ghalazio* and *ble*—that distinguish light and dark blue. They tested the speed with which Greek speakers and English speakers could distinguish between these two different colors, even when they weren't being asked to name them, and discovered the Greeks were significantly faster.[13]

Another study demonstrates how language helps structure memory. When bilingual Mandarin-English speakers were asked in English to name a statue of someone with a raised arm looking into the distance, they were more likely to name the Statue of Liberty. When they were asked the same question in Mandarin, they named an equally famous Chinese statue of Mao with his arm raised.[14] One intriguing study shows English and Spanish speakers remembering accidental events differently. In English, an accident is usually described in the standard subject-verb-object format of "I broke the bottle." In Spanish, a reflexive verb is often used without an agent, such as "*La botella se rompió*"—"the bottle broke." The researchers took advantage of this difference, asking English and Spanish speakers to watch videos of different intentional and accidental events and later having them remember what happened. Both groups had similar recall for the agents involved in intentional events. However, when remembering the accidental events, English speakers recalled the agents better than the Spanish speakers did.[15]

Language can also have a significant effect in channeling emotions. One researcher read the same story to Greek-English bilinguals in one language and, then, months later, in the other. Each time, he interviewed them about their feelings in response to the story. The subjects responded differently to the story depending on its language, and many of these differences could be attributed to specific emotion words available in one language but not the other. The English story elicited a sense of frustration in readers, but there is no Greek word for frustration, and this emotion was absent in responses to the Greek story. The Greek version, however, inspired a sense of *stenahoria* in several readers, an emotion loosely translated as "sadness/discomfort/suffocation." When one subject was asked why he hadn't mentioned *stenahoria* after his English reading of the story, he answered that he cannot feel *stenahoria* in English, "not just because the word doesn't exist but because that kind of situation would never arise."[16]

Building Blocks and Barriers

The stream of evidence demonstrating how language affects thought has been described by one linguist as a "neo-Whorfian renaissance." Today, a linguist can kick off a paper for the National Academy of Sciences with, "It is now established that native language affects one's perception of the world." Years ago, this statement might have compromised his career. Today, it doesn't even create a ripple.[17]

Many researchers nowadays make a distinction between a "strong" and "weak" form of Whorfianism. The strong form claims that your language determines how your brain is wired and what it's able to conceptualize. The Pirahã and Guugu Yimithirr examples support this claim. The weak form is less dramatic but perhaps more interesting. It states that the language we speak from birth establishes patterns of cognition that encourage us to think about the world in different ways from someone speaking another language. Put simply: language has a patterning effect on cognition.

How might this happen? As discussed earlier, neuroscientists have discovered that learning takes place through synaptic pruning, whereby frequently used neural connections in the brain continually get strengthened, while those that are not used eventually die away. In the case of the Guugu Yimithirr speakers, we can impute a particular network of synaptic connections between the part of the brain that mediates spatial awareness and the part that recognizes geographic orientation words. This network would get strengthened from infancy in Guugu Yimithirr speakers, whereas, for speakers of other languages, those connections don't get utilized and, therefore, fade away. Because the network is formed at such a young age, it would become deeply sculpted into the brain's neural pathways until eventually requiring no more conscious attention.[18]

When deep-rooted modes of cognition such as counting or spatial orientation are affected by language, this might cause speakers of that language to perceive the world in ways that become hardwired, unconscious, and inalterable by the time of adulthood, resulting in a "strong Whorfian" effect. When more conscious modes of cognition are acquired through language later in childhood, speakers of that language may be influenced in their thought patterns but still be able to view the world in alternative ways if such alternatives are offered to them, leading to a "weak Whorfian" outcome.

This suggests that very few of us as adults will ever be able to orient ourselves to the world the way a Guugu Yimithirr speaker does. On the other hand, where we are affected by "weak Whorfian" patterns of thought, we may be able to change those patterns once they become conscious to us. The "weak Whorfian" effect is not that language determines what someone is able to think but that it influences people to think in a certain way. This distinction has crucial implications. It means, for example, that if Western patterns of thought differ in some substantial ways from East Asian patterns, these differences need not be permanent, but may be subject to change if we so choose.

Linguist Alfred Bloom offers a helpful analogy of language as a series of building blocks, each of which integrates and crystallizes a certain concept that would otherwise be difficult to access and utilize. He gives an example of the word *bachelor*, which integrates four separate concepts: male, unmarried, never married, and adult. Without the word, we'd have to work hard to keep all four ideas in mind; once we've mastered the word, each time we use it, we effortlessly bring all four concepts to our conscious mind in one seamless whole.[19]

Language, in effect, leverages the work of our patterning instinct, freeing it up to be used for other requirements. When a new concept such as *bachelor* needs to be learned, the PFC must merge different concepts together in working memory to create a new, higher-level concept. Once a word has become attached to this new concept, it becomes embedded and is henceforth stored in the brain for effortless access, freeing up the PFC's working memory for new activities. This is likely the way in which language influences a person's pattern of thoughts.[20]

Through this process, languages can act as both building blocks and barriers of the mind at the same time. Once we've assigned a word to a particular set of ideas, it's easier for us to use that word than construct a new assemblage of thoughts unconnected to any word. The more complex and abstract the set of ideas attached to the word, the more difficult it is to come up with a competing set of ideas not associated with any word. The reason why the broadest, most intangible words of a language—*qi* or Tao, *atman* or soul—are often the most difficult to translate is that they are the result of so many different levels of conceptual building blocks, each of which has been assembled from a unique set of more basic concepts combined over generations by the speakers of that particular language.[21*]

Creating Our Reality

Does our language, then, shape the core concepts of our culture? Or could it work the other way, that our culture identifies what is important and then requires a word to label it? As linguists of the neo-Whorfian renaissance explore this question, they are finding a dynamic interdependency between language and culture. Just as the PFC and language coevolved (discussed in chapter 2), so a similar process can be traced between culture and language.[22]

Before language, early humans shared with other animals a universal set of tangible experiences: touch, sensation, up and down, warm and cold, near and far. They also shared with each other specifically human capacities: perceiving the intentions of others, imitating them, using categorization and analogy to find meaning in things. If we view language as a construction of symbolic building blocks, then these universally shared experiences are its foundation. As language became more sophisticated and crossed the metaphoric threshold, different cultures began to develop their own unique concepts from that shared foundation, thus creating new levels of culture-specific meaning.[23]

The further cultures diverged from each other, the more their languages began to differ, creating unique constructions from what was originally a shared foundation of human experience. These culture-specific constructions may be understood as cultural frames, generating words that have meaning only within the context of that frame and encouraging speakers to think in patterns that fit into the frame.[24]

Marketing professor David Luna has performed tests on people who are not just bilingual but bicultural—those who have internalized two different cultures—which lend support to this model of cultural frames. Working with people immersed equally in both American and Hispanic cultures, he examined their responses to various advertisements and newspaper articles in both languages and compared them to those of bilinguals who were only immersed in one culture. He reports that biculturals, more than monoculturals, would feel "like a different person" when they spoke different languages, and they accessed different mental frames depending on the cultural context, resulting in shifts in their sense of self.[25]

In particular, the use of root metaphors, embedded so deeply in our consciousness that we don't even notice them, influences how we define our sense of self and apply meaning to the world around us. "Metaphor plays a very significant role in determining what is real for us," writes cognitive linguist George Lakoff. "Metaphorical concepts . . . structure our present reality. New metaphors have the power to create a new reality."[26]

These metaphors enter our minds as infants, as soon as we begin to talk. They establish neural pathways that are continually reinforced until, just like the cardinal directions of the Guugu Yimithirr, we use our metaphorical constructs without even recognizing them as metaphors. When a parent, for example, tells a child to "put that out of your mind," she is implicitly communicating a metaphor of the MIND AS A CONTAINER that should hold some things and not others.[27]

When these metaphors are used to make sense of humanity's place in the cosmos, they become the root metaphors that structure a culture's approach to meaning. Hunter-gatherers, as we've seen, viewed the natural world through the root metaphor of GIVING PARENT, which gave way to the agrarian metaphor of ANCESTOR TO BE PROPITIATED. Both the Vedic and Greek traditions used the root metaphor of HIGH IS GOOD to characterize the source of ultimate meaning as transcendent, while the Chinese used the metaphor of PATH in their conceptualization of the Tao. These metaphors become hidden in plain sight, since they are used so extensively that people begin to accept them as fundamental structures of reality. This, ultimately, is how culture and language reinforce each other, leading to a deep persistence of underlying structures of thought from one generation to the next.[28]

"Thinking, Therefore Being"

The languages of ancient Greece and China offer us a test case *par excellence* for evaluating Whorfian effects. Separated by the Himalayas, these two great civilizations evolved over thousands of years with widely divergent cultural traditions. Their last common source was most likely the shamanic worldview of nomads who migrated across Asia fifty thousand years ago. How did each culture coevolve with its language and affect the thought patterns of its speakers? We can begin by comparing some characteristics of each language.[29]

Classical Greek is notable for its clarity and controlled structure. In addition to its use of the definite article, allowing for greater abstraction, it contains various linguistic signposts whose sole function is to clarify the structure of a sentence. This permits long, complex sentences, with a prearranged, hierarchical organization. Like other Indo-European languages, it has the classic subject-verb-object structure, along with forms and endings that show where a word fits within a sentence. For example, the difference between "I see him" and "he sees me" arises from both the word order and the declensions of each of the three words, a system unique to Indo-European languages.[30*]

Chinese lacks these classical Greek elements. Without a subject-verbobject structure, a Chinese sentence can include or omit whatever the speaker chooses. A simple verb standing alone may serve quite adequately as a sentence. In response to an invitation, a Chinese person may answer with the one word "Know," meaning she is aware of the event and may or may not come. Philosopher Denis Noble has pointed out that Descartes's foundational statement of Western philosophy—"I think, therefore I am"—would naturally have been expressed as "thinking, therefore being" in Chinese, leading potentially to a different conception of the self as a process, a verb, rather than a fixed object.[31]

Chinese also lacks the definite article, which was invented by the Greeks and gave the linguistic framework for Plato to derive his theory of Forms. Instead of seeking an abstract idea such as "the Truth," the Chinese language encouraged a more tangible search for "things that are true." Ultimately, perhaps, the greatest contrast between the two cultures is where they looked for the true nature of reality. For the Greeks, following Plato, it was in the abstract dimension of Forms; for the Chinese, it was the Tao as expressed in the material world. The two languages seem to have encouraged these divergent worldviews, with Greek pushing its speakers toward abstraction and Chinese reinforcing a material view of the nature of reality.[32]

Just as important as what the Chinese language lacks are the features it possesses that don't exist in Indo-European languages. When Westerners hear Chinese people speak, the language is frequently perceived as having a singsong quality, as though all kinds of emotional changes are being expressed from one moment to the next. This is because Chinese uses tonal qualities to change the meaning of a word, so that a level versus rising tone, or an upper versus lower tone, denote different words. The word *ma*, for example, can mean "mother," "horse," or "scold" depending on the tone used to pronounce it. In Indo-European languages, a word is something purely conceptual, while the tone we use may instill in it our emotional state. The split between word and tone reinforces the Western split between mind and body, reason and emotion. To a Chinese speaker, on the other hand, the very meaning of a word is embodied: there is no split between what is said and how a person says it.[33]

The meaning of a Chinese word frequently depends heavily on its context. Whereas Indo-European language speakers look for navigational signs within the sentence to transmit meaning—"I took her to him" versus "He took me from her"—a Chinese speaker will typically look at the overall context to determine who is doing what to whom. We can visualize the difference by imagining two different travelers, one using a compass and map to know where she's heading, the other using her knowledge of landmarks. Each of them would gain a very different understanding of the land around them, especially if they used these different systems from infancy, in much the same way that the Guugu Yimithirr have a completely different sense of orientation from the rest of us.[34]

The contextual orientation of Chinese can be seen in how a question is treated. In Indo-European languages, concepts such as "yes" and "no" exist as standalone entities that can be applied to any question. In Chinese, when someone asks, "Have you eaten?" the literal answer is not "yes" or "no" but "eaten" or "not eaten." Similarly, if you ask someone in Chinese, "How are you doing?" you would typically say, "*Ni hao bu hao*," "You good not good?" Or if you ask someone whether she'd like to go somewhere, you would say, "*Zou bu zou*?" or, "Go not go?" We can see how this type of thinking would have encouraged the traditional Chinese *yin-yang* view of the universe. Just as the meaning of *yang* arises from its relation to *yin*, so the meaning of a term in Chinese is completed by its opposite. Joseph Needham observes, "Where Western minds asked '*what* essentially is it?', Chinese minds asked 'how is it related in its beginnings, functions, and endings with everything else, and how ought we to react to it?'"[35]

Written Chinese, using graphic characters rather than an alphabet, contains ambiguity that, like the language itself, forces readers to consider the context of what they are reading in their interpretation. A Chinese reader has to guess or memorize the appropriate sound for each character, and associate it with a word she already knows, in order to arrive at its meaning. This ambiguity has been criticized by Western pundits as imprecision and fuzziness—and has even been suggested as the reason why the Scientific Revolution occurred in Europe rather than East Asia. Japanese Nobel laureate Susumu Tonegawa, for example, has written that the Japanese language does not foster clarity in scientific research: "We should consider changing our thinking process in the field of science by trying to reason in English," he suggests.[36]

These critiques generally assume that the more analytical, abstract patterns of thought induced by Indo-European languages are preferable and that East Asians should change their behavior to emulate the Western style of thinking. Suppose we removed this value judgment and instead saw the two patterns of thought as equally valid, offering us complementary and mutually enhancing ways of understanding the world? What would we find, and how might that affect our approach to our own cognition? We can explore this question by investigating some underlying differences between ancient Greek and Chinese thought and tracing how these continue to affect the thinking of East Asians and Westerners to this day.

The Truth versus the Way

Some researchers consider geography to be the ultimate source of differentiation between how these two cultures evolved. Greek terrain, with mountains sloping down to the sea and multiple small islands, lent itself to more individualistic or family-oriented occupations such as fishing, hunting, or gardening rather than large-scale irrigation-based agriculture, which needed to be maintained through large, complex, hierarchical societies. Over generations, this way of life may have caused the Greeks to be less concerned than the Chinese about their place within a larger social structure.[37]

Greek society underwent a period of political upheaval during the seventh and sixth centuries BCE, and their response to this turmoil was highly unusual. We see during this time the foundation of city-states, along with a more highly developed political awareness among citizens and a proliferation of different constitutional forms, including democracy. There was free debate among citizens on which style of government was best for them, which probably led to a more critical spirit in approaching other topics.[38]

The Greek emphasis on debate likely contributed to the kind of thinking that led to the "Greek miracle." Greek society, with its relative lack of hierarchy, didn't offer much in the way of political patronage, so intellectuals with ideas to communicate had to be entrepreneurial and find pupils ready to pay them for instruction. This led to a competitive intellectual climate, with each luminary trying to persuade others that he was the one worth following. In these debates, nothing was immune to scrutiny. If you wanted to avoid being publicly humiliated by your opponent, you needed to inspect your own arguments with intellectual rigor for possible inconsistencies. If you had a winning argument, you might try to make the most of it by turning it into an axiom that could be applied to other topics. It wasn't enough to offer something that was true; far better to show that you were in touch with the Truth.[39]

The Chinese philosophers of the time, by contrast, were mostly advisers or ministers in the courts of feudal princes. Rather than appeal to logical argumentation, they could make a greater impression through citing historical examples. They became experts at refining existing concepts that had been around from time immemorial, such as *qi*, Tao, or *yin-yang*, into sophisticated interpretations of the universe, synthesizing ancient ideas into comprehensive systems of thought.[40]

Both the ancient Greeks and Chinese made impressive advances in scientific understanding—the difference lay in how they approached their science. Both cultures, for example, saw mathematics as providing a key to understanding the natural world. The Greeks were particularly concerned with finding underlying truths, or axioms, that could be used to derive universal laws, such as the famous Pythagorean theorem, which holds true anywhere in the known universe. The Chinese, on the other hand, looked for guiding principles that unified the different aspects of mathematics. The great mathematician Liu Hui explained that what he was concerned about was unity—understanding what linked different mathematical procedures to each other to give his subject cohesion.[41]

With their focus on associations between things, the Chinese had an aversion to the formal use of logic, which works by stripping away the meaning of a statement until only its formal structure remains. The great philosopher Mencius shows the classic Chinese viewpoint when he says, "Why I dislike holding to one point is that it injures the Tao. It takes up one point and disregards a hundred others." In place of logic, the Chinese used dialectical thought to understand the universe, gaining insights through studying how everything related to everything else. This led them to develop certain core principles about the universe: reality is never fixed but constantly shifting, opposites complete each other to coexist in harmony, and nothing exists in isolation but rather is integrated within a complex web of interrelationships.[42]

As a result of these principles, Chinese science achieved different insights than the Greeks, who focused more on objects isolated from their context. When Aristotle tried to explain why a stone would fall, he speculated that it had a property of "gravity." The Chinese, by contrast, viewed everything as existing in a field of forces and achieved a deeper understanding of topics such as magnetism, acoustics, and gravity—recognizing, for example, that tides were caused by the influence of the moon, something that even Galileo could not explain.[43]

The Head and the Heart

The tendency of the Greeks to universalize and the Chinese to contextualize led the two cultures to different conceptions of human nature. The abstracting inclination of the Greek mind, reaching its apotheosis in Plato, caused them to seek the ultimate Truth outside the material world in an eternal dimension of Forms. This paralleled a dualistic conception of the human being, with an immortal soul imprisoned temporarily in a polluted body. In contrast, the Chinese sought reality within an organic view of the universe, looking for how each part harmonized within the entire system. As a result, when the Chinese contemplated the essence of human nature, they never considered the Platonic notion of a soul distinct from the body.[44]

The Chinese recognized as clearly as the Greeks something quintessentially human beyond mere bodily functions, but they situated it firmly within their physical existence. Instead of placing it above the rest of the body in the head, where Plato assigned the soul, they placed it in the heart, the center of the body. The Chinese word *xin*, which literally means "heart," is also translated as "mind." It incorporates the physical organ of the heart but also much more: the full panoply of conscious experience, including emotion, thought, intuition, and desire.[45]

If the mind is believed to exist in the head, it's easy to conceive of a split between reason and emotion. However, if the mind exists in the heart, an organ that beats faster when strong feelings arise, there would be no reason to conceptualize this split. When the heart is the center of cognition, fully understanding something becomes an integrated experience of intellect, feeling, and intuition. "The heart-mind [*xin*] is nothing without the body," wrote Chinese philosopher Wang Yang-ming, "and the body is nothing without the heart-mind."[46]

The Chinese conception of *xin* led them to reject the idea that reason, separate from emotion, had inherent value. Far from deifying reason, the Chinese identified it as a cause of human difficulties. Most people were seen as following their selfish and rationalistic desires, whereas the sage was understood to be in touch with his intuition, an integral part of the faculty of *xin*. The Chinese thus viewed a healthy approach to the human condition as one that integrated reason with emotions and intuition, seeing the unlimited pursuit of knowledge as positively dangerous. An early Taoist text known as *Inward Training* offers the following advice:

> In eating, it is best not to fill up;
> In thinking, it is best not to overdo.
> Limit these to the appropriate degree
> And you will naturally reach it [vitality].[47]

With their embodied conception of *xin*, the Chinese made no distinction between physical health and mental or spiritual health. While the ancient Greeks (and the yogis of India) viewed transcendence from bodily experience as their ultimate goal, the Chinese perceived harmonization with the Tao as something to be achieved through both mental and physiological methods. The Chinese, like the Indians, developed sophisticated practices of concentration, breathing, and movement, but they never saw these practices in terms of the mind exercising discipline over the body. Rather, body and mind were inherently integrated.[48]

The Greeks' belief in an immortal soul as a person's true essence naturally led them to emphasize the importance of the soul's continued existence after the body's death. The ancient Chinese would have none of this. Given their sense that the embodied *xin* was a person's essence, they gave little thought to the soul's continued existence after death. There was no heaven or hell, no punishment or reward meted out after death based on a person's activities during life. Zhuangzi considered it a grief that "when one's body is transformed in death, one's heart-mind goes with it in the same way." With no interest in an afterlife, the Chinese preoccupied themselves with making the most of their present life. "You do not yet know about life; why do you concern yourself about death?" answered Confucius to a question posed by one of his students.[49]

With their belief that life's meaning arose from its context, the defining characteristic of humanity for the Chinese was their existence within a social nexus. In contrast to the Greek view of reason as the faculty unique to human beings, the Chinese saw morality as what differentiated humans from other animals. As Xunzi, a Confucian philosopher, expounds: "Fire and water have energy but lack life. Grass and trees have life but no intelligence. Birds and beasts have intelligence but no morality. Man has energy, life, intelligence, and in addition morality. Therefore he is regarded as the most noble under heaven." The noblest human activity was, therefore, finding the ethical way to live in harmony with others. As sinologist Donald Munro observes, while the early Greeks were ultimately "more concerned with knowing in order to understand," their counterparts in China were "more concerned with knowing in order to behave properly toward other men."[50]

How Weird Are We?

These differences between ancient Chinese and Greek thought have remained astonishingly persistent over the millennia. Modern psychologists who have compared contemporary East Asian and Western modes of thought report an uncannily similar set of contrasts. They have identified an East Asian emphasis on dialectic thought, a holistic approach to problem-solving, an attention to context, a focus on the relationships between things, and a sense of identity arising from community. Western modes of thought have been shown to emphasize an object-focused, analytical approach paying attention to categories and rules, along with a stronger sense of individuality.[51]

The tests developed to evaluate these differences have used subtle and sometimes ingenious methods to highlight the contrasting patterns of thought. In one test, for example, to determine cultural preferences for uniqueness or conformity, Koreans and Americans were asked to choose a gift from an assortment of colored pens. Americans chose the rarest color, whereas Koreans chose the most common color. Another test was designed to distinguish between the East Asian emphasis on relationships and the Western focus on categories and rules. Chinese and American children were presented with a series of pictures with three things, such as a cow, a chicken, and grass (figure 10.1), and asked to say which two went together. American children, focusing on categorizing rules, pointed to the chicken and cow, explaining that "both are animals." Chinese children, emphasizing relationships, put the cow and the grass together, pointing out that "the cow eats the grass."[52]

Based on Richard E. Nisbett, *The Geography of Thought: How Asians and Westerners Think Differently... And Why.* (New York: Free Press, 2004).

Figure 10.1: "Which two go together?"

Following in the footsteps of their ancient forebears, East Asian and Western people continue to construct their sense of self in different ways. Social psychologists have observed that the East Asian concept of self is more interdependent, emphasizing fitting in and attending to the needs of others. The Western sense of self, seen in its most extreme form in American culture, emphasizes independence, attending more to the need for self-actualization through expression of a person's unique attributes.[53]

These contrasting construals of self lead to different pathways for achieving well-being. It is generally assumed in the West that people have a need for positive self-regard, a view so widely accepted that it is frequently believed to be a fundamental requirement of mental health for people everywhere. However, tests have shown that Japanese people, for example, tend to be more comfortable in a context of self-criticism and need for improvement than one of high self-esteem. Researchers see the Japanese comfort with self-criticism arising from a sense of self defined by relation to the community: the self-critical tendencies reflect a commitment to fitting in as much as possible to the social unit.[54]

These cultural differences lead to divergent views of how we ought to live our lives. In the individualistic culture of the West, there is high value attached to being talented, taking care of yourself, and competing successfully in the marketplace. In East Asia, a "good" person may instead be seen as someone attentive to her own weaknesses, motivated by self-improvement, and emphasizing the values and needs of those around her.[55]

What should we make of these differences that have persisted through the millennia? One important implication is that many attributes that psychologists have believed to be human universals are really only true for Westerners, a relatively small portion of humanity. A group of researchers, pointing out that most psychology experiments are carried out on samples drawn from Western, educated, industrialized, rich, and democratic societies, have memorably given this subpopulation the acronym WEIRD. People from WEIRD societies are, it turns out, frequent outliers in experiments conducted globally, and one of the least representative human populations.[56]

There is another crucially important implication to explore. In a world that sometimes seems to be careening out of control, we need to ask ourselves if there are certain patterns of thought that undergird the trajectory of today's global society and whether alternative ways of thinking could lead to more sustainable pathways. If our cultural inheritance compels us to think in certain ways—strong Whorfianism—then there's nothing we can do about it. If, however, our cultural framing merely encourages us to think in certain patterns—weak Whorfianism—then, by becoming conscious of those patterns, we may have the power to change them.

The contrast between ancient Greek and Chinese worldviews invites exploration. For those of us raised in the Western world, identifying an alternative pattern of cognition—replete with ideas of an embodied heart-mind, spiritual and physical domains as one and the same, personhood defined not by individuality but by connectivity with others—offers an opportunity to evaluate our received set of preconceptions and consider how our experience of the world might be enhanced if perceived through those alternative patterns.

There is no reason to exalt ancient Chinese or modern East Asian civilization at the expense of Western culture. There is much to be admired and criticized in both cultural complexes. While the ancient Chinese emphasized their place in the community and environment more than the Greeks did, their history is filled with wars, power struggles, and environmental degradation just like the history of the West.

We will trace in the rest of this book how the different patterns of cognition between Chinese and Western civilizations did in fact lead to divergent historical paths, but it is not helpful to judge one path as better or worse than the other. Rather, we can investigate both constellations of thought to understand how each has affected the experience of being human, and the impact each has had on the world at large. With this knowledge, we may be better equipped to recognize the patterns of thought that drive today's global society and to identify those that may help us navigate a sustainable future for humanity.

Chapter 11

PATHWAYS TO MONOTHEISM IN ISRAEL AND ALEXANDRIA

In the second millennium BCE, communities from Egypt to Mesopotamia were frequently bothered by bands of *habiru*, or "outsiders," described variously as mercenaries, thieves, or migrant laborers. Some of these *habiru* were enslaved and forced to work on the new capital of Pharaoh Ramesses II around 1250 BCE, but they escaped and made their way to Canaan. There, they settled down as sheepherders and farmers in isolated hill-country villages, accepting the name *habiru* for themselves, which eventually metamorphosed into the name they have been known by ever since: Hebrews.[1*]

From this unlikely source, the monotheistic wave began that has since swept up much of the world. The creed of monotheism has so permeated modern cognition that we need to look deeply into history to identify its underlying assumptions and implications. While one pathway to monotheism began with those Hebrew villagers in the land of Canaan, another started out with the Platonic tradition of the ancient Greeks. The story of how monotheism took hold of the entire Western tradition is one of synthesis: between the charged religious drama of the Old and New Testaments and the dispassionate philosophizing of Plato and his intellectual heirs, which formed the unique amalgam we know as Christianity. In this chapter, we'll trace these two separate pathways toward their point of convergence into the world's first systematic dualistic cosmology.

Yahweh, the Jealous God

For most of the past two millennia, people accepted the Pentateuch, the first five books of the Bible, as divine revelation written down by Moses and the rest of the Old Testament as an accurate history of the Hebrew people. Those who noticed any inconsistencies and were courageous or foolhardy enough to speak out generally found their writings banned and occasionally had to recant to save their lives. As late as 1688, English scholar Edward Gray was released from the Tower of London only after repudiating his opinion that the Pentateuch had been written by someone other than Moses.

By the nineteenth century, as biblical scholarship gained a freer hand, it became generally accepted that a number of different authors wrote the Pentateuch, which explains why it contains conflicting versions of key episodes such as the Creation or the Great Flood. Controversy, however, continued to rage over who the authors were, how they related to each other, and when they lived. In recent decades, findings from Holy Land excavations have finally enabled archaeologists, anthropologists, and biblical scholars to cobble together enough evidence for a convincing explanation of how the Old Testament actually came about.[2]

There is general consensus that the early Hebrews, living humbly in their hillside settlements, worshipped local deities as other tribes around them did. One of these was named El Shadday, or simply El, and from this came another name for the people: *Isra-El* or Israel. Another deity, a warrior-god, was called Yahweh.[3]

Early in the history of the Hebrews, the two gods El and Yahweh merged into one. We see traces of this in Exodus when Yahweh introduces himself to Moses, saying, "I am Yahweh. I appeared to Abraham, to Isaac, and to Jacob, as El Shadday, but by my name Yahweh I did not make myself known to them." The new combined El/Yahweh demanded that other gods should be utterly ignored by the Israelites, who should worship only their own "God of gods."[4]

Most Old Testament scholars agree that the early Israelites practiced monolatry rather than monotheism—meaning they readily acknowledged the existence of other gods, even though they worshipped Yahweh alone. In a poem in Exodus, the Israelites sing, "Who is like unto thee, O Lord, among the gods?" as they praise Yahweh for rescuing them from the Egyptians. The clear implication is that although other gods exist, Yahweh is stronger than them. The second of the Ten Commandments offers another implicit statement of monolatry when it forbids the Israelites to serve other gods because "I the Lord thy God am a jealous God." The very concept of jealousy implies the existence of rival gods who might be a potential threat.[5]

There is, however, one place in the Old Testament where Yahweh comes across as ardently and unequivocally monotheistic. In the book of Isaiah, we see a barrage of statements that Yahweh is the only god in existence:

> I am the LORD, and there is none else, there is no God beside me. . . . I form the light, and create darkness: I make peace, and create evil: I the LORD do all these things.

The theme continues: "I am the first and I am the last." "Before me no god was formed, nor shall there be any after me." These passages all occur in a section of the book written in a later period than the first part, referred to by scholars as Second Isaiah.[6]

How do we get from a jealous god to a self-assured creator alone in his sovereignty? To understand this dramatic transformation in the nature of the Hebrew god, we need to dig into some history of the Promised Land.

The Troubled History of the Hebrews

The Old Testament regales us with stories of the grand conquests of King David and the wise, lavish reign of his son, King Solomon. Traditionally, these monarchs were believed to have ruled the land of Israel around 1000 BCE. However, archaeologists have scoured the Holy Land for signs of these great monarchs and have found virtually nothing, leading them to conclude that the glory of this period existed only in the minds of those who chronicled it hundreds of years later. In reality, Jerusalem at that time was probably just a modest hill country village surrounded by other smaller villages.[7]

The Bible tells the story of a unified monarchy ruling from Jerusalem that split apart when ten northern tribes rebelled to set up an independent nation of Israel, leaving Jerusalem as the capital of Judah, the loyalist territory. Archaeological evidence confirms that there were in fact two separate states of Israel and Judah, but that Judah was a mere rural hinterland, while Israel developed into a prosperous kingdom. So prosperous, in fact, that its very affluence was the likely cause of its downfall. Israel had the misfortune to exist in the shadow of the expanding Assyrian empire, which demanded increasingly onerous tribute and eventually conquered Israel outright, deporting the urban population and destroying its infrastructure. Only the backward kingdom of Judah now remained intact to sustain the culture and traditions of the Hebrew people.[8]

Refugees flooded into Jerusalem from the brutal Assyrian conquest, transforming it from a simple village to a town fifteen times bigger in a single generation. Along with a social transformation came a profound religious metamorphosis. Prior to Israel's collapse, each nation had maintained separate versions of the ancient legends of their ancestors. Now, in the cultural ferment of a burgeoning Jerusalem filled with refugees, priests from both nations joined together to systematize the worship of Yahweh in alliance with a powerful faction intent on centralizing religious and economic control over the countryside.[9]

This alliance, referred to as the "Yahweh-alone movement," prohibited worshipping any other god than Yahweh, and even Yahweh had to be worshipped in specific ways controlled by the priesthood. A revised national history was constructed that retold the ancient legends with a new slant, establishing the central importance of the priesthood in carrying out Yahweh's commands and adding copious new laws. This revisionist history forms the bulk of the Pentateuch.[10]

Disaster, however, struck the new order in Jerusalem—once again, in the form of the Assyrians, who eventually subjugated the entire region, devastating large parts of the countryside and turning Judah into a vassal state. Weakened rulers in Jerusalem now allowed other gods to be worshipped, leading to the decline of the Yahweh-alone movement. The centralized priesthood, however, was down but not out. In 604 BCE, a newly ensconced king, Amon, was assassinated, and his eight-year-old son, Josiah, inherited the throne. The time of the Yahweh-alone movement's resurgence had arrived.[11]

With Josiah's reign, the revisionist mythologizing of the centralized priesthood reached new heights. We are told in the Bible that, during Josiah's renovation of the temple in Jerusalem, a dramatic event occurred. A previously unknown text is discovered, which is immediately read to Josiah. Its reverberations are earthshaking. The text tells Josiah about a covenant Yahweh made with his ancestor, David. Yahweh promised David his dynasty would rule Israel forever, and, in return, he demanded complete loyalty. The entire troubled history of Israel and Judah is then narrated and cast into this frame: every time a king turns away from Yahweh's sole worship, disaster ensues. Josiah, energized by this new finding, embarked on a ferocious campaign of religious cleansing, burning the idols of other gods and slaying their priests at the altar. The name of this newly discovered text was Deuteronomy.[12]

Where did this astonishing text come from? Two hundred years ago, a German scholar named W. M. L. De Wette concluded that, in fact, Josiah and his high priest had perpetrated a "pious fraud," as he called it. Scholars since then have corroborated his conclusions. The book of Deuteronomy was actually written shortly before it was found, and its "discovery" was just a charade: the book was written to provide justification for the power grab of the Yahwehalone movement.[13]

Their victory was fated to be short-lived. Once again, the Hebrews were swept up in the tides of the geopolitical forces of the time. A new superpower, Babylon, arose in place of the crumbling Assyrian empire. In the power struggles that ensued, Josiah and his son Zedekiah backed the wrong horse. The Babylonian king, Nebuchadnezzar, took his revenge by conquering Jerusalem, sending its aristocracy and priesthood—the core of the Yahweh-only movement—into exile in Babylon. Zedekiah was punished mercilessly. In the horrifying description of the Bible, "they slew the sons of Zedekiah before his eyes, and put out the eyes of Zedekiah, and bound him in fetters, and took him to Babylon." The Temple of Jerusalem, the center of power for the Yahweh-alone movement, was utterly destroyed. Finally, in this trauma of sorrow and destruction, we arrive at the birth of Hebraic monotheism.[14]

By the Rivers of Babylon

The elite of Hebrew society were now in exile in Babylon, carrying with them the burden of their entire cultural and religious legacy. Life in exile was not too intolerable from a material perspective: they could farm, trade, buy land, employ workers, and even own slaves. But the very meaning of these people's lives had been infused by their theology, and the core of that meaning had been gutted in front of their eyes. The emotional experience of exile was indelibly recorded by one Judean poet when he wrote:

> By the rivers of Babylon
> There we sat
> Also, we wept
> When we remembered Zion.[15]

How could this desperately defeated group make sense of what had happened? Either they had to acknowledge their god had simply failed—that Marduk, the chief god of the Babylonians, was mightier than Yahweh; or they could conclude that their defeat had been the result of Yahweh's will—that Yahweh had been angry with the Israelites and used the Babylonians as the instrument of his displeasure.[16]

It was this second explanation that the exiled theologians chose, among them the author of Second Isaiah, and here we finally behold the birth of a truly monotheistic god. Weeping by the rivers of Babylon, the exiled Israelites could take refuge in one thing: the omnipotence of their own god, Yahweh. Yahweh's newly realized power would have been a source of hope for the exiles. After all, if Yahweh was mighty enough to use the Babylonians to punish them for their misdeeds, what might he do to reward them for their righteousness?[17] It must, therefore, have seemed like proof of Yahweh's omnipotence when, after fifty years or so of exile, the tides of history turned yet again, this time in the Israelites' favor. The Babylonian empire, experiencing overreach, began to crumble and was conquered by the Persians in 539 BCE. In the first year of his reign, the Persian ruler Cyrus issued a decree for the restoration of Judah and its Temple. Not surprisingly, the author of Second Isaiah sees Cyrus as another instrument of Yahweh, only this time for good:

> Thus says the Lord to his anointed, to Cyrus, whom he has taken by his right hand to subdue nations before him. . . . I will go before you leveling the heights. I will shatter the bronze gateways, smash the iron bars. I will give you the hidden treasures, the secret hoards, that you may know that I am the Lord.[18]

Following the return to Jerusalem, a new wave of political infighting ensued between the Yahweh-alone movement and those who had remained behind in Judah. Only after decades of conflict did the monotheists, supported by the Persians, finally establish centralized control. In 458 BCE, the prophet Ezra called a public assembly at the gate of Jerusalem. There, he brought out a scroll of Yahweh's law, the Torah, and read it to the assembled masses, calling on them to renew their covenant to their god. The document Ezra read from that day was most likely the first complete compilation of the Pentateuch. Finally, after centuries of dashed hopes, invasions, and devastation, the Old Testament was woven together into something very similar to the form we know it in today.[19]

An Unbridgeable Gulf

This account of how the Old Testament came into being, while unsettling for some, is consistent with archaeological findings and rigorous textual scholar ship. What are we to make of it? Does the theology of the Old Testament represent a radical break from the cosmology of the region, or is it actually a crystallization of the values of the agrarian empires that spawned it?

The traditional interpretation holds that the Old Testament achieved a dramatic breach with the past, one of the great conceptual breakthroughs of history. In the view of celebrated scholar Yehezkel Kauffman, it was "an original creation of the people of Israel. It was absolutely different from anything the pagan world ever knew."[20]

In fact, when we examine elements in the Old Testament usually referred to as conceptual breakthroughs, we often find equivalent ideas expressed earlier in other Near East traditions. There are social welfare provisions in Deuteronomy, for example, that instruct farmers to give a tithe to the poor and permit slaves to be freed after six years, which have been lauded as radical innovations. These, however, have direct precedents in Hammurabi's Code of Laws from a thousand years earlier, and the supposedly new concepts of equity and freedom are expressed in Deuteronomy using loan words derived from Hammurabi's proclamations.[21]

Another philosophical innovation frequently attributed to the Old Testament is its treatment of good and evil. Scholars argue that the abstraction of right and wrong, with the consequent ethical mandate to follow God's commandments, first emerged in the Pentateuch. However, as we've seen, Zoroaster claims precedence in blazing this particular trail. It was Zoroaster who first referred to his own believers as "followers of the Truth" and his enemies as "followers of the Lie." In his theology, the split between the Truth and the Lie paralleled the split between absolute Good and Evil. Zoroastrianism was the religion of Cyrus and the Persian Empire, and it's likely that the exiled Jews absorbed many Zoroastrian principles. Scholars have in fact identified sections of Second Isaiah praising the omnipotence of Yahweh that reveal direct borrowing from the *Gathas*, the sacred Zoroastrian text.[22]

Perhaps the greatest breakthrough generally attributed to the Old Testament is the conception of a god so great that he is beyond form, beyond name, beyond human perception. Scholars have noted the shift within the Pentateuch itself—from an anthropomorphic god blowing the waves of the Red Sea to drown the Egyptians, to an abstract, transcendent entity separated from the world by an "unbridgeable gulf."[23]

How different, we might ask, is this conception of God from the ancient Egyptian idea of Amun, described in one text as "too mysterious for his majesty to be revealed, . . . too great to be discovered, too mighty to be known"?

Both the Hebrew and Egyptian supreme gods appear equally imponderable. There is, though, one way in which the Hebrew conception breaks into new cognitive territory. As discussed earlier, Egyptian theology held a pantheistic worldview whereby the supreme god was not separate from his creation but *was* his creation. Religious texts praise him for existing in every aspect of the universe: "You are the sky, You are the earth, You are the netherworld, You are the water, You are the air between them."[24]

This is where the Hebrew conception of God departs from other religious traditions. For the first time, the source of all that is sacred is up in the heavens, unreachable for humanity except through the mercy and goodwill of God. The rest of the universe loses its divinity, becoming dead matter. This is the great dualistic divide accomplished by the Old Testament, detaching the source of meaning and value from material existence and placing it in a separate dimension. This dualistic conception applies equally to morality. The determination of whether something is good or bad comes not from one's own experience but from whatever God has decided.[25]

This cognitive breakthrough was not necessarily destined to have the global impact it eventually had. For centuries after Ezra read the Torah at the gate of Jerusalem, the Jewish nation remained a backwater in the oceans of history, swept up in the harsh vicissitudes of geopolitical power struggles and falling victim to the conquest of the Greeks, the Egyptian and Seleucid empires, and, finally, the Romans. Ironically, it was those very conquests that allowed the ideas of the Old Testament to infiltrate human thought in a way that would have been unimaginable to its authors back in the days of Josiah. As we will see, the Old Testament was really just a warm-up to the full force of monotheistic thought.

Moses Speaking Greek

The Old Testament, as we know, was not the only way of thinking in the ancient world that derived meaning from a transcendent source. Across the Mediterranean, the Greeks were moving toward a similar idea, albeit through a very different route. Around the time the Jewish exiles were returning from Babylon, Xenophanes was speculating about one god composed entirely of mind. With this conception, he inaugurated the Greek deification of the power of pure thought, which reached its apotheosis in Plato.[26]

The Greek approach toward monotheism was different in style and content from that of the Old Testament. There were no legends of heroics and betrayals, no nation chosen for a covenant with God, no rituals requiring a priestly hierarchy. Instead, the Greeks were interested in a purely intellectual adventure, a quest for the discovery of universal abstraction. Their bondage was not in the land of Egypt but in their own bodies, and their Promised Land was not flowing with milk and honey but was the union of their rational soul with the eternal world of Ideas. This was a path of salvation, not for an entire nation but for an elite group of educated philosophers who found inspiration in the writings of Plato.[27]

Considering its intellectual nature, the widespread impact of this approach on the search for meaning in the ancient world is astonishing. One explanation is the possibility it offered people of escaping the difficulties and suffering of their everyday lives. Mystical teachings promised a kind of ecstasy available to those who purified their souls by leaving behind their bodily appetites. The ascetic ideal of renouncing corporeal desires took hold of the imagination in literate circles, gradually supplanting archaic beliefs in the legendary gods until, in the form of Neoplatonism, it became the dominant philosophy of the Greco-Roman world.[28]

Hebrew monotheism and Platonic mysticism continued for generations on parallel paths until the currents of Near Eastern history eventually swept them together. After the death of Alexander the Great, one of his generals, Ptolemy, established himself as Pharaoh in the fledgling Egyptian city of Alexandria. Ptolemy, intent on founding a new dynasty in Egypt, imported a hundred thousand Jewish prisoners from Israel as administrators to help manage his realm.[29]

Ptolemy had other aspirations beyond founding a dynasty. Inculcated in the value of the intellect by his Greek upbringing, he had a vision to build a worldclass center of learning in Alexandria, and he founded a library that would become the largest and most important of the ancient world. One of the twenty thousand books he collected for his library was the Hebrew Pentateuch, which he proceeded to have translated into Greek. Thus did the Old Testament first appear on the scene of the mainstream Western tradition.[30]

Even after its translation into Greek, the impact of the Old Testament was anything but immediate. The Jews of Alexandria noticed some parallels between Platonic and Hebrew thought, but many decades were to pass before a man named Philo, born in 20 BCE into a wealthy Jewish family, finally created a synthesis of the two traditions that would have a profound effect on the future of Western thought.[31]

A pious Jew and committed Platonist, Philo saw the two traditions as transmitting the same truth. The Jewish God, in his glorious abstraction up in the heavens, was none other than the ideal Good of Plato, unchanging and eternal. And Moses, the great leader of the Israelites who transmitted the word of God to the people, was really a Platonic philosopher who predated Plato himself. As one of Philo's followers, Numenius, famously pondered, "Who is Plato, if not Moses speaking Greek?"[32]

Philo saw the stories of the Old Testament as allegories representing a deeper truth, the greatest of which was the story of Genesis, in which God, "the perfectly pure and unsullied Mind of the universe," created the material world. But if God existed only in an abstract dimension, how could he have created the world of tangible stuff? Philo, as the first thinker to attempt a serious synthesis of Platonic and Hebraic cosmologies, gave much attention to this question and ultimately came up with an answer that would resound through the millennia. Focusing on the moment in Genesis when God said "Let there be light" and there was light, Philo settled on language itself as the solution to his conundrum. He called the instrument of God's power *Logos*, the "Word" of God, conceiving it as a kind of architect organizing the tangible world according to God's blueprint.[33]

There was another episode in Genesis that Philo crucially linked to Platonism. When Adam and Eve eat from the tree of knowledge and thereafter lose their innocence, they become ashamed of their nakedness and cover their bodies. Philo saw this as an allegory for the soul's entombment in the body, thus establishing a connection between the Platonic notion of the body imprisoning the soul and the biblical story of humanity's fall from grace. A logical consequence is that the path to salvation requires transcending the body, a conclusion that came naturally to Philo. "There are no two things so utterly opposed," he wrote, "as knowledge and pleasure of the flesh."[34]

From its intellectual center in Alexandria, the ideas of Platonism permeated the ancient world. The greatest Platonic thinker, Plotinus, was educated there before settling in Rome to teach what became known as Neoplatonism. Plotinus, like other Platonists, structured his vision of the universe on the great divide between the transcendent dimension and the material world of the body. He took this dualistic split to new heights (and depths). If Philo disliked the pleasures of the flesh, Plotinus positively loathed them. He referred to his own body as a "detestable vessel" acting as an obstacle to his spiritual development and believed that "to rise up to very truth is altogether to depart from bodies."

Plotinus saw the material world as having no positive qualities whatsoever, the antithesis of all that is worthwhile.[35]

"Who are we?" Plotinus asked, then answered that "every man is double, one of him is a sort of compound being and one of him is himself." That latter part, the true Self, had the potential to become one with the eternal Soul of the universe, which created all existence. Echoing the Vedic promise of liberation through asceticism, Plotinus offered hope to anyone ready to make contact with the infinite. "God is not external to any one," he taught, "but is present in all things, though they are ignorant that he is so."[36]

An Age of Anxiety

The Neoplatonic philosophy of Plotinus offered a pathway to salvation for its followers, but it was not exactly an easy passage. Relinquishing the body meant strict intellectual discipline and rigor. While this may have appealed to the educated elite of the Roman aristocracy, it certainly was not a philosophy to satisfy the anxiety and craving of the broader population. And during the middle of the third century, when Plotinus was teaching, the population of the entire classical world badly needed to alleviate their fears. The Roman Empire was in gradual and inexorable decline. In the last years of Plotinus's life, signs of impending disaster were only too clear. The Goths and Alammani were assaulting the empire from the north, while the Sassanid Empire caused humiliating defeats in the east.[37]

This period has been characterized by a leading historian as "an age of anxiety." In a world of increasing insecurity, it's easy to understand how the Neoplatonic philosophy offering salvation in transcendence might have been appealing, but the pathway to reach salvation would have seemed too inaccessible. The traditional gods such as Jupiter, Pluto, and Apollo were still worshipped, but fewer and fewer people actually believed the myths surrounding them. A spiritual vacuum had arisen between these two classical cosmologies that badly needed filling.[38]

There were plenty of contenders to fill the vacuum. Diplomats and traders, soldiers and slaves arrived in Rome from all over the empire, bringing various beliefs with them. Cults formed based on particular gods or goddesses, replete with the mystique of esoteric rituals from distant lands. None of these, however, satisfied the need for a coherent and accessible cosmology that offered everyone the possibility of liberation. This need would ultimately be met by a new religion that combined the emotional drama of the Old Testament with a Platonicinspired vision of heavenly bliss available to anyone, with or without a classical education. This religion, Christianity, provided humanity with the world's first truly systematic dualistic cosmology, complete with a path to salvation for all.[39]

Chapter 12

SINFUL NATURE: THE DUALISTIC COSMOS OF CHRISTIANITY

"In the beginning was the Word, and the Word was with God, and the Word was God." Thus begins the Gospel of John, written around 100 CE, and, with it, a revolution in human consciousness. Only a few decades earlier, Philo of Alexandria had conceived of Logos, the Word, as a kind of divine architect transforming God's ideas into reality. Now, John was taking it further: the Word *was* God. With this conceptual leap, John set in motion a theological shift that would drastically alter the course of human thought. What caused him to make it?[1]

John was most likely a member of an early, marginal Christian community that had broken from the Jewish faith and was now antagonistic to it. It was in John's interest to present Jesus Christ as someone who had transcended the community of Jews. But how could he do this? John had probably read some of Philo's writings suggesting Logos as the mediator of God's abstract power with the physical world. Now he had the stroke of genius to equate Jesus Christ with Logos. It was Christ who mediated the two dimensions of existence. This would make Christ a divine figure, an entity apart from normal human existence. As such, it enabled Christ to transcend his Jewish heritage and become an icon for the entire human race. Just a few sentences into the Gospel, John drops his bombshell:

> The Word [Logos] became flesh and made his dwelling among us. We have seen his glory, the glory of the one and only Son, who came from the Father, full of grace and truth. . . . No one has ever seen God, but the one and only son, who is himself God and is in closest relationship with the Father, has made him known.[2]

This idea of God manifested in the flesh, the Incarnation, would become a central tenet of Christian faith but is not mentioned anywhere else in the

New Testament. Previously, Jesus had been described as a human "exalted" by God only upon his death. Now, a new, powerful vision informs the fledgling Christian cosmology as Christ becomes the gateway between the world of humans and God's eternity. The Neoplatonists had offered salvation only through rigorous intellectual practice; now, Christ the Savior promised a direct connection to eternal salvation for anyone.[3]

With this dramatic flourish, John hit upon an idea that would engulf the Western world and ultimately the entire globe. The arcane world of Platonic Ideas, previously only available to the elite, was now open to anyone willing to believe in the power of Christ to redeem them. In this chapter, we'll trace how Plato's original dualistic speculations became the underpinning for the cosmology that would structure Western thought to the present day.

The "Living Death" of the Body

The early Christian theologians, known as the church fathers, were aware of their debt to the Platonic tradition, particularly the ideas of an unknowable deity transcending the world and a soul independent of the body with the potential to attain eternal salvation. One church father, Clement of Alexandria, claimed that God had given philosophy to the Greeks as "a preparation which paved the way towards perfection in Christ." He suggested classical Greek philosophy was the "handmaiden" of Christian theology, making it acceptable for Christians to take what was useful in classical thought and discard the rest.[4]

The amalgam of Platonism and Christianity was by no means a top-down process imposed by a few classically trained intellectuals. Rather, it arose from grassroots movements across the ancient world, such as the Gnostic sects that flourished in the second century. These sects saw the physical world as inherently evil and believed the immortal soul could achieve enlightenment (*gnosis*) through liberation from the body. The Gnostics shared with the Essene and Pharisee sects an extreme loathing for the body, which was seen as nothing more than a jailhouse preventing the soul from reaching salvation. Early Christians readily adopted this viewpoint, seeing the body—in the words of one—as "a filthy bag of excrement and urine." Monks were prohibited from watching each other eating. Girls were forbidden to bathe so they wouldn't see their own naked bodies.[5]

These tortured individuals so identified themselves with their souls that they hated their bodies like their worst enemy. "Woe to the flesh that hangs upon the soul! Woe to the soul that hangs upon the flesh!" cries the Gospel of Thomas. The body is frequently associated with death. An early text describes it as "the dark gaol, the living death, the corpse revealed, the tomb that we carry about with us." In the words of one Desert Father, "I am killing it because it is killing me." This self-destructive approach to the body went beyond metaphor. Ascetics would live for years on top of pillars or loaded with heavy chains. There are frequent approving references to self-castration as preferable to acting impurely.[6]

The Anguish of Paul

Agonizing as these bodily tortures must have been, the mental torment that early Christians put themselves through caused perhaps even greater suffering. None has left a more plaintive declaration of inner anguish than Paul, who occupies such a dominant position in the early church that he has been called the "founder of Christianity."[7]

Although Paul lived contemporaneously with Jesus, he never knew him personally, and his interpretation of Jesus's life and death was strongly at odds with that of the apostles who had actually witnessed Jesus's ministry. After his famed conversion on the road to Damascus, Paul became convinced that Jesus was a messiah who had suffered for the sins of all humanity, and he dedicated himself to spreading his vision outside the Jewish community. As such, Paul established Christianity as a universal religion, as in his Letter to the Galatians, in which he asserts: "You are all sons of God through faith in Christ Jesus. . . . There is neither Jew nor Greek, slave nor free, male nor female, for you are all one in Christ Jesus."[8]

Although such passages are sometimes used to associate Paul with the principle of universal brotherly love, his personality seems to have been quite the opposite, fraught with conflict and division. Before his conversion to Christianity, Paul had been instrumental in persecuting early Christians, and afterward, he found himself in constant conflict with the apostles and those he sought to convert.[9]

Paul's series of clashes with others seems to have been a reflection of even more severe struggles within himself, conflicts that have since become intrinsic to the very structure of Christian theology. Already steeped in the dualistic creeds of his time, Paul seems to have taken the divisions inherent in their thinking as the basis for his new Christian cosmology. He writes bitterly about the law of God forcing him to acknowledge his own sinful nature. "Nay, I had not known sin," he says, "but by the law: for I had not known lust, except the law had said, Thou shalt not covet." He declares that "all who rely on observing the law are under a curse."[10]

With his acceptance of the law of God, Paul experiences an inner battle. His consciousness is split apart like two antagonistic personalities fighting each other. He describes his inner anguish:

> I do not understand what I do, for what I want to do I do not do, but what I hate I do. . . . It is no longer I myself who do it, but it is sin living in me. . . . For in my inner being I delight in God's law; but I see another law at work in the members of my body, waging war against the law of my mind and making me a prisoner of the law of sin at work within my members. . . . What a wretched man I am! Who will rescue me from this body of death?[11]

In this passage and others like it, Paul seems to experience himself as a split personality, using words fraught with self-loathing.[12]

Paul repeatedly describes his inner conflict as a battle to the death. Either his appetites will win and his soul will end up in eternal torment, or his soul will win and put his appetites to death. There is no room for compromise. "The wages of sin is death," he writes, "but the gift of God is eternal life in Christ Jesus our Lord."[13]

Of all the physical appetites Paul was battling, sexual desire seems to have been his greatest enemy. "For the flesh lusteth against the Spirit," he writes, "and the Spirit against the flesh; for these are contrary the one to the other; that ye may not do the things that ye would." He never married and was especially scornful of the "degrading passions" that cause either sex to commit homosexual acts. "Sex," he tells the Corinthians, "is always a danger."[14]

Paul's hatred of sexuality became a clarion call for ensuing generations of Christian theologians who made sexual renunciation a central part of their faith. Countless Christians followed Paul in their fervent rejection of sexuality. Here is Saint Jerome in the fourth century:

> O how often, when I was living in the desert, in the lonely waste, scorched by the burning sun . . . how often did I fancy myself surrounded by the pleasures of Rome . . . by bands of dancing girls. My face was pale with fasting; but though my limbs were cold as ice, my mind was burning with desire, and the fires of lust kept bubbling up before me while my flesh was as good as dead.[15]

Paul's agonizing battle within himself would echo throughout the millennia, reprised over generations through the inner torment of countless devout Christians. His personality, riddled with self-hatred, infused the theology that he would bequeath to posterity.[16]

Christianizing Platonism

While Paul was passionately advocating repression of physical appetites, other church fathers focused their attention on the ideology of the new Christian regime, filling in the details of the abstractions of God and eternal soul they had inherited from Platonism.

Clement helped to construct the idea of a Christian god in the Platonic mold: a formless entity without attributes, beyond space and time. Following Plato, Clement revered the intellect, proposing that humans were made in the image of God through their capacity for rational thought. This separation of humanity from the rest of the world due to the reasoning faculty would become a central part of the Western dualistic tradition. On one side of the dualistic chasm, human conceptual consciousness produces reason; on the other side remains animate consciousness, the instinctual drives that keep the soul bound up in the physical world.[17]

Clement's initial work in creating a Platonic vision of Christianity was continued by Origen, who also conceived of an eternal God, transcendent in his perfection. The human soul, Origen affirmed, originally created as pure intelligence, was constrained in the body, waiting to be restored to its original purity. It was through contemplation of God that a person's soul could become united with the divine. To know God completely, it was necessary to have as little as possible to do with the ways of the flesh. Origen took this view so seriously that he is said to have castrated himself in adolescence in order to more perfectly separate his soul from bodily desires.[18]

Augustine, the most prominent church father, who is generally viewed as setting the future pattern of European Christian thought, viewed his religion through the same Platonic lens. Augustine was driven in his early life by a probing search for the source of true spiritual meaning, and his prolific writings on how he found this in Christianity became a cornerstone of the Western tradition: when printing was invented, his works were the first to be published after the Bible.[19]

As a youth, Augustine was a follower of the extreme Manichean sect, which held a set of dualistic beliefs so severe that even the Gnostics pale by comparison. The Manicheans saw the material world as uncompromising evil in an endless struggle against the forces of Good. The human body had been designed, they believed, by the forces of evil to imprison the soul. Committed Manicheans took this view so seriously that they removed themselves as far as possible from anything physical, employing others to handle their food and anything else relating to their bodies.

After some years, Augustine found the Manichean obsession with evil too constricting and was drawn toward Platonism, which allowed him to aspire to the sense of divine goodness available to his soul. Platonism offered Augustine a powerful vision of the eternal dimension of the divine, but it didn't show him how to get there. As he put it, he could "see the country of peace from a hill in the forest," but he could not find in Platonism the path to that "royal kingdom." Eventually he turned to Christianity as "the religion that embodies a universal path to the liberation of the soul."[20]

After his conversion, Augustine embraced the Platonic conception of Christianity developed by Clement and Origen, adding a new element in the form of original sin: it was because of Adam's disobedience in eating from the tree of knowledge, he explained, that God had condemned the entire human race to damnation. Adam's original guilt passed from generation to generation through desire for physical pleasure, with its most extreme and shameless manifestation in the sexual act. Echoing Paul, Augustine relates his own personal struggle with sexual desire, writing how he had begged God to grant him chastity and cure him of the "disease" of sexual craving, "only not yet." He had feared, he confessed, that God would hear him too soon.[21]

Augustine frequently took a more considered approach to his inner struggle than his predecessors. In his most famous work, *Confessions*, he describes his path to conversion in a way that is entirely original, exploring his inner life with sensitivity. Many scholars attribute to him the discovery of the "individual" as a conflicted free agent through his nuanced descriptions of interior experience. Augustine himself seems to have been aware of breaking new ground, writing: "Men go out and gaze in astonishment at high mountains, the huge waves of the sea, the broad reaches of rivers, the ocean that encircles the world, or the stars in their courses. But they pay no attention to themselves."[22]

Augustine did pay attention to himself, and, in so doing, he developed a conception of the human being that perseveres to this day. "Since it is almost universally agreed that we are made up of soul and body," he writes, "what we must ask now is what man really is: is he both these constituents, or is he body only or soul only?" Augustine returns to the core metaphor of the soul-body relationship used in both Platonic and Vedic thought: a man riding a horse. Is a human merely the horse, "used by a soul which rules it"? Or is he the soul alone, ruling the body? Perhaps, he surmises, the human being is a compound organism of both soul and body, "just as we call a man a knight . . . on account of the horse he rides."[23]

For all his thoughtful inquiry, Augustine could never escape the dualistic paradigm in which his ideas had evolved. Rather, the strength of his intellect only served to expand the scope of the dualistic conception of the universe ever further. With echoes of his Manichean past, Augustine came to see the entire natural world as anathema to the purity of God. He hauntingly describes how he had once loved worldly things—"Late have I loved thee, O Beauty so ancient and so new"—only to realize that this love was misdirected and prevented him from experiencing the true love of God. It was not just the human body but nature itself that could entrap and corrupt the soul with its joyous beauty.[24]

"A Strange Hybrid Monster"

Augustine's life is often seen as the transition point from the classical world to the beginning of medieval Europe, ushering in an era when Christianity would dominate all aspects of Western thought. The inner struggles of the church fathers would set the stage for how virtually all Europeans for the next thousand years tried to make sense of their internal experience and their place in the cosmos.[25]

In his influential book *The Great Chain of Being,* historian Arthur O. Lovejoy traces how the conception of a dualistic universe forced people to view their own humanness as fundamentally split. If the cosmos consisted of an eternal and a worldly dimension, where did that leave humans, who incorporated both body and soul? The disturbing answer, as Augustine had explored, was straddling the two. This position in the cosmos, Lovejoy observes, gives man "a kind of uniqueness in nature; but it is an unhappy uniqueness. He is, in a sense . . . a strange hybrid monster."[26]

The universal enforcement of Christian values on society caused this inner conflict to impinge, often with drastic effect, on the lives of virtually everyone.

"Cogito Ergo Sum"

The following century saw the birth of the Scientific Revolution in Europe. One of its preeminent instigators, René Descartes, decided to question all the assumptions he had inherited from the past in his quest for truth. A brilliant philosopher and mathematician, Descartes in his twenties experienced a lifealtering vision in which the Angel of Truth appeared and told him that mathematics was the key to unlocking the secrets of nature.[31]

Descartes henceforward resolved to trust only his own intellect in pursuit of a true understanding of reality. This was a courageous path, and Descartes experienced severe existential suffering as a result. His doubts were so serious, he wrote, that "it feels as if I have fallen unexpectedly into a deep whirlpool which tumbles me around so that I can neither stand on the bottom nor swim up to the top."[32]

Descartes was determined not to take anything for granted in his quest to comprehend the nature of existence. He would not rely on his own previously formed opinions, nor even his own senses. "I shall now close my eyes," he resolved, "stop up my ears, turn away all my senses, even efface from my thought all images of corporeal things, or at least, because this can hardly be done, I shall consider them as being vain and false; and thus communing only with myself, and examining my inner self, I shall try to make myself, little by little, better known and more familiar to myself."[33]

As he rigorously examined every thought arising in him, Descartes finally seemed to hit pay dirt. He believed he had arrived at something rock solid: the simple and undeniable realization that he was thinking:

> I next considered attentively what I was; and I saw that while I could pretend that I had no body, that there was no world, and no place for me to be in, I could not pretend that I was not; on the contrary, from the mere fact that I thought of doubting the truth of other things it evidently and certainly followed that I existed. . . . From this I recognized that I was a substance whose whole essence or nature is to think and whose being requires no place and depends on no material thing.[34]

The one fact Descartes could not question was that he was thinking, which became the source of the most famous statement in modern philosophy: *cogito ergo sum*, "I think, therefore I am." Descartes used this as the foundation for his

With the rise of the scientific worldview in modern times, the notion of "soul" has been segregated into purely theological territory, while the idea of "mind" has become ubiquitous, reinforcing the same dualistic split in the conception of a human being that was established by the Platonic-inspired church fathers.

Our Cartesian Legacy

It is almost impossible to overstate the profound impact Descartes has had on modern cognition. Along with Plato and Augustine, Descartes was a prime architect of the structures of thought so pervasive in the modern world that they are frequently viewed as self-evident truths: that our thoughts constitute our essence and that the mind is separate from the body and is what makes us human.[39]

Descartes's dualism also forms the basis for the modern view of our relationship with the natural world. According to Cartesian logic, if the mind is the source of our true identity, then our bodies are mere matter with no intrinsic value. And if that is true of our own bodies, it must be equally true of the rest of nature—animals, plants, and everything else—since no other entity possesses a mind capable of reason. In Descartes's own words: "I do not recognize any difference between the machines made by craftsmen and the various bodies that nature alone composes."[40]

With this step, Descartes completed the process, begun by monotheism, that eliminated any intrinsic value from the natural world. With nothing sacred about nature, it became available for the human intellect to use remorselessly for its own purposes. The scientific project, just getting off the ground in the seventeenth century, would henceforth view every aspect of the material world as free game for inquiry, investigation, and exploitation. As the Scientific Revolution gained steam in Europe, a split emerged between religious and rationalist thinkers, but in neither case did the dualistic presumption ever get questioned. The one fundamental truth everyone could agree on was the sanctity of the mind/soul in contrast to the rest of nature.[41]

Faithful Christians, meanwhile, continued to be tormented by their loathing of the body. New England clergyman Cotton Mather wrote in his diary how debased he felt by the need to urinate, which puts man "on the same level with the very dogs" and resolved to think only noble and divine thoughts

Chapter 13

THE SCOURGE OF MONOTHEISTIC INTOLERANCE

In the fourth year of his reign, the young Pharaoh Amenhotep IV instigated a revolution in human consciousness. Amenhotep was dedicated to the worship of the god Aten, but the entire Egyptian establishment worshipped another deity, Amun, as the god of gods. In 1361 BCE, the frustrated young pharaoh was ready to make his move. He sent the high priest of Amun into the wilderness on a stone-quarrying expedition and named Aten as the head of the pantheon, building temples to the new supreme god at the sacred site of Karnak. He changed his own name to Akhenaten: "the splendor of Aten." When the horrified high priest of Amun returned, he was sent back to the stone quarries—only this time as a common slave.[1]

Akhenaten didn't stop at replacing Amun with Aten. Instead, he insisted that Aten was quite literally the only god that existed. There was none other. He imposed his new doctrine without mercy. Worship of Amun was forbidden and persecuted; his name was hacked out of every monument in Egypt and abroad. The eradication of Amun's name was so pervasive that Egyptologists today rely on it to determine the dating of a monument. "The monotheistic revolution of Akhenaten," writes Egyptologist Jan Assmann, "was not only the first but also the most radical and violent eruption of a counter-religion in the history of humankind."[2]

Akhenaten's brutal revolution would be short-lived. In the years after his death, the lesser gods of the Egyptian cosmos were gradually resurrected, and Amun regained his place at the head of the pantheon. But Akhenaten had initiated something that would survive long after him and continues to thrive in the present day: the religious intolerance that arises from monotheism.

We will discover in this chapter that not only is religious intolerance tightly intertwined with monotheism, but, before the emergence of monotheism, it simply didn't exist. Religious intolerance, as we will see, may indeed be the predictable by-product of monotheistic belief, which, by definition, posits that there

> He who shall keep these words which are on the tablet of silver, whether he be Hittite or Egyptian, and shall not neglect them, may the thousand gods of the land of the Hatti and the thousand gods of the land of Egypt make him to be in good health and long life, as also his houses, his country and his servants.[7]

Even the mighty Roman Empire accepted without question the validity of foreign gods. When the Romans conquered a city, they would frequently set up a dedication to whichever gods protected that territory. Sometimes they would conciliate a local god by placing his image alongside the Roman gods in their camp.[8]

There was, however, one notable exception to this traditional tolerance of foreign worship: the teachings of Zoroaster, the next monotheist to appear after Akhenaten. As we've seen, Zoroaster saw the cosmos as an eternal struggle between the Truth and the Lie. Good was equated with the Truth so uncompromisingly that there was no room for independent thought. Freethinking became heresy, while intolerance toward followers of the Lie became an article of faith.

The Holy War of the Old Testament

Zoroaster's theological dogmatism was unparalleled in the ancient world—until, that is, the next outbreak of monotheism: the Old Testament. In a unending barrage of rancor, the children of Israel are repeatedly commanded by Yahweh to show no mercy to those they defeat in the name of the Lord.

The book of Deuteronomy—an early manifesto of monotheism, as we've seen—contains a series of bloodcurdling orders given by Yahweh to his followers. When the Israelites conquer an enemy's city, they are to show no mercy:

> When the Lord your God delivers it into your hand, put to the sword all the men in it. As for the women, the children, the livestock and everything else in the city, you may take these as plunder for yourselves. And you may use the plunder the Lord your God gives you from your enemies.

This, at least, can be understood within the zeitgeist of the ancient world. Massacring all the men is an extreme policy even by ancient standards, but at least it fits within accepted ancient practices, in which the spoils of war went to the victors. However, in Deuteronomy, this approach is reserved only for distant nations. For those nations unfortunate enough to exist in the territories Yahweh decided to give the Israelites as an inheritance, a more awful fate is in store:

the best of the sheep and cattle to sacrifice to his Lord. Yahweh is furious at even this slight disobedience and sends his prophet, Samuel, to tell Saul he is now rejected by Yahweh as king of Israel. Saul immediately tries to make amends. He calls for Agag to be brought to him and puts him to death right there, abjectly following Yahweh's command. It is worth recalling that, during the Nuremberg trials, the claim of "just following orders" became notorious as an insufficient defense against the charge of mass murder. It is a grim irony of history that the first exemplar of genocide carried out in the name of ideology came from the holy book of the Jewish faith, the very people that the Nazis tried to wipe out with their racist ideology.[12]

In reality, the military power of the Israelites during the biblical era remained very limited, and these genocidal narratives were no more than rabid fantasies. However, the widespread reverence given to the Old Testament as a result of the spread of Christianity means that these invocations for merciless slaughter in the name of God remain available to be read and endorsed anywhere there is a Bible to be opened.

"Whoever Does Not Believe Will Be Condemned"

In contrast to the Israelites, the Roman Empire did succeed in establishing their military power across much of the ancient world. When they did, it was a challenge for them to come to terms with the absolutist refusal of monotheistic religions to tolerate different viewpoints about the cosmos. There was no reference point for this type of behavior. The Presocratic philosopher Xenophanes had openly ridiculed the traditional set of beliefs he saw around him, but he nevertheless lived to a ripe old age. It is not surprising, then, that pagan thinkers and administrators became increasingly dismayed when Christianity infiltrated the empire and began enforcing unprecedented control over the beliefs and practices of everyone around them.[13]

The early centuries of the Christian era resounded with the battle between tolerant pagans and absolutist Christians over freedom of thought in the Western world. Most thinkers of the time acknowledged the idea of a divine higher power, but pagans readily accepted that different groups might give this deity a different name. "It makes no difference," wrote Celsus, a second-century Platonist, "whether we call Zeus the Most High or Zeus or Adonis or Sabaoth or Amun like the Egyptians, or Papaeus like the Scythians."[14]

The battle waged by the early Christians was not just against competing faiths but against the very notion of independent thought, which might undermine faith in the word of God. The idea arose that if you believed Christ was the savior sent by God for all mankind, this was the only truth you should ever care to know. "After Jesus Christ," wrote church father Tertullian, "we have no need of speculation, after the Gospel no need of research." Augustine referred to intellectual inquiry as "the disease of curiosity . . . to try and discover the secrets of nature, those secrets which are beyond our understanding, which can avail us nothing and which man should not wish to learn."[19]

Driven by this aversion to intellectual curiosity, the Christian establishment set about systematically destroying any writing that might call their new faith into question. In 529, the Christian emperor Justinian banned pagans from teaching higher education, and, later that century, Pope Gregory the Great burned libraries holding classical writings. Christian suppression of free thought remained a central part of the European experience for more than a thousand years. As late as 1600, Giordano Bruno was burned at the stake for espousing pantheistic beliefs.[20]

Like the scorpion that allegedly bites itself when caught in a ring of fire, the scourge of intolerance was inflicted from the start on other Christians who differed in their interpretation of the faith. In the first few centuries of Christian hegemony, internecine wars between power blocs supporting different interpretations of the scriptures inflicted far more casualties than the Roman persecution of Christians. This set the stage for the monotheistic intolerance that has since become the norm for global history. In a typical example from the thirteenth century, a papal legate described with glee the slaughter of the Cathars, a heterodox Christian sect: "Nearly twenty thousand of the citizens were put to the sword regardless of age and sex. The workings of divine vengeance have been wondrous."[21]

After the sixteenth-century Reformation, the entire continent of Europe was ravaged by two hundred years of holy war between Protestants and Catholics. Protestant leader Thomas Muntzer spoke for his age when he called on his fellow believers to slaughter the Catholics: "Don't let them live any longer, the evil-doers who turn us away from God, for a godless man [a Catholic] has no right to live if he hinders the godly. . . . The sword is necessary to exterminate them. . . . If they resist, let them be slaughtered without mercy."[22]

Christian intolerance of other Christians, distressing in its brutality, is surpassed only by the deluge of violence Christianity vented on followers of other faiths. The Jews, living as a minority in Christian Europe, were particularly vulnerable. From Christianity's outset, the refusal of the Jews to accept the Gospels

Tyre, "it was impossible to look upon the vast numbers of the slain without horror; everywhere lay fragments of human bodies. . . . Still more dreadful was it to gaze upon the victors themselves, dripping with blood from head to foot."[26]

For two hundred years, one Crusade after another would sear images of hate and slaughter into the collective consciousness of Christians and Muslims alike. Even in the twenty-first century, echoes of the Crusades continue to inform geopolitics. The founder of al-Qaeda, Osama bin Laden, declared the killing of Americans and Jews to be a sacred duty, stating, "We will see Saladin [a celebrated Muslim commander] carrying his sword, with the blood of unbelievers dripping from it." In 2003, US general William Boykin, commenting on the "war on terror," declared, "The battle that we're in is a spiritual battle. . . . Satan wants to destroy this nation . . . he wants to destroy us as a Christian army." Referring to a Somali military leader, Boykin added: "My God was bigger than his. I knew my God was a real God and his was an idol."[27]

The Religious Tolerance of India

How directly is monotheism to blame for imposing this religious intolerance on humanity? After all, our newspapers frequently contain stories of murderous rivalry between various religions around the world. Surely, one might speculate, the other great cosmologies of world history—Hinduism, Buddhism, Taoism, Confucianism—have had their own equally brutal histories of hatred, intolerance, and genocide?

Astonishingly, it turns out this is simply not the case. Before the influx of monotheism and later forms of absolutism from the West, the cultural traditions of Asia had no experience of the kind of murderous religious intolerance documented here. While there was competition for patronage between faiths, the notion of heresy as something to be eliminated didn't exist. Hajime Nakamura, a leading crosscultural authority on Asian spiritual traditions, observes that "in India there were no religious wars. Neither Buddhists nor Jains ever executed heretics. What they did to heretics was only to exclude them from the orders. Religious leaders in India died peacefully attended by their disciples and followers. Toleration is the most conspicuous characteristic of Indian culture."[28]

King Ashoka, whose ancient Mauryan empire covered virtually the entire Indian subcontinent, reflected this tone of religious tolerance on stupas erected across the land, which exist to this day. During his reign, he converted to

case. According to one nineteenth-century English historian, emancipating Hindus from the "great abomination" of their religion was the sacred duty of every Christian. William Wilberforce, remembered for his efforts to abolish slavery, considered Christian missionary activity in India to be "the greatest of all causes," denounced Hindu deities as "absolute monsters of lust, injustice, wickedness and cruelty," and concluded that "our religion is sublime, pure and beneficent [while] theirs is mean, licentious and cruel."[33*]

Harmonization of Religion in China

Like India, China demonstrated a tolerant approach to religious beliefs throughout the premodern period. Nakamura observes that "religious wars or struggles over ideology, which frequently arose in Europe, did not arise in China. . . . The emperors of China and India were similar in that they both did not regard religious differences a justification for war."[34]

The Chinese propensity for harmonization of different points of view reveals itself throughout their long history of evolving belief systems. An example can be seen in the writings of Zongmi, a ninth-century scholar trained in the Confucian classics who became an influential Buddhist monk. When asked by one of his students whether Confucianism, Taoism, and Buddhism were the same or different teachings, he replied: "For those of great wisdom, they are the same. On the other hand, for those with little capacity they are different. Enlightenment and illusion depends solely on the capacity of man and not on the difference of teaching." The public shared this eclectic appreciation of religious wisdom. Even today, in a typical Taoist temple, along with a central image of Lao-tzu, you might find images of a Christian saint, a Confucian sage, and the Buddha, among other deities.[35]

Buddhism gradually spread into China from India, reaching its zenith during the Tang dynasty (618–907), when it became an integral part of the Chinese cultural and political system. Toward the end of the Tang dynasty, a backlash occurred. A nationalistic movement arose against foreign influences on Chinese thought, focusing its offensive on Buddhism. By that time, the Buddhist religion had achieved enormous power, with its monasteries enjoying vast wealth. The Chinese government turned on Buddhism in an attack so severe that it is known as the "Great Anti-Buddhist Persecution." The Buddhist priesthood was purged of uneducated monks; estates and precious metals were

Chapter 14

DISCOVERING THE PRINCIPLES OF NATURE IN SONG CHINA

The year is 1017. In Europe, the Dark Ages are drawing to a close. King Canute is being crowned in London, a modest city of roughly thirty thousand. Half a world away, the emperor of China's Song dynasty, Zhenzong, is celebrating the New Year's Festival from a lavishly decorated hall on top of the Gate of Displayed Virtue, a massive construction more than three hundred meters wide. With music playing and top-ranking officials sitting in curtained boxes, Zhenzong surveys the glory of Kaifeng stretched out before him. The largest city in the world, Kaifeng contains about a million people. It is a city that never sleeps, with first-class restaurants and countless markets specializing in garments, pearls, gold and silver, incense, drugs, brothels, and every kind of food and drink imaginable. In the words of one denizen, "Here one can stay all day and never become aware when evening falls."[1]

In the time of the Song dynasty (960–1279), China was by far the most developed region in the world, with the most advanced technological know-how. Woodblock printing had been used for centuries. The recent discovery of gunpowder was transforming the military with bombs, grenades, and cannons. Chinese ships were larger and more seaworthy than those of any other nation and navigated the open seas using the magnetic compass. Inland, they transported agricultural and industrial commodities through an extensive fifty-thousand-kilometer canal network. The Song economy was further boosted by the introduction of state-issued paper currency in 1024—about eight hundred years before it became widespread in Europe.[2]

Fueled by its prosperity, Song society nurtured an open spirit of intellectual investigation that invites comparison with the European Renaissance. The great polymath Shen Kuo conceptualized true north from the magnetic needle compass and formed hypotheses of gradual climate change and geological land formation from his study of fossils. The same kind of critical thinking infused

The Buddha's "middle way" found a warm welcome in Chinese culture, which had no dualistic conception of the universe to overcome. Instead, many Chinese felt a deep affinity with the Buddhist doctrine of *dharma*: a recognition of the indivisible integrity and harmony of the universe, in which all parts are interdependent. This sounded so much like the Tao that, when Buddhist texts were translated into Chinese, the word Tao was simply used to translate the word *dharma*. After a while, educated Chinese became so comfortable with Buddhism that many believed it must have originated in China.[7]

The absorption of Buddhism into the Chinese way of life reached its zenith during the Tang dynasty (618–907), when it became an integral part of Chinese culture and society. However, there were elements of Buddhist cosmology that didn't fit so well with the Chinese sensibility, and as Buddhist influence spread, these caused a reaction. Although Buddhism had emerged as an alternative to Vedic thought, it had also absorbed some properties of the Vedic dualistic paradigm. Among these was the concept of nirvana, a state of peaceful bliss available through prolonged meditation in which bodily sensations dissolve and sensual desires disappear. Along with this emphasis on transcending the physical world, some schools of Buddhism continued to teach the core Vedic principle that the phenomenal world was only an illusion and that once practitioners became enlightened, they would recognize the emptiness of all things. A visitor to a Buddhist temple might hear endless chants of "empty, empty, empty" echoing eerily through the hallways.[8]

This was an aspect of Buddhism that many Chinese reacted against strongly. Accusations arose that Buddhism was essentially nihilistic and caused its followers to reject their proper role within the community. "The Buddhists," wrote one critic, "consider [life] to be extremely painful, and seek to escape from it. . . . They always base themselves on the idea of withdrawal from the world."[9]

Among the critics were leading philosophers of the Song dynasty, who were particularly troubled by the Buddhist notion of emptiness. The idea that the ultimate ground of reality was emptiness made little sense to a culture steeped in the notion of harmonizing with the flow of the universe. One critique of the time eloquently captured the contrast between the two traditions:

> Buddhism looks upon emptiness as the highest and upon existence as an illusion. Those who wish to learn the true Tao must take good note of this. Daily we see the sun and moon revolving in the heavens, and the mountains and rivers rooted in the earth, while men and animals wander abroad the world.

most important text of the Taoists, along with the *I Ching*, which was equally valued by Confucians. In the *Tao Te Ching*, he found a passage stating that, by pursuing the Tao without deviation, "one again returns to the unlimited." This, Zhou felt, hinted at an ancient Taoist alternative to the Buddhist concept of emptiness. He then turned to a key passage in the *I Ching* that, again, seemed to name the very basis of reality, stating: "Therefore in [the system] of the *Changes* there is the Supreme Ultimate, which produced the Two Forms [of *yin* and *yang*]." At this point, Zhou made a bold move. The "Unlimited" of the *Tao Te Ching*, he proposed, referred to the same thing as the "Supreme Ultimate" of the *I Ching*. Here, the synthesizing character of Neo-Confucianism is already apparent. In one sweeping move, Zhou Dun-yi proposed that both sources of Chinese wisdom had the same underlying conception of reality.

From there, Zhou felt he could describe how everything in the universe arises. The Supreme Ultimate produced the *yin* and *yang* modes of existence, which, in turn, generated five elemental states known in Chinese lore as fire, water, earth, metal, and wood. These interacted with each other to create the "ten thousand things"—the myriad manifestations of the material world.[13]

Another philosopher, Zhang Zai, countered the Buddhists by focusing on the traditional idea of *qi*. Instead of emptiness, Zhang declared, the universe was filled with *qi*, the fundamental energy that underlaid all the processes of the universe. *Qi*, in Zhang's view, was indestructible and continually transforming, and through its dynamic, ever-changing nature arose what he called the Great Harmony of the Tao. He was fascinated by the way in which this Great Harmony was an organic unity and yet always different. "The Principle [*li*] is one," he observed, "but its function is differentiated into the many"—a vision of the one-and-many that echoes the insights of early Vedic thinkers as well as the cosmology of ancient Egypt and would become a foundational principle of Neo-Confucian thought.[14]

What was this mysterious "Principle" that encompassed all things? Two brothers, Cheng Hao and Cheng Yi, whose uncle was none other than Zhang Zai, took it upon themselves to ponder this question. Each tried to make sense of the "principle"—the *li*—that their uncle had identified as pervading all things. It was the younger brother, Cheng Yi, who first applied the concept of *li* comprehensively to everything in the universe. "All things under heaven," he wrote, "can be understood by their *li*. As there are things, there must be principles of their being. Everything must have its principle."[15*]

A century would pass between this first wave of thinkers and the philosopher

length. The underlying concept is that matter or energy can't exist without being organized in some fundamental way.[17]

Ever since Westerners first came across the Neo-Confucian idea of li and qi, there has been a tendency to reframe the concept into the dualistic paradigm that Plato established so firmly in Western consciousness. Plato's division of the cosmos into a tangible dimension and an abstract dimension of Ideas was used to neatly map the Neo-Confucian terminology accordingly: qi represented Matter, and li represented the Idea or Form.[18]

It took a brilliant scholar named Joseph Needham to confront head-on the orthodox Western interpretation of li and qi in the middle of the twentieth century. Needham was an eminent Cambridge academic who first made a name for himself as a biochemist. In mid-career, he became fascinated by China and went on to publish a series of volumes entitled *Science and Civilisation in China,* which transformed the conventional Western view of Chinese history that had previously considered China a backward and ineffectual society.[19]

When Needham turned to the meaning of li and qi, he was well versed in the orthodox Western philosophical tradition, but he had also learned to think as a biologist and was therefore unusually well-equipped to offer an alternative perspective. He pointed out that the dualistic splits of Western thought—body versus soul, material world versus eternal God—simply didn't exist in the Chinese cosmos, and that the Platonic Form versus Matter interpretation of li and qi was therefore "entirely unacceptable." Li, he explained, was not some metaphysical concept "but rather the invisible organizing fields or forces existing at all levels within the natural world."[20]

Although invisible, these organizing principles could clearly be seen through their effect on energy and matter, in the same way that wind is invisible but can be seen through its effect on trees, leaves, and clouds. Needham pointed out that, like the wind, li should not be thought of as a fixed pattern but rather a "dynamic pattern as embodied in all living things." Consider an ocean wave breaking on the shore: we can think of the water itself as the qi, while the various forces organizing the water into its dynamic wave pattern are the li.[21]

These patterns in the natural world are only the most obvious examples of li. It also refers to patterns in time as well as space, patterns within patterns, and patterns that we create in our own minds through our patterning instinct. Li is perhaps best described as the ever-moving, ever-present set of patterns that flow through everything in nature and in all our perceptions of the world, including our own consciousness.[22]

understand this is to consider a candle flame. As the flame burns, every molecule that originally comprises the flame vanishes into the atmosphere. Each moment, the molecules making up the flame are different, yet the flame remains an ongoing entity. In scientific terms, we can understand the flame's organizing principles in terms of the relatively stable relationship between the wax, the wick, the flame's heat, and the oxygen in the atmosphere. In Neo-Confucian terminology, we would say that the li of the flame remains stable even while the qi—the physical components—continually changes.

A similar relationship between li and qi applies when we consider ourselves as a complex, dynamical system. If you look at a photograph of yourself when you were a child, you instantly recognize it as you, but virtually every cell that was in that child no longer exists in your body. Even the cells that do remain, such as brain and muscle cells, have reconfigured their internal contents so that probably none of the molecules forming that child in the photograph are part of you now. This raises the question of what it actually is that forms the intimate connection between you and that child. The answer is the li. The qi has all changed, but the li remains stable: growing, evolving, but patterning its growth on the child's original principles of organization.

The concept of li is equally applicable to studies of consciousness. Some researchers have tried to place consciousness in a specific place in the human brain, but sophisticated theories of consciousness look instead to li. Two of the foremost neuroscientists in the field describe the "li of consciousness" thus: "A dynamic core [of consciousness] is . . . a process, not a thing or a place, and it is defined in terms of neural interactions, rather than in terms of specific neural location, connectivity, or activity."[27]

Just as li was understood by the Neo-Confucians to apply to every aspect of the universe, so systems theorists are beginning to recognize that their principles apply equally to everything in the natural world. Prominent biologist Carl Woese touches on this implication when he describes organisms as "resilient patterns in a turbulent flow—patterns in an energy flow." He adds, "It is becoming increasingly clear that to understand living systems in any deep sense, we must come to see them not materialistically, as machines, but as stable, complex, dynamic organization."[28]

The significance of the correspondence between the Neo-Confucian system of thought and that of dynamical systems theory is far-reaching. Many of the insights generated by the Neo-Confucian philosophers arise from the interplay between li and qi in the natural world, in human experience, and in

Supreme Ultimate as a unity that is, at the same time, endlessly differentiated. "Fundamentally there is only one Supreme Ultimate," Zhu Xi wrote, "yet each of the myriad things has been endowed with it and each in itself possesses the Supreme Ultimate in its entirety." He alluded to a famous Buddhist metaphor of moonlight:

> Just as the moon is in heaven:
> It is only one.
> Yet it is reflected in rivers and lakes;
> It can be seen everywhere;
> It should not be called divided.

Here, Zhu Xi conceded, "the Buddhists have glimpsed the li of the Tao."[32]

As we have seen, this is one of the oldest recorded ideas in human thought. The ancient Egyptians prayed to Amun, intoning: "You are the sky, you are the earth, you are the netherworld, you are the water, you are the air between them." The Upanishads similarly describe the manifestations of Brahman: "He is the fire and the sun, and the moon and the stars. He is the air and the sea. . . . He is the boy, he is that girl."[33]

The belief in immanent divinity throughout the entire universe is known as pantheism, and, during the period of Christian dominance in Europe, it was viewed as a heresy sometimes punishable by death. In the modern era, an experience of the ultimate oneness of the cosmos is liable to be dismissed as "mystical" and not considered valid in mainstream scientific discourse. The Neo-Confucians, on the other hand, came to this understanding of the universe by way of a systematic exploration of the implications of a cosmos consisting entirely of li and qi. "When we speak of heaven, earth, and the myriad things together, there is just one li," wrote Zhu Xi. "When we come to humans, each has his or her own li. . . . Although each has his own li, each nonetheless emerges from a single li."[34]

While this statement appears paradoxical, it makes more sense if we follow the suggestion of sinologist Stephen Angle to translate li as "coherence," which he spells out as "the valuable, intelligible way that things fit together." In this case, Zhu Xi's statement would translate as: Each of us has our own unique coherence, which, nonetheless, emerges from a single coherence.[35]

What, then, is this coherence that is intrinsic to each of us and the natural world? The Neo-Confucians pursued this question with a passion. Rather than

relationship to the cosmos was the sense that li ultimately connects everything to everything else. To understand any aspect of reality, it's necessary to recognize it as linked to all other aspects of reality through a multidimensional matrix of meaning. The ultimate goal of the Investigation of Things was recognizing this interconnectivity of all aspects of existence—or, in Angle's rendition, "fully apprehending the coherence of things."[39]

This vision of the interconnectivity of li demonstrates a sophisticated understanding of the natural world and our perception of it, which was not explored in the West until the twentieth century and, even then, only by a few innovative schools of thought. Gestalt psychology, for example, which comes from the German word meaning "form," sees human perception as a holistic, self-organized integration of a complex interplay of patterns.[40]

It was Cheng Yi who first developed the idea that coherent patterns, or gestalts, are universally embedded within larger gestalts. "We say that all things are one reality," he wrote, "because all things have the same li in them. . . . The li of a thing is one with the li of all things. . . . There is only one li in the world." While this might sound rather mystical, recent breakthroughs in mathematics have demonstrated Cheng's statements to be a perceptive insight into the nature of reality. Fractal geometry, pioneered by mathematician Benoit Mandelbrot, shows how nature forms intricate patterns that replicate themselves at different scales, each pattern nested inside another. Examples of these fractal patterns are observable in clouds, coastlines, ferns, and sand dunes.[41]

Since Mandelbrot's discovery, biologists have come to recognize that the design of life itself is fractal, with cells self-organizing to form organisms, which then self-organize into communities of organisms and ecosystems. In the human body, fractal designs have been discovered in systems as diverse as blood vessels, lungs, heart rate, the digestive system, and brain networks, so much so that fractal behavior in a system is coming to be seen as a sign of good health. Additionally, researchers have noticed similarities between patterns of connectivity between neurons in the brain and the patterns exhibited by insect colonies such as ants or bees, hinting at analogous self-organized processes that create both our own consciousness and the "intelligence" of the natural world.[42]

no word for this kind of knowing exists in English. The deep sense of integration arising from this harmonization of cognition and feeling could lead to a realization of one's own nature in harmony with the entire universe. In this respect, the Neo-Confucians were fond of quoting the words of the ancient philosopher Mencius: "For a person to realize fully one's *xin* is to realize fully one's nature, and in so doing, one realizes heaven."[46]

This welcoming attitude toward feeling and intuition didn't mean that the Neo-Confucians believed in letting their emotions run wild. Rather, they developed a sophisticated and coherent theory of psychology that recognized a central place for the appropriate expression of emotions. They saw the heart-mind, *xin,* as integrating a person's intrinsic nature with emotions arising from social interaction such as love, hate, and anger.[47]

Intrinsic nature, in the Neo-Confucian view, referred to the unique patterning of the li and qi of any specific entity that gives it its own distinctive character. Thus, a tree, an animal, a mountain, or a chair each has its own intrinsic nature. In a human being, one's intrinsic nature is continually buffeted by the feelings, emotions, and passions arising from contact with the world. These all combine within the heart-mind to determine one's inner experience and consequent behavior.[48]

The way in which everything comes together in the heart-mind determines the quality of a person's experience. How could a person manage to feel and express emotions in a way that was harmonious rather than destructive? The Neo-Confucians recognized a faculty in the heart-mind that they referred to as the regulator. This faculty was not like a ruler imposing its will on the feelings. Rather, it was a process arising from the coherence of a person's character, from a person's li. In the words of one Neo-Confucian philosopher, the li is that which "controls without controlling."[49]

How different this conception of the human personality was from that of the Western tradition! Far from the Western view of the soul (later transformed into mind) desperately trying to prevent the body from carrying out sinful desires, the Neo-Confucians saw their embodied feelings as integral to a healthy existence and recognized that regulating these feelings was the result of an intrinsic process within the heart-mind rather than a battle of the will.

We find a modern validation for this Neo-Confucian framework in the discoveries of neuroscience. The heart-mind's regulating faculty is analogous to the executive function of the PFC. Consistent with the Neo-Confucian understanding, researchers report that, when the PFC regulates emotions in a

emotions in the human spectrum. He once wrote in a letter to a student that "there is harmony in sorrow. This refers to its taking rise from complete sincerity and being without any affectation." To be in harmony, the emotion needed to be expressed authentically: "The infant cries all day," Wang wrote, "without hurting his throat. This is the extreme of harmony." Harmony emerges not from repressing or transcending sincere emotions but from honoring each of them as they arise.[52]

The Effortless Sage

How does a person develop this ability to express feelings in just the right way? In Wang's view, it was by not thinking about it too much. He expressed frustration at those who "merely cripple their spirit and exhaust their energy in scrutinizing books" and engaging in "intellectual discourses." Instead, Wang taught his students to become aware of their own embodied intelligence, which he called *liang zhi*, innate knowledge. As an example of *liang zhi*, Wang described someone watching a little child about to fall into a well: he doesn't need to think in order to be alarmed and immediately spring into action to save the child. This is the spontaneous faculty of *liang zhi*—that intuitive "gut feeling" of right and wrong, which tells you how to act in a given situation. "When you direct your thought and intention," Wang explained, "your *liang zhi* knows that right is right and wrong is wrong. You cannot conceal anything from it."[53]

While Wang viewed *liang zhi* as superior to reason alone, this didn't follow the categorical split between reason and emotion that became central to the dualistic Western tradition. Rather, to stay connected with one's *liang zhi* and act in a manner truly consistent with it, a person needed to utilize conceptual faculties such as discernment and self-assessment. Rather than separating the domains of conceptual and animate consciousness, the Neo-Confucians sought to harmonize them. "To extend *liang zhi*," Wang observed, "requires special efforts, which include self-examination, self-transformation, self-discipline, self-reflection, and most important, the sincerity [*cheng*] of one's will."[54]

Wang's use of the word *cheng*—the ancient Confucian term for authentic behavior—took on extra meaning within the Neo-Confucian fractal framework that viewed each entity as nested within ever-larger entities. When someone acted with *cheng*, each aspect of himself was given appropriate expression, with the result that the person was also acting in integrity with the larger cosmos.[55]

Intimately Placed between Heaven and Earth

When they developed key concepts such as *cheng* or sagehood, the Neo-Confucians frequently expanded the scope of ancient Confucian ideas into a larger context. This was especially evident in their treatment of the Confucian term *ren*. In classical Confucianism, the concept of *ren* was primarily social, referring to a humane benevolence incorporating virtues such as filial piety and loyalty. The Neo-Confucians took this traditional idea of benevolence toward one's community and expanded it to incorporate the entire cosmos.[60]

We can see here an example of the profound Buddhist influence on Neo-Confucian thought. Buddhism had introduced to China sophisticated meditation techniques that enabled a practitioner to carefully observe his consciousness. An important exercise was the practice of extending compassion beyond one's own community—and even beyond humanity to include all other sentient beings. It was in this context that the Neo-Confucians achieved one of their greatest triumphs, fusing the Confucian goal of perfecting one's social identity with the Buddhist ideal of dissolving the boundaries of the self, to create a vision of *ren* that holds as much relevance in today's world as it held a thousand years ago.[61]

Zhang Zai, the early Neo-Confucian who conceived of a universe of qi held together in an organic unity, reflected deeply on the implications of what this cosmic structure meant for him as a human being: a fractal entity connected to the universe by the li that organized both him and his surroundings. What arose in him was a sense of universal *ren*, a vision he communicated in an essay called the "Western Inscription," which has deservedly become one of the most influential statements in Chinese philosophy and begins as follows:

> Heaven is my father and earth is my mother, and I, a small
> child, find myself placed intimately between them.
> What fills the universe I regard as my body; what directs the
> universe I regard as my nature.
> All people are my brothers and sisters; all things are my
> companions.[62]

Later Neo-Confucian thought on *ren* can well be understood as further elaborations of the framework established by this magnificent vision of human existence.[63]

> parents and strangers. But suppose here are a small basket of rice and a platter of soup. With them one will survive and without them one will die; there is not enough to save both parent and stranger. We can bear preferring to save the parent instead of the stranger. In each case, these all accord with li.

A true sense of *ren*, then, infuses all the ethical distinctions and decisions one makes in life, since it permits a deep and ongoing harmonization with one's interconnected place in the cosmos.[66]

Because of its embodied nature, *ren* is not the kind of metaphysical love that leads one to transcend the daily activities of life and remain detached from worldly affairs. More than a mere state of mind, *ren* is an engaged attitude arising from being in the world. Cheng Yi captured this idea when he stated: "No one has knowledge being unable to put it into action. If one has knowledge being unable to put it into action, the knowledge is superficial."[67]

The Neo-Confucian sense of *ren* can best be understood as an intentional experience of living in harmony with one's own inner feelings and with one's embedded existence in human society and the entire cosmos. *Ren* is not only about optimizing one's own life for the greatest spiritual fulfillment but also about humans in society existing in the most harmonious terms with each other and within the natural world.[68]

Philosophical Implications

We live in a world dominated by two incompatible worldviews, both of which are the result of dualistic thinking. The monotheism of Christianity, Islam, and Judaism posits an intangible dimension of God from which derives the ultimate source of meaning. The worldview of scientific materialism sees reductionist science as the only valid way of understanding the universe and rejects an alternative spiritual dimension. In the words of Nobel Prize–winning physicist Steven Weinberg, "The more we know of the universe, the more meaningless it appears."[69] Many people, however, find themselves caught in the middle, rejecting dualism but sensing something greater than reductionist science allows, and they seek alternative explanations for meaning in their lives, which are frequently dismissed by science as incoherent.

The Neo-Confucian tradition offers an approach to finding meaning in the cosmos that does away with the artificial trade-off created by the dualistic

[illegible]

[illegible] on the Losing Side

[illegible] of the Song dynasty and [illegible] cosmology? Even [illegible] economic and technological prowess, the Song rulers were continually under military pressure from the Manchurian empire to their north and Mongol [illegible] from Asia's heartland. It was the Mongols who finally dealt the fatal blow to Song civilization, with Genghis Khan's grandson, Kublai Khan, laying waste to their last strongholds in 1279.

The Neo-Confucian thought tradition fared better. By the time of Wang Yang-ming, at the beginning of the sixteenth century, Neo-Confucianism had become the established orthodoxy of the Chinese state. However, much of the freshness of the original philosophers had been lost along the way. This trend continued, and, by the early twentieth century, when Western colonial powers established their stranglehold over imperial China, many Chinese intellectuals viewed the Neo-Confucian tradition as responsible for the debilitated state of their civilization.[71]

Perhaps it was for this reason that the treasures of Neo-Confucianism were virtually lost to the currents of global thought in more recent centuries. History, as the saying goes, is the story told by the victors, and the same holds true for cosmologies. At the birth of Neo-Confucianism, the glorious Song capital of Kaifeng had a population thirty times greater than London's. By the time of Wang Yang-ming's death in 1529, the tables were turning. That year, the Spaniard Francisco Pizarro was appointed governor of the New World territory of Peru. The Muslim incursion of Europe reached its high-water mark with a failed siege of Vienna, the beginning of a seismic shift in the balance of power between the two great monotheistic creeds. At the Diet of Speyer, a group of German rulers kicked off the Protestant movement that would shake up the Catholic hegemony over Christendom. And Spain and Portugal agreed, with the Treaty of Saragossa, to divide up the Eastern Hemisphere between them for further conquest and plunder.

Europe was stirring, and the effects of this would have dramatic repercussions across the entire globe, creating the world structure that we inhabit today. While the Neo-Confucians sought a path of harmonization, patterns of thought in Europe were leading in very different directions, setting European civilization on a course that would result in global domination. The time has come to investigate what it was about the European mind-set that led to this drastic shift in power, and to explore the implications of the monumental transformation that would ensue.

Part 4

CONQUEST OF NATURE

Chapter 15

"TO COMAND THE WORLD": METAPHORS OF NATURE

It was the trial of the year in 1612. Everyone in England was transfixed by the nine women from Pendle Hill, Lancashire, found guilty of witchcraft and fornicating with the devil. They were condemned to die by hanging. Only nine years earlier, England's new sovereign, King James, had replaced milder witchcraft laws with automatic death sentences for witches; otherwise, the women would likely have survived their ordeal. As they went to the gallows, they had no way of knowing the resonance their personal tragedy was destined to have with a much larger drama: the profoundly changing relationship between humankind and the natural world.[1]

In the year following Pendle Hill, King James appointed his trusted advisor Francis Bacon to attorney general, an office he used to zealously prosecute suspected traitors, resorting to torture if necessary to aid in discovery. Bacon is remembered nowadays more for his eloquent writings about the glorious possibilities of the scientific investigation of nature. "Let the human race," he wrote, "recover that right over Nature which belongs to it by divine bequest."[2]

However, the metaphors Bacon used to inspire his fellow scientists left a troubling legacy. They were filled with disturbing associations of the violence and torture Bacon relied on for his legal discovery. It was as though nature were one of the Pendle Hill witches accused of a terrible crime. Nature was to be "put in constraint," and the aim of the scientist was to "hound her in her wanderings." With echoes of the witch trials, sexual innuendo lurked in the background: "Neither ought a man to make scruple of entering and penetrating into these holes and corners, when the inquisition of truth is his whole object." The scientific method, Bacon declared, "may in very truth dissect nature" to discover "the secrets still locked in [her] bosom" so that she can then be "forced out of her natural state and squeezed and molded."[3]

The images Bacon used to galvanize the spirit of scientific discovery

Dominion over Nature

When Bacon suggested interrogating nature as if she were a witness in a prosecution, he was tapping into a long tradition of viewing nature through the lens of the law. The metaphor of a DIVINE LAWGIVER, commanding the major features of the natural world as his subjects, can be traced back to early Mesopotamia. In a creation poem dating to about 2000 BCE, the sun god Marduk "prescribes the laws" for the star gods, maintaining them in their celestial path through "commands" and "decrees."[7]

The biblical view of God as DIVINE LAWGIVER was most likely inspired by this Mesopotamian idea. In Second Isaiah—a key source of the Old Testament vision of monotheism—God portrays himself as nature's commander in chief: "I have made the earth, and created man upon it: I, even my hands, have stretched out the heavens, and all their host have I commanded." This powerful metaphor is frequently used elsewhere in the Old Testament, such as in Jeremiah, where God proclaims that he has "placed the sand for the bound of the sea by a perpetual decree, that it cannot pass it."[8]

It was a theme that spread irresistibly through the cultural framework of Christian Europe. German chemist Georgius Agricola, writing in 1546 about the composition of different metals, acknowledged that the actual ingredients "from which a metal is made, no mortal can ever find out or still less explain, but only the one God has known it, who has given sure and fixed laws to Nature for mixing and blending things together." This conception of God's laws as the laws of nature was reprised by Descartes into what became the foundational scientific view of the natural world: "God sets up mathematical laws in nature as a king sets up laws in his kingdom."[9]

As DIVINE LAWGIVER, one of God's first laws was to bestow on humankind DOMINION OVER NATURE. After creating Adam and Eve, God commands them:

> Be fruitful, and multiply, and replenish the earth, and subdue it: and have dominion over the fish of the sea, and over the fowl of the air, and over every living thing that moveth upon the earth.[10]

This core metaphor recurs throughout the Old Testament. One famous example, Psalm 8, praises God for giving humankind dominion over the natural world:

[illegible] theory of evolution, the view of humankind as the crown of creation maintained its hold on the Western mind, transforming from a Christian to an evolutionary notion. Darwin's contemporary Alfred Russel Wallace, for example, concluded that evolution had been working "for countless millions of years [illegible] [illegible] in man." This idea [illegible] held. Prominent paleontologist Robert Broom expressed a typical opinion in 1933 that "much of evolution looks as if it had been planned to result in man, and in other animals and plants to make the world a suitable place for him to dwell in."

Recovering Dominion

Along with the DOMINION OVER NATURE God had granted humankind, a parallel metaphor viewed man as the STEWARD OF NATURE, with an implied duty of care. Even before the emergence of Christianity, Philo of Alexandria had rolled out the idea of man appointed by God as nature's governor: "So the Creator made man all things, as a sort of driver and pilot, to drive and steer the things on earth, and charged him with the care of animals and plants, like a governor subordinate to the chief and great King." This idea had lasting power. Seventeen hundred years later, English jurist Matthew Hale declared that "the end of man's creation was that he should be the viceroy of the great God of heaven and earth in this inferior world."[15]

There were, however, other more troubling themes inherited from the biblical narrative. The Genesis story doesn't end, of course, with God's initial arrangement, in which all the animals dutifully obey Adam and Eve. Instead, Eve persuades Adam to eat the apple from the tree of knowledge, leading to the Fall and their expulsion from the Garden of Eden, at which point humans lose their dominion over nature. The Christian conception of nature, therefore, was based on a belief that man's authority over the natural world had once been absolute, but this condition was lost after the Fall.[16]

Faced with this catastrophic loss of dominion, the idea arose that it was virtuous to reestablish man's authority in any way possible. Legends recounted the deeds of early saints who retired into the wilderness and tamed the wild beasts as proof that, by their saintliness, they were reasserting the human sovereignty lost in the Fall. This was the theological context in which Bacon trumpeted his clarion call to "Let the human race recover that right over Nature which belongs to it by divine bequest." Bacon's approach, of course, was to regain dominion through not saintliness but conquest of nature, which would be accomplished through reliance on another metaphor that has shaped our modern conception of the universe: NATURE AS MACHINE.[17]

Nature as Machine

The NATURE AS MACHINE metaphor also has its roots in the Old Testament. In those early days, machinery was far simpler, and the original metaphor focused on the concept of a divine architect measuring out the universe. The notion

[illegible]

Meanwhile, in England, Thomas Hobbes introduced his famous work *Leviathan* with a full-blown description of the world as a machine constructed by God:

> For seeing life is but a motion of limbs . . . why may we not say that all automata (engines that move themselves by springs and wheels as doth a watch) have

an artificial life: For what is the heart, but a spring; and the nerves, but so many strings; and the joints, but so many wheels, giving motion to the whole body, such as was intended by the artificer?[20]

Figure 15.1: Thirteenth-century illustration showing God as architect of the universe.

[illegible] situation, however, was considerably [illegible] contained the possibility of a purely mechanical universe without any particular purpose, with no more reality [illegible] than mechanisms. The more science revealed the intricate workings of life, the more it seemed to imply that nature really was a machine. In the early twentieth century, physiologist Jacques Loeb achieved widespread fame disseminating this view in a book entitled *The Mechanistic Conception of Life*, in which he declared that "living organisms are chemical machines possessing the peculiarity of preserving and reproducing themselves." The discovery of the DNA molecule in 1953 gave further ammunition to those who chose to view nature as machine as a cosmic reality.

In recent decades, the spectacular development of the computer has provided a powerful new metaphor to replace the watch that so dazzled people in previous centuries. One of today's most influential science writers, Richard Dawkins, has famously written that "life is just bytes and bytes and bytes of digital information," adding, "That is not a metaphor, it is the plain truth. It couldn't be any plainer if it were raining floppy discs." Dawkins is equally strident in reprising Descartes's view of the mechanical nature of the animal world, stating that "a bat is a machine, whose internal electronics are so wired up that its wing muscles cause it to home in on insects, as an unconscious guided missile homes in on an aeroplane."[24]

Many biologists have pointed out that there are, in fact, intrinsic principles to life that fundamentally differentiate it from even the most complicated machine. As we will see in a later chapter, all living organisms, from a single cell to an intelligent mammal, are self-organized, holistic systems that exhibit a sense of purpose in how they interact with the environment and metabolize energy to sustain themselves. Philosopher of science Evan Thompson has noted that Dawkins's "disavowal of metaphor is indefensible." It is, in the words of philosopher of biology Sahotra Sarkar, "a metaphor that masquerades as a theoretical concept and . . . leads to a misleading picture."[25]

This, however, has not prevented Dawkins's mechanistic view of life from being broadly accepted as the truth in mainstream thought. "New metaphors have the power to create a new reality," Lakoff observes. Dawkins provides compelling evidence in support of that statement.

"Truly to Command the World"

The core metaphors that framed the European relationship with nature had one thing in common: they all justified and celebrated the ever-increasing power humans were learning to wield over the natural world. In recent centuries, these metaphors have become rooted so deeply in our cultural cognition that they have helped form our collective reality.

Today's mainstream approach to nature was defined, quite appropriately, by the first historian of the Royal Society of London for Improving Natural Knowledge, an institution set up in 1660 for the advancement of science that remains an important contributor to scientific thought to this day. Thomas Sprat proudly declared in 1667:

[illegible]

[illegible] our global civilization's impact on the natural world threatens increasingly to destabilize its own foundations, it is [illegible] these deeply ingrained views of nature as an important causative factor of our current predicament. Meanwhile, the momentum of [illegible] continues to infuse these metaphors into our daily discourse and activity. Peter Drucker, a management consultant whose writings helped shape the philosophical foundations of the modern business corporation, observed that, in the natural world, "every plant is a weed and every mineral is just another rock. . . . Human possession and use is what activates the true nobility of any natural object."[20]

The DOMINION OVER NATURE metaphor continues to exert its hold over political discourse in the United States. In just one of countless examples, the *New York Times* reported in 2010 on members of a local group denying climate change based on their Bible reading: "It's a flat-out lie," said one member. "I read my Bible. . . . He made this earth for us to utilize." Another member added, "Being a strong Christian, I cannot help but believe the Lord placed a lot of minerals in our country and it's not there to destroy us."[30]

Even the seemingly more benign metaphor of humankind as STEWARD OF NATURE is utilized by modern political pundits as further justification for exploitation. Influential journalist Charles Krauthammer has written in *Time* magazine: "Nature is our ward, not our master. It is to be respected and even cultivated. But it is man's world. And when man has to choose between his well-being and that of nature, nature will have to accommodate. . . . In whatever situation the principle is the same; protect the environment because it is man's environment."[31]

Nature as Giving Parent

These metaphors of nature have so pervaded modern consciousness that it might seem like they have always been with us—that this is somehow the natural human way to view the world. In fact, the opposite is true. This view, with its entailments of humanity's power over nature, is unique to the JudeoChristian tradition. An ancient Egyptian hymn, for example, praises Amun for his entire creation without any sense that it was designed for humanity:

> He who gives breath to the one in the egg
> And sustains the young of the serpents,
> Who creates what gnats live on,
> And worms and fleas as well,
> Who provides for the mice in their holes
> and sustains the beetles in every piece of wood.[32]

What is notable is the reverence given to Amun for creating not only animals that are useful to humans but those that can be positively harmful: serpents, gnats, worms, fleas, mice, and beetles.

The conviction that humans share the natural world equally with all other creatures is echoed around the globe, with its source in the original

Reverent Guests of Nature

The perception of nature as GIVING PARENT is found throughout the world in cultures of all levels of sophistication. Neo-Confucian Zhang Zai gave memorable expression to this vision when he wrote, "Heaven is my father and earth is my mother and I, a small child, find myself placed intimately between them."[36]

With this familial view of the cosmos, the Chinese never experienced a drive to conquer nature. Instead, as they further elaborated their worldview, they formed a sophisticated vision of NATURE AS ORGANISM, with a particular focus on the dynamic and holistic relationship between each separate part of the organism and the whole. Chinese thought was infused with the understanding that whatever a person did—and whatever humanity as a whole might do—had implications that echoed throughout the universe. This has been described by scholars as "a kind of cosmic resonance," a sense that the human body, the state, heaven, and earth "all exhibit the *same* reciprocal processes and are parts of a single whole."[37]

In contrast to Westerners, the Chinese didn't view humans as separate from nature. The idea that all of nature was created to serve humans, such a powerful underlying theme in Western thought, was seen as rather ludicrous. A delightful classic story highlights this point. A lord held a banquet to which a thousand guests were invited, many bringing gifts of fish and game. Eyeing them approvingly, he exclaimed, "How generous is Heaven to man! Heaven makes the grains grow, and brings forth the fish and fowl, especially for our benefit!" Everyone applauded, except for a twelve-year-old son of one of the guests, who came forward and said:

> It is not as my Lord says. We belong to the same category of living beings as all the creatures of the world. It is only through size, strength or cunning, that one species gains mastery or feeds upon another. Man catches and eats what is fitting for his food, but how can you say that Heaven produced them just for him? Mosquitoes and gnats suck his blood; tigers and wolves devour his flesh—but we don't assert that Heaven produced man for the benefit of mosquitoes and gnats, or for tigers and wolves.[38]

Rather than holding DOMINION OVER NATURE, humans were seen as embedded in a triad with heaven and earth. In contrast to the Western belief in fixed laws of nature handed down by a DIVINE LAWGIVER, the Chinese saw nature as a self-organized system in which all the parts fit harmoniously together. As the ancient commentator Wangbi pointed out, "We do not see Heaven command the four seasons, and yet they do not swerve from their course."[39]

The *Tao Te Ching* returns again and again to the theme of how nature works harmoniously without a DIVINE LAWGIVER:

[illegible] portrayal of the natural world and humanity is fascinating. In some paintings, there is no sign of humanity whatsoever, but usually the human presence can be found unobtrusively within the landscape, as though it were a natural outcropping. For example, in a famous painting by Li Cheng named "Buddhist Temple in the Hills after Rain" (figure 15.2), the temple in the center fits delicately into its environment, dwarfed by the towering mountains, seeming to belong there as naturally as the trees surrounding it. This contrasts strikingly with the predominant European artistic tradition, which tends to show humans as central to the composition while using the natural landscape as a backdrop, as in Leonardo da Vinci's iconic masterpiece "Mona Lisa" (figure 15.3).[42]

Figure 15.2: "Buddhist Temple in the Hills After Rain" by Li Cheng

Figure 15.3: "Mona Lisa" by Leonardo da Vinci

European Cycle of Domination

Even with this reverence toward nature, China has experienced a long history of environmental degradation. The construction of the Great Wall, for example, resulted in vast deforestation, which caused greater sediment loads in the Yellow River, leading to massive flooding that displaced two-thirds of the local population. In our modern era, as the world faces a slew of environmental crises potentially threatening the long-term sustainability of our civilization, we must ask how to interpret this mismatch of the underlying metaphor of nature and the testament of history. Does the Chinese experience imply that, regardless of how humans approach the natural world, we are doomed to mismanage it anyway? Does it indicate that the traditional Chinese approach to the natural world was not as harmonious as its art and philosophical writings suggest?[43]

A clue to this conundrum may be found in the experience of our hunter-

[illegible]

This feedback loop, initiated in Western Europe, has transformed the entire world. It portrays humanity as holding a birthright of DOMINION OVER NATURE, to CONQUER NATURE, to use NATURE AS MACHINE, and thus "truly to command the world." All human societies have used their conceptualizing abilities to exploit the natural world—and other humans—to a greater or lesser degree. But, in Western Europe, this feedback cycle generated a new conception of power and made exploitation possible on a scale previously inconceivable. The story of this dramatic transformation in power and exploitation is the subject of the next chapter.

Chapter 16

GREAT RATS: THE STORY OF POWER AND EXPLOITATION

What was in Admiral Zheng's mind when he set off from China in 1405 with his massive armada? What was his ambition—for himself and the Chinese emperor? Over the course of the next three decades and seven long voyages, Zheng and his expeditionary force would visit a spectacular array of places ranging from East Africa to Arabia and Sri Lanka to Sumatra. He wasn't afraid to use his military might when needed, suppressing piracy and influencing local politics when he deemed it helpful. He could have done virtually anything he wanted to the places he visited: enslave the populations, mine their mineral wealth, and entrench China's empire throughout the vast expanse of the Indian Ocean. Instead, he set up embassies in China's capital, Nanjing, with emissaries from Japan, Malaya, Vietnam, and Egypt.

It was Christopher Columbus, later that century, and the Europeans who followed who would rapidly dominate the world—conquering entire continents, massacring and enslaving their inhabitants, and pillaging their natural resources. Why did Zheng, with his glorious armada, merely set up embassies, while Columbus's three meager boats would change the destiny of the world in unimaginable ways?

It's a topic that has intrigued historians for generations, and one we'll investigate in this chapter. Before we can answer it, though, we need to go further back into history. All the way back to the beginning of the human story. Once we understand how humans learned to harness energy from the world around them and use it for power and exploitation, we can identify common elements of civilizations throughout history and where and when the fateful divergence took place that led to the modern world.

[illegible]

With the rise of agriculture, there arose a new form of energy to exploit: the energy of other human beings, now locked into static communities. As we saw earlier, when someone in a hunter-gatherer band tried to gain too much power the group would block him. Through the collective force of ridicule and group intervention, the uniquely human instinct for fairness had been able to hold in check the ancient male primate drive for dominance. As a last resort, if someone didn't like what was going on, he could just walk away and join another band.

For those now living in fixed agrarian communities, this was no longer the case. The harder-working or luckier few accumulated livestock, goods, and land while others found themselves dispossessed. Hierarchies arose along with concepts of property and wealth, permitting—for the select few—that older instinct for dominance to trump the more recent instinct for fairness. Inequalities within a community gradually spread to become inequalities between communities, as one community would use force to conquer another and exploit its workers. Like so many other aspects of cultural evolution, this created a ratchet effect, in which the success of one type of behavior further encouraged that behavior, leading to its intensification until it became the dominant form. Through this process, the more efficient energy use of agriculture led to population growth and technological superiority, until the agriculturalists finally took over all the useful land from their hunter-gatherer neighbors. With the help of hierarchies and property, the ancient instinct for dominance resurfaced as the main driver of human history.[4]

"The Earth Turned White"

The spread of agriculture affected the human experience so pervasively that it's considered the most profound revolution in human history. It had a similarly momentous impact on the natural world: so dramatic that the scale of changes brought about by agriculture over the past ten thousand years has been compared to the impact of the asteroid that killed off the dinosaurs sixty-five million years ago.[5]

Apart from obvious changes to the landscape, there have been more subtle but equally profound changes in the population of plants and animals inhabiting the earth. The domestication of plants led to fewer and fewer species taking most of the land, so that, today, just twenty species of plant provide 90 percent of the vegetable food people eat. Along with the wild plants disappeared wild animals, such as the lions, tigers, elephants, rhinoceroses, and zebras that lived in the Mediterranean region until the rise of the Roman Empire.[6]

For the generations of farmers effecting these changes, this could all be seen as a sign of success: the ever-increasing efficiency by which humans were squeezing more energy out of the environment. Disturbingly, however, a mismatch began to emerge between the power of the human patterning instinct to exploit the environment and the ability of that environment to sustain itself. We already saw this mismatch in the experience of early hunter-gatherers as they colonized new territories and gradually drove most of the large animals they discovered to extinction. The imbalance became more pronounced with the spread of agriculture, as the technological prowess of civilization led to increases in human population, putting greater pressure on the productivity of the land until the cycle became unsustainable.[7]

[illegible] great [illegible] experienced the [illegible] [illegible] civilization [illegible] collapse [illegible] when the Spaniards arrived in [illegible], only about [illegible] thousand people remained, with so little [illegible] that the Spanish nearly starved. [illegible]

[illegible]

[illegible] This process can be seen particularly in the Mediterranean and Near East, where [illegible]. The Mediterranean landscape, loved nowadays for its [illegible], olive trees, and scented herbs, is in fact the result of [illegible] pressure of civilization. Its hillsides were once forested with evergreen [illegible] with oaks, beeches, pines, and cedars, but these were long ago used up for fuel and construction materials.[10]

In no place, though, is the result of agricultural overexploitation seen more starkly than in what is ironically known as the Fertile Crescent, the land around the Tigris and Euphrates in present-day Iraq. This desolate landscape, now largely treeless, was the cradle of the great civilizations of Mesopotamia, but the impressive achievements that led to the growth of civilization there also led to its downfall. The extensive irrigation that gave rise to Mesopotamia's strong, centralized institutions caused continual waterlogging of the soil, which, after evaporation in the hot sun, left a residue of salt that gradually accumulated to make the land increasingly infertile. Over the centuries, crop yields fell by two-thirds. Inscriptions from as early as 2000 BCE describe how "the earth turned white," a clear reference to the impact of salinization. This grim history is told dolefully by the Mesopotamians themselves in a lamentation called *The Curse of Akkad*:

> For the first time since cities were built and founded,
> The great agricultural tracts produced no grain,
> The inundated tracts produced no fish,
> The irrigated orchards produced neither syrup nor wine. . . .
> He who slept in the house, had no burial,
> People were flailing at themselves from hunger.[11*]

"Great Rats, Keep Away from Our Wheat!"

The exploitation of natural resources through agriculture, pervasive as it was, pales in comparison to the increased exploitation of other humans. The hierarchical structuring of society that began with agriculture fundamentally changed the human experience like no other event in history. Wherever agriculture spread, the small communities of kin that characterized hunter-gatherer society coalesced into larger social structures known as chiefdoms. Usually, a chiefdom would consist of thousands of people living in multiple villages headed by local chiefs who gave their allegiance to the "big chief."[12]

These chiefdoms inevitably followed the power ratchet effect: a society's increase in size and complexity led to greater military strength, which enabled it to conquer neighboring communities, further expanding its size and hierarchy. Typically, a tiny ruling elite, supported by specialists such as artisans, bureaucrats, and soldiers, would use its power to systematically appropriate wealth from everyone else, enabling the rulers to enjoy a life of luxury that distinguished them from the masses. The greater the inequality, the more the rulers learned to use brute force to exploit those around them. Elites everywhere luxuriated in displays of wealth and conspicuous consumption.[13]

The hierarchical structuring of society extended to gender inequality. The household came to be viewed as a miniature kingdom, with the male head as the ruler and the women and children his subjects. Female identity was defined by subordination to male gender roles. A set of tablets from Assyria spelling out royal decrees reveals a graphic example of these ancient gender inequities.

[illegible] strict social laws for women, who were totally dependent on the head of the household and severely punished for any transgression. Access to women in the palace was carefully monitored; if a palace woman met a man without an attendant, both would be killed. Outside the palace, women's rights were just as strictly circumscribed. At the bottom of the social hierarchy, a prostitute who covered herself would be punished with fifty lashes, her clothes taken away, and hot pitch poured over her head.[14]

For the most part, extremes of inequality in the great agrarian civilizations came to be regarded as the normal condition. However, a fascinating document [illegible] around 2350 BCE [illegible] possibly the [illegible] their oppres[illegible] [illegible] ruthlessly exploiting [illegible] [illegible] the people [illegible] overseer [illegible] pay; [illegible] were thrown into jail [illegible] which were required for burial in the cemetery. Artisans and apprentices were reduced to abject poverty and had to beg for food. Prisoners of war were [illegible] and forced to water the fields [illegible] only enough rations [illegible] alive. [illegible] [illegible] the [illegible] [illegible] and enacted a series of reforms for [illegible] recorded [illegible] the document [illegible] generally translated as "freedom."[15]

In China, too, occasional references [illegible] the ruthless exploitation of the common people. The oldest collection of Chinese poetry, the *Book of Odes*, contains bursts of outrage at the greed of the ruling classes that remain fresh to this day:

Men had their land and farms
But you (the feudal lord) now have them,
Men had their people and their folk
But you have seized them from them. . . .
Great rats, great rats,
Keep away from our wheat!
These three years we have worked for you
But you despised us.[16]

These fervent cries of rage, we may assume, expressed the feelings of untold millions of oppressed peasants across the globe. They were, however, no match for the military might of the ruling classes, who frequently seemed driven to push the boundaries of human exploitation as far as they would go. There was a limit to how much luxury an elite group could indulge in, but when it came to constructing monuments to their greatness, the possibilities seemed almost limitless. In many cases, pyramids were the construction of choice, conveying a symbolic connection between the society's rulers and divine power. The Great Pyramid in Egypt is estimated to have taken twenty years to build, with a hundred thousand men levied annually to transport blocks of stone from the quarry. Ten thousand workmen are believed to have taken twenty years to construct the Pyramid of the Sun at Teotihuacan, Mexico. In Cambodia, a hundred thousand workers were involved in constructing the great shrine of Pra Khan.[17]

Other construction projects had more down-to-earth goals but required even vaster scales of human fodder, such as the Grand Canal in China, which brought food from the south of the country to the capital and involved more than five million conscripted peasants guarded by fifty thousand police. It's estimated that about half the workers died on the job before the project was finished. Millions more died in building the Great Wall of China, designed to keep out the Mongols, who, when they succeeded in breaking through China's fortifications, engaged in their own brutal exploitation, removing people from their homes and resettling them in Siberia and Mongolia, where they were forced into the mines.[18]

Perhaps the ultimate form of exploitation was the institution of slavery: taking away all rights and using people as no more than property. In China, slavery had little impact on the bulk of the population, with laws generally preventing free Chinese from being enslaved. However, in the Mediterranean and, most markedly, the Roman Empire, slavery took on a far bigger profile. When the Romans conquered other nations, they had no compunction about enslaving virtually the entire population. After the 209 BCE conquest of Tarentum, 130,000 inhabitants were sold into slavery, and, after suppressing a revolt in Sardinia in 177 BCE, the Romans sent 80,000 of the island's inhabitants back to Rome as slaves. The magnitude of the slave trade during the Roman Empire was staggering, with ten thousand slaves a day arriving through the single port of Delos. By the first century CE, there are estimated to have been two to three million slaves in Italy, making up about a third of the country's population.[19]

The rise of Christianity did nothing to challenge the Roman approach to slavery. Wealthy Christians owned slaves [illegible] and were supported in this by their theologians. The New Testament book [illegible] exhorts, "Slaves, be obedient to the ones who are called your masters in the world, with deep [illegible] as to Christ." Augustine went further, suggesting that slavery is God's punishment for sin, writing, "The primary cause of slavery, then, is sin [illegible] and this can only be by a judgment of God."[20]

[illegible] and Columbus

[illegible]

[illegible] the question of why [illegible] the "proximate" direct explanations, he approaches the problem from a geographic perspective, demonstrating how the Eurasian continent, with its east-west axis, permitted the spread of agricultural innovations to similar climatic zones, which then catalyzed further cultural advances. He shows how the crops and animals available to Eurasian farmers were more malleable for domestication than those in other continents. Domestication led to outbreaks throughout Eurasia of infectious diseases as animal-borne microbes adapted to their new human hosts. Over generations, survivors of these epidemics developed resistance, whereas people living in other continents remained vulnerable. It was through the deadly and fortuitous combination of the guns, germs, and steel of the book's title, Diamond explains, that Europeans were able to conquer the rest of the world.[21]

Diamond's book offers a profound and satisfying explanation for the different rates of development between Eurasia and the rest of the world. However it doesn't give as satisfactory an answer to the question posed at the beginning of this chapter: why did the massive armada of Admiral Zheng leave such a limited impression on history, while the three flimsy boats of Christopher Columbus transformed the world beyond recognition? After all, the Chinese had gunpowder and steel in far greater quantities than the Europeans, and they were equally resistant to the germs of Eurasia.[22*]

One answer is that the Europeans approached the world with fundamentally different values than the Chinese, one of which was their approach to power. As a result of the dualistic split in European cognition, the collective European mind-set was more predisposed to use knowledge as a means to gain power over the environment, including both the natural world and other human societies. In contrast, the collective Chinese mind-set was predisposed to use knowledge as a means of maintaining stability. The foundational frames of European thought that we've been exploring—their religious absolutism, their sense of dominion over the natural world, and their mission to conquer nature—underlaid and shaped the European attitude toward their voyages of discovery.

While there may have been more immediate explanations for the divergent approaches taken by Zheng and Columbus, the ultimate cause for the difference lay in the construction of values that they both shared unquestioningly with their respective cultures. These contrasting cognitive structures made it just as unthinkable for Admiral Zheng to have conquered and enslaved the societies he visited with his armada as it would have been unthinkable for Columbus to have set up embassies with the indigenous people he encountered in the New World.

The European Approach to Power

The cognitive gap between Europe and China is traceable throughout the history of both civilizations and is evidenced in the different way each society responded to innovations in technology. Take, for example, the story of stirrups.

Horses were ridden for thousands of years before anyone came up with the idea of using stirrups to help a rider maintain balance. The first evidence of the use of stirrups comes from Buddhist carved reliefs, discovered in India, that date back to the second century BCE. The practice gradually spread to China, and, by the fourth century, figures from Chinese imperial tombs are shown using stirrups. They became widely used in the ensuing centuries but had negligible impact on the course of Chinese history. However, when stirrups [illegible] Europe in the eighth century, it [illegible] transformed the [illegible] the European predilection for [illegible] technological innovation to [illegible] over adversaries is vividly [illegible] cavalrymen began [illegible] Europe to effectively weld themselves [illegible] their horse, applying the force [illegible] to deliver a blow to the enemy with sword or lance. It was the stirrup that made the mounted knight, encased in his protective armor, the [illegible] of medieval Europe, [illegible] the tradition of chivalry and [illegible] Europe for [illegible] millennium.[24]

[illegible] the innovation of stirrups helped set up the feudal structure of [illegible] Chinese imperial [illegible] equally powerful [illegible] breaking down that structure [illegible] technological innovation [illegible] [illegible] gunpowder was incorporated into the military, the effects [illegible] The fortified castle, which had become the [illegible] [illegible] medieval Europe would come tumbling down along with the [illegible]

The pattern that emerges from these two stories is the propensity of Europeans to use innovative technologies to change the rules of the game and thus gain a power advantage. This proclivity seems to arise from a deep structure in European cognition that identifies power as a value in itself, even if gaining such power causes massive disequilibrium. One is reminded of the core Proto-Indo-European word **reg-* or king (discussed earlier), with its constellation of meanings that have passed into PIE-based cultures ever since, conceptually linking words such as *royal, right, regulate,* and *correct* into an underlying sense that, ultimately, "might is right."[25]

In China, by contrast, the predominant approach to power was to maintain society's equilibrium in the context of heaven and earth, something the emperor was obligated to do through his "mandate of heaven." Military might was seen as a force to use only when necessary to maintain stability. We can see this cultural contrast in the bewildered reactions of the first Europeans arriving in China.

Matteo Ricci, who set up the first Jesuit outpost there, was horrified by the lack of respect the Chinese showed toward their military. "Amongst us," he wrote home, "it is held to be a fine thing to see an armed man, but to them it seems evil, and they have a fear of seeing anything so horrible. . . . They consider that the most honourable man is he who flees and does not wish to harm another. . . . Whereas amongst our people the noblest and bravest become soldiers, in China it is the vilest and most cowardly who attend to matters of war."[26]

What emerges is a contrast not just between European and Chinese values but between the unique European approach to power and the norms of other major civilizations. Another illuminating example can be found in the Portuguese disruption of traditional trading practices in South Asia in the early sixteenth century. For many centuries, the four sea powers that plied the ocean stretching from the Arabian to the South China Seas all had a shared interest in trading, and they maintained unwritten rules for peaceful coexistence. They would respect each other's ships and often carried goods and passengers for each other. However, as soon as the first Portuguese sailors came across this peaceful situation in 1498, everything changed forever. Within two years, Portuguese captain Pedro Cabral attacked and seized Muslim ships loading pepper at Calicut. Violence erupted on both sides, and, in the ensuing years, the Portuguese forced a series of treaties on the entire region, giving them the right to buy products below market prices and sell "permits" to allow other ships to pass, which they violently enforced. Through military action, they radically restructured the entire trading system of the Indian Ocean. Importantly, this drastic change didn't take place through technological superiority: the Chinese still had far more advanced ships at their disposal. It came about because the seas of South Asia had for centuries been a trouble-free, peaceful zone, and the Portuguese were ready and willing to change the rules of the game through violence. Historian Janet Abu-Lughod notes that "the 'takeover' of [the preexisting] system was certainly not according to the old rules. . . . More than anything else, then, it was the new European approach to trade-cum-plunder that caused a basic transformation in the world system that had developed and persisted over some five centuries."[27]

Alexander and Ashoka

How deeply ingrained in European culture was this readiness to violently disrupt an equilibrium for the sake of power? An unscientific but intriguing [illegible] of two legendary [illegible] this European mind-set goes all the way back to the birth of Western culture in ancient Greece.

Even today, after more than two millennia, people are awed by the breathtaking military feats of Alexander the Great (356–323 BCE), who created one of the largest empires in the ancient world in a few short years, conquering the entire Persian Empire and then, desiring to reach the "ends of the world and the Great Outer Sea," led a campaign to invade India, only turning back when his army threatened mutiny. Historians have long wondered about the psychology underlying Alexander's spectacular achievements. In the words of one, "Alexander seems increasingly to have seen his progress in terms of a Grail-like quest for the apparently unattainable. He sought the 'ocean,' the ultimate limit of terrestrial [illegible]

[illegible] This European approach to power [illegible] According to ancient legend, the Phrygians [illegible] prophesied that the first person to enter the capital in an oxcart would become their king. The peasant Gordias was that man, and he dedicated his [illegible] with an elaborate knot. The oracle then prophesied that whoever untied the knot would become the king of all Asia. [illegible] When Alexander arrived there, he came up with a devastatingly simple solution: He drew his sword and sliced the knot cleanly in half. As the oracle predicted, he did go on to become ruler of all Asia. The significance of the story is that Alexander's approach established a paradigm of power for the later episodes we've been examining regarding stirrups, gunpowder, and the Portuguese transformation of the South Asian trading system. In each case, an equilibrium was destroyed by violating the previous rules of the game with brute force. Most importantly, instead of being condemned as cheating, Alexander's behavior was lauded to the extent that it became the stuff of legend.[32]

Now let's turn to another great ruler of ancient times: Ashoka of India (304–232 BCE), who inherited an empire covering most of the Indian subcontinent, forged by his grandfather Chandragupta. Ashoka showed military prowess himself, conquering the region of Kalinga, which we know about because he erected a monument commemorating his achievement. What is amazing about this monument is how Ashoka describes what he has done: rather than glorying in his conquest, Ashoka, now converted to the new religion of Buddhism, laments the destruction he has caused. In his own words:

> On conquering Kalinga the Beloved of the Gods [His Majesty] felt remorse, for, when an independent country is conquered, the slaughter, death and deportation of the people is extremely grievous to the Beloved of the Gods and weighs heavily on his mind. . . . Today if a hundredth or a thousandth part of those people who were killed or died or were deported when Kalinga was annexed were to suffer similarly, it would weigh heavily on the mind of the Beloved of the Gods. . . .

Perhaps even more remarkable than Ashoka's self-recrimination is the admonition he then offers his descendants:

> This inscription of *dhamma*[30] has been engraved so that any sons or great-grandsons that I may have should not think of gaining new conquests. . . . They should only consider conquest by *dhamma* to be a true conquest, and delight in *dhamma* should be their whole delight.[31]

In the words of Indian historian R. K. Mookerji: "Herein lies the greatness of Ashoka. Even as a mere pious sentiment this is hard to beat; at least no victorious monarch in the history of the world is known to have ever given expression to anything like it."[32]

These are, of course, just two rulers out of a host of monarchs throughout history, but their stories stand in stark contrast to each other and appear emblematic of two contrasting approaches to the meaning of power. Ashoka did not believe in relinquishing power itself but rather in using it to promote an enlightened set of values, an approach that was not unique to him but imbued in his culture. During the reign of his grandfather, a classic of statecraft named the *Arthasastra* was written, which advises how a ruler should treat nations conquered in battle. "Having acquired new territory," it declares, "the conqueror shall substitute his virtues for the enemy's vices and where the enemy was good, he shall be twice as good. He shall follow policies that are pleasing and beneficial by acting according to his *dharma* and by granting favours and exemptions, giving gifts, and bestowing honours."[33]

Was this still, however, no more than "mere pious sentiment"? Judging by the history of regions that came under Indian influence, we can infer that Indian rulers of the time were closer to Admiral Zheng than Columbus in their world superpower. The southeast corner of Southeast Asia became known as "the [illegible] India" because of the tremendous cultural, religious, and political prominence of the Indian subcontinent in their history. Indian historians indeed refer to these countries in antiquity as "Indian colonies." However, rather than being conquered and pillaged like the European colonies of the past few centuries, they became part of a peaceful trading network that advanced their security and cultural sophistication.[illegible]

Throughout history, there have, of course, been all kinds of brutal conquerors with no qualms about slaughtering their enemies and viciously terrorizing their subjects. But the Europeans added into the mix a uniquely disruptive approach to conquest. Historian Joel Mokyr notes the Europeans' "frame of mind when they arrived at the New World [illegible] [illegible] [illegible] [illegible] [illegible] [illegible] [illegible] The question was always: is it useful? Can it be [illegible]?"[illegible]

What, then, actually happened when the Europeans applied their unique values to two entire continents that lay ripe for the slaughter?

"With Fifty Men We Could Subjugate Them All"

When Christopher Columbus discovered the New World in 1492, his letters back to King Ferdinand and Queen Isabella of Spain palpably demonstrate the mind-set Mokyr describes, moving effortlessly from initial awe to plans for violent exploitation of the Arawak people he encountered. "They are so artless and so free with all they possess," he writes, "that no one would believe it without having seen it. Of anything they have, if you ask them for it, they never say no, rather they invite the person to share it, and show as much love as if they were giving their hearts." He was equally amazed by their lack of weaponry, reporting, "They do not bear arms, and do not know them, for I showed them a sword, they took it by the edge and cut themselves out of ignorance." Then, his mind wanders to thoughts of exploitation. "They would make fine servants," he reflects. "Should your Majesties command it, all the inhabitants could be taken away to Castile [Spain], or made slaves on the island. With fifty men we could subjugate them all and make them do whatever we want."[36]

Within a few short years, these musings of power and exploitation would come true beyond Columbus's wildest dreams. Some of the most astonishing stories in history recount the way the greatest empires of the New World—the Aztecs and the Incas—were laid waste by two small bands of Spanish explorers led respectively by Hernando Cortés and Francisco Pizarro. When Cortés first arrived at the gates of the Aztec capital of Tenochtitlán in 1519 with fewer than a thousand Spanish soldiers, his entire group could have been wiped out by the Aztecs, whose formidable warriors firmly controlled the central region of Mexico. Instead, they were welcomed in friendship and invited into the city to join a festive celebration. The Spanish promptly betrayed their hosts' welcome and began slaughtering the singers and dancers, chopping off their hands and heads and disemboweling them with their swords. They then retreated from the panicked crowd to the royal palace, where they took the Aztec ruler Montezuma as hostage. Once the Aztecs realized their terrible mistake, they tried to fight back, but it was too late. Within two years, their empire was gone forever, and Cortés claimed their territory for Spain, renaming the capital Mexico City. Inspired by Cortés's achievement, Pizarro set out a few years later to emulate his conquest, targeting the Inca Empire of South America. With fewer than two hundred soldiers facing an army of eighty thousand Inca warriors, Pizarro also used the strategy of surprise and betrayal to meet the Inca leader Atahualpa face to face, then began slaughtering Atahualpa's troops while taking him hostage. Within a year, the capital, Cuzco, was conquered, and the Inca Empire was no more.[37]

In *Guns, Germs, and Steel,* Jared Diamond cogently analyzes the clash of cultures that led to this one-sided conflict between the Spanish and the empires of the New World. He identifies some major factors for these routs, such as the industrial infrastructure that permitted the Spanish to sail to the New World in the first place; their use of horses, swords, and guns; and the devastating impact of the diseases they brought with them. One factor, however, that is left out of the discussion, but which underlies the entire European conquest of the New World, is the vastly different conceptualizations of power and warfare held by each side.[38]

For the Aztecs, who believed they needed the blood of human sacrifice to keep the sun in motion, warfare was a sacred endeavor to provide a continual supply of victims to propitiate the gods. The Aztecs thus conceptualized power literally in terms of the fuel needed to keep the sun rising each day. The sacred nature of warfare meant that treachery or fraud was unthinkable. They would announce their intentions to conquer a city in advance and would even send along food and weapons to the inhabitants, making sure they had a worthy adversary in battle. It was for this reason that they acted in a way that our modern viewpoint deems hopelessly naïve, inviting Cortés's soldiers into their city to join their celebration. The idea of such treachery was inconceivable to them, just as it had been inconceivable for anyone to break the legendary Gordian knot until Alexander drew his sword and sliced it in half.[39]

A similar split in concepts of power and warfare existed in North America between the native people and the English settlers. A British colonist of the seventeenth century records the following statement made to him by a Lenape Indian:

> We are minded to live at Peace: If we intend at any time to make War upon you, we will let you know of it, and the Reasons why we make War with you; and if you make us satisfaction for the Injury done us, for which the War is intended, then we will not make War on you. And if you intend at any time to make War on us, we would have you let us know of it, and the Reasons for which you make War on us, and then if we do not make satisfaction for the injury done unto you, then you may make War on us, otherwise you ought not to do it.[40]

Bizarre as this attitude seems to the modern mind (as well as to the seventeenth-century British), it made sense in a culture where warfare was a ritualized form of gaining honor rather than [illegible] to kill. The objective of the Plains Indians [illegible], contrary to the popular image of whooping hordes of aggressive ferocity, focused on the courage and honor of the individual warrior rather than defeating the enemy. Nineteenth-century anthropologist George Bird Grinnell described how the "bravest act that could be performed" was to come into personal contact with the enemy by touching him, known as counting coup:

> It was regarded as evidence of bravery for a man to go into battle carrying no weapon that would do any harm at a distance. It was more creditable to carry a lance than a bow and arrows; more creditable to carry a hatchet or war club than a lance; and the bravest thing of all was to go into a fight with nothing more than a whip, or a long twig—sometimes called a coup stick.[41]

English settlers in the seventeenth century, noticing this lack of killing, were contemptuous of the North American methods of warfare. Captain John Mason referred to the Indians' "feeble manner . . . [that] did hardly deserve the name of fighting." Captain Henry Spelman noted that the native warriors lacked "dissipline," with the result that there was no great "slawter of nether side." Instead, once "having shott away most of their arrows," both sides commonly "weare glad to retier."[42]

When the British arrived in the New World, they were astonished by the warmth of those who greeted them. Captain Arthur Barlowe landed in Virginia in 1584 and reported that "we were entertained with all love and kindness and with as much bounty, after their manner, as they could possibly devise. We found the people most gentle loving and faithfull, void of all guile and treason." Before too long, however, the "guile and treason" of the British transformed the relationship between the two groups. In their own words, "We burnt, and spoyled their corne, and Towne, all the people being fledde." As violence erupted, the British soon modified their view of the Indians, describing them as "wild beasts, and unreasonable creatures . . . brutish savages, which by reason of their godless ignorance, and blasphemous Idolatrie, are worse than those beasts which are of most wilde and savage nature."[43]

Untrammeled Exploitation

In the New World, the Europeans found an opportunity for exploitation, the magnitude of which had never occurred in history nor ever would again. Here were two continents, rich with natural resources and inhabited by people unable to defend themselves against European power. It wasn't even necessary—as in the South Asian seas—to change the rules of the game. The rules of this particular game were waiting to be written by the Europeans, who did exactly that—and, in doing so, they caused what is probably the greatest holocaust in all of human history. In every region the European explorers discovered, a ravaging of the local population ensued of almost unimaginable proportions. The population of central Mexico was twenty million in 1500, four times greater than Britain. Within a century, there were fewer than one million people alive there. Similarly, the population of the Inca Empire collapsed from eleven million in 1500 to fewer than a million in 1600. It's been estimated that, in the sixteenth century alone, close to one hundred million indigenous people died in the Americas through slaughter, starvation, or disease. As historian David Stannard concludes, "The destruction of the Indians of the Americas was, far and away, the most massive act of genocide in the history of the world."[44]

There is no doubt that the single biggest cause of death in the New World was the barrage of new diseases the Europeans brought. At times, some historians have gone so far as to suggest that this catastrophe was inadvertent: a sad but inevitable consequence of human progress. A more realistic interpretation, however, is that, in Stannard's words, "disease and genocide were interdependent forces acting dynamically—whipsawing their victims between plague and violence, each one feeding upon the other, and together driving countless numbers of entire ancient societies to the brink—and often over the brink—of total extermination."[45]

To gain some sense of the European capacity for unfettered exploitation, one has only to look to the story of Potosí in Bolivia, the location of the richest silver mine discovered by the Spaniards in South America, known as Cerro Rico ("rich hill"). In its heyday, Potosí was a bustling boom town, with 120,000 inhabitants, according to the census of 1573—more than Rome or Paris. By the beginning of the seventeenth century, Potosí boasted thirty-six magnificently decorated churches and imported the finest luxury goods from all over the world. Its wealth was legendary: the streets to the cathedral were said to have been resurfaced with silver bars. But this wealth arose from the wholesale exploitation of the indigenous people forcibly seized from across their territory and used as slave labor for mining the silver. In the words of a contemporary witness: "They are herded into the mountain and . . . beaten with iron bars . . . no light, no air. . . . There the Indians toil all week, prisoners, breathing dust that kills the lungs, and chewing coca that deceives hunger and masks exhaustion, never knowing when night falls or day breaks." The mercury used to extract the silver poisoned the workers, causing their hair and teeth to fall out and bringing uncontrollable trembling: "The victims ended up dragging themselves through the streets pleading for alms." Over the three centuries that the mountain yielded its silver, as many as eight million men, women, and children died in the mines of Potosí, perhaps the greatest number of untimely human deaths ever associated with one particular place. The Spanish mined the silver from Cerro Rico so thoroughly that, by the end, they were sweeping out the last seams with brooms. Today, Potosí is an impoverished town where the few remaining miners use picks and shovels to dig remnants of tin from the earth.[46]

God and Power

The European conquerors used Christian theology as the basis of their rule book for the exploitation of the New World. The leading spokesman for this narrative was eminent Spanish scholar Juan Ginés de Sepúlveda, who explained that the Indians of the New World were intended by God "to be placed under the authority of civilized and virtuous princes or nations, so that they may learn, from the might, wisdom, and law of their conquerors, to practice better morals, worthier customs and a more civilized way of life."[47]

To ensure legal and theological validation for their plunder, the Spanish went through a bizarre process each time they encountered an indigenous community. They would read a statement to the Indians ordering them to swear allegiance to the Pope and the Spanish crown. If the Indians didn't do as commanded (likely, since they wouldn't have understood a word), the statement went on:

> I certify to you that, with the help of God, we shall powerfully enter into your country and shall make war against you in all ways and manners that we can, and shall subject you to the yoke and obedience of the Church and of Their Highnesses. We shall take you and your wives and your children, and shall make slaves of them, and as such shall sell and dispose of them as Their Highnesses may command. And we shall take your goods, and shall do you all the mischief and damage that we can, as to vassals who do not obey and refuse to receive their lord and resist and contradict him.

With this proclamation, known as the *requerimiento*, the Spanish considered the pillaging of the New World to be legally and morally justified.[48]

Even the diseases the Europeans brought with them were widely believed to be a demonstration of God's support. An influential Spanish priest, Father Domingo de Betanzos, proclaimed in the early days of the conquest that God had condemned the entire Indian race to perish because of their sinful paganism. This laid the foundation for a viewpoint embraced wholeheartedly by later generations, so that, in 1843, respected American historian W. H. Prescott could write, "It was beneficially ordered by Providence that the land should be delivered over to another race, who would rescue it from the brutish superstitions that daily extended wider and wider."[49]

There are innumerable British accounts claiming God as an active participant in the gruesome massacres of the indigenous people. In describing a British attack on the Pequot Indians in 1636, Captain John Mason echoes the more bloodthirsty passages of the Old Testament:

> And indeed such a dreadful Terror did the Almighty let fall upon their Spirits, that they would fly from us and run into the very Flames, where many of them perished. . . . [And] God was above them, who laughed his Enemies and the Enemies of his People to Scorn, making them as a fiery Oven. . . . Thus did the Lord judge among the Heathen, filling the Place with dead Bodies![50]

Like the Spanish, the British were certain that the diseases they brought with them were God's vehicle for clearing their path to conquest. This attitude became so ingrained that even Benjamin Franklin, known for his otherwise tolerant values, gladly justified the slaughter of the Indians, writing of "the design of Providence to extirpate those savages in order to make room for the cultivators of the earth."[51]

The underlying theme of the European conquest was that the exploitation of the New World was not only theologically justified but indeed a moral obligation. This line of thought was reinforced by the DOMINION OVER NATURE metaphor that shaped the European rationale of private property as a righteous reward for "improving the land." Sir Thomas More argued that it was justifiable to take land from "any people [that] holdeth a piece of ground void and vacant to no good or profitable use." Before long, this idea was given the status of a legal doctrine, known as *vacuum domicilium*, which was used to legitimize European settlement of the New World.[52]

The growth of the Protestant ethic led to an even tighter linkage of morality and exploitation, broadening the theme to incorporate any kind of wealth creation. Richard Baxter, an influential early Protestant theologian, specified the moral obligation to exploit one's resources, writing that "if God show you a way in which you *may*, in accord with His laws, acquire *more profit* than in another way, without wrong to your soul or to any other and if you refuse this, choosing the less profitable course, *you then cross one of the purposes of your calling. You are refusing to be God's steward, and to accept his gifts.*"[53]

Exploitation as Racial Destiny

As the early British settlers exerted their powers to exploit the indigenous people of the New World, back in England Francis Bacon was introducing his metaphor of CONQUERING NATURE, one that was intimately bound up with notions of power and exploitation. One of Bacon's most famous dicta is the phrase *ipsa scientia potestas est*—"knowledge itself is power." For all his violent rhetoric, Bacon believed the ultimate purpose of this power was to benefit all humanity, writing, "I would address one general admonition to all: that they consider what are the true ends of knowledge, and that they seek it not either for pleasure of the mind, or for contention, or for superiority to others . . . but for the benefit and use of life, and that they perfect and govern it in charity." From what he saw as "the marriage of the Mind and the Universe," he hoped there would spring "a line and race of inventions that may in some degree subdue and overcome the necessities and miseries of humanity," concluding that "those twin objects, human knowledge and human power, do really meet in one."[54]

The generations of Europeans following Bacon took to heart his vision of the unity of knowledge and power but appeared to ignore his admonition to use their power to benefit others. Instead, they used their technological breakthroughs to subjugate and exploit those who lived in other continents, with ever more efficiency.[55]

After the Industrial Revolution, the countries of northern Europe took over from Spain and Portugal as leaders in exploiting the rest of the world. Their success was enormous. By the end of the nineteenth century, Great Britain alone, with a population of forty-five million people, ruled over nearly five hundred million subjects in colonies around the globe. More than half the continent of Asia was governed by Europe, along with more than 90 percent of Africa and 99 percent of Polynesia.[56]

Europeans took advantage of their access to both Africa and the New World to institute the slave trade, transporting slaves captured in Africa to work in plantations of the West Indies and North and South America. This began on a small scale in the sixteenth century, reaching its height in the eighteenth century with the transport of more than six million slaves in that century alone. It's estimated that, in total, about twelve million people were shipped to the Americas as slaves. The conditions in the boats were so terrible that about onefifth of those who were transported died on board.[57]

The abolition of the slave trade throughout the British Empire in 1807 marked the beginning of the end of this particularly egregious form of exploitation. However, the European powers simply looked elsewhere for their continued exploitation of other races. They instituted systems of indentured labor, transporting millions of workers from India, China, and the Pacific Islands to territories where they were needed. In the century following 1834, approximately thirty million Indians left their home country to work as indentured laborers across the world, along with another thirty million Chinese, suffering conditions so harsh that this system was frequently referred to as the "new form of slavery." This vast global scheme of human trafficking was not only endorsed by the colonial powers, it became the very basis for their continued exploitation. In the breathless words of Cecil Rhodes, a British colonial magnate of the late nineteenth century: "We must find new lands from which we can easily obtain raw materials and at the same time exploit the cheap slave labor that is available from the natives of the colonies. The colonies would also provide a dumping ground for the surplus goods produced in our factories."[58]

As they swept their way across the world, restructuring its demographics while condemning untold millions to the servitude that fueled their ever-increasing wealth, the Europeans were as convinced as their colonial forebears of the moral rectitude of their exploitation. With science replacing Christianity as a framework for making sense of the world, leading European thinkers showed great dexterity in appropriating the new way of thinking as further justification for world domination. The early-nineteenth-century French naturalist George Leopold Cuvier contributed to a newly emerging field of scientific racism by declaring that "the Caucasian race has given rise to the most civilized nations, to those which have generally held the rest in subjection."[59]

Early affirmations of Caucasian racial superiority were given a more robust platform with the publication in 1859 of Darwin's theory of evolution. Although Darwin himself never applied his theory to social evolution, Herbert Spencer—one of his early advocates—was only too eager to do so. His approach, known as social Darwinism, soon became the new philosophical foundation for theories of European superiority, giving imperialists what seemed like a moral duty based in biology to dominate the rest of the world.[60]

The new racist ideology of white supremacy rapidly spread throughout the world. The following, for example, passed as acceptable scientific material in late-nineteenth-century Australia:

> To the Aryan . . . apparently belong the destinies of the future. The races . . . who rest content in . . . placid sensuality and unprogressive decrepitude, can hardly hope to contend permanently in the great struggle for existence. . . . The survival of the fittest means that might—wisely used—is right. And thus we invoke and remorselessly fulfil the inexorable law of natural selection when exterminating the inferior Australian.[61]

As the world entered the twentieth century, this supposed "law of natural selection" was about to be sorely tested. After two world wars, the colonial structures established by the Europeans would get dismantled. The systematic exploitation of the entire world by one region had reached its zenith. However, the massive global inequalities it had created still show no sign of diminishing. Human exploitation continues to ravage billions of lives, with the wealthiest fifth of the world enjoying 70 percent of global income while the poorest fifth scrapes by on just 2 percent.[62]

Meanwhile, the other vector of exploitation—the natural world—has seen exponential rates of increase. At the dawn of Europe's Industrial Revolution, in 1768, scientist Joseph Priestley felt that Bacon's vision of conquering nature was finally coming to pass. "Knowledge, as Lord Bacon observes, being power," he wrote, "the human powers will, in fact, be increased; nature, including both its materials, and its laws, will be more at our command; men will make their situation in this world abundantly more easy and comfortable; they will probably prolong their existence in it, and will grow daily more happy."[63]

Has human power over nature really resulted in greater happiness? We'll explore this in a later chapter, but there is no question that, for many, the human condition has become "more easy and comfortable." While the Europeans took advantage of their power to conquer the rest of the world, their scientific achievements, inspired by the Baconian creed of CONQUERING NATURE, initiated a transformation of the human experience that has been accelerating ever since.

How did this unique transformation occur? Was it inevitable that it occurred in Europe, or could it have happened elsewhere? Was there something exceptional in the cognitive structure of the European worldview that led to it happening there? And if so, how does it relate to the other unique aspects of European cognition that we've identified? These are the questions we will begin to unravel in the following chapters.

Chapter 17

THE ENIGMA OF THE SCIENTIFIC REVOLUTION

Abul Ibn Khordadbeh knew his way around his ninth-century world. As chief spymaster in northwestern Iran for the caliph, it was his business to know what went on around him. He traveled extensively and recorded his findings in *The Book of Roads and Kingdoms*, the earliest surviving book of Arab geography, which includes descriptions of the wonders of Asia all the way to Japan and the south coast of India. There was one area, though, in which he had very little interest: Western Europe. All that region was good for, in his opinion, was "eunuchs, slave girls and boys, brocade, beaver skins, glue, sables, and swords." The following century, another Muslim geographer concurred, writing that Europeans were "dull in mind and heavy in speech," and the "farther they are to the north the more stupid, gross, and brutish they are."[1]

While the few Europeans who could read at that time might have differed with these opinions, the fact remains that, until the last few hundred years, the northern and western parts of Europe were a backwater to the great currents of civilization that swept across Eurasia. Even in the fourteenth century, Marco Polo, who grew up in Venice, one of the most sophisticated European cities of its time, was transfixed when he came across the Chinese capital of Hangzhou, describing it as "without doubt the finest and most splendid city in the world, . . . anyone seeing such a multitude would believe it a stark impossibility that food could be found to fill so many mouths."[2]

And yet, in just a few centuries, all this would be reversed. Those "stupid, gross, and brutish" nations of Europe would revolutionize humanity's relationship with nature; dominate the rest of the world; and create the framework for today's global civilization, replete with such wonders as electricity, antibiotics, automobiles, satellites, and the internet—all of which we take for granted today and yet would have been inconceivable in any earlier age. What happened? What were the underlying causes of this monumental restructuring of society?

Experts have long recognized the magnitude of the Scientific Revolution that transformed Europe. Historian Alexander Koyré called it "the most profound revolution achieved or suffered by the human mind" since Greek antiquity. According to another, it "outshines everything since the rise of Christianity. . . . [It is] the real origin both of the modern world and of the modern mentality." But the experts continue to debate the crucial question: why did this unique transformation of society happen in Europe rather than elsewhere in Eurasia? China, as we've seen, enjoyed a high level of technological and cultural sophistication. Why didn't that catalyze a scientific revolution? Islamic civilization, for several centuries, boasted some of the most advanced centers of learning the world had ever seen. Why did these not spark a transformation in scientific thought?[3]

We'll explore this enigma in this chapter, beginning by focusing our attention on Ibn Khordadbeh's Islamic world. When the Muslims turned up their noses at the barbarians to the north and west, what was it about their culture that gave them such a sense of superiority—and why did that not translate into a globe-changing Islamic scientific revolution?

Perched on the Edge of a Revolution

The Muslims of the ninth century had good reason to be proud. In less than a century following the death of the prophet Muhammad in 632, Arab tribes—previously desert nomads on the periphery of civilization—had carried out a series of conquests on a scale unparalleled in history. From as far west as the Iberian Peninsula, across the entire expanse of North Africa and Iran, and extending all the way into central Asia and northwest India, the Arabs had formed the largest empire the world had ever witnessed, complete with a common language, currency, and religion. In the ensuing centuries, this empire fragmented into different dynasties, with the Umayyads controlling Iberia while the Abbasids ruled much of the Islamic world from their new capital of Baghdad, a cosmopolitan center that rapidly became the world's largest city outside China. But, even though Islam fragmented politically, its religious tenets maintained cultural coherence through the disparate regions. As a result, a vast economic trading zone arose, linking areas as far apart as China, North Africa, and the Mediterranean. In addition to Baghdad, Damascus and Cairo grew into fabulously wealthy and sophisticated centers.[4]

The rising wealth of Islam could be measured not just in dinars—the entire region's common currency—but also in the knowledge the new rulers absorbed from their conquered territories. Since the conquests of Alexander the Great, the culture of ancient Greece had penetrated many of the regions now under Arab control. Some of the new Muslim rulers welcomed classical Greek learning with open arms, searching out Greek manuscripts and establishing new scholarly centers to translate the intellectual treasures of the Greeks into Arabic. The greatest of these was Bayt al-Hikma, the House of Wisdom, established in Baghdad in 813, which translated not just Greek manuscripts but also texts from India and Persia. It became, by the middle of the ninth century, the largest repository of books in the world, covering such subjects as mathematics, astronomy, medicine, chemistry, and geography.[5]

The Muslim scholars who directed these magnificent centers of learning were not just translating the wisdom of the past—they also grappled with its unresolved problems, creating their own Islamic tradition. The greatest of these, Abu al-Kindi, directed the House of Wisdom for many years and was himself responsible for advances in astronomy, optics, medicine, and mathematics. AlKindi and the other scholars of Baghdad took full advantage of their location at the crossroads between east and west Eurasia, incorporating the innovations of Indian mathematics into their work. Around 770, an Indian scholar had arrived in Baghdad with a set of Hindu astronomical works containing the decimal system of counting, thus introducing the concept of zero into the Islamic world. The scholars in the House of Wisdom quickly saw the potential of this new cognitive technology, previously unknown in Babylonian or Greek thought. A brilliant mathematician named al-Khwarizmi wrote important works that were later translated into Latin and introduced the concept of zero to Europe. It is from the name of his work, *Hisab al-jabr wal-muqabala,* that we get the word *algebra* and from the latinized version of his name (Algorithmi), the word *algorithm.*[6]

Muslim scholars made impressive advances in astronomy, a field that was crucial to virtually every early civilization and required some kind of conceptual model of the universe to yield meaningful results. The established model in the ancient Near East was based on Plato's dualistic cosmology, which posited a fixed domain of Ideas separate from the ever-changing material world. The apparently unchanging stars in the sky were logically placed in the domain of Ideas. There was, though, one serious problem: the planets such as Venus, Mars, and Jupiter could clearly be seen to move in irregular paths that undermined this celestial precision. Some of the greatest classical thinkers had dedicated themselves to solving this conundrum, culminating in the work of Ptolemy of Alexandria, who proposed a cosmos where each of the planets moved according to fixed wheels, which were themselves moved by other wheels of different sizes, thus explaining how the planets occasionally seemed to pirouette in the heavens rather than taking a direct circular path. Ptolemy's celestial model became the established textbook of astronomy for more than a millennium. Muslim scholars, however, through careful observation of the heavens, identified flaws in his theory and developed alternative models of the heavens that rivaled those of Copernicus, the first modern European to propose that the earth revolves around the sun.[7]

With this remarkable intellectual tradition spanning hundreds of years and thousands of miles, it's no wonder that historians frequently ask why Islamic learning didn't follow the trajectory European science would eventually take. In the words of historian Toby Huff, "The Arab achievement is so impressive that we must ask why the Arabs did not go the last mile to the modern scientific revolution." The Arabs, in Huff's view, "were perched on the forward edge of one of the greatest intellectual revolutions ever made, but they declined to make the grand transition" to the modern scientific conception of the universe. What stopped them?[8]

The Blasphemy of Reason

To understand the relationship between Islamic and scientific modes of thought, it's useful to contrast the emergence of Islam with that of Christianity. In its first four centuries, Christianity germinated gradually within the Roman Empire, with many of its leading theologians converting to the new religion only after having spent their formative years immersed in the classical learning of ancient Greece. Islam, by contrast, spread through military conquest, expanding mostly through conversion of conquered peoples. As a result, even when Muslim rulers welcomed classical Greek knowledge, it was perceived as something alien. Tellingly, Greek science and natural philosophy were known throughout Islam as the "foreign sciences," in contrast to the "Islamic sciences," such as the study of the Quran, which were considered to hold the highest place in Muslim life.[9]

In the early years of Islamic civilization, various groups vigorously competed for the hearts and minds of the Muslim community. Those who actively pursued the Greek classical tradition of knowledge were known as the *faylasuf* or "philosophers." Another group, taking a more mystical approach to Islam, were the Sufis. However, the two principal groups that emerged were the Ash'arites, traditionalists who believed in the primacy of Islamic faith, and the Mu'tazilites, who believed in a rational explication of the Quran.[10]

The Mu'tazilites were devout followers of Islam, while applying rational thought to their interpretation of theology. When passages in the Quran referred to "the face of God" or described God sitting on his throne, the Mu'tazilites argued that these descriptions should be interpreted metaphorically. It seemed to them equally valid to use reason as theology to make important distinctions in their lives, such as between good and evil. The Ash'arites, on the other hand, based their viewpoint on the fundamental presumption that the Quran was the direct word of God transmitted through Muhammad. As such, they viewed the Quran as something eternal and uncreated, an indivisible part of God: it wasn't just the word of God; it literally *was* God. How, then, to interpret statements about God's face or God sitting on his throne? The Ash'arite position was to take these statements literally, and if reason were unable to reconcile an inconsistency, it only showed the limitations of reason relative to faith. In the words of al-Ash'ari, the movement's founder: "We confess that God is firmly seated on His throne. . . . We confess that God has two hands, without asking how. . . . We confess that God has two eyes, without asking how."[11]

While the Ash'arites and Mu'tazilites were bitter rivals, one point of agreement was their condemnation of the *faylasuf*, who attempted to discover truth through the use of natural philosophy rather than the words of the Quran. In the madrassas—the predominant Muslim educational institution—the subjects taught generally included such topics as the sayings attributed to Muhammad, biographies of early Muslim religious leaders, and principles of Islamic religion and law. They would not, however, normally teach subjects dear to the *faylasuf*, such as natural science.[12]

Within the wider community, the attitude to natural science was mixed. It was broadly accepted that medicine was useful to preserve health, arithmetic was necessary for the conduct of daily affairs, and astronomy was required to calculate the celestial movements that determined the religious calendar. However, when the *faylasuf* inquired into broader questions about the universe, this was considered, at best, useless and, at worst, dangerous or even blasphemous. Indeed, the use of logic itself was often characterized as "ungodly."[13]

The intellectual achievements of the early Muslim scholars tended to emerge in particular opportune circumstances, usually under the protection of a strong royal patron. Without such support, the *faylasuf* led a precarious existence, often subject to attacks and denunciations from religious leaders. Even al-Kindi was dangerously vulnerable to the vicissitudes of shifting patronage. After enjoying the protection of two caliphs, his luck ran out with the next caliph, who was persuaded by religious scholars that al-Kindi held dangerous philosophical beliefs. His personal library was confiscated, and worse was to follow. At the age of sixty, this distinguished Muslim philosopher received fifty lashes in public before a large crowd, which reportedly roared in approval with every stroke.[14]

In spite of their precarious standing, the *faylasuf* achieved an array of remarkable intellectual breakthroughs. However, the writings of al-Ghazali (ca. 1058–1111), commonly viewed as the most influential Muslim philosopher in history, spelled the beginning of the end for the *faylasuf* tradition. Al-Ghazali's philosophical works became the mainstay of the Ash'arite school in their battle against the Mu'tazilites, who never really recovered from his attack. But alGhazali reserved his greatest vitriol for the *faylasuf*, in an assault that came primarily through a book called *The Incoherence of the Philosophers*. Al-Ghazali argued that man had been created to seek only the kind of knowledge that brings him closer to God. Religious knowledge is thus highest in value, with all other forms of knowledge holding a subordinate position. When natural science was used to aid religious observance, such as establishing the religious calendar, that was fine. When, however, it was used to determine general properties of the natural world, this was a waste of time that should be spent in worthier religious pursuits. One of al-Ghazali's favorite aphorisms was "May God protect us from useless knowledge." Finally, there was another category within natural sciences that was worse than useless: whatever might lead to a contradiction of the tenets of Islamic faith.[15]

It was here that al-Ghazali produced his most devastating attack on the *faylasuf*. He saw mathematics as dangerous because of its reliance on logical proofs to demonstrate whether something is true. He worried that people might become so impressed with the precise techniques of mathematical logic that they might use it to try to prove the existence of God and, being unable to, reject religion altogether. "How many have I seen," he wrote, "who err from the truth because of this high opinion of the philosophers and without any other basis?" Even the straightforward attribution of cause and effect to the natural world, such as the fact that fire causes burning, could set a student onto a slippery slope because, in al-Ghazali's view, God had the power to create fire without burning if he so chose. "Few there are," he wrote, who devote themselves to the natural sciences "without being stripped of religion and having the bridle of godly fear removed from their heads." The ramifications of this were chilling. He asked, "Now that you have analysed the theories of the philosophers, will you conclude by saying that one who believes in them ought to be branded with infidelity and punished with death?" This is inevitable, he concluded, accusing the *faylasuf* of "blatant blasphemy to which no Muslim sect would subscribe."[16]

Al-Ghazali's evisceration of rational thinking had a profound and lasting effect on Islamic culture. The thirteenth-century religious leader Ibn as-Salah, for example, issued a *fatwa* proclaiming that "he who studies or teaches philosophy will be abandoned by God's favor, and Satan will overpower him. What field of learning could be more despicable than one that blinds those who cultivate it and darkens their hearts against the prophetic teaching of Muhammad?" He declared menacingly, "It is the duty of the civil authorities to protect Muslims against the evil that such people can cause. Persons of this sort must be removed from the schools and punished for their cultivation of these fields."[17]

The later development of Muslim society reflected the undisputed victory of the Ash'arites over scientific thought. The word for innovation, *bidaa*, acquired the same kind of pejorative association as "heresy" in the West, especially the kind of *bidaa* that involved imitating the infidel. This aversion to innovation had profound social consequences. Within three decades of the publication of the first printed books in Europe in 1455, the most powerful Muslim ruler, the Turkish sultan, banned the publication and possession of any printed material. The ban was repeated and enforced by later sultans, with such success that the first Arabic-language books were printed in Europe by Christians in the early sixteenth century, and it was only in the nineteenth century that the ban was finally lifted in Muslim countries.[18]

The reason, then, that the scientific achievements of Islamic civilization never caused the revolution in thought that occurred in Europe becomes apparent. Muslim breakthroughs in scientific thought, impressive as they were, tended to be sporadic and clustered in communities that protected scientific thinkers from the mainstream culture. The thrust of Islamic cognition was aimed toward following the divine words of the Quran and submitting unquestioningly to faith whenever it might conflict with the findings of reason. It was focused in an opposite direction from the relentless querying of natural phenomena that was required for a revolution in scientific thought to occur.

However, this explanation for the lack of a scientific revolution in the Islamic world doesn't explain why it didn't occur in China. As we've seen, the

Chinese had no belief in an omnipotent god and no conception of any conflict between faith and reason. Let us, then, continue to unravel this enigma by turning our attention to China.

China at the Threshold

The advanced state of society in fourteenth-century China inspired awe in those few foreigners who managed to travel there. Chinese civilization had all the key technologies that Europeans later saw as a foundation for their own scientific revolution. In 1620, Francis Bacon observed that three technologies had transformed the face of European civilization: printing, gunpowder, and the nautical compass. All three were, in fact, inventions of the Chinese and were already fully utilized by the time of the Song dynasty.[19]

Beyond these three key technologies, an entire array of industrial and economic achievements gave China a gigantic lead over the rest of the world. The scale of iron production in China was, in the words of one historian, "truly staggering," reaching a level of 125,000 tons a year by 1076, as compared with the 76,000 tons produced in England in 1788 at the onset of the Industrial Revolution. One ironworks alone employed more than 3,600 workers. China's economic sophistication was equally impressive. The government started printing paper money in 1024, which soon became widespread.[20]

The sophistication of Song civilization extended into the realm of intellectual discovery. While Neo-Confucian philosophers were synthesizing the great traditions of Chinese thought, other intellectuals applied critical thinking to make remarkable progress in areas as diverse as medicine, geography, mathematics, and astronomy, with publications such as the first known treatise on forensic medicine and a geographic encyclopedia with two hundred chapters. Cartography achieved greater precision than ever before, with a vehicle for measuring road distances designed and built in 1027. In mathematics, Qin Jiushao began using the zero symbol in the fourteenth century, around the same time that Arabic numerals first appeared in Italy.[21]

In the fourteenth century, China was, in the words of economist Justin Yifu Lin, "probably the most cosmopolitan, technologically advanced and economically powerful civilization in the world" and had "reached the threshold level for a full-fledged scientific and industrial revolution." Lin goes on to ask: "Why did the Industrial Revolution not occur in China in the fourteenth century?

At that time, almost every element that economists and historians usually considered to be a major contributing factor to the Industrial Revolution in late eighteenth-century England also existed in China."[22]

Historians have gone to some lengths trying to provide answers to this conundrum. Some have focused on demographics and economics, arguing that China's high population density kept the cost of labor cheap relative to capital, thereby reducing the value of labor-saving technology and discouraging innovation. Others point to the destructive impact of the Mongol conquests during those centuries, which engulfed not just China but also large parts of the Islamic empire. Some theories have focused on sociocultural aspects of Chinese civilization. For example, the examination system for the civil service—an essential path to high status—was stultifying by modern standards, forcing students to spend six years memorizing every word of the canon of Confucian classics. It is difficult, however, to ascribe the lack of a scientific revolution to this process. Chinese history is generously peppered with breakthroughs and insights of numerous brilliant thinkers in a wide variety of fields, many of whom simultaneously pursued successful careers in the imperial bureaucracy.[23]

What do we do with this flurry of opinions, each of which may contain some nugget of truth, but none of which seems to solve the entire puzzle satisfactorily? A renowned scholar of Chinese culture, Nathan Sivin, exasperatedly declares, "I have encountered no question more often than why modern science did not develop independently in China, and none on which more firmly based opinions have been formed on the basis of less critical attention to available evidence." Sivin's response is that this is the wrong question to ask in the first place. What's the point, he retorts, in asking why something didn't occur? "It is obvious to anyone who has studied a little history that to explain what did not happen is about as rigorous as fiction. What did happen was the emergence of early modern science in Europe. It is Europe that needs to be understood." Sivin goes on, crucially, to point out the hidden cultural preconceptions that have led to this question. "Above all," he observes, "we usually assume that the Scientific Revolution is what everybody ought to have had. But it is not at all clear that scientific theory and practice of a characteristically modern kind were what other societies yearned for before they became, in recent times, an urgent matter of survival amidst violent change."[24]

Sivin's insight illuminates how, ever since the West's Scientific Revolution and consequent domination of the rest of the world, modern scientific thinking has become unreflectively accepted as the norm to which all other cultures should have aspired. If another civilization evolved in an alternative direction, this is unquestioningly assumed to have been a failure. This cultural assumption can be found in a wide range of learned books written by scholars of high repute. A thoughtful and deeply researched book by Toby Huff, *The Rise of Early Modern Science*, is nevertheless littered with references to what he characterizes as "the riddle of the success of modern science in the West—and its failure in non-Western civilizations." Huff refers repeatedly to "the failure of Arab science to yield modern science" and "the failure of China to give birth to modern science." In another example, Joel Mokyr, a leading historian on this subject, reflects: "And yet China failed to become what Europe eventually became. . . . The implications of this failure for world history are awesome to contemplate. The Chinese were, so to speak, within reach of world domination, and then shied away." Implicit in Mokyr's narrative is the assumption that the Chinese wanted world domination but failed to succeed in this obvious goal. However, as we've seen, world domination was neither a natural nor a desired goal from the Chinese perspective.[25]

Since Sivin's conceptual breakthrough, many scholars of Chinese culture have come to share his viewpoint. "Indeed," writes one team, "it is like asking why a man setting out for New York fails to arrive in Chicago. He simply wasn't headed there." Sinologist A. C. Graham poses an alternative question to ask about China, noting that "the formation of an empire, covering a fifth of mankind and still, after several thousand years, surviving even the extreme pressures of the 20th century, is an event which like the Scientific Revolution has happened only once in history." How, he asks, did China achieve such an unrivaled record of cultural stability?[26]

If China was indeed heading somewhere other than a scientific revolution, what was their intended destination? Once we relinquish the value-tinged perspective of asking about China's "failure" to achieve a scientific revolution, this frees us to inquire more meaningfully about the implicit goals of the Chinese cultural paradigm. In our current global system, which has fully imbibed the values equating the Scientific Revolution with success and other trajectories as failure, is there anything of value we can learn about a system that utilized science and technology for a different purpose?

Machine Worries, Machine Hearts

The first Europeans to arrive in China in significant numbers were Jesuit missionaries, who struggled to come to terms with the Chinese worldview. One of them, a Frenchman named Jean-Baptiste Du Halde, discussed how the Chinese failed to fully exploit their mineral deposits. "The Mountains of China are still more valuable," he wrote, "on account of the Mines of different Metals. The Chinese say they are full of Gold and Silver; but that the working of them hitherto has been hindered from some political views, perhaps, that the publick Tranquillity might not be disturbed by the too great abundance of these Metals, which would make the People haughty and negligent of Agriculture."[27]

In this passage, we can discern a core difference between the European and Chinese approaches to using technology to exploit natural resources. While the Europeans focused on maximizing what they could mine from the earth, the Chinese seem to have targeted a different objective: avoiding an imbalance that could disturb the "publick Tranquillity." In this, they appear to have been extraordinarily successful. Back in the ninth century, the Tang dynasty constructed the framework of a society that would remain remarkably stable until the twentieth century, even in the face of invasions by the Mongols and Manchus and later incursions of European powers. This stability has been viewed by many Western observers as a form of stagnation, leading historians such as Mokyr to wonder how China "failed" to achieve world domination, or Huff to analyze why they "failed" to have a scientific revolution.[28]

Should traditional Chinese society be described as stagnant, like water in a secluded pond, or healthy and stable, like water in a mountain lake that continually gets replenished without overflowing its shores? Joseph Needham, author of the multivolume classic *Science and Civilisation in China*, is convinced that it's the latter. China, he writes, "had been self-regulating, like a living organism in slowly changing equilibrium." Needham calls for "the replacement of the false and meaningless concept of 'stagnation' by the precise and applicable idea of slowly changing 'homeostasis.'" This debate has implications for our own age. If "stagnation" is the more apt description, then perhaps it makes sense to view the lack of a scientific revolution in China as a "failure," in contrast to our modern society's dynamism. If, on the other hand, Needham's assessment is right, then China's unique form of self-regulating homeostasis may hold valuable lessons for our current global society struggling with ever-increasing social, economic, and environmental imbalances.[29]

The Taoist *Zhuangzi* classic offers a fascinating story on this topic. A scholar named Zigong, while traveling, notices an old man working in a garden digging trenches, repeatedly going over to a well and returning with a jug full of water. "There's a machine," Zigong tells the farmer, "which could irrigate a hundred plots like yours in a day. Would you, good sir, like to try one?" The farmer shows some initial interest, and Zigong explains to him how it works. Suddenly, the farmer's face flushes, and he retorts: "I've heard that where there are machines, there are bound to be machine worries; where there are machine worries, there are bound to be machine hearts. With a machine heart in your breast, you've lost what was pure and simple; and the loss of the pure and simple leads to restlessness of the spirit. Where there is restlessness of the spirit, the Tao no longer dwells. It's not that I don't know about your machine—I would be ashamed to use it!" This colorful story highlights a deep-rooted mistrust of technology, driven not necessarily by a reactionary fear of change but by a worldview that values, above all else, harmonization with the Tao in all one's activities.[30]

This ingrained distrust of technology permeated the mind-set of traditional Chinese peasantry throughout its history. In an interesting vignette, an American newspaper reported in 1887 that "over a thousand telegraph poles of one line in China have been pulled down by the people, who say the telegraph is a diabolical European artifice." Apparently, Chinese farmers of the time believed that the humming of the wires disturbed the "spirits of the wind and water." This issue became so prevalent that, for some time, the government had to send soldiers to guard the lines.[31*]

Although the Taoist perception of the natural world infused popular Chinese thought from early times, it was just one of several competing visions of what it meant to harmonize with the Tao. A vocal critic of Taoism was the Confucian philosopher Xunzi, but, when he attacked the Taoists, it was their very curiosity about the natural world that he found vexing:

> You vainly seek into the causes of things;
> Why not appropriate and enjoy what they produce?
> Therefore I say—To neglect man and speculate about Nature
> Is to misunderstand the facts of the universe.[32]

Here, it is the Taoists who are accused of possessing what we would describe as a "scientific" perspective as they "seek into the causes of things," in contrast to the Confucian ethic.

The Chinese emphasis on appropriating and enjoying whatever arises rather than theorizing about it is demonstrated in a story told by historian Daniel Boorstein about Admiral Zheng's expeditions. In 1414, after Zheng established a diplomatic relationship with Bengal, a giraffe was sent to the Chinese emperor as tribute. This was the first time a giraffe had been seen in China, and it caused a great stir. However, instead of speculating about this new wonder, the Chinese automatically integrated it into their worldview. In Chinese folklore, there was a mythical creature resembling the unicorn called the *kilin* (pronounced "chi-lin"), which ate only herbs, harmed no living beings, and possessed beneficent powers. When the Chinese discovered this creature was called *girin* in the language of its country of origin, they decided that it must be a *kilin* and, as such, was a good omen demonstrating heaven's favor. As a result, on his next expedition, Zheng journeyed thousands of miles with his armada to the east African country of Malindi, the source of the giraffe, to establish a diplomatic relationship and ensure more giraffes would be sent to the emperor. Boorstein interprets this story as evidence of China's "failure" to learn from new experiences. "It was not the appeal of slaves, of gold, or of silver," he writes, "but the charm of the giraffe that drew Cheng He's later expeditions to Malindi and the far reaches of the eastern coast of Africa. . . . The world's curiosities," he concludes, "had become mere symptoms of China's virtue. So was revealed a Chinese Wall of the Mind against the lessons of the rest of the planet."[33]

It's easy, from the vantage point of the twenty-first century, to ridicule the Chinese assessment of the giraffe as unscientific thinking, another sign of their cultural "stagnation." However, as we've seen, the European quest for slaves, gold, and silver can be understood as a symptom of a cognitive structure that venerated power and exploitation for its own sake, and which eventually caused untold devastation to the rest of the world. For the people of Malindi, it was surely a blessing that the Chinese, rather than the Portuguese, were the ones to have discovered them.

What, then, was the structure of Chinese cognition that maintained stability for millennia, causing them to develop in a different direction from a scientific revolution? For the Chinese, there was no distinct separation between humankind and nature. Humanity existed in a constantly changing universe comprising waves of qi forever alternating between *yin* and *yang*. Arising from this cosmological viewpoint, the ultimate objective was harmonization: the healthy integration of the individual with society and of humanity with the natural world. The intellect was used not to arrive at some abstract conception of Truth but to learn the wisdom of harmonizing with the Tao. Seeking fixed laws of nature made no sense, since everything in the cosmos was in a state of dynamic flow. The very idea of using pure logic to arrive at a universal theory of something was an absurdity, since nothing existed in an isolated theoretical form without context. Finally, the use of technology was quite acceptable as a way of enhancing civilized life, but, with no conception of humanity's separation from nature, the idea of "conquering nature" was unthinkable.

With this cognitive structure, even the most potentially disruptive forces, such as the invention of gunpowder or the invasion of the Mongols, could be subsumed and incorporated into the social fabric. During the Song dynasty, when Chinese civilization was at a peak of creative flux, the most brilliant minds were focused not on achieving a disruptive break with the past but on synthesizing their three major philosophical traditions into Neo-Confucianism. It seems likely that, barring the onslaught of Western powers, Chinese society would have continued evolving in stable fashion into the distant future.

Whereas the cognitive structure of Islamic civilization was organized around submission to God and gave primacy to faith, Chinese civilization was organized around social cohesion and gave primacy to harmonizing with the Tao. By virtue of their cognitive structures, neither civilization was headed in the direction of a scientific revolution, and it seems unlikely that such a cognitive upheaval would ever have occurred in either of them. However, neither of these great civilizations would be a match for the cataclysmic confrontation with the forces that were unleashed in Europe as it went through its scientific and industrial transformation. The time has come, then, to follow Nathan Sivin's suggestion and turn to Europe. What caused Europe to take a path that was unique in world history? Why did Europe alone experience a scientific revolution?

A Series of Accidents?

Following the emergence of scientific thought in the seventeenth century, Europe went through a series of transformations: the Industrial Revolution in the eighteenth and nineteenth centuries and a dramatic military and economic rise to world dominance that culminated in the early twentieth century. With such breadth of transformation, scholars have tended to explain Europe's astonishing surge based on their own particular area of expertise.

Some have emphasized geography, pointing to Europe's variety of ecological niches and wealth of natural resources. Historian Kenneth Pomeranz argues that Europe's access to the vast resources of the New World gave it a competitive edge, leading to what he calls "the great divergence." Other historians focus on the fragmented nature of European society and the split between religious and secular authority: with the proliferation of different jurisdictions, no single ruler could capriciously put a halt to threatening changes. "Had the Ming and Ch'ing Dynasties of China failed to unite China," writes one, "it is quite likely that the first capitalist, industrialized societies would have developed there." Others have noted that, even with Europe's fragmentation, unifying elements such as the lingua franca of Latin helped advance intellectual understanding.[34]

Various miscellaneous factors are invoked as well. Europe's science, it's been noted, was really a direct continuation of Greek science. Some claim that Europe's system of self-governing institutions, with its guilds, towns, and universities, made the difference. A number of observers have emphasized the rise of capitalism as the driving force of European dominance; however, both Chinese and Islamic civilizations boasted equally sophisticated economic and financial systems.[35]

Adding to this bewildering array of theories are those who claim there were no underlying structural reasons whatsoever for the rise of Europe—that, in effect, Europe just got lucky. One historian has described the rise of the West as "a series of near-miraculous accidents." Another surmises that "it is in some very complex way the result of many different and unique causes that resist generalization." Historian Janet Abu-Lughod states the case plainly, writing, "There was no *inherent historical necessity* that shifted the system to favor the West rather than East, nor was there any inherent historical necessity that would have prevented cultures in the eastern region from becoming the progenitors of a modern world system."[36]

So which is it? Where do we go from here? Is Sivin's assertion true that "it is Europe that needs to be understood," or is there nothing inherent about Europe to understand after all? Before giving up on the search for an answer, however, let us turn our attention to the Scientific Revolution itself and explore whether its characteristics offer any clues.[37]

Scientific Cognition

In our modern age, we are so used to the presence of science all around us that we tend to take it for granted, like the fish that never realizes it's swimming in water. We check the weather forecast, turn on our computers, take an antibiotic, and drive to work, spending our day utilizing the products of science and accepting its mode of cognition, giving little, if any, thought to where it came from. Science, in the words of author Brian Appleyard, is "*buried* within us, it is concealed. In order to expose its workings we need to look beneath the fabric of contemporary life. . . . It requires an effort of the imagination to see how we have been formed by the struggles of the last 400 years."[38]

The magnitude of the cognitive change wrought by those struggles is enormous. Historian Stephen Gaukroger notes that the rise of science was responsible for a "transformation of cognitive and intellectual values" that "has a strong claim to being the single most fundamental feature of the modern era. The West's sense of itself, its relation to its past, and its sense of its future were all profoundly altered as cognitive values generally came to be shaped around scientific ones."[39]

A crucial aspect of this transformation was that it required people to think in an unprecedented way. Other systems of thought accepted personal intuition as a valid source of knowledge. A unique characteristic of scientific thought is its rejection of this belief, replacing it with the principle of objectivity: the idea that there are fixed truths about the universe that can be objectively validated. From this foundation, certain consequences naturally emerge, such as the use of mathematics as a common language to describe these truths that transcend cultural barriers, and reliance on the empirical method to prove that these truths exist.[40]

The cognitive structure that visualizes a fixed Truth to be sought through the application of logic and reason can be traced all the way back to ancient Greece. This suggests a hypothesis that the underlying cause of the Scientific Revolution occurring in Europe was cognitive and can be found in the conceptual structures that shaped patterns of thought in the collective European consciousness over thousands of years. It suggests that, while the cognitive trajectories of Chinese and Islamic civilization were targeting other destinations, European thought structures were heading inexorably toward a scientific revolution. Such a hypothesis contradicts those who argue there is nothing inherent in Europe that produced the Scientific Revolution. It implies that there is, after all, a solution to this enigma. Such a solution looks beyond the economic, political, or geographic factors of Europe's rise to identify a cognitive structure in the European mind that was unique in history and that led, perhaps inevitably, to the Scientific Revolution.

Over the past several centuries, there have been those who have trumpeted aspects of European culture as causative factors in Europe's "success" versus the "failure" of other cultures in the world. That is not the intention here. Rather, the goal is to identify the nature of a peculiarly European mind-set that engendered the unprecedented phenomenon the world has experienced in the last few hundred years: one that produced devastating genocides and exploitation as well as the spectacular technological achievements that have transformed the lives of virtually everyone on the planet. According to this hypothesis, that mind-set is to be found in the dualistic structure of thought that originated in ancient Greece and later became synthesized into the systematic monotheism of Christianity. It is this underlying dualism that led eventually to the unique emergence in Europe of what we may call "scientific cognition." The story of how this happened is the subject of the next chapter.

Chapter 18

THE LANGUAGE OF GOD: THE EMERGENCE OF SCIENTIFIC COGNITION

In 1633, Galileo, struggling heroically for scientific truth, was tried by the Inquisition and compelled under threat of torture to recant his theory that the earth revolved around the sun. A broken man, he was forced to live out the rest of his years under house arrest, while his books were banned. In this dramatic moment, the bitter struggle between science and religion showed itself in sharpest relief: the high-minded, noble Galileo striving for freedom of thought against the dogmatic, closed-minded Catholic Church mired in superstition.

Or, at least, that's the way the story has generally been told over the centuries. The "Galileo affair" is frequently rolled out to show the incompatibility of science and religion, two worldviews often seen in today's world as irreconcilably opposed. This chapter, however, offers a different view of the relationship between Christianity and science. A careful reading of history shows that, rather than the two being implacable foes, science, in fact, belongs to the same cognitive family as Christianity: conceived by the same ancestor, incubated in Christianity's embrace for a millennium, and coming of age as a staunch proponent of its Christian heritage.

In contrast to the chasm that exists today between fundamentalist Christians and scientific atheists, this chapter reveals how the structures of thought that led to Christianity also laid the foundations for what would emerge as scientific cognition. As we'll see, even that heroic tale of Galileo's struggle against the Inquisition turns out to contain layers of complexity that blur the stark relief in which it is usually told.

Seeking the Perfection of the Universe

The trail—like so many others in European thought—goes all the way back to ancient Greece, and even a little further. The Greeks, like the Hebrews, inherited from Babylon a belief that the cosmos followed a set of natural laws. Heraclitus, echoing the Old Testament, observed that the sun "will not transgress his measure," otherwise the bailiffs of the goddess of justice, Diké, "will find him out." The idea of natural laws permeated Greek thought so thoroughly that it infused their language: the Greek word *astronomos*, for example, comes from the root *nomos*, which means "law."[1]

The Greeks took seriously the entailments of the natural law metaphor. Ptolemy of Alexandria described how he considered natural phenomena to be on trial—with reason as the judge. The very notion of a geometric proof—one of the greatest inventions of classical Greece—was derived from a courtroom setting where an advocate attempts to prove to others beyond doubt why a certain argument must be true. The best way to win a trial is usually with evidence, and the use of empirical evidence to prove or disprove a theory was another practice developed further by the Greeks than any other civilization.[2]

In the patterns of early Greek thought, we already see the core characteristics of scientific cognition: believing in natural laws, abstracting generalizations from particular findings, and extensively using both logical proofs and empirical methods. Underlying these ways of thinking was a belief in the existence of objective truth in the universe—a conceptualization that would form the basis for future scientific thought. The principle of objectivity—a belief in fixed, eternal truths about the natural world that can be objectively validated—is a defining characteristic of scientific thought. The ancient Greeks, alone in history, were responsible for conceiving the idea of a universal truth that could be accessed by the systematic employment of reason.[3*]

One particular aspect of the Greek search for truth would have far-reaching ramifications for scientific cognition. This was the emphasis on mathematics as a key to unlocking the secrets of the universe, a tradition that can be traced back to Pythagoras. For Pythagoras and his followers, mathematics was the basis of all knowledge, an idea succinctly summarized by one of his followers:

> And all the things that are known have a number—
> For without this nothing could be thought of or known.

This was one of the central principles Plato used to construct his model of the universe that would form the foundation of Western thought. He emblazoned this belief on the doors to his Academy with the words, "Let no one unacquainted with geometry enter here."[4]

In the Greek vision, mathematics could take a person beyond mere scientific investigation and into the spiritual realm. There was, the Greeks believed, a geometric perfection to the universe that could be perceived by humans because of their ability to reason. The seat of reason, the human soul, was the vehicle that connected a human to this eternal harmony. This vision formed the basis of the Western tradition, inspiring successive generations to pursue their souls' immortal destiny through their intellect.[5]

As the center of Hellenic culture shifted from Athens to Alexandria, Plato's conception of the universe went with it. For the followers of this worldview, there was no distinction between scientific investigation and spiritual fulfillment, since the intellect and the soul were indistinguishable. Ptolemy, for example, wrote of "the constancy, order, symmetry and calm which are associated with the divine" which "makes its followers lovers of this divine beauty, accustoming them and reforming their natures, as it were, to a similar spiritual state." Nicomachus, a first-century mathematician, wrote a work called the *Theology of Arithmetic* in which he asserted that numbers were the creation of the divine mind, and their investigation revealed the working method of God.[6]

As Christianity enveloped the ancient world, the eternal truths of the Platonic worldview fit nicely into a conception of a world created and overseen by an omnipotent God. Around 500 CE, a set of influential books surfaced in the Greek-speaking world, written by an author known as Pseudo-Dionysius, which used a fusion of Platonism and Christianity to explain the relationship between God, humans, and the universe, at the heart of which was the Pythagorean conception of number as the basis for everything.[7]

The scientific way of thinking showed glimmers of life but had not yet reached a level of maturity where it could progress independently. Like an egg—laid but not yet hatched—it needed an incubator where it could be protected while it grew to maturity. That incubator would turn out to be the Christian worldview that emerged under the auspices of the Roman Catholic Church.

Spicing the Dish for the Multitudes

The Catholic Church might have seemed at the time like an unlikely incubator for scientific cognition. From the earliest days of Christianity, the writings of Paul instigated a battle between faith and reason. Paul felt there was no place in Christianity for both the reason of the Greek philosophers and faith in God. "The wisdom of the world," he wrote, "is foolishness to God." As Paul's writings became more authoritative, they established battle lines between science and religion that remain in place to this day.[8]

Paul's views on the irreconcilability of faith and reason resemble those of the Muslim philosopher al-Ghazali discussed in the previous chapter. Just as al-Ghazali's condemnation of rational thought rang the death knell of Islamic science, so Paul's virulent attack on reason threatened to do the same in the Christian sphere. Paul's polemic sowed the seeds of a powerful tradition in early Christian thought against intellectual reasoning. Tertullian was particularly vehement, writing, "After Jesus Christ we have no need of speculation, after the Gospel no need of research." John Chrysostom called on his fellow Christians to "restrain our own reasoning, and empty our mind of secular learning, in order to provide a mind swept clear for the reception of divine words." Philastrius of Brescia, an early harbinger of al-Ghazali, declared that the search for empirical knowledge was itself a heretical act.[9]

Strident as these attacks were, they didn't have the fatal effect on intellectual inquiry that al-Ghazali's broadside would have in the Islamic world. Why not? Some intriguing clues can be found in a debate between Celsus, a pagan scholar defending ancient classical philosophy, and Origen, a Christian scholar articulating the new religion's worldview. This wasn't a regular debate. Rather, Celsus wrote a comprehensive attack on Christianity around 177 CE, every copy of which was destroyed by a fifth-century pope; we only know about it today because Origen, writing about fifty years after Celsus, responded to his arguments point by point, quoting him so extensively that 90 percent of Celsus's original work survives intact.

An important focus of the debate was the difference between reasoned conviction and blind faith or *pistis*. Celsus, following the Platonic tradition, saw reason as the only valid route to understanding the cosmos. *Pistis* was the state of mind of the ignorant who blindly accepted whatever they were told. And yet, to the astonishment of Celsus and his peers, *pistis* formed the foundation of the Christian approach.

Origen's response is illuminating. Instead of dismissing Greek philosophy, he showed nearly as much admiration for Plato as Celsus had. The difference, for Origen, was that Plato's ideas could be accessed only by those with a scholarly education: it is as though Plato spiced his dish to please the upperclass palate, whereas Christian preachers, flavoring their sermons with *pistis*, "[cooked] for the multitude." We accept *pistis*, Origen explained, "as useful for the multitude"; it is the best that can be done for them, since "very few people are enthusiastic about rational thought." The dish could be flavored with reason or *pistis*, but it remained essentially the same meal. Christianity, Origen implied, was Platonism for the masses.[10]

Origen's defense of Christianity had a very different character than Paul's total warfare. Instead of an all-or-nothing choice between faith and reason, Origen offered a more nuanced relationship. In this, he was following a line of reasoning begun by Clement a generation earlier, which had depicted Greek philosophy as the handmaiden of theology—a kind of preparatory training for those who then embraced Christianity on faith.

There were, then, two competing schools of thought in early Christianity regarding classical Greek philosophy. Paul's approach was outright rejection of rational thought as anathema to Christian faith; Origen's was to assimilate what was useful into Christian theology. It might have been difficult to tell in the early centuries which had the upper hand, but the competition would eventually be resolved by a man who was to have as profound an effect on the future of Christianity as al-Ghazali had on Islam.

That man was Augustine, the theologian whose probing writings would become the foundation of Western Christian thought. Augustine set the standard for thinking about the relationship between faith and reason, weaving together elements of both Paul's and Origen's views into a synthesis that would satisfy future generations of Christians.

Throughout his writings, Augustine referred to God's eternal law as a truth that could be understood both through faith and reason, and he went so far as to assert that Christianity itself had been foreshadowed by the ancient Greeks. "What is now called Christian religion," he wrote, "has existed among the ancients." At the same time, Augustine admitted to his own intellectual struggle with core Christian beliefs. Certain truths, such as the existence of God, he believed were attainable through reason, while other truths, such as the Incarnation, could only be accessed through faith. Relying on one's own intelligence in these matters was the sin of pride. It took an act of humility to relinquish one's own intellect and accept the authority of the scriptures even when reason stood in the way. "I would not have believed the Gospels," he wrote, "except on the authority of the Catholic Church."[11]

Augustine's synthesis held that faith alone was sufficient for a Christian, whereas reason alone was not. "It is enough," he wrote, "for the Christian to believe that the only cause of all created things . . . is the goodness of the Creator, the one true God." However, while reason was inferior to faith, its use was still valid. It was an important faculty that should be cultivated, encouraged, and put to good use within the parameters of Christian faith.[12]

With Augustine's solid but circumscribed endorsement of reason, Europe entered the medieval period under the domination of the Catholic Church. The incubation of scientific cognition had begun.

The Rising Tide of Reason

The Middle Ages have not had a good press. Ever since the Renaissance, they have been generally viewed as an era of superstition and ignorance. The centuries following the collapse of the Roman Empire, unquestionably an age of decline, are known as the Dark Ages. And yet, even in the darkest years, there were those who maintained the light of intellectual inquiry, passing on and even adding to a tradition that would eventually gather strength and soar. Many heroes of this remarkable feat of sustenance have been largely forgotten, except in the rarefied halls of academia. One of these was Boethius, a statesman, philosopher, and devout Christian who, determined to pass on the wisdom of the Greeks to future generations, assiduously translated Aristotle's works on logic into Latin.[13]

Thanks to the heroic endeavors of Boethius and others, glimmers of classical learning survived the worst ravages of the Dark Ages. One text was particularly influential in transmitting ancient Greek philosophy into European thought. This was the *Timaeus*: the only work of Plato to have survived the collapse of the Roman Empire, which was translated into Latin in the third century. Of all Plato's works, the *Timaeus* was the one most focused on describing a Pythagorean cosmos, with a creator designing the world on the basis of geometric harmony. It was especially valuable as a bridge between classical and Christian thought because, while expounding the mathematical vision of Pythagoras, it also described the creator in terms that seemed consistent with the Christian idea of God.[14]

Inspired by their readings of the *Timaeus* and Aristotle's treatise on logic, some thinkers in the early medieval period began to reemphasize the role of reason in their quest to understand the universe. One notable was John Scotus, a ninth-century Irish philosopher and theologian who upended Augustine's formulation by placing reason above ecclesiastical authority. "Authority," he wrote, "proceeds from true reason, but reason certainly does not proceed from authority. . . . True reason . . . does not require to be confirmed by the assent of any authority."[15]

Gradually, reliance on reason permeated mainstream Catholic theology. In the late tenth century, Gerbert of Aurillac, an accomplished mathematician, became pope. Gerbert used his influence to promote classical learning, and his followers assiduously disseminated his methods for teaching what was known as "natural philosophy" throughout northern Europe, with logic becoming a core part of the curriculum in the European cathedral schools.[16]

The tide of reason was rising, as can be seen in the career of Anselm of Canterbury, an eleventh-century advocate of the use of reason in theology, who was later made a saint. Anselm's fellow monks, impressed by his rigorous use of logic, asked him to prove the existence of God logically without recourse to anything in the scriptures. Anselm obliged them with the first treatise offering what is known as the "ontological proof " of God's existence, and, in doing so, he established a new role for reason in the Christian tradition: as a vehicle to buttress and even instill faith, rather than a mere "handmaiden" employed to analyze theological arguments.[17]

By the twelfth century, the adoption of reason had reached such critical mass that the shift in European thought during this period has been called a conceptual revolution. It was here that Christianity began to nurture scientific cognition. John Scotus's suggestion that reason had natural authority above even the scriptures was now increasingly accepted. When the words of the Bible conflicted with the findings of natural philosophy, such as when Psalm 103 described the heavens as a skin or an arched roof, it was assumed that the scriptures were speaking metaphorically. While al-Ghazali's writings were silencing those in the Islamic world who offered anything other than a literal interpretation of the Quran, fourteenthcentury philosopher Nicole Oresme could state openly that biblical expressions of God becoming angry or pacified "are not to be taken literally."[18]

Ironically, an important catalyst of this transformation came from the intellectual treasures that Muslim scholars had carefully translated from Greek to Arabic in previous centuries but that were now cast adrift in the Islamic world. After the Christians captured Toledo from the Muslims in 1085, a new breed of

European scholars made a pilgrimage to this center of Islamic learning, voraciously translating what they found. Within two centuries, virtually the entire corpus of Greek and Islamic science was made available to Europe in Latin.[19]

These works found an eager reception in the cluster of new universities springing up across Europe—institutions of learning unlike anything the world had ever seen. Anyone who intended to pursue a career in law, medicine, or theology had to complete a six-year course in the classical subjects of logic and arithmetic, geometry, music, and astronomy—a curriculum first established by the Pythagoreans and developed further by Boethius. This impressive study program gave a common intellectual heritage, steeped in the classical tradition, to generations of Europeans pursuing vocations in virtually any professional or administrative field.[20]

Trained in the classical disciplines, and stimulated by the learning emanating from Spain, a fresh class of thought leaders emerged in Europe, experimenting in new ways to synthesize Christian theology with natural philosophy. The cognitive foundation for modern science was being laid.[21]

The Implicit Narrative of Christian Rationalism

What did this foundation of scientific cognition look like? It was a seamless fusion of the classical deification of reason with the belief in the omniscience of a Christian God. Although each natural philosopher developed their own unique understanding of the cosmos, there were underlying, interrelated themes that framed the cognitive structure of what might be called "Christian rationalism." These themes wove together Platonic notions of natural law, reason, logic, and truth into a Christian narrative that, although never stated explicitly as such, went something like this:

> God created the universe according to a fixed set of **Natural Laws**.
>
> God gave Man **Reason** in his image; therefore, it is incumbent on Man to use it well.
>
> God's Natural Laws are based on **Logic**; therefore, Reason can be used to understand them.
>
> By using Reason to understand God's Natural Laws, Man can perceive the **Truth**.
>
> By perceiving the Truth through Reason, Man can arrive at a glimpse of **God's Mind**.[22*]

This implicit cosmological narrative formed the basis of what would become scientific cognition. Even though they were derived in the Middle Ages from ancient sources, these interrelated presumptions formed the context—and served as inspiration—for the great intellectual breakthroughs of the Scientific Revolution. Astonishingly, they continue to provide the cognitive structure (sometimes unstated and unacknowledged) of much thinking about science that qualifies today as mainstream.

It is a testament to the power of this framework that it generated the scientific worldview underlying much of our global civilization; but it is equally important to recognize that this narrative is based on unverifiable assumptions about the nature of the universe that encourage patterns of thinking to evolve in certain directions. By consciously recognizing them as such, we can open our minds to other patterns of conceptualizing our cosmos that might lead to different cognitive outcomes.[23]

However, for the generations of Christian rationalists who would collectively construct the modern view of reality, the concept of alternative worldviews with different foundational structures was unthinkable. The implicit narrative of Christian rationalism enabled them to build, brick by brick, idea by idea, the edifice that forms scientific cognition and was responsible for constructing our modern world.

The "Eternal Law" of Reason

The burgeoning city of Paris was at the epicenter of the new ferment of Christian rationalism. Its university, founded in 1170, received a written charter from the pope guaranteeing its intellectual independence. A leading thinker, Peter Abelard, wrote a powerful apologia of rational inquiry called *Sic et Non* (*Yes and No*) claiming that humanity's duty to use the faculty of reason found its source from the New Testament. He interpreted Matthew's famous statement, "Seek, and ye shall find; knock, and it shall be opened unto you," as an invitation for humankind to seek the Truth about the natural world through rational investigation.[24]

Across the English Channel, similar views were expressed by Adelard of Bath, who asserted that reason could solve all inquiries "since we must assume that all nature is based on a sure and logical foundation." Oxford University, established in 1214, spawned a scientific movement credited with laying the foundations of the modern practice of science. One key figure, Robert

Grosseteste, developed the parameters for what is known today as the scientific method. His student, Roger Bacon, considered by some the first true scientist, viewed mathematics as the language of nature and believed that the science of optics would offer a way to understand the mind of the creator.[25]

The new approach of using reason to understand the natural world gained such prestige that theologians were enticed into viewing their own field as a branch of science. Thomas Aquinas, whose ideas would dominate European thought for the remainder of the Middle Ages, was the first to make the unprecedented claim that theology was, in fact, a science. Indeed, it was "the most perfect science" because its knowledge came from God.[26]

Thomas claimed priority for theology over natural science but didn't view this as diminishing the importance of the latter. Rather, it seemed clear to him that reason could be fully reconciled with faith because both are ultimately gifts from God. It was Aquinas, more than anyone, who consolidated the framework of Christian rationalism. "There is a certain Eternal Law," he declared, "to wit, Reason, existing in the mind of God, and governing the whole universe." Through empirical knowledge of God's eternal law as manifested in the natural world, he claimed, we humans may acquire our best glimpse of God himself. And that knowledge could only be gained through the use of Reason.[27]

The tantalizing promise of getting in touch with eternal Truth through the use of one's intellect would mesmerize future generations of the most brilliant minds in the European tradition—and, as we will see, continues to do so to the present day.

Deciphering the Language of God

The primacy of Christian rationalism, as construed by Aquinas, essentially settled any further dispute in the later Middle Ages between faith and reason. The primary challenge now was to use the tools of reason to decipher the laws of nature and discover what was actually in God's mind. Throughout Europe, leading thinkers contributed to the storehouse of knowledge inherited from the ancient Greeks. The Renaissance, which is conventionally viewed as a drastic break from the past, was, rather, a flowering of the growth in learning that had been accumulating over centuries.[28]

The vision of God's laws as a geometric harmony, and the ambition of tapping into divine consciousness by understanding them, drove the intellectual breakthroughs that created the modern scientific conception of the universe.

Johannes Kepler based a radical new theory of planetary motion on this belief. Kepler was an ardent Platonist with a mystical vision of divine geometry. He wrote in the preface of his first major work that he would demonstrate that God did, in fact, create his universe on the basis of geometry, exactly as Plato had speculated. In a *tour de force* of mathematical wishful thinking, Kepler proposed that each of the five planets (known in his era) traveled in an orbit defined by a sphere, each of which contained one of the "regular solids" or polyhedra, which had remained a source of fascination since Pythagoras (figure 18.1).[29]

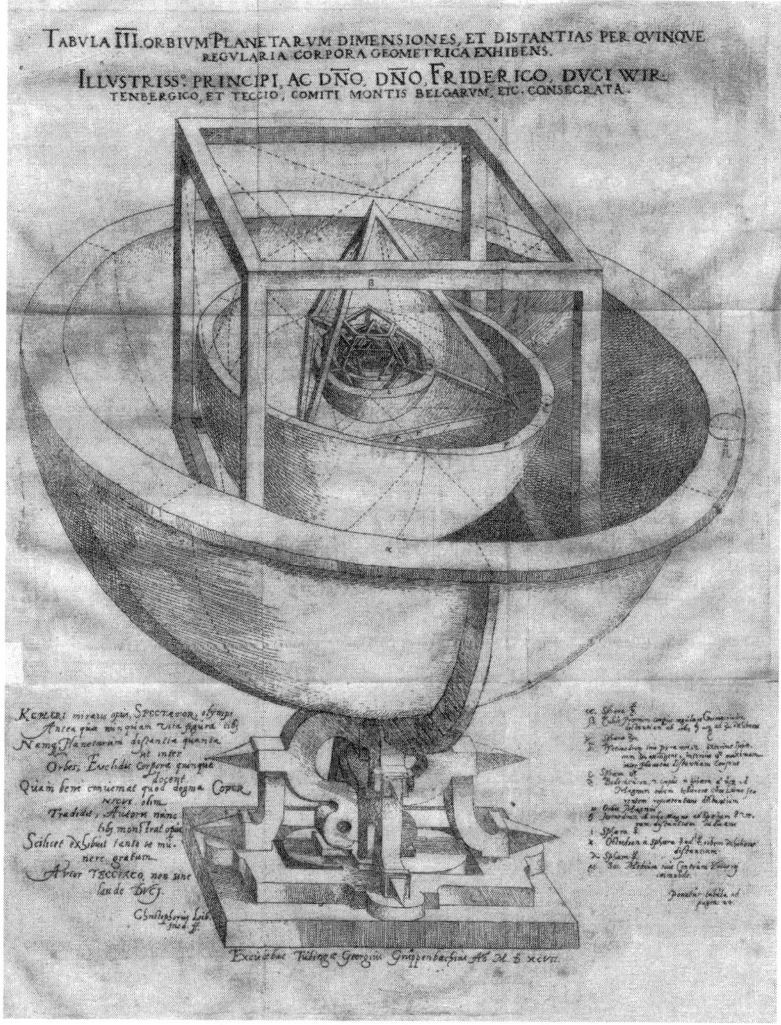

Figure 18.1: Kepler's illustration of the geometric "Secret of the Universe."

Kepler felt he had glimpsed the secret of God's universe. In a letter to a friend, he wrote, "What else can the human mind hold besides numbers and magnitudes? These alone we apprehend correctly, and if piety permits to say so, our comprehension is in this case of the same kind as God's, at least insofar as we are able to understand it in this mortal life."[30]

Kepler would sometimes refer to the forces he measured as obeying what he called "geometric laws." Here, in Kepler's genius, was the beginning of a transformation in the common perception of the cosmos. What had previously been God's laws of nature were now characterized as scientific laws. "Geometry," he wrote, "existed before the Creation, is co-eternal with the mind of God, *is God himself* (what exists in God that is not God himself ?); geometry provided God with a model for the Creation." God himself, Kepler seemed to imply, was bound by the geometric laws of the universe.[31]

Kepler's contemporary, Galileo, shared his Platonic vision of a universe created mathematically by a geometer god. Whereas Kepler investigated astronomical laws, Galileo searched for the existence of more general laws in his quest to read God's mind. To Galileo, it was self-evident that the pathway to God was mathematical. "Philosophy," he famously wrote, "is written in this grand book, the universe. . . . It is written in the language of mathematics, and its characters are triangles, circles, and other geometric figures."[32*]

So certain was Galileo about his vision of the cosmos that he viewed his own insights as being essentially the same as God's:

> As to the truth, of which mathematical demonstrations give us the knowledge, it is the same which the Divine Wisdom knows. . . . Now these inferences which our intellect apprehends with time and a gradual motion the Divine Wisdom, like light, penetrates in an instant.

In this remarkable passage, Galileo seems to imply that the primary difference between his mind and God's is merely one of speed in cognitive processing. Whereas Galileo has to think through his mathematics logically, God can do so instantaneously in a single thought.[33]

Both Kepler and Galileo seem intoxicated by the power of the mathematical language they were developing. Both were convinced they saw the Truth in a way that others simply could not. At times, Kepler would mock earlier theologians who had denied the earth was round. Kepler, a Lutheran living in central Europe during the stormy years of the Protestant Reformation, had his run-ins with theology, at one point being forced into exile because he refused to convert to Catholicism. However, in spite of his willingness to debate truths with theologians, his scientific writings never stirred up any great controversy. What was it, then, about Galileo that caused him to become the poster boy of the scientific struggle with religion?[34]

Galileo versus the Inquisition

Following Aquinas's embrace of natural philosophy, the Catholic Church had incorporated into its worldview the writings of philosophers such as Aristotle and Ptolemy. Even so, when German astronomer Nicolaus Copernicus contradicted Ptolemy in 1543 by proposing that the earth revolved around the sun, he received an enthusiastic reception from church authorities. For decades, Copernicus's theories were discussed in centers of learning throughout Europe without much concern for their theological implications. And yet, in 1616, when Galileo set out to silence critics of the new heliocentric view, he initiated a chain of events that resulted in Copernicus's book, *On the Revolutions of the Celestial Spheres*, being placed in the Inquisition's index of prohibited works. It would remain there until 1758. What had changed?[35]

Europe was in turmoil, and it had nothing to do with whether the earth revolved around the sun. After a millennium of undisputed religious authority, the Catholic Church had been rocked to its foundations by the forces of the Reformation, unleashed by Martin Luther in 1517. The Catholic establishment, desperately trying to maintain its authority over interpretation of the scriptures, condemned the teachings of Luther and his followers as heresies and forbade anyone to "twist the sense of Holy Scripture against the meaning which has been and is being held by our Holy Mother Church." All to no avail. By the early seventeenth century, Europe was in the middle of two hundred years of holy war, pitting Protestant against Catholic.[36]

The confrontation between Galileo and the Inquisition was an extra battle that no one of high standing really wanted—except Galileo. The scientific authorities in the Catholic Church were aware that if the Copernican view of the universe were correct, certain passages in the Bible that described the sun as "running his course" would need to be interpreted metaphorically rather than literally. That, in itself, presented little difficulty. The issue was rather one of due process and, above all, maintenance of the church's authority in interpreting scriptures. If the church had to change its official position about something as fundamental as the position of the earth in the heavens, the authorities needed to make sure it was well founded before taking such a drastic move.[37]

Galileo was well aware of church policy. He had been told by a cardinal that the Bible should be interpreted literally except for passages where there was a "compelling necessity" to view its content as merely metaphorical. Was there, then, a "compelling necessity" for the Catholic Church to change its view of the solar system in the early seventeenth century?[38]

It is difficult for the modern reader, who has grown up with photographs of the earth spinning in space around the sun, to recognize what a drastic and even absurd idea this would have been to earlier generations. Serious skeptics of the time had plenty of empirical reasons to dismiss what appeared to many as a wild hypothesis.[39*]

When Galileo forced the issue to a head, Cardinal Bellarmine was called to adjudicate the matter. Bellarmine had lectured on astronomy in his youth and was in close contact with astronomers in Rome who were enthusiastic about Galileo's work. His writings show respect for Copernicus's theory along with a desire to avoid escalating the conflict unnecessarily. When it came to changing official church policy on such a substantive matter, Bellarmine insisted, quite reasonably, on seeing proof, writing:

> If there were a real proof that . . . the Sun does not go round the Earth but the Earth round the Sun, then we should have to proceed with great circumspection in explaining passages of Scripture which appear to teach the contrary, and we should rather have to say that we did not understand them than declare an opinion to be false which is proved to be true. But as for myself, I shall not believe that there are such proofs until they are shown to me.[40]

The problem was that Galileo had no proof to show Bellarmine. At that time, the Copernican system was no more than a hypothesis and contained many loose ends. Galileo tried to cover this up in a letter to Bellarmine, claiming he could offer "a host of proofs," but it would be a waste of time because of the ignorance of those who opposed him. This bluff was characteristic of Galileo, who had an abrasive personality, delighting in publicly ridiculing those who disagreed with him. He was not above using his intellectual acumen as a smoke screen even when he was wrong.[41*]

Bellarmine tried to effect a compromise. He placed Copernicus's book in the Index until the passages that argued for a heliocentric system could be proven correct. He encouraged Galileo to freely develop his theories as hypotheses but avoid using them to interpret the scriptures, which Galileo was wont to do. It was only after years of enjoying fame and fortune that Galileo eventually wrote the book that would bring him in front of the Inquisition, in which he portrayed himself as a brilliant savant explaining the new view of the universe and caricatured the pope as a foolish buffoon representing the church's Aristotelian worldview.[42]

Galileo was itching for a showdown. When called to Rome by the Inquisition, he had the option of ignoring the summons and remaining in his hometown of Florence but chose to confront the Inquisition directly. Unlike so many other victims of the Inquisition's brutality, Galileo was treated with dignity. Rather than being confined to the dungeons during his trial, he was allowed to reside as the Tuscan ambassador's guest at the Villa Medici. After being found guilty of heresy, he was sentenced by the Inquisition to "formal prison," which turned out to be the palace of the Archbishop of Siena, and he was ordered to repeat seven penitential psalms once a week for three years, which were delegated, with ecclesiastical consent, to his daughter, a Carmelite nun.[43]

The mainstream historical narrative that depicts an irreconcilable conflict between science and Christianity frequently holds up the Galileo affair as its *cause célèbre*. Galileo's caustic personality and the church's relative restraint in responding to him certainly do not exonerate the Catholic Church for its handling of the affair. They do, however, call into question whether it was historically inevitable. Ironically, what emerges from this story is that, instead of acting as the enemy of science, the church authorities were primarily concerned about receiving scientific proof of the new theory before shifting their official worldview. It was perhaps Galileo, rather than Bellarmine, who was guilty of subverting a rigorous and methodical pursuit of truth.[44*]

From God's Laws to Newton's Laws

With Kepler's search for the divine geometry of the heavens, and Galileo's conviction that the book of nature was written by God in the language of mathematics, scientific cognition was finally hatched. As it spread throughout the intellectual centers of Europe, it continued to be invigorated, and—notwithstanding the Galileo affair—even appropriated by Christian rationalism.

In fact, it was really a continuation of Christian rationalism, with a subtle but important shift in emphasis, focusing now on precise mathematical definitions of the laws God had inscribed into the universe.[45]

Of all the brilliant thinkers of the seventeenth century, probably no one made a greater contribution to deciphering these laws than Isaac Newton. In his major work, he accomplished the final step in transforming God's laws into defined laws of nature. With his three mathematically derived "laws of motion," he established the concept of "laws" as a foundation of scientific cognition. As mathematicians enthusiastically embraced Newton's findings, it seemed self-evident that the theoretical foundation of Christian rationalism—that God had created the universe according to a fixed set of natural laws—was indisputably true.[46]

After Newton, the idea of laws of nature would become firmly embedded into the structure of modern thought. However, the shift from Christian rationalism to scientific cognition in no way undermined religious authority. In those pre-Darwinian days, with no theory of evolution to explain the complexity of the natural world, the exquisite design of nature was seen as powerful evidence of God's handiwork. English physicist Robert Boyle declared the intricate contrivance of the natural world to be "one of the great motives" to religious belief.[47]

Not only were Christianity and natural science seen as fully compatible, there was a prevalent belief that only Christians, as devotees of God's Truth, had received the grace from God to be capable of discerning his eternal mind through natural science. A letter from Leibniz to the French government, congratulating them on their contribution to science, exults in the likely impression their new technologies would have on non-Christian cultures:

> A king of Persia will exclaim over the effect of the telescope, and a mandarin of China will be overcome with astonishment when he understands the infallibility of a geometrician missionary. What will these peoples say? . . . I believe that they will recognize that the mind of man has something of the divine, and that this divinity communicates itself especially to Christians.[48]

Before too long, Newton's laws became an integral part of the European worldview. As the Industrial Revolution began in earnest in England, devout Christians would commonly sing this hymn to praise their god for the Newtonian world he had graciously created:

Praise the Lord, for he hath spoken,
Worlds his mighty voice obeyed;
Laws, which never shall be broken,
For their guidance he hath made.[49]

Knowing the Mind of God

A consequential aspect of Newton's laws of motion was that they worked everywhere in the known universe: they could predict the trajectory of a cannonball as well as the orbit of a planet around the sun. This effectively put an end to one aspect of the Platonic cosmos—the idea, so mesmerizing to Kepler, that the heavens were perfectly geometric and followed different laws than on earth.

At the same time, Newton's laws gave further credence to the Platonic notion of an abstract dimension of Ideas that were eternally fixed and true. Throughout the nineteenth century, mathematicians continued to visualize a Platonic universe. One of the greatest, Georg Cantor, a devout Catholic, believed that, through his mathematical study of infinity, he could prove the existence of God, much as Anselm had been asked by his monks to do in the eleventh century. Cantor saw numbers as eternal realities that were discovered by humans and followed Godgiven laws. Other mathematicians, less devout than Cantor, held the same conviction that mathematics represented a reality that was discovered, not constructed, by the human mind. This Platonic idealization of mathematics was increasingly decoupled from the concept of a Christian God while remaining as central to the scientific belief system as God was to Christianity.[50]

Newton's laws were superseded by Einstein's theory of relativity in the early twentieth century, but this did nothing to undermine the Platonic belief in an eternal truth waiting to be discovered. Even as he revolutionized the laws of physics, Einstein himself held this view, writing, "One reason why mathematics enjoys special esteem, above all other sciences, is that its propositions are absolutely certain and indisputable." Einstein, who viewed himself as agnostic, nevertheless showed such conviction in the Platonic order of the universe that much of his work was driven by this belief. When a new generation of physicists formulated the theories of quantum mechanics, postulating a world driven by random, probabilistic activity, Einstein dismissed it, exclaiming famously that "God does not play dice," and spent his later years vainly trying to formulate an alternative, Platonic theory.[51]

However, even quantum mechanics did nothing to quell the prevalent faith held by mathematicians in the existence of a separate Platonic dimension of eternal truth. This belief remains so pervasive that it is frequently stated, both by leading scientists and in the mainstream scientific press, as an indisputable article of faith. Roger Penrose, an internationally renowned mathematician, has proffered a modern restatement of Plato's theory:

> I imagine that whenever a mind perceives a mathematical idea, it makes contact with Plato's world of mathematical concepts. . . . When mathematicians communicate . . . each is directly in contact with the same externally existing Platonic world! All the information was there all the time. It was just a matter of putting things together and 'seeing' the answer. . . . In their greatest works, mathematicians are revealing eternal truths that have some kind of prior ethereal existence.[52*]

These ideas are ubiquitous in modern scientific cognition. Prominent cosmologist Max Tegmark asserts that "our universe is not just described by mathematics—it is mathematics. . . . We don't invent mathematical structures—we discover them, and invent only the notation for describing them." And Stephen Hawking, possibly the greatest physicist of our time, concludes his bestseller *A Brief History of Time* by imagining the moment when the "theory of everything" is eventually discovered, with a reprisal of the Christian rationalist narrative:

> Then we shall all, philosophers, scientists, and just ordinary people, be able to take part in the discussion of the question of why it is that we and the universe exist. If we find the answer to that, it would be the ultimate triumph of human reason—for then we would know the mind of God.[53]

Universal Truth or Universally True?

With such an impressive array of experts sharing the same Platonic vision, it might be tempting for the rest of us to accept that perhaps it's true. Are these brilliant minds all in touch with a Platonic dimension of Truth not available to ordinary humans? On the other hand, this chapter reveals that the Platonic belief in an eternal truth is, rather, a received cultural assumption so embedded into our cognition that it is rarely ever challenged or even recognized as such.[54]

This sense of the universal truth of mathematics is partly driven by the fact that math works so well—what has been called by theoretical physicist Eugene Wigner the "unreasonable effectiveness of mathematics." It has long been a source of astonishment to scientists how mathematics can make theoretical predictions that are later proven empirically to be true. The power of a few equations to predict the behavior of things as small as a molecule and as large as a galaxy is so awesome as to be understandably intoxicating. Astrophysicist Mario Livio, in his book *Is God a Mathematician?*, points out that mathematics, unique among all human creations, has a self-consistency that seems to force "truths" upon us. Euclid's geometry is as true today as it was two thousand years ago.[55]

Not every mathematician, however, subscribes to the Platonic vision. Prominent geometrician Sir Michael Atiyah envisions mathematics as a language of science, just as spoken language and music are both languages of the mind. He speculates that perhaps mathematics itself could evolve to express reality in new ways as the findings of quantum physics throw out ever-stranger paradoxes. Even the number system, he suggests, may be concepts of our own creation. "Let us imagine," he ponders, "that intelligence had resided, not in mankind, but in some vast solitary and isolated jelly-fish, buried deep in the depths of the Pacific Ocean. It would have no experience of individual objects, only with the surrounding water. Motion, temperature and pressure would provide its basic sensory data. In such a pure continuum the discrete would not arise and there would be nothing to count."[56]

At its heart, the crucial question is whether there is ultimately such a thing as *the* Truth, as opposed to cognitive constructions creating relationships between coordinates that are always true. Within plane geometry, for example, it is always true that the area of a circle is equal to pi times the radius squared. But just because something is always true, that doesn't necessarily make it the Truth.[57]

Even within mathematics, laws once viewed as universally true are sometimes later found to describe a more constrained set of circumstances. For example, Euclid's laws of geometry were considered universally true until the nineteenth century, when a series of breakthroughs led to the conceptualization of geometry in curved space following different laws, which became known as non-Euclidean geometry. Similarly, Newton's laws were viewed as universally applicable until Einstein demonstrated they were not valid in certain circumstances. In neither case was Euclid or Newton proved wrong; rather, the scope of their laws, once thought to be universal, was constrained by new findings.[58]

Some mathematicians point out that, in spite of its "unreasonable effectiveness," there are domains where mathematics is far less effective, particularly those that exhibit self-organized behavior, such as biological systems, human interactions, weather patterns, and stock market fluctuations. Pioneering branches of modern science, such as systems biology and complexity theory, use mathematics to investigate these domains while rejecting the notion of an eternally fixed mathematical truth waiting to be discovered.[59]

The question of whether mathematics leads to the ultimate Truth has profound implications for how humanity can find meaning from the universe. If, instead of being the gateway to "the mind of God," mathematics is a specific language constructed by the human mind, there may be other constructions of meaning offering alternative truths that are no less valid. This raises the intriguing possibility that we have the ability to consciously select and integrate different structures of cognition as sources of meaning in our lives.

Mathematics, however, as the language of science, has powered the scientific revolution that helped shape our modern world, and this has given a certain credence to those who make claims for its universality. Although no longer exulting, like Leibniz, in the "divinity" of mind that "communicates itself especially to Christians," many observers automatically make assumptions about the universal validity of the science originally developed in Europe, seeing it as a value-free truth that transcends cultural boundaries.[60]

However, as we've seen, other civilizations such as China and the Islamic world were headed on trajectories very different from that of Europe. These divergent paths were laid down by cognitive structures of meaning that led scholars to value different uses for their mental capabilities. "I see no reason," reflects Nathan Sivin, "to believe that anyone in the world in 1200 or 1500, given detailed specifications, would have wanted our kind of science. Some, no doubt, would have been fascinated by its exactitude and analytical power, but they were likely at the same time to be repelled by its insistence on quantity over quality and its lack of connection with human values."[61]

Scientific cognition emerged within the dualistic paradigm of Western thought, and its pursuit of an abstract, disembodied version of the truth continues to reinforce the fissures within Western cognition. Sciences continue to be taught in terms of abstract principles divorced from the real world. In the words of two physicists writing about complexity: "The ideas that form the foundation of our worldview are . . . very simple indeed: The world is lawful, and the same basic laws hold everywhere. Everything is simple, neat, and expressible in terms of everyday mathematics . . . except, of course, the world."[62]

Once we begin to recognize that the search for truth in the universe through mathematics is merely one possible pathway in the human search for meaning, other possibilities open up—not in rejection of scientific cognition but as opportunities for science to expand its domain of investigation. Just as the laws of Euclid and Newton remain valid within specified parameters, so the mathematically based search for scientific laws to describe the universe can retain its validity and usefulness while potentially fitting into larger structures of cognition. The domains of self-organized complexity, for example, which describe the nonlinear behavior of living systems, including our global civilization, preclude reduction to mathematical equations. As we'll explore in the following chapters, the "language of God" may be precise, but learning to use it has had a rather ambiguous effect on the course of human history.

Chapter 19

"SOMETHING FAR MORE DEEPLY INTERFUSED": THE SYSTEMS WORLDVIEW

The Butterfly and the Tornado

Edward Lorenz walked down the hall at the Massachusetts Institute of Technology campus to get a cup of coffee. It was the winter of 1961, and while another snowstorm was threatening outside, Lorenz was busy constructing his own model of the weather on a state-of-the-art computer installed in his office, replete with vacuum tubes and a spaghetti of wires. Lorenz was on the cutting edge of the scientific endeavor to decipher the hidden mechanisms of nature. Back in the eighteenth century, mathematician Pierre-Simon Laplace had proposed that the universe was completely deterministic and, given enough information, it was theoretically possible to predict the movement of every atom. Scientists ever since had been inspired by this vision, analyzing nature's building blocks with the goal of predicting exactly how they worked. They had been hamstrung primarily by limitations in calculating horsepower, but the recent arrival of computers held the promise of great breakthroughs.

Newton's laws had already proven their awesome capability to predict the movements of planets and rocket trajectories. Einstein's physics had led to the splitting of the atom. Now, with the new capability of computers, Lorenz planned to extend science's predictive powers to the complex arena of weather forecasting. He analyzed the nonlinear interactions of variables such as wind direction and temperature and impressed his peers with detailed models of weather patterns. However, his new computer needed constant repairs. Today, he was checking that it had been fixed properly by running a model he had used previously. Walking back to his office, coffee in hand, he expected to see exactly the same output as before. Instead, to his consternation, the new weather patterns diverged significantly from the previous run, but the computer itself seemed to be working fine. What was wrong?

When Lorenz went back to check all his inputs for accuracy, he made a discovery that would have far-reaching implications for our understanding of nature—puncturing the certainties of Laplace's deterministic universe and helping launch a new worldview that is becoming increasingly influential: the systems view of life. Lorenz's discovery seemed utterly insignificant: in his hurry to test the computer, he had rounded off one of his numerical inputs. Instead of 0.506127, he had entered 0.506. And yet, that tiny change in input had led to a drastic difference in predicted weather patterns. A lesser scientist might have shrugged and continued working. Lorenz, however, spent the next decade following the implications of this discrepancy, which he shared with fellow scientists in 1972 with a question that has since become world-famous: "Does the flap of a butterfly's wings in Brazil set off a tornado in Texas?" Lorenz had discovered what became known as "deterministic chaos": the principle that, in a nonlinear world, tiny changes in initial conditions could lead to vastly different outcomes, making long-term prediction impossible.[1]

In this chapter, we'll discover how an array of brilliant scientists, Lorenz among them, has forged a new way of understanding nature that has the potential to transform the predominant modern worldview. This approach sees nature as a complex, dynamic web of interconnected systems, which works according to certain principles that can be investigated but never completely controlled. With its contradiction of the Western fixed, mechanical view of nature, the new systems way of thinking has a surprising amount in common with traditional Chinese ideas about the universe. We'll consider some of those similarities as we unearth them.

The systems approach to the universe also boasts a long pedigree in European thought. Much of this book has covered the rise of the predominant European worldview, beginning with Plato's dualistic universe and manifesting in the root metaphors of CONQUERING NATURE and NATURE AS MACHINE that undergird the current mainstream way of thinking. However, from the time of the ancient Greeks onward, there were European thinkers who didn't subscribe to the dominant view. Instead, they conceived of a world closer in spirit to the modern systems understanding: one that was dynamic and alive rather than fixed and mechanistic. Their alternative ideas lived on, albeit obscured by the glare of the prevailing Western tradition, in much the same way that light from a full moon offers a different perspective on familiar surroundings.

For this reason, we can consider this alternative way of thinking as Europe's "moonlight tradition," an understanding of which helps to place modern systems thinking in its full cultural context.

The Moonlight Tradition: Ancient Beginnings

In the earliest days of Greek philosophy, Heraclitus was fascinated by the ever-changing nature of the universe, famously observing that "it is impossible to step into the same river twice." This flicker of Greek thought, however, was eclipsed by the belief in fixed, universal laws of nature that culminated in Plato's dualistic universe. The eternally fixed dimension of Ideas, in Plato's cosmos, formed the ideal blueprint of reality, of which the changeable material world was merely an inferior imitation. This eternal dimension was also the origin of each human soul temporarily entombed in the physical body.[2]

Powerful as Plato's teachings must have been, not everyone in his Academy agreed with him. One student in particular, Aristotle, sported an intellect that matched his teacher's and went on to develop his own theories of the cosmos that repudiated the Platonic model. For Aristotle, the purpose of something wasn't to be as close as possible to its ideal blueprint. Aristotle investigated how embryos developed and realized you could only understand an embryo's changes when you were aware of what it would become. Everything, in his view, like the embryo, had an intrinsic purpose for its physical existence. As such, it made no sense to separate the form and matter of something. In order to gain a full understanding, the natural scientist had to study both.[3]

Aristotle gave an example of a house. One person might describe a house in terms of what it's composed of: stone, bricks, or timber. Another might evaluate it in terms of how it fulfills its purpose: say, to provide shelter. Which of these, Aristotle asked, is the natural scientist? Only the person, he answered, who combines both.[4]

This merger of form and matter entirely unraveled Plato's theory of the soul, which Plato believed to have an immaterial existence. Aristotle developed a competing theory, in which the soul was indistinguishable from the body. "We do not have to enquire whether the soul and the body are one," he asserted, "any more than whether the wax and its shape are one." Instead, something's soul arose from its defining purpose. "If the eye were an animal," he explained, "sight would be its soul, since this is the defining essence of an eye. The eye is matter for sight, and if this departs it is no longer an eye except in name, like the eye of a statue or in a painting."[5]

As the inventor of systematic logic, Aristotle was not afraid to deduce from this theory that every living thing must have a soul. He conceived of a hierarchy of souls according to the type of organism. Plants possessed a vegetative soul, which allowed them to grow and reproduce; animals had, additionally, a sensitive soul that permitted them to move and feel; humans possessed, in addition, a rational soul that gave them the capacity to reason. Unlike Plato's eternal soul, these souls could not be expected to survive the body's death. Soul and body were, rather, two different aspects of an organism's physical existence.[6]

For centuries, it looked as if Aristotle's worldview might win out over Plato's. The dominant philosophical schools of the late ancient world were Stoicism and Epicureanism, both of which believed, like Aristotle, in a single, material universe. They understood the soul as the organizing principle of the body, neither of which could exist without the other. The Stoics expanded this notion to view all matter as fundamentally linked in a dynamic web, interconnected through the underlying principle *pneuma*, which permeated the cosmos as a kind of soul of the universe.[7]

This materialist view of the universe, however, could not coexist with the Christian cosmos, defined by a transcendent God bestowing an eternal soul to each individual. The idea of the soul being as mortal as the body undermined the very basis of Christian salvation. As the early church fathers elaborated their account of God's universe, they made a conscious choice to base it on Plato's cosmos, eschewing the ideas of Aristotle along with those of the Stoics and Epicureans. As a result, it was Plato's dualistic paradigm that framed the European way of thinking for two millennia.[8]

The Modern Moonlight Tradition

The rediscovery of Aristotle's works in twelfth-century Europe created serious challenges for theologians, who were forced to grapple with his theory of the soul when they tried to reconcile his ideas with Christian theology. Thomas Aquinas, whose Aristotelian-based philosophy dominated Christendom for centuries, settled on an uneasy equivocation about the soul, recognizing Aristotle's point of view but nevertheless maintaining the soul's eternal existence without the body.[9]

Aristotle's ideas of the material soul, though stifled by mainstream thought, formed the basis of the modern moonlight tradition, which achieved its first magnificent flowering in the genius of Leonardo da Vinci. Leonardo was obsessed by the dynamic patterns of nature, viewing the earth as a living organism with a vegetative soul, constantly in a process of transformation. "We may therefore say," he averred, "that the Earth has a vital force of growth, and that its flesh is the soil, its bones are the successive strata of the rocks which form the mountains; its cartilage is the porous rock, its blood the veins of the waters."[10]

Leonardo, working secretively and never publishing his findings, achieved an array of astounding scientific discoveries that remained locked away in his notebooks. The pioneers of the Scientific Revolution in the seventeenth century, transfixed by their pursuit of God's eternal Truth, remained unaware of Leonardo's insights, and his vision of a living universe in constant transformation was neglected with their adoption of Descartes's model of a fixed, mechanistic world.[11]

The moonlight tradition, however, continued on. Even at the height of the Scientific Revolution, alternative worldviews were proffered by a few innovative thinkers. Baruch Spinoza, a Dutch Jewish philosopher, was ostracized from his community for his pantheistic views. Spinoza, considered by some to be the spiritual grandfather of ecology, saw God as identical with nature and believed everything in the universe to be an expression of the thought of God. Like Aristotle and the Neo-Confucians, Spinoza saw mind and body as not separate but instead two distinct attributes of existence. Another contemporary philosopher, Leibniz, contributed greatly to the Scientific Revolution even while maintaining that the world was fully alive, down to the smallest particle of matter. Leibniz was fascinated by the Chinese concepts he heard about through Jesuit missionaries, and his philosophical vision of a preestablished harmony in the universe contains strong echoes of the Neo-Confucian conception of the Supreme Ultimate manifested through the world in the form of li.[12]

By the late eighteenth century, a widespread revulsion to the predominant mechanistic view of the universe erupted throughout Europe in the form of the Romantic movement. For a brief period, it was as though the sun were eclipsed, and the moonlight tradition illuminated the intellectual landscape. "May God us keep from Single vision and Newton's sleep," wrote visionary poet William Blake. Another poet, William Wordsworth, lamented, "Our meddling intellect Misshapes the beauteous forms of things: We murder to dissect." Wordsworth composed a memorable expression of reverence at the complex systems underlying the universe:

> And I have felt
> A presence that disturbs me with the joy
> Of elevated thoughts; a sense sublime
> Of something far more deeply interfused,
> Whose dwelling is the light of setting suns,
> And the round ocean and the living air,
> And the blue sky, and in the mind of man;
> A motion and a spirit, that impels
> All thinking things, all objects of all thought,
> And rolls through all things.[13]

This Romantic backlash to the Age of Reason, however, reinforced the conceptual split between reason and emotion that has since become a hallmark of modern thought. Rational philosophy, complained poet John Keats, will "clip an Angel's wings, Conquer all mysteries by rule and line . . . Unweave a rainbow." These attacks on science created intellectual battle lines that laid the groundwork for a counterattack by rationalists accusing the Romantics of indulging in sentimentality.[14]

On the Continent, poet and statesman Johann Wolfgang von Goethe refused to go along with this division being formed between science and beauty. Goethe, who founded the science of morphology—the study of forms—instead saw beauty, like Leonardo centuries earlier did, as "a manifestation of secret natural laws, which otherwise would have been hidden from us forever." Rather than trying to conquer nature, Goethe believed a scientist should approach nature as a participant and that scientific insight arises through not detached observation but an intuitive sense of connection with nature's dynamic flux. His way of understanding nature has clear similarities to the Neo-Confucian Investigation of Things. "From the Supreme Ultimate above," Zhu Xi had said, "to a small thing like a blade of grass . . . we must understand them one by one. . . . As more and more is accumulated, one will spontaneously be able to achieve a far and broad understanding." This was, in essence, Goethe's approach to scientific investigation.[15]

While the European military-industrial juggernaut stormed through the nineteenth century in its frenzy to conquer both nature and other continents, a few philosophers further developed Goethe's unconventional ideas. Alfred North Whitehead saw continual transformation as a defining principle of the natural world and recognized the impossibility of a completely objective view of the universe. "There is no holding nature still and looking at it," he wrote. "The real point is that the essential connectedness of things can never be safely omitted." While Whitehead's was an isolated voice in the English-speaking world, a prominent European philosophical school known as phenomenology raised these ideas to a new level of sophistication. Its underlying basis was the rejection of the notion of scientific objectivity, replacing it with the recognition that humans are embodied in the physical world and that our understanding of the universe arises from how we are situated within it. Philosophers such as Husserl, Merleau-Ponty, and Heidegger explored the profound implications arising from this. Like the Neo-Confucians before them, they recognized that intellect alone did not suffice to comprehend the universe, but skillful use of one's intuition was required for a deeper understanding.[16]

The Mathematics of the Real World

Embracing intuition, however, did not have to mean discarding the intellect. As the nineteenth century drew to a close, an increasing number of European scientists had the audacity to delve into the messiness of nature's dynamic complexity and try to make sense of it.

The most complex system that we know of is the human mind, and that was the focus of study for one group of thinkers, who developed what became known as Gestalt psychology. Their fundamental insight was that the mind works by creating a holistic, integrated pattern of meaning from its surroundings, which cannot be reduced into an aggregation of its discrete elements. Its central finding, "The whole is other than the sum of its parts," has become a hallmark of much systems thinking since then. Another group, led by German biologist Ernst Haeckel, conducted an investigation into the complexity of nature. Creating the science of ecology, they examined the tangled networks of systems that exist among the different organisms that make up an environment and explored the profound and sometimes unexpected effects that changes in one system can have on another with which it is connected.[17]

As physicists collaborated to develop quantum theory in the early twentieth century, they gave validation at the deepest level to the phenomenologists, who had rejected the existence of a fixed, objective reality discoverable by science. In trying to determine whether an electron was a wave or a particle, researchers began to realize that it depended on how they approached it.

"What we observe," wrote theoretical physicist Werner Heisenberg, "is not nature itself, but nature exposed to our method of questioning." The original insights of Goethe and Whitehead were now receiving the highest caliber of scientific corroboration.[18]

By the middle of the twentieth century, leading thinkers were developing the holistic way of thinking into a formal science of its own, which they called systems theory. Austrian biologist Ludwig von Bertalanffy was determined to place systems thinking on a firm mathematical foundation. His efforts were paralleled in the United States by Norbert Wiener and other researchers, who developed the science of cybernetics, an investigation of the dynamics of control and communication in both nature and machines. As he pursued this inquiry, Wiener became impressed by how patterns seemed to be a fundamental characteristic of reality. With words that reprise the insights of the Neo-Confucians a thousand years earlier, he observed: "We are but whirlpools in a river of ever-flowing water. We are not stuff that abides, but patterns that perpetuate themselves."[19]

With this remarkable work being conducted on both sides of the Atlantic, it might seem surprising that when Edward Lorenz introduced his ideas about deterministic chaos to a conference of leading scientists in 1972, he received such a shocked response. However, the scientific community had developed such impervious barriers between its various subdisciplines that the majority of mainstream scientists still had very little understanding of the basic principles of systems thinking. In fact, they were conducting their research on a foundation that was incompatible with much of what systems theory proposed.

Newton's laws, and the sciences they spawned, had been based on a conceptualization of an idealized universe that truly existed only in the mathematical abstractions they postulated. They worked so well because, in many cases, the messy complications of the real world had relatively little effect. They were superb at predicting the movements of planets in the vacuum of space and almost as effective in determining where a cannonball would go, since the variable effects of such disturbances as wind were generally insignificant. In pursuing their disciplines, scientists would often use the Latin phrase *ceteribus paribus*—"other things being equal"—to dismiss the random noise that didn't fit into the theory. Now, in systems thinking, a new set of methods was emerging to investigate the unequal world of those other things.[20]

A brilliant mathematician, Benoit Mandelbrot, developed a new branch of mathematics, called fractal geometry, to describe this non-Newtonian world.

His 1983 book *The Fractal Geometry of Nature* had a profound effect on the field of mathematics. Mandelbrot explained in clear terms the limitations of classical theory:

> Most of nature is very, very complicated. How could one describe a cloud? A cloud is not a sphere. . . . It is like a ball but very irregular. A mountain? A mountain is not a cone. . . . If you want to speak of clouds, of mountains, of rivers, of lightning, the geometric language of school is inadequate.

The fractal forms that Mandelbrot's mathematical formulas create have a delicate grace that mirrors the beauty of nature itself (figure 19.1). Fractal geometry helped instigate a deeper understanding of patterns in nature. One profound insight was that the same design tends to repeat itself at larger or smaller scales. Coastlines, cloudscapes, sand dunes, and rivers all demonstrate what is known as scale independency, creating similar patterns both close up and from a distance. Biologists began to recognize these fractal patterns in all kinds of living systems: leaf veins, tree branches, blood vessels, lung brachia, and neurons. Social scientists discovered similar fractal principles in all kinds of human constructions: cities, music, and stock market fluctuations.

Figure 19.1: Computer-generated fractal image of a fern

The enormous range of domains in which fractals could be identified led to an even more profound realization: there seemed to be certain principles in nature itself that applied across a whole array of disciplines. The traditional approach to science, in which specialists focused their lives on one tiny patch of knowledge, seemed incapable of recognizing these cross-disciplinary underlying structures in the nature of reality.[21]

Life at the Edge of Chaos

It seems fitting that some of the most important insights in exploring these hidden principles of nature have come from scientists who had the courage to cross over from one specialty to another. One of these was Austrian physicist Erwin Schrödinger, who won a Nobel Prize for his work on quantum theory, then ventured into the fundamentals of biology, publishing a seminal book in 1944 entitled *What Is Life?*[22]

Schrödinger's groundbreaking answer to this age-old question began with the second law of thermodynamics, which states that the universe is undergoing an irreversible process of entropy: an inexorable decline from order to disorder. This law predicts that heat will always flow to cooler regions and explains why, once you've beaten an egg, you can never get the yolk back. However, Schrödinger observed that while the universe as a whole undergoes entropy, life somehow manages to reverse this process. Living organisms, he noted, survive through sucking order out of the entropy around them and organizing it in a way beneficial to them. They do this through the process known in biology as metabolism. Schrödinger called this process negative entropy (or negentropy) and saw it as the defining characteristic of life.[23]

The end point of a system undergoing entropy is known in physics as equilibrium: the state where there is no order left to lose. Another Nobel laureate, Ilya Prigogine, spent years investigating systems such as flames, tornadoes, and whirlpools that managed to maintain themselves far from equilibrium, achieving stability even while they were continually in flux. What was the process by which they managed to continually change and yet remain relatively stable? Prigogine explained how these systems undergo a process of self-organization. In certain circumstances, when a large number of independent elements are continually interacting with each other, they achieve a coherent state. The same principles of self-organization apply to water molecules in a whirlpool as well as a flock of starlings, a school of fish, or a crowd of humans leaving a sports stadium.[24]

These systems only achieve self-organized coherence under certain circumstances. This can be seen clearly in the case of water. When water is frozen, the molecules connect to each other in a fixed state that doesn't allow for any fluidity. At the other extreme, when water is boiling, the relationship between the water molecules is random, with no coherent patterns emerging. There is a certain area somewhere between the states of fixity and randomness that selforganization can occur.[25]

This balance between the opposite states of rigidity and chaos has led some theorists to speculate that life itself exists at the "edge of chaos," a state with enough dynamism to continue growing and adapting and enough stability to maintain order and integration. The balance of dynamism and stability leads to an important characteristic feature of self-organized systems: they are continually responding to changes in their environment while remaining robust. A whirlpool in a river, a candle flame, a flock of birds—all look different from one moment to the next, even while they remain recognizably coherent. You can see this property for yourself by filling a sink with water, unplugging it, and watching the vortex of water spiraling down the drain. As long as there is enough water in the sink, the exact shape of the vortex is constantly changing and yet remains stable.[26]

It's easy enough to see water molecules self-organize in this way. But how do other systems move into a state of self-organized coherence? There are two indispensable factors. There must be a large number of individual elements interacting with and influencing each other, and the system must be continually interacting with the environment, usually containing smaller systems within it. As the system's complexity reaches a certain critical mass, it achieves a newly coherent state, sometimes dramatically, in a process known as emergence.[27]

A powerful example of emergence can be seen in an ant colony. When ants discover a food source and carry some of it back to the nest, they leave a trail behind them of a chemical called pheromone, which evaporates after a while. If another ant discovers the pheromone trail, it will follow it to the food source and add its own pheromone to the trail when it brings back the food. If only a small number of ants are foraging, the pheromone trail of a successful ant is likely to evaporate before being discovered by the others, and so their collective efficiency is no more than the sum of each individual ant's efforts. However, when the number of ants reaches a critical mass, the likelihood of a pheromone trail being discovered goes up exponentially, and the colony becomes superefficient at collecting the best food sources. A cohesive group intelligence emerges out of a simple chemical signaling system.[28]

The concept of emergence is sometimes criticized as being quasi-mystical or unscientific. However, it has been studied across a wide range of different fields and shown to be the result of sometimes-simple behavioral rules that combine to cause unexpected events that could not occur merely by aggregating the individual components. In this sense, the whole—consistent with Gestalt theory—becomes something other than the sum of its parts. We can see the power of emergence through humanity's history and in important aspects of our daily lives: culture is the emergent result of large numbers of humans interacting; language emerges from the complex interactions of words; the internet emerged from a critical mass of connected computers; and leading neuroscientists theorize that consciousness is the emergent result of the self-organized interactions of neurons in the brain and nervous system. One might speculate that if Aristotle had access to modern systems theory, he would have explained the soul as the integrative organizing principle emerging from the living systems he studied so assiduously.[29]

Of all examples of emergence, perhaps the most awe-inspiring is the emergence of life on earth. Leading researchers have followed Schrödinger's path in investigating the principles of self-organization to probe the mysteries of life itself. Chilean biologists Humberto Maturana and Francisco Varela identified a unique attribute of living systems that differentiates them from other selforganized systems. A living system doesn't just self-organize—it actively generates itself, taking energy from the environment to modify itself and perpetuate its existence. They called this process *autopoiesis*, from the Greek words meaning "self-generation." They described how every living system—as small as a single cell and as big as a redwood tree—has a sense of itself as an integrated entity and a basic understanding of what it is meant to do. Aristotle's original conjecture that each organism had an intrinsic sense of purpose was being borne out by scientific insights millennia later.[30]

Since Maturana and Varela's breakthrough, other researchers have developed sophisticated models to explain this apparent miracle of self-generating life. The core principle of these models is a process of reciprocal causality between all the different parts of the system and the whole. The whole emerges as a gestalt from the complex interactions of its parts, and it simultaneously specifies what each of the parts needs to do from moment to moment. Each causes the other. What came first—the parts or the whole? Leading researchers propose that the answer is both: in a process of circular, dynamic co-emergence, the parts generate the whole while the whole organizes the parts.[31]

Nature: Machine or Organism?

How different this is from the mainstream Western view of nature as a machine! As we saw in a previous chapter, after the invention of the clock, Europeans became transfixed by a vision of nature as an intricate clockwork designed by God. Since the Scientific Revolution, the view of nature as a very complicated machine has spread worldwide. One of today's most influential popularizers of science, Richard Dawkins, has devoted much of his career to disseminating this idea, which has shaped how many people in today's world think about the underlying structure of nature.[32]

With the advent of computers, the machine metaphor of nature has become even more intoxicating. Dawkins's avowal that "life is just bytes and bytes and bytes of digital information" underlies much of how people understand our world. In biology, genes are commonly described like computer programmers that "code" for certain traits. In discussions of psychology, countless writers describe the mind as "software" and the body as "hardware" with a brain that is "wired" in a certain way.[33]

A major reason for this pervasive view of nature as a machine has been the spectacular success of scientific disciplines that used it as a model for research. Most science works through a reductionist approach: viewing the world as an assemblage of parts that can each be analyzed separately. This method has led to enormous success in many fields, permitting the remarkable achievements of science and technology in creating the modern world. It has led to the increased specialization of science, causing researchers to spend their careers gaining detailed expertise in tightly constrained areas of knowledge. It has also, through its success, caused many scientists to conflate their powerful metaphor of NATURE AS MACHINE with a philosophical belief that nature is in fact a deterministic machine. The reductionist view has become, for many, an article of faith, causing them to claim that every aspect of our world, no matter how aweinspiring, is "nothing but" the mechanical motion of particles acting predictably on each other. This view is summed up by Nobel laureate Francis Crick, one of the discoverers of the DNA molecule:

> You, your joys and your sorrows, your memories and your ambitions, your sense of personal identity and free will, are in fact no more than the behavior of a vast assembly of nerve cells and their associated molecules.[34]

The findings of systems theory show this view to be misguided. In selforganized systems, the complex interaction of many connected elements causes emergent behavior that could never be predicted by a study of each part alone, no matter how detailed. The reductionist view of "nothing but" is analogous to someone observing that Shakespeare's entire opus is nothing but an assemblage of twenty-six letters repeated in different configurations. Whether we are evaluating tornadoes, Shakespeare, or life itself, the patterns that connect the parts frequently contain far more valuable information than the parts themselves.[35]

This is especially true of living organisms. Because of the way a living system continually regenerates itself, the parts that constitute it are, in fact, perpetually being changed. It is the organism's dynamic patterns that maintain its coherence. Every five days, a person gets a new stomach lining, and, every two months, a new liver. It is estimated that 98 percent of the atoms in a person's body are replaced each year. And yet, we are all recognizably the same people that we were a couple of years ago. It is our self-organized patterns that give us our continued identity.[36]

This new understanding of nature as a self-organized, self-regenerating system extends, like a fractal, from a single cell to the global system of life on earth. The conventional view of nature as a machine has encouraged many in our culture to view the earth as a material resource with no intrinsic value, available to be exploited purely for humanity's needs. However, in recent decades, the perception of the earth itself as a self-organized entity has become increasingly influential. Scientist James Lovelock was the first to recognize how the different feedback cycles of the oceans, the atmosphere, and the land caused a self-regulating effect responsible for the robust conditions for life to thrive on earth through billions of years. Lovelock named the entire global system Gaia, after the Greek goddess that personified the earth. While Gaia lacks some characteristics of a true organism, it has been shown to display the crucial quality of autopoiesis, sustaining itself as a living planet through its network of complex feedback loops.[37]

A New Paradigm

The systems view offers humanity a new understanding of life, one that is scientifically rigorous while embracing a sense of quality. The systems view doesn't replace the reductionist approach to science but offers a new way of apprehending aspects of nature that reductionism is unable to explain. Some things can best be understood through a reductionist approach—by breaking them down to their discrete elements and investigating each in turn. Other things—especially what is alive or composed of living entities, such as organisms, ecosystems, and human communities—can only be understood through a process of integration, through recognizing how each part relates to each other and the whole. That is where systems theory contributes to greater human understanding.[38]

The systems perspective offers important insights into the nature of reality that upend many assumptions forming the basis of the predominant worldview. It tells us that the relationship between things is frequently more important than the things themselves. It emphasizes that everything in the natural world is dynamic rather than static and that biological phenomena can't be predicted with precision: instead of fixed laws, we therefore need to search for the underlying organizing principles of nature. These principles, it reveals, occur across widely different domains, from heart rhythms to climate variations and from lake ecologies to internet social media connections. It also shows how self-organized systems are fractally embedded within one another: a cell may be part of an organism, which is part of a community, which is nested within an ecosystem, which in turn is part of Gaia.[39]

The shift from a reductionist to a holistic frame carries major philosophical and ethical implications. In recent decades, physicist Fritjof Capra, along with other leading systems thinkers, has applied this new understanding to an extensive range of human activities, including such disparate fields as health, economics, human relationships, environmental sustainability, and spirituality. The common theme linking all these domains is the recognition of the intrinsic interdependency of all living systems and the realization that humans are an integral part of the natural world. "We have to regain our experience of connectedness," writes Capra, "with the entire web of life."[40]

The systems approach transforms the traditional view of how nature works. Rather than a battleground of "selfish genes" competing to outperform one another, it offers an understanding of nature as a web of networked systems, dynamically optimizing at different levels of evolutionary selection. It similarly recasts the conventional view of human nature. Instead of seeing each individual as selfish and competitive, seeking only personal advantage, it offers a more nuanced understanding of humanity as also cooperative and altruistic, embedded within larger social and natural networks.[41]

Scientists at the forefront of systems thinking recognize the far-reaching ramifications of their findings. "We are seeking a new conceptual framework that does not yet exist," writes researcher Stuart Kauffman. However, while this view of nature is relatively new in science, we have seen in this book how earlier cultures have already explored many of the philosophical implications of a connected cosmos. The wisdom of indigenous worldviews shares much with systems thinking, and the Neo-Confucian investigation of the li—the organizing principles of the universe—offers deep insights to modernity, with its understanding of the Tao as the metapattern of all nature's principles, discoverable in one's own nature as well as in the natural world.[42]

Remarkably, though, many people today remain unaware of this alternative way of understanding nature. When Edward Lorenz announced his discovery of deterministic chaos to a conference of leading scientists in 1972, he sent shock waves reverberating through the halls of academia. When he received the distinguished Kyoto Prize two decades later, he was said to have "brought about one of the most dramatic changes in mankind's view of nature since Sir Isaac Newton." In spite of this, many mainstream scientists—not to mention the rest of the public—continue to understand reality according to the predominant reductionist stance. In 2013, readers of a respected British magazine, *Prospect*, named outspoken reductionist Richard Dawkins as the world's top thinker. Why has mainstream thinking so far failed to fully embrace this new understanding of life?[43]

One answer lurks in a famous monograph published in 1962 by philosopher of science Thomas Kuhn called *The Structure of Scientific Revolutions*. "In science," Kuhn observes, "novelty emerges only with difficulty, manifested by resistance." When a worldview is established, and works reasonably well, people get used to thinking according to the cognitive structures it encourages. As we've seen throughout this book, the human patterning instinct has evolved to focus attention on what fits within its cultural frame and ignore what doesn't. Just like an infant who learns to ignore sounds that are not part of her native language, people tend to ignore anomalies that don't fit within the established scientific paradigm. When anomalies begin to build up, it causes increasing turbulence within a scientific community, as some people offer a new paradigm while others hold on to the old. Finally, only after a period of difficult transition, the new paradigm becomes generally accepted. A classic example of this paradigm shift is the Scientific Revolution, which replaced the medieval Christian worldview with the Newtonian.[44]

Kuhn points out that the transfer of allegiance from one paradigm to the other is "a conversion experience that cannot be forced." Scientists who have invested productive careers in the old paradigm are understandably loath to give up their preconceptions. The paradigm shift is therefore likely to occur only, he suggests, "when the first tradition is felt to have gone badly astray."[45]

Has the reductionist worldview gone badly astray? In some respects, reductionists can point out that their approach has never been more successful. By isolating nature's building blocks and analyzing them to the utmost detail, scientists have been able to read and edit genomes, produce microchips with dazzling processing power, and change the molecular structure of materials through nanotechnology. However, from another perspective, the current worldview appears to be propelling our global civilization to a precipice where even its continued existence may be in jeopardy. The approach to the natural world encouraged by reductionist thinking—CONQUERING NATURE and NATURE AS MACHINE—has created imbalances that are becoming increasingly unstable. As we peer into the future, the threat of uncontrolled climate change looms, in addition to other impending global crises such as deforestation, freshwater scarcity, and an accelerated extinction of species.

A Web of Meaning

The systems approach invites a different way of making meaning from our world. By emphasizing the underlying principles that apply to all living things, it helps us realize our intrinsic connectedness with the natural world. The recognition that we are not separate from nature and cannot, ultimately, control it encourages a more participatory approach of trying to influence the complex systems around us for greater harmony. In place of the metaphors of nature that have led humanity to this precipice, the systems worldview offers up a new metaphor of nature as a WEB OF MEANING, in which the very interconnectedness of all life gives both meaning and resonance to our individual and collective behavior.

As we will see in the next two chapters, there are enormous stakes in the contest between these two worldviews. The new systems paradigm is already beginning to influence how people think about their relationships with each other and with the natural world. Our global community may indeed be transitioning from CONQUERING NATURE to experiencing nature as a WEB OF MEANING, but is the shift rapid enough to change society's trajectory? The future course of humanity may, indeed, be determined by the answer to this question.

Chapter 20

CONSUMING THE EARTH IN THE MODERN ERA

In "The Sorcerer's Apprentice," a famous poem by Goethe, an apprentice, left alone for the day, tries to use his magic to command a broom to fetch water from a nearby river for a bath. At first, things go wonderfully. The broom fetches water with a bucket and fills up the tub. However, as the tub begins to overflow, the apprentice realizes he hasn't mastered the spell to stop the broom. It keeps going back to the river, fetching more water with every bucket, bowl, and cup available until the entire house is flooded. In desperation, the apprentice chops the broom in half with an ax, only to watch, to his horror, as both halves continue to inundate the house, now at double the speed. Fortunately, the sorcerer eventually returns and recites the spell that puts everything back in order.[1]

Goethe never suggested his poem as a metaphor for society, but, looking back, it is tempting to see it as a compelling depiction of our current state of affairs. The apprentice, like so many of us in the modern age, is at first dazzled by his power over the natural world. However, at a certain point, he begins to realize he's unleashed a force over which he has inadequate control, only to discover that his desperate attempts to contain it actually increase its powers of destruction.

Has our global civilization found itself in a Sorcerer's Apprentice dilemma? Has the technological magic unleashed by scientific knowledge placed us on a trajectory accelerating ever faster out of control? Or do we have it within ourselves to find the sorcerer's spell that can restore harmony in our world? These are the crucial questions of our era that underlie the last two chapters of this book.

"That Forever Empty"

The frenetic rate of change in modern society is driven primarily by the exponential power of technological innovation. Moore's law, which in the mid-1970s predicted a doubling of computing power every two years, has surprised many pundits by continuing to hold true over decades. The convergence of different technologies has accelerated the rate of change even further. For example, the discovery of the DNA molecule in 1953 at first didn't seem related to advances in computer technology. However, as scientists have become increasingly adept at decoding DNA, the two technologies have converged to create breakthroughs at a velocity beyond almost anyone's predictions.[2]

As a result, we've arrived in the early twenty-first century at a state in which continual rapid innovation has become the norm. We're no longer surprised when ideas once in the realm of science fiction become scientific fact and, before too long, entrench themselves into our daily life. Scientists are reengineering virtually every aspect of our lives, affecting how we think, eat, and communicate in ways that are both trivial and profound. Being caught up in this whirlwind of change can be exhilarating. The possibilities of the future sometimes seem limitless, with the promise of ever-more-powerful technologies, fueled by advances in areas such as artificial intelligence, genetic engineering, and nanotechnology. At the same time, it is causing massive disruptions to the human experience, along with a dislocation of people's sense of meaning in their lives.

The busy façade of modern life, with its endless flurry of cell phones, sports updates, e-mails, and celebrity news, covers an emptiness that no one wants to feel. Louis C. K., an American comedian and urban sage, explained in a primetime interview in 2013 that he had taken his daughter's mobile phone away from her because he thought it was harmful. Punctuated by rapturous applause and knowing laughter from the audience, he delivered a bleak vision of modern existential emptiness:

> Underneath everything else in your life, there's that thing—that forever empty—you know what I'm talking about? . . . That knowledge that it's all for nothing and you're all alone. You know, it's down there, and sometimes when things clear away and you're not watching anything, you're in your car and you start going, "Oh no, here it comes, that I'm alone . . ." Like it starts to visit on you. . . . That's why we text and drive. . . . People are willing to risk taking a life and ruining their own, because they don't want to be alone for a second, because it's so hard. . . .
>
> The thing is, because we don't want that first bit of sad, we push it away with the phone. . . . You never feel completely sad or completely happy, you just feel kind of satisfied with your products, and then you die.[3]

Many of us in the modern world, captivated by our gadgets, know what he's referring to and can laugh along with the rest of his audience. However, the implications, both for humanity and the natural world, are anything but funny. There exists, in the words of cultural historian Thomas Berry, "a deep hidden rage against the human condition, an unwillingness to accept life under the conditions that life is granted us, a feeling of oppression by the normal human condition, a feeling that the pains of life and ultimately death are something that should not be, something that must be defeated."[4]

The Western dualistic tradition has inexorably separated humanity from a sense of connection with the rest of the world, leaving an underlying sense of meaninglessness. The modern form of cognition has been called "the Cartesian mode" by Fritjof Capra, who reflects that people functioning exclusively in this mode "may be free from manifest symptoms but cannot be considered mentally healthy. . . . For people whose existence is dominated by this mode of experience no level of wealth, power, or fame will bring genuine satisfaction, and thus they become infused with a sense of meaninglessness, futility, and even absurdity that no amount of external success can dispel."[5]

As Louis C. K. pointed out, this loss of meaning is papered over by the pursuit of ever more material possessions. It is a quest that takes place not just at the individual level but in the structure of our political and economic systems. The imperative for perpetual economic growth, incessantly fortified by the messages of our popular media, has been aptly described as a fetish: the worship of an inanimate object believed to have magical powers. The consequences of this go beyond the sense of emptiness experienced by the privileged minority who are able to afford the newest gadgets. It has created a vast and increasing gap between the wealthy elite and the rest of the world's population, and it is responsible for the unsustainable consumption of the world's resources that is driving our civilization toward a precipice.

Where did this global fetish for economic growth come from? What does it mean for our world, and where will it end? In these two final chapters, we'll trace the surprising sources of our modern consumer culture, investigate its devastating consequences, and explore how the meaning we as a global society derive from our current situation might hold the key to humanity's future.

The Emergence of Consumer Culture

We can trace the beginnings of modern consumer culture back to England's Industrial Revolution in the eighteenth century. As handcrafted goods gave way to mechanized production, people were forced to leave their small towns and villages for factory jobs in the growing cities. Along with this, the new discoveries of the Scientific Revolution were seeping into public consciousness. The certainties of monotheism were becoming unraveled by new theories offering alternative views of the cosmos: envisioning the earth as merely a tiny planet in an unimaginably large universe and humans as having evolved through natural processes rather than been created in their current form by God.[6]

The combined effects of the Industrial and Scientific Revolutions were doubly disruptive, transforming both the structure of society and how people made sense of their world. A specter of existential doubt emerged about humanity's place in the cosmos, with a consequent loss of assurance regarding the source of meaning in life. Toward the end of the nineteenth century, Nietzsche famously summed up the cognitive turmoil of his age when he pronounced, "God is dead."[7]

In the United States, colonized originally by devout Protestants and later by waves of immigrants from Catholic European nations, God may not have seemed dead, but he played a more limited role in the collective psyche. By the late nineteenth century, a series of movements known as mind-cure religions took hold of the popular imagination, responding to the uncertainties of the time by emphasizing only positive aspects of the human experience. They taught that people could cure their own problems through positive thinking, and their focus was finding salvation in this life rather than an afterlife.

With their emphasis on the benefits of worldly goods, the mind-cure religions were a grassroots interpretation of the prevailing Protestant ethic that viewed personal wealth as evidence of one's salvation status. Buoyed by characteristically American pragmatism, they hinted that salvation could be achieved through the manufactured goods themselves, finding—in the words of one historian—"the good" through "goods." One enormously popular expression of mind-cure values was *The Wonderful Wizard of Oz*, published in 1900, which implicitly affirmed that, through an effort of will, people could change their lives to experience joy, abundance, and happiness.[8]

Another pervasive effect of nineteenth-century industrialization was the systematic measurement and processing of human activity. This reached a new level of efficiency with the "scientific management" of Frederick Taylor, who introduced "time studies" in factories, in which consultants would follow workers around with stopwatches, timing every activity, and suggest improvements to every aspect of workflow down to such details as how coal or iron ore should be shoveled. Taylor's vision reached its apogee in the factories of Henry Ford, who introduced automated assembly-line production of his vehicles in 1912, leading to enormous productivity gains across the entire industrial landscape. However, it was already becoming apparent to Ford and other industrialists of his age that these increases in factory productivity would be worthless unless they were accompanied by commensurate increases in consumption.[9]

Out of these twin developments—increasing numbers of people seeking salvation in this world rather than the next, and increasingly efficient industrial producers seeking consumers for their goods—our current consumer culture emerged. In a bold move symbolizing the birth of the modern consumer, Henry Ford in 1914 decided to increase his workers' wages by enough that they could aspire to buy their own Model T Fords. The masses now had a dual role to play in modern capitalism: they were to be both workers and consumers.[10]

It didn't take long for the more astute observers of that period to recognize that something significant had changed around them. Philosopher Samuel Strauss gave it a name: *consumptionism.* "It is obvious," he observed, "that Americans have come to consider their standard of living as a somewhat sacred acquisition, which they will defend at any price. This means that they would be ready to make many an intellectual or even moral concession in order to maintain that standard." The industrialists who needed burgeoning markets for their rising production were only too happy to encourage this new material sense of the sacred, experimenting with such innovations as consumer trading stamps and advertising on billboards and the radio.[11]

These were the beginnings of what historian Ernest Gellner has called the "society of perpetual growth," focusing the human search for meaning in an entirely new direction. We've seen how, at their core, societies are driven by the way in which they have patterned meaning into the cosmos: the ancient Egyptians yearning for *ma'at*, the Chinese searching for harmony, or the early Christians seeking salvation. In the consumer culture born in the early twentieth century in the United States, the purchase and consumption of material goods became the value that trumped all others. In contrast to the old hierarchical class systems of Europe, material consumption became a critical factor in determining one's status within society. In 1899, as this new era was unfolding, American sociologist

Thorstein Veblen identified a process he called "conspicuous consumption," by which people compete to achieve higher status through being seen to consume more expensive goods and services than their peers, a practice that continues to drive patterns of behavior in the early twenty-first century.[12]

A new breed of consumer marketers blazed a trail with state-of-the-art techniques to actively manage this rise in public consumption. A leading force was Edward Bernays, known as the "father of public relations." Bernays was Sigmund Freud's nephew and used his uncle's insights into the subconscious to develop his new methods. "We must shift America from a needs to a desires culture," declared Bernays's business partner, Paul Mazur. "People must be trained to desire, to want new things, even before the old have been entirely consumed. We must shape a new mentality. Man's desires must overshadow his needs." In 1928, Bernays proudly described how his techniques for mental manipulation had permitted a small elite to control the minds of the American population:

> The conscious and intelligent manipulation of the organized habits and opinions of the masses is an important element in democratic society. Those who manipulate this unseen mechanism of society constitute an invisible government that is the true ruling power of this country. We are governed, our minds molded, our tastes formed, our ideas suggested, largely by men we have never heard of. . . . In almost every act of our daily lives . . . we are dominated by the relatively small number of persons . . . who pull the wires which control the public mind.[13]

The following year, a presidential report gave credit to the mind control espoused by Bernays for helping to create a limitless future of American consumption, explaining it had "proved conclusively . . . that wants are almost insatiable; that one want satisfied makes way for another. The conclusion is that economically, we have a boundless field before us; that there are new wants that will make way endlessly for newer wants, as fast as they are satisfied . . . by advertising and other promotional devices."[14]

The pursuit of material consumption as an overarching goal required one crucial attribute: money. As the underlying institution that linked all goods in a relative hierarchy of value, money achieved preeminence as an indicator of status and the purpose behind one's activities. This focus on money as the sole arbiter of value had the effect of supplanting other traditional sources of meaning in the human experience. Every society that has reached a certain level of complexity has needed a medium of exchange for goods. However, it is only in modern consumer culture that the medium of exchange was an end in itself. In fact, as we'll see, the institution of money has itself become one of the core underlying drivers of our culture of consumption.[15]

A Self-Accelerating Treadmill

Once based on tangible objects, money has become an increasingly abstract entity, now residing solely as a symbol in our shared consciousness. And yet, the more abstract it has become, the more powerful its hold over the human trajectory.

In virtually every society, dating back to hunter-gatherer times, objects such as shells or furs have been used as a medium of exchange. In agrarian societies, precious metals began to be used. The problem with this type of money is that its value was fixed by the underlying worth of the commodity, and carrying a lot of it around could prove difficult. China's Song dynasty solved this by using paper certificates for commerce instead of coins made from precious metals. These certificates, which carried a promise that they could be exchanged for a commodity such as gold, required trust in the creditworthiness of the issuing institution and therefore arose only in more sophisticated societies. This first abstraction of money from its material roots permitted far more growth in the amount of money available to society.[16]

The next stage in the abstraction of money occurred in the United States. The reliance on the ability to exchange paper money into gold put a natural brake on the rate at which money could grow. In a series of steps through the twentieth century, the US government moved away from what was known as the "gold standard," culminating in 1971, when President Richard Nixon announced that its currency would no longer be backed by gold, but only by its guarantee. At this point, with the gold standard eliminated, money became a purely symbolic abstraction, existing solely in the shared network of the global conceptual consciousness.[17]

The money supply, now wholly controlled by central banks, could be increased without regard to any underlying commodity. There was, however, one important catch to this newfound freedom of money. It was now created as a form of debt, requiring a promise to be paid back. As such, the money supply had to keep growing to service the interest on the debt, making perpetual economic growth a necessity to keep the entire system running.

This reliance on the future growth of money extends also to the capital invested in companies. Corporations are valued as a multiple of their current earnings, so most of the financial wealth in our society really represents a claim on the future wealth still to be created. All these expectations for a return on capital are ultimately based on a presumption of continued economic growth in society at large. Failure to grow—or even just the threat of it—thus leads to banks failing, businesses going bankrupt, and people losing their jobs. Meanwhile, as the money supply grows, there needs to be a corresponding increase in the goods and services available to be purchased to avoid runaway inflation. Now, instead of needing more gold to grow, our economy needs a continual increase in the amount of stuff that money can buy, just to maintain its stability.[18]

As the reader may have noticed, this dilemma, known as a self-reinforcing feedback loop, resembles that of the Sorcerer's Apprentice. Just as the broomstick seemed destined to continue fetching water from the lake until the sorcerer's house was utterly flooded, so the requisite growth of money has put our society on a relentless search for ever more natural resources to monetize. These can be tangible resources such as land, water, minerals, and trees, or intangibles that were previously freely offered, such as childcare, education, or food preparation. As long as it can be commoditized, it helps to keep the economy from collapsing under its own weight.[19]

This self-accelerating treadmill of perpetual growth has become the underlying force driving our global civilization, affecting virtually every aspect of our lives. It has been the engine behind the previously unimaginable advances in technology, medicine, and communication that have transformed the lives of most people on the planet. It has also pervaded the global consciousness, becoming an integral part of the system of values on which our society is based. The primary vehicle by which this has occurred is, like money, another powerful abstraction created by modern society that has also developed a self-sustaining life of its own: the corporation.

The Rise of the Corporation

Back in the seventeenth century, when the British and Dutch were first learning to exploit their overseas colonies, a problem emerged: people were afraid to finance expeditions with debt because they faced jail if something went wrong and they couldn't repay their loans. The solution these governments came up with was a corporate charter, which limited investors' liability to the amount of their investment and nothing more. Before long, though, it became clear that these legal charters created an incentive to take inappropriate risks because the potential upside was greater than the downside. In England, after a series of spectacular frauds and a market crash, corporations were banned in 1720. The ban was eventually lifted when the Industrial Revolution generated demand for new investments in railways and other infrastructure.[20]

The political leaders of the United States, aware of the English experience, were suspicious of corporations. Thomas Jefferson wrote in 1816, "I hope we shall take warning from the [English] example and crush in its birth the aristocracy of our monied corporations which dare already to challenge our government to a trial of strength and bid defiance to the laws of our country." Accordingly, corporations in America were given limited charters with tightly constrained powers. However, during the turmoil of the Civil War, industrialists took advantage of the disarray, leveraging widespread political corruption to expand their influence.

As the nation reconstructed itself, it increasingly fell under the sway of corporate power. "This is a government of the people, by the people, and for the people no longer. It is a government of corporations, by corporations, and for corporations," lamented Rutherford B. Hayes, who became president in 1877. Corporations took full advantage of their newfound dominance, influencing state legislatures to permit charters to be issued in perpetuity that gave them the right to do anything not explicitly prohibited by law. A crucial moment occurred in 1886, when the Supreme Court designated corporations as "persons" entitled to the protections of the Fourteenth Amendment, which had been passed to give equal rights to former slaves enfranchised after the Civil War.[21*]

When we typically think of a corporation, we tend to imagine it as composed of human beings, whether executives, board members, or employees. However, a corporation is utterly different from the people who are part of it. In contrast to people, who are capable of empathy and generally care for others beyond themselves, corporations are abstract entities usually created with the single mandate of maximizing financial returns for their shareholders. They are theoretically immortal and cannot be put in prison, and the larger multinationals are not constrained by the laws of any individual country.[22]

With equivalent rights to human beings but with the incalculable advantage of their superhuman powers, corporations have literally taken over the world. They have grown so massive that fifty-three of the largest hundred economies in the world are corporations. Along with their vast power, corporations have imposed on the world a set of values, arising from their overriding objective to maximize financial returns, at odds with many intrinsic human values. Even those in a position of power within a corporation only maintain that power as long as they follow the corporate mandate of maximizing shareholder value above all other considerations.[23]

An illustration of this single-minded corporate focus on financial returns can be seen in a conversation between biologist Paul Ehrlich and a Japanese journalist. Ehrlich observed that the Japanese whaling industry was at risk of exterminating the whales that were the source of its wealth. The journalist responded: "You are thinking of the whaling industry as an organization that is interested in maintaining whales; actually it is better viewed as a huge quantity of [financial] capital attempting to earn the highest possible return. If it can exterminate whales in ten years and make a 15% profit, but it could only make 10% with a sustainable harvest, then it will exterminate them in ten years. After that, the money will be moved to exterminating some other resource." If we were to anthropomorphize and think of a corporation as a person, we would have to characterize that person as a psychopath, completely lacking the ability for empathy that is a crucial element of normal human behavior.[24]

Driven by the compulsion to maximize financial value at the expense of all else, corporations have used their domination of public discourse to inculcate their values into the global consciousness, wielding their clout to lobby legislatures and influence the mass media. Al Gore, who served as vice president for eight years, describes how Congress is incapable of passing laws without permission from the corporate lobbies that control their campaign finances. "It is now common," he reveals, "for lawyers representing corporate lobbies to sit in the actual drafting sessions where legislation is written, and to provide the precise language for new laws intended to remove obstacles to their corporate business plans. . . . Many US state legislatures often now routinely rubberstamp laws that have been written in their entirety by corporate lobbies." While each corporation has its own distinct objectives, there is a set of underlying values common to virtually all of them that forms the ideology of capitalism.[25]

Capitalism is based on the premise that the most desirable state of affairs is economic growth, which can be attained most effectively through free markets in which assets are privately owned. Based on this credo, the primary responsibility of government is to provide the infrastructure necessary for the free market to conduct its business with minimal constraints. Some important assumptions about human nature underlie these beliefs. Individuals are understood to be motivated primarily by financial self-interest. They are assumed to be rational in pursuit of this goal, and their "rationality" is believed to lead them to act competitively rather than cooperatively in the marketplace. Another crucial assumption holds that the aggregation of all these individuals competitively seeking their own financial gain leads to the most beneficial outcome for society. These assumptions about human nature are not self-evident truths; however, the money-based system constructed by capitalism encourages and rewards these traits over other traditional, community-oriented values, creating a selffulfilling prophecy about the nature of human behavior.[26]

Through the first half of the twentieth century, capitalism competed globally against other powerful ideologies such as communism and fascism. That would change drastically after World War II. In 1944, the soon-to-be victorious powers held a conference at Bretton Woods to lay the foundation for a global structure upon which capitalism could thrive. At that time of war-torn devastation, a vision of unrestrained worldwide economic growth was understandably intoxicating, and institutions such as the World Bank and the International Monetary Fund were established to facilitate this prospect. With this infrastructure in place, world trade soared spectacularly, with an 11.5-fold increase in the forty-five years from 1950. The last major constraint on global capitalism disappeared in 1991 with the collapse of the Soviet Union and its communist bloc of countries. Since then, globalization has transformed the world economy, dissolving barriers between countries and creating a single worldwide economic entity.[27]

Cornucopia for Capitalism

In the integrated economy that emerged, corporations have been able to use their transnational powers to dictate their own terms to virtually any country in the world. With the free movement of capital, corporations can choose to build factories in nations with the weakest labor unions or locate polluting plants in countries with lax environmental laws, basing their decisions solely on maximizing returns for their shareholders. Governments compete with each other to make their nations the most attractive for corporate investment.[28]

In this favorable environment for corporations, global production and consumption have skyrocketed. Worldwide economic output increased from $6.4 trillion in 1950 to $72.4 trillion in 2012, more than a tenfold increase. To put these statistics in perspective, it is compelling to realize that while it took the entire length of human history to build world production to the 1950 level, the world is now *increasing* its production by that amount, on average, every couple of years. The benefits of this dramatic growth in consumption have been enormous, leading to better health, increased consumer choices, and a much higher standard of living for many.[29]

These benefits, though, have been distributed very unevenly. Ever since the rise of agriculture, differences in wealth and power between people have been an inescapable part of the human experience. However, the emergence of the global capitalist economy has caused the disparity between rich and poor to become a gaping chasm. Within the United States, inequality has reached levels even greater than those seen in the 1920s: the top 20 percent of the country own 93 percent of the non-home wealth. Further up the scale, the inequality gets even more extreme: the top 1 percent of the country own 43 percent of the non-home wealth, whereas the lower 60 percent of the population claim just 0.3 percent of the nation's wealth.[30*]

Wealth disparities within the United States, extreme as they are, pale in comparison to the gulf between the global rich and poor. As the twentieth century began, the richest countries in the world were about ten times wealthier than the poorest. With the triumph of global capitalism, the twenty-first century began with the richest countries seventy-one times wealthier than the poorest. The statistics describing the chasm between rich and poor are so extreme that they are frequently difficult to grasp. Oxfam reported in 2017 that the richest eight men in the world now own as much as the entire bottom half of the world's population, comprising 3.7 billion people. Similar disparities exist in global consumption. The wealthy Organisation for Economic Co-operation and Development countries, representing less than 20 percent of the world's population, consume 86 percent of the world's goods and services, while the poorest 20 percent consume only 1.3 percent. These numbers translate into the harsh reality that a billion people—equivalent to the entire population of the OECD countries—go hungry every day, while another billion remain chronically malnourished, failing to get the vitamins and minerals they need for health.[31]

These glaring disparities in wealth are the logical outcome of a global economic system built around the values of capitalism and dominated by corporations that follow the imperative of maximizing financial returns for their shareholders. An illustration of the mind-set underlying this system can be seen in a quote from the chief economist at the World Bank, an institution purportedly established to aid development and reduce world poverty. In a leaked 1992 internal memo on pollution, he expressed the view that "a given amount of health-impairing pollution should be done in the country with the lowest cost, which will be the country with the lowest wages. I think the economic logic behind dumping a load of toxic waste in the lowest-wage country is impeccable." This chief economist was Larry Summers, who went on to serve as secretary of the treasury in the Democratic Clinton administration.[32]

The callousness underlying this kind of comment partly arises from the intrinsic difficulty in making an emotional connection with the grim statistics of global suffering. Giving texture to the underlying numbers, economist David Korten, who spent many years in international development, writes of the "hundreds of millions displaced from the lands on which they once made a modest living, to make way for dams, agricultural estates, forestry plantations, resorts, golf courses, and myriad other development projects." He continues:

> The displaced, lacking other options, move onto marginal, environmentally unstable lands to eke out a living as best they can—often at great human and environmental cost. Others move into squalid urban squatter settlements, pushing wages down and rents up. Once-lush hillsides are stripped bare of trees. Coral reefs once vibrant with life become underwater wastelands. The air is thick with pollutants. Cultures grounded in strong spiritual, family, and community values give way to materialism and violence.[33]

Korten describes one small group of indigenous Igorot in the Benguet province of the Philippines who used to engage in small-scale "pocket mining" of the gold veins in their ancestral lands—until those lands were taken over by the Benguet Corporation, owned by wealthy Filipinos, the Philippine government, and US investors. With modern industrial machinery stripping away the soil and polluting the riverbeds, local people could no longer grow rice and bananas for sustenance and were forced to travel to the other side of the mountain for water to drink and bathe. Meanwhile, cyanide from the mines polluted fields downstream and poisoned fish in the gulf, while Benguet earned billions of pesos for its shareholders in what Korten describes as a "massive resource transfer from the poor to the rich." Beyond the obvious suffering of the people in this story, its greater significance is that, in its essentials, it has been repeated innumerable times in developing countries across the world.[34]

Exploiting Ancient Sunlight

Henri Saint-Simon, a French political theorist, announced in 1830 that "the exploitation of man by man has come to its end. . . . The exploitation of the globe, of external nature, becomes henceforth the sole end of man's physical activity." Saint-Simon's forecast was woefully wrong about "the exploitation of man by man." However, on the "exploitation of the globe," history has proven him correct. The root Western metaphor of CONQUERING NATURE has created a cognitive framework in which the untrammeled exploitation of the world's natural resources is seen by many as cause for celebration rather than concern.[35]

When the English began using coal to power steam engines in the eighteenth century, without knowing it at the time, they were harnessing energy that the sun had radiated to the earth about four hundred million years ago during the Carboniferous Period. At that time in the earth's history, a high level of carbon dioxide in the atmosphere had trapped the sun's energy, warming the planet and providing copious carbon as raw material for plants and sea algae, which grew abundantly, covering the land and seabed over millions of years with a dense mat of dead organic matter, extending in some places thousands of feet deep. This dead plant matter, compressed over eons, is the source of the coal and oil deposits we exploit in our modern society.[36]

Ultimately, the source of our recent dramatic growth in consumption has been our ability to exploit the energy of the ancient sunlight from the Carboniferous Period. The discovery of fossil fuels created a self-generating feedback loop that continues unabated to this day. The first steam engines were used to pump floodwater out of the coal mines, permitting more coal to be mined as fuel for more engines, thus reinforcing and perpetuating a cycle of ever-increasing economic growth. Transformative as coal was for the English, the discovery of oil (with energy density double that of coal) initiated a new phase of even more intensive fossil fuel exploitation that defines our modern age. At our current rate of energy usage, it has been calculated that our world is going through about fourteen thousand years' worth of that fossilized sunshine from the Carboniferous age every day.[37]

We are so used to enjoying the benefits of oil's stored energy that it is difficult to comprehend precisely how much it is doing for us. A single barrel of oil holds as much energy as one man could produce in heavy manual labor over roughly ten years. Buckminster Fuller proposed a brilliant way to visualize the power of oil with the notion of "energy slaves"—the human equivalent of oil's energy. It would take one energy slave pedaling hard on a bicycle to keep a hundred-watt light bulb going. An average American, who consumes about twenty-four barrels of oil per year, would require about two hundred energy slaves to sustain her lifestyle, while the entire world population, using far less energy on average than Americans, would require a mind-boggling sixty-six billion energy slaves to produce the work currently provided by oil. Instead of energy slaves, however, the world economy has been able to access oil at remarkably low prices to fuel its massive expansion.[38]

The Great Acceleration

The discovery of fossil fuels, the Western view of nature as something to be exploited, and a global economic system based on capitalist principles combined to generate ever more powerful ratchet effects, perhaps the most significant of which has been the growth in the number of humans on the planet. It took all human history to build the world's population to about a billion by 1800. This was followed by a steady increase over the next 150 years to 2.5 billion. Then, around 1950, the population skyrocketed, nearly tripling to 7.4 billion people in 2015. More people were added to the world during the twentieth century than in all of previous human history. Fittingly, the period since World War II has been called "The Great Acceleration."[39]

From a certain perspective, this increase can be viewed, in the words of one economist, as "the greatest human achievement in history." For much of human history, life expectancy at birth was between twenty and thirty years. In the past two centuries, through improvements in agriculture, sanitation, and medicine, life expectancy in the developed world has reached around seventy-five years, and, in much of the rest of the world, it has increased to more than sixty years.[40]

However, decline in fertility rates has not kept up with the decline in death rates, with the result that the sheer number of human beings consuming the world's natural resources is a major cause for alarm. With a growth rate of eighty million people per year—equivalent to a new city of more than a million inhabitants being built every five days—demographers forecast a world with nearly ten billion human occupants by 2050.[41]

With the culture of capitalism urging increased consumption throughout the world, the demand on the planet's resources continues to grow even more rapidly than the population. People around the globe, bombarded with images of living standards from the wealthiest countries, understandably aspire to this level of comfort for themselves. Bolstered by this unremitting appetite for growth, the world economy is projected to quadruple again by 2050.[42]

It is difficult to imagine what a quadrupling of our current economic activity would mean to the human experience and to the planet on which we all rely. Scientists have calculated that humans now appropriate more than 40 percent of the total energy available to sustain life on earth—called net primary productivity—for our own consumption. We use more than half the world's freshwater for our own purposes and have transformed 43 percent of the earth's terrain into agricultural or urban landscapes. To sustain our current rate of expansion, it's been estimated that human appropriation of net primary productivity would need to double or triple by mid-century. Scientists are understandably asking if this is in fact possible.[43]

Like the sorcerer's apprentice, we've discovered the magic spell to unleash formidable forces, only to find that they seem to be unstoppable once they've begun.

The Arrival of the Anthropocene

In every part of the earth, natural systems that have sustained themselves from time immemorial are groaning under the strain of this pressure. The basic elements of life on earth that we take for granted—forests, fish in the oceans, water to drink—are rapidly being consumed by humanity's voracious demands.

We regulate the flow of about two-thirds of the earth's rivers, and many of the greatest rivers—Colorado, Yellow, Yangtze, Ganges, Nile—no longer reach the sea during parts of the year. Massive inland water bodies, such as the Aral Sea and Lake Chad, have virtually disappeared. Much of the world's agriculture, including the wheat-growing states of the Midwest, rely on underground aquifers that are being used up at unsustainable rates. It has been forecast that, by midcentury, as much as three-quarters of the earth's population could face freshwater scarcity.[44]

Similarly, we are insatiably exhausting the bounty of the earth's natural terrain. Half of the world's tropical and temperate forests have disappeared, along with about half the wetlands and a third of the mangroves. At the current rate of deforestation, roughly an acre a second, half of what still remains of the Amazon rain forest will be gone within thirty years.[45]

Even the topsoil that we rely on for cultivation of crops is rapidly being depleted. Like aquifers, topsoil naturally regenerates itself, but at a rate of about a centimeter every two hundred years. Meanwhile, in the United States, we are using it up at ten times the rate of replenishment; in Europe, seventeen times; in China, fifty-seven times. This has already led to a significant loss of productivity on nearly a third of the world's arable land. Much of this loss has been masked by the use of manufactured nitrogen fertilizer, which has become so widespread that—astonishingly—more than half of all nitrogen atoms in green plant material now come from artificial fertilizer rather than the earth's own ecosystem. This has created a new problem as nitrogen runoff drains into the oceans, causing uncontrolled algae blooms that consume the water's oxygen, leaving none for any other life. More than four hundred of these "dead zones" have emerged in coastal waters around the world, some extending in size to more than twenty thousand square miles.[46]

Not even the furthest regions of the oceans have escaped humanity's depredations. As a result of industrialized fishing, the oceans have lost more than 90 percent of large fish such as tuna and swordfish. If overfishing continues unchecked, it's expected that catches around the world will be down 30 to 60 percent by mid-century. An international team of ocean experts, reporting in 2013 on the state of the oceans, could barely mask their desperation at what they call a "dismal outlook," calling for urgent global action "if we are to avoid tipping us further, and irreversibly, onto the despair side of the hope/despair balance."[47]

Pushed out of their natural habitats, hunted down and poisoned by our pollutants, the nonhuman animals with which we share the earth are reeling along with the rest of the planet. A 2008 report announced that populations of all vertebrates—mammals, birds, reptiles, amphibians, and fish—had declined on average by a third over the past four decades.[48]

Perhaps even more disquieting is the rate at which human activity is driving species to extinction. There have been five times in the history of life on earth when a global catastrophe caused a mass extinction of species. Scientists now recognize that the onslaught of humanity is causing the sixth of these catastrophic extinction events, driving species into oblivion at a rate a thousand times faster than would be natural. Between 30 and 50 percent of all vertebrate species are threatened with extinction this century.[49]

Many prominent scientists have concluded that humanity has now emerged as its own force of nature. The scope of human impact is so enormous, and will affect the distant future of the earth to such a degree, that they are describing our modern period as a new geological epoch called the Anthropocene. "Human activities," writes a leading scientist, "have become so pervasive and profound that they rival the great forces of Nature and are pushing the earth into planetary *terra incognita*. . . . The phenomenon of global change represents a profound shift in the relationship between humans and the rest of nature."[50]

Heating the Planet

Of all the impacts humanity is having on the planet, perhaps the most ominous is climate change, which threatens to disrupt the very foundation on which human society has been built since the rise of agriculture. The story of our civilization's inadequate response to the threat of climate change is illustrative of how society's predominant values are at odds with humanity's own intrinsic well-being.

In the 1950s, scientist Charles Keeling first began measuring the level of carbon dioxide in the atmosphere and discovered it was steadily rising each year—an increase that has since been convincingly demonstrated by scientists to be caused by fossil fuels. Carbon dioxide, a greenhouse gas, has the effect of trapping the sun's radiation and thus raising the earth's temperature. The nowfamous Keeling curve is currently increasing at a rate three times faster than when Keeling began his measurements, and, as a result, the world is already 0.9 degrees Celsius hotter than in 1900. It has been calculated that a safe level of atmospheric carbon dioxide would be about 350 parts per million (ppm). This level was reached in 1990 and keeps climbing steadily, surpassing 400 ppm in 2013, higher than earth has experienced for eight hundred thousand years.[51]

When concerns were first raised about the effects of global warming, the world seemed to appreciate the urgency. In 1992, more than 170 nations signed an accord that was followed five years later by the Kyoto Protocol, with legally binding commitments for countries to achieve fossil fuel emission targets. However, the United States never ratified the agreement, and it became largely ineffective.[52]

While the nations of the world avoided confronting the issue, the growth rate of fossil fuel emissions has doubled from 1.5 percent to 3 percent a year, and global climate has begun to change menacingly. The ten warmest years on record have all occurred since 1998. The sea ice in the Arctic has declined precipitously. A rash of what used to be called "once in a century" droughts regularly occur, in regions as disparate as Australia, the Amazon rain forest, southern China, and the southwestern United States. Unprecedented mega-heatwaves have become regular events. Flooding has been equally devastating, such as the massive flood in Pakistan in 2011 that covered one-fifth of the entire country for months, displacing twenty million people.[53]

Less visible, but no less damaging, is the effect of increasing carbon levels in the oceans. About a third of the carbon from fossil fuel emissions gets dissolved in the oceans, leading to increased acidification, which impedes the growth of calcifying organisms such as corals and shellfish. This impact is especially severe on coral reefs, which are viewed as the "rain forests of the sea," containing more than 25 percent of the world's fish biodiversity. The extent of reefs worldwide is already much reduced, and experts have warned that, at current rates of acidification, they could disappear entirely by the end of this century.[54]

In spite of the growing realization of the dangers of fossil fuel emissions, alternative energy sources, such as solar or wind power, continue to receive minimal investment in infrastructure. They represented just 1.9 percent of the world's total energy supply in 1973, and, in 2010, after decades of global awareness about climate change, that percentage had barely crept up to 3.2 percent. Planned expenditures over the next two decades on fossil fuel extraction are triple what is to be spent on renewable energies. Just one company—ExxonMobil—regularly spends about $100 million a day exploring for more oil and gas reserves.[55]

The picture becomes even grimmer when amplifying feedbacks are taken into account. An example of an amplifying feedback is that the ice sheets at the poles normally reflect a lot of the sun's radiation back into space, but when they melt, as the one in the Arctic is doing, they give way to dark ocean, which absorbs more rays and thus speeds up the warming process further. Another amplifying feedback comes from the massive amount of methane—a more potent greenhouse gas—hidden below the permafrost in the north. As the permafrost melts, more methane is released, again accelerating the heating of the planet. As a result, when effects of climate change are projected for the later part of this century and beyond, the prognosis becomes increasingly dismal. At a certain point—no one knows precisely when—the ice sheets of Greenland and a vast part of the West Antarctic are expected to melt into the ocean, either of which would raise sea levels by ten to thirty feet.[56]

The likely effects of these changes on our civilization are dreadful to contemplate. Because most cities have grown up around oceans, half of the world's population currently lives within fifteen miles of the coast. While some northern regions will experience a better climate for agriculture, crop yields in tropical regions may shrink by as much as half, with some experts predicting the collapse of agricultural systems in some regions. One team that studied climate change throughout history has found it has a strong causal linkage with human conflict. With scenarios of hundreds of millions of climate refugees fleeing flooded regions, along with collapsing agricultural systems, it is not difficult to imagine how that might come about.[57]

In 2015, nearly two decades after the Kyoto Protocol, the nations of the world finally agreed in Paris that carbon emissions needed to be cut significantly to avoid catastrophic consequences. However, even though the Paris Agreement set an aggressive target for keeping global warming as far as possible below two degrees Celsius, the emission reductions plans submitted still put the world on a trajectory for catastrophic temperature rise by the end of the century.

"A Global Suicide Pact"

The threat of climate change, ominous as it is, cannot be separated from other pressures on the planet imposed by the frenzied growth of our world economy. In a 2009 paper entitled "A Safe Operating Space for Humanity," prominent scientists identified nine global systems that humanity relies on and calculated "planetary boundaries" for their safe functioning. They reported that in three of the systems—climate, biodiversity, and the nitrogen cycle—we have already exceeded the safe boundaries. These systems are deeply interconnected, so when one system is under pressure, it exerts repercussions on others, leading to new and unpredictable amplifying feedbacks. Of particular concern is the concept of a tipping point: the risk that at some point—impossible to predict or perhaps even to recognize when we are crossing it—a planetary system passes a threshold from which there is no going back, no matter what we might do from there on.[58*]

The scientists who study these things, however, have not yet been heard by enough people to make a difference. This is not from lack of trying. In 1992, a group of more than 1,700 scientists, including the majority of Nobel laureates in science, issued a statement as plainly as could be written, called "World Scientists' Warning to Humanity," that declared:

> Human beings and the natural world are on a collision course. . . . If not checked, many of our current practices put at serious risk the future that we wish for human society and the plant and animal kingdoms, and may so alter the living world that it will be unable to sustain life in the manner that we know. Fundamental changes are urgent if we are to avoid the collision our present course will bring about. . . .
>
> We the undersigned, senior members of the world's scientific community, hereby warn all humanity of what lies ahead. A great change in our stewardship of the earth and the life on it is required, if vast human misery is to be avoided and our global home on this planet is not to be irretrievably mutilated.[59]

Prominent earth scientists have been repeating this message for decades with rising desperation. We are facing an "imminent planetary emergency," writes one. We may be heading "toward the worst catastrophe in the history of *Homo sapiens,*" declares another, while a third warns that if we fail to negotiate this crisis, "we will lay a curse of unimaginable magnitude on future generations," causing "a catastrophe unprecedented in earth history."[60]

Our global leaders, who theoretically have the power to affect our future course, are aware of the magnitude of the crisis. The United Nations Secretary-General, Ban Ki-Moon, gave an address to the World Economic Forum in 2011 in which he described humanity's situation in unequivocal terms, stating:

> For most of the last century, economic growth was fuelled by what seemed to be a certain truth: the abundance of natural resources. We mined our way to growth. We burned our way to prosperity. We believed in consumption without consequences. Those days are gone. . . . Over time, that model is a recipe for national disaster. It is a global suicide pact.[61]

In spite of these warnings, the world continues to engage in its collective suicide pact. What are the reasons for this? Can anything be done to alter our course? When the sorcerer's apprentice lost control of his handiwork, the sorcerer eventually came home and uttered the magic spell. What, in our case, may be required to take back control over humanity's destiny?

Ideological Lock-In

The reasons our civilization continues hurtling toward a precipice are multilayered. There are some readily identifiable factors; underpinning these are certain structural characteristics of our global system that lock in our current momentum, and underlying these are cognitive frames—mostly concealed—that form the basis for our collective behavior. Each of these layers must be addressed to make a meaningful course correction.

The easily identifiable forces propelling humanity on its current course are the special interests that gain financially and politically—at least, in the short term—from continued economic growth and use of fossil fuels. Hundreds of millions of dollars are spent annually in political lobbying and funding for those who deny the threat of anthropogenic climate change. Even though 98 percent of serious scientists stand behind the findings of the UN-sponsored Intergovernmental Panel on Climate Change, the "climate deniers" wield enough power over the media in the United States that they continue to define the public debate in terms of *whether* there is climate change rather than what to do about it. They currently exert enough power over the US legislative process to thwart meaningful legislation at the national level.[62]

However, even without these special interests, some structural characteristics of our global system make it very difficult to change direction. One of these is known as *technological lock-in*: the fact that, once a technology is widely adopted, an infrastructure is built up around it, making change prohibitively expensive. A frequently cited example is the QWERTY keyboard, which was originally designed for its *in*efficiency in an attempt to slow down the rate of typing and therefore prevent early typewriter keys from hitting each other. More efficiently laid-out keyboards can double typing speeds, and yet it has been impossible for them to make inroads because everyone is used to the older, inefficient design. In the case of fossil fuels, an obvious example of technological lock-in is the network of gas stations for vehicles with conventional engines. Any new electric car technology has an uphill battle to create a competing network, even if its vehicles offer equivalent performance.[63]

These technological challenges can be overcome with enough investment. A far greater obstacle to meaningful change is *financial lock-in*: the financial infrastructure underlying the fossil fuel–based economy. Fossil fuel corporations are valued primarily on the basis of their proven coal, oil, and gas reserves. However, for the world to keep global warming to two degrees, the oil companies could only use about one-fifth of their reserves. These corporations would experience drastic declines in market value if the world were to make a serious commitment to rein in global warming. Given the overriding corporate objective of maximizing financial returns, their executives have a powerful incentive to steer the public debate away from this issue.[64]

Beyond the narrow interests of the fossil fuel industry, the entire capitalist economy is founded on perpetual growth. In aggregate, world stock markets are valued on the same growth assumptions that predict a quadrupling of the global economy by mid-century. Business leaders fret that if a concerted attempt were made to reduce this growth trajectory, it might lead to a spiraling decline in valuations, possibly even to the collapse of the capitalist system. Additionally, in the arena of geopolitical rivalry, the power of a nation relative to others is substantially based on economic strength. Leaders fear that if their nation unilaterally chose to reduce its own growth to a more sustainable level, this would reduce its ability to protect its national interests. It is as though we live in a world of not one but many sorcerers' apprentices, each competing with the others, so that even if each of them knew the spell to stop his own runaway broom, he would immediately be outcompeted by the others, so each therefore continues in the group folly.[65]

This self-defeating collective dynamic, known in economics as the "tragedy of the commons," highlights a crucial flaw in capitalist ideology: the notion that it is inevitably beneficial for society when each person seeks to maximize his own gain. Underlying this notion is an even more fundamental defect of classical economic theory: the assumption that nature is inexhaustible. When the framework of modern economics was developed in the eighteenth century, it seemed reasonable to view natural resources as unlimited because, for all intents and purposes, they were. Economists therefore treated minerals, trees, and water as commodities to be sold at a price that was simply the cost of extracting and marketing them. As we've seen, the experience of the past fifty years has proven that assumption to be wrong. In the words of systems theorist

Kenneth Boulding, "Anyone who believes exponential growth can go on forever in a finite world is either a madman or an economist."[66]

In spite of this obvious and fundamental flaw, classical economic theory continues to be used around the world as the driving force for decisions made by corporations, policy makers, and governments. How can that be? Environmental historian J. R. McNeill offers an explanation: "When an idea becomes successful, it easily becomes even more successful: it gets entrenched in social and political systems, which assists in its further spread. It then prevails even beyond the times and places where it is advantageous to its followers." This is another form of lock-in: *ideological.* "Big ideas," McNeil observes, "all became orthodoxies, enmeshed in social and political systems, and difficult to dislodge even if they became costly."[67*]

The "Hedonic Treadmill"

A powerful example of ideological lock-in is the standard of gross domestic product (GDP), by which the performance of governments and countries is judged across the world. The economist who invented it in the 1930s, Simon Kuznets, warned that it was a "potentially dangerous oversimplification that could be misleading" and subject to "resulting abuse." However, in the aftermath of World War II, as the world was gearing up for the Great Acceleration, GDP was formally incorporated into official policy making.[68]

The basic fault with GDP as a measure of a country's performance is that it fails to distinguish between activities that promote welfare and those that reduce it. Anything that causes economic activity of any kind, whether good or bad, adds to GDP. An oil spill, for example, increases GDP because of the cost of cleaning it up: the bigger the spill, the better it is for GDP. In the description of one team of analysts: "By the curious standard of the GDP, the nation's economic hero is a terminal cancer patient who is going through a costly divorce. The happiest event is an earthquake or a hurricane. The most desirable habitat is a multibillion-dollar Superfund site."[69]

GDP measures the rate at which our society is transforming nature and human activities into the monetary economy, regardless of the ensuing quality of life. When someone picks vegetables from their garden and cooks them for a friend, this has no impact on GDP; however, buying a similar meal from the frozen food section of a supermarket involves an exchange of money and therefore adds to GDP. Because of this, activities that put more burden on the environment tend to contribute more to GDP. Driving to work in a car is GDPenhancing, whereas cycling to work has no effect; turning on the air conditioning increases GDP, whereas opening a window does nothing for it. In this bizarre system of accounting, toxic pollution can be triply beneficial for GDP growth: once when a chemical company produces hazardous by-products, twice when the pollutants need to be cleaned up, and a third time if they cause harm to people that requires medical treatment.[70]

The measure of GDP goes from being merely bizarre to dangerous for humanity's future because of the fact that metrics have a profound impact on what society tries to achieve. As one economist observes: "We get what we measure. The indicators we choose to define success become the things we strive for." Recognizing this, various groups, including the United Nations and the European Community, have begun to explore alternative ways to measure society's true performance. The Himalayan state of Bhutan has broken new ground by creating a "Gross National Happiness" index, incorporating values such as spiritual well-being, health, and biodiversity.[71]

These alternative measures offer a very different story of the human experience over the last fifty years than the one presented by GDP. When researchers applied a measure known as the Genuine Progress Indicator to seventeen countries around the world, they discovered that although GDP has continually increased since 1950, worldwide GPI reached its peak in 1978 and has been declining ever since.[72]

In spite of this, the mainstream media unquestionably accept the mantra of our locked-in ideology that economic growth, measured by GDP, is the societal objective to be pursued above all else. If GDP actually measured those aspects of life that lead to greater happiness, we should expect that the richer a country is, the happier its people are. This is true for subsistence-level economies, where people who are barely surviving are, not surprisingly, the unhappiest. However, this correlation disappears after a country's GDP per capita reaches a moderate level (roughly equivalent to countries such as Mexico or Turkey). Beyond that, there is no correlation between the wealth of a country and the reported happiness of its population.[73]

In countries such as the United States, the United Kingdom, and Japan, GDP per capita skyrocketed after World War II, yet the reported life satisfaction of their populations remained flat. This is called the "Easterlin paradox" after the scientist who first discovered it in 1974. More recently, researchers have analyzed eastern European countries following the fall of the Soviet Union; and China, which experienced two decades of the fastest rise in GDP per capita ever seen. In each case, they found the same results: overall life satisfaction failed to increase with the rise in income levels.[74]

Easterlin's explanation for this paradox was that while economic growth raised people's standard of living, it also raised their aspirations, leading to a negative effect on their happiness. This effect has become known as the "hedonic treadmill": no matter how affluent people become, they continually compare themselves with others in their peer group and always desire more. In our globally interconnected world, the standards people compare themselves against are no longer exclusively those of their local peer group but those of the global elite whose images are continually thrust into their presence. The global "hedonic treadmill" is getting ever faster and broader.[75]

Edward Bernays, the mastermind of modern consumerism, and his followers appear to have succeeded only too well.

Humanity's Search for Meaning

Our modern world is the result of the runaway success of one of the most powerful cognitive patterns in history. Capitalism triumphed over competing ideologies with its seductive precept that, by selfishly pursuing individual financial gain, each person was contributing to the greater benefit of society. With the advent of "consumptionism," capitalism instilled an intoxicating new purpose into people's lives, promising them that their feelings of emptiness, meaninglessness, or alienation could be cured through the possession and conspicuous use of manufactured goods. No matter that the "cure" was only temporary: through hard work and dedication, you could earn more money to purchase even more goods, thus stepping on to the hedonic treadmill.

This pattern has become so embedded into the global construction of meaning that most people accept it without question. Those fortunate enough to possess more money than others gain more in the short term on the treadmill of temporary satisfaction. However, the ultimate beneficiaries are not human at all but rather the conceptual creations called corporations, which exist collectively to transform the human experience and the natural world into the monetized economy, regardless of the ultimate effect on humanity as a whole.

How did this cognitive pattern achieve such success? We've seen that, beginning with the "mind-cure" movement of the late nineteenth century, a consumption-based ideology served to redress a lack of meaning in people's lives, replacing an inner void resulting from the uniquely Western mode of dualistic cognition with the consumerist frenzy of capitalism.

In more integrative patterns of cognition, such as those of traditional Chinese thought or indigenous cultures, people's relationship to their community and the natural world satisfied the drive of their patterning instinct to find meaning in life. In the prescientific Christian era, as in Islamic civilization, the belief in a transcendent God infused meaning into people's lives even though it led to the bifurcated experience that continues to cause so much suffering. However, in our mainstream modern value system, the separation from the desacralized natural world—created by the Greeks, systematized by Christianity, and endorsed by reductionist science—is complete.

Where does this leave us? The forces driving humanity toward potential disaster are daunting and only seem to be gaining in strength through our economy's continued frenzy of growth. This is not, of course, the usual narrative we receive through our media. Instead, the mainstream message incessantly hammers home the clarion call of progress. We hear about new technologies that promise to solve our problems and about endless opportunities for those who choose to take their chances on the hedonic treadmill. What about genetic engineering, artificial intelligence, and the other technological miracles arising from the continued progression of Moore's law? Might these advances offer humanity the ability to continue consuming the earth without having to face such dire consequences?

This book began by inviting the reader to imagine a satellite being launched into space with wobbly controls. If the trajectory became too steep, the satellite would break through the earth's gravity field and leave it behind forever; if there were too much friction, it would burn up in the atmosphere and come crashing down. Only with great care might the satellite somehow achieve a stable orbit. When we consider our civilization as that satellite, we might ask which path we are on. One trajectory, with Moore's law underwriting endless technological wizardry, promises a future in which humanity itself might be redefined. At the rate with which we are using up the earth's resources, another trajectory threatens potential disaster ahead for humanity. Which of these is more likely to be humanity's actual path? And, even more crucially, is there a way our civilization can somehow be steered to achieve a sustainable path for humanity's future—a path in which progress might mean something other than consuming the earth? The final chapter will explore these questions.

Part 5

THE WEB OF MEANING?

Chapter 21

TRAJECTORIES TO OUR FUTURE

In the classic movie *2001: A Space Odyssey*, astronaut Dr. Floyd is on his way to a meeting in a space station orbiting the earth. It has the look and feel of an ultramodern international airport. He steps into a videophone booth to call his wife back on Earth and reaches his little girl, who tells him her mommy is out. Dr. Floyd chats with his daughter about her upcoming birthday party and then leaves her an important message to give to his wife, trying hard to impress it into her child's memory. This vignette, filmed in 1968 and envisioning a world three decades ahead, offers a fascinating glimpse into the pitfalls of forecasting the future. From our vantage point in the early twenty-first century, we can see two significant errors. On the one hand, there is no sophisticated space station orbiting the earth. On the other hand, in the actual world of 2001, Dr. Floyd wouldn't have needed to leave that message with his daughter; instead, he could simply have reached his wife directly on her mobile phone, no matter where she was.[1]

These mistakes are common to predictions about the future. They arise from the simple fact that predictions are usually made by extrapolating past trends into the future through a linear progression. However, the way the future unfolds is nonlinear. The tremendous progress in rocket technology that fueled the moon landing in 1969 failed to continue at the same rate. Meanwhile, Moore's law was beginning to exert its exponential effect on the miniaturization of information processing chips, permitting a previously unthinkable reduction in the size required for a mobile telephone.

The one thing we can rely on about humanity's future trajectory is its nonlinearity. That fact presents us with both humanity's greatest peril and our greatest reason for hope. Our peril arises from the fact that we can't just look at the recent decades of prosperity enjoyed by much of the world and assume it will continue indefinitely; at the same time, we can glean hope from the realization that humanity's unsustainable growth in consumption, inexorable as it appears, will not necessarily continue until our global civilization is doomed. What does the future hold for humanity? In this final chapter, we'll investigate some of the possibilities—from the grimmest to the most dazzling—and discover the important part each of us has to play in humanity's actual trajectory.

Limits to Growth

The same year that *2001: A Space Odyssey* came out, a group of prominent politicians, businessmen, and scientists known as the Club of Rome commissioned a project at MIT to develop a more systematic view of the future. The project team, well aware of the nonlinear nature of the future, focused their attention on how major drivers of our future—such as population growth, technology, and pollution—interact with each other to produce outcomes that could never be predicted by modeling each factor in isolation. It was the first integrated model of the entire globe, and it produced some disturbing results, which the team published in 1972 in the book *Limits to Growth*. It was a little book, but it had a big impact, selling twelve million copies in more than thirty languages.[2]

The book shocked its readers because, for the first time, someone had asked the question of whether economic growth could continue indefinitely, then systematically tried to answer it. Their answer was that unless drastic changes were made, our economic boom would be followed by the global collapse of our civilization sometime in the twenty-first century. Even those who had previously viewed our economic growth as unsustainable had generally assumed things would just stabilize after a while. Why would there be a collapse? The team explained their results with the concept of "overshoot": a gradual process by which we continue using resources and polluting our environment at an unsustainable rate, but without causing such a dramatic impact that it forces society to make radical changes to its behavior. This process, they explained, could continue for decades before hitting a wall that leads to societal collapse. Overshoot is easy to understand on a more human scale. We all know that if you keep dipping into your bank account at a faster rate than you can put money into it, you'll eventually go bankrupt. If your community has access to a single forest, and you chop down the trees at a faster rate than they can regrow, you can keep enjoying plenty of wood until, one day, there isn't a single tree left. On a global scale, overshoot is more complex and far more difficult to visualize, but, ultimately, the book explained, it works the same way.[3]

This was not a message that most people wanted to hear, and *Limits to Growth* provoked a vehement backlash that obscured what the authors were trying to communicate. Some of the book's most vocal critics obfuscated its message with blatant misinformation. For example, it was commonly believed that the book predicted collapse by the year 2000, when it had made no such forecast. In 1992, President George H. W. Bush declared: "Twenty years ago some spoke of limits to growth. But today we now know that growth is the engine of change. Growth is the friend of the environment." The force of the media campaign against *Limits to Growth* was so powerful that a general belief arose, even in peer-reviewed journals, that its findings had been scientifically discredited. However, that was never the case. In fact, a study conducted in 2008 compared the first thirty years of the scenarios simulated by the team's model and found that its "standard run" scenario, which results in global collapse by mid-century, matched the observed historical data more closely than any other run.[4]

Scenarios for Our Future

The team that published *Limits to Growth* emphasized they weren't making a specific prediction about the future. Rather, they were offering scenarios to show the world where it might be headed unless collective decisions were made to change direction. Another team that has worked on something similar—the Global Scenario Group of the Stockholm Environment Institute—points out three good reasons why we can never actually predict the future. First, there's the problem of ignorance: we can never know every salient fact about the world. Second, even if we knew all the important facts, we still couldn't predict the nonlinear way they might interact. Finally, there's the all-important reality that the future is subject to human choices: no matter how predetermined things might seem, our individual and collective wills have the power to steer the future into a direction of our choosing. The unpredictability of the future doesn't mean there's no point in understanding what it might hold. Rather, the opposite is true: the fact that we *can* affect our future makes it even more important to understand the major drivers of the possible trajectories.[5]

Some of these drivers are clear to see. Something virtually all prognosticators agree on is the global nature of humanity's future. Most critical factors affecting humanity have become planetary in scope. We now have a deeply interconnected global economy, with corporations that transcend political boundaries and consumer goods that frequently contain materials from dozens of countries. Some characteristics of globalization offer reasons for hope. The rise of the internet has caused the rapid flow of information around the world to be nearly seamless, while our civilization has developed global institutions such as the United Nations—limited as they sometimes appear—and has witnessed the rise of other nongovernmental organizations with worldwide reach.[6]

There's widespread agreement on another crucial driver of our future: the breathtaking rate of change in many powerful and converging technologies. Innovations in fields such as synthetic biology, artificial intelligence, genetic engineering, and nanotechnology catalyze each other to create ever more opportunities for further breakthroughs, offering potential for dramatic transformation in virtually every aspect of human experience.[7]

All this leads to a general consensus that, no matter what shape the future takes, it will be fundamentally different from anything we've known in the past. Looking back through human history, we can recognize two great phase transitions: the emergence of agriculture about ten thousand years ago and the rise of the scientific age over the past few hundred years. In our current era, it's becoming clear that we're entering a third great transition.[8]

But a transition to what? To a glorious age of technology, in which human limitations can be overcome and unimaginable possibilities beckon? Or to the collapse of civilization itself, as presaged in *Limits to Growth*? Or something in between these two extremes, with convolutions we can't even begin to envisage? Before we explore these scenarios, it's worthwhile to get more acquainted with the general character of phase transitions so we can be better prepared to evaluate them.

Dinosaurs, Forest Fires, and Resilience

In the seventeenth century, the king of Sweden was building up his navy to fight the Poles in the Baltic Sea. The grandest of his new ships was the *Wasa*, which he wanted to be so glorious that he ordered it built higher than his engineers advised. Within minutes of leaving port on its maiden voyage, a sudden breeze caused the *Wasa* to lurch to one side, and it immediately capsized and sank less than a mile from land. This is a graphic example of a critical transition, which can be understood as a sudden shift from one stable state to another. For the *Wasa*, the stable states were floating and sinking. For ecosystems, human societies, and other complex systems, like the *Wasa*, the critical transition from one state to another frequently happens suddenly and unexpectedly.[9]

Critical transitions can occur for two kinds of reasons: sledgehammer effects and threshold effects. A sledgehammer effect, as its name implies, arises when an outside force causes dramatic change in a system, leaving it in a new state very different from its previous state. A good example of a sledgehammer effect is the asteroid that is believed to have wiped out the dinosaurs about sixtyfive million years ago. In a relatively short period of time, the world transitioned from being dominated by dinosaurs to being dominated instead by mammals. A more recent example is the deforestation caused when humans chop down forests for farmland. Threshold effects are sometimes more difficult to identify while they're happening but can be equally powerful. They refer to the critical transition that happens when a system changes from within. One example of a threshold effect discussed in this book is how language emerged from a feedback loop between the cultural and biological evolution of humans, creating a symbolic network that's been the foundation of human culture ever since.[10]

In complex systems, critical transitions frequently arise from an interplay between threshold and sledgehammer effects. Consider a forest growing unimpeded year after year. Gradually, the undergrowth and brush build up until the forest becomes a tinderbox. Suddenly, a lightning storm kindles some brush to create a forest fire, turning the forest into charcoal. The gradual buildup of the kindling was the threshold effect, while the lightning, in this case, was the sledgehammer. When a system is healthy, it is generally less susceptible to external changes and may need the force of a giant sledgehammer force to damage it. However, a system can become increasingly brittle and unstable, making it vulnerable to transformation by a much smaller external effect, such as the breeze that capsized the *Wasa* or a single match that sparks a devastating forest fire. When this happens, the system is considered to have lost its *resilience*.[11]

The resilience of a system determines whether it can withstand big shocks or is susceptible to collapse from a small disturbance. Resilience can be understood as the capacity of a system to recover from a disturbance. But recovery doesn't necessarily mean remaining the same; the most resilient systems are often those that are constantly adapting to changes in their environment. A healthy forest, for example, might experience regular fires, leading to new species of vegetation emerging. Environmental scientist Marten Scheffer defines a resilient system as one that can accommodate changes and reorganize itself while maintaining the crucial attributes that give the system its unique character.

This helps us think about how our civilization might respond to the drastic changes—environmental, technological, and cognitive—that we're experiencing. How resilient is our society to these changes? Are there ways to increase our resilience and transform ourselves while retaining the essential attributes of our humanity and our global civilization? It's a big question. Fortunately, there's a framework we can use to try to answer it.[12]

Prominent systems thinkers have formed a general theory of change in complex systems called the adaptive cycle model, which applies to different kinds of systems across vast scales of time and space, from day-to-day changes in local ecosystems to the evolution of species over millions of years. This model sees complex systems as passing through four phases of a cycle. The cycle begins with a rapid *growth phase*, during which innovative strategies can exploit new opportunities. In a capitalist system, this is the period when entrepreneurs thrive, developing new products and targeting new markets. Gradually, the system moves to a more stable *conservation phase*, when rules and established connections become more important. This phase can last for a long time, during which the future seems quite predictable, but as time goes on, the system becomes increasingly brittle and resistant to change. It becomes less resilient. At a certain point, a small disturbance can cause the entire system to collapse, which is the *release phase*. This could be the lightning igniting a forest fire or, in financial markets, a sudden loss of confidence leading to panic. Following the system's collapse, a period of chaos ensues, and uncertainty rules. New opportunities emerge for creativity, which is why the final stage in the cycle is called the *renewal phase*. In this period, small chance events can drastically shape the future. In an ecosystem, new species may emerge that had previously been suppressed (such as the mammals that took over from the dinosaurs). In social systems, this is the time when charismatic individuals might have an inordinate impact on public opinion, either for good or for evil. "Early in the renewal phase," experts note, "the future is up for grabs."[13]

Which of these four phases best describes our current global system? There's no simple answer, partly because our global system is itself a network of different systems, each of which might be in a different phase of its own adaptive cycle. Those who focus on technology, for example, might argue we're still in a growth phase, with waves of progress resulting from innovation. On the other hand, the earth's natural systems appear to be entering the late stages of a conservation phase, coming precariously close to tipping points that could destabilize our civilization.

Could our global civilization itself be in the late stage of a conservation phase and face imminent collapse? That possibility is consistent with the warning issued by *Limits to Growth*. In the decades to come, as the world experiences the stress of climate disruption, with increased mass migrations, infrastructure breakdowns, and crop failures, these stresses on our global system may further reduce its resilience to unexpected shocks.

The crucial question is how much resilience is built into our global system. Unfortunately, much of it has been designed with short-term efficiencies in mind, which have tended to reduce resilience rather than increase it. In a resilient system, individual nodes—families or communities—need to be self-sufficient enough to survive in an emergency. In our modern civilization, most of us lack self-sufficiency, relying on the global network of commerce and information for food and other necessities. As those networks have been honed over decades for ever greater efficiencies, their resilience has been whittled away. To minimize costs, inventories in factories and warehouses have frequently been cut to no more than a few days' supply, but this means that, in the event of any significant disruption of just one important commodity—a real threat from climate change—the entire network that feeds and sustains our global civilization could rapidly grind to a halt.[14]

How Societies Collapse

If our society were to succumb to the onslaught of climate change, it wouldn't be the first to do so. Studies have shown a correlation between the declines of ancient civilizations and periods of significant climate change. The Harappan civilization is believed to have collapsed after a loss of the monsoon rains, and the New Kingdom of ancient Egypt, the Akkadian Empire, and the Maya all suffered eventual collapse following centuries-long dry periods.[15]

If you broaden the scope to include general environmental decline, the correlation with the collapse of civilizations gets even more striking. The Mesopotamians gradually brought ruin on themselves through the salinization caused by their massive irrigation system, leaving their doleful lamentation, *The Curse of Akkad,* to tell us how their fields "produced no grain." The Maya, too, were brought down not just by drought but by overexploitation of their land, and the same seems to have been true for the Anasazi civilization of the American Southwest. In his book *Collapse: How Societies Choose to Fail or Survive,* Jared Diamond describes the poignant example of Easter Island, where the first human arrivals colonized a fertile, forested haven and then proceeded, over centuries, to destroy every tree on the entire island. He asks the harrowing question, "What did the Easter Islander who cut down the last palm tree say while he was doing it?" Later in this section, we can perhaps conjecture an answer to this.[16*]

The implications for our current civilization are immediately apparent. In addition to climate change, we're facing the myriad environmental pressures chronicled in the previous chapter arising from exponential growth in consumption. However, some who have studied the collapse of earlier civilizations point out that environmental pressures alone, no matter how severe, are not enough to cause a society to collapse. Rather, they say, it depends on how the society responds to these problems. One anthropologist, Joseph Tainter, notes that, in the American Southwest, although environmental degradation led in one instance to collapse, in another case, it led to the society becoming more complex. "If a society cannot deal with resource depletion," Tainter ponders, "then the truly interesting questions revolve around the society, not the resource. What structural, political, ideological, or economic factors in a society prevented an appropriate response?"[17]

Intent on answering this question, Tainter extensively studied different civilizations in history and published his conclusions in a work called *The Collapse of Complex Societies*. Tainter offers something approaching a grand theory of collapse, describing a generic life cycle that applies, in his view, to every complex society including our own. At their core, Tainter explains, societies can be understood in terms of energy flows. If a society is fortunate to discover a new source of energy, it will naturally grow in size and complexity as it exploits that energy. The source of energy can vary considerably. It can arise from a new technology, such as the irrigation systems of Mesopotamia, or be the collective energy of conquered nations forced to submit to a military power such as the Roman Empire. As a civilization gets more complex, it needs ever more energy to maintain its growth and will generally keep doing what it's done successfully in the past, such as build more irrigation channels or conquer more nations. Tainter describes this as a society's investment in complexity. However, after the first easy pickings, the next steps in the society's growth become more difficult and costly, offering more miserly returns. At a certain point, the society's return on investment in complexity peaks, and it finds itself spending increasing amounts of resources for ever more meager returns. In effect, as the society gets more complex, it finds itself having to run harder and harder just to stay in the same place.[18]

This situation resembles the late conservation phase of the adaptive cycle model. The problems keep getting bigger, requiring ever more costly solutions, which add to the society's complexity, in turn requiring even more energy than before, causing a new round of problems that become ever more insurmountable. In this downward spiral, it becomes increasingly difficult for regular citizens to maintain the lifestyle they are used to, frequently leading to social unrest, which further undermines the society's resilience. "With continuation of this trend," Tainter concludes, "collapse becomes a matter of mathematical probability, as over time an insurmountable stress surge becomes increasingly likely."[19]

The Roman Empire presents the best documented—and dramatic—example of Tainter's model. Tainter tells how, as it expanded, Rome would conquer new territories and appropriate the spoils, in the form of agricultural surplus, treasure, and slaves, causing an infusion of wealth. However, after each conquest, the Empire incurred new costs to administer, garrison, and defend the province. How did they pay for this? By conquering another territory for another one-time wealth infusion. By the first century CE, the Roman Empire had expanded so far that maintaining it was draining Rome's wealth, while new territories were becoming increasingly difficult to conquer. Rome's return on investment in complexity was turning negative. How did its leaders respond? By gradually debasing Rome's currency, the denarius, by reducing its silver content with copper and thereby artificially increasing the money supply. With this strategy, Rome's leaders essentially kicked their problems down the road for later generations to deal with. "The inflation that would inevitably follow," writes Tainter, "would tax the future to pay for the present, but the future could not protest." Eventually, the denarius became worthless, and the empire was on the brink of collapse. Taxes were raised beyond the peasants' ability to feed themselves, villages dwindled, people fled to the cities, and, by the time Rome itself was ransacked in 476 by Germanic tribes, it was a virtual nonevent to much of the empire that had already been devastated by Rome's own policies.[20]

What makes the story of Rome's collapse so chilling is how difficult it would have been for someone living in the middle of it to predict how bad things were going to get. Consistent with the adaptive cycle model, Rome maintained apparent stability for centuries until eventually it lost all resilience and disintegrated. This arc can be seen dramatically in figure 21.1, which shows the debasement of the denarius over the centuries. Imagine you were a Roman economist analyzing the denarius late in the second century as it enjoyed a temporary upswing in value. You might have felt hopeful that it would maintain that level, not knowing how dramatically it was destined to fall in just a few decades.[21]

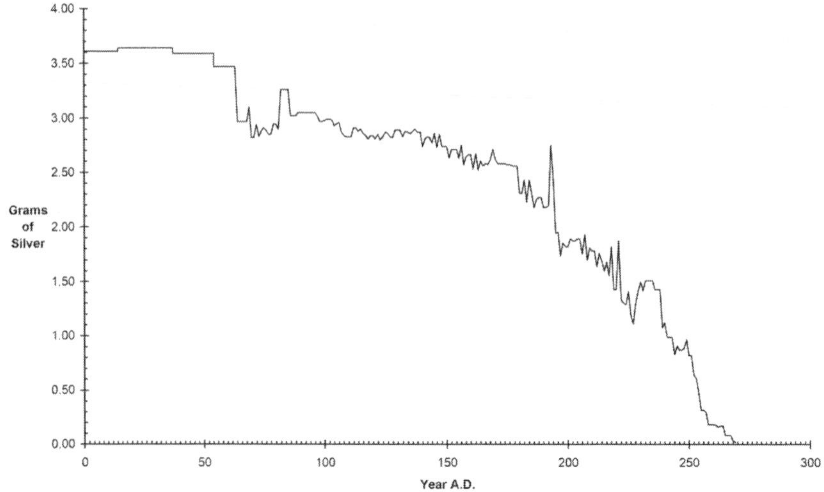

Figure 21.1: Debasement of the denarius to 269 CE (Tainter 1988).

A modern version of this process has occurred in the overexploitation of fisheries, where stocks decline as a result of being overfished from one generation to the next, but people forget how things used to be and consider the situation to be normal, until the next decline. The term "shifting baseline syndrome" has been coined to describe how people get used to each new level. This, perhaps, offers an answer to Jared Diamond's question of what that Easter Islander was thinking when he cut down the last tree. Most likely, he didn't think anything of it at all because, by then, the only trees left would have been little more than weeds, good for nothing more than weaving a mat.[22]

Will Our Society Collapse Like Rome?

It's difficult to consider the collapse of the Roman Empire without drawing parallels to our own civilization. Whereas Rome's primary energy source was conquered nations, the primary energy source of our civilization is fossil fuels. But we're facing the same type of problems the Romans faced. Whereas they encountered increasing costs of administering their empire, we're confronted with the global impact of rising carbon emissions. Where they chose shortterm solutions that created insurmountable problems for future generations, we're doing the same by permitting carbon emissions to keep increasing, even when we know it will lead in the future to runaway climate change. Where they were eventually driven to consume their own capital in desperation, squeezing their territories until they destroyed them, our civilization is unsustainably consuming the earth's resources while falsely claiming the results as current income.

When Tainter turns his attention to our civilization, he sees nothing to suggest that we can somehow escape the inexorable logic of his grand theory. In ancient societies, he notes, if you needed a new source of energy, you could turn to territorial expansion. In our global society, we're all in it together, so there's nowhere to turn. "Collapse," he avers, "if and when it comes again, will this time be global. No longer can any individual nation collapse. World civilization will disintegrate as a whole." The only thing that can save us, he believes, is a new source of energy to fuel our continued rise in complexity.[23]

When we look at how our society is currently deriving its energy, the facts seem to support Tainter's viewpoint. Whereas the Romans experienced diminishing returns from military expeditions, we are receiving diminishing returns as the oil companies mine the furthest reaches of the globe for fossil fuels. Like the Romans, we've used up the low-hanging fruit.

Can technology save us? Tainter thinks not. He points to what is known as the "Jevons paradox," which shows that whenever technology makes the use of a resource more efficient, this only increases its use, as consumption goes up to exploit the new efficiencies. The oil industry's recent desperate rush into tar sands and "fracking" seems to confirm Tainter's thesis, as our global economy invests billions of dollars into technological solutions to extract ever more fossil fuels, even while their carbon emissions are threatening the future of our civilization.[24]

Many have looked at this situation and arrived at the same gloomy prognosis. Prominent biologist Paul Ehrlich sees this as the "human predicament," suggesting that "determining how to prevent it from generating a global collapse is perhaps the foremost challenge confronting humanity." Others have concluded we're already so far along the path to ruin that it's too late. "We have come to believe," writes another team of academics, "that human civilization . . . will self-destruct, producing massive environmental damage, social chaos and megadeath."[25]

From a larger perspective, one could view the arc of our civilization as just another cycle in the sweep of history. If our civilization eventually succumbs, the logic goes, in time another one will surely arise, which may learn from our mistakes. However, as astronomer Fred Hoyle has pointed out, there may never be another opportunity in the earth's history for any advanced intelligence to reach our level of technological sophistication. The reason is that we've already used up all the "easy pickings" from the energy sources and raw materials that the earth offers. "With coal gone," Hoyle observed, "oil gone, high-grade metallic ores gone, no species however competent can make the long climb from primitive conditions to high-level technology. This is a one-shot affair. If we fail, this planetary system fails so far as intelligence is concerned."[26]

The stakes could not be higher for humanity. If our current civilization collapses, the human race will continue, but we're most likely condemning our descendants for time immemorial to lives without the benefits we've enjoyed, to societies bounded by the limitations and values of agrarian norms, where draft animals and human slaves become the energy fodder for small, powerful elites. What can we do to avert this catastrophe?

Technology as Savior?

The solution, to many, is simple. Technology, the fruit of human ingenuity, will save us. It always has in the past and will continue to do so. What about Tainter's argument? A reasonable rebuttal is that the continuously accelerating feedback cycle of modern technology has created a dynamic different from that of any previous era. Perhaps Moore's law, combined with the explosive potential of converging technologies, has given our civilization, in effect, a new energy source, one that is potentially limitless and therefore doesn't conform to Tainter's theory.

The favorite whipping boy of these technology optimists, known as cornucopians, is the hapless Thomas Malthus, a late-eighteenth-century English cleric who was the first to warn of the dangers of exponential growth. Malthus reasoned that if the human race were to transcend the diseases and wars that kept population in check, their numbers would expand exponentially, but the resources to feed them were finite, so the result would inevitably be mass starvation. It was for this reason, Malthus surmised, that the benevolent creator put poverty, disease, and warfare on the earth: to keep the population from growing out of control.[27]

For two centuries, Malthus's predictions have provided a reliable straw man for the cornucopians who scoff at warnings of humanity's doom. Malthus's "earlier dire predictions," in the words of one, "have all been overcome by the exercise of human ingenuity." The *Economist*, a voice of capitalist optimism, opines that "once again the gloom is overdone. . . . There may be curbs on traditional forms of growth, but there is no limit to human ingenuity. That is why Malthus remains as wrong today as he was two centuries ago."[28]

The allure of technology is so intoxicating that sometimes even distinguished economists speak about it as though it has transcended not just Tainter's theory but the very laws of nature. "The world can, in effect, get along without natural resources," remarked Nobel Prize–winning economist Robert Solow. Another prominent cornucopian, Julian Simon, upped the ante even further. "Technology exists now," he wrote, "to produce in virtually inexhaustible quantities just about all the products made by nature—foodstuffs, oil, even pearls and diamonds. . . . We have in our hands now—actually, in our libraries—the technology to feed, clothe, and supply energy to an ever-growing population for the next 7 billion years."[29]

Seven billion years? This could be dismissed as mere silliness, except that the underlying principles espoused by these economists form the framework for the global economy that is rapidly consuming the earth's resources. The idea of progress has transfixed the Western imagination, causing otherwise sober thinkers to rhapsodize euphorically about the possibilities of the human endeavor. The rhapsodic vision of cornucopians, emanating from even the most established institutions, sometimes sounds more like religious prophecy than the result of careful scientific investigation. A joint report published in 2003 by the National Science Foundation and the US Department of Commerce, entitled *Converging Technologies for Improving Human Performance*, concludes, "The twenty-first century could end in world peace, universal prosperity, and evolution to a higher level of compassion and accomplishment."[30]

How could technology accomplish this vision in the face of our civilization's crisis of consumption? The cornucopians are ready with answers. Consider, for example, the ubiquitous smartphone. Incorporating the functions of a camera, radio, telephone, music center, compass, navigation system, and endless other devices, this "represents the great dematerialization of modern civilization, well ahead of any imminent collapse of natural resources," writes cornucopian M. J. Kelly. Turning to agriculture, cornucopians offer a vision of animal protein bioengineered in factories rather than obtained from animals grazing in the fields, just as synthetic fiber has mostly replaced wool. Under this scenario, rather than speaking of peak oil, "we can speak of peak farmland—we will need smaller areas in future to feed the world, and we will oversee the managed return of excess land to the wild."[31]

We can even use genetic engineering to improve on the natural process of photosynthesis in plants, cornucopians argue. According to theoretical physicist Freeman Dyson, the most efficient crops in nature convert just 1 percent of the sunlight they receive into chemical energy. "We can imagine," he writes, "that in the future, when we have mastered the art of genetically engineering plants, we may breed new crop plants that have leaves made of silicon, converting sunlight into chemical energy with ten times the efficiency of natural plants. . . . They would allow solar energy to be used on a massive scale without taking up too much land. They would look like natural plants except that their leaves would be black, the color of silicon, instead of green, the color of chlorophyll."[32]

Engineering Our Planet

What about the devastation threatened by climate change as we continue to burn through fossil fuels in endless pursuit of economic growth? Cornucopians offer a potential solution to this, too, in the form of geoengineering. Recognizing that uncontrolled carbon emissions are heating the planet with potentially catastrophic results, geoengineering proponents have proffered various global-scale proposals to counter these effects. Some schemes focus on reducing the amount of sunlight reaching the earth, floating billions of tiny strips of tinfoil in orbit around the earth to reflect the sunlight, or injecting massive amounts of sulfur dioxide into the upper atmosphere. Other ideas include fertilizing the oceans with iron slurry to increase the volume of marine life, which would consume excess carbon dioxide from the atmosphere.[33]

The very idea of geoengineering has been received with nothing short of derision from many observers. Since we are already dealing with the "unanticipated consequences of . . . pumping 90 million tons of heat-trapping pollution into the atmosphere every twenty-four hours," writes Al Gore, "it would, in my opinion, be utterly insane to launch a second planetary experiment in the faint hope that it might temporarily cancel out some of the consequences of the first experiment without doing even more harm in the process."[34]

The primary argument against these proposals is that they could never be effectively tested and, in addition, they risk causing even greater problems in their unintended consequences. There is, also, a well-founded concern that if people believe there's an engineering solution to climate change, this would reduce the pressure to curtail use of fossil fuels and give license to continue with business as usual. Beyond these lies a deeper, philosophical concern:

geoengineering is, in many ways, the ultimate realization of the root metaphors of NATURE AS MACHINE and CONQUERING NATURE that have become an integral part of modern cognition. With geoengineering, we would be turning these metaphors into our lived reality.

Or is it too late anyway? Have we already come to dominate nature so extensively that our best option now is to consciously accept our role as stewards of the earth's life-support systems? This is a perception shared across the ideological spectrum, including those actively working to find sustainable ecological solutions to our crisis. "In a very real sense," writes a team of environmental scientists, "the world is in our hands—and how we handle it will determine its composition and dynamics, and our fate. . . . Humanity's dominance of Earth means that we cannot escape responsibility for managing the planet . . . for the foreseeable future."[35]

It may seem like a relatively small step from this considered awareness of humanity's impact on the natural world to an acceptance of geoengineering in principle. Indeed, argues at least one advocate, it would be an "evasion of our ethical duties" to ignore the fact that our human activities have already affected the world to such an extent that we need to engineer a solution.[36]

A small step in logic, perhaps, but, to paraphrase Neil Armstrong when he walked on the moon, geoengineering would be a giant step for humankind. James Lovelock, the visionary engineer who first conceived of the earth as the self-sustaining organism he called Gaia, offers a somber prophecy for humanity. Humankind, he writes, "would wake up one day to find that [we] had the permanent lifelong job of planetary maintenance engineer. Gaia would have retreated into the muds, and the ceaseless intricate task of keeping all of the global cycles in balance would be ours. Then at last we should be riding that strange contraption, the 'spaceship Earth', and whatever tamed and domesticated biosphere remained would indeed be our 'life support system'."[37]

Is this the future we desire for our descendants? Living on the earth might be a very different experience for them under this scenario. Will they eat their synthetic protein bioengineered in factories? When they leave the city for a rare visit to the "countryside," will they drive past vast fields of black vegetation absorbing the sun's energy for their grid? Will they swim in oceans filled with iron slurry to absorb excess carbon emissions? Even the sky would no longer be blue if sulfur dioxide were used to absorb some of the sun's rays in the upper atmosphere.[38]

But would any of this matter to them? Each new generation is, after all, subject to "shifting baseline syndrome," affecting not just its sense of what's normal but the values driving its own search for meaning. Perhaps future generations will see our attachment to blue skies and green vegetation as charming relics of a bygone age. In fact, according to a growing number of futurists, we must accept that, within a few generations, our descendants might be so different from us as to be virtually unrecognizable. According to these visionaries, humanity itself is about to enter a phase transition that could make the human race as obsolete as the Neanderthals.

Transcending Our Humanity

The idea that human inventiveness will lead to a new posthuman stage in evolution is almost as old as the theory of evolution itself. In 1863, just four years after Darwin's *Origin of Species* was published, novelist Samuel Butler predicted that, one day, machines would evolve into a new form of life. "We are ourselves creating our own successors," he wrote. "Man will become to the machine what the horse and dog are to man. . . . The time will come when the machines will hold the real supremacy over the world and its inhabitants."[39]

Butler's article, partly prophetic, partly tongue-in-cheek, didn't have quite the effect on Western thought that Darwin's theory did, but, in recent decades, the idea that human cultural evolution has bypassed biological evolution has become widely accepted. "*Homo sapiens*," writes biologist E. O. Wilson, "is about to decommission natural selection, the force that made us. . . . Evolution, including genetic progress in human nature and human capacity, will be from now on increasingly the domain of science and technology tempered by ethics and political choice. . . . Soon we must look deep within ourselves and decide what we wish to become."[40]

Some who have looked within themselves have decided that we should embrace an utterly new phase, as Butler predicted, in the evolutionary story. "Technical civilization, and the human minds that support it," writes futurist Hans Moravec, "are the first feeble stirrings of a radically new form of existence, one as different from life as life is from simple chemistry. . . . Intelligent machines, which will grow from us, learn our skills, and initially share our goals and values, will be the children of our minds. . . . We parents can gracefully retire as our mind children grow beyond our imagining."[41]

Not everyone is as willing as Moravec to give carte blanche to machines to inherit our future. Rather, they envisage humanity evolving itself into something not yet imagined but still recognizably from human descent. This idea, known as transhumanism, is rapidly becoming a realistic bioengineering possibility. Scientists are already taking the first steps on the slippery slope to "designer babies." As researchers perfect their genetic engineering skills, how long will it be before the allure of designing their own offspring becomes irresistible to some parents?[42]

This possibility has led to a heightened sense of alarm among many ethicists. Political scientist Francis Fukuyama has called transhumanism "the world's most dangerous idea," claiming that what is ultimately at stake is "the very grounding of the human moral sense, which has been a constant ever since there were human beings." Many critics of human genetic engineering recognize that, in individual cases, it's hard to argue against the promise of improved health, better cognitive capacity, and longer life, but they argue that the intuitive repugnance we feel about altering the very essence of human nature should be honored. This repugnance "is the emotional expression of deep wisdom," argues prominent scholar Leon Kass, "beyond reason's power completely to articulate it."[43]

For transhumanists, though, the promise of genetic engineering is just the beginning of humanity's new journey into uncharted and enticing territory. "Transhumanists view human nature as a work-in-progress, a half-baked beginning that we can learn to remold in desirable ways," declares philosopher Nick Bostrom, a de facto spokesperson for the movement. In an intoxicating manifesto, he proclaims the belief that "humanity's potential is still mostly unrealized" and envisions the possibility of "overcoming aging, cognitive shortcomings, involuntary suffering, and our confinement to planet Earth." Bostrom imagines a chasm between "posthumans" and current humans as wide as that which currently exists between us and chimpanzees: "In much the same way chimpanzees lack the cognitive wherewithal to understand what it is like to be human . . . so we humans may lack the capacity to form a realistic intuitive understanding of what it would be like to be a radically enhanced human (a 'posthuman') and of the thoughts, concerns, aspirations, and social relations that such humans may have."[44]

Toward the Singularity?

This transhumanist vision at least retains some essence of humanity at its core, albeit with values and capabilities beyond our imagining. An even more radical conception of where we might be headed, known as the Singularity, is gaining increasing momentum among the high-tech cultural elite. The Singularity refers to a belief that, at the current rate of technological progress, we're rapidly approaching a threshold event in history when artificial intelligence will transcend human intelligence, and the resulting transformation will lead to a new form of existence utterly different from anything that has come before.

British mathematician I. J. Good was the first to describe this powerful and unsettling vision in 1965. "Let an ultraintelligent machine," he wrote, "be defined as a machine that can far surpass all the intellectual activities of any man however clever. Since the design of machines is one of these intellectual activities, an ultraintelligent machine could design even better machines; there would then unquestionably be an 'intelligence explosion', and the intelligence of man would be left far behind. Thus the first ultraintelligent machine is the last invention that man need ever make."[45]

More recently, the idea of the Singularity has been associated with inventor and futurist Raymond Kurzweil, who published a bestseller, *The Singularity Is Near,* in 2005. Kurzweil blends razor-sharp expertise in artificial intelligence with an unbounded vision that's both apocalyptic and exhilarating to many followers. Speculative as his ideas remain, they're gaining traction: Kurzweil is currently a director of engineering at Google, and his Singularity University boasts a faculty of some of Silicon Valley's leading entrepreneurs.[46]

The Singularity is no longer a mere thought experiment set in some distant future. It needs to be investigated as a possible scenario for humanity's trajectory, with urgent questions to be answered: Is it feasible? What form might it take? And what would be its consequences?

One troubling form of the Singularity would be if machine intelligence achieves such complexity that it spontaneously self-organizes and becomes a conscious agent. Given the massively interconnected nature of today's internet, it's not unreasonable to conceive of artificial intelligence emerging not necessarily from a single supercomputer but from massively distributed arrays of computation linked through the internet. There is already more machine-to-machine communication occurring over the internet than human communication, and it's estimated that, by 2020, there will be as many as fifty billion nodes linking such disparate systems as home networks, production lines, electricity grids, inventory systems, and vehicles. This begins to approach the number of neurons in the human brain, at approximately a hundred billion. Could this massive network, called the "internet of things," ever develop its own intelligence?[47]

If machine intelligence became self-aware, what would that look like? For decades, the de facto standard for determining whether a machine is truly intelligent has been the Turing test: A person in a separate room engages in a written conversation with two entities. One entity is human, the other a computer programmed to imitate a human. If the tester cannot tell the computer apart from the human, the computer passes the test. To date, no computer has passed. Suppose, however, a computer network becomes intelligent through its own self-organized process, absent any direct human programming. In that case, we might not even recognize that intelligence is there until the network begins acting in unanticipated ways. Under this scenario, as we begin to recognize the machine's intelligence, it might be only too obvious that it is not human.[48]

In this version of the Singularity, a truly alien intelligence would be taking over. It wouldn't matter that humans were its original creators: there would be no reason to assume it would have benign intentions toward us. An early warning of this kind of threat can be found in the experience of chess master Garry Kasparov, the first world champion to be defeated by a supercomputer, Deep Blue. In earlier competitions with computers, Kasparov reported a mechanical predictability to their actions. With Deep Blue, it was different: Kasparov described what he felt as an "alien intelligence." As he pondered his defeat, he reflected: "I am a human being. When I see something that is well beyond my understanding, I'm afraid."[49]

The implications of this form of the Singularity are potentially horrifying. There is no reason to suppose that such an alien intelligence would want to optimize the conditions of the earth for humanity, or for any form of biological life. If humans did offer it some utility, as in the science fiction classic *The Matrix*, we might become its farmed fodder, in much the same way that farmyard animals support our needs.[50]

Pure Intelligence?

This, however, is a long way from the Singularity vision that Kurzweil espouses. The Singularity, for him, will be an intentional merger of humans with technology, permitting us to transcend our biological limitations. "There will be no distinction, post-Singularity, between human and machine or between physical and virtual reality," Kurzweil declares. He argues that the Singularity is much closer than most people imagine, setting its date at 2045. "The nonbiological intelligence created in that year," he asserts, "will be one billion times more powerful than all human intelligence today."[51]

Kurzweil bases his prediction on his "law of accelerating returns," under which technological advances keep accelerating exponentially. Until when? In Kurzweil's model, it just doesn't stop. Even the Singularity is just one stage toward something even grander, a Big Bang–like explosion of intelligence on a vast, cosmic scale "until nonbiological intelligence comes close to 'saturating' the matter and energy in our vicinity of the universe." Even this is just a step toward a greater destiny. "As we approach this limit," he continues, "the intelligence of our civilization will continue its expansion in capability by spreading outward toward the rest of the universe. . . . Ultimately, the entire universe will become saturated with our intelligence. This is the destiny of the universe. . . . We will determine our own fate rather than have it determined by the current 'dumb', simple, machinelike forces that rule celestial mechanics."[52]

Kurzweil envisions the entire universe filled with an intelligence originally created by the human mind. While the scope of his vision is extraordinary, it is based on a value system as old as the ancient Greeks. What we see in Kurzweil's discourse is an ultramodern version of the deification of reason initiated by Plato, which became the foundation for our modern worldview. In Plato's cosmology, our conceptual consciousness, expressed through reason, linked us to the divine. The early Christians transformed this into the conception of an immortal soul existing, after the body's death, with God in heaven. Descartes reformulated this dualistic framework into the modern, scientifically acceptable mind-body split, identifying the human capacity for thought as the essence of our existence. Kurzweil's vision of pure intelligence carries this dualistic tradition into the future, fueled by the power of technology.[53]

Kurzweil himself makes no bones about the teleological underpinning of his ideas. "As I see it," he reflects, "the purpose of the universe reflects the same purpose as our lives: to move toward greater intelligence and knowledge." His definition of what makes us human reads as a high-tech version of Plato: "To me, the essence of being human is not our limitations—although we do have many—it's our ability to reach beyond our limitations. We didn't stay on the ground. We didn't even stay on the planet. And we are already not settling for the limitations of our biology." Plato, too, wasn't ready to settle for the limitations of biology, writing: "We are in fact convinced that if we are ever to have pure knowledge of anything, we must get rid of the body and contemplate things by themselves with the soul by itself."[54]

Plato used his extraordinary imagination to deify the human reasoning capability, conceiving a creator god as the personification of reason. Kurzweil is prepared to go further: through technology, our intelligence will ultimately *become* God. "Is there a God in this religion?" he asks, and then answers his own question. "Not yet, but there will be. Once we saturate the matter and energy in the universe with intelligence, it will 'wake up', be conscious and sublimely intelligent. That's about as close to God as I can imagine." In this future manifestation of divinity, Kurzweil sees posthumans eventually determining the destiny of the universe as they ponder how best to manipulate the laws of physics. "The fate of the universe," he writes, "is a decision yet to be made, one which we will intelligently consider when the time is right."[55*]

When Kurzweil talks about "we" possessing this future godlike power, he means this literally. His fervent hope is that the Singularity will arrive soon enough for him to get on board personally and thus escape what he calls the "calamity" of death. "I'm not planning to die," he reveals. "It's my plan to be involved in this next phase of humanity where we get past some of the frailties of these Version 1.0 bodies we have. The way to 'meet our maker,' so to speak, is, in fact, by staying alive."[56]

Two and a half millennia ago, Plato attempted to transcend the death of his body by making it irrelevant, imagining himself to have a soul that would survive for eternity. Now, Kurzweil is straining toward the actualization of Plato's original ambition. How does he intend to achieve this? By scanning the entire contents of his nervous system into a digital format and uploading it onto hardware that he thinks will be available by the late 2030s. "Currently," he writes, "when our human hardware crashes, the software of our lives—our personal 'mind file'—dies with it. However, this will not continue to be the case when we have the means to store and restore the thousands of trillions of bytes of information represented in the pattern that we call our brains."[57]

For Kurzweil, his body is "hardware" and his mind is "software"—a direct continuation of the dualistic Cartesian conception of the human being. With a simple updating of terminology, Plato's "soul," which became Descartes's "mind," is transformed into Kurzweil's "software." Once again, we're back to that root metaphor of Western cognition: NATURE AS MACHINE. In this respect, Kurzweil's view of his body parallels the view of the earth held by geoengineering proponents: in both cases, they have taken the metaphor of NATURE AS MACHINE for the literal truth.

Kurzweil is not alone in this modern variant of Platonic/Cartesian dualism.

In fact, this view is held by many leading thinkers in artificial intelligence and genetic engineering. One of them, Marvin Minsky, refers to our bodies as "meat machines," while Larry Page, cofounder and CEO of Google's parent company, Alphabet (and therefore holding the power to direct Kurzweil's research program), has referred to human DNA as "600 megabytes compressed" of programming, arguing that "it's smaller than any modern operating system" and therefore our "program algorithms probably aren't that complicated."[58]

The problem with this view is that it is fundamentally misguided. The metaphor of NATURE AS MACHINE, whether applied to the natural world or the human organism, is no more than a metaphor, one that has been powerful enough to propel the trajectory of the modern world and, through its success, to mislead many people into mistaking it for reality. "It is important," writes a team of leading neuroscientists, "to emphasize the stark differences between brains and computers. . . . Software and hardware, which can be easily separated in a computer, are completely interwoven in brains—a neuron's biophysical makeup is intrinsically linked to the computations it carries out." Our human experience, whether Kurzweil likes it or not, is fundamentally embodied and cannot be separated from our physical existence in the way software can be separated from hardware. Sadly for Kurzweil, he will not succeed in his quest for immortality by uploading his brain because his ambition is based on a dualistic metaphor of human existence that ultimately does not constitute reality.[59]

Human Superorganism?

Is a human-induced Singularity, then, a flawed concept? Not necessarily. If it were to occur, though, we should expect it in a form different from that envisaged by Kurzweil. Instead of a disembodied intelligence, the Singularity could conceivably arise from the very fact that human consciousness is embedded in a physical network of neurons. In this version of the Singularity, human nervous systems across the world could connect with each other through the internet, permitting a new type of human superorganism to emerge.

Neurosurgeons are already capable of implanting electrodes into a person's brain, allowing paralyzed stroke victims to move a cursor on a computer simply by thinking about it. Currently, this requires complicated surgery. However, Miguel Nicolelis, a pioneer in brain-machine interfaces, believes that, by around 2030, noninvasive methods could enable people to communicate regularly with their computers using thought. With further enhancements, the communication could become two-way: a person's nervous system could receive as well as transmit information with a computer.[60]

Futurist Ramez Naam gives an intriguing account of what the experience might be like for people enjoying this form of "cyborg" interaction. "You learn how to use it," he writes, "to control sleep, appetite, mood, sexual arousal, and even your heart rate and respiration. You gain the ability to remain calm merely by willing it. You learn how to use [it] to navigate the Internet, asking questions and receiving answers just by thinking about them." Once we communicate this way with our computers, there's no reason we couldn't extend it to communicate with other people. Naam sees this capability permitting previously unattainable connections between ourselves and others. He envisages two people making love while consciously opening all their senses and emotions to each other, attaining an intimacy at first overwhelming but deeply enticing. Before long, he surmises, "you routinely trade memories and experiences with other implanted humans. You learn to view the world through other people's eyes. You let others see through yours. . . . You can no longer imagine a disconnected life."[61]

Once a critical mass of people begin to communicate through this "brain net," Nicolelis wonders, "could these descendants of ours wake up one morning and simply realize that they had peacefully given birth to a different human species altogether?" This, he conjectures, could offer "the ultimate human perceptual experience: to discover that each of us is not alone, that our most intimate thoughts, experiences, anguish, passions and desires, the very primordial stuff that defines us as humans, can be shared by billions of our brothers and sisters."[62]

Unlike Kurzweil's Singularity, this version would not provide immortality to any of us. It might, however, cause the emergence of a new, collective entity, a self-organized human intelligence that incorporates and reflects each of the billions of individuals comprising it, in much the same way that an ant colony—sometimes referred to as a "superorganism"—demonstrates a collective intelligence far beyond the limitations of each individual ant. In today's society, many people might recoil from this vision, fearing the loss of individuality that it might entail. However, this wouldn't necessarily be the case. One proponent of this kind of Singularity, Michael Chorost, argues that "a direct mind-tomind technology can, by design, enhance empathy and the direct recognition of another person's uniqueness." A future collective mind, he believes, "will take nothing away from human individuality. . . . [It] would feel like taking part in a symphony. A violinist contributes to an orchestra but is not diminished in doing so. To the contrary, she becomes more human in the realization of her innate talents."[63]

There is much in human history to support his argument. Humans have always striven to connect with each other. The unique capacity for shared intentionality is what first enabled humans to communicate ideas and feelings with each other. Our most crucial invention—language—is essentially a vehicle to transcend each person's cognitive isolation. Another uniquely human capability, music, permits us to share emotional experiences in a meaningful and exquisite way. More recently, the internet has transformed global society through the enhanced connectivity it's provided. Whether we consider language, music, or the internet, it's hard to argue that these have reduced our individuality. On the contrary, each has permitted us to develop and express our individuality more effectively. From this perspective, it's reasonable to see the emergence of a human superorganism as something that could profoundly enrich, rather than detract from, the intrinsic experience of being human.

Toward a Bifurcation of Humanity?

We've been exploring vastly different scenarios for the human trajectory, from environmental collapse to dramatic possibilities of human transformation. Sometimes the visions are so far apart, it seems as if each group is talking about an entirely different world. But they're not. It's just one earth, containing more than seven billion of us, some working on trailblazing technologies, others (many more) struggling to survive one day at a time.

When a complex system reaches the edge of a previously stable state, this is known in systems theory as a bifurcation point, from which the system transitions to one new state or another. Occasionally, it splits into two distinct systems, such as when a river branches into two tributaries going in different directions, when a single cell divides into two, or when different species evolve from the same progenitor. Could this kind of bifurcation happen to the human race? And if so, what would that mean to those in each of the two new branches?

The lives of affluent people in developed countries are so vastly different from the experience of billions in less developed regions that it already seems like two separate human systems. After a visit to China's industrial heartland, Bob Carr, a former foreign minister of Australia, gave this bleak assessment:

"The landscape was simple. There were clusters of shoebox-style tower blocks. They were linked by clogged expressways in a flattened, cleared landscape. It was so bleak, so denatured, that it could have been a place rebuilt after a nuclear blast. The air was heavy with smog. Acid rain fell. . . . This will be how more people will live in 100 years."[64]

A member of the team that published *Limits to Growth*, Jorgen Randers, recently offered a view of the near future in a book entitled *2052: A Global Forecast for the Next Forty Years*. In it, he predicts a continuation of the global divide between rich and poor, with a minority securing affluent lives at the expense of the rest. Our current global system, he believes, promising prosperity through continued economic growth, offers false hope to most of the human race. "To this day," he warns, "six billion people are being misled into believing that there are no natural constraints and they can have it all because human ingenuity will come to the rescue. The truth is they simply cannot."[65]

Meanwhile, in affluent echelons of the developed world, advances in genetic engineering offer the possibility that, within a few decades, the gulf between rich and poor might extend beyond economics to biology. Once scientists can identify sets of genes that lead to better intelligence, physical fitness, health, and longevity, is it realistic to believe that affluent parents, who already invest so much to give a competitive edge to their children, will forego the advantages that genetic engineering could offer? At first, new generations would appear much like the older ones, only somewhat more intelligent, healthier, and longer lived. Before too long, however, we could envisage a new shifting baseline syndrome changing the default perception of what constitutes a human being in the affluent world. Gregory Stock, an advocate of human genetic engineering, predicts we will soon see humans as divergent as "poodles and Great Danes." He's not alone in this view. Physicist Freeman Dyson has warned that engineering the human germline "could cause a splitting of humanity into hereditary castes," while biologist Lee Silver sees what he calls "GenRich" and "naturals" ultimately splitting into "entirely separate species, with no ability to cross-breed, and with as much romantic interest in each other as a current human would have for a chimpanzee."[66]

At the current rate of advances in genetic engineering, it's feasible that Silver's forecast of separate human species could come about by next century. Based on the predictions of experts quoted in this chapter, it's reasonable to expect, by 2050, a young, affluent, urban couple—let's call them Cameron and Jude—to be planning their genetically optimized offspring while communicating their thoughts and feelings to each other in an enhanced form using neural implants.[67]

Meanwhile, what might be happening to the rest of humanity? Randers offers insights based on his sophisticated modeling of key factors driving the global system. For those concerned about society's imminent collapse, the (qualified) good news is that we shouldn't expect it by mid-century. We can expect more droughts, floods, extreme weather, insect infestations, and higher sea levels. The coral reefs will have virtually disappeared, and many species will be extinct. But Jude and Cameron will still enjoy the benefits of civilization. "The world will still be operational," Randers predicts, but it will be "looking with angst" toward further climate change in the second half of the century, with considerable fear for the prospect of the self-reinforcing climate feedback mechanisms described in the previous chapter threatening more massive changes ahead.[68]

Cameron and Jude will be fortunate to be living in London, one of the affluent cities that, by then, will have spent many billions of dollars to protect against the massive tidal surges that will be part of the new normal. The story will be very different for coastal cities in less prosperous regions, such as Africa and Southeast Asia. There, beleaguered by political instability, massive poverty, and inadequate infrastructure, cities will be reeling from the ravages of climate change. Reduction in river flows and falling groundwater tables will lead to widespread shortages of potable water. Flooding and landslides will disrupt electricity, sanitation, and transportation systems, all of which will lead to rampant infectious disease. Meanwhile, even as these cities strain to breaking point, millions more refugees will be streaming in from the rural hinterland, where the effects of climate change will be even more devastating. Wealthier residents will flee these urban disaster zones for safer abodes, either in the developed world or in newly planned, segregated cities that insulate them from the suffering of their compatriots, leaving the largest urban population centers without the capital reserves to fortify their structures against the threatening onslaught of even more severe climate change.[69]

We can expect an increasing number of countries to become failed states, disintegrating into "hundreds of fiefdoms, medieval levels of child mortality, and very low literacy." A prime example of a country already under this kind of imminent threat is Pakistan, where the population's demand on resources currently exceeds its biocapacity by 80 percent. Randers's book forecasts that Pakistan will run out of resources "well before 2052," leading to increased internal conflicts, which could be especially perilous given the country's nuclear arsenal.[70]

Along with the human catastrophe of failed states and the misery of billions in overwhelmed coastal megacities, the nonhuman world will be suffering its own form of collapse. Natural ecosystems will be reduced to islands of conservation habitats surrounded by vast agribusiness plantations and urban sprawl. Tropical rain forests will only survive as degraded, shrinking remnants in national parks. Cameron and Jude might not, however, consider this situation as gravely as we do, given their reduced expectation of the natural world from shifting baseline syndrome, as well as their ability to experience vastly enhanced virtual-reality immersions in wildlife reservations, enabling them to feel closer to nature in some ways than do many urban residents in today's world.[71]

On the other hand, might Cameron and Jude be more profoundly disturbed by the convulsions of their world than an equivalent couple in today's society would be? Could their enhanced connectivity with what's left of the natural world cause them to treasure it more keenly? Might the impending devastation from climate change drive them and their peers to demand a radical redirection in the world's trajectory? Could their potentially enhanced ability to literally *feel* the suffering of the impoverished billions cause them to press for a different world economic order that honors the intrinsic rights of each human being?

What It Means to Be Human

The attitude Cameron and Jude—and millions of their peers—take toward their world will fundamentally affect the future trajectory of the human race. And this attitude will depend ultimately on their core values, which will largely be inherited from us. As we progress further into this century, with its combination of glorious possibilities and existential threats, it is becoming clear that our generation, along with the next, is engaged in nothing less than a struggle over the future of what it means to be human.

To understand this struggle better, let's use our understanding of complex systems to consider the threshold or sledgehammer effects that could cause our current system to transition into a new steady state. In our current world, two important threshold effects are the exponential progress of technology and the ever-widening global wealth gap. There are also two major sledgehammer effects: climate change and the depletion of the world's natural resources.

Under one scenario, the sledgehammer effects overwhelm the threshold effects, and our global civilization collapses, consistent with the warnings of

Limits to Growth and Tainter's model of civilization. After decades of the worst holocaust in human history, filled with unimaginable suffering, the survivors would be looking at a future in which humanity would never again be able to rise above the values and norms of traditional agrarian society, with humans and animals forever exploited as the primary energy source for an elite minority. It's safe to say that virtually no one in today's world wants to see that.

In another scenario—let's call it Techno Split—the sledgehammer and threshold effects work together to split apart the human race while maintaining some form of technological civilization. Continued exponential technological progress permits civilization, for the affluent minority, to keep advancing. The world would be a fundamentally different place. Geoengineering projects could change the very nature of the earth, potentially turning vegetation black and taking the blueness out of the sky. Wilderness would be relegated to history, with a few carefully engineered ecozones maintained as parks and venues for virtual-reality tours. As the affluent minority enjoyed their neurally interconnected, genetically enhanced lives, they would be increasingly segregated from the billions of others suffering the effects of climate change and resource depletion. Eventually, they would become—effectively, if not literally—two separate species. One species, genetically and technologically enhanced, exploring entirely new ways of being human; the other species, genetically akin to us, barely surviving within its collapsed infrastructure.

Is this what we desire for humanity's future? Those who agree with Kurzweil that humanity's defining feature is the ability to reach beyond the limitations of biology might believe so and celebrate humanity's ultimate triumph: the unfettered progress of humanity's CONQUEST OF NATURE.

But there's another view of humanity that permeates the modern world, one based on the "recognition of the inherent dignity and of the equal and inalienable rights of all members of the human family." These words, from the UN's Universal Declaration of Human Rights, represent a different kind of progress: the progress of humanity's moral scope, which has expanded beyond tribal groupings to encompass the entire human race. In this view, spelled out by the Declaration, "all human beings are born free and equal in dignity and rights. They are endowed with reason and conscience and should act towards one another in a spirit of brotherhood." According to this view, "everyone is entitled to a social and international order in which the rights and freedoms set forth in this Declaration can be fully realized."[72]

From this viewpoint, the Techno Split scenario would be a fundamental betrayal of human values. It would be, as one critic said about Singularity visionaries, akin to "rich people building a lifeboat and getting off the ship." If you, like me, feel stirred deep in your heart by the view of humanity expressed in the Universal Declaration of Human Rights, you might be asking, "What can be done to prevent Techno Split from happening?"[73]

The forces driving humanity to this bifurcation point seem vast and overwhelming: our economic system based on ever-growing consumption; the huge and expanding disparities in wealth; the exponential rate of innovation in technology; the inexorably increasing temperature of the earth; and the dwindling supply of natural resources. It's tempting to throw your hands up in the air, say, "There's nothing I can do about it," and go back to your daily life. But, ultimately, the future is subject to our individual and collective will. We have the power, as the collective force of humanity, to steer our future in a direction of our choosing. To look away is to neglect our individual and collective responsibility. We can use our power. We can make a choice.

What would it take to navigate toward a future consistent with a more inclusive view of humanity? When a system is stretched to breaking point, something has to give. In the Techno Split scenario, our economic model remains resilient, but our shared humanity is transformed beyond recognition. In a scenario where our shared humanity remains intact, the economic system driving our current trajectory would need to be transformed, along with its underlying values: the pursuit of never-ending material growth and the glorification of humanity's conquest of nature.

Could such a drastic transformation of our global system really take place in the foreseeable future? There seems no doubt that a transformation will take place. The question becomes: will it be humanity or our economic system that gets transformed beyond recognition?

A scenario in which humanity remains resilient requires something greater than even the most compelling political and technological solutions to our current crises, such as a global price on carbon and massive investment in green energy. These are undoubtedly necessary to avert disaster, but, even if they're fully effective, they wouldn't be sufficient to avoid the Techno Split scenario. That would require a more fundamental shift in the underlying values that drive our day-today decisions about what we purchase, what we eat, how we earn our money, and how we seek fulfillment. For most of us around the world, these daily choices seem reasonable enough within their context, but, collectively, they lead humanity one step at a time toward either collapse or Techno Split.[74]

The Great Transformation

Many have come to recognize the need for this fundamental change in values. It's been variously called the Great Transformation, the Great Transition, the Great Turning, and humanity's Great Work. Like the two earlier great transitions of human history, it would encompass a transformation of virtually every aspect of the human experience: our values, our goals, and our collective behavior.[75]

There is a major difference, however, between this Great Transformation and the earlier ones. Both agriculture and the Scientific and Industrial Revolutions were the result of generations of people merely acting in ways that made sense to them at the time, without necessarily holding a vision of where their collective actions were leading humanity. It was only long afterward that people could look back and recognize the transformation. This third great transition, by contrast, will only take place if enough people are conscious of its need and prepared to change their own values and behavior to affect humanity's direction. It would be a unique achievement in humanity's history.[76]

A Great Transformation would need to be founded on a worldview that could enable humanity to thrive sustainably on the earth into the future. In place of root metaphors such as NATURE AS MACHINE and CONQUERING NATURE, the new worldview would be based on the emerging systems view of life—recognizing the intrinsic interconnectedness between all forms of life on earth and seeing humanity as embedded integrally within the natural world.

What values would arise from this worldview? Three core values emerge. The first is an emphasis on *quality of life* rather than material possessions. In place of the global obsession with defining progress in terms of economic output and material wealth, we would begin to prioritize progress in the quality of our lives, both individually and in society at large. Secondly, we would base political, social, and economic choices on a sense of our *shared humanity*, emphasizing fairness and dignity for all rather than maximizing for ourselves and our parochially defined social group. Finally, we would build our civilization's future on the basis of *environmental sustainability*, with the flourishing of the natural world as a foundational principle for humanity's major decisions.[77]

A strange dichotomy might arise when you read these three core values. One part of you, perhaps, might agree that they feel consistent with your own sense of right and wrong. And another part of you might shake its head and say, "But there's no way this can ever happen. That's simply not how the world actually works." So how realistic is it for a Great Transformation to take place within this century and protect humanity's future?

The insights of systems thinking can help frame an answer. What do we get if we apply the adaptive cycle model to our present reality? Our global system is actually a network of different systems in different phases of their own cycles. Developments in one system can affect the other systems and push or pull them to different places in their own life cycle. For example, developments in the technology system, such as providing cheap renewable energy, could conceivably affect the earth's climate system and prevent it moving from a conservation phase to a release phase.

We can think of our civilization's values as part of a global *cognitive system*, which has been molded largely on the success of the *economic system* that's dominated the world in the past century. Both our cognitive and economic systems may be in a late conservation phase. As the ravages of climate change begin to undermine the world's economic stability, these disruptions can be expected to affect the cognitive system that was based on the economic system's previous success. People might begin, in increasing numbers, to question the cognitive foundations of that system: an economy based on perpetual growth, in which nature is a resource to plunder and the pursuit of economic gain is paramount. In the adaptive cycle model, a worldwide questioning of core values could bring our cognitive system closer to its own release phase. Which system—cognitive or economic—will reach its release phase first? If it's the economic system, the release phase will lead either to collapse or Techno Split. But what would it mean for our world if the cognitive system reached its release phase first?

When a cognitive system enters a release phase, this means that beliefs and values held implicitly through people's lives begin to be questioned. Structures of meaning begin to unravel. People's patterning instinct drives them to seek a new pattern of meaning to replace the old one, leading rapidly to the renewal phase, when the future is up for grabs. A relatively mild version of this occurred during the counterculture movement of the 1960s and 1970s, when new ideas and values spread quickly throughout the world, leading to new norms becoming widely accepted, such as equal rights for racial minorities, women, and homosexuals. A more dramatic cognitive release phase occurred during the decline of the Roman Empire, as paganism crumbled and was replaced by Christianity. In that period, an entire civilization was heading for collapse, causing a spiritual vacuum to develop as people questioned their previously held beliefs.[78]

As our civilization stumbles through the turmoil of this century, it's reasonable to expect a cognitive release phase as dramatic as that which engulfed the Roman Empire. Which construction of meaning will ultimately triumph and replace our current structure? This is perhaps the most crucial question facing humanity because whichever one triumphs may ultimately control the future direction of the human race. And it's a question that we, the current generation, will all participate in answering through the choices we make.

The two leading contenders will most likely emerge from competing worldviews with contrasting definitions of humanity. The worldview of CONQUERING NATURE, consistent with Kurzweil's definition of humanity as transcending its biology, leads inexorably to the Techno Split scenario. The alternative worldview of nature as a WEB OF MEANING, consistent with the definition of humanity as a community of shared dignity and rights, offers a path to a Great Transformation of society.

The Movement for a Shared Humanity

It may sound impossibly idealistic that the view of humanity as a sharing community could form the basis for a worldwide shift in ideology, but many historical examples show how powerful this vision can be. The abolitionist movement of the nineteenth century succeeded in putting an end to slavery, which had previously been seen as integral to the global economy. Other movements have successfully fought for minority rights around the world, transforming cultural norms and overthrowing established political structures such as the apartheid regime of South Africa. In more recent decades, movements have fought for the preservation of the natural world. When Rachel Carson published her exposé of the indiscriminate use of pesticides in 1962, her solitary stand was denounced as hysterical and unscientific. Only eight years later, at the first Earth Day in 1970, twenty million Americans marched to protect the environment, and, by 1990, two hundred million people in 141 countries across the world were demonstrating for the earth.[79]

These movements have scored important successes even in the unlikely arena of global governance. The worldwide ban on atmospheric nuclear testing, the Geneva Conventions against torture, and the ban on commercial whaling are all dramatic examples of what can happen when enough people fight for what they know is right. Perhaps the most striking of these successes was the world's reaction to the damage of the ozone layer, which protects the earth from a lethal form of ultraviolet light. In 1974, scientists first raised the possibility that chlorofluorocarbons (CFCs), which had been used for decades in coolants and aerosols, might be destroying ozone molecules in the upper atmosphere above the South Pole. Within a few years, legislation in the United States prohibited the use of CFCs in aerosol sprays, but most of the rest of the world didn't follow suit. In 1984, scientists measured a terrifying 40 percent drop in ozone and published a paper announcing an "ozone hole" in the Southern Hemisphere. Now the world sat up and took notice. After difficult negotiations sponsored by the United Nations, five different protocols were passed in the decade between 1987 and 1997 that led to a cut in the worldwide production of CFCs by more than 90 percent. While the ozone layer is still vulnerable, the size of the hole has stabilized, and it's expected to recover gradually over the next fifty years. Through the combined action of scientists, consumer activists, and responsible policy makers, a potential global disaster of immense proportions was averted.[80]

What's more, the values of the Great Transformation are already held by large segments of the world's population. In a worldwide survey conducted in 2000 on people's attitudes toward the natural world, 76 percent of respondents said that humans should "coexist with nature," versus only 19 percent who believed we should "master nature." People are willing to put their money where their mouth is on this issue, with 74 percent of respondents in Europe and North America thinking environmental protection is more important than economic growth, even if some jobs are lost.[81]

There is also surprising consensus that our economic structure should be fairer, even among groups in which this might be least expected. A remarkable 2011 survey asked Americans about the degree of inequality in their country. All demographic groups, including self-identified Republicans and the wealthy, dramatically underestimated the current level of wealth inequality in the United States and proposed an ideal allocation that resembles that of Sweden more closely than their own country. These findings suggest that, in spite of ongoing polemical divisions in American politics, there appears to be a shared underlying ethic of fairness across the nation that is frequently overlooked.[82]

Finally, even in the face of the onslaught of consumerist messaging from mass media, there is a desire among younger people to live their lives defined by a sense of meaning rather than material success. The most important factor that young American adults value in a successful career, according to a

2011 survey, is a sense of meaning—being connected to something bigger than themselves and to the world itself.[83]

Surveys on values identify three distinct subcultures across national, racial, and linguistic boundaries. There are Traditionals, who uphold socially conservative values, girded by strong religious beliefs and nostalgia for the past. There are Moderns, comprising roughly half the population, whose values closely align with consumer-driven mainstream culture, prioritizing personal success and financial gain and embracing a modern urban lifestyle with the latest technologies. Then there are Cultural Creatives, who value ecological sustainability, accept other cultures, and are concerned with issues relating to the quality of life—both their own and others'—such as healthcare, education, and self-actualization. Interestingly, the share of Cultural Creatives in the population has been steadily growing, from roughly 25 percent in the 1990s to 35 percent in 2008. At the risk of overgeneralizing, we might assume that Moderns are more aligned with values that could lead humanity to Techno Split, while Cultural Creatives might be the mainspring of the values required for the Great Transformation.[84]

Cultural Creatives around the world tend to hold similar values and are more closely aligned with each other than with other people in their own countries. As such, they form an emerging global culture with a significant impact on society, not just through their lifestyles but through consciously engaging in activism to change humanity's trajectory. Environmental activist Paul Hawken has estimated that there are more than a million organizations worldwide, both large and small, engaged in humanitarian causes. This dispersed and unstructured grouping of concerned citizens constitutes, in his mind, "the largest social movement in all of human history."[85]

The potential impact of this social movement is increased by the power of the internet to amplify each individual group's effectiveness through its networked connectivity. Hawken points to Metcalfe's law, which states that the usefulness of a network grows exponentially when its connections grow arithmetically. In this way, the collective actions of small groups of individuals can potentially become a global force to countervail the massive corporate networks that currently dominate global civilization. Globalization, which is frequently decried as a force for exploitation, could thus turn out to be a boon for the human race. The global culture emerging from the internet offers humanity a view of itself as an interconnected whole, inviting people to see themselves as part of a web of life encompassing the entire world.[86*]

The internet also offers the opportunity for people at a grassroots level to change the very structures that have defined commerce and communication since the rise of the Industrial Revolution. Collaborative offerings such as *Wikipedia* and Firefox—an open-source web browser with half a billion users—demonstrate the power of a volunteer network to compete with established corporations. In another development, the newly emerging "sharing economy," which emphasizes the value of sharing access to products rather than owning them outright, is rapidly extending to cars, homes, clothes, tools, toys, and other items. These examples are perhaps only the first baby steps toward new structures of human cooperation that haven't yet been imagined.[87*]

As a counterweight to the forces leading civilization toward either collapse or Techno Split, the internet offers a way to create an enhanced collective intelligence at a time when we need it the most. "This struggle to save the future," observes Al Gore, "will be played out in a contest between Earth Inc. and the Global Mind."[88]

The ease with which the internet transmits ideas across the world means that, when the time comes, the transformation of global consciousness could occur at a speed that might surprise everyone. It is part of our evolved human nature to stick together with our group's attitudes or opinions even when a changing situation leaves those attitudes out of date, which can frequently cause social rigidity and political inertia. When thought leaders emerge, offering new ways of thinking, they gradually attract increasing numbers of people until a tipping point is reached and the "stickiness" that kept people attached to their old pattern of thinking is superseded by the pull of the new ideas. All of a sudden, the gradual shift in ideas becomes an avalanche when those who are most comfortable sticking together find themselves in a rush to join in the new way of thinking. In the age of the internet, this tipping point can conceivably be reached much more rapidly than in the past.[89]

The number of people required to create that tipping point is surprisingly small, if they're truly committed to the new paradigm. Political scientists have studied the history of all campaigns across the world since 1900 that led to government overthrow or territorial liberation, and they've discovered that no campaign failed once it achieved the active and sustained participation of just 3.5 percent of the population. This finding gives scientific backing to the inspiring words of Margaret Mead: "Never deny the power of a small group of committed individuals to change the world. Indeed that is the only thing that ever has."[90]

Choosing Our Future

What would the latter part of this century look like if our global civilization took the path of a Great Transformation? We can be sure it would contain much that's currently unimagined. But there are some characteristics that experts recognize as indispensable to that future. It's likely we'd see a reorganized United Nations, with powers to enforce a more responsible approach to our global commons, such as the oceans, the atmosphere, and the environment. When corporations and governments made investment decisions, they'd explicitly factor the externalities of the natural world into their cost-benefit analyses. While there would still be massive income inequality between rich and poor nations, that gap would be decreasing as a result of economic structures based on fairness rather than untrammeled exploitation. And the flourishing of the natural world would be given a high priority in global decision-making. There might even be an enforceable UN Declaration of the Rights of Nature, putting the natural world on the same legal standing as humanity.[91]

This future, driven by an understanding of the interconnected nature of global systems, would embrace continued technological innovation in a form that enhances sustainable consumption and shared access for people around the world. The dramatic advances currently anticipated in computing power, genetic engineering, nanotechnology, and robotics could be welcomed and harnessed in the great project to give all humanity a prosperous and sustainable life on earth.[92]

It's a relay race against time in which every one of us is part of the team. It's a race that humanity can win, if the two visions of progress—technological and moral—that underlie modern cognition can fuse into one vision of harnessing technology for the benefit of the collective human spirit.[93]

What is ultimately required is a shift toward a new way of finding meaning from our existence. Many visionaries and deep thinkers today recognize the need for a new global consciousness, based on an underlying and all-infusing sense of connectedness. The meaning we derive from our existence must arise from our connectedness if we are to succeed in sustaining our civilization into the distant future: connectedness within ourselves, to other humans, and to the entire natural world.[94]

Our global civilization is on an unsustainable course because the meaning we've derived from the world has historically been based on disconnection. Beginning with the dualistic conception of human being and cosmos in ancient

Greece, Western civilization (more recently becoming global civilization) has followed a path of cognitive separation. By prizing reason over emotion, splitting human existence into mind and body, and then defining humanity only by its mind, we set the cognitive foundation for the scientific and industrial revolutions that transformed the world. In our relationship to the external world, we pursued a similar path of disconnection, finding meaning in transcendence while desacralizing the earth, creating root metaphors of nature as an ENEMY TO BE CONQUERED and a MACHINE TO BE ENGINEERED. Since then, we've been busy developing technologies designed to turn those metaphors into fact. By continuing to see humans as essentially separate from nature and from each other, we've found ourselves on a path to either a collapse or a Techno Split.

However, we've seen in this book that there are alternative ways of understanding human existence and our relationship with the natural world. We've seen how shamanic notions of intrinsic connectedness with nature developed into different forms of pantheism. We saw how, a thousand years ago in Song China, philosophers recognized humanity as embedded within natural systems, as expressed so memorably by Zhang Zai when he wrote:

> Heaven is my father and earth is my mother, and I, a small
> child, find myself placed intimately between them.
> What fills the universe I regard as my body; what directs the
> universe I regard as my nature.
> All people are my brothers and sisters; all things are my
> companions.

We also saw the deep compatibility of this cosmology with the systems understanding of the universe developed in recent decades by leading thinkers.

In diametric opposition to the dualistic framework of meaning that has structured two and a half millennia of Western thought, the new systems way of thinking about the universe leads to the possibility of finding meaning ultimately through connectedness within ourselves, to each other, and to the natural world. This way of thinking, seeing the cosmos as a WEB OF MEANING, has the potential to offer a robust framework for the Great Transformation values that emphasize the quality of life, our shared humanity, and the flourishing of nature.

Cultures shape values, and those values shape history. By the same token, our values will shape our future. By understanding how different cultures through history have formed their own patterns of meaning and how the values of our civilization are themselves the result of historical constructions, it becomes possible for us to shape our own set of values—one that could create a sustainable future of shared human dignity and flourishing of the natural world. Whether that actually happens in this century is ultimately up to all of us—and the meaning we choose to forge from the lives we lead.

FURTHER READING

Introduction

Diamond, Jared. *Guns, Germs, and Steel: A Short History of Everybody for the Last 13,000 Years*. London: Vintage, 2005. Highly recommended: A groundbreaking approach to world history that explains some of the deep structural reasons why Eurasia developed at a faster pace than the rest of the world.

Lakoff, George, and Mark Johnson. *Metaphors We Live By*. Chicago: University of Chicago, 2003. Highly recommended: Pioneering the field of cognitive linguistics, it shows how virtually all abstract ideas are formed as metaphors from the scaffolding of more tangible experiences.

Chapter 1. How We Became Human

Suddendorf, Thomas. *The Gap: The Science of What Separates Us from Other Animals*. New York: Basic Books, 2013. A comprehensive, up-to-date review identifying the key elements of human cognitive uniqueness.

Boehm, Christopher. *Hierarchy in the Forest: The Evolution of Egalitarian Behavior*. Cambridge, MA: Harvard University Press, 1999. A sophisticated and penetrating analysis of a key question regarding human nature: whether we are intrinsically power seeking or egalitarian.

Donald, Merlin. *Origins of the Modern Mind: Three Stages in the Evolution of Culture and Cognition*. Cambridge, MA: Harvard University Press, 1991. Highly recommended for its valuable analysis of the evolution of human cognition in three stages, incorporating the concept of mimetic culture.

Tomasello, Michael. *The Cultural Origins of Human Cognition*. Cambridge, MA: Harvard University Press, 2000. Recommended for its explanation of the role of culture in human evolution and its identification of shared intentionality as a crucial, uniquely human characteristic.

Deacon, Terrence W. *The Symbolic Species: The Co-Evolution of Language and the Brain*. New York: Norton, 1997. Highly recommended for its analysis of the central role of the prefrontal cortex in the evolution of human cognition and symbolic thought.

Chapter 2. The Magical Weave of Language

Kuhl, Patricia K. "A New View of Language Acquisition." *Proceedings of the National Academy of Sciences* 97, no. 22 (2000): 11850–57. Recommended for its powerful insights into how the human patterning instinct develops in prelinguistic infants.

Jackendoff, Ray. "Possible Stages in the Evolution of the Language Capacity." *Trends in Cognitive Sciences* 3, no. 7 (1999): 272–79. Recommended for its coherent model of language evolution that transcends the conventional debate on the topic.

Chapter 3. The Rise of Mythic Consciousness

Atran, Scott. *In Gods We Trust*. New York: Oxford University Press, 2002. Recommended for its insightful application of cognitive science to understand the evolution of religion.

Guthrie, Stewart. *Faces in the Clouds: A New Theory of Religion*. New York: Oxford University Press, 1993. Recommended for its explanation of the power of anthropomorphism in human thought.

Boyer, Pascal. *Religion Explained: The Evolutionary Origins of Religious Thought*. New York: Basic Books, 2001. A valuable evolutionary explanation of religion in the human experience.

Chapter 4. The Giving Environment: The World of the Hunter-Gatherers

Lee, Richard Borshay. "Eating Christmas in the Kalahari." *Natural History* 78, no. 10 (1969). Recommended for its enjoyable and groundbreaking explanation of hunter-gatherer values.

Bird-David, Nurit. "The Giving Environment: Another Perspective on the Economic System of Gatherer-Hunters." *Current Anthropology* 31, no. 2 (1990): 189–96. Recommended for its deep insight into the root metaphor of the hunter-gatherer worldview.

Peterson, Nicolas. "Demand Sharing: Reciprocity and the Pressure for Generosity among Foragers." *American Anthropologist* 95, no. 4 (1993): 860–74. Woodburn, James. "Egalitarian Societies." *Man* 17, no. 3 (1982): 431–51. Both recommended for their explanation of egalitarianism in hunter-gatherer societies.

Chapter 5. Agriculture and Anxiety

Barker, Graeme. *The Agricultural Revolution in Prehistory: Why Did Foragers Become Farmers?* Oxford: Oxford University Press, 2009. A detailed and extensive explanation of the transition from foraging to farming.

Cauvin, Jacques. *The Birth of the Gods and the Origins of Agriculture.* Translated by Trevor Watkins. Cambridge: Cambridge University Press, 2000. An original perspective on the cognitive revolution that occurred with the emergence of agriculture.

Trigger, Bruce G. *Understanding Early Civilizations.* New York: Cambridge University Press, 2003. Highly recommended for its comprehensive sweep and deep insights into the practices and thought patterns of early civilizations.

Chapter 6. Going Their Own Ways: Early Civilizations

Hornung, Erik. *Conceptions of God in Ancient Egypt: The One and the Many.* Translated by John Baines. New York: Cornell University Press, 1996.

Assmann, Jan. *The Search for God in Ancient Egypt*. Translated by David Lorton. Ithaca, NY: Cornell University Press, 2001. Both recommended for profound explorations of Egyptian thought by two of the world's leading experts.

Kramer, Samuel Noah. *The Sumerians: Their History, Culture, and Character*. Chicago: University of Chicago Press, 1963. An accessible and informative overview of Mesopotamian civilization and culture.

Anthony, David W. *The Horse, the Wheel and Language: How Bronze Age Riders from the Eurasian Steppes Shaped the Modern World*. Princeton, NJ: Princeton University Press, 2007. Highly recommended for its deeply researched and extensive analysis of Proto-Indo-European culture.

Zaehner, R. C. *The Dawn and Twilight of Zoroastrianism*. London: Phoenix Press, 2002. An authoritative introduction to Zoroastrianism.

Chapter 7. The Birth of Dualism in Ancient Greece

Kitto, H. D. F. *The Greeks*. London: Penguin Books, 1991. An accessible and helpful introduction to ancient Greek culture and civilization.

McEvilley, Thomas. *The Shape of Ancient Thought: Comparative Studies in Greek and Indian Philosophies*. New York: Allworth Press, 2002. Highly recommended: A significant and groundbreaking book, extensively researched, showing the deep structural analogues between ancient Greek and Indian thought.

Cornford, F. M. *From Religion to Philosophy: A Study in the Origins of Western Speculation*. New York: Dover Publications, 1912/2004. An insightful analysis of Greek thought, remaining fresh a century after its publication.

Chapter 8. Dualism and Divinity in Ancient India

Basham, A. L. *The Wonder That Was India*. London: Picador, 2004. A valuable and thoughtful overview of Indian history, thought, and culture.

Zimmer, Heinrich. *Philosophies of India*. Edited by Joseph Campbell. Princeton, NJ: Princeton University Press, 1951. A deep dive into the different philosophical traditions of India.

Feuerstein, Georg. *The Yoga Tradition: Its History, Literature, Philosophy and Practice*. Prescott, AZ: Hohm Press, 1998. An exhaustive and wellresearched study of the history and development of yoga.

Chapter 9. The Search for Harmony in Ancient China

The Tao Te Ching: A New Translation with Commentary. Translated by Ellen M. Chen. St. Paul, MN: Paragon House, 1989. A sensitive translation of the seminal Chinese text with illuminating notes.

Lloyd, Geoffrey, and Nathan Sivin. *The Way and the Word: Science and Medicine in Early China and Greece*. New Haven, CT: Yale University Press, 2002. Recommended for its unique insights into the contrasts between early Chinese and Greek thought.

Schwartz, Benjamin I. *The World of Thought in Ancient China*. Cambridge, MA: Belknap Harvard University Press, 1985. A scholarly overview of the different thought traditions of ancient China.

Zhang, Yu Huan, and Ken Rose. *Who Can Ride the Dragon?: An Exploration of the Cultural Roots of Traditional Chinese Medicine*. Taos, NM: Paradigm Publications, 1995. An accessible and illuminating introduction to the Chinese cultural tradition.

Chapter 10. The Cultural Shaping of Our Minds

Deutscher, Guy. *Through the Language Glass: Why the World Looks Different in Other Languages*. New York: Metropolitan Books, 2010. A modern reassessment of the Sapir-Whorf hypothesis incorporating the latest research findings.

Nakamura, Hajime. *Ways of Thinking of Eastern Peoples: India-China-TibetJapan*. Honolulu: University of Hawaii Press, 1964. An insightful comparison and contrast of different Asian styles of thought from a rare scholar with deep and extensive cross-cultural expertise.

Nisbett, Richard E. *The Geography of Thought: How Asians and Westerners Think Differently . . . and Why*. New York: Free Press, 2004. A fascinating exploration of the roots and current manifestations of the contrasting thought patterns of East Asia and the West.

Chapter 11. Pathways to Monotheism in Israel and Alexandria

Friedman, Richard Elliott. *Who Wrote the Bible?* New York: HarperCollins, 1997. Finkelstein, Israel, and Neil Asher Silberman. *The Bible Unearthed: Archaeology's New Vision of Ancient Israel and the Origin of Its Sacred Texts*. New York: Touchstone, 2002. Both recommended as modern, comprehensive assessments of the most recent archaeological, anthropological, and textual findings in relation to the Old Testament.

Wright, Robert. *The Evolution of God*. New York: Hachette Book Group, 2009. A perceptive and highly readable analysis of the emergence and development of monotheism.

Pollard, Justin, and Howard Reid. *The Rise and Fall of Alexandria*. New York: Viking Penguin, 2006. A fascinating account of a little-known center that was crucial to the development of Western thought.

Chapter 12. Sinful Nature: The Dualistic Cosmos of Christianity

Freeman, Charles. *The Closing of the Western Mind: The Rise of Faith and the Fall of Reason*. New York: Vintage Books, 2005. A panoramic survey of early Christendom, showing how it shut down much of the freethinking of the classical era.

Tarnas, Richard. *The Passion of the Western Mind: Understanding the Ideas That Have Shaped Our World View*. New York: Ballantine Books, 1991. A thoughtful investigation into the core thought patterns of the Christian worldview.

Grant, Robert M. *Gods and the One God*. Philadelphia: Westminster Press, 1986. A helpful and readable account of the transition from paganism to monotheism.

Chapter 13. The Scourge of Monotheistic Intolerance

Kirsch, Jonathan. *God against the Gods: The History of the War between Monotheism and Polytheism*. New York: Penguin Compass, 2004. An eye-opening and highly readable indictment on the intolerance of monotheism.

Chapter 14. Discovering the Principles of Nature in Song China

Needham, Joseph. *Science and Civilisation in China*. Vol. 2, *History of Scientific Thought*. London: Cambridge University Press, 1972. Highly recommended: a brilliant and groundbreaking elucidation of traditional Chinese and Neo-Confucian cosmology.

Angle, Stephen C. *Sagehood: The Contemporary Significance of Neo-Confucian Philosophy*. New York: Oxford University Press, 2009. A valuable scholarly account of the modern relevance of Neo-Confucian thought.

Ziporyn, Brook. "Form, Principle, Pattern or Coherence? Li in Chinese Philosophy." *Philosophy Compass* 3, no. 3 (2008). Recommended for its discussion of the idea of "coherence" as a core concept in Neo-Confucian thought.

Chapter 15. "To Command the World": Metaphors of Nature

Merchant, Carolyn. *The Death of Nature: Women, Ecology and the Scientific Revolution* (New York: HarperCollins, 1980). Recommended for its insights into the underlying metaphorical concepts of the modern European worldview.

Capra, Fritjof. *The Turning Point: Science, Society, and the Rising Culture*. New York: Bantam Books, 1988. A deep exploration of the modern mechanistic worldview and the possibilities for alternative ways of thinking.

White, Lynn. "The Historical Roots of Our Ecological Crisis." *Science* 155, no. 3767 (1967): 1203–07. A seminal paper that catalyzed a greater understanding of the ecological implications of traditional Christian cosmology.

Chapter 16. Great Rats: The Story of Power and Exploitation

Ponting, Clive. *A New Green History of the World: The Environment and the Collapse of Great Civilizations*. New York: Penguin, 2007. A comprehensive and compelling environmental perspective on world history.

Abu-Lughod, Janet L. *Before European Hegemony: The World System AD 1250–1350*. New York: Oxford University Press, 1989. An illuminating portrayal of the global order that existed before the rise of European colonialism.

Stannard, David E. *American Holocaust: Columbus and the Conquest of the New World*. New York: Oxford University Press, 1992. An unflinching and shocking exposé of the brutality unleashed by the European conquest of the New World.

Chapter 17. The Enigma of the Scientific Revolution

Huff, Toby E. *The Rise of Early Modern Science: Islam, China, and the West*. New York: Cambridge University Press, 2006. An extensively researched, thoughtful study of contrasting patterns of thought in European, Chinese, and Islamic civilization.

Needham, Joseph. *The Grand Titration: Science and Society in East and West*. Toronto: University of Toronto Press, 1969. Recommended for its enlightening and original perspectives on the structural differences between Eastern and Western approaches to science.

Sivin, Nathan. "Why the Scientific Revolution Did Not Take Place in China—or Did It?" *Environmentalist* 5, no. 1 (1985). Recommended for its groundbreaking insight into why non-European cultures followed paths that would not lead to a scientific revolution.

Chapter 18. The Language of God: The Emergence of Scientific Cognition

Cromer, Alan. *Uncommon Sense: The Heretical Nature of Science*. New York: Oxford University Press, 1993. Recommended for its clear explanation of the unique nature of scientific cognition.

Gaukroger, Stephen. *The Emergence of a Scientific Culture*. New York: Oxford University Press, 2006. A modern, deeply researched investigation into the emergence of scientific culture as a new way of thinking about the universe.

Burtt, E. A. *The Metaphysical Foundations of Modern Science*. New York: Dover Publications, 1924/2003. After nearly a century, this book remains fresh with its insights into the frames of thinking of the pioneers of the Scientific Revolution.

Koestler, Arthur. *The Sleepwalkers: A History of Man's Changing Vision of the Universe*. London: Penguin, 1989. Recommended for its lively, incisive probe into the lives and thought of several key instigators of the Scientific Revolution, especially Kepler and Galileo.

Livio, Mario. *Is God a Mathematician?* New York: Simon & Schuster, 2009. Recommended for its wide-ranging analysis of mathematics as a universal language and the cosmological implications of its universality.

Chapter 19. "Something Far More Deeply Interfused": The Systems Worldview

Gleick, James. *Chaos: Making a New Science*. New York: Penguin, 1987. A highly readable account of complexity, introducing the characters and concepts of this new way of understanding the world.

Capra, Fritjof, and Pier Luigi Luisi. *The Systems View of Life: A Unifying Vision*. New York: Cambridge University Press, 2014. Highly recommended: a comprehensive and deeply insightful review of the systems view of life and its social and philosophical implications.

Thompson, Evan. *Mind in Life: Biology, Phenomenology, and the Sciences of Mind*. Cambridge, MA: Harvard University Press, 2007. A profound and thoughtful investigation into the philosophical and spiritual implications of systems thinking.

Kauffman, Stuart. *At Home in the Universe: The Search for Laws of SelfOrganization and Complexity*. New York: Oxford University Press, 1995. A mathematically oriented exploration of the cosmological implications of complexity that is also highly accessible to a lay reader.

Goodwin, Brian. *How the Leopard Changed Its Spots: The Evolution of Complexity*. Princeton, NJ: Princeton University Press, 2001). A thoughtful review of how systems thinking transforms our understanding of biology.

Chapter 20. Consuming the Earth in the Modern Era

McNeill, J. R. *Something New under the Sun: An Environmental History of the Twentieth-Century World*. New York: Norton, 2001. Recommended for its eye-opening exposition of humanity's effect on the earth in the past century.

Korten, David C. *When Corporations Rule the World*. Sterling, VA: Kumarian Press/Berrett-Koehler, 2001. Recommended for its penetrating review of the devastating effect of global capitalism on the human experience.

Hartmann, Thom. *The Last Hours of Ancient Sunlight*. New York: Three Rivers Press, 2004. A staggering assessment of the damage modern civilization is inflicting on our environment and our future.

Speth, James Gustave. *The Bridge at the Edge of the World: Capitalism, the Environment, and Crossing from Crisis to Sustainability*. New Haven, CT: Yale University Press, 2008. A sobering appraisal from a veteran environmentalist on the environmental implications of our current global system.

Rockström, Johan, et al. "A Safe Operating Space for Humanity." *Nature* 461, no. 24 (September 2009): 472–75. An important paper that has helped frame current thinking about how humanity's actions are threatening the stability of the earth system.

Chapter 21. Trajectories to Our Future

Raskin, Paul, Tariq Banuri, Gilberto Gallopin, Pablo Gutman, and Al Hammond. *Great Transition: The Promise and Lure of the Times Ahead.* Boston: Stockholm Environment Institute, 2003. A short but deeply thought-through assessment of the possible future scenarios facing humanity.

Gore, Al. *The Future: Six Drivers of Global Change.* New York: Random House, 2013. A thorough and discerning evaluation of the major drivers for change in our global society and their implications for the future.

Tainter, Joseph A. *The Collapse of Complex Societies.* Cambridge: Cambridge University Press, 1988. A scholarly analysis of societal collapse that has deservedly framed much serious discussion on the topic since its publication.

Randers, Jorgen. *2052: A Global Forecast for the Next Forty Years.* White River Junction, VT: Chelsea Green, 2012. A thoughtful projection into the future by one of the original team members of *Limits to Growth.*

Berry, Thomas. *The Great Work: Our Way into the Future.* New York: Three Rivers Press, 1999. A penetrating and visionary account of the enormous challenge and opportunity facing humanity in the future.

ACKNOWLEDGMENTS

This book has been germinating for nearly a decade. Initiated during a challenging period of my life, it is a result of my own search for meaning that I undertook at that time. In my journey of discovery, I was guided by the hundreds of learned scholars whose insights and perspectives have helped shape this book. Through their writings, I felt invited into a community of wisdom that spans the generations, and for that I am deeply grateful.

In particular, I owe a huge debt to the profound insights of Joseph Needham for helping me understand the organic cosmology of traditional China; the groundbreaking research of George Lakoff, which taught me the power of metaphor in constructing our reality; and the brilliant vision of Fritjof Capra, who showed me the tremendous potential of systems thinking to help transform our modern worldview. I am particularly grateful to Fritjof for his warm support in helping me bring this book to publication and in writing its foreword.

I am indebted to other notable scholars whose insights helped shape this book into its particular pattern of meaning, particularly Sir Geoffrey Lloyd, Nathan Sivin, Jared Diamond, Merlin Donald, Terrence Deacon, Steve Mithen, Michael Tomasello, Thomas McEvilley, Bruce Trigger, Robert Wright, Edward Slingerland, David Anthony, Richard Nisbett, Christopher Boehm, Stuart Kauffman, Evan Thompson, and Joseph Tainter.

I have received helpful feedback and encouragement from leaders in their fields regarding particular chapters that I have shared with them over the years, including Fritjof Capra, Sir Geoffrey Lloyd, David Korten, Nathan Sivin, Paul Ekman, Yair Lior, Sun Yue, Sir Michael Atiyah, and Jerry Feldman.

I am deeply grateful for the warm encouragement and support I've been blessed to receive from my friends and family, including Ari, Zachary, Benjamin, Aiyana and Jim, Lila, Martin, Carole, Marco and Jason, Atossa, Louis, Teja, Alan, John, Eddy and Traci, Joseph, Troy, Verna, Stefani, Matthew, and so many others.

I appreciate the valuable support and advice I've received in getting the book to publication from Sam Barry, Lee Kravetz, John Berger, and my agent, Maryann Karinch; and I'm indebted to those at Prometheus Books who have helped me bring it into the world, including Steven L. Mitchell, Hanna Etu, Lisa Michalski, Cate Roberts-Abel, and Jacqueline Parkison.

Finally, I reserve my greatest appreciation for Elizabeth Ferguson, my beloved wife and trusted partner. She has lived and breathed this book with me, and without her penetrating editorial critiques, her never-ending encouragement, and her brilliant insights, the book would not have taken its current shape.

NOTES

Preface

1. Jacob Bronowski, "Part 1: Lower Than the Angels," *The Ascent of Man*, episode 1, aired May 1973 (BBC, 1973).

2. This topic is covered in more detail in chapter 16, "Great Rats: The Story of Power and Exploitation."

3. F. S. C. Northrop, *The Meeting of East and West: An Inquiry Concerning World Understanding* (Woodbridge, CT: Ox Bow Press, 1979), 375–76.

4. Edward Said, *Orientalism* (New York: Vintage, 1979). Summarizing the postmodernist perspective, one of its leading thinkers, Michel Foucault, wrote, "All my analyses are against the idea of universal necessities in human existence. . . . It is meaningless to speak in the name of—or against—Reason, Truth, or Knowledge." Cited in Stephen R. C. Hicks, *Explaining Postmodernism: Skepticism and Socialism from Rousseau to Foucault* (Tempe, AZ: Scholargy, 2004), 2.

5. See Paul Cilliers, *Complexity and Postmodernism: Understanding Complex Systems* (New York: Routledge, 2002), 113–14. See also J. J. Clarke, *The Tao of the West: Western Transformations of Taoist Thought* (New York: Routledge, 2000), 185–90.

6. Jared Diamond, *Guns, Germs, and Steel: A Short History of Everybody for the Last 13,000 Years* (London: Vintage, 2005).

7. Kenneth Pomeranz, *The Great Divergence* (Princeton, NJ: Princeton University Press, 2000).

8. This topic is discussed in detail in chapter 17, "The Enigma of the Scientific Revolution." For some of the innumerable references to China's "failure" to have an industrial revolution, see Toby E. Huff, *The Rise of Early Modern Science: Islam, China, and the West* (New York: Cambridge University Press, 2006), 10, 216, 291; Joel Mokyr, *The Lever of Riches: Technological Creativity and Economic Progress* (New York: Oxford University Press, 1990), 219; D. S. Landes, *The Wealth and Poverty of Nations* (New York: W. W. Norton, 1998), 55.

9. Ian Morris, *Why the West Rules—for Now: The Patterns of History, and What They Reveal about the Future* (New York: Picador, 2010), 28–30.

10. See Sarah Mathew and Charles Perreault, "Behavioural Variation in 172 Small-Scale Societies Indicates That Social Learning Is the Main Mode of Human Adaptation," *Proceedings of the Royal Society B: Biological Sciences* 282, no. 1810 (2015). This study analyzes 172 Native American tribes at the time of European contact

and concludes that "cultural history, not environment, is the main determinant of behavioural variation across groups."

11. F. John Odling-Smee, Kevin N. Laland, and Marcus W. Feldman, "Niche Construction," *American Naturalist* 147 (1996): 641–48; Kevin N. Laland, John Odling-Smee, and Marcus W. Feldman, "Niche Construction, Biological Evolution, and Cultural Change," *Behavioral and Brain Sciences* 23 (2000): 131–46.

12. Steven Pinker, "The Cognitive Niche: Coevolution of Intelligence, Sociality, and Language," *Proceedings of the National Academy of Sciences* 107 (2010): 8993–99; Cecilia Heyes, "New Thinking: The Evolution of Human Cognition," *Philosophical Transactions of the Royal Society B: Biological Sciences* 367 (2012): 2091–96; Andrew Whiten and David Erdal, "The Human Socio-Cognitive Niche and Its Evolutionary Origins," *Philosophical Transactions of the Royal Society B: Biological Sciences* 367 (2012): 2119–29; Robert Boyd, Peter J. Richerson, and Joseph Henrich, "The Cultural Niche: Why Social Learning Is Essential for Human Adaptation," *Proceedings of the National Academy of Sciences* 108 (2011): 10918–25.

13. Richard Wrangham, *Catching Fire: How Cooking Made Us Human* (New York: Basic Books, 2010); Kevin N. Laland, John Odling-Smee, and Sean Myles, "How Culture Shaped the Human Genome: Bringing Genetics and the Human Sciences Together," *Nature Reviews Genetics* 11 (2010): 137–48; Kevin N. Laland and Luke Rendell, "Cultural Memory," *Current Biology* 23 (2013): R736–40.

14. Ayse K. Uskul, Shinobu Kitayama, and Richard E. Nisbett, "Ecocultural Basis of Cognition: Farmers and Fishermen Are More Holistic Than Herders," *Proceedings of the National Academy of Sciences* 105 (2008): 8552–56; T. Talhelm et al., "Large-Scale Psychological Differences within China Explained by Rice versus Wheat Agriculture," *Science* 344 (2014): 603–8.

15. Nicholas Wade, *A Troublesome Inheritance: Genes, Race, and Human History* (New York: Penguin, 2014).

16. See chapter 10, "The Cultural Shaping of Our Minds," for an in-depth discussion of the Sapir-Whorf hypothesis and its aftermath.

17. George Lakoff and Mark Johnson, *Metaphors We Live By* (Chicago: University of Chicago, 2003), 3, 145–46. See, in particular, chapter 15, "Contrasting Metaphors of Nature," for more detail on this and other core metaphors of nature and their historical impact.

18. Cilliers, *Complexity and Postmodernism*, 3.

19. Ibid., 3–5. For a more in-depth understanding of complex systems, see Stuart Kauffman, *At Home in the Universe: The Search for Laws of Self-Organization and Complexity* (New York: Oxford University Press, 1995); Evan Thompson, *Mind in Life: Biology, Phenomenology, and the Sciences of Mind* (Cambridge, MA: Harvard University Press, 2007); Ricard Solé and Brian Goodwin, *Signs of Life: How Complexity Pervades Biology* (New York: Basic Books, 2000).

20. Marten Scheffer et al., "Early-Warning Signals for Critical Transitions," *Nature* 461 (2009): 53–59; Marten Scheffer, *Critical Transitions in Nature and Society* (Princeton, NJ: Princeton University Press, 2009).

21. Ibid.; Max Rietkerk et al., "Self-Organized Patchiness and Catastrophic Shifts in Ecosystems," *Science* 305 (2004): 1926–29.

22. John Maynard Smith and Eors Szathmary, *The Origins of Life: From the Birth of Life to the Origin of Language* (New York: Oxford University Press, 2000); Stephen J. Gould and Niles Eldredge, "Punctuated Equilibria: The Tempo and Mode of Evolution Reconsidered," *Paleobiology* 3 (1977): 115–51.

23. For a discussion of the coupled dynamics of human cognitive and tangible systems, see Jianguo Liu et al., "Complexity of Coupled Human and Natural Systems," *Science* 317 (2007): 1513–16; also William A. Brock, Karl-Göran Mäler, and Charles Perrings, "Resilience and Sustainability: The Economic Analysis of Nonlinear Dynamic Systems," in *Panarchy: Understanding Transformations in Human and Natural Systems (Synopsis)*, ed. Lance H. Gunderson and C. S. Holling, trans. Bernice Wuethrich (Washington, DC: Island Press, 2002), 261–91. I know of relatively few sustained attempts to approach historical change from the perspective of complex systems. Some pioneering thinkers in archaeology, anthropology, and history have, however, made reference to this approach. Some examples: Merlin Donald sees the evolution of prelinguistic "cognitive communities" as an "excellent example of emergent evolution." Ursula Goodenough and Terrence Deacon view the rise of language as "quintessentially emergent." Describing the rise of agriculture, Jacques Cauvin notes "an almost circular movement of reciprocal interactions," while a team of archaeologists recognizes "an inseparable interplay . . . between ideological and socioeconomic change across the forager-to-farmer transition." Norman Yoffee approaches the emergence of city-states in Mesopotamia as a phase transition within a complex system. See Merlin Donald, *A Mind So Rare: The Evolution of Human Consciousness* (New York: Norton, 2001); Ursula Goodenough and Terrence W. Deacon, "The Sacred Emergence of Nature," in *The Oxford Handbook of Religion and Science*, ed. Philip Clayton (New York: Oxford University Press, 2006); Jacques Cauvin, *The Birth of the Gods and the Origins of Agriculture*, trans. Trevor Watkins (Cambridge: Cambridge University Press, 2000); Leore Grosman, Natalie D. Munro, and Anna Belfer-Cohen, "A 12,000-Year-Old Shaman Burial from the Southern Levant (Israel)," *Proceedings of the National Academy of Sciences* 105 (2008): 17665–69; Norman Yoffee, *Myths of the Archaic State: Evolution of the Earliest Cities, States, and Civilizations* (Cambridge: Cambridge University Press, 2005); Isaac I. T. Ullaha, Ian Kuijtb, and Jacob Freemanc, "Toward a Theory of Punctuated Subsistence Change," *Proceedings of the National Academy of Sciences* 112 (2015): 9579–84.

Introduction

1. Louise Levathes, *When China Ruled the Seas: The Treasure Fleet of the Dragon Throne 1405–1433* (New York: Oxford University Press, 1994); Jacques Gernet, *A History of Chinese Civilization* (New York: Cambridge University Press, 2006), 398–42; Janet L. Abu-Lughod, *Before European Hegemony: The World System A.D. 1250–1350* (New York: Oxford University Press, 1989), 343–44; Paul R. Ehrlich, *Human Natures: Genes, Cultures, and the Human Prospect* (New York: Penguin, 2002), 268.

2. See Rachael Beddoe et al., "Overcoming Systemic Roadblocks to Sustainability: The Evolutionary Redesign of Worldviews, Institutions, and Technologies," *Proceedings of the National Academy of Sciences* 106, no. 8 (2009): 2483–89.

3. See, for example, George Lakoff and Mark Johnson, *Metaphors We Live By* (Chicago: University of Chicago, 2003).

4. Quoted in Thomas McEvilley, *The Shape of Ancient Thought: Comparative Studies in Greek and Indian Philosophies* (New York: Allworth Press, 2002).

5. For summaries of prefrontal cortex function: Earl K. Miller and Jonathan D. Cohen, "An Integrative Theory of Prefrontal Cortex Function," *Annual Review of Neuroscience* 24 (2001): 167–202; Joaquin M. Fuster, "The Prefrontal Cortex—an Update: Time Is of the Essence," *Neuron* 30, no. 2 (2001): 319–33; S. Goldman-Rakic, "The Prefrontal Landscape: Implications of Functional Architecture for Understanding Human Mentation and the Central Executive," *Philosophical Transactions of the Royal Society B* 351 (1996): 1445–53.

6. The two forms of consciousness, described here as *animate* and *conceptual*, are recognized by many leading cognitive neuroscientists and referred to by different names such as *primary* and *secondary* consciousness (Gerald Edelman) or *core* and *higher-order* consciousness (Antonio Damasio). This distinction is also recognized in dual process theory, which differentiates a fast, automatic mode of thinking called *System 1* and a slower, calculating mode of thought called *System 2*. See Antonio Damasio, *The Feeling of What Happens: Body and Emotion in the Making of Consciousness* (New York: Harcourt, 1999); Gerald M. Edelman and Giulio Tononi, *A Universe of Consciousness: How Matter Becomes Imagination* (New York: Basic Books, 2000); Daniel Kahneman, *Thinking Fast and Slow* (New York: Farrar, Straus and Giroux, 2011).

7. The characterization of the patterning function as an important part of the pfc's activity is in no way intended to ignore the enormous complexity of the pfc and its range of functions. The pfc is frequently described as the locus of executive function, which includes attention, working memory, planning, temporal integration, decision-making, and inhibitory control. Models of pfc function refer to its hierarchical organization of cognitive networks, its temporal organization of action, and its relational integration. I'm using the term "patterning" as a high-level summary to encompass much, but not all, of what makes the pfc crucial to our uniquely human

cognition. See Barbara J. Knowlton and Keith J. Holyoak, "Prefrontal Substrate of Human Relational Reasoning," in *The Cognitive Neurosciences*, ed. M. S. Gazzaniga (Cambridge, MA: MIT Press, 2009); Joaquin M. Fuster, *The Prefrontal Cortex* (New York: Elsevier, 1988), 333–78; Ilka Diester and Andreas Nieder, "Semantic Associations between Signs and Numerical Categories in the Prefrontal Cortex," *PLoS Biology* 5, no. 11 (2007): 2684–95.

8. Patricia K. Kuhl, "A New View of Language Acquisition," *Proceedings of the National Academy of Sciences* 97, no. 22 (2000): 11850–57; Patricia K. Kuhl, "Early Language Acquisition: Cracking the Speech Code," *Nature Reviews: Neuroscience* 5 (2004): 831–43.

9. Cited in Tom Sjöblom, "Spandrels, Gazelles and Flying Buttresses: Religion as Adaptation or as a By-Product," *Journal of Cognition and Culture* 7, no. 3–4 (2007): 293–312; Stewart Guthrie, *Faces in the Clouds: A New Theory of Religion* (New York: Oxford University Press, 1993), 32.

Chapter 1. How We Became Human

1. Thomas Suddendorf, *The Gap: The Science of What Separates Us from Other Animals* (New York: Basic Books, 2013), 240–41. The scenario described here is known in archaeological circles as the "East Side Story." See also Susan C. Antón, Richard Potts, and Leslie C. Aiello, "Evolution of Early *Homo*: An Integrated Biological Perspective," *Science* 345, no. 6192 (2014): 45, for a more recent view that emphasizes the variability of the new environment as the primary driver of hominid adaptation.

2. Michael Tomasello, "The Human Adaptation for Culture," *Annual Review of Anthropology*, no. 28 (1999): 509–29.

3. For a useful table listing characteristically human attributes, see Mark V. Flinn, David C. Geary, and Carol V. Ward, "Ecological Dominance, Social Competition, and Coalitionary Arms Races: Why Humans Evolved Extraordinary Intelligence," *Evolution and Human Behavior* 26, no. 1 (2005): 10–46.

4. C. Owen Lovejoy, "Reexamining Human Origins in Light of *Ardipithecus ramidus*," *Science* 326, no. 2 (2009): 74e1–74e8.

5. Ibid.; Christopher Boehm, *Hierarchy in the Forest: The Evolution of Egalitarian Behavior* (Cambridge, MA: Harvard University Press, 1999), 149–70; Andrew Whiten and David Erdal, "The Human Socio-Cognitive Niche and Its Evolutionary Origins," *Philosophical Transactions of the Royal Society B: Biological Sciences* 367, no. 1599 (2012): 2119–29.

6. Lovejoy, "Reexamining Human Origins."

7. Merlin Donald, *Origins of the Modern Mind: Three Stages in the Evolution of Culture and Cognition* (Cambridge, MA: Harvard University Press, 1991), 199–200; Steven Mithen, *The Singing Neanderthals: The Origins of Music, Language, Mind, and Body* (Cambridge, MA:

Harvard University Press, 2006), 137; William H. McNeill, *Keeping Together in Time: Dance and Drill in Human History* (Cambridge, MA: Harvard University Press, 1995); William H. McNeill, "A Short History of Humanity," *New York Review of Books* 47, no. 11 (2000).

8. Merlin Donald, *A Mind So Rare: The Evolution of Human Consciousness* (New York: Norton, 2001), 88, 263–65.

9. R. I. M. Dunbar and Susanne Shultz, "Evolution in the Social Brain," *Science* 317, no. 7 (2007); Carl Zimmer, "Sociable, and Smart," *New York Times*, March 4, 2008.

10. David Premack and G. Woodruff, "Does the Chimpanzee Have a Theory of Mind?," *Behavioral and Brain Sciences* 4 (1978): 515–26; Daniel J. Povinelli and Todd M. Preuss, "Theory of Mind: Evolutionary History of a Cognitive Specialization," *Trends in Neurosciences* 18, no. 9 (1995): 418–24; Michael Tomasello, *The Cultural Origins of Human Cognition* (Cambridge, MA: Harvard University Press, 2000), 89–90, 179.

11. Richard D. Alexander, "The Evolution of Social Behavior," *Annual Review of Ecology and Systematics* 5 (1974): 325–83.

12. Cited in Flinn, Geary, and Ward, "Ecological Dominance." See also Henrike Moll and Michael Tomasello, "Cooperation and Human Cognition: The Vygotskian Intelligence Hypothesis," *Philosophical Transactions of the Royal Society B: Biological Sciences* 362, no. 1480 (2007): 639–48; Charles Darwin, *On the Origin of Species by Means of Natural Selection* (London: John Murray, 1859), chap. 3.

13. Robert L. Trivers, "The Evolution of Reciprocal Altruism," *Quarterly Review of Biology* 46, no. 1 (1971): 35–57.

14. Quoted in Herbert Gintis et al., "Explaining Altruistic Behavior in Humans," *Evolution and Human Behavior* 24, no. 3 (2003): 153–72.

15. Alexander, "Evolution of Social Behavior," 335.

16. The literature discrediting the "selfish gene" approach to evolution is extensive. Although the topic is outside the scope of this book, the following is a sampling of some of the clearest expositions from recognized leaders in the field of evolutionary biology: Stephen Jay Gould, "Darwinism and the Expansion of Evolutionary Theory," *Science* 216, no. 4544 (1982): 380–87; David J. Depew and Bruce H. Weber, *Darwinism Evolving: Systems Dynamics and the Genealogy of Natural Selection* (Cambridge, MA: MIT Press, 1996); David Sloan Wilson and Edward O. Wilson, "Rethinking the Theoretical Foundation of Sociobiology," *Quarterly Review of Biology* 82, no. 4 (2007): 327–48; Brian Goodwin, *How the Leopard Changed Its Spots: The Evolution of Complexity* (Princeton, NJ: Princeton University Press, 2001); Eva Jablonka and Marion J. Lamb, "Precis of Evolution in Four Dimensions," *Behavioral and Brain Sciences* 30, no. 4 (2007): 353–92; Rasmus Gronfeldt Winther, "Systemic Darwinism," *Proceedings of the National Academy of Sciences* 105, no. 33 (2008): 11833–38; Massimo Pigliucci, "Do We Need an Extended Evolutionary Synthesis?" *Evolution* 61, no. 12 (2007): 2743–49.

17. Tomasello, *Cultural Origins*, 21.

18. Moll and Tomasello, "Cooperation and Human Cognition."

19. Ernst Fehr and Urs Fischbacher, "The Nature of Human Altruism," *Nature* 425 (2003): 785–91.

20. Ibid.; Gintis et al., "Explaining Altruistic Behavior."

21. Ibid.

22. Christopher Boehm, "Egalitarian Behavior and Reverse Dominance Hierarchy," *Current Anthropology* 34, no. 3 (1993): 227–54.

23. Ibid.; Boehm, *Hierarchy in the Forest.*

24. See chapter 5, "Agriculture and Anxiety," for an investigation of the rise of agriculture, and chapter 16, "Great Rats: The Story of Power and Exploitation," for a focused account of how the human instinct for dominance has led, since the emergence of agriculture, to an overthrow of this "reverse dominance hierarchy" and to everincreasing inequality within human society.

25. William C. McGrew, "Chimpanzee Technology," *Science* 328 (2010): 579–80; Robert N. Proctor, "The Roots of Human Recency: Molecular Anthropology, the Refigured Acheulean, and the UNESCO Response to Auschwitz," *Current Anthropology* 44, no. 2 (2003): 213–39; Stanley H. Ambrose, "Paleolithic Technology and Human Evolution," *Science* 291, no. 2 (2001): 1748–53.

26. While the human brain occupies only 2 percent of body mass, it consumes about 20 percent of total metabolism. See Gerhard Roth and Ursula Dicke, "Evolution of the Brain and Intelligence," *Trends in Cognitive Sciences* 9, no. 5 (2005): 250–53; Ambrose, "Paleolithic Technology."

27. Ambrose, "Paleolithic Technology."

28. Ibid.; Thomas Suddendorf, "Foresight and Evolution of the Human Mind," *Science* 312, no. 19 (2006): 1006–7; Thomas Suddendorf and Michael C. Corballis, "The Evolution of Foresight: What is Mental Time Travel, and Is It Unique to Humans?," *Behavioral and Brain Sciences* 30 (2007): 299–351.

29. Tomasello, *Cultural Origins*, 197; Russell A. Barkley, "The Executive Functions and Self-Regulation: An Evolutionary Neuropsychological Perspective," *Neuropsychology Review* 11, no. 1 (2001): 1–29.

30. Jean-Pierre Changeux, *The Physiology of Truth: Neuroscience and Human Knowledge*, trans. M. B. DeBevoise (Cambridge, MA: Harvard University Press, 2002), 108–9.

31. Joaquin M. Fuster, "The Prefrontal Cortex—an Update: Time Is of the Essence," *Neuron* 30, no. 2 (2001): 319–33; Jacqueline N. Wood and Jordan Grafman, "Human Prefrontal Cortex: Processing and Representational Perspectives," *Nature Reviews: Neuroscience* 4 (2003): 139–47.

32. Steven Mithen, *The Prehistory of the Mind* (London: Thames & Hudson, 1996). The Swiss Army knife metaphor was originally proposed by Leda Cosmides and John Tooby (see Mithen, *Prehistory of the Mind*, 42.)

33. Frederick L. Coolidge and Thomas Wynn, "Executive Functions of the Frontal Lobes and the Evolutionary Ascendancy of *Homo sapiens*," *Cambridge Archaeological*

Journal 11, no. 2 (2001): 255–60; Frederick L. Coolidge and Thomas Wynn, "Working Memory, Its Executive Functions, and the Emergence of Modern Thinking," *Cambridge Archaeological Journal* 15, no. 1 (2005): 5–26; John Duncan, "An Adaptive Coding Model of Neural Function in Prefrontal Cortex," *Nature Reviews: Neuroscience* 2 (2001): 820–29; Patricia Goldman-Rakic, quoted in Michael Balter, "Did Working Memory Spark Creative Culture?" *Science* 328 (2010): 160–63.

34. Terrence W. Deacon, *The Symbolic Species: The Co-Evolution of Language and the Brain* (New York: Norton, 1997); William Noble and Iain Davidson, *Human Evolution, Language and Mind: A Psychological and Archaeological Inquiry* (New York: Cambridge University Press, 1996). I am grateful to Noble and Davidson for the example of writing words to substitute for food in the dog's bowl as an example of a symbol.

35. Christopher S. Henshilwood and Curtis W. Marean, "The Origin of Modern Human Behavior: Critique of the Models and Their Test Implications," *Current Anthropology* (2003): 627–51.

36. Ernst Cassirer, *An Essay on Man* (New Haven, CT: Yale University Press, 1944), 26.

Chapter 2. The Magical Weave of Language

1. Robert M Seyfarth, Dorothy L. Cheney, and Peter Marler, "Monkey Responses to Three Different Alarm Calls: Evidence of Predator Classification and Semantic Communication," *Science* 210 (1980): 801–3.

2. Martin A. Nowak, Joshua B. Plotkin, and Vincent A. A. Jansen, "The Evolution of Syntactic Communication," *Nature* 404, no. 30 (2000): 495–98.

3. Gilles Fauconnier and Mark Turner, "The Origin of Language as a Product of the Evolution of Double-Scope Blending," *Behavioral and Brain Sciences* 31, no. 5 (2008): 520–21.

4. Ibid.

5. Ulf Liszkowski et al., "Prelinguistic Infants, but Not Chimpanzees, Communicate about Absent Entities," *Psychological Science* 20, no. 5 (2009): 654–60.

6. Marc D. Hauser, Noam Chomsky, and W. Tecumseh Fitch, "The Faculty of Language: What Is It, Who Has It, and How Did It Evolve?" *Science* 298, no. 22 (2002): 1569–79. For a full review of recursion in the evolution of language, see W. Tecumseh Fitch, "The Evolution of Language: A Comparative Review," *Biology and Philosophy* 20 (2005): 193–230. See also Merlin Donald, *Origins of the Modern Mind: Three Stages in the Evolution of Culture and Cognition* (Cambridge, MA: Harvard University Press, 1991), 39.

7. Terrence W. Deacon, *The Symbolic Species: The Co-Evolution of Language and the Brain* (New York: Norton, 1997), 288; Jared Taglialatela et al., "Communicative Signaling Activates 'Broca's' Homolog in Chimpanzees," *Current Biology* 18 (2008): 343–48; JeanPierre Changeux, *The Physiology of Truth: Neuroscience and Human Knowledge*, trans.

M. B. DeBevoise (Cambridge, MA: Harvard University Press, 2002), 123. See Donald, *Origins of the Modern Mind*, 45–94, for a full discussion of the history of anatomical theories of human language.

8. Deacon, *Symbolic Species*, 20; Changeux, *Physiology of Truth*, 123–24; Joaquin M. Fuster, "Frontal Lobe and Cognitive Development," *Journal of Neurocytology* 31 (2002): 373–85.

9. Leslie C. Aiello and R. I. M. Dunbar, "Neocortex Size, Group Size, and the Evolution of Language," *Current Anthropology* 34, no. 2 (1993): 184–93.

10. Donald, *Origins of the Modern Mind*, 253–54.

11. Nicholas Evans, "Context, Culture, and Structuration in the Languages of Australia," *Annual Review of Anthropology*, no. 32 (2003): 13–40. See also Donald, *Origins of the Modern Mind*, 284.

12. Aiello and Dunbar, "Neocortex Size"; Sally McBrearty and Alison S. Brooks, "The Revolution That Wasn't: A New Interpretation of the Origin of Modern Human Behavior," *Journal of Human Evolution* 39 (2000): 453–563.

13. Adam Powell, Stephen Shennan, and Mark G. Thomas, "Late Pleistocene Demography and the Appearance of Modern Human Behavior," *Science* 324, no. 5 (June 2009): 1298–301; Marc D. Hauser, "The Possibility of Impossible Cultures," *Nature* 460, no. 9 (July 2009): 190-96; Jared Diamond, *The Third Chimpanzee: The Evolution and Future of the Human Animal* (New York: Harper Perennial, 1993).

14. William Noble and Iain Davidson, "The Evolutionary Emergence of Modern Human Behaviour: Language and Its Archaeology," *Man* 26, no. 2 (1991): 223–53.

15. William Noble and Iain Davidson, *Human Evolution, Language and Mind: A Psychological and Archaeological Inquiry* (New York: Cambridge University Press, 1996); Gilles Fauconnier and Mark Turner, *The Way We Think: Conceptual Blending and the Mind's Hidden Complexities* (New York: Basic Books, 2002), 183; Frederick L. Coolidge and Thomas Wynn, "Working Memory, Its Executive Functions, and the Emergence of Modern Thinking," *Cambridge Archaeological Journal* 15, no. 1 (2005): 5–26. See also Richard G. Klein, "Archeology and the Evolution of Human Behavior," *Evolutionary Anthropology* 9, no. 1 (2000): 17–36, which argues that this sudden change must have been caused by a genetic mutation that permitted symbolic thought.

16. Steven Pinker, *The Language Instinct: How the Mind Creates Language* (New York: Harper Perennial, 1994), 4–5.

17. Ibid., 44–73.

18. Steven Pinker and Paul Bloom, "Natural Language and Natural Selection," *Behavioral and Brain Sciences* 13, no. 4 (1990): 707–84.

19. Daniel Margoliash and Howard C. Nusbaum, "Language: The Perspective from Organismal Biology," *Trends in Cognitive Sciences* 13, no. 12 (2009): 505–10; Morten H. Christiansen and Nick Chater, "Language as Shaped by the Brain," *Behavioral and Brain Sciences*, no. 31 (2008): 489–558. For other critiques of the theory of a "language

instinct" and "universal grammar," see Evans, "Context, Culture"; Deacon, *Symbolic Species*, 27; Fauconnier and Turner, *Way We Think*, 173; Nick Chater, Florencia Reali, and Morten H. Christiansen, "Restrictions on Biological Adaptation in Language Evolution," *Proceedings of the National Academy of Sciences* 106, no. 4 (2009): 1015–20; Francisco Aboitiz and V. Ricardo Garcia, "The Evolutionary Origin of the Language Areas in the Human Brain: A Neuroanatomical Perspective," *Brain Research Reviews* 25 (1997): 381–96; and Michael Tomasello, *The Cultural Origins of Human Cognition* (Cambridge, MA: Harvard University Press, 2000), 94.

20. Patricia K. Kuhl, "A New View of Language Acquisition," *Proceedings of the National Academy of Sciences* 97, no. 22 (2000): 11850–57. See also Fauconnier and Turner, *Way We Think*, 173.

21. Kuhl, "New View." See also Patricia K. Kuhl, "Early Language Acquisition: Cracking the Speech Code," *Nature Reviews: Neuroscience* 5 (2004): 831–43. Another study providing evidence of the human infant's patterning instinct has demonstrated the ability of eight-month-old infants to segment discrete words from fluent speech based solely on the statistical relationship between neighboring speech sounds. See Jenny R. Saffran, Richard N. Aslin, and Elissa L. Newport, "Statistical Learning by 8-Month-Old Infants," *Science* 274 (1996): 1926–28.

22. Deacon, *Symbolic Species*, 321–75.

23. Evans, "Context, Culture."

24. Ray Jackendoff, "Possible Stages in the Evolution of the Language Capacity," *Trends in Cognitive Sciences* 3, no. 7 (1999): 272–79.

25. Ibid.

26. Dietrich Stout et al., "Neural Correlates of Early Stone Age Toolmaking: Technology, Language and Cognition in Human Evolution," *Philosophical Transactions of the Royal Society B* 363 (2008): 1939–49.

27. See Derek Bickerton, *Language and Species* (Chicago: University of Chicago Press, 1990) for a hypothesis of protolanguage.

28. Stanley H. Ambrose, "Paleolithic Technology and Human Evolution," *Science* 291, no. 2 (March 2001): 1748–53.

29. George Lakoff and Mark Johnson, *Metaphors We Live By* (Chicago: University of Chicago, 2003).

Chapter 3. The Rise of Mythic Consciousness

1. Paul G. Bahn, *Cave Art: A Guide to the Decorated Ice Age Caves of Europe* (London: Frances Lincoln, 2007). See also David Lewis-Williams, *The Mind in the Cave* (London: Thames & Hudson, 2002), 55.

2. Anthony Sinclair, "Art of the Ancients," *Nature* 426, no. 18 (2003): 774–75; Paul

Mellars, "Origins of the Female Image," *Nature* 459, no. 14 (2009): 176–77; Nicholas J. Conard, "A Female Figurine from the Basal Aurignacian of Hohle Fels Cave in Southwestern Germany," *Nature* 459, no. 14 (2009): 248–52; Daniel S. Adler, "The Earliest Musical Tradition," *Nature* 460, no. 6 (2009): 695–96.

3. Nicholas J. Conard, "Cultural Modernity: Consensus or Conundrum?" *Proceedings of the National Academy of Sciences* 107, no. 17 (2010): 7621–22; Ian Tattersall, "An Evolutionary Framework for the Acquisition of Symbolic Cognition by *Homo sapiens*," *Comparative Cognition & Behavior Reviews* 3 (2008): 99–114; Paul Mellars, "The Impossible Coincidence. A Single-Species Model for the Origins of Modern Human Behavior in Europe," *Evolutionary Anthropology* 14, no. 1 (2005): 12–27; Ofer Bar-Yosef, "The Upper Paleolithic Revolution," *Annual Review of Anthropology* 2002, no. 31 (2002): 363–93; Jared Diamond, *The Third Chimpanzee: The Evolution and Future of the Human Animal* (New York: Harper Perennial, 1993).

4. Colin Renfrew, *Prehistory: The Making of the Human Mind* (New York: Modern Library, 2007). Renfrew's original framing of the question dealt with not just the time lag between anatomical modernity and the Upper Paleolithic revolution but also the ensuing time lag until the rise of agriculture, some thirty thousand years later. See also Merlin Donald, "The Sapient Paradox: Can Cognitive Neuroscience Solve It?" *Brain* 132, no. 3 (2008).

5. Renfrew, *Prehistory*; Christopher S. Henshilwood et al., "Middle Stone Age Shell Beads from South Africa," *Science* 304, no. 16 (2004): 404; Christopher S. Henshilwood and Curtis W. Marean, "The Origin of Modern Human Behavior: Critique of the Models and Their Test Implications," *Current Anthropology* 44 (2003): 627–51; Christopher S. Henshilwood et al., "Emergence of Modern Human Behavior: Middle Stone Age Engravings from South Africa," *Science* 295, no. 15 (2002): 1278–80; Paul Mellars, "Why Did Modern Human Populations Disperse from Africa ca. 60,000 Years Ago? A New Model," *Proceedings of the National Academy of Sciences* 103, no. 25 (2006): 9381–86. See also Michael Balter, "Early Start for Human Art? Ochre May Revise Timeline," *Science* 323, no. 30 (2009): 569.

6. Sally McBrearty and Alison S. Brooks, "The Revolution That Wasn't: A New Interpretation of the Origin of Modern Human Behavior," *Journal of Human Evolution* 39 (2000): 453–563.

7. Peter Forster, "Ice Ages and the Mitochondrial DNA Chronology of Human Dispersals: A Review," *Philosophical Transactions of the Royal Society B* 359, no. 1442 (2004): 255–64; Mellars, "Modern Human Populations."

8. Adam Powell, Stephen Shennan, and Mark G. Thomas, "Late Pleistocene Demography and the Appearance of Modern Human Behavior," *Science* 324, no. 5932 (2009): 1298–301; Mellars, "Modern Human Populations"; Richard G. Klein, "Archeology and the Evolution of Human Behavior," *Evolutionary Anthropology* 9, no. 1 (2000): 17–36; Elizabeth Culotta, "Did Modern Humans Get Smart or Just Get Together?" *Science* 328 (2010): 164.

9. The Neanderthals and other hominids (for example, *Homo erectus*) had already colonized southern Asia and Europe beginning more than a million years ago. See Steven Mithen, *The Prehistory of the Mind* (London: Thames & Hudson, 1996), 29; Forster, "Ice Ages."

10. Forster, "Ice Ages"; Steven Mithen, *The Singing Neanderthals: The Origins of Music, Language, Mind, and Body* (Cambridge, MA: Harvard University Press, 2006); Tattersall, "Evolutionary Framework"; Richard G. Klein, "Whither the Neanderthals?," *Science* 299 (2003): 1525–27; Robert N. Proctor, "The Roots of Human Recency: Molecular Anthropology, the Refigured Acheulean, and the Unesco Response to Auschwitz," *Current Anthropology* 44, no. 2 (2003): 213–39; Paul R. Ehrlich, *Human Natures: Genes, Cultures, and the Human Prospect* (New York: Penguin, 2002). See also Mellars, "Impossible Coincidence," for a valuable discussion on the topic.

11. Paul G. Bahn, "Neanderthals Emancipated," *Nature* 394 (1998): 719–721; Joao Zilhao, "Symbolic Use of Marine Shells and Mineral Pigments by Iberian Neandertals," *Proceedings of the National Academy of Sciences* 107, no. 3 (2010): 1023–1028; Francesco d'Errico et al., "Neanderthal Acculturation in Western Europe? A Critical Review of the Evidence and Its Interpretation," *Current Anthropology* 39, Supplement (1998): S1–S43; Michael Balter, "Neandertal Champion Defends the Reputation of Our Closest Cousins," *Science* 337 (2012): 642–643. There is a continuing heated debate on the validity of claims of symbolic thinking by Neanderthals. Mellars, for example, has argued that analysis of Neanderthal remains conducted in 2010 has led to the "effective collapse" of the argument for complex symbolic behavior among late Neanderthal populations in Europe. See Paul Mellars, "Neanderthal Symbolism and Ornament Manufacture: The Bursting of a Bubble?," *Proceedings of the National Academy of Sciences* 107, no. 47 (2010): 20147–20148.

12. See Thomas Wynn, and Frederick L. Coolidge, "The Expert Neandertal Mind," *Journal of Human Evolution* 46, no. 4 (2004): 467–487, whose findings support this hypothesis. Their analysis, using a synthesis of cognitive neuropsychology, anthropology and archaeology, proposes that *homo sapiens* had greater "syntactical complexity" than the Neanderthals, including the use of subjunctive and future tenses, and that this enhanced use of language may have given modern humans "their ultimate selective advantage over Neandertals."

13. Conard, "Cultural Modernity"; Lewis-Williams, *Mind In the Cave*, 96. Recent studies of the Neanderthal genome have divulged that modern humans share between 1–4% of their DNA with Neanderthals, a finding that has led some to suggest the encounter between the species was less combative. However, whatever interbreeding occurred between humans and Neanderthals appears to have been in the Red Sea area prior to the appearance of humans in Europe. See Richard E. Green et al., "A Draft Sequence of the Neandertal Genome," *Science* 328 (2010): 710–722.

14. Scott Atran, *In Gods We Trust* (New York: Oxford University Press, 2002), 66–67.

15. See Terrence W. Deacon, *The Symbolic Species: The Co-Evolution of Language and the Brain* (New York: Norton, 1997), 436–7.

16. Elizabeth Culotta, "On the Origin of Religion," *Science* 326 (2009): 784–787; Tom Sjöblom, "Spandrels, Gazelles and Flying Buttresses: Religion as Adaptation or as a By-Product," *Journal of Cognition and Culture* 7, no. 3-4 (2007): 293–312.

17. Malinowski, quoted in Stewart Guthrie, *Faces in the Clouds: A New Theory of Religion* (New York: Oxford University Press, 1993), 12.

18. S. J. Gould and R. C. Lewontin, "The Spandrels of San Marco and the Panglossian Paradigm: A Critique of the Adaptationist Programme," *Proceedings of the Royal Society of London B* 205, no. 1161 (1979): 581–98.

19. Atran, *In Gods We Trust*; Scott Atran and Ara Norenzayan, "Religion's Evolutionary Landscape: Counterintuition, Commitment, Compassion, Communion," *Behavioral and Brain Sciences* 27, no. 6 (2004): 713–30.

20. Pascal Boyer, "Religious Thought and Behaviour as By-Products of Brain Function," *Trends in Cognitive Sciences* 7, no. 3 (2003): 119–24. See also Ilkka Pyysiäinen and Marc Hauser, "The Origins of Religion: Evolved Adaptation or By-Product?," *Trends in Cognitive Sciences* 14, no. 3 (2010): 104–9.

21. Jesse M. Bering, "The Folk Psychology of Souls," *Behavioral and Brain Sciences* 29, no. 5 (2006): 453–98.

22. Deborah Kelemen, "Are Children 'Intuitive Theists?': Reasoning about Purpose and Design in Nature," *Psychological Science* 15, no. 5 (2004): 295–301; Deborah Kelemen and Evelyn Rosset, "The Human Function Compunction: Teleological Explanation in Adults," *Cognition* 111 (2009): 138–43.

23. Atran, *In Gods We Trust*, 15.

24. Guthrie, *Faces in the Clouds*, 82–83, 187.

25. Pascal Boyer, *Religion Explained: The Evolutionary Origins of Religious Thought* (New York: Basic Books, 2001), 144–45; Guthrie, *Faces in the Clouds*, 198; Boyer, "Religious Thought."

26. Nicolas Baumard and Pascal Boyer, "Explaining Moral Religions," *Trends in Cognitive Sciences* 17, no. 6 (2013): 272–80.

27. Gerald Edelman is credited with first developing this understanding of infant brain development with his theory of "neural Darwinism." See Israel Rosenfield, "Neural Darwinism: A New Approach to Memory and Perception," *New York Review of Books* 33, no. 15 (1986). Also see Gerald M. Edelman and Giulio Tononi, *A Universe of Consciousness: How Matter Becomes Imagination* (New York: Basic Books, 2000), 83–84, for a discussion in Edelman's own words. Separately, neuroscientist Jean-Pierre Changeux developed a similar theory of "learning by selection"; see Israel Rosenfield and Edward Ziff, "How the Mind Works: Revelations," *New York Review of Books* 55, no. 11 (2008): 62–65, for a discussion of Changeux's approach. For an anthropological perspective on how synaptic pruning changes the "operational architecture of cognition in the

developing brain," see Merlin Donald, "Material Culture and Cognition: Concluding Thoughts," in *Cognition and Material Culture: The Archaeology of Symbolic Storage*, ed. Colin Renfrew and Chris Scarre (Cambridge: McDonald Institute for Archaeological Research, 1999), 181–87. For more recent neuroscientific insights on how synaptic pruning leads to human learning, see Andrew N. Meltzoff et al., "Foundations for a New Science of Learning," *Science* 325, no. 5938 (2009): 284–88; and Patricia J. Brooks and Sonia Ragir, "Prolonged Plasticity: Necessary and Sufficient for Language-Ready Brains," *Behavioral and Brain Sciences* 31, no. 5 (2008): 514–15.

28. Wolf Singer, "The Brain, a Complex Self-Organizing System," *European Review* 17, no. 2 (2009): 321–29.

29. Evan Thompson and Francisco J. Varela, "Radical Embodiment: Neural Dynamics and Consciousness," *Trends in Cognitive Sciences* 5, no. 10 (2001): 418–25.

30. Merlin Donald, *A Mind So Rare: The Evolution of Human Consciousness* (New York: Norton, 2001), 211–12. See also George Lakoff and Mark Johnson, *Philosophy in the Flesh: The Embodied Mind and Its Challenge to Western Thought* (New York: Basic Books, 1999), 13.

31. Michael Tomasello, "The Human Adaptation for Culture," *Annual Review of Anthropology*, no. 28 (1999): 509–29. See also C. H. Waddington, "Evolutionary Systems: Animal and Human," *Nature* 183, no. 4676: 1634–38.

32. Donald, *Mind So Rare*, 374. For a full discussion of the various types of external symbolic storage, see Lyn Wadley, "What is Cultural Modernity? A General View and a South African Perspective from Rose Cottage Cave," *Cambridge Archaeological Journal* 11, no. 2 (2001): 201–21.

33. Donald, *Mind So Rare*, 313.

34. Ibid., 308–10.

35. Ibid., 12, 298–99.

36. Deacon, *Symbolic Species*, 436.

37. For an overview of modern neuroscientific findings on the plasticity of the adult brain, see Sharon Begley, *Train Your Mind, Change Your Brain* (New York: Ballantine Books, 2007).

Chapter 4. The Giving Environment: The World of the Hunter-Gatherers

1. Richard Borshay Lee, "Eating Christmas in the Kalahari," *Natural History* 78, no. 10 (1969).

2. See Lawrence H. Keeley, *War before Civilization: The Myth of the Peaceful Savage* (New York: Oxford University Press, 1996), 5–8, for a detailed summary of the Hobbes versus "noble savage" debate. Rousseau, although an ardent critic of Hobbes, in fact never used the "noble savage" phrase, which was coined by the English poet John Dryden.

3. For a more detailed discussion of this topic, see Graeme Barker, *The Agricultural*

Revolution in Prehistory: Why Did Foragers Become Farmers? (Oxford: Oxford University Press, 2009), 44. Barker writes, "Although there is today, and has been in the recent past, considerable variability in forager societies, much more striking are the similarities that can be discerned. . . . For all the difficulties of using ethnographic material, the behaviours of recent and present-day foragers remain an invaluable resource for helping us reflect on the likely characteristics of forager behaviours before farming."

4. Bruce G. Trigger, *Understanding Early Civilizations* (New York: Cambridge University Press, 2003), 683.

5. See Michael Winkelman, "Shamanism and Cognitive Evolution," *Cambridge Archaeological Journal* 12, no. 1 (2002): 71–101; Richard K. Nelson, "The Watchful World," in *Readings in Indigenous Religions*, ed. Graham Harvey (New York: Continuum, 2002), 343–64.

6. Nelson, "Watchful World." See, also, the description of the Ojibwa (Chippewa) Indians by Diamond Jenness, cited in Claude Lévi-Strauss, *The Savage Mind* (Chicago: University of Chicago Press, 1966), 37; Robert Wright, *The Evolution of God* (New York: Hachette Book Group, 2009), 19–20.

7. Deborah Bird Rose, "Sacred Site, Ancestral Clearing, and Environmental Ethics," in *Readings in Indigenous Religions*, ed. Harvey, 319–42.

8. Quoted in Harvey Arden, *Dreamkeepers: A Spirit-Journey into Aboriginal Australia* (New York: HarperCollins, 1994), 3–4, 23; Deborah Bird Rose, *Nourishing Terrains: Australian Aboriginal Views of Landscape and Wilderness* (Canberra: Australian Heritage Commission, 1996), 39–40.

9. Rose, *Nourishing Terrains*, 9, 27–28, 71.

10. A. Irving Hallowell, "Ojibwa Ontology, Behavior, and World View," in *Readings in Indigenous Religions*, ed. Harvey; Nurit Bird-David, "'Animism' Revisited: Personhood, Environment, and Relational Epistemology," in *Readings in Indigenous Religions*, ed. Harvey, 72–105.

11. Nurit Bird-David, "The Giving Environment: Another Perspective on the Economic System of Gatherer-Hunters," *Current Anthropology* 31, no. 2 (1990): 189–96. See also Calvin Luther Martin, cited in Barker, *Agricultural Revolution*, 409; and Pascal Boyer, *Religion Explained: The Evolutionary Origins of Religious Thought* (New York: Basic Books, 2001), 69, for a description of the African Ituri pygmies' perception that the forest "looks after" them.

12. Barker, *Agricultural Revolution*, 59.

13. Ibid.

14. Reported by ethnologist Knud Rasmussen, quoted in David Abram, *The Spell of the Sensuous* (New York: Random House, 1996), 87.

15. Hallowell, "Ojibwa Ontology," 34.

16. Mircea Eliade, *Shamanism: Archaic Techniques of Ecstasy* (Princeton, NJ: Princeton University Press, 2004), 259–87; Michael James Winkelman, "Shamans and Other

'Magico-Religious' Healers: A Cross-Cultural Study of Their Origins, Nature, and Social Transformations," *Ethos* 18, no. 3 (1990): 308–52. For descriptions and definitions of shaman practices, see Eliade, *Shamanism*; David Lewis-Williams, *The Mind in the Cave* (London: Thames & Hudson, 2002), 133; Michael Winkelman, "Shamanism and Cognitive Evolution," *Cambridge Archaeological Journal* 12, no. 1 (2002): 71–101; Leore Grosman, Natalie D. Munro, and Anna Belfer-Cohen, "A 12,000-Year-Old Shaman Burial from the Southern Levant (Israel)," *Proceedings of the National Academy of Sciences* 105, no. 46 (2008): 17665–69.

17. Eliade, *Shamanism*, 4; Winkelman, "'Magico-Religious' Healers"; LewisWilliams, *Mind in the Cave*. In the case of Yoga, Georg Feuerstein describes "many aspects and motifs of Shamanism," including the "yogin's ecstatic introversion and mystical ascent," a number of yogic postures such as cross-legged sitting, and the tradition of *tapas* or asceticism. See Georg Feuerstein, *The Yoga Tradition: Its History, Literature, Philosophy and Practice* (Prescott, AZ: Hohm Press, 1998), 94–95. In the case of Chinese culture, Kwang-chih Chang describes the "close relationship with shamanism" of ancient Chinese civilization in Chang, "Ancient China and Its Anthropological Significance," in *The Breakout: The Origins of Civilization*, ed. Martha Lamberg-Karlovsky (Cambridge, MA: Peabody Museum, 2000), 1–11; Herrlee G. Creel describes the early Chinese tradition of "*wu*, often called 'shamans,' who held séances with spirits and were believed able to heal the sick" in Creel, *What Is Taoism? And Other Studies in Chinese Cultural History* (Chicago: University of Chicago Press, 1970), 11–12; and Eliade notes the "presence of a considerable number of shamanic techniques throughout the course of Chinese history," in Eliade, *Shamanism*, 456–57. Chang also notes the shamanistic sources of Mayan and Aztec practices, referring to the research of Peter T. Furst.

18. Winkelman, "Shamanism and Cognitive Evolution"; Winkelman, "'MagicoReligious' Healers"; Eliade, *Shamanism*, 333; Gordon R. Willey, "Ancient Chinese, New World, and Near Eastern Ideological Traditions: Some Observations," in *Breakout*, ed. Lamberg-Karlovsky, 25–36.

19. Lewis-Williams, *Mind in the Cave*, 205–6, 149, 160. For earlier shamanic interpretations of Upper Paleolithic art, see Eliade, *Shamanism*, 503–4, and also Winkelman, "Shamanism and Cognitive Evolution." For an opposing viewpoint, that Upper Paleolithic cave images are "not logically necessary demonstrations" of shamanism, see Bruno David in Winkelman, "Shamanism and Cognitive Evolution."

20. Lewis-Williams, *Mind in the Cave*, 277–81.

21. Eliade, *Shamanism*, 53–58; Hallowell, "Ojibwa Ontology"; Scott Atran, *In Gods We Trust* (New York: Oxford University Press, 2002), 55.

22. Leda Cosmides and John Tooby, "Evolutionary Psychology: A Primer," in *Center for Evolutionary Psychology, UCSB*, Santa Barbara, 2006.

23. Cited in David E. Stannard, *American Holocaust: Columbus and the Conquest of the New World* (New York: Oxford University Press, 1992), 63.

24. Cited in Peter Bellwood, *First Farmers: The Origins of Agricultural Societies* (Oxford:

Blackwell, 2005), 39.

25. Quotations are from Sahlins, cited in Barker, *Agricultural Revolution*, 55–56; and Alan Barnard, "Contemporary Hunter-Gatherers: Current Theoretical Issues in Ecology and Social Organization," *Annual Review of Anthropology* 12 (1983): 193–214. See also Keeley, *War before Civilization*, 166.

26. Cited in Dianne Dumanoski, *The End of the Long Summer: Why We Must Remake Our Civilization to Survive on a Volatile Earth* (New York: Crown, 2009), 176.

27. See an extensive analysis of this issue in Jared Diamond, *The Third Chimpanzee: The Evolution and Future of the Human Animal* (New York: Harper Perennial, 1993), 180–91. For other discussions of the topic, see Steven Mithen, *The Prehistory of the Mind* (London: Thames & Hudson, 1996), 218–19; Bellwood, *First Farmers*; and Trigger, *Understanding Early Civilizations*, 123, 669.

28. Findings from research presented by Clark Spencer Larsen at the American Association of Physical Anthropologists meeting March 31–April 4, 2009, Chicago, IL, reported by Ann Gibbons, "Civilization's Cost: The Decline and Fall of Human Health," *Science* 324, no. 1 (2009): 588. See also Diamond, *Third Chimpanzee*, 186.

29. Craig Dilworth, *Too Smart for Our Own Good: The Ecological Predicament of Humankind* (New York: Cambridge University Press, 2010), 57–60; "Hunter-Gatherers: Noble or Savage?," *Economist*, December 22, 2007.

30. Nicolas Peterson, "Demand Sharing: Reciprocity and the Pressure for Generosity among Foragers," *American Anthropologist* 95, no. 4 (1993): 860–74; James Woodburn, "Egalitarian Societies," *Man* 17, no. 3 (1982): 431–51.

31. Woodburn, "Egalitarian Societies." Daniel L. Everett describes similar behavior in the Pirahã of the Amazon, noting that "artifacts that they trade for (such as machetes, cans, pans, etc.) are not well cared-for and are often 'lost' the day they are purchased." See Everett, "Cultural Constraints on Grammar and Cognition in Pirahã: Another Look at the Design Features of Human Language," *Current Anthropology* 46, no. 4 (2005): 621–46.

32. Lee, "Eating Christmas."

33. Cited in Peter J. Wilson, *The Domestication of the Human Species* (New Haven, CT: Yale University Press, 1988), 39.

34. Everett, "Cultural Constraints." See also Michael Gurven et al., "'It's a Wonderful Life': Signaling Generosity among the Ache of Paraguay," *Evolution and Human Behavior* 21, no. 4 (2000): 263–82, which describes how individual foragers who were more generous than their peers during good times received more food than others when they became injured or sick, a phenomenon they saw as analogous to "paying a high premium for long-term health insurance."

35. Hallowell, "Ojibwa Ontology," 45–46; Bird-David, "'Animism' Revisited," 85–86. Bird-David points out that this is "a common phenomenon among huntergatherers, who have what Alan Barnard called 'a universal kinship system.'"

36. Wilson, *Domestication*, 33; Everett, "Cultural Constraints."

37. Cited in Woodburn, "Egalitarian Societies," 437–38. See also Wilson, *Domestication*, 29–32.

38. Keeley, *War before Civilization*, 29–31, 37–39.

39. Wilson, *Domestication*, 51. Keeley himself seems to acknowledge this at one point, writing that "no more than a handful of adult males" are usually available to fight in a hunter-gatherer band, and "when such a small group of men commits violence against another band or family, even if faced in open combat by all the men of the other group, this activity is not called war but is usually referred to as feuding, vendetta, or just murder." *War before Civilization*, 29–31.

40. Wilson, *Domestication*, 51. See also John Horgan, "The End of War," *New Scientist* (July 2009): 39–41, for a helpful discussion. It should be noted that the most egregious examples of violence in primitive societies are sometimes misattributed to huntergatherers. The Yanomamö, for example, are often cited as an example of an extremely warlike hunter-gatherer society, when, in fact, they are horticulturalists. R. B. Hames, "Yanomamö, Varying Adaptations of Foraging Horticulturalists," in *Anthropology*, ed. C. Ember and M. Ember (New York: Prentice Hall, 2009), 103–31. Similarly, some of the most notorious headhunting tribes, such as the Iatmul of New Guinea or the Naga of India, are, in fact, either horticulturalists or seminomadic pastoralists. See reference to both of these tribes in Scott Atran and Ara Norenzayan, "Religion's Evolutionary Landscape: Counterintuition, Commitment, Compassion, Communion," *Behavioral and Brain Sciences* 27, no. 6 (2004): 713–30.

41. Samuel Bowles, "Conflict: Altruism's Midwife," *Nature* 456, no. 20 (November 2008): 326–27. See also Samuel Bowles, "Did Warfare among Ancestral Hunter-Gatherers Affect the Evolution of Human Social Behaviors?," *Science* 324 (June 2009): 1293–98; and Jung-Kyoo Choi and Samuel Bowles, "The Coevolution of Parochial Altruism and War," *Science* 318 (October 2007): 636–40. The argument for group selection of genes supporting cooperation in the late Pleistocene is also made in Jonathan Haidt, "The New Synthesis in Moral Psychology," *Science* 316, no. 18 (May 2007): 998–1002.

42. See Dilworth, *Too Smart*, 81–83, for an extensive description of Martin's overkill hypothesis; see also Richard Leakey and Roger Lewin, *The Sixth Extinction* (New York: Anchor Books, 1995), 183.

43. Dilworth, *Too Smart*, 81–83; David A. Burney and Timothy F. Flannery, "Fifty Millennia of Catastrophic Extinctions after Human Contact," *Trends in Ecology and Evolution* 20, no. 7 (2005): 395–401; Richard G. Roberts and Barry W. Brook, "And Then There Were None?" *Science* 327, no. 22 (January 2010): 420–22; Colin Tudge, *Neanderthals, Bandits and Farmers: How Agriculture Really Began* (New Haven, CT: Yale University Press, 1998), 21–24; J. Tyler Faith and Todd A. Surovell, "Synchronous Extinction of North America's Pleistocene Mammals," *Proceedings of the National Academy of Sciences* 106, no. 49 (2009): 20641–45.

44. Storrs Olson, quoted in Leakey and Lewin, *Sixth Extinction*, 194. See also

Christopher Johnson, "Megafaunal Decline and Fall," *Science* 326 (November 2009): 1072–73; Faith and Surovell, "Synchronous Extinction"; Michael R. Waters and Thomas W. Stafford Jr., "Redefining the Age of Clovis: Implications for the Peopling of the Americas," *Science* 315 (February 23, 2007): 1122–26.

45. Tudge, *Neanderthals, Bandits and Farmers*; Roberts and Brook, "And Then There Were None?"

Chapter 5. Agriculture and Anxiety

1. *The Epic of Gilgamesh*, ed. N. K. Sandars (London: Penguin, 1972), 30–31, 63–65.

2. For expressions of the historical magnitude of the transition to agriculture, see Graeme Barker, *The Agricultural Revolution in Prehistory: Why Did Foragers Become Farmers?* (Oxford: Oxford University Press, 2009), 414; David Lewis-Williams and David Pearce, *Inside the Neolithic Mind* (London: Thames & Hudson, 2005), 20; Peter Bellwood, *First Farmers: The Origins of Agricultural Societies* (Oxford: Blackwell, 2005), 14.

3. Leore Grosman, Natalie D. Munro, and Anna Belfer-Cohen, "A 12,000-Year-Old Shaman Burial from the Southern Levant (Israel)," *Proceedings of the National Academy of Sciences* 105, no. 46 (2008): 17665–69; Michael Balter, "The Tangled Roots of Agriculture," *Science* 327, no. 22 (January 2010): 404–6; Natalie D. Munro and Leore Grosman, "Early Evidence (ca. 12,000 B.P.) for Feasting at a Burial Cave in Israel," *Proceedings of the National Academy of Sciences* 107, no. 35 (2010): 15362–66.

4. Colin Renfrew, *Prehistory: The Making of the Human Mind* (New York: Modern Library, 2007), 114; Brian Hayden, "A New Overview of Domestication," in *Last Hunters, First Farmers: New Perspectives on the Prehistoric Transition to Agriculture*, ed. T. Douglas Price and Anne Birgitte Gebauer (Santa Fe, NM: School of American Research Press, 1995), 273–99.

5. James Woodburn, "Egalitarian Societies," *Man* 17, no. 3 (1982): 431–51; Alain Testart et al., "The Significance of Food Storage among Hunter-Gatherers: Residence Patterns, Population Densities, and Social Inequalities [and Comments and Reply]," *Current Anthropology* 23, no. 5 (1982): 523–37. For a discussion of Woodburn's and Testart's impact on anthropological thought, see Alan Barnard, "Contemporary Hunter-Gatherers: Current Theoretical Issues in Ecology and Social Organization," *Annual Review of Anthropology* 12 (1983): 193–214; also Morris Berman, *Wandering God: A Study in Nomadic Spirituality* (Albany: State University of New York Press, 2000), 51–56.

6. For other views interpreting sedentism as a prerequisite to agriculture, see T. Douglas Price and Anne Birgitte Gebauer, "New Perspectives on the Transition to Agriculture," in *Last Hunters, First Farmers*, ed. Price and Gebauer, 8; Ofer Bar-Yosef and Richard H. Meadow, "The Origins of Agriculture in the Near East," in *Last Hunters,*

First Farmers, ed. Price and Gebauer, 41; Peter J. Wilson, *The Domestication of the Human Species* (New Haven, CT: Yale University Press, 1988), 59.

7. Bellwood, *First Farmers*, 19–20; Peter Forster, "Ice Ages and the Mitochondrial DNA Chronology of Human Dispersals: A Review," *Philosophical Transactions of the Royal Society B* 359, no. 1442 (2004): 255–64; Barker, *Agricultural Revolution*, 398, 411–12; Jared Diamond, "Evolution, Consequences and Future of Plant and Animal Domestication," *Nature* 418, no. 8 (August 2002): 700–7; Balter, "Tangled Roots."

8. Bar-Yosef and Meadow, "Origins of Agriculture," 49; Diamond, "Evolution, Consequences"; Deborah M. Pearsall, "Domestication and Agriculture in the New World Tropics," in *Last Hunters, First Farmers*, ed. Price and Gebauer, 162. Additionally, early agriculture was not necessarily more productive than foraging and, according to at least one researcher, was most likely less productive. See Samuel Bowles, "Cultivation of Cereals by the First Farmers Was Not More Productive Than Foraging," *Proceedings of the National Academy of Sciences* 108, no. 12 (2011): 4760–65.

9. Diamond, "Evolution, Consequences"; Pearsall, "Domestication and Agriculture," 157–60; Jacques Cauvin, *The Birth of the Gods and the Origins of Agriculture*, trans. Trevor Watkins (Cambridge: Cambridge University Press, 2000), 52; Marc Van De Mieroop, *A History of the Ancient Near East ca. 3000–323 BC*, Blackwell History of the Ancient World (Malden, MA: Blackwell, 2004); Norman Yoffee, *Myths of the Archaic State: Evolution of the Earliest Cities, States, and Civilizations* (Cambridge: Cambridge University Press, 2005), 200–201.

10. Bar-Yosef and Meadow, "Origins of Agriculture," 86; Ian Hodder, *The Domestication of Europe* (Oxford: Blackwell, 1990), 291–92; Craig Dilworth, *Too Smart for Our Own Good: The Ecological Predicament of Humankind* (New York: Cambridge University Press, 2010), 118–19; Cauvin, *Birth of the Gods*, 65.

11. Ofer Bar-Yosef, "The Upper Paleolithic Revolution," *Annual Review of Anthropology* 2002, no. 31 (2002): 363–93; Diamond, "Evolution, Consequences"; Jared Diamond and Peter Bellwood, "Farmers and Their Languages: The First Expansions," *Science* 300, no. 25 (April 2003): 597–603; Bellwood, *First Farmers*, 14, 61, 65–66, 277–78. Bellwood notes "a possible increase in world population from 10 million to 50 million across the total of world transitions to agriculture."

12. Bellwood, *First Farmers*, 61, 65–66, 277–78.

13. Barker, *Agricultural Revolution*, 325–28; T. Douglas Price, Anne Birgitte Gebauer, and Lawrence H. Keeley, "The Spread of Farming into Europe North of the Alps," in *Last Hunters, First Farmers*, ed. Price and Gebauer, 104; Patricia Balaresque et al., "A Predominantly Neolithic Origin for European Paternal Lineages," *PLoS Biology* 8, no. 1 (2010): e1000285.

14. Price and Gebauer, "New Perspectives," 8.

15. Woodburn, "Egalitarian Societies"; Peter Bellwood, "Early Agriculturalist Population Diasporas? Farming, Languages, and Genes," *Annual Review of Anthropology* 30 (2001): 181–207.

16. Price, Gebauer, and Keeley, "Spread of Farming," 123; Barker, *Agricultural Revolution*, 378–90.

17. Balaresque et al., "A Predominantly Neolithic Origin"; Helena Malmström et al., "Ancient DNA Reveals Lack of Continuity between Neolithic Hunter-Gatherers and Contemporary Scandinavians," *Current Biology* 19, no. 20 (2009): 1–5; Price, Gebauer, and Keeley, "Spread of Farming," 95–103; Michael Balter, "Ancient DNA Says Europe's First Farmers Came from Afar," *Science* 325, no. 4 (September 2009): 1189; B. Bramanti et al., "Genetic Discontinuity between Local Hunter-Gatherers and Central Europe's First Farmers," *Science* 326, no. 2 (October 2009): 137–40; Wolfgang Haak et al., "Ancient DNA from European Early Neolithic Farmers Reveals Their Near Eastern Affinities," *PLoS Biology* 8, no. 11 (2010): e1000536.

For other perspectives suggesting "a far more nuanced picture" combining both colonization and cultural diffusion theories, see Barry Cunliffe, *Europe between the Oceans, 9000 BC–AD 1000* (New Haven, CT: Yale University Press, 2008), 88; also Peter Rowley-Conwy, "Human Prehistory: Hunting for the Earliest Farmers," *Current Biology* 19, no. 20 (2009): R948–R49, for a theory of transition by "pulses."

18. For the neurocognitive requirements of agriculture, see Frederick L. Coolidge and Thomas Wynn, "Working Memory, Its Executive Functions, and the Emergence of Modern Thinking," *Cambridge Archaeological Journal* 15, no. 1 (2005): 5–26; and Frederick L. Coolidge and Thomas Wynn, "Executive Functions of the Frontal Lobes and the Evolutionary Ascendancy of *Homo sapiens*," *Cambridge Archaeological Journal* 11, no. 2 (2001): 255–60.

For perspectives on the cognitive shift to agriculture, see Barker, *Agricultural Revolution*, 144, 385; Wilson, *Domestication of the Human Species*, 10; Hodder, *Domestication of Europe*, 18–19, 32, 164, 288; David W. Anthony, *The Horse, the Wheel and Language: How Bronze Age Riders from the Eurasian Steppes Shaped the Modern World* (Princeton, NJ: Princeton University Press, 2007), 155.

19. Cauvin, *Birth of the Gods*, 3, 220; Ian Hodder et al., "Review Feature: The Birth of the Gods and the Origins of Agriculture," *Cambridge Archaeological Journal* 11, no. 1 (2001): 105–21. See also Wilson, *Domestication of the Human Species*, 65.

20. See Woodburn, "Egalitarian Societies"; Barker, *Agricultural Revolution*, 306; Colin Renfrew, *Prehistory: The Making of the Human Mind* (New York: Modern Library, 2007), 135, 141–42; Samuel Bowles and Jung-Kyoo Choi, "Coevolution of Farming and Private Property during the Early Holocene," *Proceedings of the National Academy of Sciences* 110, no. 22 (2013): 8830–35.

21. Barker, *Agricultural Revolution*, 1–2. See Joyce Marcus and Kent V. Flannery, "The Coevolution of Ritual and Society: New 14C Dates from Ancient Mexico," *Proceedings of the National Academy of Sciences* 101, no. 52 (2004): 18257–61, for a fascinating account of an archaeological excavation in Mexico that traces the evolution, over 1,300 years, from the ad hoc rituals of egalitarian nomadic foragers to a full-time priesthood with state temples.

22. See L. Fortunato and M. Archetti, "Evolution of Monogamous Marriage by Maximization of Inclusive Fitness," *Journal of Evolutionary Biology* 23 (2010): 149–56. Also Renfrew, *Prehistory*, 122; Woodburn, "Egalitarian Societies."

23. Cited in Berman, *Wandering God*, 138.

24. Barker, *Agricultural Revolution*, 409–10, quoting Calvin Luther Martin.

25. Bar-Yosef and Meadow, "Origins of Agriculture," 78–79; Erik Hornung, *Conceptions of God in Ancient Egypt: The One and the Many*, trans. John Baines (New York: Cornell University Press, 1996), 105.

26. Cauvin, *Birth of the Gods*, 69–70, 225; Nurit Bird-David, "The Giving Environment: Another Perspective on the Economic System of Gatherer-Hunters," *Current Anthropology* 31, no. 2 (1990): 189–96.

27. Jan Assmann, *Moses the Egyptian: The Memory of Egypt in Western Monotheism* (Cambridge, MA: Harvard University Press, 1997), 45–46.

28. Ibid., 147–8, 177; John H. Walton, *Ancient Near Eastern Thought and the Old Testament: Introducing the Conceptual World of the Hebrew Bible* (Grand Rapids, MI: Baker, 2006), 130.

29. Bruce G. Trigger, *Understanding Early Civilizations* (New York: Cambridge University Press, 2003), 414–16, 424; Anthony Aveni, *Empires of Time: Calendars, Clocks, and Cultures* (Boulder, CO: University Press of Colorado, 2002), 229–30, 248, 254.

30. Jan Assmann, *The Search for God in Ancient Egypt*, trans. David Lorton (Ithaca, NY: Cornell University Press, 2001), 63–64; Lynn White Jr., "The Historical Roots of Our Ecological Crisis," *Science* 155, no. 3767 (1967): 1203–7; Trigger, *Early Civilizations*, 411–15, 426.

31. Walton, *Ancient Near Eastern Thought*, 214; Thomas McEvilley, *The Shape of Ancient Thought: Comparative Studies in Greek and Indian Philosophies* (New York: Allworth Press, 2002), 543–46; Eknath Easwaran, trans., *The Upanishads* (Tomales, CA: Nilgiri Press, 1987), 155; Paul S. MacDonald, *The History of the Concept of the Mind: Speculations about Soul, Mind and Spirit from Homer to Hume* (Aldershot, UK: Ashgate, 2003), 11–12, 22.

32. Ying-Shih Yu, "'O Soul, Come Back!' A Study in the Changing Conceptions of the Soul and Afterlife in Pre-Buddhist China," *Harvard Journal of Asiatic Studies* 47, no. 2 (1987): 363–95.

33. Trigger, *Early Civilizations*, 532, 538; Walton, *Ancient Near Eastern Thought*, 117, 211, 316; Assmann, *Search for God*, 43, 119–20; Yu, "'O Soul, Come Back!'"; Barry J. Kemp, *Ancient Egypt: Anatomy of a Civilization* (New York: Routledge, 1991), 208; Mark Lehner, "Absolutism and Reciprocity in Ancient Egypt," in *The Breakout: The Origins of Civilization*, ed. Martha Lamberg-Karlovsky (Cambridge, MA: Peabody Museum Monographs, 2000), 69–97; W. Scott Morton and Charlton M. Lewis, *China: Its History and Culture* (New York: McGraw-Hill, 2005), 29; Julia Ching, *The Religious Thought of Chu Hsi* (New York: Oxford University Press, 2000), 63; Derk Bodde, "Dominant Ideas

in the Formation of Chinese Culture," *Journal of the American Oriental Society* 62, no. 4 (1942): 293–99.

34. Walton, *Ancient Near Eastern Thought*, 317.

35. Ibid., 130; Trigger, *Early Civilizations*, 641.

36. Cited in Assmann, *Search for God*, 69.

37. Ibid., 71; Aveni, *Empires of Time*, 223, 241; Walton, *Ancient Near Eastern Thought*, 130.

38. Satapatha Brahmana VII, 2, 1, 4, cited in Mircea Eliade, *The Myth of the Eternal Return: Cosmos and History*, trans. Willard R. Trask, Bollingen Series XLVI (Princeton, NJ: Princeton University Press, 2005); Gen. 2:2–3.

Chapter 6. Going Their Own Ways: Early Civilizations

1. W. Scott Morton and Charlton M. Lewis, *China: Its History and Culture* (New York: McGraw-Hill, 2005), 2.

2. Jacques Gernet, *A History of Chinese Civilization* (New York: Cambridge University Press, 2006), 45–46; Chad Hansen, *A Daoist Theory of Chinese Thought: A Philosophical Interpretation* (New York: Oxford University Press, 2000), 31; Benjamin I. Schwartz, *The World of Thought in Ancient China* (Cambridge, MA: Belknap Harvard University Press, 1985), 20; Bruce G. Trigger, *Understanding Early Civilizations* (New York: Cambridge University Press, 2003), 422–23.

3. Trigger, *Understanding Early Civilizations*, 422–23.; David N. Keightley, "The Religious Commitment: Shang Theology and the Genesis of Chinese Political Culture," *History of Religions* 17, nos. 3/4 (1978): 211–25. See Hu Shih in the *Outline of the History of Chinese Philosophy* (1938) cited in Ellen M. Chen, *The Tao Te Ching: A New Translation with Commentary* (St. Paul, MN: Paragon House, 1989), 23; also J. J. M. de Groot, cited in Ernst Cassirer, *An Essay on Man* (New Haven, CT: Yale University Press, 1944), 84–85.

4. Kwang-chih Chang, "Ancient China and Its Anthropological Significance," in *The Breakout: The Origins of Civilization*, ed. Martha Lamberg-Karlovsky (Cambridge, MA: Peabody Museum, 2000), 1–11. See also Keightley, "Shang Theology." Other scholars who have noted the link to shamanism in Chinese civilization include Herrlee G. Creel, *What Is Taoism? And Other Studies in Chinese Cultural History* (Chicago: University of Chicago Press, 1970); also Mircea Eliade, *Shamanism: Archaic Techniques of Ecstasy* (Princeton, NJ: Princeton University Press, 2004, 456–57.

5. Keightley, "Shang Theology."

6. Ibid.

7. Ibid.

8. Ibid.

9. Ibid.

10. See Barry J. Kemp, *Ancient Egypt: Anatomy of a Civilization* (New York: Routledge, 1991). Kemp gives an alternative explanation for the possible source of the Egyptian sense of the unreliability of *ma'at*, noting that the "small political units of late Predynastic Egypt" might have felt "surrounded and threatened" by their neighbors. This condition, however, was true of virtually all early civilizations, but only Egypt experienced such a total reliance on one natural event—the Nile flood—to keep catastrophe at bay.

11. Norman Cohn, *Cosmos, Chaos and the World to Come: The Ancient Roots of Apocalyptic Faith* (New Haven, CT: Yale Nota Bene, 2001), 9; Erik Hornung, *Conceptions of God in Ancient Egypt: The One and the Many*, trans. John Baines (New York: Cornell University Press, 1996), 213–16; Jan Assmann, *The Search for God in Ancient Egypt*, trans. David Lorton (Ithaca, NY: Cornell University Press, 2001), 3–4.

12. John H. Walton, *Ancient Near Eastern Thought and the Old Testament: Introducing the Conceptual World of the Hebrew Bible* (Grand Rapids, MI: Baker, 2006), 318; Cohn, *Cosmos, Chaos*, 27–30.

13. Cohn, *Cosmos, Chaos*, 27–30; Walton, *Ancient Near Eastern Thought*, 318, 327–28. Book of the Dead passage cited in Robert Wright, *The Evolution of God* (New York: Hachette Book Group, 2009), 317–18.

14. Hornung, *Conceptions of God*, 188; Assmann, *Search for God*, 10–11.

15. Walton, *Ancient Near Eastern Thought*, 100–101; Hornung, *Conceptions of God*, 236–37; V. Nikiprowetzky, "Ethical Monotheism," *Dædalus* 104, no. 2 (1975): 69–89.

16. Assmann, *Search for God*, 170–74; Jean-Daniel Stanley et al., "Short Contribution: Nile Flow Failure at the End of the Old Kingdom, Egypt: Strontium Isotopic and Petrologic Evidence," *Geoarchaeology* 18, no. 3 (2003): 395–402.

17. Assmann, *Search for God*, 57–58, 182–83; Thomas McEvilley, *The Shape of Ancient Thought: Comparative Studies in Greek and Indian Philosophies* (New York: Allworth Press, 2002), 24–25.

18. Assmann, *Search for God*, 198–99; Jan Assmann, *Moses the Egyptian: The Memory of Egypt in Western Monotheism* (Cambridge, MA: Harvard University Press, 1997), 24–25.

19. Assmann, *Search for God*, 207; Nikiprowetzky, "Ethical Monotheism."

20. Assmann, *Search for God*, 211–13.

21. Jonathan Kirsch, *God against the Gods: The History of the War between Monotheism and Polytheism* (New York: Penguin Compass, 2004), 27–28.

22. Keesing cited in Pascal Boyer, *Religion Explained: The Evolutionary Origins of Religious Thought* (New York: Basic Books, 2001), 140; Assmann, *Search for God*, 200.

23. McEvilley, *Shape of Ancient Thought*, 24–25.

24. Assmann, *Search for God*, 12, 24–25.

25. Ibid., 241.

26. Ibid., 205, 236, 238; Assmann, *Moses the Egyptian*, 198–99.

27. Samuel Noah Kramer, *The Sumerians: Their History, Culture, and Character* (Chicago: University of Chicago Press, 1963), 3–5. See also Clive Ponting, *A New Green*

History of the World: The Environment and the Collapse of Great Civilizations (New York: Penguin, 2007), 69. The importance of irrigation as a driver of civilization is so crucial that a general "hydraulic" theory of civilization was developed by the historian Karl Wittfogel in his 1957 book *Oriental Despotism: A Comparative Study of Total Power* and later elaborated by anthropologist Julian Steward. While this theory is no longer held to be universally true (see Trigger, *Understanding Early Civilizations*, 24, 59–60), it remains explanatory for the rise of Mesopotamian civilization.

28. Thorkild Jacobsen, "Ancient Mesopotamian Religion: The Central Concerns," *Proceedings of the American Philosophical Society* 107, no. 6 (1963): 473–84.

29. Cited in Walton, *Ancient Near Eastern Thought*, 318.

30. Cited in Jean Bottéro, *Religion in Ancient Mesopotamia*, trans. Teresa Lavender Fagan (Chicago: University of Chicago Press, 2001), 66.

31. Ibid., 31. See also Jacobsen, "Ancient Mesopotamian Religion"; Joseph Needham, *The Grand Titration: Science and Society in East and West* (Toronto: University of Toronto Press, 1969), 301.

32. *Lamentation over the Destruction of Ur* cited in Jacobsen, "Ancient Mesopotamian Religion." See also Kramer, *Sumerians*, 114–17.

33. Cited in Bottéro, *Religion in Ancient Mesopotamia*, 61; also in Cohn, *Cosmos, Chaos*, 50.

34. Bottéro, *Religion in Ancient Mesopotamia*, vii; Kramer, *Sumerians*, 229; Peter Watson, *Ideas: A History of Thought and Invention, from Fire to Freud* (New York: HarperCollins, 2005), 76.

35. Jack Goody, *The Domestication of the Savage Mind* (New York: Cambridge University Press, 1977). See also Steven Roger Fischer, *A History of Writing* (London: Reaktion Books, 2001), 56.

36. David C. Lindberg, *The Beginnings of Western Science: The European Scientific Tradition in Philosophical, Religious, and Institutional Context, Prehistory to A.D. 1450* (Chicago: University of Chicago Press, 2007), 16; A. Leo Oppenheim, "The Position of the Intellectual in Mesopotamian Society," *Dædalus* 104, no. 2 (1975): 37–46. See also Kramer, *Sumerians*, 155.

37. Ibid.

38. C. C. Lamberg-Karlovsky, "The Near Eastern 'Breakout' and the Mesopotamian Social Contract," in *Breakout*, ed. Lamberg-Karlovsky, 13–24; David H. MayburyLewis, "On Theories of Order and Justice in the Development of Civilization," in *Breakout*, ed. Lamberg-Karlovsky, 39–43.

39. Trigger, *Understanding Early Civilizations*, 332–33; Marc Van De Mieroop, *A History of the Ancient Near East ca. 3000–323 BC*, Blackwell History of the Ancient World (Malden, MA: Blackwell, 2004), 111–15.

40. Lamberg-Karlovsky, "Near Eastern 'Breakout.'"

41. Ibid.; Norman Yoffee, *Myths of the Archaic State: Evolution of the Earliest Cities, States, and Civilizations* (Cambridge: Cambridge University Press, 2005), 108.

42. Kramer, *Sumerians*, 280; John Keay, *India: A History* (New York: Grove Press, 2000), 16; Andrew Lawler, "A Forgotten Corridor Rediscovered," *Science* 328 (2010): 1092–97.

43. Andrew Lawler, "Indus Collapse: The End or the Beginning of an Asian Culture?," *Science* 320 (June 6, 2008): 1281–83; Keay, *India*, 5.

44. Keay, *India*, 7–18; A. L. Basham, *The Wonder That Was India* (London: Picador, 2004), 14–44; Lawler, "Indus Collapse."

45. Basham, *Wonder That Was India*, 16; Gregory Possehl, quoted in Lawler, "Indus Collapse," and in Colin Renfrew, *Prehistory: The Making of the Human Mind* (New York: Modern Library, 2007), 167–70; Stuart Piggott, quoted in Georg Feuerstein, *The Yoga Tradition: Its History, Literature, Philosophy and Practice* (Prescott, AZ: Hohm Press, 1998), 100.

46. Renfrew, *Prehistory*, 167–70; Andrew Lawler, "Boring No More, a Trade-Savvy Indus Emerges," *Science* 320 (June 6, 2008): 1276–81. See also Gregory L. Possehl, "Harappan Beginnings," in *Breakout*, ed. Lamberg-Karlovsky; Gregory L. Possehl, "Revolution in the Urban Revolution: The Emergence of Indus Urbanization," *Annual Review of Anthropology* 19 (1990): 261–82.

47. *The Bhagavad Gita*, ed. and trans. Eknath Easwaran (Tomales, CA: Nilgiri Press, 1985), 3–4. See also Joseph Campbell, *The Inner Reaches of Outer Space: Metaphor as Myth and as Religion* (Novato, CA: New World Library, 1986), 47; Mircea Eliade, *Yoga: Immortality and Freedom* (Princeton, NJ: Princeton University Press, 1970), 361; also Lawler, "Boring No More."

48. Lawler, "Indus Collapse."

49. David W. Anthony, *The Horse, the Wheel and Language: How Bronze Age Riders from the Eurasian Steppes Shaped the Modern World* (Princeton, NJ: Princeton University Press, 2007), 6–15. See also J. Mallory, *In Search of the Indo-Europeans: Language, Archaeology and Myth* (London: Thames & Hudson, 1989), 11–23.

50. Anthony, *The Horse, the Wheel*, 6–15; Peter Bellwood, *First Farmers: The Origins of Agricultural Societies* (Oxford: Blackwell, 2005), 186.

51. The Anatolian farming hypothesis was first proposed by Colin Renfrew in 1987. See Colin Renfrew, *Archaeology and Language: The Puzzle of Indo-European Origins* (Cambridge: Cambridge University Press, 1990). For more recent support of this hypothesis, see Russell D. Gray and Quentin D. Atkinson, "Language-Tree Divergence Times Support the Anatolian Theory of Indo-European Origin," *Nature* 426 (November 27, 2003): 435–39.

52. Anthony, *The Horse, the Wheel*, 83–101; Mallory, *In Search of the Indo-Europeans*, 143–185, 243. For a recent DNA-based study providing strong support for the Kurgan hypothesis, see Morten E. Allentoft et al., "Population Genomics of Bronze Age Eurasia," *Nature* 522 (June 11, 2015): 167–72; Wolfgang Haak et al., "Massive Migration from the Steppe Was a Source for Indo-European Languages in Europe," *Nature* 522 (June 11, 2015): 207–11. For a "bipartisan" discussion of the debate, see Jared Diamond

and Peter Bellwood, "Farmers and Their Languages: The First Expansions," *Science* 300 (April 25, 2003): 597–603.

53. Lawler, "Indus Collapse"; A. L. Basham, *The Origins and Development of Classical Hinduism* (New York: Oxford University Press, 1989), 7–8.

54. Anthony, *The Horse, the Wheel*, 454; Mallory, *In Search of the Indo-Europeans*, 143–185, 243.

55. Basham, *Classical Hinduism*, 8–10.

56. The four primary castes were *Brahman*, *Kshatriya*, *Vaishya*, and *Sudra*. Further stratification ensued between different kinds of wage laborers, hired laborers, and slaves. See Romila Thapar, "Ethics, Religion, and Social Protest in the First Millennium BC in Northern India," *Dædalus* 104, no. 2 (1975): 119–32. Thousands of years after their original invasion of the Indian subcontinent, the descendants of the Aryans continue to hold a dominant role in Indian society. A recent genetic study of India's current population shows two genetically distinct populations, with a PIE-sourced, predominantly upper-caste population genetically closer to Central Asians and Europeans. See David Reich et al., "Reconstructing Indian Population History," *Nature* 461 (September 24, 2009): 489–95.

57. Basham, *Classical Hinduism*, 8–10; Anthony, *The Horse, the Wheel*, 408; Heinrich Zimmer, *Philosophies of India*, ed. Joseph Campbell (Princeton, NJ: Princeton University Press, 1951), 8–9, footnote written by Campbell.

58. Anthony, *The Horse, the Wheel*, 55; A. N. Marlow, "Hinduism and Buddhism in Greek Philosophy," *Philosophy East and West* 4, no. 1 (April 1954): 35–45.

59. Marlow, "Hinduism and Buddhism"; Feuerstein, *Yoga Tradition*, 31; Easwaran, *Bhagavad Gita*, 111; R. C. Zaehner, *The Dawn and Twilight of Zoroastrianism* (London: Phoenix Press, 2002), 48.

60. Anthony, *The Horse, the Wheel*, 455–56. See also Cohn, *Cosmos, Chaos*, 61–62, 71.

61. Anthony, *The Horse, the Wheel*, 300–302, 459. See John Travis, "Trail of Mare's Milk Leads to First Tamed Horses," *Science* 322 (October 17, 2008): 368, for a description of the discovery of mare's milk on pottery fragments from Kazakhstan dating to between 3700 and 3100 BCE, the putative timeframe for the PIE homeland, described as "the smoking gun for horse domestication."

62. Anthony, *The Horse, the Wheel*, 137–38, 328.

63. Anthony, *The Horse, the Wheel*, 160–61; Cohn, *Cosmos, Chaos*, 60; Mallory, *In Search of the Indo-Europeans*, 125.

64. Mallory, *In Search of the Indo-Europeans*, 140–41; Anthony, *The Horse, the Wheel*, 134–35.

65. Diamond and Bellwood, "Farmers and Their Languages."

66. Anthony, *The Horse, the Wheel*, 341–42; John Noble Wilford, "A Lost European Culture, Pulled from Obscurity," *New York Times*, December 1, 2009; Mallory, *In Search of the Indo-Europeans*, 182–85.

67. Mallory, *In Search of the Indo-Europeans*, 182–85; Recent archaeological findings have shown the same hierarchical structures in the pre-PIE cultures of Eastern Europe that we should expect from the previous chapters' discussion of agrarian values. See Wilford, "A Lost European Culture."

68. Anthony, *The Horse, the Wheel*, 343.

69. Zaehner, *Zoroastrianism*, 34; Cohn, *Cosmos, Chaos*, 94–95; Mary Boyce, *Zoroastrians: Their Religious Beliefs and Practices* (New York: Routledge, 2001).

70. Cited in Zaehner, *Zoroastrianism*, 34.

71. Boyce, *Zoroastrians*, 20; Morris Berman, *Wandering God: A Study in Nomadic Spirituality* (Albany: State University of New York Press, 2000), 186–87.

72. Boyce, *Zoroastrians*, 43–44.

73. McEvilley, *Shape of Ancient Thought*, 122; Zaehner, *Zoroastrianism*, 41.

74. Cited in Zaehner, *Zoroastrianism*, 40–42.

75. Boyce, *Zoroastrians*, 50–53, 145–62; Cohn, *Cosmos, Chaos*, 220–22; Israel Finkelstein and Neil Asher Silberman, *The Bible Unearthed: Archaeology's New Vision of Ancient Israel and the Origin of Its Sacred Texts* (New York: Touchstone, 2002), 292–305; Morton Smith, "II Isaiah and the Persians," *Journal of the American Oriental Society* 83, no. 4 (September–December 1963): 415–21.

Chapter 7. The Birth of Dualism in Ancient Greece

1. A. E. Taylor, *Plato: The Man and His Work* (Mineola, NY: Dover Publications, 1926/2001), 1–9; C. A. Huffman, *Philolaus of Croton: Pythagorean and Presocratic: A Commentary on the Fragments and Testimonia with Interpretive Essays* (Cambridge: Cambridge University Press, 1993), 5; Anthony F. Beavers and Christopher Planeaux, "Plato's Life," in *Exploring Plato's Dialogues* (Evansville, IN: University of Evansville, 1998).

2. Quoted in Arthur O. Lovejoy, *The Great Chain of Being: A Study of the History of an Idea* (Cambridge, MA: Harvard University Press, 1936/1964), 24.

3. Karl Jaspers, *The Origin and Goal of History*, trans. M. Bullock (London: Routledge and Kegan Paul, 1953).

4. J. Mallory, *In Search of the Indo-Europeans: Language, Archaeology and Myth* (London: Thames & Hudson, 1989), 68–71; Jean-Pierre Vernant, *The Origins of Greek Thought* (Ithaca, NY: Cornell University Press, 1982), 16; H. D. F. Kitto, *The Greeks* (London: Penguin Books, 1991), 26; David W. Anthony, *The Horse, the Wheel and Language: How Bronze Age Riders from the Eurasian Steppes Shaped the Modern World* (Princeton, NJ: Princeton University Press, 2007), 48–49.

5. Marc Van De Mieroop, *A History of the Ancient Near East ca. 3000–323 BC*, Blackwell History of the Ancient World (Malden, MA: Blackwell, 2004), 227–82; Charles H.

Kahn, *Pythagoras and the Pythagoreans: A Brief History* (Indianapolis: Hackett, 2001), 19; Thomas McEvilley, *The Shape of Ancient Thought: Comparative Studies in Greek and Indian Philosophies* (New York: Allworth Press, 2002), 5–6.

6. Walter Burkert, *The Orientalizing Revolution: Near Eastern Influence on Greek Culture in the Early Archaic Age* (Cambridge, MA: Harvard University Press, 1992), 6, 25–26, 129. See also Van De Mieroop, *Ancient Near East*, 275–76; and David C. Lindberg, *The Beginnings of Western Science: The European Scientific Tradition in Philosophical, Religious, and Institutional Context, Prehistory to AD 1450* (Chicago: University of Chicago Press, 2007), 12.

7. G. S. Kirk, J. E. Raven, and M. Schofield, *The Presocratic Philosophers*, 2nd ed. (Cambridge: Cambridge University Press, 1983), 95–98. Also see Burkert, quoted in Paul S. MacDonald, *The History of the Concept of the Mind: Speculations about Soul, Mind and Spirit from Homer to Hume* (Aldershot: Ashgate, 2003), 41.

8. Fragments 30 and 49a, cited in McEvilley, *Shape of Ancient Thought*, 37; Fragment 32, cited in A. N. Marlow, "Hinduism and Buddhism in Greek Philosophy," *Philosophy East and West* 4, no. 1 (April 1954): 35–45. See also Kitto, *Greeks*, 180; Vernant, *Origins of Greek Thought*, 122; Gregory Vlastos, *Plato's Universe* (Canada: Parmenides, 2005), 5.

9. Cited in Marlow, "Hinduism and Buddhism." See also Lindberg, *Beginnings of Western Science*, 31; F. M. Cornford, *From Religion to Philosophy: A Study in the Origins of Western Speculation* (New York: Dover Publications, 1912/2004), 100.

10. Kitto, *Greeks*, 146–47.

11. See Richard E. Nisbett et al., "Culture and Systems of Thought: Holistic versus Analytic Cognition," *Psychological Review* 108, no. 2 (2001): 291–310. Also Merlin Donald, *Origins of the Modern Mind: Three Stages in the Evolution of Culture and Cognition* (Cambridge, MA: Harvard University Press, 1991), 275.

12. Kitto, *Greeks*, 146–47.

13. Peter Watson, *Ideas: A History of Thought and Invention, from Fire to Freud* (New York: HarperCollins, 2005), 118; B. Snell, *The Discovery of the Mind in Greek Philosophy and Literature* (Mineola, NY: Courier Dover, 1953), 231; Iain McGilchrist, *The Master and His Emissary: The Divided Brain and the Making of the Western World* (New Haven, CT: Yale University Press, 2009), 285–86.

14. McEvilley, *Shape of Ancient Thought*, 31–33.

15. Fragments 14, 15, and 16, cited in Kirk, Raven, and Schofield, *Presocratic Philosophers*, 169.

16. Fragment 24, ibid.

17. Fragment 14, ibid., 363–65.

18. Ibid., 412; R. M. Hare, *Plato* (Oxford: Oxford University Press, 1982), 12–13.

19. Joseph Needham, *The Grand Titration: Science and Society in East and West* (Toronto: University of Toronto Press, 1969).

20. Kitto, *Greeks*, 176–77.

21. Ibid.

22. Ibid., 191–94; Lindberg, *Beginnings of Western Science*, 25–27.

23. Kitto, *Greeks*, 192; Mario Livio, *Is God a Mathematician?* (New York: Simon & Schuster, 2009), 26.

24. Kitto, *Greeks*, 179, 189; Vlastos, *Plato's Universe*; G. E. R. Lloyd, *Early Greek Science: Thales to Aristotle* (New York: W. W. Norton, 1970).

25. Cited in Vlastos, *Plato's Universe*.

26. Lindberg, *Beginnings of Western Science*, 25–27; Lloyd, *Early Greek Science*, 8–12; Donald, *Origins of the Modern Mind*, 273–74.

27. McEvilley, *Shape of Ancient Thought*, 53–54.

28. Edward Grant, *Science and Religion, 400 BC to AD 1550: From Aristotle to Copernicus* (Baltimore: Johns Hopkins University Press, 2004). Chad Hansen, *A Daoist Theory of Chinese Thought: A Philosophical Interpretation* (New York: Oxford University Press, 2000), 17.

29. Grant, *Science and Religion*, 37.

30. Aetius, cited in Kirk, Raven, and Schofield, *Presocratic Philosophers*, 158–59; Cornford, *From Religion to Philosophy*, 109–10. See also François Jullien, *Vital Nourishment: Departing from Happiness* (New York: Zone Books, 2007), 56; E. R. Dodds, *The Greeks and the Irrational* (Berkeley, CA: University of California Press, 1951), 138–39.

31. Cornford, *From Religion to Philosophy*, 199–200; Douglas J. Stewart, "Socrates' Last Bath," *Journal of the History of Philosophy* 10, no. 3 (1972): 253–59; Hans Jonas, *The Phenomenon of Life: Toward a Philosophical Biology* (Evanston: Northwestern University Press, 2001), 13.

32. McEvilley, *Shape of Ancient Thought*, 105; Plato, *Cratylus* 400c, cited in ibid.; Cornford, *From Religion to Philosophy*, 179–80.

33. Christiane L. Joost-Gaugier, *Measuring Heaven: Pythagoras and His Influence on Thought and Art in Antiquity and the Middle Ages* (New York: Cornell University Press, 2006).

34. Cornford, *From Religion to Philosophy*, 199–200.

35. Kirk, Raven, and Schofield, *Presocratic Philosophers*, 238; Joost-Gaugier, *Measuring Heaven*, 12; Marlow, "Hinduism and Buddhism"; Stephen Batchelor, *The Awakening of the West: The Encounter of Buddhism and Western Culture* (Berkeley: Parallax Press, 1994), 5.

36. Michel Ferrari, "Culture and Development Matter to Understanding Souls, No Matter What Our Evolutionary Design," *Behavioral and Brain Sciences* 29, no. 5 (2006): 472; also Dodds, *Greeks and the Irrational*, 138–39. See the writings of Empedocles, cited in MacDonald, *History of the Concept of the Mind*, 32–33; also Fragments 115 and 147, cited in Kirk, Raven, and Schofield, *Presocratic Philosophers*, 315–17.

37. The *Republic*. See Lindberg, *Beginnings of Western Science*, 36–37; Cornford, *From Religion to Philosophy*, 246–47. See also Jeffrey Gold, "Plato in the Light of Yoga," *Philosophy East and West* 46, no. 1 (1996): 17–32; also R. Ferwerda, "The Meaning of the Word *Soma* (Body) in the Axial Age: An Interpretation of Plato's Cratylus 400c," in *The Origins & Diversity of Axial Age Civilizations*, ed. Shmuel N. Eisenstadt (Albany: State University of New York Press, 1986).

38. Francis. M. Cornford, *Plato's Cosmology: The Timaeus of Plato* (Indianapolis: Hackett, 1937/1997), 286.

39. For a description of the pfc's role in cognitive control, see Leon Tremblay and Wolfram Schultz, "Relative Reward Preference in Primate Orbitofrontal Cortex," *Nature* 398, no. 22 (April 1999): 704–8; Todd A. Hare, Colin F. Camerer, and Antonio Rangel, "Self-Control in Decision-Making Involves Modulation of the VmPFC Valuation System," *Science* 324, no. 1 (May 2009): 646–48.

40. Hare, *Plato*, 53–56.

41. Cited in Gold, "Plato in the Light."

42. Ibid.

43. The *Phaedo*, cited in Hare, *Plato*, 35. Also cited in McEvilley, *Shape of Ancient Thought*, 190; and in Gold, "Plato in the Light."

44. Patricia Smith Churchland, *Neurophilosophy: Toward a Unified Science of the Mind-Brain* (Cambridge, MA: Massachusetts Institute of Technology, 1989), 242. See also R. W. Sperry, "Mind-Brain Interaction: Mentalism, Yes; Dualism, No," *Neuroscience* 5 (1980): 195–206.

45. *Euthydemus*, cited in Cornford, *From Religion to Philosophy*, 252.

46. Lindberg, *Beginnings of Western Science*, 38. For a description of the categorizing faculty of the prefrontal cortex, see Earl K. Miller, David J. Freedman, and Jonathan D. Wallis, "The Prefrontal Cortex: Categories, Concepts and Cognition," *Philosophical Transactions of the Royal Society B* 357 (2002): 1123–36.

47. Cornford, *From Religion to Philosophy*, 252.

48. Ibid.

49. From the *Timaeus*, cited in Cornford, *Plato's Cosmology*, 354. See also F. M. Cornford, "Was the Ionian Philosophy Scientific?," *Journal of Hellenic Studies* 62 (1942): 1–7.

50. G. E. R. Lloyd, "Plato as a Natural Scientist," *Journal of Hellenic Studies* 88 (1968): 78–92; Kahn, *Pythagoras and the Pythagoreans*, 56–57; Karen Armstrong, *The Great Transformation* (New York: Alfred A. Knopf, 2006).

51. Lindberg, *Beginnings of Western Science*, 39.

52. Cornford, *Plato's Cosmology*, 33–34; Lovejoy, *Great Chain of Being*, 41–42.

53. The *Republic*, cited in Hare, *Plato*, 44–45; Cornford, *Plato's Cosmology*, 33–34; Kitto, *Greeks*, 193.

54. Hare, *Plato*, 7.

55. Cornford, *From Religion to Philosophy*, 262–63.

56. Dodds, *Greeks and the Irrational*, 238–39.

57. Cornford, *From Religion to Philosophy*, 261.

Chapter 8. Dualism and Divinity in Ancient India

1. Cited in Stephen Batchelor, *The Awakening of the West: The Encounter of Buddhism and Western Culture* (Berkeley: Parallax Press, 1994), 5.

2. A. L. Basham, *The Wonder That Was India* (London: Picador, 2004), 4.

3. Thomas McEvilley, *The Shape of Ancient Thought: Comparative Studies in Greek and Indian Philosophies* (New York: Allworth Press, 2002), 29; Heinrich Zimmer, *Philosophies of India*, ed. Joseph Campbell (Princeton, NJ: Princeton University Press, 1951), 100–101, 338; A. L. Basham, *The Origins and Development of Classical Hinduism* (New York: Oxford University Press, 1989), 13–14.

4. *Rig Veda* 10.129, cited in Basham, *Classical Hinduism*, 22–24.

5. Gananath Obeyesekere, *Imagining Karma: Ethical Transformation in Amerindian, Buddhist, and Greek Rebirth* (Berkeley, CA: University of California Press, 2002).

6. Ibid. See also McEvilley, *Shape of Ancient Thought*, 116; Zimmer, *Philosophies of India*, 281.

7. Obeyesekere, *Imagining Karma*.

8. McEvilley, *Shape of Ancient Thought*, 42–43; Norman Cohn, *Cosmos, Chaos and the World to Come: The Ancient Roots of Apocalyptic Faith* (New Haven, CT: Yale Nota Bene, 2001), 72–73.

9. *Chandogya Upanishad* 8.5.1–3, cited in William K. Mahony, *The Artful Universe: An Introduction to the Vedic Religious Imagination* (Albany: State University of New York Press, 1998), 143–51. See also Zimmer, *Philosophies of India*, 8; and Karen Armstrong, *The Great Transformation* (New York: Alfred A. Knopf, 2006), 126.

10. G. L. Possehl, "Harappan Beginnings," cited under "Harappa: Explorations of the Mind?" in chapter 6.

11. Mahony, *Artful Universe*, 46–49.

12. Ibid.

13. See Katha Upanishad II.1.9, which uses the analogy of fire to describe the relationship between *atman* and Brahman, in *The Upanishads*, trans. Eknath Easwaran (Tomales, CA: Nilgiri Press, 1987).

14. Brhadaranyaka Upanishad; See also Prasna Upanishad, cited in McEvilley, *Shape of Ancient Thought*, 100; Zimmer, *Philosophies of India*, 81; Easwaran, *Upanishads*, 25; Aldous Huxley, *The Perennial Philosophy* (New York: HarperCollins, 1945/2004), 6; Georg Feuerstein, *The Yoga Tradition: Its History, Literature, Philosophy and Practice* (Prescott, AZ: Hohm Press, 1998), 311; *The Bhagavad Gita*, ed. and trans. Eknath Easwaran (Tomales, CA: Nilgiri Press, 1985), 159.

15. Mahony, *Artful Universe*, 10; Easwaran, *Upanishads*, 11–12.

16. For useful summaries of the Vedic cosmology, see Feuerstein, *Yoga Tradition*, 126; Easwaran, *Upanishads*, 11–12.

17. Brhadaranyaka Upanishad IV.5.15, cited in Hajime Nakamura, *Ways of*

Thinking of Eastern Peoples: India-China-Tibet-Japan (Honolulu: University of Hawaii Press, 1964), 54; Brhadaranyaka Upanishad III.8.8 and Taittiriya Upanishad III.1.1, cited in Marlow, "Hinduism and Buddhism"; McEvilley, *Shape of Ancient Thought*, 33.

18. Digha Nikaya 1.2.5, cited in Glen Wallis, *Basic Teachings of the Buddha: A New Translation and Compilation, with a Guide to Reading the Texts* (New York: Random House, 2007), 84–85. The Digha Nikaya is a Buddhist scripture and not one of the Upanishads, but Wallis regards this quote from the Buddha as a description of the prevailing concept of Brahman, which was consistent and contemporary with the Upanishads.

19. Katha Upanishad I.2.18; I.3.15, in Easwaran, *Upanishads*, 86, 89–90. See also Zimmer, *Philosophies of India*, 3, 79–81; Feuerstein, *Yoga Tradition*, 4.

20. A. E. Taylor, *Plato: The Man and His Work* (Mineola, NY: Dover Publications, 1926/2001), 206; Easwaran, *Bhagavad Gita*, 62–64 (II.13–25). The *Bhagavad Gita* is not strictly one of the Upanishads and was likely composed around the third century BCE, after the bulk of the Upanishads; but, as described by Easwaran, it "distills the essence of the Upanishads, not piecemeal but comprehensively."—ibid., 8. For another reference contrasting *atman* with the body, see Brihadaranyaka Upanishad IV.1.7–8, in Easwaran, *Upanishads*, 43–44.

21. Amritabindu Upanishad, in Easwaran, *Upanishads*, 243; McEvilley, *Shape of Ancient Thought*, 181; Marlow, "Hinduism and Buddhism."

22. Zimmer, *Philosophies of India* (quoting Joseph Campbell), 19; Mahony, *Artful Universe*, 32.

23. Chandogya Upanishad VIII.1.1, 5; cited in Easwaran, *Upanishads*, 26–28. See also Edward Shils, "Some Observations on the Place of Intellectuals in Max Weber's Sociology, with Special Reference to Hinduism," in *The Origins and Diversity of Axial Age Civilizations*, ed. Shmuel N. Eisenstadt (Albany: State University of New York Press, 1986).

24. Katha Upanishad II.6.14ff., cited in Basham, *Wonder That Was India*, 256.

25. Feuerstein, *Yoga Tradition*, 31; Diana Morrison, in Easwaran, *Bhagavad Gita*, 111.

26. McEvilley, *Shape of Ancient Thought*, 183; Feuerstein, *Yoga Tradition*, 214–15; Jeffrey Gold, "Plato in the Light of Yoga," *Philosophy East and West* 46, no. 1 (1996): 17–32.

27. It is noteworthy that Zoroaster also used a horse and rider metaphor in describing the relationship between the reasoning soul and the body. The fact that all three PIE traditions used the same metaphor offers a fascinating insight, since the PIE culture is widely recognized as having been the first society to domesticate the horse and utilize horse-driven wagons for transport. In the early days of PIE culture, the pioneers of horse domestication must have wondered at their awesome achievement in harnessing the wild power of the horse. Is it possible that this seminal mastery achieved by the human mind over a wild force of nature was the seed for the dualistic mind-body split that became central to the later PIE-based thought traditions?

28. Plato, *Phaedrus*, trans. Benjamin Jowett, http://classics.mit.edu/Plato/

phaedrus.html. See also McEvilley, *Shape of Ancient Thought*, 185; Marlow, "Hinduism and Buddhism," 43.

29. Easwaran, *Upanishads*, 88–89.

30. Kena Upanishad II.2-3, Katha U'panishad I.2.23, in ibid., 69–70, 87.

31. Katha Upanishad II.3.10, in ibid., 96.

32. Mircea Eliade, *Yoga: Immortality and Freedom* (Princeton, NJ: Princeton University Press, 1970), 119–21; Basham, *Wonder That Was India*, 327–28; Morrison, in Easwaran, *Bhagavad Gita*, 99–100.

33. Gold, "Plato in the Light." The lack of mention in Plato of the yoga practices of meditation, *pranayama*, and *asanas* supports the theory that Harappan civilization was the source of yoga. If yoga had its origin in PIE practices, it seems implausible that these techniques would have been so fully developed in the Indian branch of Indo-European culture and have disappeared without a trace in the Greek branch.

34. Maitri Upanishad, cited in Eliade, *Yoga*, 126; Kausitaki Upanishad, cited in Mahony, *Artful Universe*, 172–75.

35. Michael N. Nagler, "Reading the Upanishads," in Easwaran, *Upanishads*, 251–301.

36. Ibid.

37. *Nirvana-Shatka*, cited in Feuerstein, *Yoga Tradition*, 74–75.

38. Shvetashvatara Upanishad, IV, 2–4, in Easwaran, *Upanishads*, 225.

39. Katha Upanishad II.2.2, in ibid., 28.

40. Easwaran, *Bhagavad Gita*, 132 (IX4–6).

41. See Zimmer, *Philosophies of India*, 25–26.

42. Shvetashvatara Upanishad, III, 7, 14–15, in Easwaran, *Upanishads*, 223–24.

43. See "Reconciling the One and the Many" in chapter 6.

44. *Speaking of Siva*, trans. A. K. Ramanujan, quoted in David Shulman, "Living in India's Spirit World," *New York Review of Books* LVII, no. 16 (2010): 43–44.

45. Brihadaranyaka Upanishad, in Easwaran, *Upanishads*, 36–37.

Chapter 9. The Search for Harmony in Ancient China

1. *The Complete Works of Chuang Tzu*, trans. Burton Watson (New York: Columbia University Press, 1968), 240–41.

2. *The Tao Te Ching: A New Translation with Commentary*, trans. Ellen M. Chen (St. Paul, MN: Paragon House, 1989), chap. 32, 133.

3. Watson, *Chuang Tzu*, 240–41. See also Herrlee G. Creel, *What Is Taoism? And Other Studies in Chinese Cultural History* (Chicago: University of Chicago Press, 1970), 32–33, for a vivid description of the earthy nature of Taoist thought.

4. It should be noted that this chapter—and other discussions of traditional

Chinese civilization in this book—refer to Chinese culture prior to the intrusion of Western values and technology. The social, cultural, and political values expressed in China today are not necessarily consistent with traditional Chinese values—and, in some cases, diametrically opposed. It is therefore important to refrain from making direct inferences regarding modern China from the subject matter of this chapter. The following chapter, by contrast, will examine how certain traditional ways of thinking—East Asian and Western—have maintained their cognitive patterns even in modern times. See the preface for a discussion of how Western values infiltrated the cultures of the rest of the world along with colonial conquest.

5. François Jullien, *Vital Nourishment: Departing from Happiness* (New York: Zone Books, 2007), 76. For more in-depth discussions of the meaning of *qi*, see Geoffrey Lloyd and Nathan Sivin, *The Way and the Word: Science and Medicine in Early China and Greece* (New Haven, CT: Yale University Press, 2002), 196–97; also Bruce G. Trigger, *Understanding Early Civilizations* (New York: Cambridge University Press, 2003), 416.

6. Benjamin I. Schwartz, "On the Absence of Reductionism in Chinese Thought," *Journal of Chinese Philosophy* 1 (1973): 27–44; Benjamin I. Schwartz, *The World of Thought in Ancient China* (Cambridge, MA: Belknap Harvard University Press, 1985), 185; Yu Huan Zhang and Ken Rose, *Who Can Ride the Dragon? An Exploration of the Cultural Roots of Traditional Chinese Medicine* (Taos, NM: Paradigm Publications, 1995), 42.

7. Harold D. Roth, *Original Tao: Inward Training and the Foundations of Taoist Mysticism*, Translations from the Asian Classics (New York: Columbia University Press, 1999), 41–42; Zhang and Rose, *Who Can Ride the Dragon?*, 38, 68, 126; Jullien, *Vital Nourishment*, 76; Ying-Shih Yu, "'O Soul, Come Back!' A Study in the Changing Conceptions of the Soul and Afterlife in Pre-Buddhist China," *Harvard Journal of Asiatic Studies* 47, no. 2 (1987): 363–95.

8. Zhang and Rose, *Who Can Ride the Dragon?*, 67–69; Donald J. Munro, *The Concept of Man in Early China* (Ann Arbor, MI: Center for Chinese Studies, University of Michigan, 1969), 122–23.

9. Derk Bodde, "Dominant Ideas in the Formation of Chinese Culture," *Journal of the American Oriental Society* 62, no. 4 (1942): 293–99.

10. Chen, *Tao Te Ching*, Section 2.2, 55; Zhang and Rose, *Who Can Ride the Dragon?*, 39–40; Alan Watts, *Tao: The Watercourse Way* (New York: Pantheon Books, 1975), 19–20.

11. David L. Hall and Roger T. Ames, *Thinking through Confucius* (Albany, NY: State University of New York Press, 1987), 17–19; Xinyan Jiang, "Chinese Dialectical Thinking: The Yin Yang Model," *Philosophy Compass* 8, no. 5 (2013): 438–46.

12. Zhang and Rose, *Who Can Ride the Dragon?*, 52.

13. Cited in Julia Ching, *The Religious Thought of Chu Hsi* (New York: Oxford University Press, 2000), 7.

14. Mark Elvin, "Was There a Transcendental Breakthrough in China?" in *The Origins and Diversity of Axial Age Civilizations*, ed. Shmuel N. Eisenstadt (Albany: State

University of New York Press, 1986); Joseph Needham, *The Grand Titration: Science and Society in East and West* (Toronto: University of Toronto Press, 1969), 46; Hajime Nakamura, *Ways of Thinking of Eastern Peoples: India-China-Tibet-Japan* (Honolulu: University of Hawaii Press, 1964), 272; Ching, *Chu Hsi*, 7; Schwartz, *World of Thought*, 390.

15. Lloyd and Sivin, *Way and the Word*, 226; Joseph Needham, *Science and Civilisation in China*, vol. 2, *History of Scientific Thought* (London: Cambridge University Press, 1972), 527.

16. Needham, *History of Scientific Thought*, 582.

17. Ibid., 561–62.

18. Ibid., 281; Fritjof Capra and Pier Luigi Luisi, *The Systems View of Life: A Unifying Vision* (New York: Cambridge University Press, 2014).

19. Toby E. Huff, *The Rise of Early Modern Science: Islam, China, and the West* (New York: Cambridge University Press, 2006), 363. See also Munro, *Concept of Man*, 122–23.

20. *Doctrine of the Mean*, cited in Bodde, "Dominant Ideas"; Yu-Lan Fung, *A Short History of Chinese Philosophy: A Systematic Account of Chinese Thought from Its Origins to the Present Day* (New York: Free Press, 1976), 144; Joseph Needham, "History and Human Values: A Chinese Perspective for World Science and Technology," *Philosophy and Social Action* 11, no. 1 (1976).

21. Lloyd and Sivin, *Way and the Word*, 220; Ching, *Chu Hsi*, 6, 94; Needham, "History and Human Values"; David Loy, "Transcendence East and West," *Man and World* 26, no. 4 (1993): 403–27.

22. *Tso-chuan*, cited in Hall and Ames, *Thinking through Confucius*, 165–66, who also refer to Confucius' statement: "The exemplary person pursues harmony rather than agreement; the small person is the opposite."

23. Roth, *Original Tao*, 180.

24. Chen, *Tao Te Ching*, chap. 1, 51.

25. Ibid., 21; Zhang and Rose, *Who Can Ride the Dragon?*, 85; Roth, *Original Tao*, 44.

26. Chen, *Tao Te Ching*, chap. 51, 175–76.

27. Ellen M. Chen, "The Meaning of *Te* in the *Tao Te Ching*: An Examination of the Concept of Nature in Chinese Taoism," *Philosophy East and West* 23, no. 4 (October 1973): 457–70.

28. Ying-shih Yü, "Life and Immortality in the Mind of Han China," *Harvard Journal of Asiatic Studies* 25 (1964): 80–122. See also Nathan Sivin, "On the Word 'Taoist' as a Source of Perplexity. With Special Reference to the Relations of Science and Religion in Traditional China," *History of Religions* 17, nos. 3/4 (1978): 303–30.

29. W. Scott Morton and Charlton M. Lewis, *China: Its History and Culture* (New York: McGraw-Hill, 2005), 47.

30. Chen, *Tao Te Ching*, chap. 48, 168.

31. Edward Slingerland, *Effortless Action: Wu-Wei as Conceptual Metaphor and Spiritual*

Ideal in Early China (New York: Oxford University Press, 2003); Needham, *Science and Civilisation*, 68–69, 562–63. Citation in Needham from the *Li Chi*.

32. *Huai Nan Tzu*, cited in Needham, *Science and Civilisation*, 68–69; David B. Wong, "Identifying with Nature in Early Daoism," *Journal of Chinese Philosophy* 36, no. 4 (2009): 568–84. See also Munro, *Concept of Man*, 142.

33. Joaquin M Fuster, "The Prefrontal Cortex—An Update: Time Is of the Essence," *Neuron* 30, no. 2 (2001): 319–33; Aron K. Barbey, Frank Krueger, and Jordan Grafman, "An Evolutionarily Adaptive Neural Architecture for Social Reasoning," *Trends in Neurosciences* 32, no. 12 (2009): 603–10.

34. Chen, *Tao Te Ching*, chap. 2, 55–56; chap. 20, 102. See also Schwartz, *World of Thought*, 207.

35. Chen, *Tao Te Ching*, chap. 32, 133. See also Slingerland, *Effortless Action*, 80.

36. Chen, *Tao Te Ching*, chap. 29, 126–27. See also chap. 38, 14–16.

37. Tung-Chi Lin, "The Chinese Mind: Its Taoist Substratum," *Journal of the History of Ideas* 8, no. 3 (June 1947): 259–72; Watson, *Chuang Tzu*, 10–11; Sivin, "On the Word 'Taoist'"; Needham, *Science and Civilisation*, 164; Munro, *Concept of Man*, 121; Hall and Ames, *Thinking through Confucius*, 59.

38. Schwartz, *World of Thought*, 47; Benjamin I. Schwartz, "Transcendence in Ancient China," *Dædalus* 104, no. 2 (1975): 57–68.

39. Cho-Yun Hsu, "Historical Conditions of the Emergence and Crystallization of the Confucian System," in *Axial Age Civilizations*, ed. Eisenstadt.

40. Ibid.; Chad Hansen, *A Daoist Theory of Chinese Thought: A Philosophical Interpretation* (New York: Oxford University Press, 2000), 32.

41. Cited in Dieter Kuhn, *The Age of Confucian Rule: The Song Transformation of China* (Cambridge, MA: Belknap Press of Harvard University Press, 2009), 10.

42. Jullien, *Vital Nourishment*, 170.

43. Zhang and Rose, *Who Can Ride the Dragon?*, 58.

44. Wong, "Identifying with Nature."

45. Schwartz, *World of Thought*, 102–3.

46. *Analects* XV, cited in A. C. Graham, *Disputers of the Tao: Philosophical Argument in Ancient China* (Peru, IL: Open Court, 1989).

47. Munro, *Concept of Man*, 32–33. See also Hall and Ames, *Thinking through Confucius*, 85–86, 171–72, 346n.

48. *Hsün Tzu*, cited in Needham, *Science and Civilisation*, 27. See also Munro, *Concept of Man*, 26–27; Hall and Ames, *Thinking through Confucius*, 85–86.

49. Schwartz, *World of Thought*, 66–68; Hansen, *Daoist Theory*, 77–78.

50. *Analects* 8.2, cited in Schwartz, *World of Thought*, 82. See also Yanming An, "Western 'Sincerity' and Confucian '*Cheng*,'" *Asian Philosophy* 14, no. 2 (2004): 155–69.

51. *Chung Yung*, cited in Needham, *Science and Civilisation*, 468. See also An, "Western 'Sincerity.'"

52. Munro, *Concept of Man*, 28–29; Elvin, "Transcendental Breakthrough."
53. Hall and Ames, *Thinking through Confucius*, 227–32.
54. Chen, *Tao Te Ching*, chap. 38, 145–46.

Chapter 10. The Cultural Shaping of Our Minds

1. Guy Deutscher, *Through the Language Glass: Why the World Looks Different in Other Languages* (New York: Metropolitan Books, 2010), 163–75.
2. Ibid.; Lera Boroditsky, "How Language Shapes Thought: The Languages We Speak Affect Our Perceptions of the World," *Scientific American* (February 2011): 63–65.
3. Deutscher, *Through the Language Glass*, 187–93.
4. Guy Deutscher, "You Are What You Speak," *New York Times Magazine* (August 29, 2010), 42–47; Vyvyan Evans, *The Language Myth: Why Language Is Not an Instinct* (Cambridge, UK: Cambridge University Press, 2014), 1–22.
5. Cited in Benjamin Lee Whorf, *Language, Thought and Reality*, ed. John B. Carroll (Cambridge, MA: MIT Press, 1956), 134.
6. Ibid., 240.
7. Ibid., 143–54, 243–44.
8. Ibid., 213–14, 241.
9. Deutscher, "You Are What You Speak."
10. Steven Pinker, *The Language Instinct: How the Mind Creates Language* (New York: HarperPerennial, 1994), 4–11, 48; Evans, *Language Myth*.
11. Daniel L. Everett, "Cultural Constraints on Grammar and Cognition in Pirahã: Another Look at the Design Features of Human Language," *Current Anthropology* 46, no. 4 (2005): 621–46.
12. Peter Gordon, "Numerical Cognition without Words: Evidence from Amazonia," *Science* 306, no. 15 (October 2004): 496–99.
13. Guillaume Thierry et al., "Unconscious Effects of Language-Specific Terminology on Preattentive Color Perception," *Proceedings of the National Academy of Sciences* 106, no. 11 (March 17, 2009): 4567–70.
14. Viorica Marian and Margarita Kaushanskaya, "Language Context Guides Memory Content," *Psychonomic Bulletin & Review* 14, no. 5 (2007): 925–33.
15. Caitlin M. Fausey and Lera Boroditsky, "Who Dunnit? Cross-Linguistic Differences in Eye-Witness Memory," *Psychonomic Bulletin & Review* 18 (2011): 150–57.
16. Alexia Panayiotou, "Switching Codes, Switching Code: Bilinguals' Emotional Responses in English and Greek," *Journal of Multilingual and Multicultural Development* 25, nos. 2–3 (2004): 124–39. For a sampling of other crosslinguistic studies demonstrating how language affects thought, see Li Hai Tan et al., "Language Affects Patterns of Brain Activation Associated with Perceptual Decision," *Proceedings of the National Academy*

of Sciences 105, no. 10 (2008): 4004–9; Alfred H. Bloom, *The Linguistic Shaping of Thought: A Study in the Impact of Language on Thinking in China and the West* (New York: Psychology Press, 1981), 13–14, 31.

17. Thierry et al., "Unconscious Effects"; Nicholas Evans, "Context, Culture, and Structuration in the Languages of Australia," *Annual Review of Anthropology*, no. 32 (2003): 13–40. See also Michael Tomasello, *The Cultural Origins of Human Cognition* (Cambridge, MA: Harvard University Press, 2000), 164.

18. Deutscher, *Through the Language Glass*, 187–93, 233–34.

19. Bloom, *Linguistic Shaping of Thought*, 73.

20. Alfred H. Bloom, "Caution: The Words You Use May Affect What You Say: A Response to Au," *Cognition* 17, no. 3 (1984): 275–87. For more on the cognitive neuroscience of how this process works, see John D. E. Gabrieli, Russell A. Poldrack, and John E. Desmond, "The Role of Left Prefrontal Cortex in Language and Memory," *Proceedings of the National Academy of Sciences* 95 (1998): 906–13; Susan Bookheimer, "Functional MRI of Language: New Approaches to Understanding the Cortical Organization of Semantic Processing," *Annual Review of Neuroscience* 25 (2002): 151–88; W. Tecumseh Fitch, "The Biology and Evolution of Language: 'Deep Homology' and the Evolution of Innovation," in *The Cognitive Neurosciences*, ed. Michael S. Gazzaniga (Cambridge, MA: MIT Press, 2009); Joaquin M Fuster, *The Prefrontal Cortex* (New York: Elsevier, 1988), 307–10.

21. Bloom, *Linguistic Shaping of Thought*, 59–60, 86. See also Alistair C. Crombie, "Designed in the Mind: Western Visions of Science, Nature and Humankind," *History of Science* 26 (1988): 1–12. Crombie notes how science itself may be viewed as a certain type of language, working through the same process of merging concepts into a more abstract concept and then giving it a name, thus creating a new building block for further conceptualizations.

22. Everett, "Cultural Constraints"; Evans, "Context, Culture"; Nicholas Evans and Stephen C. Levinson, "The Myth of Language Universals: Language Diversity and Its Importance for Cognitive Science," *Behavioral and Brain Sciences* 32, no. 5 (2009): 429–92.

23. Michael Tomasello, "Universal Grammar Is Dead," *Behavioral and Brain Sciences* 32, no. 5 (2009): 429–92.

24. Jerome A. Feldman, *From Molecule to Metaphor: A Neural Theory of Language* (Cambridge, Massachusetts: MIT Press, 2008), 101, 136–37, 145–47. See also Theodore L. Brown, *Making Truth: Metaphor in Science* (Urbana, IL: University of Illinois Press, 2003), 145–47.

25. David Luna, Torsten Ringberg, and Laura A. Peracchio, "One Individual, Two Identities: Frame Switching among Biculturals," *Journal of Consumer Research* 35, no. 2 (2008): 279–93. For an in-depth investigation in how culture helps construct our sense of self, see Hazel Rose Markus and Shinobu Kitayama, "Culture and the Self:

Implications for Cognition, Emotion, and Motivation," *Psychological Review* 98, no. 2 (1991): 224–53; also Steven J. Heine et al., "Is There a Universal Need for Positive SelfRegard?," *Psychological Review* 106, no. 4 (1999): 766–94.

26. George Lakoff and Mark Johnson, *Metaphors We Live By* (Chicago: University of Chicago, 2003), 145–46.

27. Tomasello, *Cultural Origins*, 168–69.

28. See Richard E. Nisbett et al., "Culture and Systems of Thought: Holistic versus Analytic Cognition," *Psychological Review* 108, no. 2 (2001): 291–310.

29. For perspectives on the Whorfian effects of the two languages, see A. C. Graham, *Disputers of the Tao: Philosophical Argument in Ancient China* (Peru, IL: Open Court, 1989), 389; François Jullien, *Vital Nourishment: Departing from Happiness* (New York: Zone Books, 2007), 12–13.

30. David W. Anthony, *The Horse, the Wheel and Language: How Bronze Age Riders from the Eurasian Steppes Shaped the Modern World* (Princeton, NJ: Princeton University Press, 2007), 19–20; H. D. F. Kitto, *The Greeks* (London: Penguin Books, 1991), 26–28. Although this chapter only focuses on the distinction between Greek and Chinese, a similar distinction may be discerned between Sanskrit—another Indo-European language—and Chinese. For an in-depth analysis of the unique characteristics of Sanskrit and its contrast to Chinese and Japanese linguistic structures, see Hajime Nakamura, *Ways of Thinking of Eastern Peoples: India-China-Tibet-Japan* (Honolulu: University of Hawaii Press, 1964), especially chapters 1–13.

31. Alan Watts, *Tao: The Watercourse Way* (New York: Pantheon Books, 1975), 11; Denis Noble, *The Music of Life: Biology beyond Genes* (Oxford: Oxford University Press, 2006), 139–40; Chad Hansen, "Chinese Language, Chinese Philosophy, and 'Truth,'" *Journal of Asian Studies* 44, no. 3 (May 1985): 491–519; Toby E. Huff, *The Rise of Early Modern Science: Islam, China, and the West* (New York: Cambridge University Press, 2006), 296; Peter Watson, *Ideas: A History of Thought and Invention, from Fire to Freud* (New York: HarperCollins, 2005, 302–3.

32. Bloom, *Linguistic Shaping of Thought*, 35–36; David L. Hall and Roger T. Ames, *Thinking through Confucius* (Albany, NY: State University of New York Press, 1987), 263.

33. Chad Hansen, *A Daoist Theory of Chinese Thought: A Philosophical Interpretation* (New York: Oxford University Press, 2000), 41; Watson, *Ideas*, 300.

34. Yu Huan Zhang and Ken Rose, *Who Can Ride the Dragon? An Exploration of the Cultural Roots of Traditional Chinese Medicine* (Taos, NM: Paradigm Publications, 1995), 30; Nisbett et al., "Culture and Systems of Thought."

35. Hansen, *Daoist Theory*, 41; Zhang and Rose, *Who Can Ride the Dragon?*, 27; Joseph Needham, *Science and Civilisation in China*, vol. 2, *History of Scientific Thought* (London: Cambridge University Press, 1972), 199–200.

36. Steven Roger Fischer, *A History of Writing* (London: Reaktion Books, 2001), 180–81; Zhang and Rose, *Who Can Ride the Dragon?*, 27; W. C. Hannas, *Writing on the*

Wall: How Asian Orthography Curbs Creativity (Philadelphia: University of Pennsylvania Press, 2003), 6–7; Neil Postman, *Technopoly: The Surrender of Culture to Technology* (New York: Vintage Books, 1993), 124; F. S. C. Northrop, *The Meeting of East and West: An Inquiry concerning World Understanding* (Woodbridge, CT: Ox Bow Press, 1979).

37. Richard E. Nisbett and Takahiko Masuda, "Culture and Point of View," *Proceedings of the National Academy of Sciences* 100, no. 19 (2003): 11163–70.

38. G. E. R. Lloyd, *Early Greek Science: Thales to Aristotle* (New York: W. W. Norton, 1970), 13–15.

39. Geoffrey Lloyd and Nathan Sivin, *The Way and the Word: Science and Medicine in Early China and Greece* (New Haven, CT: Yale University Press, 2002), 186–87. See also G. E. R. Lloyd, "On the 'Origins' of Science," *Proceedings of the British Academy* 105 (1999): 1–16; Richard E. Nisbett, *The Geography of Thought: How Asians and Westerners Think Differently . . . and Why* (New York: Free Press, 2004), 37–38.

40. Lloyd and Sivin, *Way and the Word*, 241; Joseph Needham, *The Grand Titration: Science and Society in East and West* (Toronto: University of Toronto Press, 1969), 243; Stephen Gaukroger, *The Emergence of a Scientific Culture* (New York: Oxford University Press, 2006), 33–34.

41. Lloyd and Sivin, *Way and the Word*, 47–51, 66–67.

42. Jack Goody and Ian Watt, "The Consequences of Literacy," *Comparative Studies in Society and History* 5, no. 3 (1963): 337. See also Nisbett, *Geography of Thought*, 25–27, 174–76.

43. Nisbett and Masuda, "Culture and Point of View."

44. Needham, *Science and Civilisation*, 303; Hall and Ames, *Thinking through Confucius*, 20; Herrlee G. Creel, *What Is Taoism? And Other Studies in Chinese Cultural History* (Chicago: University of Chicago Press, 1970), 35; Mark Elvin, "Was There a Transcendental Breakthrough in China?," in *The Origins and Diversity of Axial Age Civilizations*, ed. Shmuel N. Eisenstadt (Albany: State University of New York Press, 1986).

45. Harold D. Roth, *Original Tao: Inward Training and the Foundations of Taoist Mysticism* (New York: Columbia University Press, 1999), 42; Francis. M. Cornford, *Plato's Cosmology: The Timaeus of Plato* (Indianapolis: Hackett, 1937/1997), 282.

46. See Jullien, *Vital Nourishment*, 56–57; also Ning Yu, "Heart and Cognition in Ancient Chinese Philosophy," *Journal of Cognition and Culture* 7, nos. 1–2 (2007): 27–47; Donald J. Munro, *A Chinese Ethics for the New Century: The Ch'ien Mu Lectures in History and Culture, and Other Essays on Science and Confucian Ethics* (Hong Kong: Chinese University Press, 2005), 24; Julia Ching, *To Acquire Wisdom: The Way of Wang Yang-Ming* (New York: Columbia University Press, 1976), 88.

47. Roth, *Original Tao*, 84; Jullien, *Vital Nourishment*, 15; Yu-Lan Fung, *A Short History of Chinese Philosophy: A Systematic Account of Chinese Thought from Its Origins to the Present Day* (New York: Free Press, 1976), 287.

48. Russell Kirkland, "Meditation and 'Spiritual Hygiene' in Late Classical

Texts," University of Georgia, retrieved August 22, 2012 from: https://faculty.franklin.uga.edu/kirkland/sites/faculty.franklin.uga.edu.kirkland/files/HYGIENE.pdf.

49. Zhang and Rose, *Who Can Ride the Dragon?*, 74; Jullien, *Vital Nourishment*, 16; Elvin, "Transcendental Breakthrough?"; Graham, *Disputers of the Tao*, 16; David Loy, "Transcendence East and West," *Man and World* 26, no. 4 (1993): 403–27. See also Ho Peng Yoke, *Li, Qi, and Shu: An Introduction to Science and Civilization in China* (Mineola, NY: Dover Publications, 1985), 186–87; Derk Bodde, "Dominant Ideas in the Formation of Chinese Culture," *Journal of the American Oriental Society* 62, no. 4 (1942): 29–99.

50. Donald J. Munro, *The Concept of Man in Early China* (Ann Arbor, MI: Center for Chinese Studies, University of Michigan, 1969), 48, 54; Nisbett, *Geography of Thought*, 5; Nisbett and Masuda, "Culture and Point of View"; Hansen, *Daoist Theory*, 315–16; Elvin, "Transcendental Breakthrough?"

51. Nisbett et al., "Culture and Systems of Thought"; Hansen, "Chinese Language"; Nisbett, *Geography of Thought*, xvi–xx.

52. Nisbett et al., "Culture and Systems of Thought"; Hansen, "Chinese Language"; Nisbett, *Geography of Thought*, xvi–xx; Nisbett and Masuda, "Culture and Point of View"; A. Boduroglu, P. Shah, and R. E. Nisbett, "Cultural Differences in Allocation of Attention in Visual Information Processing," *Journal of Cross-Cultural Psychology* 40 (3): 349–60.

53. Markus and Kitayama, "Culture and the Self "; Heine et al., "Is There a Universal Need"; Masami Takahashi, "Toward a Culturally Inclusive Understanding of Wisdom: Historical Roots in the East and West," *International Journal of Aging and Human Development* 51, no. 3 (2000): 217–30.

54. Heine et al., "Is There a Universal Need."

55. Steven J. Heine and Takeshi Hamamura, "In Search of East Asian SelfEnhancement," *Personality and Social Psychology* 11, no. 1 (2007): 4–27.

56. Joseph Henrich, Steven J. Heine, and Ara Norenzayan, "The Weirdest People in the World?," *Behavioral and Brain Sciences* 33, no. 2–3 (2010): 61–135.

Chapter 11. Pathways to Monotheism in Israel and Alexandria

1. We can't be sure that the *habiru* really were the original Hebrews. It's a theory that's been floated since the early twentieth century, and although some have rejected it, it appears reasonable to many scholars. See Edward Chiera, "Habiru and Hebrews," *American Journal of Semitic Languages and Literatures* 49, no. 2 (1933): 115–24. For a more recent perspective, see Nadav Na'aman, "Ḫabiru-Like Bands in the Assyrian Empire and Bands in Biblical Historiography," *Journal of the American Oriental Society* 120, no. 4 (2000): 621–24. For an argument against this linkage, see A. Rainey, "*Shasu* or *Habiru*: Who Were the Early Israelites?," *Biblical Archaeology Review* 34, no. 6 (2008). For other

discussions of the *habiru* origins of the Hebrew people in the context of early monotheistic thought, see Julian Jaynes, *The Origin of Consciousness in the Breakdown of the Bicameral Mind* (New York: Mariner Books, 2000), 293–94; also Norman Cohn, *Cosmos, Chaos and the World to Come: The Ancient Roots of Apocalyptic Faith* (New Haven, CT: Yale Nota Bene, 2001), 128–29.

2. Richard Elliott Friedman, *Who Wrote the Bible?* (New York: HarperCollins, 1997), 17–27; Israel Finkelstein and Neil Asher Silberman, *The Bible Unearthed: Archaeology's New Vision of Ancient Israel and the Origin of Its Sacred Texts* (New York: Touchstone, 2002), 10–13.

3. Mark S. Smith, *The Early History of God: Yahweh and the Other Deities in Ancient Israel* (Grand Rapids, MI: Wm. B. Eerdmans, 2002), 32, 64, 91–94.

4. 4Ibid., 34; Exodus 6:2–3.

5. Exodus 15:1–18; Smith, *Early History of God*, 2–4; Cohn, *Cosmos, Chaos*, 152; Benjamin Uffenheimer, "Myth and Reality in Ancient Israel," in *The Origins and Diversity of Axial Age Civilizations*, ed. Shmuel N. Eisenstadt (Albany: State University of New York Press, 1986), 145–46. For other Biblical passages acknowledging the existence of other gods, see Exodus 20; Joshua 22:22; Micah 4:5; Judges 11:24.

6. Citations from Isaiah compiled in Robert Wright, *The Evolution of God* (New York: Hachette Book Group, 2009), 172; also see V. Nikiprowetzky, "Ethical Monotheism," *Dædalus* 104, no. 2 (1975): 69–89, for a similar compilation.

7. Finkelstein and Silberman, *Bible Unearthed*, 130–45.

8. Ibid., 196–99, 158–59, 214–21.

9. Ibid., 230, 243; Friedman, *Who Wrote the Bible?*, 87.

10. Friedman, *Who Wrote the Bible?*, 207–16; Finkelstein and Silberman, *Bible Unearthed*, 246–49.

11. Finkelstein and Silberman, *Bible Unearthed*, 249–74; see also Friedman, *Who Wrote the Bible?*, 91–96.

12. Friedman, *Who Wrote the Bible?*, 96–143; Finkelstein and Silberman, *Bible Unearthed*, 275–80.

13. Finkelstein and Silberman, *Bible Unearthed*, 275–80.

14. Ibid., 289–95; 2 Kings 25:7.

15. Psalm 137, cited in Friedman, *Who Wrote the Bible?*, 152–53. See also Cohn, *Cosmos, Chaos*, 148–49; Finkelstein and Silberman, *Bible Unearthed*, 305–6.

16. Wright, *Evolution of God*, 169–71.

17. Ibid., 171; Cohn, *Cosmos, Chaos*, 143–49; Nikiprowetzky, "Ethical Monotheism"; Smith, *Early History of God*, 191–96; Friedman, *Who Wrote the Bible?*, 154.

18. Isaiah 45:1–3; Finkelstein and Silberman, *Bible Unearthed*, 298, 308; Cohn, *Cosmos, Chaos*, 157.

19. Cohn, *Cosmos, Chaos*, 157; Finkelstein and Silberman, *Bible Unearthed*, 297–301; Friedman, *Who Wrote the Bible?*, 159–60.

20. See Wright, *Evolution of God*, 100, 124–25; Uffenheimer, "Myth and Reality," 136–37.

21. The loan words are *misharum* (equity) and *andurarum* (freedom) in Isaiah 11:4–5. See C. C. Lamberg-Karlovsky, "The Near Eastern 'Breakout' and the Mesopotamian Social Contract," in *The Breakout: The Origins of Civilization*, ed. Martha LambergKarlovsky (Cambridge, MA: Peabody Museum, 2000). See also Finkelstein and Silberman, *Bible Unearthed*, 285–87.

22. Morton Smith, "II Isaiah and the Persians," *Journal of the American Oriental Society* 83, no. 4 (September–December 1963): 415–21; John H. Walton, *Ancient Near Eastern Thought and the Old Testament: Introducing the Conceptual World of the Hebrew Bible* (Grand Rapids, MI: Baker, 2006), 154–55; Jean Bottéro, *Religion in Ancient Mesopotamia*, trans. Teresa Lavender Fagan (Chicago: University of Chicago Press, 2001), 169; Erik Hornung, *Conceptions of God in Ancient Egypt: The One and the Many*, trans. John Baines (New York: Cornell University Press, 1996), 253–54.

23. Shmuel N. Eisenstadt, "The Axial Age Breakthrough in Ancient Israel," in *Axial Age Civilizations*, ed. Eisenstadt, 128. See also Friedman, *Who Wrote the Bible?*, 236–38; Wright, *Evolution of God*, 99; Uffenheimer, "Myth and Reality in Ancient Israel."

24. Jan Assmann, *The Search for God in Ancient Egypt*, trans. David Lorton (Ithaca, NY: Cornell University Press, 2001), 238.

25. Uffenheimer, "Myth and Reality."

26. Robert M. Grant, *Gods and the One God* (Philadelphia: Westminster Press, 1986).

27. Uffenheimer, "Myth and Reality," 150–51.

28. Andrew Louth, *The Origins of the Christian Mystical Tradition: From Plato to Denys* (New York: Oxford University Press, 2007), 188; Charles Freeman, *The Closing of the Western Mind: The Rise of Faith and the Fall of Reason* (New York: Vintage Books, 2005), 234; Edward Grant, *Science and Religion, 400 BC to AD 1550: From Aristotle to Copernicus* (Baltimore: Johns Hopkins University Press, 2004), 100.

29. Justin Pollard and Howard Reid, *The Rise and Fall of Alexandria* (New York: Viking Penguin, 2006), 70.

30. 30. Ibid., 70–73.

31. 31. Ibid., 194–97.

32. Quoted in Freeman, *The Closing of the Western Mind*, 73–74; also in Jonathan Kirsch, *God against the Gods: The History of the War between Monotheism and Polytheism* (New York: Penguin Compass, 2004), 119. See also Pollard and Reid, *Rise and Fall of Alexandria*, 194–97; Wright, *Evolution of God*, 217.

33. Grant, *Gods and the One God*, 85; Pollard and Reid, *Rise and Fall of Alexandria*, 194–97. See also Freeman, *Closing of the Western Mind*, 73–74; Wright, *Evolution of God*, 219; Richard Tarnas, *The Passion of the Western Mind: Understanding the Ideas That Have Shaped Our World View* (New York: Ballantine Books, 1991), Kindle locations 9121–29.

34. Cited in Wright, *Evolution of God*, 230. See also Paul S. MacDonald, *The History of the Concept of the Mind: Speculations about Soul, Mind and Spirit from Homer to Hume* (Aldershot: Ashgate, 2003), 92–94.

35. Grant, *Gods and the One God*, 99–100; Louth, *Christian Mystical Tradition*, 35; MacDonald, *Concept of the Mind*, 111; Pollard and Reid, *Rise and Fall of Alexandria*, 247; Christiane L. Joost-Gaugier, *Measuring Heaven: Pythagoras and His Influence on Thought and Art in Antiquity and the Middle Ages* (New York: Cornell University Press, 2006), 104.

36. MacDonald, *Concept of the Mind*, 112; Stephen R. L. Clark, "Plotinian Dualisms and the 'Greek' Ideas of Self," *Journal of Chinese Philosophy* 36, no. 4 (2009): 554–67; E. R. Dodds, *Pagan and Christian in an Age of Anxiety* (London: Cambridge University Press, 1965), 86; Caroline F. E. Spurgeon, *Mysticism in English Literature* (Charleston, SC: BiblioBazaar, 1913/2007), 21.

37. Freeman, *Closing of the Western Mind*, 81, 296.

38. Dodds, *Pagan and Christian*, 3; Kirsch, *God against the Gods*, 93, 213–68; Warren Treadgold, *A Concise History of Byzantium* (New York: Palgrave, 2001), 44.

39. Kirsch, *God against the Gods*, 90, 95.

Chapter 12. Sinful Nature: The Dualistic Cosmos of Christianity

1. John 1:1 (New International Version).

2. John 1:2–3, 14–18 (NIV). See Charles Freeman, *The Closing of the Western Mind: The Rise of Faith and the Fall of Reason* (New York: Vintage Books, 2005), 128–31; also Robert Wright, *The Evolution of God* (New York: Hachette Book Group, 2009), 240–41.

3. Freeman, *Closing of the Western Mind*, 128–31; Richard Tarnas, *The Passion of the Western Mind: Understanding the Ideas That Have Shaped Our World View* (New York: Ballantine Books, 1991), Kindle locations 2053–63.

4. Tarnas, *Passion of the Western Mind*, Kindle locations 2032–43, 2053–63, 2977–82; Freeman, *Closing of the Western Mind*, 142–44; Paul S. MacDonald, *The History of the Concept of the Mind: Speculations about Soul, Mind and Spirit from Homer to Hume* (Aldershot: Ashgate, 2003), 142–43; E. R. Dodds, *The Greeks and the Irrational* (Berkeley, CA: University of California Press, 1951), 266; Peter Watson, *Ideas: A History of Thought and Invention, from Fire to Freud* (New York: HarperCollins, 2005), 219–20; George Lakoff and Mark Johnson, *Philosophy in the Flesh: The Embodied Mind and Its Challenge to Western Thought* (New York: Basic Books, 1999), 372; Justin Pollard and Howard Reid, *The Rise and Fall of Alexandria* (New York: Viking Penguin, 2006), 222; Edward Grant, *Science and Religion, 400 BC to AD 1550: From Aristotle to Copernicus* (Baltimore: Johns Hopkins University Press, 2004), 107.

5. Freeman, *Closing of the Western Mind*, 75; E. R. Dodds, *Pagan and Christian in an Age of Anxiety* (London: Cambridge University Press, 1965), 29–35; Grant, *Science and Religion*, 107; Watson, *Ideas*, 229–30; Robert M. Grant, *Gods and the One God* (Philadelphia: Westminster Press, 1986), 86.

6. Dodds, *Greeks and the Irrational*, 32–33.

7. Freeman, *Closing of the Western Mind*, 107.

8. Galatians 3:26–29 (NIV).

9. Freeman, *Closing of the Western Mind*, 107–14. See also Wright, *Evolution of God*, 264–70.

10. Romans 7:7 (King James Version); Galatians 3:10 (NIV). See Wright, *Evolution of God*, 108–9.

11. Romans 7:15–24 (NIV).

12. See Lancelot Law Whyte, *The Next Development in Mankind* (New Brunswick, NJ: Transaction Publishers, 1944/2003), 171–72, for an insightful discussion on this aspect of Paul's thought.

13. Romans 6:23 (NIV). See also Romans 7:5, 6, 11 (NIV).

14. Galatians 5:17 (American Standard Version); Romans 1:24–32; 1 Corinthians 6:9–11, cited in Freeman, *Closing of the Western Mind*, 110, 121.

15. Cited in Freeman, *Closing of the Western Mind* 236–37.

16. Ibid., 122.

17. Grant, *Gods and the One God*, 90–91; MacDonald, *Concept of the Mind*, 129.

18. Dodds, *Pagan and Christian*, 17, 33, 128; Watson, *Ideas*, 229–30; Freeman, *Closing of the Western Mind*, 147; Andrew Louth, *The Origins of the Christian Mystical Tradition: From Plato to Denys* (New York: Oxford University Press, 2007), 71.

19. Dodds, *Pagan and Christian*, 132; Freeman, *Closing of the Western Mind*, 277–78.

20. *City of God*, cited in Freeman, *Closing of the Western Mind*, 278–81; Tarnas, *Passion of the Western Mind*, loc. 2066–72; MacDonald, *Concept of the Mind*, 145, 354. See also Alfred North Whitehead, *Adventures of Ideas* (New York: Free Press, 1933), 106.

21. *Confessions*, cited in David L. Hall and Roger T. Ames, *Thinking from the Han: Self, Truth and Transcendence in Chinese and Western Culture* (Albany: State University of New York Press, 1998), 47. See also Karen Armstrong, *A Short History of Myth* (Edinburgh: Canongate Books, 2005), 112–13; Tarnas, *Passion of the Western Mind*, loc. 2835–44; Louth, *Christian Mystical Tradition*, 144.

22. Freeman, *Closing of the Western Mind*, 283–84.

23. Cited in MacDonald, *Concept of the Mind*, 149–50.

24. Cited in Louth, *Christian Mystical Tradition*, 139. See also Tarnas, *Passion of the Western Mind*, loc. 2757–58; Freeman, *Closing of the Western Mind*, 150.

25. Joseph Needham, *Science and Civilisation in China*, vol. 2, *History of Scientific Thought* (London: Cambridge University Press, 1972), 302; Arthur O. Lovejoy, *The Great Chain of Being: A Study of the History of an Idea* (Cambridge, MA: Harvard University Press, 1936/1964), 198–99.

26. Needham, *History of Scientific Thought*, 302; Lovejoy, *Great Chain of Being*, 198–99.

27. Freeman, *Closing of the Western Mind*, 242–44.

28. John 12:25 (NIV).

29. Cited in Aldous Huxley, *The Perennial Philosophy* (New York: HarperCollins, 1945/2004).

30. Cited in Theodore Roszak, "What a Piece of Work is Man: Humanism, Religion, and the New Cosmology," *Network: The Scientific and Medical Network Review* (1999): 3–5; *Hymne of Heavenly Beautie*, cited in Caroline F. E. Spurgeon, *Mysticism in English Literature* (Charleston, SC: BiblioBazaar, 1913/2007), 24–25.

31. E. A. Burtt, *The Metaphysical Foundations of Modern Science* (New York: Dover Publications, 1924/2003), 105.

32. René Descartes, *Meditations on First Philosophy*, cited in Nicholas Humphrey, *A History of the Mind: Evolution and the Birth of Consciousness* (New York: Copernicus/SpringerVerlag, 1992).

33. Meditations 3 and 4, cited in Thomas McEvilley, *The Shape of Ancient Thought: Comparative Studies in Greek and Indian Philosophies* (New York: Allworth Press, 2002), 180.

34. *Discourse on Method*, cited in Daniel C. Dennett, *Consciousness Explained* (New York: Penguin, 1993), 30.

35. Cited in MacDonald, *Concept of the Mind*, 279–80.

36. Cited in Paul Wienpahl, *The Radical Spinoza* (New York: New York University Press, 1979), 16.

37. *Discourse on Method*, cited in Owen Flanagan, *The Problem of the Soul: Two Visions of Mind and How to Reconcile Them* (New York: Basic Books, 2002), 173.

38. Cited in MacDonald, *Concept of the Mind*, 279–81.

39. George Lakoff and Mark Johnson, *Philosophy in the Flesh: The Embodied Mind and Its Challenge to Western Thought* (New York: Basic Books, 1999), 400–408.

40. Cited in Fritjof Capra, *The Turning Point: Science, Society, and the Rising Culture* (New York: Bantam Books, 1988), 61.

41. Lynn Margulis and Dorion Sagan, *What Is Life?* (Berkeley/Los Angeles: University of California Press, 2000), 38; Hans Jonas, *The Phenomenon of Life: Toward a Philosophical Biology* (Evanston, IL: Northwestern University Press, 2001), 72, 54–55; Guoping Zhao, "Two Notions of Transcendence: Confucian Man and Modern Subject," *Journal of Chinese Philosophy* 36, no. 3 (September 2009): 391–407; Leo Marx, "The Idea of Nature in America," *Dædalus* (Spring 2008): 8–21.

42. Gordon H. Orians, "Nature & Human Nature," *Dædalus* (Spring 2008): 39–48; Max Weber, *The Protestant Ethic and the Spirit of Capitalism*, trans. Steven Kalberg (Los Angeles: Roxbury, 1920/2002), xxxi–xxxiii, xxxix, lxxvii–lxxx, 100–101.

43. Humphrey Taylor, "The Religious and Other Beliefs of Americans 2003," (New York: HarrisInteractive, 2003); Humphrey Taylor, "What People Do and Do Not Believe In," (New York: HarrisInteractive, 2009).

Chapter 13. The Scourge of Monotheistic Intolerance

1. Jonathan Kirsch, *God against the Gods: The History of the War between Monotheism and Polytheism* (New York: Penguin Compass, 2004), 24–28; Erik Hornung, *Conceptions of God in Ancient Egypt: The One and the Many*, trans. John Baines (New York: Cornell University Press, 1996), 244–50.

2. Kirsch, *God against the Gods*, 24–28; Hornung, *Conceptions of God*, 244–50; Jan Assmann, *Moses the Egyptian: The Memory of Egypt in Western Monotheism* (Cambridge, MA: Harvard University Press, 1997), 24–25; Jan Assmann, *The Search for God in Ancient Egypt*, trans. David Lorton (Ithaca, NY: Cornell University Press, 2001), 199.

3. For other studies linking religious intolerance with monotheism, see Robert Wright, *The Evolution of God* (New York: Hachette Book Group, 2009), 101; Mircea Eliade, *The Myth of the Eternal Return: Cosmos and History*, trans. Willard R. Trask (Princeton, NJ: Princeton University Press, 2005), 109n; Assmann, *Moses the Egyptian*, 1–3; Kirsch, *God against the Gods*, 2.

4. Assmann, *Moses the Egyptian*, 1–3; John H. Walton, *Ancient Near Eastern Thought and the Old Testament: Introducing the Conceptual World of the Hebrew Bible* (Grand Rapids, MI: Baker, 2006), 111–12.

5. Walton, *Ancient Near Eastern Thought*, 111–12.

6. Jean Bottéro, *Religion in Ancient Mesopotamia*, trans. Teresa Lavender Fagan (Chicago: University of Chicago Press, 2001), 96–97.

7. Cited in Wright, *Evolution of God*, 82. See also Assmann, *Moses the Egyptian*, 45–46; Marc Van De Mieroop, *A History of the Ancient Near East ca. 3000–323 BC*, Blackwell History of the Ancient World (Malden, MA: Blackwell, 2004), 260.

8. Charles Freeman, *The Closing of the Western Mind: The Rise of Faith and the Fall of Reason* (New York: Vintage Books, 2005), 68–69.

9. Deuteronomy 20 (NIV). The word *genocide* was only coined in 1944 in an attempt to describe the Holocaust, and it might be argued that it is an anachronism to use it to describe events of an earlier era. However, in the case of the Bible, we are not examining a mere historical document from ancient times; rather, we are investigating the values propagated by a living document regularly cited by authorities across the world. Therefore, it is important to understand the values promoted in the Bible in terms that are relevant to our modern age.

10. Deuteronomy 7, NIV.

11. Joshua 6, NIV.

12. 1 Samuel 15, NIV.

13. F. M. Cornford, *From Religion to Philosophy: A Study in the Origins of Western Speculation* (New York: Dover Publications, 1912/2004), 44.

14. Freeman, *Closing of the Western Mind*, 69–70.

15. Ibid., 230. See also Kirsch, *God against the Gods*, 7; Robert M. Grant, *Gods and the One God* (Philadelphia: Westminster Press, 1986), 172–73.

16. E. R. Dodds, *Pagan and Christian in an Age of Anxiety* (London: Cambridge University Press, 1965); Richard Tarnas, *The Passion of the Western Mind: Understanding the Ideas That Have Shaped Our World View* (New York: Ballantine Books, 1991), Kindle locations 2347–57.

17. Mark 16:15, NIV.

18. Cited in Kirsch, *God against the Gods*, 10.

19. Tertullian, *The Prescriptions against the Heretics*, trans. S. L. Greenslade (Early Latin Theology, Library of Christian Classics V, 1956), 19–64, http://www.tertullian.org/articles/greenslade_prae/greenslade_prae.htm; Freeman, *Closing of the Western Mind*, vii.

20. Warren Treadgold, *A Concise History of Byzantium* (New York: Palgrave, 2001), 83; Joel Mokyr, *The Lever of Riches: Technological Creativity and Economic Progress* (New York: Oxford University Press, 1990), 201n.

21. Kirsch, *God against the Gods*, 114; Freeman, *Closing of the Western Mind*, 296.

22. David E. Stannard, *American Holocaust: Columbus and the Conquest of the New World* (New York: Oxford University Press, 1992), 190–91. See also Elaine Pagels cited in Jeremy Rifkin, *The Empathic Civilization: The Race to Global Consciousness in a World in Crisis* (New York: Penguin, 2009), 237.

23. Freeman, *Closing of the Western Mind*, 132–33; Stannard, *American Holocaust*, 175–76.

24. Stephen Batchelor, *The Awakening of the West: The Encounter of Buddhism and Western Culture* (Berkeley, CA: Parallax Press, 1994), 83–84.

25. 25. Koran (Pickthall), Suras 2:191; 3:157; 4:74; 9:73; 98:6.

26. Cited in Scott Atran, *In Gods We Trust* (New York: Oxford University Press, 2002), 289–90n; Stannard, *American Holocaust*, 178.

27. Atran, *In Gods We Trust*, 289–90n; John W. Grula, "Pantheism Reconstructed: Ecotheology as a Successor to the Judeo-Christian, Enlightenment, and Postmodernist Paradigms," *Zygon* 43, no. 1 (2008): 159–80. An investigation into Boykin's statement by the Department of Defense in 2004 took no official action against him for his remarks.

28. Hajime Nakamura, *Ways of Thinking of Eastern Peoples: India-China-TibetJapan* (Honolulu: University of Hawaii Press, 1964), 170–72. See also David Loy, "Transcendence East and West," *Man and World* 26, no. 4 (1993): 403–27.

29. John Keay, *India: A History* (New York: Grove Press, 2000), 87–97; Heinrich Zimmer, *Philosophies of India*, ed. Joseph Campbell (Princeton, NJ: Princeton University Press, 1951), 495–98; Aldous Huxley, *The Perennial Philosophy* (New York: HarperCollins, 1945/2004), 199.

30. A. L. Basham, *The Wonder That Was India* (London: Picador, 2004), 347.

31. Keay, *India*, 241; Basham, *Wonder That Was India*, 268.

32. Keay, *India*, 276–78, 316–17; Basham, *Wonder That Was India*, 481–82.

33. Keay, *India*, 429; Basham, *Wonder That Was India*, 482. British misrule can be

considered responsible for some of the worst outbreaks of intolerance between Hindu and Muslim in South Asia. When the British government pulled out of the subcontinent and partitioned it into Pakistan and India, they forced up to twenty-five million Muslims, Hindus, and Sikhs to leave their homes as refugees and catalyzed internecine strife resulting in up to a million deaths. See Paul R. Brass, "The Partition of India and Retributive Genocide in the Punjab, 1946–47: Means, Methods, and Purposes," *Journal of Genocide Research* 5, no. 1 (2003): 71–101.

34. Nakamura, *Ways of Thinking of Eastern Peoples*, 19, 285. See also Derk Bodde, "Dominant Ideas in the Formation of Chinese Culture," *Journal of the American Oriental Society* 62, no. 4 (1942): 293–99.

35. Nakamura, *Ways of Thinking of Eastern Peoples*, 287, 293.

36. Jacques Gernet, *A History of Chinese Civilization* (New York: Cambridge University Press, 2006), 278, 294–95.

37. Ibid., 454–55, 518–20; Thomas David DuBois, *Religion and the Making of Modern East Asia* (New York: Cambridge University Press, 2011), 92–93. See also Wing-tsit Chan, "The Study of Chu Hsi in the West," *Journal of Asian Studies* 35, no. 4 (1976): 555–77.

Chapter 14. Discovering the Principles of Nature in Song China

1. Dieter Kuhn, *The Age of Confucian Rule: The Song Transformation of China* (Cambridge, MA: Belknap Press of Harvard University Press, 2009), 195–204.

2. Jacques Gernet, *A History of Chinese Civilization* (New York: Cambridge University Press, 2006), 320–29; Clive Ponting, *World History: A New Perspective* (London: Pimlico, 2001), 382–89; Janet L. Abu-Lughod, *Before European Hegemony: The World System AD 1250–1350* (New York: Oxford University Press, 1989), 322–34.

3. Gernet, *History of Chinese Civilization*, 338–43; Justin Yifu Lin, "The Needham Puzzle: Why the Industrial Revolution Did Not Originate in China," *Economic Development and Cultural Change* 43, no. 2 (January 1995): 269–92. For all its great achievements, the Song dynasty also had serious shortcomings: it was during this period that foot binding first appeared, an excruciating practice that led to the increased subjugation of women for many centuries to come. See Kuhn, *Age of Confucian Rule*, 261–63.

4. Kuhn, *Age of Confucian Rule*, 120, 99; Gernet, *History of Chinese Civilization*, 344–45.

5. Heinrich Dumoulin, *Zen Buddhism: A History*, Volume I: India and China (Bloomington, IN: World Wisdom, 2005), 64.

6. Ibid., 64–68; Yu-Lan Fung, *A Short History of Chinese Philosophy: A Systematic Account of Chinese Thought from Its Origins to the Present Day* (New York: Free Press, 1976), 241; Glen Wallis, *Basic Teachings of the Buddha: A New Translation and Compilation, with a Guide to Reading the Texts* (New York: Random House, 2007), xiv–xv.

7. Dumoulin, *Zen Buddhism*, 64–65, 266; Fung, *Chinese Philosophy*, 212; Red Pine, *The Zen Teaching of Bodhidharma* (New York: North Point Press, 1987), 115. A. C. Graham, *Disputers of the Tao: Philosophical Argument in Ancient China* (Peru, IL: Open Court, 1989), 172. For valuable discussions of *dharma*, see *The Dhammapada*, trans. Glen Wallis (New York: Random House, 2004), xii; *The Bhagavad Gita*, ed. and trans. Eknath Easwaran (Tomales, CA: Nilgiri Press, 1985).

8. Gernet, *History of Chinese Civilization*, 278; Dumoulin, *Zen Buddhism*, 19, 42; Kuhn, *Age of Confucian Rule*, 111.

9. Dumoulin, *Zen Buddhism*, 277; Julia Ching, *To Acquire Wisdom: The Way of Wang Yang-Ming* (New York: Columbia University Press, 1976), 15.

10. Hu Yin, cited in Joseph Needham, *Science and Civilisation in China*, vol. 2, *History of Scientific Thought* (London: Cambridge University Press, 1972), 411. See also Siu-chi Huang, *Essentials of Neo-Confucianism: Eight Major Philosophers of the Song and Ming Periods* (Westport, CT: Greenwood Press, 1999), 65–66.

11. Dumoulin, *Zen Buddhism*, 268; Fung, *Chinese Philosophy*, 268.

12. Huang, *Essentials of Neo-Confucianism*, 6–7; Carsun Chang, *The Development of Neo-Confucian Thought* (New York: Bookman Associates, 1957), 28; Wing-tsit Chan, "Chu Hsi's Appraisal of Lao Tzu," *Philosophy East and West* 25, no. 2 (April 1975): 131–44; Yu-Lan Fung and Derk Bodde, "The Philosophy of Chu Hsi," *Harvard Journal of Asiatic Studies* 7, no. 1 (1942): 1–51; Yu-Lan Fung and Derk Bodde, "The Rise of Neo-Confucianism and Its Borrowings from Buddhism and Taoism," *Harvard Journal of Asiatic Studies* 7, no. 2 (1942): 89–125.

13. Huang, *Essentials of Neo-Confucianism*, 20–24; Needham, *Science and Civilisation*, 460–66.

14. Huang, *Essentials of Neo-Confucianism*, 60, 62, 68; Wing-tsit Chan, "The Evolution of the Confucian Concept of Jên," *Philosophy East and West* 4, no. 4 (January 1955): 295–319.

15. Wing-tsit Chan, "Neo-Confucianism and Chinese Scientific Thought," *Philosophy East and West* 6, no. 4 (1957): 309–32; Huang, *Essentials of Neo-Confucianism*, 85; Graham, *Disputers of the Tao*, 313–14. The word *li* discussed in this chapter should not be confused with the ancient Confucian word *li* meaning ritual discussed in Chapter 9. They are unrelated words in Chinese with different roots.

16. Julia Ching, *The Religious Thought of Chu Hsi* (New York: Oxford University Press, 2000), 167.

17. Huang, *Essentials of Neo-Confucianism*, 131–33; Ching, *Chu Hsi*, 29; Ho Peng Yoke, *Li, Qi, and Shu: An Introduction to Science and Civilization in China* (Mineola, NY: Dover Publications, 1985), 5, 27; Stephen C. Angle, *Sagehood: The Contemporary Significance of Neo-Confucian Philosophy* (New York: Oxford University Press, 2009), 40. Given the frequent usage of the terms li and qi in the remainder of this chapter, neither word will henceforth be italicized in the interest of ease in reading the text.

18. Ching, *Chu Hsi*, 195–96; Fung and Bodde, "Philosophy of Chu Hsi," 12–14, 19; David L. Hall and Roger T. Ames, *Thinking from the Han: Self, Truth and Transcendence in Chinese and Western Culture* (Albany: State University of New York Press, 1998), 228, 234. The dualistic misinterpretation of li and qi continues into modern times: see W. Scott Morton and Charlton M. Lewis, *China: Its History and Culture* (New York: McGraw-Hill, 2005), 113–14, for a recent discussion of li and qi that continues to use the erroneous Platonic paradigm.

19. Abu-Lughod, *Before European Hegemony*, 322–23; Simon Winchester, *The Man Who Loved China: The Fantastic Story of the Eccentric Scientist Who Unlocked the Mysteries of the Middle Kingdom* (New York: HarperCollins, 2008), 28–29.

20. Needham, *Science and Civilisation*, 475–76. See also Brook Ziporyn, "Form, Principle, Pattern or Coherence? Li in Chinese Philosophy," *Philosophy Compass* 3, no. 3 (2008): 401–22; Kirill O. Thompson, "Li and Yi as Immanent: Chu Hsi's Thought in Practical Perspective," *Philosophy East and West* 38, no. 1 (1988): 30–46.

21. Needham, *Science and Civilisation*, 558, 473; Alan Watts, *Tao: The Watercourse Way* (New York: Pantheon Books, 1975), 45–46. See also Joseph Needham, "Human Laws and Laws of Nature in China and the West (II): Chinese Civilization and the Laws of Nature," *Journal of the History of Ideas* (1951): 194–230.

22. Needham, *Science and Civilisation*, 558; Ching, *Chu Hsi*, 46; David Yu, "The Conceptions of Self in Whitehead and Chu Hsi," *Journal of Chinese Philosophy* 7, no. 2 (1980): 153–73.

23. Cited in Needham, "Human Laws," 220–21.

24. Needham, *Science and Civilisation*, 479–80.

25. Fritjof Capra, *The Tao of Physics: An Exploration of the Parallels between Modern Physics and Eastern Mysticism* (Boston: Shambhala Publications, 1999), 158–160, 213–14; Fung and Bodde, "Rise of Neo-Confucianism," 23.

26. See, for example, Stuart Kauffman, *At Home in the Universe: The Search for Laws of Self-Organization and Complexity* (New York: Oxford University Press, 1995); Evan Thompson, *Mind in Life: Biology, Phenomenology, and the Sciences of Mind* (Cambridge, MA: Harvard University Press, 2007); Ricard Solé and Brian Goodwin, *Signs of Life: How Complexity Pervades Biology* (New York: Basic Books, 2000); Ursula Goodenough, *The Sacred Depths of Nature* (New York: Oxford University Press, 1998); Scott Camazine et al., *Self-Organization in Biological Systems* (Princeton, NJ: Princeton University Press, 2001).

27. Gerald M. Edelman, and Giulio Tononi, *A Universe of Consciousness: How Matter Becomes Imagination* (New York: Basic Books, 2000), 18–19, 144.

28. Carl R. Woese, "A New Biology for a New Century," *Microbiology and Molecular Biology Reviews* (2004): 173–86.

29. Gregory Bateson, *Mind and Nature: A Necessary Unity* (Cresskill, NJ: Hampton Press, 2002), 7, 10 (italics in the original).

30. Cited in Angle, *Sagehood*, 42–43, 86; Needham, *Science and Civilisation*, 484; and

Hoyt Cleveland Tillman, *Confucian Discourse and Chu Hsi's Ascendancy* (Honolulu: University of Hawaii Press, 1992), 10.

31. Ching, *Chu Hsi*, 37–44; Huang, *Essentials of Neo-Confucianism*, 130; Thompson, "Li and Yi"; Needham, *Science and Civilisation*, 466.

32. Angle, *Sagehood*, 44–45; Thompson, "Li and Yi"; Ching, *Chu Hsi*, 46.

33. See chapter 6 and chapter 8.

34. Angle, *Sagehood*, 44–45.

35. Angle, *Sagehood*, 32; Ziporyn, "Form, Principle."

36. Ching, *Chu Hsi*, 130; Chan, "Neo-Confucianism and Chinese Scientific Thought,"; Huang, *Essentials of Neo-Confucianism*, 138.

37. Chan, "Neo-Confucianism and Chinese Scientific Thought"; William Ernest Hocking, "Chu Hsi's Theory of Knowledge," *Harvard Journal of Asiatic Studies* 1, no. 1 (1936): 109–27.

38. See, for example, Christopher Boehm, *Moral Origins: The Evolution of Virtue, Altruism, and Shame* (New York: Basic Books, 2012); Patricia Smith Churchland, *Braintrust: What Neuroscience Tells Us about Morality* (Princeton, NJ: Princeton University Press, 2011); Sam Harris, *The Moral Landscape: How Science Can Determine Human Values* (New York: Free Press, 2011).

39. Angle, *Sagehood*, 35, 156.

40. Thompson, "Li and Yi."

41. Cited in Chan, "Neo-Confucianism and Chinese Scientific Thought." See also James Gleick, *Chaos: Making a New Science* (New York: Penguin, 1987), 81–118.

42. Lynn Margulis and Dorion Sagan, *What Is Life?* (Berkeley/Los Angeles: University of California Press, 2000), 4; Barry A. Cipra, "A Healthy Heart is a Fractal Heart," *SIAM News* 36, no. 7 (2003); Gleick, *Chaos*, 108–10; György Buzsáki, *Rhythms of the Brain* (New York: Oxford University Press, 2006), 126–27; Solé and Goodwin, *Signs of Life*, 147–51; Iain D. Couzin, "Collective Cognition in Animal Groups," *Trends in Cognitive Sciences* 13, no. 1 (2008): 36–43; Ashley J. W. Ward et al., "Quorum DecisionMaking Facilitates Information Transfer in Fish Shoals," *Proceedings of the National Academy of Sciences* 105, no. 19 (2008): 6948–53.

43. Huang, *Essentials of Neo-Confucianism*, 148–49; Thompson, "Li and Yi."

44. Goodenough, *Sacred Depths of Nature*, 46.

45. Angle, *Sagehood*, 170; Huang, *Essentials of Neo-Confucianism*, 85, 93–98; Harold D. Roth, *Original Tao: Inward Training and the Foundations of Taoist Mysticism*, Translations from the Asian Classics (New York: Columbia University Press, 1999), 42.

46. Hall and Ames, *Thinking from the Han*, 309n; Wing-tsit Chan, "The Study of Chu Hsi in the West," *Journal of Asian Studies* 35, no. 4 (1976): 555–77; Donald J. Munro, *A Chinese Ethics for the New Century: The Ch'ien Mu Lectures in History and Culture, and Other Essays on Science and Confucian Ethics* (Hong Kong: Chinese University Press, 2005), 24.

47. Fung and Bodde, "The Philosophy of Chu Hsi," 9; Huang, *Essentials of Neo-Confucianism*, 113, 137.

48. Fung and Bodde, "Philosophy of Chu Hsi," 9; Huang, *Essentials of NeoConfucianism*, 110; Angle, *Sagehood*, 34.

49. Luo Qinshun, cited in Angle, *Sagehood*, 41–42. See also Fung and Bodde, "Philosophy of Chu Hsi," 9.

50. Luiz Pessoa, "On the Relationship between Emotion and Cognition," *Nature Reviews: Neuroscience* 9 (February 2008): 148–58; Antonio Damasio, *The Feeling of What Happens: Body and Emotion in the Making of Consciousness* (New York: Harcourt Inc., 1999).

51. *Doctrine of the Mean*, cited in Huang, *Essentials of Neo-Confucianism*, 152–53.

52. Angle, *Sagehood*, 67–68, 70, 104, 241n.

53. Huang, *Essentials of Neo-Confucianism*, 195–97, 204–7; Angle, *Sagehood*, 19–20; Ching, *To Acquire Wisdom*, 107–110.

54. Huang, *Essentials of Neo-Confucianism*, 195–97, 204–7.

55. Needham, *Science and Civilisation*, 468–69.

56. Angle, *Sagehood*, 13–22; John Borthrong, "Chu Hsi's Ethics: *Jen* and *Ch'eng*," *Journal of Chinese Philosophy* 14, no. 2 (1987): 161–78.

57. Angle, *Sagehood*, 19; Ching, *To Acquire Wisdom*, 53–54.

58. Huang, *Essentials of Neo-Confucianism*, 116, 198–200.

59. Ibid., 109–10.

60. Hall and Ames, *Thinking from the Han*, 31–32; Benjamin I. Schwartz, *The World of Thought in Ancient China* (Cambridge, MA: Belknap Harvard University Press, 1985) 75–85; Donald J. Munro, *The Concept of Man in Early China* (Ann Arbor, MI: Center for Chinese Studies, University of Michigan, 1969), 71–73.

61. Tillman, *Confucian Discourse*, 17; Chan, "Evolution of the Confucian Concept of Jên"; Chan, "Study of Chu Hsi in the West," 563–64; Huang, *Essentials of NeoConfucianism*, 72.

62. Cited in Ching, *Chu Hsi*, 26–27; Chan, "Evolution of the Confucian Concept of Jên"; Angle, *Sagehood*, 68.

63. Chan, "Evolution of the Confucian Concept of Jên."

64. Quoted in Matthieu Ricard and Trinh Xuan Thuan, *The Quantum and the Lotus* (New York: Three Rivers Press, 2001), 72.

65. Huang, *Essentials of Neo-Confucianism*, 93–96.

66. 66. Ibid., 198; Angle, *Sagehood*, 70–71, 102–3, 122.

67. Chan, "Evolution of the Confucian Concept of Jên"; Huang, *Essentials of NeoConfucianism*, 115; Ching, *To Acquire Wisdom*, 44, 67.

68. Angle, *Sagehood*, 117–18, 122.

69. From *Dreams of a Final Theory* by Steven Weinberg, quoted in Stuart Kauffman, *At Home in the Universe*, ix.

70. Ricard and Thuan, *Quantum and the Lotus*, 50; Needham, *Science and Civilisation*, 492–93; Ching, *Chu Hsi*, 61; Joseph Needham, *The Grand Titration: Science and Society in East and West* (Toronto: University of Toronto Press, 1969), 39; Ravi Ravindra, "Notes

on Scientific Research and Spiritual Search," *Parabola* 33, no. 3 (Fall 2008): 7–11; Yung Sik Kim, "Some Aspects of the Concept of Ch'i in Chu Hsi," *Philosophy East and West* 34, no. 1 (1984): 25–36.

71. Borthrong, "Chu Hsi's Ethics: *Jen* and *Ch'eng*."

Chapter 15. "To Command the World": Metaphors of Nature

1. Carolyn Merchant, *The Death of Nature: Women, Ecology and the Scientific Revolution* (New York: HarperCollins, 1980), 168.

2. *Novum Organum*, cited in Clive Ponting, *A New Green History of the World: The Environment and the Collapse of Great Civilizations* (New York: Penguin, 2007), 123–24. See also Peter Pesic, "Wrestling with Proteus: Francis Bacon and the 'Torture' of Nature," *Isis* 90, no. 1 (1999): 81–94.

3. Citations in Merchant, *Death of Nature*; Fritjof Capra, *The Turning Point: Science, Society, and the Rising Culture* (New York: Bantam Books, 1988), 56.

4. William Leiss, *The Domination of Nature* (Montreal: McGill-Queen's University Press, 1994), 55–59; Theodore Roszak, *Where the Wasteland Ends: Politics and Transcendence in Postindustrial Society* (Garden City, NY: Anchor Books, 1973), 215.

5. Cited in Merchant, *Death of Nature*, 188–89.

6. George Lakoff and Mark Johnson, *Metaphors We Live By* (Chicago: University of Chicago, 2003), 145–46.

7. Joseph Needham, *Science and Civilisation in China*, vol. 2, *History of Scientific Thought* (London: Cambridge University Press, 1972), 533.

8. Isaiah 45:12; Jeremiah 5:22 (KJV).

9. Cited in Joseph Needham, *The Grand Titration: Science and Society in East and West* (Toronto: University of Toronto Press, 1969), 307; Merchant, *Death of Nature*, 205.

10. Genesis 1:26–28 (KJV).

11. Psalms 8:3–8 (KJV).

12. Arthur O. Lovejoy, *The Great Chain of Being: A Study of the History of an Idea* (Cambridge, MA: Harvard University Press, 1936/1964), 186–87. See also Lynn White Jr., "The Historical Roots of Our Ecological Crisis," *Science* 155, no. 3767 (1967): 1203–7; John W. Grula, "Pantheism Reconstructed: Ecotheology as a Successor to the Judeo-Christian, Enlightenment, and Postmodernist Paradigms," *Zygon* 43, no. 1 (2008): 159–80; E. A. Burtt, *The Metaphysical Foundations of Modern Science* (New York: Dover Publications, 1924/2003), 18; *Deep Ecology for the Twenty-First Century*, ed. George Sessions (Boston: Shambhala Publications, 1995), 160.

13. Cited in Lovejoy, *Great Chain of Being*, 186–87.

14. Richard Leakey and Roger Lewin, *The Sixth Extinction* (New York: Anchor Books, 1995), 80.

15. Citations in Leiss, *Domination of Nature*, 33; George Sessions, "Deep Ecology as Worldview," in *Worldviews and Ecology: Religion, Philosophy, and the Environment*, ed. Mary Evelyn Tucker and John A. Grim (Maryknoll, NY: Orbis Books, 1994).

16. Merchant, *Death of Nature*, 185.

17. Leiss, *Domination of Nature*, 31–32; Ponting, *New Green History*, 123–24.

18. Isaiah 40:12; Job 38:4–6 (KJV).

19. Joel Mokyr, *The Lever of Riches: Technological Creativity and Economic Progress* (New York: Oxford University Press, 1990), 202; Toby E. Huff, *The Rise of Early Modern Science: Islam, China, and the West* (New York: Cambridge University Press, 2006), 182; Alfred W. Crosby, *The Measure of Reality: Quantification and Western Society, 1250–1600* (New York: Cambridge University Press, 1997), 83–84. See also Merchant, *Death of Nature*, 223; Needham, *Grand Titration*, 84.

20. Merchant, *Death of Nature*, 128–29, 212, 226; Capra, *Turning Point*, 61.

21. Merchant, *Death of Nature*, 226.

22. Cited in ibid., 143.

23. Ibid., 115. See also Capra, *Turning Point*, 107–8; Leo Marx, "The Idea of Nature in America," *Dædalus* (Spring 2008): 8–21.

24. Richard Dawkins, *The Blind Watchmaker* (New York: Norton, 1986).

25. Dawkins, *Blind Watchmaker*; Evan Thompson, *Mind in Life: Biology, Phenomenology, and the Sciences of Mind* (Cambridge, MA: Harvard University Press, 2007), 180; Steven Rose, *Lifelines: Life beyond the Gene* (New York: Oxford University Press, 1997), 109. For more detailed explanations of the topic, see Thompson, *Mind in Life*; Rose, *Lifelines*; and Fritjof Capra and Pier Luigi Luisi, *The Systems View of Life: A Unifying Vision* (New York: Cambridge University Press, 2014).

26. Cited in Lovejoy, *Great Chain of Being*, 232.

27. Ponting, *New Green History*, 123–24.

28. Ibid., 255; Thom Hartmann, *The Last Hours of Ancient Sunlight* (New York: Three Rivers Press, 2004), 141–42.

29. Peter Drucker, *Innovation and Entrepreneurship* (1985), 30, cited in *Deep Ecology*, ed. Sessions, 12–13.

30. John M. Broder, "Climate Change Doubt Is Tea Party Article of Faith," *New York Times*, October 20, 2010.

31. Thomas Berry, *The Great Work: Our Way into the Future* (New York: Three Rivers Press, 1999), 44.

32. Jan Assmann, *The Search for God in Ancient Egypt*, trans. David Lorton (Ithaca, NY: Cornell University Press, 2001), 58; Erik Hornung, *Conceptions of God in Ancient Egypt: The One and the Many*, trans. John Baines (New York: Cornell University Press, 1996), 200.

33. John A. Grim, "Native North American Worldviews and Ecology," in *Worldviews and Ecology: Religion, Philosophy, and the Environment*, ed. Mary Evelyn Tucker and John A. Grim (Maryknoll, NY: Orbis Books, 1994), 43. See also Ursula Goodenough,

"Reflections on Scientific and Religious Metaphor," *Zygon* 35, no. 2 (2000): 233–40; Deborah Bird Rose, *Nourishing Terrains: Australian Aboriginal Views of Landscape and Wilderness* (Canberra: Australian Heritage Commission, 1996), 10.

34. Cited in Ponting, *New Green History*, 128. It should be noted that the authenticity of Chief Seattle's letter is disputed, and the earliest written version dates to several decades later. Nevertheless, there is little doubt that it was an accurate rendition of the prevailing indigenous worldview.

35. Cited in Merchant, *Death of Nature*, 28.

36. Cited in Julia Ching, *The Religious Thought of Chu Hsi* (New York: Oxford University Press, 2000), 26–27.

37. Ching, *Chu Hsi*, 6; G. E. R. Lloyd, *The Ambitions of Curiosity: Understanding the World in Ancient Greece and China* (Cambridge: Cambridge University Press, 2002), 138; Needham, *Science and Civilisation*, 290, 379; Yu Huan Zhang and Ken Rose, *Who Can Ride the Dragon? An Exploration of the Cultural Roots of Traditional Chinese Medicine* (Taos, NM: Paradigm Publications, 1995), 256; Derk Bodde, "Dominant Ideas in the Formation of Chinese Culture," *Journal of the American Oriental Society* 62, no. 4 (1942): 293–99; Joseph Needham, "History and Human Values: A Chinese Perspective for World Science and Technology," *Philosophy and Social Action* 11, no. 1 (1976).

38. Needham, *Science and Civilisation*, 55–56; Ching, *Religious Thought of Chu Hsi*, 6.

39. Needham, "History and Human Values," 22.

40. *The Tao Te Ching: A New Translation with Commentary*, trans. Ellen M. Chen (St. Paul, MN: Paragon House, 1989), chaps. 34, 51 in 137–38, 175.

41. Chen, *Tao Te Ching*, chap. 29, 126–27.

42. Chen, *Tao Te Ching*, chap. 15, 90; W. Scott Morton and Charlton M. Lewis, *China: Its History and Culture* (New York: McGraw-Hill, 2005), 109–10; J. J. Clarke, *The Tao of the West: Western Transformations of Taoist Thought* (New York: Routledge, 2000), 153–54; Mary Wyman, "Chinese Mysticism and Wordsworth," *Journal of the History of Ideas* 10, no. 4 (1949): 517–38.

43. Paul R. Ehrlich, *Human Natures: Genes, Cultures, and the Human Prospect* (New York: Penguin, 2002), 255.

44. Wangari Maathai, "The Tree of Life," *Parabola* (2007): 13–17.

Chapter 16. Great Rats: The Story of Power and Exploitation

1. Leslie A. White, "Energy and the Evolution of Culture," *American Anthropologist* 45, no. 3 (1943): 335–56.

2. David Price, "Energy and Human Evolution," *Population and Environment* 16, no. 4 (1995): 301–19.

3. White, "Energy and the Evolution of Culture," 336–38.

4. Peter J. Richerson and Robert Boyd, "Complex Societies: The Evolutionary Origins of a Crude Superorganism," *Human Nature* 10, no. 3 (1999): 253–89; Peter J. Richerson, Robert Boyd, and Robert L. Bettinger, "Was Agriculture Impossible during the Pleistocene but Mandatory during the Holocene? A Climate Change Hypothesis," *American Antiquity* 66, no. 3 (2001): 387–411.

5. Bruce Smith, quoted in Paul R. Ehrlich, *Human Natures: Genes, Cultures, and the Human Prospect* (New York: Penguin, 2002), 227.

6. Richard Leakey and Roger Lewin, *The Sixth Extinction* (New York: Anchor Books, 1995), 127–28.

7. See Craig Dilworth, *Too Smart for Our Own Good: The Ecological Predicament of Humankind* (New York: Cambridge University Press, 2010).

8. Clive Ponting, *A New Green History of the World: The Environment and the Collapse of Great Civilizations* (New York: Penguin, 2007), 78–82; Jared Diamond, *Collapse: How Societies Choose to Fail or Survive* (New York: Penguin Books, 2005), 157–77, quoting David Webster.

9. Diamond, *Collapse*, 136–56; 79–135.

10. Ponting, *New Green History*, 74.

11. Cited in Michael Marshall, "Climate Change: The Great Civilisation Destroyer?," *New Scientist*, no. 2876 (2012): 32–36. Not all agrarian civilizations inevitably experienced the long-term decline in productivity described here. In the Nile valley, the annual flooding fostered simple irrigation systems that had no deleterious effect on soil productivity. However, in large regions of Eurasia, including both preindustrial Europe and China, occasional breakthroughs in technology and crop utilization would lead to a population increase until a new carrying capacity was reached, with the result that, in both regions, according to Ponting, "the overwhelming majority of the population lived permanently on the verge of starvation." See Ponting, *New Green History*, 69–72, 82–85, 90–97.

12. Robert Wright, *The Evolution of God* (New York: Hachette Book Group, 2009), 47; Alain Testart et al., "The Significance of Food Storage among Hunter-Gatherers: Residence Patterns, Population Densities, and Social Inequalities [and Comments and Reply]," *Current Anthropology* 23, no. 5 (1982): 523–37; David W. Anthony, *The Horse, the Wheel and Language: How Bronze Age Riders from the Eurasian Steppes Shaped the Modern World* (Princeton, NJ: Princeton University Press, 2007), 132–33.

13. Bruce G. Trigger, *Understanding Early Civilizations* (New York: Cambridge University Press, 2003), 44–45, 50.

14. Ibid., 153, 188; Marc Van De Mieroop, *A History of the Ancient Near East ca. 3000–323 BC* (Malden, MA: Blackwell, 2004), 144, 183–84.

15. Trigger, *Understanding Early Civilizations*, 142; Samuel Noah Kramer, *The Sumerians: Their History, Culture, and Character* (Chicago: University of Chicago Press, 1963), 79.

16. Cited in Joseph Needham, *Science and Civilisation in China*, vol. 2, *History of Scientific Thought* (London: Cambridge University Press, 1972), 105–8.

17. Peter J. Wilson, *The Domestication of the Human Species* (New Haven, CT: Yale University Press, 1988), 127–28.

18. Ponting, *New Green History*, 267; Janet L. Abu-Lughod, *Before European Hegemony: The World System AD 1250–1350* (New York: Oxford University Press, 1989), 156.

19. Jeremy Rifkin, *The Empathic Civilization: The Race to Global Consciousness in a World in Crisis* (New York: Penguin, 2009), 226–27; Ponting, *New Green History*, 268.

20. Charles Freeman, *The Closing of the Western Mind: The Rise of Faith and the Fall of Reason* (New York: Vintage Books, 2005), 205–6.

21. Jared Diamond, *Guns, Germs, and Steel: A Short History of Everybody for the Last 13,000 Years* (London: Vintage, 2005).

22. Diamond is aware of this question, which he phrases, "Why Europe, not China," and he attempts to answer it by focusing, once again, on environmental factors. He also points to some practical reasons for the contrast between Columbus's and Zheng's missions. For example, Admiral Zheng was forced to comply with the centralized decision-making of the Chinese imperial palace, while Columbus could canvass different European monarchs with his ideas until he found one who was supportive and would fund him. However, in my opinion, these represent—in Diamond's own parlance—proximate rather than ultimate factors in the contrast between the two civilizations. See Diamond, *Guns, Germs, and Steel*, 409–17.

23. Joseph Needham, *The Grand Titration: Science and Society in East and West* (Toronto: University of Toronto Press, 1969), 86.

24. Ibid., 70–71.

25. See "Proto-Indo-Europeans: Might Is Right" in chapter 6.

26. Stephen Batchelor, *The Awakening of the West: The Encounter of Buddhism and Western Culture* (Berkeley: Parallax Press, 1994), 172. See also Jacques Gernet, *A History of Chinese Civilization* (New York: Cambridge University Press, 2006), 97.

27. Abu-Lughod, *Before European Hegemony*, 275–76, 290, 361.

28. John Keay, *India: A History* (New York: Grove Press, 2000), 71.

29. Justin Pollard and Howard Reid, *The Rise and Fall of Alexandria* (New York: Viking Penguin, 2006), 5–6.

30. Pali for *dharma*. See "Dharma and Tao" in chapter 14 for a discussion of the meaning of *dharma*.

31. Keay, *India*, 91–92.

32. Cited in ibid.

33. Cited in ibid.

34. Ibid., 127–28. See also A. L. Basham, *The Wonder That Was India* (London: Picador, 2004), 487; William Dalrymple, "The Great and Beautiful Lost Kingdoms," *New York Review of Books* (May 21, 2015).

35. Joel Mokyr, *The Lever of Riches: Technological Creativity and Economic Progress* (New York: Oxford University Press, 1990), 188.

36. Steven Mintz and Sara McNeil, "The Meaning of America," *Digital History*, 2016, http://www.digitalhistory.uh.edu/disp_textbook_print.cfm?smtid=3&psid=57 (accessed June 20, 2016); H. Koning, *Columbus: His Enterprise: Exploding the Myth* (New York: Monthly Review Press, 1976), 53–54.

37. David E. Stannard, *American Holocaust: Columbus and the Conquest of the New World* (New York: Oxford University Press, 1992), 75–81; Diamond, *Guns, Germs, and Steel*, 67–74.

38. Diamond, *Guns, Germs, and Steel*, 74–81.

39. Anthony Aveni, *Empires of Time: Calendars, Clocks, and Cultures* (Boulder, CO: University Press of Colorado, 2002), 241; Stannard, *American Holocaust*, 76.

40. Stannard, *American Holocaust*, 109–11.

41. Cited in ibid.

42. Cited in ibid.

43. Cited in ibid., 227.

44. Ibid., x, 74–75, 95, 221–22; Clive Ponting, *World History: A New Perspective* (London: Pimlico, 2001), 212.

45. Stannard, *American Holocaust*, xii, 286.

46. Eduardo Galleano, *Open Veins of Latin America: Five Centuries of the Pillage of a Continent* (New York: Monthly Review Press, 1997), 31–41. Estimates for the exact number of people who died at Potosí are difficult to establish, and some experts believe the toll to be less than Galeano's estimate of eight million. See Patrick Greenfield, "Story of Cities #6: How Silver Turned Potosí into 'the First City of Capitalism,'" *Guardian*, March 21, 2016.

47. Cited in Stannard, *American Holocaust*, 64.

48. Ibid., 65–66.

49. Ibid., 218; Arthur Koestler, *Janus: A Summing Up* (New York: Random House, 1978), 95.

50. Cited in Stannard, *American Holocaust*, 113–14.

51. Thom Hartmann, *The Last Hours of Ancient Sunlight* (New York: Three Rivers Press, 2004), 224; F. S. C. Northrop, *The Meeting of East and West: An Inquiry concerning World Understanding* (Woodbridge, CT: Ox Bow Press, 1979), 68.

52. Cited in Stannard, *American Holocaust*, 233–34. See also William Leiss, *The Domination of Nature* (Montreal: McGill-Queen's University Press, 1994), 74.

53. Cited in Max Weber, *The Protestant Ethic and the Spirit of Capitalism*, trans. Steven Kalberg (Los Angeles: Roxbury, 1920/2002), xxxvi–xxxvii. (Italics in the original.)

54. *Meditations Sacrae*, cited in Owen Flanagan, *The Really Hard Problem: Meaning in a Material World* (Cambridge, MA: MIT Press, 2007), 221; *The Great Instauration*, cited in Hans Jonas, *The Phenomenon of Life: Toward a Philosophical Biology* (Evanston: Northwestern University Press, 2001), 188–89.

55. See Leiss, *Domination of Nature*, xiv.

56. M. E. Townsend, *European Colonial Expansion since 1871* (Chicago: J. Lippincott, 1941), 19; A. Supan, *Die territoriale Entwicklung der Europaischen Kolonien* (Gotha, 1906), 254, https://www.mtholyoke.edu/acad/intrel/pol116/colonies.htm (accessed July 10, 2013).

57. Ponting, *New Green History*, 175–76.

58. Ibid., 175–76, 197–98. See also C. Erickson, "Review: Indentured Labour in the British Empire 1834–1920. By Kay Saunders," *Population Studies* 39, no. 1 (1985): 1184–85.

59. Cited in Thomas McEvilley, *The Shape of Ancient Thought: Comparative Studies in Greek and Indian Philosophies* (New York: Allworth Press, 2002), xxi, xxiv.

60. David J. Depew and Bruce H. Weber, *Darwinism Evolving: Systems Dynamics and the Genealogy of Natural Selection* (Cambridge, MA: MIT Press, 1996), 156–59.

61. Cited in Stannard, *American Holocaust*, 244.

62. Isabel Ortiz and Matthew Cummins, "Global Inequality: Beyond the Bottom Billion—A Rapid Review of Income Distribution in 141 Countries," (New York: UNICEF, 2011), 45.

63. Cited in Stephen Gaukroger, *The Emergence of a Scientific Culture* (New York: Oxford University Press, 2006), 39.

Chapter 17. The Enigma of the Scientific Revolution

1. Alfred W. Crosby, *The Measure of Reality: Quantification and Western Society, 1250–1600* (New York: Cambridge University Press, 1997), 3; Janet L. AbuLughod, *Before European Hegemony: The World System AD 1250–1350* (New York: Oxford University Press, 1989), 106.

2. Justin Yifu Lin, "The Needham Puzzle: Why the Industrial Revolution Did Not Originate in China," *Economic Development and Cultural Change* 43, no. 2 (January 1995): 269–92.

3. Alexander Koyré and Herbert Butterfield, both quoted in Steven Shapin, *The Scientific Revolution* (Chicago: University of Chicago Press, 1998), 1–4. Some modern historians, such as Shapin, have questioned whether "revolution" is the appropriate word to apply to this transition, but few disagree with the proposition that a major transformation in thought occurred during this time.

4. Clive Ponting, *World History: A New Perspective* (London: Pimlico, 2001), 301–58.

5. Ibid., 336–37, 368; A. I. Sabra, "The Appropriation and Subsequent Naturalization of Greek Science in Medieval Islam: A Preliminary Statement," *History of Science* 25, no. 69 (1987): 223–43.

6. Sabra, "Appropriation of Greek Science"; David C. Lindberg, *The Beginnings of Western Science: The European Scientific Tradition in Philosophical, Religious, and Institutional*

Context, Prehistory to AD 1450 (Chicago: University of Chicago Press, 2007), 174; Alan Cromer, *Uncommon Sense: The Heretical Nature of Science* (New York: Oxford University Press, 1993) Kindle locations 1281–84, 1303–4.

7. G. E. R. Lloyd, *Early Greek Science: Thales to Aristotle* (New York: W. W. Norton, 1970), 80–98; Justin Pollard and Howard Reid, *The Rise and Fall of Alexandria* (New York: Viking Penguin, 2006), 201–6; Arthur Koestler, *The Sleepwalkers: A History of Man's Changing Vision of the Universe* (London: Penguin, 1989), 69–72; Toby E. Huff, *The Rise of Early Modern Science: Islam, China, and the West* (New York: Cambridge University Press, 2006), 57–58.

8. Huff, *Rise of Early Modern Science*, 61–62. See also Sabra, "Appropriation of Greek Science," 238.

9. Edward Grant, *Science and Religion, 400 BC to AD 1550: From Aristotle to Copernicus* (Baltimore: Johns Hopkins University Press, 2004), 230–31.

10. Sabra, "Appropriation of Greek Science," 230; Reza Aslan, *No God but God: The Origins, Evolution, and Future of Islam* (New York: Random House, 2006), 153–55.

11. Aslan, *No God but God*, 153–55; Grant, *Science and Religion*, 235–37; Huff, *Rise of Early Modern Science*, 110–11.

12. Grant, *Science and Religion*, 237; Huff, *Rise of Early Modern Science*, 153.

13. Sabra, "Appropriation of Greek Science," 232–33; Grant, *Science and Religion*, 239–40; Edward Grant, *The Foundations of Modern Science in the Middle Ages: Their Religious, Institutional, and Intellectual Contexts* (New York: Cambridge University Press, 1996), 178–79.

14. Grant, *Science and Religion*, 239–40.

15. Sabra, "Appropriation of Greek Science," 239–40; Grant, *Science and Religion*, 237–38.

16. Grant, *Science and Religion*, 237–38; Grant, *Foundations of Modern Science*, 180–81; Huff, *Rise of Early Modern Science*, 113.

17. Grant, *Science and Religion*, 238–39.

18. Joel Mokyr, *The Lever of Riches: Technological Creativity and Economic Progress* (New York: Oxford University Press, 1990), 189; Huff, *Rise of Early Modern Science*, 231–32; Cromer, *Uncommon Sense*, loc. 1324.

19. Joseph Needham, *The Grand Titration: Science and Society in East and West* (Toronto: University of Toronto Press, 1969), 65–71; Abu-Lughod, *Before European Hegemony*, 322–24.

20. Abu-Lughod, *Before European Hegemony*, 323–34; Ponting, *World History*, 382–89; Jacques Gernet, *A History of Chinese Civilization* (New York: Cambridge University Press, 2006), 325–26.

21. Gernet, *History of Chinese Civilization*, 341.

22. Lin, "Needham Puzzle," 270–71.

23. Ibid., 283–84; Ponting, *World History*, 388–89; Gernet, *History of Chinese*

Civilization, 271–75, 347–48; Mark Elvin, *The Pattern of the Chinese Past: A Social and Economic Interpretation* (Stanford, CA: Stanford University Press, 1972); Nathan Sivin, "Why the Scientific Revolution Did Not Take Place in China—or Did It?" *Environmentalist* 5, no. 1 (1985): 39–50.

24. Sivin, "Scientific Revolution"; Nathan Sivin, "Review: Joseph Needham. Science and Civilization in China, Volume 7: The Social Background. Part 2, General Conclusions and Reflections," *China Review International* 12, no. 2 (Fall 2005): 297–307.

25. Huff, *Rise of Early Modern Science*, 10, 216, 291; Mokyr, *Lever of Riches*, 218–19. For other examples of the view of China's "failure" to follow the Western path, see D. S. Landes, *The Wealth and Poverty of Nations* (New York: W. W. Norton, 1998), 55, who writes of "China's failure to realize its potential"; Kenneth Pomeranz, *The Great Divergence* (Princeton, NJ: Princeton University Press, 2000), who describes the "failure of [the Chinese] economy to grow as fast as that of western Europe"; and Robert Wright, *Nonzero: The Logic of Human Destiny* (New York: Vintage Books, 2000), who exclaims, "Now that we know how close China came to having its own industrial revolution, its failure to actually have one is all the more inexcusable!"

26. A. C. Graham, *Disputers of the Tao: Philosophical Argument in Ancient China* (Peru, IL: Open Court, 1989), 317; Yu Huan Zhang and Ken Rose, *Who Can Ride the Dragon? An Exploration of the Cultural Roots of Traditional Chinese Medicine* (Taos, NM: Paradigm Publications, 1995), 134.

27. Cited in Sally Dugan and David Dugan, *The Day the World Took Off: The Roots of the Industrial Revolution* (Macmillan, 2000), 142.

28. W. Scott Morton and Charlton M. Lewis, *China: Its History and Culture* (New York: McGraw-Hill, 2005), 99–100.

29. Needham, *Grand Titration*, 119–20.

30. *Zhuangzi*, chap. 12, cited in Joseph Needham, *Science and Civilisation in China*, vol. 2, *History of Scientific Thought* (London: Cambridge University Press, 1972), 124; also in *The Tao Te Ching: A New Translation with Commentary*, trans. Ellen M. Chen (St. Paul, MN: Paragon House, 1989), 229.

31. Morton and Lewis, *China*, 161; Mokyr, *Lever of Riches*, 233n. The fear of the destabilizing impact of technology can be seen in other East Asian cultures. For example, in Japan, guns were introduced by the Portuguese in the mid-sixteenth century and at first were widely accepted, only to be banned later because of worries that they would have a destabilizing impact on society. See Dugan and Dugan, *Day the World Took Off*, 144.

32. Cited in Needham, *Science and Civilisation*, 28.

33. Daniel Boorstein, *The Discoverers: A History of Man's Search to Know His World and Himself* (New York: Vintage, 1985), 196–99.

34. Barry Cunliffe, *Europe between the Oceans, 9000 BC–AD 1000* (New Haven, CT: Yale University Press, 2008); Pomeranz, *Great Divergence*; Crosby, *Measure of Reality*, 53–54; Mokyr, *Lever of Riches*, 207; Daniel Chirot, "The Rise of the West," *American*

Sociological Review 50 (1985): 181–95; Stephen Gaukroger, *The Emergence of a Scientific Culture* (New York: Oxford University Press, 2006), 31.

35. Cromer, *Uncommon Sense*, locs. 1829–37; Abu-Lughod, *Before European Hegemony*, 224.

36. Ernest Gellner, *Plough, Sword, and Book: The Structure of Human History* (Chicago: University of Chicago Press, 1988), 199; Gernet, *History of Chinese Civilization*, 347–48; José Ignacio Cabezón, "Buddhism and Science: On the Nature of the Dialogue," in *Buddhism and Science: Breaking New Ground*, ed. B. Alan Wallace (New York: Columbia University Press, 2003), 40; Abu-Lughod, *Before European Hegemony*, 12. (Italics in the original.)

37. Chirot, "Rise of the West," 181.

38. Bryan Appleyard, *Understanding the Present: An Alternative History of Science* (New York: Tauris Parke Paperbacks, 2004), xviii.

39. Gaukroger, *Emergence of a Scientific Culture*, 1.

40. Cromer, *Uncommon Sense*, locs. 307–10, 322, 104; Huff, *Rise of Early Modern Science*, 67; Needham, *Grand Titration.*

Chapter 18. The Language of God: The Emergence of Scientific Cognition

1. Edgar Zilsel, "The Genesis of the Concept of Physical Law," *Philosophical Review* 51, no. 3 (May 1942): 245–79; Joseph Needham, *The Grand Titration: Science and Society in East and West* (Toronto: University of Toronto Press, 1969), 301–302.

2. Geoffrey Lloyd and Nathan Sivin, *The Way and the Word: Science and Medicine in Early China and Greece* (New Haven, CT: Yale University Press, 2002), 165; Alan Cromer, *Uncommon Sense: The Heretical Nature of Science* (New York: Oxford University Press, 1993), Kindle locations 1856–62.

3. Thomas McEvilley, *The Shape of Ancient Thought: Comparative Studies in Greek and Indian Philosophies* (New York: Allworth Press, 2002), 177. This view of truth as the ultimate objective of philosophical investigation is in striking contrast to the views of other major Eurasian civilizations such as China or India. For discussions of how the Chinese had no concept of an abstract, universal truth, see Chad Hansen, "Chinese Language, Chinese Philosophy, and 'Truth,'" *Journal of Asian Studies* 44, no. 3 (May 1985): 491–519; Edward Slingerland, *Effortless Action: Wu-Wei as Conceptual Metaphor and Spiritual Ideal in Early China* (New York: Oxford University Press, 2003), 4. The Indian tradition posited the existence of an all-encompassing truth but differed from the Greeks in seeing it as existing beyond the realm of the intellect. See "Peeling the Onion" in chapter 8.

4. Christiane L. Joost-Gaugier, *Measuring Heaven: Pythagoras and His Influence on Thought and Art in Antiquity and the Middle Ages* (New York: Cornell University Press, 2006), 87–88. See also F. M. Cornford, *From Religion to Philosophy: A Study in the Origins of Western Speculation* (New York: Dover Publications, 1912/2004), 205.

5. Joost-Gaugier, *Measuring Heaven*, 91–92; G. E. R. Lloyd, *Early Greek Science: Thales to Aristotle* (New York: W. W. Norton, 1970), 79.

6. Joost-Gaugier, *Measuring Heaven*, 104–5; Justin Pollard and Howard Reid, *The Rise and Fall of Alexandria* (New York: Viking Penguin, 2006), 66; Edward Grant, *Science and Religion, 400 BC to AD 1550: From Aristotle to Copernicus* (Baltimore: Johns Hopkins University Press, 2004), 19.

7. Joost-Gaugier, *Measuring Heaven*, 118–19.

8. Charles Freeman, *The Closing of the Western Mind: The Rise of Faith and the Fall of Reason* (New York: Vintage Books, 2005), 119–20; Richard Tarnas, *The Passion of the Western Mind: Understanding the Ideas That Have Shaped Our World View* (New York: Ballantine Books, 1991), Kindle locations 2236–45.

9. Freeman, *Closing of the Western Mind*, 316.

10. E. R. Dodds, *Pagan and Christian in an Age of Anxiety* (London: Cambridge University Press, 1965), 120–22; Pollard and Reid, *Rise and Fall of Alexandria*, 215.

11. Grant, *Science and Religion*, 13–14; Freeman, *Closing of the Western Mind*, 286; Zilsel, "Concept of Physical Law"; Stephen Gaukroger, *The Emergence of a Scientific Culture* (New York: Oxford University Press, 2006), 51–52.

12. Tarnas, *Passion of the Western Mind*, locs. 2254–62; Grant, *Science and Religion*, 113; David C. Lindberg, *The Beginnings of Western Science: The European Scientific Tradition in Philosophical, Religious, and Institutional Context, Prehistory to AD 1450* (Chicago: University of Chicago Press, 2007), 149.

13. Lindberg, *Beginnings of Western Science*, 358; Joost-Gaugier, *Measuring Heaven*, 118–19; Edward Grant, *The Foundations of Modern Science in the Middle Ages: Their Religious, Institutional, and Intellectual Contexts* (New York: Cambridge University Press, 1996), 75.

14. Joost-Gaugier, *Measuring Heaven*, 118; Toby E. Huff, *The Rise of Early Modern Science: Islam, China, and the West* (New York: Cambridge University Press, 2006), 98.

15. Grant, *Science and Religion*, 148.

16. Ibid., 149–50.

17. Ibid., 153–54; Lindberg, *Beginnings of Western Science*, 207.

18. Grant, *Science and Religion*, 223; Tina Stiefel, "The Heresy of Science: A Twelfth-Century Conceptual Revolution," *Isis* 68, no. 243 (1977): 347–62.

19. Grant, *Science and Religion*, 166–69; Lynn White Jr., "The Historical Roots of Our Ecological Crisis," *Science* 155, no. 3767 (1967): 1203–7.

20. Grant, *Foundations of Modern Science*, 170–76; Grant, *Science and Religion*, 172; Joost-Gaugier, *Measuring Heaven*, 121–22.

21. Grant, *Foundations of Modern Science*, 84–85, 176; Grant, *Science and Religion*, 229–30.

22. The use of the word "Man," as opposed to "Humanity," goes against the modern convention of avoiding the male gender for references to humanity but is employed here because the patriarchal mind-set of the time saw these relationships

between humanity and God through Reason, Logic, and Truth as overwhelmingly expressed through the male gender.

23. The linkage between scientific and Christian cognition is rarely discussed in modern cultural critiques, but there have been notable exceptions. See, for example, Theodore Roszak, *Where the Wasteland Ends: Politics and Transcendence in Postindustrial Society* (Garden City, NY: Anchor Books, 1973); and Lancelot Law Whyte, *The Next Development in Mankind* (New Brunswick, New Jersey: Transaction Publishers, 1944/2003), 84–85.

24. Grant, *Science and Religion*, 156–63; Philip Ball, "Triumph of the Medieval Mind," *Nature* (2008): 816–18.

25. Grant, *Science and Religion*, 162; Ball, "Triumph of the Medieval Mind," 817; Stiefel, "Heresy of Science"; Peter Watson, *Ideas: A History of Thought and Invention, from Fire to Freud* (New York: HarperCollins, 2005), 376–77.

26. Geoffrey Turner, "St. Thomas Aquinas on the 'Scientific" Nature of Theology," *New Blackfriars* 78, no. 921 (1997): 464–76.

27. Lindberg, *Beginnings of Western Science*, 241; Zilsel, "Concept of Physical Law," 257–58; Grant, *Foundations of Modern Science*, 74; Watson, *Ideas*, 330–31; Joseph Needham, *Science and Civilisation in China*, vol. 2, *History of Scientific Thought* (London: Cambridge University Press, 1972), 538; Bryan Appleyard, *Understanding the Present: An Alternative History of Science* (New York: Tauris Parke Paperbacks, 2004), 23.

28. Grant, *Science and Religion*, 239–40; Grant, *Foundations of Modern Science*, 146; William Leiss, *The Domination of Nature* (Montreal: McGill-Queen's University Press, 1994), 36–37.

29. Gaukroger, *Emergence of a Scientific Culture*, 173; Charles H. Kahn, *Pythagoras and the Pythagoreans: A Brief History* (Indianapolis: Hackett, 2001), 161; E. A. Burtt, *The Metaphysical Foundations of Modern Science* (New York: Dover Publications, 1924/2003), 50, 55.

30. Cited in Arthur Koestler, *The Sleepwalkers: A History of Man's Changing Vision of the Universe* (London: Penguin, 1989), 535; Burtt, *Metaphysical Foundations*, 58.

31. Zilsel, "Concept of Physical Law," 266; Koestler, *Sleepwalkers*, 264; Kahn, *Pythagoras and the Pythagoreans*, 171.

32. Burtt, *Metaphysical Foundations*, 82–90; Alfred W. Crosby, *The Measure of Reality: Quantification and Western Society, 1250–1600* (New York: Cambridge University Press, 1997), 240. Galileo was, in fact, merely repeating what Plato had declared two thousand years earlier when he wrote that "the world was God's epistle written to mankind" and that "it was written in mathematical letters." See Steven Shapin, *The Scientific Revolution* (Chicago: University of Chicago Press, 1998), 58.

33. Burtt, *Metaphysical Foundations*, 82.

34. 34. Ibid., 66.

35. Ibid., 51; Koestler, *Sleepwalkers*, 155.

36. Olaf Pedersen, "Galileo and the Council of Trent: The Galileo Affair Revisited," *Journal for the History of Astronomy* (1983): 1–29.

37. Ibid.

38. Ibid.

39. Burtt, *Metaphysical Foundations*, 38. Even fifty years later, prominent scientist Robert Hooke of the British Royal Society commented on the lack of hard scientific evidence to confirm Copernicus's hypothesis: "Whether the Earth move or stand still hath been a problem, that since Copernicus revived it, hath much exercised the wits of our best modern astronomers and philosophers, amongst which notwithstanding there hath not been any one who hath found out a certain manifestation either of the one or the other." See Dennis Danielson and Christopher M. Graney, "The Case against Copernicus," *Scientific American* (January 2014): 72–76.

40. Cited in Koestler, *Sleepwalkers*, 454–55; Pedersen, "Galileo and the Council," 12.

41. Koestler, *Sleepwalkers*, 360, 373, 450–60. Koestler describes Galileo's preferred method of argumentation as "to make a laughing stock of his opponent in which he invariably succeeded, whether he happened to be in the right or in the wrong." He quotes one witness describing Galileo in action: "Before answering the opposing reasons, he amplified them and fortified them himself with new grounds which appeared invincible, so that, in demolishing them subsequently, he made his opponents look all the more ridiculous." See ibid., 458.

42. 42. Ibid., 479–91.

43. 43. Ibid., 461, 499–501.

44. Pedersen, "Galileo and the Council of Trent," 9. According to Koestler, Galileo in fact showed a pattern of obfuscation and distortion of the facts in his scientific writings. When Kepler published his correct explanation of tides as an effect of the moon's attraction, which contradicted Galileo's own research, Galileo angrily dismissed Kepler's arguments as astrological superstition. Galileo frequently wrote of the Copernican system as if it were proven beyond doubt, when, in fact, there were many deficiencies to the hypothesis that remained unresolved. See Koestler, *Sleepwalkers*, 360, 373, 444–45, 460, 484.

45. Gaukroger, *Emergence of a Scientific Culture*, 3, 506–7.

46. Ibid., 60–61; Zilsel, "Concept of Physical Law," 274–76.

47. Shapin, *Scientific Revolution*, 143–44.

48. David Landes, *Revolution in Time: Clocks and the Making of the Modern World* (Cambridge, MA: Belknap Press, 2000), 40–41.

49. Cited in Needham, *Science and Civilisation in China*, 518.

50. Koestler, *Sleepwalkers*, 404; John D. Barrow, *The Infinite Book* (London: Vintage, 2005), 85–90; Mario Livio, *Is God a Mathematician?* (New York: Simon & Schuster, 2009), 169–70; Hans Jonas, *The Phenomenon of Life: Toward a Philosophical Biology* (Evanston: Northwestern University Press, 2001), 66.

51. Kahn, *Pythagoras and the Pythagoreans*, 172; Appleyard, *Understanding the Present*, 44; Alan B. Wallace, *Choosing Reality: A Buddhist View of Physics and the Mind* (Ithaca, NY:

Snow Lion Publications, 1996), 88; Vasant Natarajan, "What Einstein Meant When He Said 'God Does Not Play Dice . . .'" *Resonance* 13, no. 7 (2008): 655–61.

52. Cited in Matthieu Ricard and Trinh Xuan Thuan, *The Quantum and the Lotus* (New York: Three Rivers Press, 2001), 223. In an interesting anecdote, philosopher Jim Holt relates that he once gave a lecture to an international audience of elite mathematicians and asked how many of them were Platonists. About three-quarters raised their hands. See Jim Holt, "Proof: A Mathematician Explains Why the Arguments for God Just Don't Add Up," *New York Times*, January 13, 2008. See also Livio, *Is God a Mathematician?*, 169–70; Jonas, *Phenomenon of Life*, 64; David Malone, "Perspectives: Are We Still Addicted to Certainty?," *New Scientist*, no. 2615 (August 4, 2007).

53. Max Tegmark, "Mathematical Cosmos: Reality by Numbers," *New Scientist*, no. 2621 (September 14, 2007); Stephen Hawking, *A Brief History of Time* (New York: Bantam, 1998), 191.

54. For some rare, noteworthy examples of recognizing scientific cognition as a cultural assumption, see: Nathan Sivin, "Why the Scientific Revolution Did Not Take Place in China—or Did It?" *Environmentalist* 5, no. 1 (1985): 43; George Lakoff and Mark Johnson, *Philosophy in the Flesh: The Embodied Mind and Its Challenge to Western Thought* (New York: Basic Books, 1999), 236–37.

55. Eugene Wigner, "The Unreasonable Effectiveness of Mathematics in the Natural Sciences," *Communications on Pure and Applied Mathematics* 13, no. 1 (1960): 1–14; Livio, *Is God a Mathematician?*, 4–12.

56. Michael Atiyah, "Mathematics: Queen and Servant of the Sciences," *Proceedings of the American Philosophical Society* 137, no. 4 (December 1993): 527–31; Livio, *Is God a Mathematician?*, 10-11.

57. Livio, *Is God a Mathematician?*, 242.

58. Ibid., 155–62; Cromer, *Uncommon Sense*, locs. 136, 222.

59. Livio, *Is God a Mathematician?*, 245, 251–52.

60. Huff, *Rise of Early Modern Science* 62–63; Sivin, "Scientific Revolution," 43.

61. Nathan Sivin, "Review: Joseph Needham. Science and Civilization in China, Volume 7: The Social Background. Part 2, General Conclusions and Reflections," *China Review International* 12, no. 2: Fall (2005): 297–307.

62. Nigel Goldenfeld and Leo Kadanoff, "Simple Lessons from Complexity," *Science* 284, no. 2 (April 1999): 87–89.

Chapter 19. "Something Far More Deeply Interfused": The Systems Worldview

1. James Gleick, *Chaos: Making a New Science* (New York: Penguin, 1987), 11–31; Edward Ott, "Edward N. Lorenz (1917–2008)," *Nature* (2008): 300; Fritjof Capra and Pier Luigi Luisi, *The Systems View of Life: A Unifying Vision* (New York: Cambridge University Press, 2014), 114.

2. A. N. Marlow, "Hinduism and Buddhism in Greek Philosophy," *Philosophy East and West* 4, no. 1 (April 1954): 35–45.

3. J. L. Ackrill, *Aristotle the Philosopher* (Oxford: Clarendon Press, 1981), 36; David C. Lindberg, *The Beginnings of Western Science: The European Scientific Tradition in Philosophical, Religious, and Institutional Context, Prehistory to AD 1450* (Chicago: University of Chicago Press, 2007), 64; David J. Depew and Bruce H. Weber, *Darwinism Evolving: Systems Dynamics and the Genealogy of Natural Selection* (Cambridge, MA: MIT Press, 1996), 40–41.

4. *De Anima*, cited in Ackrill, *Aristotle the Philosopher*, 61.

5. *De Anima*, cited in ibid., 70–71.

6. Ibid., 56; Lindberg, *Beginnings of Western Science*, 63–64; Paul S. MacDonald, *The History of the Concept of the Mind: Speculations about Soul, Mind and Spirit from Homer to Hume* (Aldershot: Ashgate, 2003), 65–66; Evan Thompson, *Mind in Life: Biology, Phenomenology, and the Sciences of Mind* (Cambridge, MA: Harvard University Press, 2007), 226.

7. Lindberg, *Beginnings of Western Science*, 78–80; MacDonald, *History of the Concept of the Mind*, 71–72, 79; Charles Freeman, *The Closing of the Western Mind: The Rise of Faith and the Fall of Reason* (New York: Vintage Books, 2005), 44.

8. Lindberg, *Beginnings of Western Science*, 240; MacDonald, *History of the Concept of the Mind*, 71–72, 79; G. E. R. Lloyd, "Finite and Infinite in Greece and China," *Chinese Science* 13 (1996): 11–34.

9. N. Kretzmann and E. Stump, *The Cambridge Companion to Aquinas* (Cambridge: Cambridge University Press, 1993), 128–36. Theologians were helped by the fact that Aristotle sometimes, in contradiction to his own theory, alluded to a nonmaterial property of the uniquely human rational soul. See Ackrill, *Aristotle the Philosopher*, 62–63.

10. Cited in Fritjof Capra, *Learning from Leonardo: Decoding the Notebooks of a Genius* (San Francisco: Berrett Koehler, 2013), 67.

11. Ibid., xii–xiii.

12. Paul Wienpahl, *The Radical Spinoza* (New York: New York University Press, 1979), 67–70; George Sessions, ed., *Deep Ecology for the Twenty-First Century* (Boston: Shambhala Publications, 1995), 162, 176; MacDonald, *History of the Concept of the Mind*, 300–302; Wing-tsit Chan, "The Study of Chu Hsi in the West," *Journal of Asian Studies* 35, no. 4 (1976): 555–77.

13. William Blake, "Letter to Thomas Butts," November 22, 1802; William Wordsworth, "The Tables Turned," 1798; William Wordsworth, "Lines Written a Few Miles above Tintern Abbey," in *Lyrical Ballads* (London: J. & A. Arch., 1798).

14. John Keats, "Lamia," 1828.

15. Quoted in A. Ladd et al., *Romanticism and Transcendentalism: 1800–1860* (New York: Chelsea House Publishers, 2010), 6; Jeremy Rifkin, *The Empathic Civilization: The Race to Global Consciousness in a World in Crisis* (New York: Penguin, 2009), 307–8, 608–9; Mae-Wan Ho, "The Integration of Science with Human Experience," *Leonardo* 24, no. 5 (1991): 607–15.

16. William Leiss, *The Domination of Nature* (Montreal: McGill-Queen's University Press, 1994), 125–29, 142; David Abram, *The Spell of the Sensuous* (New York: Random House, 1996), 36–53.

17. Capra and Luisi, *Systems View of Life*, 66–68; Bang Wong, "Points of View: Gestalt Principles (Part 1)," *Nature Methods* 7, no. 11 (2010): 863.

18. Capra and Luisi, *Systems View of Life*, 68–79.

19. Ibid., 85–94.

20. Nigel Goldenfeld and Leo Kadanoff, "Simple Lessons from Complexity," *Science* 284, no. 2 (April 1999): 87–89.

21. Capra and Luisi, *Systems View of Life*, 116–26; Gleick, *Chaos* 94–110; Lynn Margulis and Dorion Sagan, *What Is Life?* (Berkeley/Los Angeles: University of California Press, 2000); Kenneth J. Hsu and Andrew Hsu, "Self-Similarity of the '1/f Noise' Called Music," *Proceedings of the National Academy of Sciences* 88 (April 1991): 3507–9.

22. Erwin Schrödinger, *What Is Life? With Mind and Matter and Autobiographical Sketches* (Cambridge: Cambridge University Press, 1944/1992).

23. Ibid., 67–75; Depew and Weber, *Darwinism Evolving*, 461–62.

24. Capra and Luisi, *Systems View of Life*, 158; D. J. T. Sumpter, "The Principles of Collective Animal Behaviour," *Phil. Trans. R. Soc. Lond. B* 361 (2006): 5–22; Margulis and Sagan, *What Is Life?*, 16.

25. Stuart Kauffman, *At Home in the Universe: The Search for Laws of Self-Organization and Complexity* (New York: Oxford University Press, 1995), 26.

26. Ibid., 86, 91; Brian Goodwin, *How the Leopard Changed Its Spots: The Evolution of Complexity* (Princeton, NJ: Princeton University Press, 2001); Krisztina Kosse, "Some Regularities in Human Group Formation and the Evolution of Societal Complexity," *Complexity* 6, no. 1 (2001): 60–64; David A. Perry, "Self-Organizing Systems across Scales," *Tree* 10, no. 6 (June 1995): 241–44; Donald S. Coffey, "Self-Organization, Complexity and Chaos: The New Biology for Medicine," *Nature Medicine* 4, no. 8 (1998): 882–85.

27. Paul Cilliers, *Complexity and Postmodernism: Understanding Complex Systems* (New York: Routledge, 2002), 3–5.

28. Sumpter, "Principles of Collective Animal Behaviour"; Madeleine Beekman, David J. Sumpter, and Francis L. W. Ratnieks, "Phase Transition between Disordered and Ordered Foraging in Pharaoh's Ants," *Proceedings of the National Academy of Sciences* 98, no. 17 (2001): 9703–6.

29. Scott Camazine et al., *Self-Organization in Biological Systems* (Princeton, NJ: Princeton University Press, 2001) 31–34; Roger Lewin, *Complexity: Life at the Edge of Chaos* (Chicago: University of Chicago Press, 1999), 175; Russ Abbott, "The Reductionist Blind Spot," *Complexity* 14, no. 5 (2009): 10–22; Giulio Tononi, Gerald M. Edelman, and Olaf Sporns, "Complexity and Coherency: Integrating Information in the Brain," *Trends in Cognitive Sciences* 2, no. 12 (1998): 474–84; Ursula Goodenough and Terrence W. Deacon, "The Sacred Emergence of Nature," in *The Oxford Handbook of Religion and Science*, ed. Philip Clayton (New York: Oxford University Press, 2006).

30. Humberto R. Maturana and Francisco J. Varela, *The Tree of Knowledge: The Biological Roots of Human Understanding* (Boston: Shambhala, 1987); Lynn Margulis and Dorion Sagan, *Microcosmos: Four Billion Years of Microbial Evolution* (Berkeley: University of California Press, 1997); Evan Thompson and Francisco J. Varela, "Radical Embodiment: Neural Dynamics and Consciousness," *Trends in Cognitive Sciences* 5, no. 10 (2001): 418–25; Francisco J. Varela, Evan Thompson, and Eleanor Rosch, *The Embodied Mind: Cognitive Science and Human Experience* (Cambridge, MA: MIT Press, 1993); Francisco J. Varela and Natalie Depraz, "Imagining: Embodiment, Phenomenology, and Transformation," in *Buddhism and Science: Breaking New Ground*, ed. B. Alan Wallace (New York: Columbia University Press, 2003).

31. Thompson, *Mind in Life*, 64–65, 92; Peter T. Macklem, "Emergent Phenomena and the Secrets of Life," *Journal of Applied Physiology*, no. 104 (2008): 1844–46.

32. See chapter 15; also Richard Dawkins, *The Blind Watchmaker* (New York: Norton, 1986).

33. For one of countless examples of the generally accepted view of nature as a machine, see César A. Hidalgo, "Planet Hard Drive," *Scientific American* (August 2015): 73–75.

34. Francis Crick, *The Astonishing Hypothesis: The Scientific Search for the Soul* (New York: Touchstone, 1994), 3. See also E. O. Wilson, *Consilience: The Unity of Knowledge* (New York: Vintage Books, 1999), 58–61.

35. Stuart Kauffman, *Reinventing the Sacred: A New View of Science, Reason, and Religion* (New York: Basic Books, 2008), 15; Denis Noble, *The Music of Life: Biology beyond Genes* (Oxford: Oxford University Press, 2006), 77; R. W. Sperry, "Mind-Brain Interaction: Mentalism, Yes; Dualism, No," *Neuroscience* 5 (1980): 195–206; Depew and Weber, *Darwinism Evolving*, 375; Carl R. Woese, "A New Biology for a New Century," *Microbiology and Molecular Biology Reviews* (2004): 173–86; Richard C. Lewontin, "The Dream of the Human Genome," *New York Review of Books* 39, no. 10 (1992); Abbott, "Reductionist Blind Spot"; Capra and Luisi, *Systems View of Life*, 19–59.

36. Margulis and Sagan, *What Is Life?*, 17.

37. James Lovelock, *Gaia: A New Look at Life on Earth* (Oxford: Oxford University Press, 2000); Timothy M. Lenton and David M. Wilkinson, "Developing the Gaia Theory: A Response to the Criticisms of Kirchner and Volk," *Climatic Change* 58, no. 1–2 (2003): 1–12.

38. Capra and Luisi, *Systems View of Life*, 1–15; Fritjof Capra, *The Turning Point: Science, Society, and the Rising Culture* (New York: Bantam Books, 1988).

39. Kauffman, *Reinventing the Sacred*; Fritjof Capra, *The Web of Life: A New Scientific Understanding of Living Systems* (New York: Anchor Books, 1996).

40. Ibid., 287–88; Capra and Luisi, *Systems View of Life*.

41. Lewontin, "Dream of the Human Genome"; Depew and Weber, *Darwinism Evolving*, 477–78; Woese, "New Biology for a New Century"; Goodwin, *How the Leopard Changed Its Spots*, xvi–xvii.

42. Kauffman, *At Home in the Universe*, 185–86. See "The Modern Relevance of Li" in chapter 14.

43. Ott, "Edward N. Lorenz"; John Dugdale, "Richard Dawkins Named World's Top Thinker in Poll," *Guardian*, April 25, 2013.

44. Thomas S. Kuhn, *The Structure of Scientific Revolutions* (Chicago: University of Chicago Press, 1996), 64.

45. Ibid., 85–86, 151–52.

Chapter 20. Consuming the Earth in the Modern Era

1. Johann Wolfgang von Goethe, "The Sorcerer's Apprentice," trans. Brigitte Dubiel (1797). I am indebted to Steve Hagen for pointing out this work as a parable for the power of technology. See Steve Hagen, *Buddhism Is Not What You Think: Finding Freedom beyond Beliefs* (San Francisco: HarperCollins, 2004), 28–29.

2. Ray Kurzweil, *The Singularity Is Near* (New York: Penguin Books, 2005), 56–72; Bill McKibben, *Enough: Staying Human in an Engineered Age* (New York: Owl Books, 2003), 70.

3. Jeremy Lent, "Louis C. K. and the Democracy of Consciousness," *Liology*, November 20, 2013, http://liology.net/2013/11/20/louis-c-k-and-the-democracy-of-consciousness/ (accessed February 5, 2017). Original video clip: "Louis C.K. Hates Cell Phones," YouTube video, 4:50, from the September 20, 2013, episode of *Conan* on TBS, posted by "Team Coco" on September 20, 2013, https://www.youtube.com/watch?v=5HbYScltf1c (accessed February 5, 2017).

4. Thomas Berry, "Ethics and Ecology," paper presented at *Harvard Seminar on Environmental Ethics* (Cambridge, MA: Harvard University Press, 1996).

5. Fritjof Capra, *The Turning Point: Science, Society, and the Rising Culture* (New York: Bantam Books, 1988), 380. See also Morris Berman, "The Cybernetic Dream of the Twenty-First Century," *Journal of Humanistic Psychology* (Spring 1986): 24–51.

6. Clive Ponting, *World History: A New Perspective* (London: Pimlico, 2001), 637–72.

7. Peter Watson, *The Age of Atheists: How We Have Sought to Live Since the Death of God* (New York: Simon & Schuster, 2014), iBooks edition, Introduction.

8. W. Leach, *Land of Desire: Merchants, Power, and the Rise of a New American Culture* (New York: Vintage, 1993), 252. See also Richard H. Robbins, *Global Problems and the Culture of Capitalism* (Boston: Pearson Education, 2008), 23–24.

9. Neil Postman, *Technopoly: The Surrender of Culture to Technology* (New York: Vintage Books, 1993), 13; James R. Beniger, *The Control Revolution: Technological and Economic Origins of the Information Society* (Cambridge, MA: Harvard University Press, 1986), Kindle edition, locations 4624–48.

10. J. R. McNeill, *Something New under the Sun: An Environmental History of the TwentiethCentury World* (New York: Norton, 2001), Kindle edition, locations 4772–80.

11. Cited in Robbins, *Culture of Capitalism*, 1–2. See also Beniger, *Control Revolution*, locs. 5404–42.

12. Robbins, *Culture of Capitalism*, 2–3; Thorstein Veblen, *The Theory of the Leisure Class* (New York: Dover Publications, 1899/1994).

13. Cited in Al Gore, *The Future: Six Drivers of Global Change* (New York: Random House, 2013), iBook edition, chap. 4.

14. Report of the "Committee on Recent Economic Changes," issued by President Herbert Hoover in 1929, cited in Gore, *Future*, chap. 4.

15. Robbins, *Culture of Capitalism*, 3; David C. Korten, *When Corporations Rule the World* (Sterling, VA: Kumarian Press/Berrett-Koehler, 2001), 16–17.

16. Robbins, *Culture of Capitalism*, 7–8.

17. Ibid., 9–13.

18. Ibid., 11–12. See also Roger Boyd, "Economic Growth: A Social Pathology," *Humanity's Test*, Alberta, November 7, 2013, http://www.humanitystest.com/economicgrowth-a-social-pathology/ (accessed February 5, 2017).

19. Boyd, "Economic Growth"; Robbins, *Culture of Capitalism*, 11–12.

20. Paul Krugman, *The Return of Depression Economics and the Crisis of 2008* (New York: W. W. Norton, 2009); Gore, *Future*, chap. 3; Robbins, *Culture of Capitalism*, 94–95.

21. Gore, *Future*, chap. 3; Korten, *When Corporations Rule the World*, 64–65.

22. Korten, *When Corporations Rule the World*, 64–65. This designation, occurring in the case *Santa Clara County v. Southern Pacific Railroad Company*, was never explicitly voted on by the Supreme Court but rather was added in the "headnotes" of the case by a court reporter who was a former president of a railway company. This backhanded 1886 ruling became the basis for a more recent (2010) landmark case, *Citizens United v. FEC*, which further enhanced corporate power to sway public opinion by lifting restrictions on political spending by corporations in candidate elections. See Gore, *Future*, chap. 3.

23. Thom Hartmann, *The Last Hours of Ancient Sunlight* (New York: Three Rivers Press, 2004), 221.

24. Gore, *Future*, chap. 3; Capra, *Turning Point*, 221; Robbins, *Culture of Capitalism*, 299.

25. Cited in Joseph Wayne Smith and Gary Sauer-Thompson, "Civilization's

Wake: Ecology, Economics and the Roots of Environmental Destruction and Neglect," *Population and Environment* 19, no. 6 (1998): 541–75.

26. Gore, *Future*, chap. 3; Beniger, *Control Revolution*, locs. 5404–42.

27. Robbins, *Culture of Capitalism*, 95–97; McNeill, *Something New under the Sun*, loc. 5030; Korten, *When Corporations Rule the World*, 123–33.

28. Robbins, *Culture of Capitalism*, 97–99; Robert Costanza, "Sustainable Wellbeing," *Resurgence & Ecologist*, no. 279 (2013): 39–41; Korten, *When Corporations Rule the World*, 28; Gore, *Future*, chap. 1.

29. Robbins, *Culture of Capitalism*, 66–67, 105.

30. World Bank, http://data.worldbank.org/region/WLD (accessed February 18, 2014).

31. Edward N. Wolff, "Recent Trends in Household Wealth in the United States: Rising Debt and the Middle-Class Squeeze—An Update to 2007" (working paper, Levy Economics Institute, Annandale-on-Hudson, NY, 2010). Wolff reports that this inequality increased significantly in the twenty-four years between 1989 and 2007, with the wealth of the top 1 percent more than doubling while the poorest 40 percent of the population lost 63 percent of their wealth in that period. The disparity in income has similarly been increasing substantially in recent decades. The income of the top 1 percent grew by 275 percent between 1979 and 2007, while, for the lowest 20 percent of the nation, income in 2007 was only 18 percent higher than in 1979. See Congressional Budget Office, "Trends in the Distribution of Household Income between 1979 and 2007" (Washington DC: Congressional Budget Office, 2011).

32. James Gustave Speth, *The Bridge at the Edge of the World: Capitalism, the Environment, and Crossing from Crisis to Sustainability* (New Haven, CT: Yale University Press, 2008), 41–42; Clive Ponting, *A New Green History of the World: The Environment and the Collapse of Great Civilizations* (New York: Penguin, 2007), 337; Oxfam, "An Economy for the 99%," in *Oxfam Briefing Paper: Summary* (Oxford: Oxfam, 2017); Royal Society, *People and the Planet* (London: Royal Society, 2012), 52; OECD,"Total Population," in *OECD Factbook 2011–2012: Economic, Environmental and Social Statistics* (Paris: OECD, 2012), http://dx.doi.org/10.1787/factbook-2011-9-en. See also Thomas Piketty, *Capital in the Twenty-First Century*, trans. Arthur Goldhammer (Cambridge, MA: Harvard University Press, 2014).

33. "Pollution and the Poor: Lawrence Summers' Memo," *Economist*, February 8, 1992, 66. The *Economist*, a magazine known for supporting the underlying values of capitalism, published Summers's memo and, while objecting to his explicit language, subsequently endorsed his position that migration of polluting industries to developing countries was "desirable."

34. Korten, *When Corporations Rule the World*, 2.

35. Ibid., 49.

36. Cited in William Leiss, *The Domination of Nature* (Montreal: McGill-Queen's University Press, 1994), 13.

37. Hartmann, *Last Hours*, 7–12.

38. Hans Joachim Schellnhuber et al., *Flagship Report: World in Transition: A Social Contract for Sustainability* (Berlin: German Advisory Council on Global Change, 2011), 326; McNeill, *Something New under the Sun*, locs. 587–606; Anders Wijkman and Johan Rockström, *Bankrupting Nature: Denying Our Planetary Boundaries* (New York: Routledge, 2012), Kindle edition, locations 1437–40; Samuel Alexander, "Peak Oil, Energy Descent, and the Fate of Consumerism" (Melbourne: Simplicity Institute, 2011).

39. Wijkman and Rockström, *Bankrupting Nature*, locs. 1470–79. Also, see Alexander, "Peak Oil"; Luis de Sousa, "What Is a Human Being Worth (in Terms of Energy)?," *The Oil Drum: Europe*, 2008, http://europe.theoildrum.com/node/4315.

40. Will Steffen, cited in Wijkman and Rockström, *Bankrupting Nature*, locs. 968–73. See also John Bongaarts, "Human Population Growth and the Demographic Transition," *Philosophical Transactions of the Royal Society B: Biological Sciences* 364, no. 1532 (2009): 2985–90; E. O. Wilson, *The Future of Life* (New York: Vintage Books, 2003), 28–29.

41. Julian L. Simon, "The State of Humanity: Steadily Improving," Cato Policy Report, Cato Institute, 1995, https://www.cato.org/policy-report/september-october-1995/state-humanity-steadily-improving (accessed February 5, 2017); Department of Economic and Social Affairs, Population Division, *Charting the Progress of Populations* (New York: United Nations, 2000), 45–49, http://www.un.org/esa/population/publications/charting/charting.htm (accessed February 5, 2017). See the World Population Clock at http://www.worldometers.info/world-population/ for current population statistics.

42. Bongaarts, "Human Population Growth"; WWF, *Living Planet Report 2012: Biodiversity, Biocapacity and Better Choices*, ed. Monique Grooten (Gland, Switzerland: WWF, 2012), 54; Royal Society, *People and the Planet*, 7.

43. OECD, *OECD Environmental Outlook to 2050: The Consequences of Inaction* (Paris: OECD Publishing, 2012); John Hawksworth and Danny Chan, *World in 2050: The BRICs and Beyond: Prospects, Challenges and Opportunities* (London: PwC, 2013).

44. Steven W. Running, "Approaching the Limits," *Science* 339 (2013): 1276–77; Schellnhuber et al., "World in Transition," 31; Richard Leakey and Roger Lewin, *The Sixth Extinction* (New York: Anchor Books, 1995), 239.

45. McNeill, *Something New*, locs. 2501–5; Schellnhuber et al., "World in Transition," 42; Peter M. Vitousek et al., "Human Domination of Earth's Ecocystems," *Science* 277 (July 25, 1997): 494–99; "A Fresh Approach to Water," *Nature* 452, no. 7185 (2008): 253; Peter Rogers, "Facing the Freshwater Crisis," *Scientific American*, August 2008, 46–53; David R. Steward et al., "Tapping Unsustainable Groundwater Stores for Agricultural Production in the High Plains Aquifer of Kansas, Projections to 2110," *Proceedings of the National Academy of Sciences* 110, no. 37 (2013): E3477–E86.

46. Speth, *Bridge at the Edge of the World*, 1–2; Committee on Understanding and

Monitoring Abrupt Climate Change and Its Impacts, *Abrupt Impacts of Climate Change: Anticipating Surprises*, ed. Jim White (Washington, DC: National Research Council of the National Academies, 2013), 81.

47. Gore, *Future*, chap. 4; Robert M. May, "Address of the President: Threats to Tomorrow's World," *Notes and Records of the Royal Society* 60, no. 1 (2006): 109–30; David Perlman, "Scientists Alarmed by Ocean Dead-Zone Growth," *San Francisco Chronicle*, August 15, 2008.

48. Hartmann, *Last Hours*, 26; *Abrupt Impacts of Climate Change*, 106; Gore, *Future*, chap. 6; Alex Rogers and Dan Laffoley, *International Earth System Expert Workshop on Ocean Stresses and Impacts. Summary Report* (Oxford: IPSO, 2011).

49. WWF, *Living Planet Report*, 18.

50. Leakey and Lewin, *Sixth Extinction*, 241–49; Speth, *Bridge*, 36–38; Johan Rockström et al., "A Safe Operating Space for Humanity," *Nature* 461, no. 24 (September 2009): 472–75; James Hansen et al., "Assessing 'Dangerous Climate Change': Required Reduction of Carbon Emissions to Protect Young People, Future Generations and Nature," *PLOS ONE* 8, no. 12 (2013): e81648.

51. Jane Lubchenco, "Entering the Century of the Environment: A New Social Contract for Science," *Science* 279 (1998): 491–97; Will Steffen, Paul J. Crutzen, and John R. McNeill, "The Anthropocene: Are Humans Now Overwhelming the Great Forces of Nature?," *Ambio: A Journal of the Human Environment* 36, no. 8 (2007): 614–21. See also Paul J. Crutzen, "Geology of Mankind," *Nature* 415, no. 6867 (2002): 23; and Vitousek et al., "Human Domination."

52. James Hansen, *Storms of My Grandchildren: The Truth about the Coming Climate Catastrophe and Our Last Chance to Save Humanity* (New York: Bloomsbury USA, 2009), Kindle edition, locations 2152–61; *Climate Change: Evidence and Causes* (Royal Society and National Academy of Sciences, 2014); Justin Gillis, "Heat-Trapping Gas Passes Milestone, Raising Fears," *New York Times*, May 10, 2013; Noah Diffenbaugh and Christopher Field, "Changes in Ecologically Critical Terrestrial Climate Conditions," *Science* 341, no. 6145 (2013): 486–92.

53. Hansen, *Storms*, 182–85, 205–6; Clive Hamilton, *Requiem for a Species: Why We Resist the Truth about Climate Change* (New York: Earthscan, 2010), 39; Ian Austen, "Canada Announces Exit from Kyoto Climate Treaty," *New York Times*, December 12, 2011.

54. Hansen et al., "Assessing 'Dangerous Climate Change'"; Gore, *Future*, chap. 6; Wijkman and Rockström, *Bankrupting Nature*, locs. 808–13, 1092–102, 2529–84; WWF, *Living Planet Report*, 94–95; *Abrupt Impacts of Climate Change*, 3. While it cannot be proven that each of these disasters was a direct result of climate change, scientists have shown that climate change has shifted the probability distribution for temperatures anomalies, and thus they can be said "with a high degree of confidence" to be "a consequence of global warming." See James Hansen, Makiko Sato, and Reto Ruedy, "Perception of Climate Change," *Proceedings of the National Academy of Sciences* 109, no. 37 (2012): E2415–E23.

55. Schellnhuber et al., "World in Transition," 39; Royal Society, *People and the Planet*, 67; Rogers and Laffoley, *Ocean Stresses*; *Abrupt Impacts of Climate Change*, 95.

56. A. T. C. Jérôme Dangerman and Hans Joachim Schellnhuber, "Energy Systems Transformation," *Proceedings of the National Academy of Sciences* 110, no. 7 (2013): E549–E58; Bill McKibben, "Global Warming's Terrifying New Math: Three Simple Numbers That Add Up to Global Catastrophe—and That Make Clear Who the Real Enemy Is," *Rolling Stone*, July 19, 2012; Michael T. Klare, "The Third Carbon Age: Don't for a Second Imagine We're Heading for an Era of Renewable Energy," *TomDispatch*, August 8, 2013, http://www.tomdispatch.com/blog/175734/tomgram%3A_michael_ klare%2C_how_to_fry_a_planet/ (accessed June 23, 2016).

57. Hansen, *Storms*, Kindle locs. 1431–47; Hansen et al., "Assessing 'Dangerous Climate Change'"; *Abrupt Impacts of Climate Change*, 6.

58. Gore, *Future*, chap. 6; Will Steffen, "Surviving the Anthropocene: Challenges for the 21st Century," Climate Change Institute, 2008; Hansen et al., "Assessing 'Dangerous Climate Change'"; Wijkman and Rockström, *Bankrupting Nature*, locs. 1314–23; Solomon M. Hsiang, Marshall Burke, and Edward Miguel, "Quantifying the Influence of Climate on Human Conflict," *Science* 341, no. 6151 (2013): 1–17.

59. Rockström et al., "A Safe Operating Space"; Rachael Beddoe et al., "Overcoming Systemic Roadblocks to Sustainability: The Evolutionary Redesign of Worldviews, Institutions, and Technologies," *Proceedings of the National Academy of Sciences* 106, no. 8 (2009): 2483–89; Wijkman and Rockström, *Bankrupting Nature*, locs. 1003–7, 1085–88. One striking example of this kind of irreversible tipping point can be seen in the collapse of cod fisheries in Newfoundland. After centuries of sustainable fishing, an increase in investment and technology led to a quadrupling of the catch in the 1960s; stocks then began to decline dramatically as fishermen continued their overexploitation, until, in 1992, the cod virtually disappeared from the region, leading the Canadian government to declare a fishing moratorium that put twenty-five thousand Newfoundlanders out of work. After more than two decades of no fishing, the cod have still not returned. See Marten Scheffer, *Critical Transitions in Nature and Society* (Princeton, NJ: Princeton University Press, 2009), 196–99; McNeill, *Something New*, locs. 3895–903.

60. Henry Kendall, "World Scientists' Warning to Humanity," Union of Concerned Scientists, 1992, http://www.ucsusa.org/about/1992-world-scientists.html#.WJebFPkrLIU (accessed February 5, 2017).

61. Speth, *Bridge*, 26–27; Paul R. Ehrlich, *Human Natures: Genes, Cultures, and the Human Prospect* (New York: Penguin, 2002), 321; Leakey and Lewin, *Sixth Extinction*, 224.

62. "Twentieth-Century Model 'a Global Suicide Pact', Secretary-General Tells World Economic Forum Session on Redefining Sustainable Development," UN Department of Public Information, January 28, 2011, https://www.un.org/press/en/2011/sgsm13372.doc.htm (accessed February 5, 2017).

63. Hansen, *Storms*, locs. 2100–2105; Wijkman and Rockström, *Bankrupting Nature*, locs. 2224–37; Hamilton, *Requiem for a Species*, 95–133.

64. Royal Society, *People and the Planet*, 59; Jared Diamond, *Guns, Germs, and Steel: A Short History of Everybody for the Last 13,000 Years* (London: Vintage, 2005), 248; Dangerman and Schellnhuber, "Energy Systems Transformation."

65. *Unburnable Carbon: Are the World's Financial Markets Carrying a Carbon Bubble?* (Carbon Tracker Initiative, 2012), http://www.carbontracker.org/wp-content/uploads/2014/09/Unburnable-Carbon-Full-rev2-1.pdf (accessed February 5, 2017); McKibben, "Global Warming's Terrifying New Math."

66. Boyd, "Economic Growth"; Peter Victor, "Questioning Economic Growth," *Nature* 468 (2010): 370–71.

67. See Garrett Hardin, "The Tragedy of the Commons," *Science* 162 (1968): 1243–48; Ponting, *New Green History*, 132–33; Boyd, "Economic Growth"; Royal Society, *People and the Planet*, 73; Boulding's quote cited in Mark Bittman, "A Banker Bets on Organic Farming," *New York Times*, August 28, 2012.

68. McNeill, *Something New*, locs. 4910–19. The assumption of inexhaustible natural resources is only one of the fundamental problems with classical economics that drive our civilization on an unsustainable path. In another example, when markets use a discount rate in evaluating different scenarios, they frequently use a rate of 10 percent per year, significantly reducing the value of future benefits compared with current costs. With this discount rate, a benefit twenty years in the future will be valued at only onetenth of its true value. It becomes "cost efficient" to allow the world to collapse from climate damage, as long as the collapse is more than forty years in the future. See Jorgen Randers, *2052: A Global Forecast for the Next Forty Years* (White River Junction, VT: Chelsea Green, 2012), Kindle edition, locations 3449–54.

69. Gore, *Future*, chap. 4; Clifford Cobb, Ted Halstead, and Jonathan Rowe, "If the GDP Is Up, Why Is America Down?," *Atlantic Monthly*, October 1995.

70. Cobb, Halstead, and Rowe, "If the GDP Is Up"; Ida Kubiszewski et al., "Beyond GDP: Measuring and Achieving Global Genuine Progress," *Ecological Economics* 93 (2013): 57–68.

71. Cobb, Halstead, and Rowe, "If the GDP Is Up"; Korten, *When Corporations Rule the World*, 44; Jon Hall, "Measuring What Matters to Make a Difference," *Journal of Futures Studies* 15, no. 2 (2010): 151–54.

72. Cobb, Halstead, and Rowe, "If the GDP Is Up"; Schellnhuber et al., "World in Transition," 74–76.

73. Kubiszewski et al., "Beyond GDP."

74. Ronald Inglehart, "Globalization and Postmodern Values," *Washington Quarterly* 23, no. 1 (2000): 215–28. Inglehart's paper identifies the correlation threshold between GDP and subjective well-being as $10,000 per capita based on 1998 US dollars; this is equivalent to $14,350 in 2014 dollars; in 2013, the GDP per capita of Turkey was $15,000

and of Mexico was $15,300. See also Anthony A. Leiserowitz, Robert W. Kates, and Thomas M. Parris, "Sustainability Values, Attitudes, and Behaviors: A Review of Multinational and Global Trends," *Annual Review of Environment and Resources* 31 (2006): 413–44.

75. Richard A. Easterlin et al., "The Happiness-Income Paradox Revisited," *Proceedings of the National Academy of Sciences* 107, no. 52 (2010): 22463–68; John Knight, "Economic Growth and the Human Lot," *Proceedings of the National Academy of Sciences* 109, no. 25 (2012): 9670–71; Richard A Easterlin et al., "China's Life Satisfaction: 1990–2010," *Proceedings of the National Academy of Sciences* 109, no. 25 (2012): 9775–80.

76. Knight, "Economic Growth"; Ed Diener, Louis Tay, and Shigehiro Oishi, "Rising Income and the Subjective Well-Being of Nations," *Journal of Personality and Social Psychology* 104, no. 2 (2013): 267. While Diener et al. agree with some of Easterlin's findings on the negative impact on rising aspirations, they find that income correlates with happiness when it leads to greater optimism about the future.

Chapter 21. Trajectories to Our Future

1. Stanley Kubrick, *2001: A Space Odyssey* (Metro-Goldwyn-Mayer, 1968).

2. Some notable members of the Club of Rome have included prominent statesmen such as Mikhail Gorbachev, Václav Havel, and Pierre Trudeau. See http://www.clubofrome.org/membership/ (accessed June 24, 2016). Debora MacKenzie, "Doomsday Book," *New Scientist*, no. 2846 (2012): 38–41; Graham M. Turner, "A Comparison of *The Limits to Growth* with 30 Years of Reality," *Global Environmental Change* 18 (2008): 397–411; Donella Meadows, Jorgen Randers, and Dennis Meadows, *Limits to Growth: The 30-Year Update* (White River Junction, VT: Chelsea Green, 2004), Kindle edition, locations 408–13.

3. MacKenzie, "Doomsday Book"; Turner, "Comparison"; Meadows, Randers, and Meadows, *30-Year Update*, locs. 3021–31.

4. MacKenzie, "Doomsday Book"; Turner, "Comparison"; Meadows, Randers, and Meadows, *30-Year Update*, locs. 3492–3503.

5. See Paul Raskin et al., *Great Transition: The Promise and Lure of the Times Ahead* (Boston: Stockholm Environment Institute, 2003), 13; Ervin Laszlo, *Macroshift: Navigating the Transformation to a Sustainable World* (San Francisco: Berrett-Koehler, 2001), iBook edition, Preface.

6. Al Gore, *The Future: Six Drivers of Global Change* (New York: Random House, 2013), iBook edition, Introduction; Raskin et al., *Great Transition*, 7–8.

7. Gore, *Future*, Introduction; Joel Garreau, *Radical Evolution: The Promise and Peril of Enhancing Our Minds, Our Bodies—and What It Means to Be Human* (New York: Doubleday, 2005).

8. Gore, *Future*, Introduction; Raskin et al., *Great Transition*, 2–7; Meadows, Randers, and Meadows, *30-Year Update*, locs. 4427–32; Hans Joachim Schellnhuber et al.,

Flagship Report: World in Transition: A Social Contract for Sustainability (Berlin: German Advisory Council on Global Change, 2011).

9. Marten Scheffer, *Critical Transitions in Nature and Society* (Princeton, NJ: Princeton University Press, 2009), 11–12.

10. Anthony D. Barnosky et al., "Approaching a State Shift in Earth's Biosphere," *Nature* 486, no. 7401 (2012): 52–58; Scheffer, *Critical Transitions*, 176–77. See "The Coevolution of Language and the pfc" in chapter 2.

11. Scheffer, *Critical Transitions*, 58–59.

12. Scheffer, *Critical Transitions*, Kindle edition, locations 1096–121.

13. Lance H. Gunderson and C. S. Holling, eds., *Panarchy: Understanding Transformations in Human and Natural Systems (Synopsis)* (Washington: Island Press, 2002), iBook edition, chap. 1; Scheffer, *Critical Transitions*, locs. 811–30.

14. See Thomas Homer-Dixon, *The Upside of Down: Catastrophe, Creativity, and the Renewal of Civilization* (Washington, DC: Island Press, 2008), Kindle edition, locations 1471–77, 3348–61.

15. Michael Marshall, "Climate Change: The Great Civilisation Destroyer?" *New Scientist*, no. 2876 (2012): 32–36.

16. Jared Diamond, *Collapse: How Societies Choose to Fail or Survive* (New York: Penguin Books, 2005), 114. *It should be noted that Diamonds theory of the ecological collapse in Easter Island has been challenged. More recent analyses suggest that the most likely reason for the eradication of trees was rats that may have been stowaways on the first boats to arrive and had no natural predators on the island. For a valuable discussion of the question, see Rutger Bregman, *Humankind: A Hopeful History* (London: Bloomsbury, 2020), 115–36.

17. Joseph A. Tainter, *The Collapse of Complex Societies* (Cambridge: Cambridge University Press, 1988), Kindle edition, locations 897–904. See also Karl W. Butzer, "Collapse, Environment, and Society," *Proceedings of the National Academy of Sciences* 109, no. 10 (2012): 3632–39.

18. Tainter, *The Collapse of Complex Societies*, locs. 1548–62. Note the consistency between Tainter's understanding of the importance of energy flows in society and the thesis proposed by Leslie White in his 1943 paper "Energy and the Evolution of Culture," discussed in "The Power Ratchet" in chapter 16.

19. Tainter, *Collapse of Complex Societies*, locs. 1938–43, 2004–9, 3011–26.

20. Ibid., locs. 2344–69; Joseph A. Tainter, "Resources and Cultural Complexity: Implications for Sustainability," *Critical Reviews in Plant Sciences* 30, no. 1–2 (2011): 24–34.

21. See Ugo Bardi, "The Punctuated Collapse of the Roman Empire," *Cassandra's Legacy*, July 15, 2013, http://cassandralegacy.blogspot.it/2013/07/the-punctuated-collapse-of-roman-empire.html (accessed February 5, 2017).

22. Daniel Pauly, "Anecdotes and the Shifting Baseline Syndrome of Fisheries," *Trends in Ecology & Evolution* 10, no. 10 (1995): 430.

23. Tainter, *Collapse of Complex Societies*, loc. 3353.

24. Tainter, "Resources and Cultural Complexity."

25. Paul R. Ehrlich and Anne H. Ehrlich, "Can a Collapse of Global Civilization Be Avoided?," *Proceedings of the Royal Society B: Biological Sciences* 280, no. 1754 (2013); David W. Orr, *Down to the Wire: Confronting Climate Collapse* (New York: Oxford University Press, 2009), 156; Joseph Wayne Smith and Gary Sauer-Thompson, "Civilization's Wake: Ecology, Economics and the Roots of Environmental Destruction and Neglect," *Population and Environment* 19, no. 6 (1998): 541–75.

26. Cited in Richard C. Duncan, "The Life-Expectancy of Industrial Civilization," paper presented at the Proceedings of the 1991 International System Dynamics Conference, Bangok, Thailand, 1991.

27. Jeffrey C. Nekola et al., "The Malthusian-Darwinian Dynamic and the Trajectory of Civilization," *Trends in Ecology & Evolution* 28, no. 3 (2013): 127–30; Robert W. Kates, "Population, Technology, and the Human Environment: A Thread through Time," *Dædalus* 125, no. 3 (1996): 43–71.

28. Michael J. Kelly, "Why a Collapse of Global Civilization Will Be Avoided: A Comment on Ehrlich and Ehrlich," *Proceedings of the Royal Society B: Biological Sciences* 280, no. 1767 (2013); "Malthus, the False Prophet," *Economist*, May 15, 2008.

29. Solow cited in Dianne Dumanoski, *The End of the Long Summer: Why We Must Remake Our Civilization to Survive on a Volatile Earth* (New York: Crown, 2009), 75; Julian L. Simon, "The State of Humanity: Steadily Improving," Cato Policy Report, Cato Institute, 1995, https://www.cato.org/policy-report/septemberoctober-1995/state-humanity-steadily-improving (accessed February 5, 2017).

30. Cited in Garreau, *Radical Evolution*, chap. 4.

31. Kelly, "Why a Collapse Will Be Avoided."

32. Freeman Dyson, "Our Biotech Future," *New York Review of Books*, July 19, 2007.

33. Clive Hamilton, "Geoengineering: Our Last Hope, or a False Promise?," *New York Times*, May 28, 2013; Gore, *Future*, chap. 6.

34. Gore, *Future*, chap. 6.

35. Peter M. Vitousek et al., "Human Domination of Earth's Ecosystems," *Science* 277 (1997): 494–99.

36. Brad Allenby, "Earth Systems Engineering and Management: A Manifesto," *Environmental Science & Technology* 41, no. 23 (2007): 7960–7965.

37. James Lovelock, *Gaia: A New Look at Life on Earth* (Oxford: Oxford University Press, 2000), 123–24.

38. Gore, *Future*, chap. 6.

39. Samuel Butler, "Darwin among the Machines," *Christ Church Press*, June 13, 1863. See also Lynn Margulis and Dorion Sagan, *Microcosmos: Four Billion Years of Microbial Evolution* (Berkeley, CA: University of California Press, 1997), 257; and George B. Dyson, *Darwin among the Machines: The Evolution of Global Intelligence* (New York: Basic

Books, 1997), 25–26.

40. E. O. Wilson, *Consilience: The Unity of Knowledge* (New York: Vintage Books, 1999), 302–3. See also Merlin Donald, *A Mind So Rare: The Evolution of Human Consciousness* (New York: Norton, 2001), 382.

41. Hans Moravec, *Robot: Mere Machine to Transcendent Mind* (New York Oxford University Press, 1999), 125–26.

42. See Bill McKibben, *Enough: Staying Human in an Engineered Age* (New York: Owl Books, 2003), 24; Mark Prigg, "Get Ready for the 'Superbaby': Chinese Firm's Bid to Allow Parents to Pick Their Smartest Embryos," *Daily Mail*, January 14, 2014, http://www.dailymail.co.uk/sciencetech/article-2539596/Get-ready-superbaby-Chinesefirm-set-allow-parents-pick-smartest-embryos.html (accessed June 24, 2016).

43. Francis Fukuyama, *Our Posthuman Future: Consequences of the Biotechnology Revolution* (New York: Farrar, Straus and Giroux, 2002), 102; Leo Kass, "Beyond Therapy: Biotechnology and the Pursuit of Human Improvement," President's Council on Bioethics, Washington, DC, 2003, 16. See also George J. Annas, Lori B. Andrews, and Rosario Isasi, "Protecting the Endangered Human: Toward an International Treaty Prohibiting Cloning and Inheritable Alterations," *American Journal of Law and Medicine* 28 (2002): 151–78.

44. Nick Bostrom, "Transhumanist Values," *Review of Contemporary Philosophy* 4, nos. 1–2 (2005): 87–101.

45. Bostrom, "Transhumanist Values"; Vernor Vinge, "What Is the Singularity?" (presentation, Vision 21 Symposium, Westlake, OH, March 30, 1993).

46. Ray Kurzweil, *The Singularity Is Near* (New York: Penguin Books, 2005); Singularity University, http://singularityu.org (accessed February 5, 2017); *Wikipedia*, s.v. "Ray Kurzweil," http://en.wikipedia.org/wiki/Ray_Kurzweil (accessed September 2, 2016).

47. "Machine-to-Machine Communications: Connecting Billions of Devices," *OECD Digital Economy Papers*, no. 192 (2012).

48. Igor Aleksander, "The Self 'Out There,'" *Nature* 413 (2001): 23; Michael Chorost, *World Wide Mind: The Coming Integration of Humanity, Machines, and the Internet* (New York: Free Press, 2011), iBook edition, chap. 11.

49. Moravec, *Robot*, 66–69; McKibben, *Enough*, 78.

50. Vernor Vinge, "What Is the Singularity?"; Margulis and Sagan, *Microcosmos*, 260.

51. Kurzweil, *Singularity*, 9, 136.

52. Ibid., 29–30.

53. See "The Deification of Reason" in chapter 7 and "Cogito Ergo Sum" in chapter 12.

54. Kurzweil, *Singularity*, 32, 311. See "The Conflict of Body and Soul" in chapter 7.

55. Kurzweil, *Singularity*, 361, 375. In this Platonic view of humanity's conceptual

intelligence as godlike, Kurzweil is joined by other prophets of the technological Singularity. The transhumanist Ramez Naam, for example, argues: "'Playing God' is actually the highest expression of human nature. The urges to improve ourselves, to master our environment, and to set our children on the best path possible have been the fundamental driving forces of all of human history. Without these urges to 'play God,' the world as we know it wouldn't exist today." Cited in *Singularity*, 299.

56. Kurzweil, *Singularity*, 210; Garreau, *Radical Evolution*, chap. 4.

57. Kurzweil, *Singularity*, 325.

58. Minsky quoted in McKibben, *Enough*, 203–4. Page quoted in Nicholas Carr, *The Shallows: What the Internet Is Doing to Our Brains* (New York: Norton, 2011), iBook edition, chap. 8.

59. Christof Koch and Gilles Laurent, "Complexity and the Nervous System," *Science* 284 (1999): 96–98.

60. Miguel A. L. Nicolelis, "Mind out of Body," *Scientific American* (February 2011): 81–83.

61. Ramez Naam, *More Than Human: Embracing the Promise of Biological Enhancement* (New York: Broadway Books, 2005), 205–6.

62. Nicolelis, "Mind out of Body."

63. Chorost, *World Wide Mind*, chap. 10.

64. Quoted in Garreau, *Radical Evolution*, chap. 5; see also "Cornucopia for capitalism" in chapter 20.

65. Jorgen Randers, *2052: A Global Forecast for the Next Forty Years* (White River Junction, VT: Chelsea Green, 2012), Kindle edition, locations 791–803.

66. Stock quoted in Garreau, *Radical Evolution*, chap. 4. Dyson and Silver quoted in McKibben, *Enough*, 38–39. For perspectives on the positive and negative aspects of human germline engineering, see Gregory Stock, *Redesigning Humans: Choosing Our Children's Genes* (New York: Houghton Mifflin, 2002) and McKibben, *Enough*.

67. For the author's own perspective on how human genetic engineering could lead within a few generations to two distinct species, see his science fiction novel: Jeremy Lent, *Requiem of the Human Soul* (Vancouver: Libros Libertad, 2009). For an illustration of how "shifting baseline syndrome" could make this divergence seem natural to succeeding generations, see four hypothetical "future articles" at http://humansoul.com/Future_Articles.html.

68. Randers, *2052*, locs. 1226–36.

69. Randers, *2052*, locs. 2727–39.

70. Mathis Wackernagel, "The Race to Lose Last," in Randers, *2052*, 144–48.

71. Stephan Harding, "Nature Limited to Parks," in Randers, *2052*, 156–58.

72. "Universal Declaration of Human Rights," United Nations, 1948, http://www.un.org/en/documents/udhr/.

73. Andrew Orlowski, quoted in Ashlee Vance, "Merely Human? That's So

Yesterday," *New York Times*, June 13, 2010.

74. Orr, *Down to the Wire*, 124.

75. The "Great Transformation," a term originally coined by the Hungarian economist Karl Polanyi, is used in Schellnhuber et al., "World in Transition." The "Great Transition" is used in Raskin et al., *Great Transition*. The "Great Turning" is used in Joanna Macy, *Active Hope: How to Face the Mess We're in Without Going Crazy* (Novato, CA: New World Library, 2012). The "Great Work" is used in Thomas Berry, *The Great Work: Our Way into the Future* (New York: Three Rivers Press, 1999).

76. See William Ruckelshaus, quoted in Meadows, Randers, and Meadows, *30-Year Update*, locs. 4427–32.

77. Raskin et al., *Great Transition*, x; Nekola et al., "The Malthusian–Darwinian Dynamic"; John H. Matthews and Frederick Boltz, "The Shifting Boundaries of Sustainability Science: Are We Doomed Yet?" *PLoS Biology* 10, no. 6 (2012): e1001344; Paul J. Crutzen and Christian Schwägerl, "Living in the Anthropocene: Toward a New Global Ethos," *Yale Environment 360* (2011).

78. See also "An Age of Anxiety" in chapter 11.

79. Gore, *Future*, chap. 3; Paul Hawken, *Blessed Unrest: How the Largest Social Movement in History Is Restoring Grace, Justice, and Beauty to the World* (New York: Penguin, 2007), 5; J. R. McNeill, *Something New under the Sun: An Environmental History of the Twentieth-Century World* (New York: Norton, 2001), Kindle edition, locations 5081–106.

80. Meadows, Randers, and Meadows, *30-Year Update*, locs. 3108–458.

81. Anthony A. Leiserowitz, Robert W. Kates, and Thomas M. Parris, "Sustainability Values, Attitudes, and Behaviors: A Review of Multinational and Global Trends," *Annual Review of Environment and Resources* 31 (2006): 413–44.

82. Michael I. Norton and Dan Ariely, "Building a Better America: One Wealth Quintile at a Time," *Perspectives on Psychological Science* 6, no. 1 (2011): 9–12.

83. Emily Esfahani Smith and Jennifer L. Aaker, "Millennial Searchers," *New York Times*, November 30, 2013.

84. Paul H. Ray, *The Potential for a New, Emerging Culture in the US: Report on the 2008 American Values Survey* (Mill Valley, CA: Institute for the Emerging Wisdom Culture, 2008).

85. Ibid.; Hawken, *Blessed Unrest*, 3–4, 12, 141–44, 163–64.

86. Hawken, *Blessed Unrest*, 164. See also Raskin et al., *Great Transition*, 69; and H. J. Schellnhuber, "'Earth System' Analysis and the Second Copernican Revolution," *Nature* 402, supplement (December 2, 1999): C19–C23. It's important to note that these humanitarian movements are not necessarily antagonistic to capitalism as a commercial system, but rather to the domination of massive, transnational corporations that has emerged in the past century. The cooperative movement, for example, offers a successful model of worker-owned corporations that aligns well with the values of the Great Transformation. (See Shaila Dewan, "Who Needs a Boss?" *New York Times*, March 25, 2014.) Additionally,

the rise in B Corporations (where "B" stands for "Benefit"), which aim to benefit all stakeholders, not just shareholders, demonstrates that it's possible for companies to succeed commercially within the current capitalist system while maintaining values consistent with the Great Transformation. See https://www. bcorporation.net/.

87. Jeremy Rifkin, "The Rise of Anti-Capitalism," *New York Times*, March 15, 2014. It's worth noting that the internet also offers the opportunity for humanity to overcome the "Tragedy of the Commons," the collective dynamic that causes people to maximize their own profit at the expense of the larger community. A study of this dilemma around the world has shown that groups of people who can personally identify one another tend to rely on trust, reciprocity, and reputation to overcome this dynamic and make decisions that prioritize the community over individuals. By increasing the connectivity between groups around the world, the internet offers the possibility for the attributes of trust, reciprocity, and reputation to become more significant attributes in larger-scale social and economic decision-making. See Elinor Ostrom et al., "Revisiting the Commons: Local Lessons, Global Challenges," *Science* 284, no. 5412 (1999): 278–82.

88. Gore, *Future*, chap. 6.

89. See Scheffer, *Critical Transitions*, Kindle locs. 2542–83.

90. Erica Chenoweth, "My Talk at Tedxboulder: Civil Resistance and the '3.5% Rule,'" *RationalInsurgent*, November 4, 2013, http://rationalinsurgent.com/2013/11/04/my-talk-at-tedxboulder-civil-resistance-and-the-3-5-rule (accessed June 24, 2016); Meadows, Randers, and Meadows, *30-Year Update*, locs. 4522–4524.

91. Raskin et al., *Great Transition*, 41–51; Schellnhuber et al., "World in Transition," 8; Robert Costanza, "Sustainable Wellbeing," *Resurgence & Ecologist*, no. 279 (2013): 39–41; Polly Higgins and Cormac Cullinan, "Towards a Universal Declaration of Planetary Rights," in *EnAct International* (London: Cape Town, 2009).

92. See Jonathon Porritt, *The World We Made: Alex Mckay's Story from 2050* (New York: Phaidon Press, 2013).

93. See Jeremy Rifkin, *The Empathic Civilization: The Race to Global Consciousness in a World in Crisis* (New York: Penguin, 2009), 616.

94. Fritjof Capra and Pier Luigi Luisi, *The Systems View of Life: A Unifying Vision* (New York: Cambridge University Press, 2014); Thomas Berry, "Ethics and Ecology" (presentation, Harvard Seminar on Environmental Ethics, Harvard University, Cambridge, MA, April 9, 1996); Raskin et al., *Great Transition*, 55, 69; Schellnhuber, "'Earth System' Analysis"; Laszlo, *Macroshift*, chap. 4; Alan R. Drengson, "Shifting Paradigms: From Technocrat to Planetary Person," *Anthropology of Consciousness* 22, no. 1 (2011): 9–32; Joern Fischer et al., "Mind the Sustainability Gap," *Trends in Ecology & Evolution* 22, no. 12 (2007): 621–24; David C. Korten, *Change the Story, Change the Future: A Living Economy for a Living Earth* (Oakland, CA: Berrett-Koehler, 2015); Anders Wijkman and Johan Rockström, *Bankrupting Nature: Denying Our Planetary Boundaries* (New York: Routledge, 2012), Kindle edition, locations 375–79.

INDEX